Oracle Press™

Oracle9*i*
Performance Tuning
Tips & Techniques

"Rich Niemiec offers hundreds of hints, tips, and tricks of the trade that can be useful to any DBA wanting to achieve maximum performance of Oracle applications. No Oracle library would be complete without this book."
—Ken (Dr. DBA) Jacobs, Vice President of Product Strategy for Server Technologies, Oracle Corporation

"Rich Niemiec has a burning passion for Oracle technology that blossoms in his writing. Having spent a lifetime in the software industry and with 15 years of experience on Oracle alone, Rich is an 'Oracle' of Oracle."
—Mark Jarvis, Chief Marketing Officer, Oracle Corporation

"Rich is the undisputed expert in Oracle database technology and tuning. This book will become a 'must have' for all database professionals who are serious about their trade."
—David A. Anstey, President, POCSOL, Inc. USA and President, Oracle Development Tools User Group (ODTUG)

ORACLE®

Oracle Press™

Oracle9*i* Performance Tuning Tips & Techniques

Richard J. Niemiec

McGraw-Hill/Osborne

New York   Chicago   San Francisco
Lisbon   London   Madrid   Mexico City   Milan
New Delhi   San Juan   Seoul   Singapore   Sydney   Toronto

McGraw-Hill/Osborne
2100 Powell Street, 10th Floor
Emeryville, California 94608
U.S.A.

To arrange bulk purchase discounts for sales promotions, premiums, or fund-raisers, please contact **McGraw-Hill/Osborne** at the above address. For information on translations or book distributors outside the U.S.A., please see the International Contact Information page immediately following the index of this book.

Oracle9*i* Performance Tuning Tips & Techniques

1234567890 FGR FGR 019876543
ISBN 0-07-222473-8

Publisher
Brandon A. Nordin

Vice President & Associate Publisher
Scott Rogers

Acquisitions Editor
Lisa McClain

Project Editor
Lisa Wolters-Broder

Acquisitions Coordinator
Athena Honore

Technical Editor
Janet Stern

Copy Editor
Chrisa Hotchkiss

Proofreader
Susie Elkind

Indexer
Irv Hershman

Computer Designers
Mickey Galicia, Elizabeth Jang

Illustrators
Michael Mueller, Lyssa Wald

Series Design
Jani Beckwith

Cover Series Designer
Damore Johann Design, Inc.

This book was composed with Corel VENTURA™ Publisher.

"Perhaps, in order to really become free, we have to move from struggling to hear God's Voice to letting God's Voice speak through us."

Rabbi Jonathan Kraus

To Regina, the love of my life...

The journey with you has been one of great love and great friendship. You were the missing puzzle piece that I finally found. With this crucial piece, I was able to start fitting all the other unconnected pieces and finally complete the picture of life. Because of you there is always happiness in my world.

After a long trip, yours are the eyes I long to see first.

After a burdensome day, yours is the only hug that makes me forget.

Your sweetness carries me through life in every season.

Thank you for all of the love, joy and happiness that you have showered my life with... it's like a rainbow from heaven. You have always given me all that I want, all that need and all that's important in my life. God blessed me with his greatest gift when he sent you into my life.

Your passion drives strength into my hopes and dreams.

Your smile is there to guide my steps through trials and tribulations.

We weather the storms together, you and I.

The tiny moments with you make up the best parts of my life. You are my best friend in life, and even though I've traveled all around the globe, you're still the most wonderful person I've ever met.

To Jacob, Lucas, Hollyann and Melissa...

You are the other four great people in my life. Thanks for your love, energy, fun, and caring. You are each incredible in your own way. In your eyes, I see the love of God shine into the world and into my life. He has blessed me greatly.

Contents

ACKNOWLEDGMENTS xxiii
INTRODUCTION xxvii

1 Oracle9i–An Introduction to Oracle9i New Features (DBA & Developer) 1
New Oracle9i Administrative Features 3
    Migration Notes 3
    SVRMGRL and Connect Internal Desupport 4
    Security Enhancements with the DBCA and the SYS Account 4
    Server Parameter Files (SPFILE) 4
    Automatic Undo Management (AUM) 5
    Resumable Space Allocation 6
    Default Temporary Tablespaces 7
    Oracle Managed Files 7
    Dynamic Memory Management 8
    Multiple Database Block Size Support 9
    Cursor Sharing 10
    Self-Tuning PGA 10
    Online Table Redefinition 10
    Miscellaneous Administrative Features 11
New Oracle9i Architectural Features 11
    New Partitioning Options and Features 12
    Extraction of Object Metadata 12
    Automatic Segment Space Management 13
    New Indexing Features 13
New Oracle9i Data Warehousing Features 15
    External Tables 15
    View Constraints 15
    Multitable Insert Statements 15
New Oracle9i SQL and PL/SQL Features 16
    Associative Arrays 17
    Oracle CASE Statements and Expressions 17
    Oracle MERGE Statements 18

Support for ANSI/ISO SQL 1999 Compliance 18
Other Miscellaneous SQL and PL/SQL Features 19
New Oracle9i Backup and Recovery Features 21
Fast Start Fault (Time-Based) Recovery 21
Flashback Query 22
New RMAN Features 22
New Log Miner Features 23
Oracle9i *Data Guard* 23
Real Application Clusters (RAC) 23
Parallel Databases 24
Architecture of Oracle RAC 25
Internal Workings of Oracle RAC system 27
SCN Processing 29
Conclusion 30
Tips Review 31
References 32

2 Basic Index Principles (Beginner Developer and Beginner DBA) **33**
Basic Index Concepts 34
Concatenated Indexes 36
The Oracle ROWID 37
Suppressing Indexes 38
Using the NOT EQUAL Operators (, !=) 38
Using IS NULL or IS NOT NULL 39
Using Functions 40
Comparing Mismatched Data Types 41
Selectivity 41
The Clustering Factor 42
The Binary Height 43
Using Histograms 45
Fast Full Scans 47
Skip-Scans 47
Types of Indexes 49
B-tree Indexes 49
Bitmap Indexes 50
HASH Indexes 53
Index-Organized Tables 55
Reverse Key Indexes 55
Function-Based Indexes 56
Partitioned Indexes 57
Fast Index Rebuilding 60
Tips Review 60
References 62

3 Disk I/O and Fragmentation (DBA) **63**
Using Disk Arrays 64
Available RAID Levels 65
Simplifying Setup and Maintenance 65

Is the Disk Array Made for a 24-Hour Shop? 66
Considering the Cost 66
Distributing Key Data Files Across Available Hardware Disks 66
Storing Data and Index Files in Separate Locations 67
Avoiding I/O Disk Contention 68
Moving Data Files to Balance File I/O 70
Using Locally Managed Tablespaces 71
Creating Tablespaces as Locally Managed 71
Migrating Dictionary-Managed Tablespaces to Locally Managed 72
Viewing File/Tablespace Information Using Enterprise Manger 73
Avoiding Disk Contention by Using Partitions 73
Getting More Information About Partitions 76
Other Types of Partitions 77
Other Partitioning Options 80
Using Index Partitioning 83
Exporting Partitions 84
Eliminating Fragmentation 84
Using the Correct Extent Size 86
Creating a New Tablespace and Moving Data to It 86
Exporting and then Reimporting the Table 88
Avoiding Chaining by Setting Percents Correctly 89
Rebuilding the Database 90
Using UNDO Management 92
Determining Whether Redo Log File Size Is a Problem 93
Determining the Size of Your Log Files and Checkpoint Interval 94
Increasing Chances of Recovery: Committing After EachBatch 96
Using Rollback Segments 96
Avoiding Contention Among Rollback Segments 97
Monitoring Rollback Segment Waits and Contention 97
Increasing Rollback Segments 97
Isolating Large Transactions to Their Own Rollback Segments 98
Using the Simpler Approach: Undo Tablespace 99
Monitoring UNDO Space 100
Killing Problem Sessions 100
Sorting in Memory to Reduce Disk I/O 101
Having Multiple Control Files on Different Disks and Controllers 103
Using Raw Devices to Improve I/O for Write-Intensive Data 103
Advantages of Using Raw Devices 103
Drawbacks of Using Raw Devices 104
Examining Other Disk I/O Precautions and Tips 104
Considering Issues in the Planning Stages 104
Tips Review 105
References 106

4 Tuning the Database with Initialization Parameters (DBA) **107**
Identifying Crucial init.ora Parameters 108
Changing the init.ora File Without a Restart 109
Viewing the init.ora Parameters with Enterprise Manager 110

Increasing Performance by Tuning the DB_CACHE_SIZE 111
    Using V$DB_CACHE_ADVICE in Tuning DB_CACHE_SIZE 113
    Keeping the Hit Ratio for the Data Cache above 95 Percent 115
    Monitoring the V$SQLAREA View to Find Slow Queries 115
Setting DB_BLOCK_SIZE to Reflect the Size of Your Data Reads 119
    Tuning the SHARED_POOL_SIZE for Optimal Performance 120
    Using Oracle Multiple Buffer Pools 129
    Tuning the PGA_AGGREGATE_TARGET for Optimal Use of Memory 132
    Modifying the Size of Your SGA to Avoid Paging and Swapping 132
    Understanding the OPTIMIZER_MODE: Cost-Based vs. Rule-Based
        Optimization 134
    Creating Enough Dispatchers 135
    Twenty-Five Important Initialization Parameters 137
    Finding Undocumented init.ora Parameters 138
    Understanding the Typical Server 139
    Modeling a Typical Server 140
Tips Review 141
References 143

5 Enterprise Manager and Tuning Pack (DBA and Developer) **145**
The Enterprise Manager Console 147
The Instance Folder 148
    Instance Management-The Status Screen 148
    Instance Management–Startup Options 148
    Instance Management–The Initialization Parameters 148
    Instance Management–Examine a Single Session 148
    Instance Management–Memory Advisors 149
The Schema Folder 150
    Schema Management–Examine Specific Tables 151
    Schema Management–Examine Specific Indexes 153
    Schema Management–Examine SYS Information 154
    Schema Management–Examine Packages, Procedures, and Triggers 156
The Security Folder 157
    Security Management–Creating a Profile 157
The Storage Folder 160
The Oracle SQL Scratchpad and SQL*Plus Worksheet 161
Performance Manager 163
    Performance Manager–The Database Health Overview Chart 163
    Performance Manager–The Buffer Cache Hit Ratio 165
    Performance Manager–The Library Cache Hit Ratio 167
    Performance Manager–The Data Dictionary Cache Hit Ratio 168
    Performance Manager–The SQL Area 169
    Performance Manager–The Memory Sort Hit Ratio 169
    Performance Manager–The System I/O Rate 170
    Performance Manager–Database Instance Information 171
    Performance Manager–Building Your Own Charts 173
    Performance Manager–Top Charts and Sessions 175

Oracle Tuning Pack–SQL Analyze 179
    SQL Analyze–The EXPLAIN PLAN 180
    SQL Analyze–Execution Statistics 182
    SQL Analyze–Comparing Different Plans 184
    SQL Analyze–The Tuning Wizard 185
The Index Tuning Wizard 188
Oracle Tuning Pack–Oracle Expert 189
    Oracle Expert–Focusing on a Schema 190
    Oracle Expert–Setting Up the Rules for the Tuning Session 191
    Oracle Expert–Making Changes and Measuring the Impact 192
    Oracle Expert–Examine the Recommendations 193
    Oracle Expert–Drilling Down to Recommendation Detail 194
    Oracle Expert–Recommended Systemwide Changes 195
Oracle Tuning Pack–The Tablespace Map 196
The Oracle Expert Analysis Report 197
Business Impact Reporting 198
    Service-Level Reporting 198
    Application Health Assessment 199
Tips Review 201
References 204

6 Using EXPLAIN, TRACE, TKPROF, and STORED OUTLINES (Developer & DBA) **205**
The Oracle TRACE Utility 206
    Simple Steps for TRACE with a Simple Query 207
    The Sections of a TRACE Output 212
    A More Complex TKPROF Output 213
    Digging into the TKPROF Output 215
    Using EXPLAIN PLAN Alone 216
    EXPLAIN PLAN—Read It Top to Bottom or Bottom to Top? 220
    Reading the EXPLAIN PLAN 221
    Yet Another EXPLAIN PLAN Output Method: Building the Tree Structure 226
    Another Example Using the Tree Approach 227
    Tracing/EXPLAINing Problem Queries in Developer Products 230
    Important Columns in the PLAN_TABLE Table 230
    Helpful Oracle-Supplied Packages 232
    INIT.ORA Parameters for Undocumented TRACE 233
    Using Stored Outlines 235
Tips Review 241
References 243

7 Basic Hint Syntax (Developer and DBA) **245**
Top Hints Used 247
Available Hints and Groupings 248
Specifying a Hint 250
Specifying Multiple Hints 251
Using an Alias 251
Using Hints 252

Using the CHOOSE Hint 252
Using the RULE Hint 253
Using the FIRST_ROWS Hint 254
Using the ALL_ROWS Hint 255
Using the FULL Hint 255
Using the INDEX Hint 256
Using the NO_INDEX Hint 257
Using the INDEX_JOIN Hint 258
Using the AND_EQUAL Hint 259
Using the INDEX_COMBINE Hint 259
Using the INDEX_ASC Hint 260
Using the INDEX_DESC Hint 260
Using the INDEX_FFS Hint 261
Using the ORDERED Hint 261
Using the LEADING Hint 263
Using the ORDERED_PREDICATES Hint 263
Using the ROWID Hint 264
Using the NO_EXPAND Hint 265
Using the DRIVING_SITE Hint 266
Using the USE_MERGE Hint 267
Using the USE_NL Hint 267
Using the USE_HASH Hint 268
Using the PUSH_SUBQ Hint 269
Using the PARALLEL Hint 270
Using the NOPARALLEL Hint 271
Using the APPEND Hint 271
Using the NOAPPEND Hint 272
Using the CACHE Hint 272
Using the NOCACHE Hint 273
Using the CLUSTER Hint 274
Using the HASH Hint 274
Using the CURSOR_SHARING_EXACT Hint 275
Problems with Hints 275
Hints at a Glance 276
Tips Review 277
References 279

8 Query Tuning (Developer and Beginner DBA) 281
Querying V$SQLAREA and V$SQL 283
Selecting from the V$SQLAREA View to Find the Top Queries 283
Selecting from the V$SQL View to Find the Top Queries 284
Determining When to Use an Index 285
Forgetting the Index 285
Creating an Index 286
Checking the Index on a Table 287
Indexing Properly 287
Fixing a Bad Index 288

Indexing the SELECT and WHERE 290
Using the Fast Full Scan 291
Making Queries "Magically" Faster 292
Caching a Table in Memory 293
Using Multiple Indexes (Use the Most Selective) 294
Using the Index Merge 296
Handling Suppressed Indexes 297
Using Function-Based Indexes 298
Understanding the "Curious" OR 299
Using the EXISTS Function 300
Tips Review 301
References 302

9 Table Joins and Other Advanced Tuning **303**
Join Methods 305
    NESTED LOOPS Joins 305
    SORT-MERGE Joins 306
    CLUSTER Joins 307
    HASH Joins 308
    Index Joins 308
Table Join Initialization Parameters 312
    SORT-MERGE Join Parameters 312
    HASH Join Parameters 312
Comparing the Primary Join Methods 312
A Two-Table Join: Equal-Sized Tables (Cost-Based) 313
A Two-Table INDEXED Join: Equal-Sized Tables (Cost-Based) 316
Forcing a Specific Join Method 319
Eliminating Join Records (Candidate Rows) in Multitable Joins 321
A Two-Table Join Between a Large and Small Table 323
Three-Table Joins: Not as Much Fun (Cost-Based) 326
Bitmap Join Indexes 328
    Bitmap Indexes 329
Third-Party Product Tuning 334
Tuning Distributed Queries 338
When You Have Everything Tuned 340
Miscellaneous Tuning Snippets 341
    Real Application Clusters (RAC) 341
    Red Hat is Red Hot: Linux Is Making a Move 342
    External Tables 343
    Snapshot Too Old: Developer Coding Issue 348
    Set Event to Dump Every Wait 348
    Block Dumps: The Last Word (Extremely Advanced Only) 350
Tuning Using Simple Mathematical Techniques 351
    Traditional Mathematical Analysis 352
    Seven-Step Methodology 352
    Pattern Interpretation 359
    Mathematical Techniques Conclusions 364

More Mathematical Techniques: Apply Control Theory 365
Tips Review 375
References 376

10 Using PL/SQL to Enhance Performance (Developer and DBA) **379**
Using DBMS_APPLICATION_INFO for Real-Time Monitoring 381
Using Log Timing Information in a Database Table 383
Reducing PL/SQL Program Unit Iterations and Iteration Time 386
Using ROWID for Iterative Processing 389
Standardizing on Data Types, IF Statement Order, and PLS_INTEGER 391
    Ensuring the Same Data Types in Comparison Operations 391
    Ordering IF Conditions Based on the Frequency of the Condition 393
    Using the PLS_INTEGER PL/SQL Data Type for Integer Operations 394
Reducing the Calls to SYSDATE 395
Reducing the Use of the MOD Function 397
Pinning Objects in the Shared Pool 399
    Pinning (Caching) PL/SQL Object Statements into Memory 400
    Pinning All Packages 400
Identifying PL/SQL Objects that Need to Be Pinned 401
Using and Modifying DBMS_SHARED_POOL.SIZES 402
    Finding Large Objects 403
Getting Detailed Object Information from DBA_OBJECT_SIZE 404
    Getting Contiguous Space Currently in the Shared Pool 404
Finding Invalid Objects 405
Finding Disabled Triggers 406
Using PL/SQL Tables for Fast Reference Table Lookups 408
Finding and Tuning SQL When Objects Are Used 410
Using the Time Component When Working with DATE Data Types 413
Tuning and Testing PL/SQL 416
Examining the Implications of PL/SQL Object Location 417
Using Rollback Segments to Open Large Cursors 418
    Using Active Transaction Management to Process Large Quantities of Data .. 419
Using Temporary Database Tables for Increased Performance 420
Integrating a User Tracking Mechanism to Pinpoint Execution Location 421
Limiting the Use of Dynamic SQL 421
Looking at Some Examples for Beginners 422
    Creating PL/SQL Code 422
    Creating a Procedure 423
    Executing the Procedure from PL/SQL 423
    Creating a Function 423
    Executing the get_cust_name Function from SQL 424
    Creating a Package 424
    Using PL/SQL in a Database Trigger 425
Tips Review 425
References 426

11 Using Parallel Features to Improve Performance (DBA) **427**
Basic Concepts of Parallel Operations 428

Parallel DML and DDL Statements and Operations 430
Parallel DML Statements and Operations Since Oracle9i 431
Parallelism and Partitions 432
Inter- and Intraoperation Parallelization 432
    Examples of Using Inter- and Intraoperations (PARALLEL and
    NOPARALLEL Hints) 433
Creating Table and Index Examples Using Parallel Operations 435
    Real-World Example of Distributing Data for Effective Parallel Operations ... 436
Parallel DML Statements and Examples 437
    Parallel DML Restrictions 438
    Parallel DML Statement Examples 438
Monitoring Parallel Operations via the V$ Views 440
    V$PQ_TQSTAT 440
    V$PQ_SYSSTAT 441
    V$PQ_SESSTAT 444
Using EXPLAIN PLAN and AUTOTRACE on Parallel Operations 445
Tuning Parallel Execution and the Oracle9i Initialization Parameters .. 450
Parallel Loading 456
Performance Comparisons and Monitoring Parallel Operations 457
Other Parallel Notes 460
Tips Review 460
References 462

12 The V$ Views (Developer & DBA) **463**
V$ View Creation and Access 465
    Obtaining a Count and Listing of All V$ Views 467
    Finding the X$ Tables Used to Create the V$ Views 469
    Finding the Underlying Objects That Make Up the DBA_ views 470
    Using Helpful V$ Scripts 471
    Summary of Memory Allocated (V$SGA) 475
    Detail of Memory Allocated (V$SGASTAT) 475
    Finding init.ora Settings in V$PARAMETER 476
    Determining Hit Ratio for Data (V$SYSSTAT) 477
    Determining Hit Ratio for the Data Dictionary (V$ROWCACHE) 478
    Determining Hit Ratio for the Shared SQL and PL/SQL (V$LIBRARYCACHE) . 479
    Identifying PL/SQL Objects That Need to Be Kept (Pinned) 479
    Finding Problem Queries by Querying V$SQLAREA 480
    Finding Out What Users Are Doing and Which Resources They Are Using .. 481
    Finding Out Which Objects a User Is Accessing 482
    Using Indexes 484
    Identifying Locking Issues 485
    Killing the Problem Session 486
    Finding Users with Multiple Sessions 487
    Finding Disk I/O Issues 488
    Finding Rollback Segment Contention 490
    Determining Whether Freelists Is Sufficient 491
    Checking Privileges and Roles 492
    V$ View Categories 494

Tips Review 498
References 500

13 The X$ Tables (Advanced DBA) 501
Introducing the X$ Tables 502
    Misconceptions About the X$ Tables 504
    Granting Access to View the X$ Tables 504
Creating V$ Views and X$ Tables 506
    Obtaining a List of the X$ Tables That Make Up the V$ Views 507
Obtaining a List of All the X$ Tables 508
Obtaining a List of All the X$ Indexes 509
Using Hints with X$ Tables and Indexes 510
Shared Pool 511
Queries to Monitor the Shared Pool 512
    ORA-04031 Errors 512
    Large Allocations Causing Contention 513
    Fragmentation 514
    Low Free Memory in Shared and Java Pools 515
    Library Cache Hit Ratio 515
    High Number of Hard Parses 517
    Latch Waits and/or Sleeps 517
    Miscellaneous 518
Redo 519
Initialization Parameters 520
Buffer Cache/Data Blocks 523
    Buffer Statuses 524
    Segments Occupying Block Buffers 525
    Hot Data Blocks/Latch Contention and Wait Events 527
Instance/Database 531
Effective X$ Table Use and Strategy 532
Related Oracle Internals Topics 532
    Traces 532
    Events 533
    Dumps 533
    Oradebug 534
X$ Table Groups 535
X$ Table and Non-V$ Fixed View Associations 555
Common X$ Table Joins 557
    New 9i *X$* Tables 560
    Undocumented Fixed Views 561
    Future Version Impact 562
Tips Review 562
References 562

14 Using STATSPACK to Tune Waits and Latches (Advanced DBA) 565
Installing STATSPACK 566
    Security of the PERFSTAT Account 567
    Post-Installation 567

Gathering Statistics 568
Running the Statistics Report 572
Interpreting the STATSPACK Output 572
The Header Information 572
The Load Profile 573
Instance Efficiency 574
Top Wait Events 576
Top SQL Statements 582
Instance Activity Statistics 583
Tablespace and File I/O Statistics 587
Additional Memory Statistics 588
Rollback/UNDO Statistics 589
Latch Statistics 591
Dictionary and Library Cache Statistics 595
SGA Memory Statistics 597
Nondefault init.ora Parameters 599
Top 10 Things to Look for in STATSPACK Output 600
Managing the STATSPACK Data 600
Upgrading STATSPACK 601
Uninstalling STATSPACK 601
Tips Review 602
References 603

15 Performing a Quick System Review (DBA) **605**
The Total Performance Index (TPI) 606
The Education Performance Index (EPI) 607
The System Performance Index (SPI) 608
The Memory Performance Index (MPI) 610
Buffer Hit Ratio 610
Dictionary Cache Hit Ratio 612
Library Cache Hit Ratio 613
Sorting in Memory Hit Ratio 613
Percent of Data Buffers Still Free 614
Top 10 Memory Abusers as a Percent of All Statements 615
Top 25 Memory Abusers Statements Tuned 616
Pinning/Caching Objects 617
The Disk Performance Index (DPI) 618
Top 25 Disk-Read Abuser Statements Tuned 619
Top 10 Disk-Read Abusers as Percent of All Statements 620
Tables/Indexes Separated 621
Chaining in Mission-Critical Tables 621
Key Oracle Files Separated 622
Rollback Segment Balance 622
Temporary Segment Balance 623
The Total Performance Index (TPI) 624
An Overall System Review Example 625
Rating System 625
Example System Review Rating Categories 626

Items Requiring Immediate Action 628
Other Items Requiring Action 628
The System Information List 628
Memory-Related Values 629
Disk-Related Values 629
CPU-Related Values 630
Backup and Recovery–Related Information 630
Naming Conventions and/or OFA Standards and Security Information 631
DBA Knowledge Rating 631
Tips Review 632
References 633

16 Monitoring the System Using UNIX Utilities (DBA) **635**
UNIX Utilities 636
Using sar to Monitor CPU Usage 636
Using top to Find the Worst User on the System 638
Using uptime to Monitor CPU Load 640
Using mpstat to Identify CPU Bottlenecks 640
Combining ps with Selected V$ Views 641
Using sar to Monitor Disk I/O Problems 645
Using iostat to Identify Disk I/O Bottlenecks 645
Using sar and vmstat to Monitor System Paging/Swapping 648
Using ipcs to Determine Shared Memory 651
Using vmstat to Monitor System Load 652
Monitoring Disk Freespace 653
Monitoring Network Performance 654
Tips Review 657
References 657

A Key init.ora Parameters (DBA) **659**
Desupported init.ora Parameters 660
Deprecated init.ora Parameters 661
Top Twenty-Five init.ora Parameters 662
Top Ten init.ora Parameters to Remember 663
Top Thirteen Undocumented init.ora Parameters 664
Listing of Documented init.ora Parameters (V$PARAMETER) 666
Listing of Undocumented init.ora Parameters (x$ksppi/x$ksppcv) 678
Top Ten Reasons Not to Write a Book 678
Tips Review 679
References 679

B The V$ Views (DBA and Developer) **681**
Creation of V$ and GV$ Views and *X$* Tables 682
The Oracle9i (9.2.0.1.0) GV$ Views 683
The Oracle9*i* (9.2.0.1.0) V$ Views 686
The Oracle9i Scripts of the *X$* Tables Used to Create the V$ Views 690

C The X$ Tables (DBA) 767
Oracle9*i* X$ Tables Ordered by Name 768
Oracle9*i* X$ Indexes 772
Oracle9*i* X$ Tables Cross Referenced to V$ Views 783
Oracle9*i* GV$ Views Cross Referenced to X$ Tables 791
Oracle9*i* X$ Tables Not Referenced by a GV$ View 800

Index 803

Acknowledgements

"You must be the change you wish to see in the world."
Mahatma Gandhi

I really thought that an update to this book would be a simple task. TUSC commitments, IOUG commitments, and tough economic conditions all added to the complexity of getting this task accomplished. I really ended up enduring many weekends and nights in several painful 100–120-hour weeks to get this update done. That effort would not have been nearly enough had I not had the help of many other people that contributed greatly. The following people also put in the extra hours during these very tough times to make this effort a success.

Brad Brown and Joe Trezzo are still the best two partners that you could ever have. They are like brothers to me and are always there when I need them. Thanks; you guys are the best! Lisa Price was my primary editor. Lisa, you are the best editor on the planet. You really were the one that kept the ball rolling and made this happen. You are one of those rare people in life that helped lessen the burden of this extraordinary task. Janet Stern of Oracle Corporation was the primary technical editor. Janet, a heartfelt thanks for an incredible editing job. You were absolutely fantastic as you definitely took the book to another level! I can't thank you enough for your efforts. You are one of the best out there!

Athena Honore was my acquisitions coordinator at McGraw-Hill/Osborne. Athena, thanks for all of your help in driving the process to fruition. Your strength propelled us many times. Lisa Wolters-Broder was my project editor. Lisa, thanks for your incredible positive spirit that helped carry us through the latter part of this process. Lyssa Wald was the illustration supervisor. Thanks for getting the equations right. Lisa McClain, acquisitions editor, managed the entire effort of the book and kept us on track. Thanks for your efforts; this one got finished in half the time of the last one. Scott Rogers, Osborne's vice president and associate publisher—he gets the right information into the hands of the people that build the systems that run this world. You are the man!

Kevin Aiken was an additional technical editor. Kevin, thanks for your detailed review to help get this to the next level. Also, thanks for tireless checking all of the scripts. Steve Adams was an additional technical editor for some of the tougher chapters. Steve, thanks for taking the time to help in your specialty areas! Marcel Kratochvil was an additional technical editor. Marcel, thanks for your help early on in driving the 9i material of the book. Bruce Scott–Thanks for taking the time with me in doing the Select article interview and sending me the rare Oracle founders picture.

Robert Freeman–Thanks for your help in getting the new features chapter complete. He wrote most of the new Chapter 1 single-handedly. Madhu Tumma–Thanks for your great section on RAC that I added to Chapter 1. Kevin Loney–Thanks for your work in updating Chapter 2 and 11 and providing the statspack installation information in Chapter 14. Bill Callahan–Outstanding job updating a very difficult chapter, Chapter 3. Randy Swanson–Great job in updating Chapter 4 and simplifying this area to the key initialization parameters to focus on. Valerie Kane and David LeRoy–Thanks for your efforts in getting me all of these screen shots as well as editing the verbiage. Oracle again provided me the content for Chapter 5. Mark Riedel–Thanks for the update to Chapter 6, especially the addition of stored outlines. Joe Holmes–Thanks for updating your advanced information in Chapter 9. Maurizio Bonomi–Thanks for the addition on Control Theory to Chapter 9. Roger Schrag–Thanks for your original information on joins to Chapter 9. Bob Taylor–Great job checking and updating Chapter 10 for Oracle9i. Chris Ostrowski–Thanks for going through the TUSC scripts and checking them against Oracle9i for Chapter 12. Bob Yingst–Thanks for passing along some of the V$ scripts for Chapter 12. Kevin Gilpin–Outstanding job re-working one of the hardest chapters in the book—Chapter 13—and also adding some scripts for chapter 12. John Vincenzo–Outstanding job updating Chapter 16 once again. Mark Jarvis–From the fast track of Formula 1 to Oracle Corporation… not much of a change for you. Thanks for all your help! Ken Jacobs–Thanks for your support of the Oracle product through the eyes of the customer. Andy Mendelsohn–Thanks for getting answers to some of the really tough questions. Kate Kerner and Katy Ryan—thanks for making my IOUG life easier.

Very special thanks goes to these people who help manage TUSC throughout this process (in addition to Broe): Tony Catalano, Jeff Ellington, Bruno Ierullo, Dave Kaufman, Bill Lewkow, Dan Rabinowitz, Burk Sherva, Jake Van der Vort, and Dave Ventura. Thanks to Sheila Reiter and Barb Dully of TUSC who are always there when we need them. Thanks Larry Ellison, Bob Miner, Bruce Scott, and Ed Oates for the great database!

Thanks to the following people that in some way contributed to this version of the book in addition to those above: Olga Akerman, Diane Ansah, David Anstey, Eyal Aronoff, Mike Ault, Janet Bacon, Kamila Bajaria, Bernie Balliard, Greg Bogode, Don Burleson, Pat Callahan, Rachel Carmichael, Tony Catalano, Axel Chagnot, Daniel Collins, Martin Pena, Craig Davis, Dr. Paul Dorsey, Lucy Eppolito, Lance Fang, Robin Fingerson, Kim Floss, Sergio Frank, David Gaston, Paul Gilreath, Mark Greenhalgh, K. Gopalakrishnan, Doug Held, Gerry Hills, Nguyen Hoang, Pat Holmes, Lydia Griffey, Andy Hamilton, Scott Heaton, Mike Holder, Amy Horvat, Santosh Jadhav, Lance James, Tony Jedlinski, Ron Jedlinski, Jeremy Judson, Shaharidan Karim, Dave Kaufman, Mike Killough, Peter Koletzke, Thomas Kyte, Bill Lewkow, Matt Malcheski, Connor McDonald, Ronan Miles, Cary Milsap, Sitansu Mittra, Ken Morse, Shankar Mukherjee, Pradeep Navalkar, Stanley Novinsky, Albert Nashon Owino, Cetin Ozbutun, Rob Palmatier, Venkatesh Prakasam, Preston Price, Ron Priester, Greg Pucka, Chris Racicot, Sazzadur Rahman, Heidi Ratini, Dennis Remmer, Bert Spencer, Mohamed Sabir, Sabina Schoenke, Burk Sherva, Felipe Teixeira de Souza, Graham Thornton, Gaja Krishna Vaidyanatha, Jake Van der Vort, Vince Vasquez, Dave Ventura, Rob Wall, Tom Wood, Pedro Ybarro, Ghazi Ben Youssef, and Dr. Oleg Zhooravlev.

Thanks to the following people at TUSC who make it possible for us to write books: Lynn Agans, Anwer Ahmed, Brian Anderson, Martin Andrea, Joel Anonick, Diane Ansah, Michael Ault, Janet Bacon, Kamila Bajaria, Roger Behm, Ashok Bhuvanagiri, Gregory Bogode, Michael Bonofiglio, Dean Bouchard, James Broniarczyk, Eric Broughton, Bradley Brown, Mark Bullen, Paul Burke, Michael Butler, Damir Calic, Patrick Callahan, Karen Callaghan, William Callahan, Alain Campos, Peter Cargill, Brian Carignan, Michael Castro, Anthony Catalano, Deqiao Chen, Michelle Chesterfield, Kiran Chimata, Emily Clark, Holly Clawson, Judy Corley, Janet Dahmen, Terrence Daley, Rodney Davis, Susan Difabio, Douglas Dikun, Barbara Dully, Jeffrey Ellington, Matthew Engels, Brett Feldmann, Kevin Fiedler, Daniel Filkins, Robin Fingerson, David Fornalsky, Vicky Foster, Leon Francisco, Sergio Frank, Robert Freeman, Darren Fulton, Jennifer Galloway, Craig Gauthier, Bradley Gibson, Kevin Gilpin, Steven Glubka, Gary Goebel, Scott Goff, Joe Graham, Jason Grandy, Chelsea Graylin, Kathleen Greenhalgh, Mark Greenhalgh, John Gregory, Matt Grove, Paula Hahn, Rex Halbeisen, Andrew Hamilton, Steven Hamilton, Donald Hammer, Wes Handy, Dave Hathway, Scott Heaton, Mike Henderson, Michael Holder, Christopher Holland, Ronald Holleman, Amy Horvat, Leslie Hutchings, Bruno Ierullo, Mohammad Jamal, Celeste Jenkins, Douglas Kadoski, Mohammad Kanaan, David Kaufman, Teri Kemple, Prabhjot Khurana, Michael Killough, Karen King, Olen Kline, Charles Krutsinger, Felix Lacap, Lynn Lafleur, Patricia Lee, Ronald Lemanske, Alexander Levin, Bill Lewkow, Andrew Limouris, Mike Linde, Eric Linneman, Lawrence Linnemeyer, Ryan Litwin, Scott Lockhart, Kevin Loney, Antonia Lopez, Douglas Lundin, Kevin Maher, Tim Mahoney, Matthew Malcheski, Daniel Marsh, Daniel Martino, Kevin Marvicsin, Gillian McGee, Kimberly McGinley, Sean McGuire, Wayne McGurk, Charlene Mo, David Muehlius, Paul Murray, Joseph Nibert, Christos Nikolaides, Shaun O'Brien, Michael O'Mara, Christopher Ostrowski, Robert Palmatier, John Parker, Mark Pelzel, Allen Peterson, Gregg Petri, Cory Pfohl, Nadica Podgurski, Robin Pond, Lisa Price, Preston Price, Gilbert Quesea, Dan Rabinowitz, John Rago, Heidi Ratini, Pamela Real, Robert Reczek, Sheila Reiter, Mark Riedel, Jennifer Riefenberg, Christopher Rizzo, Nancy Robbins, Christopher Savory, Scott Schmidt, Alan Schneider, Sabina Schoenke, Chad Scott, Kerry Scott, Larrel Scott, Charles Seaks, Julie Shaw, Raymond Shaw, Kevin Sheahan, Burkhard Sherva, Mick Simenc, Tony Solosky, Edward Stayman, Kevin Start, Jack Stein, Kathy Suchy, Thomas Suhrhoff, Ray Surapaneni, Randy Swanson, Linda Talacki, Zhichen (Jenny) Tao, Bob Taylor, Jack Taylor, Wayne Taylor, Christopher Thoman, John Thompson, Graham Thornton, David Trch, Joseph Trezzo, Joseph Tseng, Joel Tuisl, James Turner, Razi Ud-Din, James Urban, Jason Van Ausdall, Jake Van Der Vort, James Vaughn Jr., Vince Vazquez, David Ventura, Jonathan Vincenzo, Jack Wachtler, Robert Wall, Aisha Walls-Coleman, James Walsh, Kimberly Washington, Michael Williams, Chuck Wisely, Daniel Wittry, Thomas Wood, Robert Yingst, Amy Zahnen, Richard Zapata, and Qi Zhou.

Thanks to the following people who have helped out in other ways: Sandra Hill, Floyd & Georgia Adams, Kristen Brown, Lori Trezzo, Sohaib Abbasi, Michael Abbey, Ian Abramson, Jeff & Donna Ackerman, Steve & Becky Adams, Joe Arozarena, Paster James C. Austin, Randy Baker, Abed BenBrahim, John Beresniewicz, Oliver Bernhard, Ronny Billen, Keith Block, Gary Bloom,

George Bloom, Melanie Bock, David Bohan, A.W. Bolden, Rene Bonvanie, Gary Bradshaw, Ted Brady, Aldo Bravo, J. Birney & Julia Brown, Sam & Rhonda Bruner, Bill Burke, Ashley Burkholder, Jeremy Burton, Andrew Busch, Jeff Butcher, Clyde Bryant, Dan Cameron, Bogdan Capatina, Joe Carbonara, Katie Carlson, Rachel Carmichael, Monty Carolan, Radu Caulea, Christina Cavanna, Bob Christensen, Edward Chu, Vikram Churamani, Joan Clark, Ray J. Clark, Rich Clough, Kevin Clukey, Rachel Cohen, Dr. Ken Coleman, Larry Collins, Lee Collins, Jim Conlon, Mike Corey, Peter Corrigan, Jason Couchman, Stephen Covey, Shanda Cowan, Sharon Daley, Barb Darrow, Mary Ann Davidson, Tom Davidson, Luis Davila, Leigh Cantrell Day, Tony DeMeo, Sohan DeMel, Jose DiAvilla, Bill & Barbara Dinga, Joe Dougherty Jr., Kris & Lisa Downey, Brenda Dreier, Carl Dudley, Matt Eberz, Kristy Edwards, Eileen Egan, Lisa Elliot, Buff Emslie, Dan Erickson, Chick Evans, Dr. Tony Evans, Darcy Evon, Mark Farnham, Tony Feisel, Jorge Ferreira, Kelly Ferris, Julie Ferry, Stephen Feurenstein, Ted & Joan File, Lee Fisher, Charlie Fishman, Tim & Jan Fleming, Flip, Andy Flower, Karen Foley, Heidi Fornalsky, Kate Freeman, Karen Gainey, Mike Gangler, Julie Geer-Brown, Kevin Gerhard, Len Geshan, George Gilbert, Sally Gluckman, Mark Gokman, Laverne Gonzales, Dennis Gottlieb, Cammi Granato, Tony Granato, Kent Graziano, Alan Greenspan, Carrie Greeter, Sarah Grigg, Ken Guion, Mark Gurry, Stephanie Guthrie, Rebecca Hahn, John Hall, Mike Hartstein, Jeff Henley, Bob Hill, James Hobbs, Kristin Hollins, Pat Holmes, Napoleon Hopper Jr., Rich Horbaczewski, Dan Hotka, Roger Jackson, Jeff Jacobs, Tony Jambu, Don Jaskulske & Dianne Innes-Jaskulske, Samantha Johns, Steve Johnson, Jeff Jonas, Michael Jordan, Jeremy Judson, Mark Jungerman, Emily Kao, Ari Kaplan, Stephen Karniotis, Maralynn Kearney, Dan Kelleher, Robert Kennedy, Kate Kerner, Ann Kilhoffer-Reichert, Martin Luther King Jr., Vick Khachadourian, George Koch, Fran Koerner, Kaarina Koskenalusta, Larry Kozlicki, Paul C. Krause, Fred Krauss, Mark Krefta, Ron Krefta, Dave Kreines, Thomas Kurian, Mark Kwasni, Paul Lam, Jennifer Lamson, Marva Land, Ray Lane, Karen Langley, Carl Larson, John Lartz, Brian Laskey, Herve Lejeune, Steve Lemme, Rich Levin, Cheng Lim, Quan Logan, Dave Luhrsen, Tony Mack, Ann Mai, Manzo, Julie Marple, Donna McConnell, Stephen McConnell, Kirk McGowan, Ehab & Andrea Mearim, Margaret Mei, Kuassi Mensah, Regina Midkiff, Jeff Mills, Jal Mistri, John Molinaro, Solveig Morkeberg, Steve Muench, Minelva Munoz, Cassie Naval, Scott Nelson, Robin North, Julie O'Brian, Jon O'Connell, Ann O'Neill, Francisco Martinez Oviedo, Cindy Niemiec, Dr. Dave & Dawn Niemiec, Mike Niemiec, Robert & Cookie Niemiec, Dr. Ted & Paula Niemiec, Merrilee Nohr, Rita Palanov, Jeri Palmer, Jignesh Patel, Arlene Patton, Ray Payne, Ricky Penick, Dr. Mary Peterson, Michael Pettigrew, Chuck Phillips, John Ramos, Gary Raymond, Frank Ress, Arnold Ridgel, Anne Ristau, George Roberts, Mike Rocha, Ulka Rodgers, Charlie Rose, Chuck Rozwat, Leslie Rubin, Steve Rubin, Mike Runda, Joe Russell, Mike Russell, Theresa Rzepnicki, Terry Savage, Douglas Scherer, David Scott, Kevin Scruggs, Mike Serpe, Allen Shaheen, Lewei Shang, Dr. Austin Shelley, Julie Silverstein, Judy Sim, Julie Sowers, Anthony Speed, Jeff Spicer, Katy Ryan, Rick Stark, Cassandra Staudacher, Leslie Steere, Bob Strube Sr., Bob Strube Jr., Burt & Dianna Summerfield, Cyndie Sutherland, Inna Suvorov, Matt Swann, Michael Swinarski, Andy Sze, Matthew Szulik, David Teplow, Marlene Theriault, Eugene (EGBAR) & Adrienne (Sky's the Limit) Trezzo, David Tuson, Oleg Wasynczuk, Bill Weaver, Jim Weber, Mike Weber, Huang Wei, Erich Wessner, Steve Wilkenson, John Wilmott, Marcus Wilson, Jeremiah Wilton, Oprah Winfrey, Ron Wohl, Randy Womack, Marcia Wood, Jacqueline Woods, Chris Wooldridge, Don Woznicki, Janet Yingling Young, Tony Ziemba, Mary Ann Zirelli, Edward Zhu, Chris Zorich, and Andreas Zwimpfer. Lastly, thanks to *your name goes here* for buying this book and being dedicated to improving your own skills (or if I forgot your name above).

Introduction

"I have come to the frightening conclusion that I am the decisive element. It is my personal approach that creates the climate. It is my daily mood that makes the weather. I possess tremendous power to make life miserable or joyous. I can be a tool of torture or an instrument of inspiration; I can humiliate or humor; hurt or heal. In all situations, it is my response that decides whether a crisis is escalated or de-escalated, and if a person is humanized or de-humanized. If I treat people as they are, I make them worse. If I treat people as they ought to be, I help them become what they are capable of becoming."

Goethe

A Work in Progress

Each of us should bear the labels "imperfect" and "under construction." We are all works in progress, continually being formed by the challenges that shape our character. Throughout history there have been tough economies and wars that tested us. Forever will history's tests and opportunities be the measure of how far we've come. Are your challenges strengthening your character? Are your challenges helping you understand where you still need work? Listen to your behavior when times are tough and you'll know where to refine your character for the better.

We are continually reminded, too, that every country is a work in progress. Like us, these countries seem to learn from similar mistakes, often over and over again. Technology is also a work in progress that is always being advanced, making life better for all of us. Advances in technology have also brought about uncertainty and even fear. But technology can eliminate uncertainty, improve productivity, and move the world forward. It is our job to move technology forward in our lifetime, and make life better for those who come after us.

Individual freedom continues to drive innovation and technology. The United States has been a rare experiment in self-rule, where individual freedoms and a diversity of people from every nation around the globe has led to tremendous innovation over the past century. Freedom has brought about some of the greatest advances in history. The industrial revolution was the first of many waves in advances that improved the standard of living for countless people. America is still imperfect, still a work in progress. Our real enemies continue to be fear and lapses of character. America's founding fathers built a strong foundation for us to work with, despite its imperfections, which can also teach us how to build a great team in business today.

In his 2001 Pulitzer Prize-winning novel *Founding Brothers*, author Joseph Elliot unlocks the ingredients of a great team. He studied what he calls the eight most prominent political leaders of the new republic: Abigail Adams, John Adams, Aaron Burr, Benjamin Franklin, Alexander Hamilton, Thomas Jefferson, James Madison, and George Washington.

Elliot writes: "The achievement of the revolutionary generation was a collective enterprise that succeeded because of the diversity of personalities and ideologies present in the mix. Their interactions and juxtapositions generated a dynamic form of balance, an equilibrium." They pulled together with the common belief "that character matters."

The Art of Virtue, by Benjamin Franklin, is a great book that I think helps define the importance of character.

"And because in old age the only solid satisfaction is the reflection of a long life spent in meaning well," wrote Franklin, who also believed that, "In this life, the only constant and durable source of happiness, is in acts of humanity, friendship, generosity, and benevolence. Since the foundation of all happiness is thinking rightly, and since correct action is dependent on correct opinion, we cannot be too careful in choosing the value system we allow to govern our thoughts and actions."

Your thoughts lead to actions, your actions form habits, your habits form your character, and your character determines your destiny. Think positively and about how you will succeed, and you will! It's never too late to start moving toward what you want to be in life.

Tough times and tests of fortitude will come calling from time to time to show you what you've become and how well your character is being formed. Will you see what you've hoped you would become? Will your test be your next lesson not learned, or will it be your finest moment?

Have you ever wondered where all of our heroes have gone? The answer is that they are all around you, waiting for you to pull the best out of them. Learn from history, and put together your own great team.

While technical proficiency in your chosen profession is paramount to success, character traits are equally important to the success of a person, team, or business. Books on leaders and leadership have been around for a long time, yet never before has the need for leaders in the world been so great. The World Wide Web is becoming the main medium for world transactions. Global leaders are now needed to navigate an ever-demanding world stage.

In 1920, Eleanor Roosevelt entered the world stage when she got the right to vote. In 1948, just 28 years later, she spearheaded the Declaration of Human Rights that gave human rights to all people across the globe for the first time in history. The year 2000 saw the maturation of an Internet technology that continues to mount an ever-growing wave that is rippling around the world. This technology is just beginning to revolutionize the delivery of information and education across the globe. Take the time to educate and do it with character, and you can help educate the next Eleanor, who will make life better for us all. The hopes and dreams of many depend on our ability to implement technology to better provide the vehicle to educate the world's population and provide increasing productivity. We need to make this tech's finest moment worldwide!

Oracle Celebrates 25 Years

Oracle celebrated its 25th anniversary in 2002 as a multi-billion-dollar company that has literally driven every business to web-based computing. It's amazing to look back on the history of Oracle Corporation and the diverse team that has led to its success. Larry Ellison has been the driving factor of Oracle the company, but Bob Miner was the driving factor behind Oracle the product. America is all about freedom, resilience, and opportunity. Larry is one of the greatest examples of what is possible in a free society.

The Pieces of the Oracle Puzzle

Prior to forming Oracle, Bob Miner was Larry Ellison's manager, where they worked together on a CIA project code-named "Oracle." Ed Oates, another founder of Oracle, happened to be walking by Bob Miner's door when Larry Ellison mentioned his (Larry's) wife's name. She turned out to be Ed Oates' lab partner from high school. Bruce Scott, who would be hired upon the formation of the company, is the "Scott" in scott/tiger (Tiger was Bruce's daughter's cat). Bruce is now the founder and CEO of Pointbase.

The Early Years at Oracle, Through the Eyes of Bruce Scott

"While Larry was at Precision Instruments, the company needed to do a $400,000 consulting project. For three or four engineers, that was a lot of money back then, as wages were about 1/10 of what they are now. Larry landed the deal. Larry was not part of the new company when it was founded; he was still at Precision Instruments. The new company was called Software Development Labs (SDL). We had three employees when we started in August of 1977. Bob Miner was the president; Ed Oates and I were both software engineers. We did 90 percent of the work on this two-year project in the first year, so we had the next year to work on Oracle. Ed finished the other 10 percent of the project over the next year, while Bob and I started to write the Oracle database.

"When we completed the Precision Instruments work, we had about $200,000 in the bank. We decided that we wanted to be a product company rather than a consulting company. Bob wanted to build an ISAM product for the PDP11. He felt there was a need for an access layer. Larry wasn't interested in that at all. Larry had been following what IBM was doing, and he found a paper on the System/R based on Codd's 1970 paper on relational databases. It described the SQL language, which was at the time called SEQUEL/2. Larry brought us the paper and asked if we could build this. We thought that it would be easy enough to do. So, we started. I was 24 years old at the time, Bob was about 15 years older than me, and Larry was about 10 years older than me. I left Oracle in 1982 after about five and a half years of working there. When I left, we had just finished version 3 of the database. Roughly half the code was mine and half was Bob's. I believe that a lot of the parser code in the current database may still be mine."

Bruce Scott has also said that his best day was Oracle's first users' conference. This was a customer conference that we put on. It was in 1982, and it drew about 25-50 people. It was beginning to catch on. Here's a timeline of how things progressed.

Oracle RDBMS History Over the Years

- 1970–Dr. Edgar Codd publishes his theory of relational data modeling.

- 1977–Software Development Laboratories (SDL) formed by Larry Ellison, Bob Miner, Ed Oates, and Bruce Scott with $2,000 of start-up cash. Larry and Bob come from Ampex where they were working on a CIA project code-named "Oracle." Bob and Bruce begin work on the database.

- 1978–The CIA is their first customer, yet the product is not released commercially as of yet. SDL changes its name to Relational Software Inc. (RSI).

- 1979–RSI ships the first commercial version, Version 2 (there is no V1 shipped on fears that people won't buy a first version of software) of the database written in Assembler Language. The first commercial version of the software is sold to Wright-Patterson Air Force Base. It is the first commercial RDBMS on the market.

- 1981–The first tool, Interactive Application Facility (IAF), which is a predecessor to Oracle's future SQL*Forms tool, is created.

- 1982–RSI changes its name to Oracle Systems Corporation (OSC) and then simplifies the name to Oracle Corporation.

- 1983–Version 3, written in C (which makes it portable) is shipped. Bob Miner writes one half, while also supporting the Assembler based V2, and Bruce Scott writes the other half. It is the first 32-bit RDBMS.

- 1984–Version 4 released. First tools released, (IAG –genform, IAG-runform, RPT). First database with read consistency. Oracle ported to the PC.

- 1985–Version 5 and 5.1 are released, First Parallel Server database on VMS/VAX.

- 1986–Oracle goes public on March 12 (the day before Microsoft and 8 days after Sun). The stock opens at $15 and closes at $20.75. Oracle Client/Server is introduced; first client/server database. Oracle5.1 is released.

- 1987–Oracle is the largest DBMS company. Oracle Applications group started. First SMP (symmetrical multiprocessing) database introduced.

- 1987–Rich Niemiec along with Brad Brown and Joe Trezzo join Oracle (historical for the reasons related to this book) and implement the first production client/server application running Oracle.

- 1988–Oracle V6 released. First row-level locking. First hot database backup. Oracle moves from Belmont to Redwood Shores, Calif. PL/SQL introduced.

- 1992–Oracle V7 is released.

- 1993–Oracle GUI client/server development tools introduced. Oracle Applications moved from character mode to client/server.

- 1994–Bob Miner, the genius behind the Oracle database technology, dies of cancer.

- 1995–First 64-bit database.

- 1996-Oracle7.3 released.

- 1997–Oracle8 is introduced. Oracle Application Server is introduced. Applications for the web introduced. Oracle is the first web database. Oracle BI tools such as Discoverer are introduced for data warehousing. Tools have native Java support.

- 1998–First major RDBMS (Oracle8) ported to Linux. Application 11 shipped. Oracle is the first database with Java support.

- 1999–Oracle 8i released. Integrates Java/XML into development tools. Oracle is the first database with native XML support.

- 2000–Oracle9i Application Server released at it becomes the first database with middle-tier cache. Launches E-Business Suite, wireless database with OracleMobile, Oracle9i Application Server Wireless, and Internet File System (iFS).

- 2001–Oracle9i (9.1) released. Oracle is the first database with Real Application Clusters (RAC).

- 2002–Oracle9i Release 2 (9.2) released.

I asked Bruce Scott what made Oracle successful in his mind. Bruce said, "I've thought about this a lot. I really think that it was Larry. There were a lot of other databases, like Ingres, out there that we beat. It was really Larry's charisma, vision, and his determination to make this thing work no matter what. It's just the way Larry thinks. I can give you an example that exemplifies his thought process: We had space allocated to us and we needed to get our terminals strung to the computer room nextdoor. We didn't have anywhere to really string the wiring. Larry picks up a

hammer, crashes a hole in the middle of the wall, and says there you go. It's just the way he thinks: make a hole—make it happen somehow. It was Larry, the right thing, and the right time."

Larry Ellison is the genius behind Oracle, the company, and Bob Miner was the genius behind Oracle, the product. The combination of the diverse team Oracle has had over the years is the secret of their success!

Happy Birthday, Oracle!

Changes Made in the New Version of the Book

The primary goal of this book is to help beginner and intermediate Oracle professionals understand and better tune Oracle systems. Many expert topics are also covered, but the objective is primarily to assist professionals who are frustrated and looking for simple tips to help improve performance. This book has one simple goal: to provide an arsenal of tips you can use in various situations to make your system faster. For those who read the first book, here are some of the changes and/or additions for each of the chapters:

- Chapter 1: Re-written completely for basic Oracle9i new features.

- Chapter 2: Added coverage of bitmap indexes and other 9i features.

- Chapter 3: Added Locally Managed objects and expanded entire chapter.

- Chapter 4: Targeted new Oracle9i features and simplified for Oracle9i.

- Chapter 5: Added all new screen shots for the Oracle9i version of Enterprise Manager.

- Chapter 6: Updated for Oracle9i added Stored Outlines.

- Chapter 7: Added new hints in Oracle9i and updated previous ones.

- Chapter 8: Updated and tested for Oracle9i.

- Chapter 9: Updated and tested for Oracle9i; added Kalman Filter.

- Chapter 10: Expanded (nearly doubled) as PL/SQL tuning influence expands.

- Chapter 11: Updated for Oracle9i.

- Chapter 12: Expanded to show many more V$ view queries.

- Chapter 13: This chapter is much-revised with help from Kevin Gilpin and Steve Adams.

- Chapter 14: Updated for STATSPACK (previously estat/bstat).

- Chapter 15: Rebuilt and retested system reviews based on feedback from previous one.

- Chapter 16: UNIX Chapter updated to include Linux.

- Appendix A: Updated for Oracle9i with updated queries and new Top 25.

- Appendix B: Updated for Oracle9i with updated queries.

- Appendix C: Updated for Oracle9i with updated queries.

In Memory

Lastly, I would be remiss if I didn't include something on the World Trade Center because it is an event that will mark this period in time. This event was also close to home for the Oracle community. I was asked to keynote the New York Oracle Users Group (NYOUG). The meeting was to be scheduled for September 11, 2001. The directions were to take the train to the World Trade Center and then walk two blocks to the meeting. The meeting would also have speakers and organizers that included many of the experts in the world of Oracle: John Beresniewicz, Rachel Carmichael, Jason Couchman, Dr. Paul Dorsey, Ari Kaplan, Kevin Loney, Ulka Rodgers, Douglas Scherer, Marlene Theriault, and Gaja Krishna Vaidyanatha. Fortunately, they were not able to get the meeting booked for the 11th and they had to move it to September 12th instead. Many of us were very lucky because we were not booked to fly to New York until later in the afternoon. Still, having a plane ticket to New York on 9-11 was very eerie. The Oracle User Group world was very close to some heavy losses. I was so thankful when I had heard that all of the people above were safe from harms way that day. Probably the most encouraging thing I saw concerning the NYOUG was just one week later. It was a request keynote at the now re-scheduled NYOUG meeting. Already, they were bouncing back and ready to try to schedule the next meeting… what resilience! I tip my hat to the NYOUG.

Unfortunately, we also had a client in the World Trade Center. We had been developing a disaster recovery plan for them over the summer. Fortunately, the project was over and Kevin Loney (who was the person developing the plan) no longer was working there. He had been working on the floor that was hit by the first plane. The recovery of the data went fine; the recovery for those who survived will continue for a long time to come. The hardest lesson that we learned, that we had not previously considered, was that the staff might not be available to recover the system after the disaster. We always thought that at least the staff would be available (at the minimum via phone support) to assist in the off-site recovery. Perhaps the hardest part following a disaster is working with those who did survive. Recovering the system may no longer be their priority. We learned that off-site people (in addition to off-site hardware and software) are needed to take the entire recovery task on, and they must be trained and ready. I tip my hat to Kevin for carrying this company through this; it was difficult just listening to his some of his phone message updates.

Oracle did, however, lose several of its own. We will always remember the following people in our hearts and in our prayers: Todd Beamer, Francis X. Deming, Steve Morris, Deepa Pakkala, Nitin Parandkar, Jeff Simpson, Harshad Thatte, and Ken Zelman.

The IOUG conference that followed this event in the spring of 2002 was the toughest one ever. Because the conference was only six months after 9-11, there was still a lot of uncertainty.

Then, everything was put in perspective, as the convention people took us into a meeting prior to the opening of the conference, and told us to be prepared to make a decision on what to do in case anything major happened in the world. It was a simple precaution, but one that weighed heavy on my mind. Things went fine. Finally, the end of the week arrived; a tiring, harrowing, never-ending experience was finally winding down. I was heading to my last presentation, "Uncommon Leaders"; I just had to talk about the incredible conference committee, SBA staff, board members, and the uncommon leaders who did the little things that carried us through the week. I had meetings before the presentation, then it was on to the last-minute questions. I found myself left with two wonderful minutes prior to the presentation to "clear the mechanism," as I often do to clear my mind free of any other thoughts… or so I thought.

Then Steve Lemme comes up and whispers in my ear, "A small commuter plane hit a building overseas; it may be nothing, but they said to be prepared to make a decision on short notice." It was a poignant moment. The event turned out to be a non-issue, and the conference was a great success. I learned how many volunteers it really takes to make a success during tough times—all of them. It will take all of us, working together as a team with all of our diverse strengths, to drive the next generation of technology.

References

Founding Brothers, Joseph Elliot
The Book of Virtue, Benjamin Franklin
"Rich Niemiec Interviews Bruce Scott," Select Magazine, 2001
"Retrospective: Still Growing after all these Years," Rich Niemiec, Oracle Magazine, 2001
History of Oracle, Donita Klement, 1999

CHAPTER
1

Oracle9i–An Introduction
to Oracle9i New Features
(DBA & Developer)

First, I want to note that this book is primarily focused on helping beginner and intermediate Oracle professionals understand and better tune Oracle systems. Many expert topics are also covered, but the objective is primarily to assist professionals who are frustrated and looking for simple tips to help improve performance. This book has one simple goal: to provide an arsenal of tips you can use in various situations to make your system faster.

In the last edition of this book, Chapter 1 was an all-encompassing discussion on tuning for those who didn't have time to read the whole book. Many people complained that this information was duplicated in other chapters (wasting paper), or worse, some people read only the first chapter and thought they understood tuning. Even worse, some people read a single tip (or never read the book at all) and claimed that the entire book was based on hit ratios alone instead of the 1000+ tips that were contained within. Nothing is further from the truth. I am always looking for a way to better help you and to dispel myths like these.

With that in mind, the first chapter of this edition focuses on what's new in Oracle9*i*. The rest of the chapters gradually increase in complexity and provide a plethora of tips to help you in your tuning adventures. I am sure that you will encounter at least some information that you won't find elsewhere.

If you still want a single method or an all-encompassing way of tuning (in a single chapter), I provide two such chapters for those who don't have the time to read the whole book. The first is Chapter 14 on Statspack: an incredible tool that includes most of the common scripts most experts use to tune a system. This chapter took the most time and testing on the rewrite. The second is Chapter 5 on Enterprise Manager: the tool of the future that provides a graphical way to tune your system, giving you the incredible ability to view and tune multiple systems through one window.

For those of you who want the full effect of the book, let's start with the Oracle9*i* new features. The chapters that follow dive deeper into the features that focus on performance tuning.

The topics covered in this chapter include the following:

- New Oracle9*i* administrative features

- New Oracle9*i* architectural features

- New Oracle9*i* data warehousing features

- New Oracle9*i* SQL and PL/SQL features

- New Oracle9*i* backup and recovery features

- New Oracle9i Real Application Clusters (RAC)

Oracle9*i* is the latest version of the Oracle RDBMS. It comes in the form of releases 1 and 2. In Oracle9*i*, Oracle has introduced new features and functionality throughout the database engine, and it has also enhanced the functionality of many supporting products such as RMAN and OEM. This chapter provides an initial introduction to these new features so you can take advantage of them when opportunity permits.

WARNING
Because these features are new, you should use them cautiously and test them completely until you are sure they work without causing your database problems. If you have access to Metalink, we strongly advise you to determine whether any known problems exist with the feature you are preparing to use. Google.com (although quite broad) is another good place to search for current information on Oracle features and functionality.

New Oracle9i Administrative Features

Oracle9i introduces a number of new administrative features that can make the database administrator's life very easy. This section discusses a number of these new features, including the following:

- Migration Notes
- SVRMGRL and Connect Internal Desupport
- Security enhancements associated with the Database Creation Assistant and the SYS account
- Server parameter files (SPFILE)
- Automatic Undo Management
- Resumable Space Allocation (one of our favorite new features)
- Default temporary tablespaces
- Oracle-Managed Files
- Dynamic memory management
- Multiple database block size support
- Cursor sharing
- Self-tuning PGA
- Online table redefinition
- Miscellaneous administrative features

Let's look at each of these features in a bit more detail.

Migration Notes

Migrating to Oracle9i is reasonably straightforward in most cases. If you are migrating from Oracle version 8 or 8i, then all that is required is the execution of a few scripts to migrate the database. Oracle9i supports migration from an Oracle7 environment only if you are currently on Oracle version 7.3.4. A migration from Oracle 7.3.4 requires that you use the Database Migration Assistant or the mig utility. Oracle9i has larger space and memory requirements than previous versions of Oracle; make sure you take these requirements into consideration prior to migrating.

TIP
Oracle9i has larger space and memory requirements than previous versions of Oracle.

SVRMGRL and Connect Internal Desupport

As predicted, the Server Manager utility (svrmgrl) is no longer available in Oracle9i. Now, database administration is done via SQL*Plus or OEM. Also, Connect Internal is no longer available in Oracle9i. To perform administrative activities on the database (like shutdown or startup), you need to log in using an account that is assigned SYSDBA privileges, using the AS SYSDBA login syntax. Here is an example of logging in to the SYS account as SYSDBA using SQL*Plus (but don't log on this way; do it interactively, or your passowrd could be seen as a ps-f command):

```
sqlplus "sys/password as sysdba"
```

Other variations on the login syntax exist depending on whether you are connecting locally or to a remote server/database. Oracle9i now comes with a new privilege called the GRANT ANY OBJECT PRIVILEGE, which facilitates this ability. So the correct name of the privilege is GRANT ANY OBJECT PRIVILEGE. The syntax follows:

```
GRANT grant any object privilege TO user;
```

WARNING
Of course, be careful granting this privilege to other accounts because it is very powerful.

Security Enhancements with the DBCA and the SYS Account

After creating a database by using the Database Creation Assistant (DBCA), you will be prompted to enter new SYS and SYSTEM passwords of the database being created. Also, most user/schemas that are created by the DBCA, except SYS and SYSTEM, will be locked. Also note that SYS can now grant privileges on any object in the database. You no longer have to grant privileges to SYS to allow it to manage the grants on your objects.

Server Parameter Files (SPFILE)

Oracle9i offers to manage your database initialization file for you automatically in the form of a server parameter file (SPFILE). Rather than having to edit the database initialization file when you want to make a change, you simply issue an alter system command to change the value in the

SPFILE. When changing dynamic parameters, you can opt to either dynamically change the value for the current instance but leave the SPFILE alone, you can change it in the SPFILE and not impact the instance, or you can change the parameter value in both the instance and the SPFILE. If the parameter were static, then you would change only the SPFILE. The following is an example of changing a parameter in both the SPFILE and the instance:

```
Alter system set open_cursors=1000 scope=both;
```

Note the SCOPE keyword: this is the key. Table 1-1 lists the three options for SCOPE.

You can reset a parameter to its default value with the alter system reset command. Additionally, you can open and read an SPFILE because most of the settings are visible in it. You should not manually alter the SPFILE via any kind of text editor, however, because Oracle includes information in the header and footer of the SPFILE to ensure its integrity.

You can convert an SPFILE to a text parameter file with the create pfile from spfile command. Conversely, you can convert a text parameter file to a SPFILE with the create spfile from pfile command. If you are running RAC, Oracle9*i* allows your different instances to share the same initialization parameter file (SPFILE or text). You can define global parameters for all databases, or specific parameters for a specific database within the same parameter file. See Chapter 4 for a more detailed discussion.

TIP
If you can't figure out why your system isn't using the value in your init.ora file, you probably have an SPFILE overriding it.

Automatic Undo Management (AUM)

Rollback segment administration is simplified in Oracle9*i* with the introduction of Automatic Undo Management. With this feature, the allocation and management of rollback segments becomes Oracle's responsibility. This feature is fairly easy to use. Simply follow these steps:

1. Create an UNDO tablespace with the create undo tablespace command or even at database creation time. Note that you can create multiple UNDO tablespaces, but only one can be in use at a time.

Option	Description
Memory	Makes the change only for the instance. If the parameter is not dynamic, an error is returned.
Spfile	Makes the change only in the SPFILE.
Both	Makes the change in the instance and the SPFILE. If the parameter is static, an error is returned.

TABLE 1-1. *Options for Changing Database Parameters with the alter system Command*

2. Modify the database initialization parameters particular to automated UNDO. These parameters include UNDO_MANAGEMENT, UNDO_TABLESPACE, and optionally, UNDO_SUPPRESS_ERRORS.

3. Restart the database.

When using Automatic Undo Management, Oracle sizes and creates the rollback segments automatically. Generally, it creates ten UNDO segments and adds additional UNDO segments as the system load requires. See Chapter 3 for additional information.

TIP
Be cautious of Automatic Undo Management in the early versions of Oracle 9.0. (This applies to 9.0.1 and 9.0.2.) A bug in Automated Undo Management can prevent your database from starting and forces you to recover it.

Resumable Space Allocation

How many times have you started a bulk SQL*Loader process or imported data into a table in your database, but the load failed because you ran out of space? Load failure caused by lack of available space can be a huge problem. Typically, you have a limited window in which to perform the load. Often, space-related failures occur in the middle or toward the end of the load, which is a big problem because you don't have enough time to restart the load. Oracle9*i* comes to the rescue with resumable space allocation.

With resumable space allocation, certain space-related errors cause the session encountering the error to suspend for a specified amount of time, allowing the DBA to correct the problem. You can use resumable space allocation to suspend the session in the following circumstances:

- You are running out of tablespace space.

- You have reached a max extent condition in the table or an associated index.

- You have exceeded a tablespace quota.

Most Oracle DML statements can use resumable space allocation features, although some restrictions apply regarding objects in dictionary-managed tablespaces. Even parallel processing can take advantage of this feature. Also, the Oracle Import utility and SQL*Loader utilities have new parameters that allow you to take advantage of this feature.

To use resumable space allocation, you must enable it on a session-by-session basis using the alter session enable resumable command. By default, if the space condition is not corrected after two hours, the transaction fails. You can configure a larger or smaller value if necessary. Once enabled, Oracle automatically detects the space condition and suspends the session. Oracle writes an entry to the alert log that the session has been suspended. Additionally, the DBA_RESUMABLE view maintains a record of all currently suspended sessions. Once the DBA has corrected the space problem, the suspended session automatically resumes its operation at the point of suspension.

Oracle also provides an AFTER SUSPEND system trigger event, which allows you to automate your response to a session suspend condition. Further, the DBMS_RESUMABLE package is provided to allow for management of resumable space allocation from within SQL or PL/SQL.

TIP
You can use resumable space allocation to suspend/resume a session that would otherwise fail with a space-related error.

Default Temporary Tablespaces

In previous versions of Oracle, users were assigned SYSTEM as the default temporary tablespace. This could lead to problems if the DBA was not careful to assign the user to the correct temporary tablespace when creating the account. Oracle9*i* solves this problem with the introduction of the default temporary tablespace. When a default temporary tablespace is defined, Oracle assigns that tablespace to each new user account as it's created. Of course, if you define a temporary tablespace for that user account, then that setting overrides the default setting.

You define an Oracle default tablespace by using the alter database default temporary tablespace command. You can also define the default temporary tablespace for the database within the confines of the create database command. If you want to change the currently defined default temporary tablespace, simply use the alter database default temporary tablespace command. All users assigned to the old default temporary tablespace will now be assigned to the newly defined default temporary tablespace. Users assigned to other temporary tablespaces will remain unchanged.

Oracle Managed Files

Oracle-Managed Files (OMF) is a new feature that allows the database to manage just about all facets of Oracle database file administration. With OMF configured properly, you don't need to define the names or locations of Oracle files or the size of the file, and you don't need to worry about removing the datafile after you have created it. You just need to configure a few parameters, and Oracle does the rest. OMF manages creation of your database REDO logs and controls files and database datafiles for you automatically. If you drop a tablespace made up of OMF datafiles, Oracle removes those datafiles from the file system.

To configure OMF, you must set these parameters:

Parameter Name	Description
db_create_file_dest	Defines the location that OMF uses to create all database datafiles. This parameter is dynamic.
db_create_online_log_dest_*n*	Allows you to define up to five different locations for multiplexed online REDO logs and control files. This parameter is dynamic.

TIP
You can use Oracle-Managed Files (OMF) to simplify database management.

Dynamic Memory Management

Sometimes you need to modify the memory allocation of your Oracle database SGA. You might want to add memory to the database default buffer cache, or maybe the shared pool; you might even want to remove memory from one of these structures. Until Oracle9*i*, the database had to be shut down before you could modify memory allocations. Oracle9*i* offers the ability to dynamically alter many memory configurations via the alter system command. Table 1-2 lists the memory cache areas that can be dynamically altered.

Note that some memory areas are still not dynamic. This includes the JAVA_POOL. Also, if you continue to use the DB_BLOCK_BUFFERS, BUFFER_POOL_KEEP, and BUFFER_POOL_ RECYCLE parameters, you will not be able to dynamically alter these memory areas either.

An additional parameter called SGA_MAX_SIZE is used to define the maximum amount of memory that can be allocated to the SGA. This parameter defaults to the total amount of memory allocated to the SGA when the database is first started. You can override this default by setting the SGA_MAX_SIZE parameter, but this task requires you to shut down and restart the database instance.

Cache Description	Parameter Name	Description
Default database data buffer cache	DB_CACHE_SIZE (New parameter in 9*i*)	Defines the size of the default database cache. Can be defined in bytes, kilobytes (KB), or megabytes (MB). Note that you allocate the default database buffer cache in bytes and not buffers, as with the DB_BLOCK_BUFFERS setting. The DB_BLOCK_ BUFFERS parameter is depreciated in Oracle9*i* in favor of this parameter.
Shared memory data buffer subcache definition	DB_NK_CACHE_SIZE (New parameter in 9*i*)	Defines the size of a database memory cache of size nK. These cache sizes come in powers of 2 (2KB, 4KB, 8KB, 16KB). The amount of memory allocated to the cache can be defined in bytes, kilobytes (KB), or megabytes (MB). This memory is not allocated from the SGA, but is allocated from free memory.
Keep cache area	DB_KEEP_CACHE_SIZE (New parameter in 9*i*)	Defines the size of the keep buffer pool. Can be defined in bytes, kilobytes (KB), or megabytes (MB). The BUFFER_POOL_KEEP parameter is depreciated in Oracle9*i* in favor of this parameter. This memory is not allocated from the SGA, but is allocated from free memory.
Recycle cache area	DB_RECYCLE_CACHE_SIZE (New parameter in 9*i*)	Defines the size of the keep buffer pool. Can be defined in bytes, kilobytes (KB), or megabytes (MB). The BUFFER_POOL_RECYCLE parameter is depreciated in Oracle9*i* in favor of this parameter. This memory is not allocated from the SGA, but is allocated from free memory.
Shared pool	SHARED_POOL_SIZE	Defines the size of the shared pool.
Large pool	LARGE_POOL_SIZE	Defines the size of the large pool.

TABLE 1-2. *Dynamic Database Parameters*

Finally, be aware that if you set the SGA_MAX_SIZE parameter on most platforms, Oracle acquires memory equivalent to SGA_MAX_SIZE from the operating system at database startup. Thus, even though your total SGA may have only 300MB allocated, if SGA_MAX_SIZE is set to 500MB, Oracle acquires 500MB from free memory.

WARNING
Be cautious setting SGA_MAX_SIZE so that you don't take memory away from user sessions or applications, and that you don't cause swapping to occur. Dynamic memory management is covered in great detail in Chapter 4.

TIP
You can use dynamic memory management to tune a database while the system is running, including altering the memory within the System Global Area (SGA).

Multiple Database Block Size Support

In previous versions of Oracle, the database was a single, consistent block size. Once that block size was fixed, that was it—the database block size was set in stone unless you re-created the database. This was problematic in many cases. For example, if you wanted to transport tablespaces between databases of different block sizes, you could not. Further, in certain conditions, hybrid databases might benefit from database data residing in tablespaces of differing block sizes.

To solve this problem, Oracle9*i* allows you to assign different block sizes to each individual tablespace (except SYSTEM, Temporary, and UNDO or Rollback segment tablespaces) as the tablespace is created. Additionally, tablespaces that are transported into the database can be a different block size than the default database block size.

We have already discussed the different shared memory subcache definitions. You will need to create shared memory subcaches before you can transport in or create a tablespace with a block size other than the default block size.

The ability to create and/or transport tablespaces with multiple block sizes has numerous applications. For hybrid databases, tablespaces with smaller block sizes may be more efficient for OLTP access, whereas those with larger block sizes may be more efficient for reporting purposes. Also, in the past it would sometimes be difficult to transport tablespaces between OLTP systems and data warehouse or reporting systems because of differing block sizes of the databases. This is no longer the case. See Chapter 4 for additional details.

WARNING
Oracle development does not support the notion of using multiple block sizes for performance tuning. The nonstandard block caches are not optimized.

TIP
With Oracle9i, each tablespace can have a different block size, thus making block size selection a less critical selection before the database is created.

Cursor Sharing

Oracle8*i* introduced a feature called cursor sharing that provided the ability of the optimizer to convert literals within SQL statements into bind variables in certain situations. As a result, SQL statements that are alike (except literal values) can share a given cursor. This has the impact of reducing the overall time to parse the SQL statement and, perhaps most importantly, reducing fragmentation of the shared SQL area of the shared pool. Unfortunately, one of the end results of cursor sharing and the use of bind variables is that the optimizer has a difficult time determining the selectivity of the data in the columns associated with the bind variable. This can lead to suboptimal execution plans. You use the parameter CURSOR_SHARING=FORCE to enable cursor sharing.

Oracle9*i* now adds modifications to cursor sharing. If you set CURSOR_SHARING=SIMILAR, the optimizer will be able to analyze the distribution of the data in the columns. (Use the analyzed statistics of the table, columns, associated indexes, and any histograms you may have generated, and determine if the parsed execution plan will be optimal. If the plan does appear to be optimal, then the parsed SQL statement will be used. See Chapter 4 for additional details.)

TIP
The initialization parameter CURSOR_SHARING can be set to minimize issues with the shared pool.

Self-Tuning PGA

Oracle9*i* can now self-tune the PGA for a given session. Previously, the DBA had a number of different parameters to choose from when tuning the memory allocated to an Oracle server session. Now, Oracle can use just one parameter, PGA_AGGREGATE_TARGET, to define the total amount of physical memory that should be made available for use by all dedicated server processes. Using this value, Oracle then derives values for parameters such as SORT_AREA_SIZE, HASH_AREA_SIZE, BITMAP_MERGE_AREA_SIZE, and CREATE_BITMAP_AREA_SIZE. Note that you can still tune individual parameters if you wish. Chapter 4 provides a detailed discussion of this topic.

Online Table Redefinition

Using the new DBMS_REDEFINITION package, you can redefine a table online, while the data in that table is still available for users to query or execute DML against. You can move the entire table, specific partitions, or any number of combinations of operations during the redefinition. Other operations might include renaming columns, moving the table to a new tablespace, converting the table to an IOT or into a partitioned table, and so on. A number of rules and limitations exist regarding online table redefinition, as you might expect.

Miscellaneous Administrative Features

A number of other administrative features are new to Oracle9*i*. You can now instruct Oracle to remove database datafiles when dropping a tablespace by using the new INCLUDING CONTENTS AND DATAFILES clause of the drop tablespace command. Here is an example:

```
DROP TABLESPACE old_data INCLUDING CONTENTS AND DATAFILES;
```

Oracle9*i* now also gives the DBA the option to prohibit any nologging operation on the database with the new FORCE LOGGING clause of the alter database or create database commands. This option is great to have if you are administering a standby database environment.

If your database has ever crashed on you in the middle of a hot backup, you know what a pain it can be to get all of the database datafiles out of hot backup mode. Oracle9*i* comes to the rescue with the alter database end backup command. Now just one command takes all the database datafiles out of hot backup mode.

Oracle9*i* also makes it easier to convert from LONG data types to LOB data types. This is facilitated through the `alter table command`, as seen here:

```
alter table my_table modify (text_column clob);
```

WARNING
Be mindful of the additional disk space requirements that accompany this conversion. You will need about twice the space of the original LONG to perform the conversion.

Another nice new feature is that SYS has truly become a privileged administrative account. Prior to Oracle9*i*, the SYS account could not grant direct access rights to objects it did not own, unless the owner of the object gave SYS the rights to do so. But in Oracle9*i*, SYS can now grant and revoke access to any object in the database at will. This new feature is closely associated with the new Oracle9*i* privilege GRANT ANY OBJECT PRIVILEGE, which can be granted to any users to allow them to administer grants throughout the database.

One final point you might be interested in is that the system tablespace can now be locally managed in Oracle9*i*R2. In fact, if you use the Database Creation Assistant in 9*i*R2, it creates the system tablespace as a locally managed tablespace by default. Note that if you make the system tablespace locally managed, no other tablespaces in the database will be able to be dictionary managed.

NOTE
If you make the system tablespace locally managed, you will not be able to create any dictionary-managed tablespaces in the database.

New Oracle9*i* Architectural Features

Oracle9*i* offers new architectural features that can help improve the performance of your database if used properly. Some of these features, out of the box, have the potential to affect your database performance without you having to do a thing. This section discusses these new features, including the following:

- New partitioning options and features
- Extraction of object metadata
- Automatic segment space management
- New indexing features

New Partitioning Options and Features

Oracle9*i* comes with some new partitioning options that you will want to know about. First, Oracle9*i* introduces a new type of partitioning called *list partitioning*: you can define a list of values associated with a partition key column and assign those values to a specific partition.

For example, if you had a retail operation in all 50 states and you often performed lookups on your customers by state, you might want to use list partitioning to partition your customer information by state.

Oracle9*i*R2 builds on the list-partitioning feature by allowing you to build range-partitioned tables that are subpartitioned using the list partition method. Also, 9*i*R2 offers an option to create a MAXVALUE partition for a list-partitioned table, which was not available in 9*i*R1. Also in 9*i*R2, Oracle has made split-partition operations more efficient. Chapter 3 discusses partitioning in detail.

TIP
Oracle9i allows greater flexibility and provides better functionality for partitioning than previous versions of Oracle.

Extraction of Object Metadata

Many DBAs have either crafted their own scripts to extract DDL from the database data dictionary, or they have purchased a tool to do it for them. Oracle9*i* simplifies the job of extracting database object DDLs by introducing the DBMS_METADATA package. It allows you to extract the DDL for objects within the database in straight text format, or you can opt to extract it in XML format. Listing 1-1 provides an example of the use of DBMS_METADATA extracting the table SCOTT.EMP.

```
SQL> set pages 0
SQL> set long 100000
SQL> Select dbms_metadata.get_ddl('TABLE', 'EMP','SCOTT') from dual;

CREATE TABLE "SCOTT"."EMP" ( "EMPNO" NUMBER(4,0), "ENAME" VARCHAR2(10), "JOB"
VARCHAR2(9), "MGR" NUMBER(4,0),
"HIREDATE" DATE, "SAL" NUMBER(7,2), "COMM" NUMBER(7,2),
"DEPTNO" NUMBER(2,0), CONSTRAINT "PK_EMP" PRIMARY KEY ("EMPNO") USING INDEX
PCTFREE 10 INITRANS 2 MAXTRANS 255 STORAGE(INITIAL 16384 NEXT 16384 MINEXTENTS 1
MAXEXTENTS 505 PCTINCREASE 50 FREELISTS 1 FREELIST GROUPS 1 BUFFER_POOL DEFAULT)
TABLESPACE "SYSTEM" ENABLE, CONSTRAINT "FK_DEPTNO" FOREIGN KEY ("DEPTNO")
```

```
REFERENCES "SCOTT"."DEPT" ("DEPTNO") ENABLE NOVALIDATE)
PCTFREE 10 PCTUSED 40 INITRANS 1 MAXTRANS 255 NOCOMPRESS LOGGING
STORAGE(INITIAL 65536 NEXT 1048576 MINEXTENTS 1
MAXEXTENTS 2147483645  PCTINCREASE 0
FREELISTS 1 FREELIST GROUPS 1 BUFFER_POOL DEFAULT)
TABLESPACE "USERS";
```

Listing 1-1: Using DBMS_METADATA to extract SCOTT.EMP

TIP
*Use the DBMS_METADATA package to extract DDL from the
database data dictionary.*

Automatic Segment Space Management

In previous versions, Oracle tracked block availability with freelists that tracked all blocks that
were available to write to. The method of tracking free space in a segment could be contentious
at times, and caused performance problems. Although freelist space management is still available
(and is the default setting), Automatic Segment Space Management (ASSM) is a new feature in
Oracle9i that is designed to simplify free space management of segments and reduce the contention
that can accompany the use of freelists. ASSM can be enabled only within a locally managed
tablespace, and all segments within a tablespace designated to use ASSM must use ASSM. To
create a tablespace that uses ASSM, use the SEGMENT SPACE MANAGEMENT AUTO parameter
of the create tablespace command.

   When you create a segment in a tablespace using ASSM, Oracle creates a series of bitmap
blocks known as bitmapped blocks (BMBs), which are stored in the segment being created
(typically at the beginning, but other BMBs can be added anywhere in the segment as needed).
The BMBs are kept current by Oracle as data in the segment is being modified, and the BMBs are
used to track data block space allocation.

   ASSM eliminates the need for freelists and freelist groups commonly associated with a Real
Application Cluster (RAC) environment. ASSM leads to better performance in many cases, particularly
if your segments contain rows that vary in size. In a Real Application Clustered environment,
segments built using ASSM can perform much better than those using freelist space management.

   Should you use ASSM? It isn't the silver bullet for all your problems, but if your problems
revolve around freelist contention, ASSM may well be your answer.

TIP
*Free space management is simplified by the introduction of Automatic
Segment Space Management (ASSM).*

New Indexing Features

Several new features related to indexing appear in Oracle9i. This section addresses those features,
including skip scanning of indexes, bitmap join indexes, and creation of bitmap indexes on
index-organized tables. Chapter 2 discusses indexing for beginners.

Skip Scanning of Indexes

Oracle9i has changed the indexing rules. Now it can perform an index skip scan operation. The skip scan operation allows the Oracle optimizer to consider any column within an index for an index scan operation, even if that column is not on the leading edge of the index. This new feature has some implications that you should consider. When you are migrating, you might find your SQL queries getting different execution plans (and hopefully running faster because of this). Therefore, the execution plan of some of your hand-crafted and hinted SQL queries might change as well. So test carefully and make sure this feature will not negatively impact your database.

Bitmap Join Indexes

Oracle9i offers some new indexing options that can help you improve your database performance. A bitmap join index creates an index that is, for all practical purposes, a prejoin of columns from two or more different tables represented in the form of a bitmap. If you have table joins that involve columns with a relatively small number of distinct values, then a bitmap join index might work for you.

Mapping Tables and Bitmap Indexes on Index-Organized Tables

Oracle9i now allows you to create bitmap indexes on index-organized tables (IOT). To create a bitmap index on an IOT, you must first create a mapping table on the table. The mapping table translates the bit in the index to a logical ROWID in the IOT. You create a mapping table when you create the IOT by using the MAPPING TABLE clause of the create table command, as seen in Listing 1-2.

```
create table tusc_employee
( emp_no   number primary key,
  ename    varchar2(50)  )
organization index
mapping table tablespace users;
```

Listing 1-2: Using the MAPPING TABLE clause of the `create table` command

Note that to add a mapping table to an existing IOT, you must rebuild the IOT and create the mapping table at that time.

One of the main purposes of mapping tables is to support another new Oracle9i feature: the ability to create secondary bitmap indexes on IOTs. You can create multiple bitmap indexes on a single IOT in Oracle9i, all of which are supported by the single mapping table.

Other New 9i Index Features

Oracle9i has added the following additional index functionality features:

- You can now create, rebuild, or coalesce IOT secondary indexes online.

- Parallel DML on IOTs is now supported.

- You can now move IOTs with overflow segments online in Oracle9i.

- You can now monitor index usage with the MONITORING USAGE clause of the alter index command. The monitoring of an index is binary in nature; in other words, you only know if the index has been used, not how many times it has been used or how recently.

New Oracle9*i* Data Warehousing Features

The following data warehouse features are new in Oracle9*i*:

- External tables
- View constraints
- Multitable INSERT statements

External Tables

Oracle9*i* allows you to access external files from within the database directly through the use of the new external table feature. An external table is defined within the database, and it points to a physical datafile that is present on the server where the database operates. You create an external table with the create table command, using the new ORGANIZATION EXTERNAL clause. Once the table is defined, you can access it with normal SQL SELECT statements. Note that you cannot currently create any indexes on external tables. If you wish to remove an existing external table, just drop it with the drop table command.

View Constraints

Query rewrite depends on the definition of constraints between related tables to work properly. This has been a problem in the past because you could not create constraints on views; thus, if a view were built on a dimension or fact table and was used in a SQL statement, Oracle could not take advantage of query rewrite (and thus, perhaps, take advantage of a materialized view).

To solve this problem, Oracle9*i* introduces view constraints. You can now define primary key, unique key, and foreign keys on a view when you issue the create view command. Alternatively, you can add constraints to the view through the alter view command. Note that any constraint that is defined will not be validated, and that NOT NULL constraints are inherited from the base table.

Multitable Insert Statements

Often, source data is destined for more than one table. In these cases, before Oracle9*i*, multiple INSERT statements would be required, which resulted in additional unnecessary I/O to the source table in order to populate the different tables. Oracle9*i* introduces multitable INSERT statements, which come in three different forms:

- **Unconditional**   Inserts the given data into multiple tables without restriction.
- **Pivoting**   Inserts data from a denormalized structure into one or more tables.
- **Conditional**   Provides for conditional control of each insert based on established specific criteria.

Listing 1-3 shows one type of multitable INSERT statement: a pivoting INSERT statement.

```
Insert all
Into all_sales values(store_id, 'Q1', sales_q1)
```

```
Into all_sales values(store_id, 'Q2', sales_q2)
Into all_sales values(store_id, 'Q3', sales_q3)
Into all_sales values(store_id, 'Q4', sales_q4)
Select store_id, sales_q1, sales_q2,
sales_q3, sales_q4
from quarterly_sales_by_store where year='2001'
```

Listing 1-3: Using a pivoting INSERT statement

In this case, we are taking a flattened, denormalized table called QUARTERLY_SALES_BY_ STORE and creating records in the ALL_SALES table in a more normalized fashion. Listing 1-4 shows an example of the QUARTERLY_SALES_BY_STORE table and the resulting ALL_SALES table after the query has been executed.

```
SQL> select * from quarterly_sales_by_store
STORE_ID SALES_Q1 SALES_Q2 SALES_Q3 SALES_Q4 YEAR
-------- -------- -------- -------- -------- ----
       1      100      200      300      600 2001
       2      200      400      600     1200 2001

SQL> select * from all_sales;
 STORE_NUM QU      SALES
---------- -- ----------
         1 Q1        100
         2 Q1        200
         1 Q2        200
         2 Q2        400
         1 Q3        300
         2 Q3        600
         1 Q4        600
         2 Q4       1200
```

Listing 1-4: Querying the QUARTERLY_SALES_BY_STORE table and results

TIP
Oracle9i introduces some powerful data warehousing features, such as external tables and multitable inserts.

New Oracle9*i* SQL and PL/SQL Features

Oracle9*i* has added much new functionality in the SQL and PL/SQL arena. New features discussed in this section include the following:

- Associative arrays
- Oracle CASE statements and expressions
- Oracle MERGE statements
- Support for ANSI/ISO SQL 1999 compliance

Associative Arrays

Until Oracle9*i*, we could associate a numeric datatype as the index to an array of a PL/SQL table via the INDEX BY BINARY_INTEGER option only when defining that PL/SQL table. Oracle9*i* now allows you to index on a Varchar datatype using the INDEX BY VARCHAR2(N) option. Here is a snippet of PL/SQL code where this is done:

```
type v_test_table is table of number
index by varchar2(100);
```

NOTE
This is an Oracle9iR2 feature.

Oracle CASE Statements and Expressions

Oracle8*i* offered a CASE statement within SQL, but no such statement was available in PL/SQL. Within PL/SQL, Oracle9*i* offers two variations of the case command, simple and searched. CASE statements do not return a value, whereas CASE expressions do return a value. Both types of case commands are available in two flavors: simple or searched. A simple `case` command evaluates only a single value, whereas a searched case value can evaluate multiple values. Listing 1-5 shows an example of the use of the case command in the form of a simple CASE expression.

```
Create or replace function calculate_values (p_input   varchar2)
Return number
Is
V_return number;
Begin
    V_return:=case p_input
         When 'EXPENSE' then 1
         When 'INCOME' then 2
         ELSE  3
    End;
    Return v_return;
End;
```

Listing 1-5: Using the `case` command in the form of a simple CASE expression

In this example, we pass a value p_input into the function. The CASE statement then evaluates the p_input value and assigns a value to the v_return variable. Listing 1-6 shows an example of a searched CASE statement.

```
Create or replace function calculate_values
(p_input   varchar2, p_number number)
Return number
Is
```

```
V_return number;
Begin
    case
        When p_input ='EXPENSE' and p_number < 1000
            Then v_return:=0;
        When p_input ='EXPENSE' and p_number < 5000
            Then v_return:=20;
        When p_input ='EXPENSE' and p_number >= 5000
            Then v_return:=40;
        Else v_return:=100;
    End case;
    Return v_return;
End;
```

Listing 1-6: Using a searched CASE statement

Oracle MERGE Statements

During different load processes, you may want to insert a record if one doesn't already exist or update a record if it already exists. Previously, you would need to write PL/SQL to perform such an operation. The new MERGE statement is designed for just such a situation. The MERGE statement allows you to insert a record into a table if it doesn't already exist, and it allows you to update an existing record in a table during the execution of the statement. Listing 1-7 shows the use of a MERGE statement.

```
Merge into all_sales_data a
Using mtd_sales_data b
On (a.sale_id=b.sale_id)
When matched then
    Update set a.sale_amt=b.sale_amt, a.store_num=b.store_num
When not matched then
    Insert (sale_id, store_num, sale_amt)
    Values (b.sale_id, b.store_num, b.sale_amt);
```

Listing 1-7: Using a MERGE statement

TIP
Oracle9i introduces the merge command, also known as the upsert command because it updates the record if it's there and inserts the record if it's not there.

Support for ANSI/ISO SQL 1999 Compliance

Oracle has added the following new SQL operators to comply with the ANSI/ISO SQL 1999 standard:

- **Cross join**   Produces a cross product of two tables, resulting in a Cartesian join
- **Natural join**   Performs a join based on like columns in two tables

- **Using** Allows specification of columns to be used as the equijoin when performing the join

- **On** Restricts the result set returned by a statement

- **Left outer join** Performs a left outer join

- **Right outer join** Performs a right outer join

- **Outer join** Performs an outer join on both tables

- **Inner join** Performs an inner join on both tables

Note that even though the outer join SQL 1999 syntax is included in Oracle9i, the old outer join operator (+) is still available.

Other Miscellaneous SQL and PL/SQL Features

A host of new features exist in 9i that deserve mention. This section covers cached execution plans, the DBMS_XPLAN, time zones, LOB support, PL/SQL native complication, character vs. byte semantics, and fine-grained auditing.

Looking at Cached Execution Plans

Sometimes explain plan output can be wrong—not often, but it can happen. If you want to see the real execution plan that Oracle is using for a given query, you can use the new V$SQL_PLAN view. This view, looking much like the Oracle PLAN_TABLE view, contains the execution plans for all SQL statements currently in the shared SQL area. It also contains address information so you can join to V$SQLAREA if you need to get at the text of the SQL statement or its execution statistics of the given SQL statements.

Generating an Explain Plan Using DBMS_XPLAN

Every DBA has his or her own script to format the results of the plan table. The problem is, you have to maintain those scripts, and you have to tote them around with you to different work sites if you are consulting. Oracle9iR2 solves this problem with DBMS_XPLAN. You can use it to display and format the execution plan for you! Listing 1-8 shows a simple example.

```
SQL> Explain plan set statement_id='TUSC' for Select * from emp;
Explained.
SQL> select * from table(dbms_xplan.display);

PLAN_TABLE_OUTPUT
--------------------------------------------------------------------
| Id  | Operation            | Name  | Rows  | Bytes | Cost  |
--------------------------------------------------------------------
|   0 | SELECT STATEMENT     |       |    15 |   495 |     2 |
|   1 |   TABLE ACCESS FULL  | EMP   |    15 |   495 |     2 |
--------------------------------------------------------------------
Note: cpu costing is off
9 rows selected.
```

Listing 1-8: Using DBMS_XPLAN

TIP

You can use DBMS_XPLAN to display a common format of a query's execution plan.

New Date and Time Datatypes, Functions, and Functionality

Oracle9i introduces the concept of time zone offsets to the database. Thus, you can establish which time zone your server is and record times based on an offset from the server time zone. You can also set the time zone at the session level, allowing applications to establish a time zone setting when they execute.

Oracle9i also introduces several new date and time datatypes to provide an additional level of precision regarding elapsed time, with a possible precision of up to nine digits. This precision is limited by the precision of the underlying operating system.

Table 1-3 lists the new date and time datatypes available in Oracle9i.

In addition to the new date/time datatypes, Oracle has introduced a host of new functions related to date and time. These include functions to manipulate the new date/time datatypes previously listed and to deal with the new time zone features in Oracle9i.

TIP

Oracle9i introduces new data/time datatypes to better handle time zones.

Better Support for LOBs

Oracle9i now provides native support for LOBs of up to 32KB. Consequently, character-based functions such as SUBSTR now work with LOBs of up to 32KB. Also, you can use the alter table command to effortlessly convert LONGs within a table to LOBs. Be aware that some significant temporary space requirements are associated with the conversion of a LONG column to a LOB.

Datatype	Description
Timestamp	Provides for a greater degree of time measurement than SYSDATE.
Timestamp with Time Zone	Provides for a greater degree of time measurement than SYSDATE, along with a representation of the time zone offset from the currently set time zone.
Timestamp with Local Time Zone	Provides for a greater degree of time measurement than SYSDATE. The output time is adjusted to reflect the time for the currently set time zone.
Interval day to second	Stores a period of time in days, hours, minutes, and seconds.
Interval year to month	Stores a period of time in months and years.

TABLE 1-3. *New Oracle9i Date and Time Datatypes*

PL/SQL Native Compilation

Oracle9*i* supports native compilation of PL/SQL stored procedures. Therefore, you can compile PL/SQL procedures with your C compiler, and they will work much faster. You need to set parameters to indicate to Oracle that you wish to compile the procedure natively. You can even use native compilation on Oracle-supplied PL/SQL packages.

Character vs. Byte Semantics

Oracle9*i* allows you to define storage of a character type using either the length of the character or bytes. This has application in multibyte character codesets (such as Unicode) to ensure that a character column can store the number of characters required.

Fine-Grained Auditing

Oracle9*i* allows you to audit all SELECT access against a specific table. Auditing occurs after you create specific audit policies that define the degree of auditing that should occur. The criteria defined in an audit policy can be granular down to the selection of a specific column or columns and based on a range of values. When Oracle executes SQL statements, the audit policies are checked to see if the SQL statement merits auditing. If so, a record is written to the DBA_FGA_ AUDIT_TRAIL table for the DBA or security staff to review later.

New Oracle9*i* Backup and Recovery Features

Several new features are present in Oracle9*i*, which can change the performance of backup and/or recovery:

- Fast start fault (time-based) recovery

- Flashback query

- New RMAN features

- New LogMiner features

- Oracle9*i* Data Guard

Fast Start Fault (Time-Based) Recovery

Fast start fault recovery (FSFR) is a new Oracle9*i* feature that is designed to reduce the overall time it takes to perform crash or instance recovery. You configure FSFR by setting the FAST_START_ MTTR_TARGET parameter, defined in seconds (0 to 3600), in the database parameter file or SPFILE. Based on this setting, Oracle dynamically derives other database parameter settings so that the requested mean time to recover (mttr) will be as close to the requested time as possible. FAST_ START_MTTR_TARGET replaces several parameters used in Oracle8*i* and earlier, such as DB_ BLOCK_MAX_DIRTY_TARGET (which is now an obsolete parameter), FAST_START_IO_TARGET, and LOG_CHECKPOINT_INTERVAL. Any of these parameters can be set manually to override the derived values that Oracle assigns to them based on the setting of FAST_START_MTTR_TARGET.

Flashback Query

Oracle9*i* offers the ability to look back into the past to see how the data looked at a specific point in time. This functionality is known as *flashback query*. With flashback query, you first define a point in time (or SCN) to flash back to at the session level using the DBMS_FLASHBACK package. Once you have defined the point in time that you wish to flash back to, all subsequent queries for that session produce results that reflect the committed state of the object being queried at approximately that flashback point in time. Once you have completed your flashback queries, you then disable flashback query, and all rows subsequently returned will represent the current temporal state of the database. Oracle9*i*R2 adds additional functionality to flashback query by allowing you to specify a flashback time for a specific individual SQL statement via the new AS OF clause.

Note that we indicated the rows returned were from approximately the flashback time requested. Oracle does round the flashback time or SCN number to 5-minute increments. Also, you can flash back only approximately five days because of internal restrictions that Oracle has placed on referencing the time and SCN. Finally, if you want to use flashback query, all of the UNDOs generated from the point in time to which you wish to flash back must be available. Oracle uses this UNDO to generate the read-consistent images that it needs to construct the flashback data. If this UNDO is not available, the flashback query returns an error. You must be using Automatic Undo Management.

TIP
Flashback query can be used to fix user errors.

New RMAN Features

RMAN has come a long way since its first introduction in Oracle8. Oracle9*i* offers a RMAN that is very functional and feature rich. For example, RMAN in Oracle9*i* offers configurable default parameters. By configuring default values for channels, and level of parallelism, a run block is often no longer needed when backing up the database. Now, database backups are often as simple as using the backup database command. Oracle9*i* also allows you to back up your database and the archive logs together in one operation with the backup database plus archivelog command.

Some sites like to back up their database to disk, and then later back up those backup set pieces to tape. Orace9*i* RMAN simplifies this task because it now has the ability to back up backup sets. Using optional arguments, you can define which backup sets you want backed up based on time or date of the backup, or other criteria.

Recovery of the control file and the database SPFILE is now much easier with the ability to automatically back up these critical components with every backup. Simply issue the configure controlfile autobackup on command, and Oracle includes the control file and database SPFILE (if one is being used) at the end of every backup. Also, if you have enabled automated backups of your control file, Oracle backs up the control file only to disk every time a change you make to the database impacts the control file.

Oracle also simplifies recovery of the control file, even when you are not using a recovery catalog. Just set the database DBID, and in some cases, allocate a channel to the backup device, and Oracle searches for the most current backup of the database control file.

A final new Oracle9i RMAN feature worth mentioning is Block Media Recovery. This functionality allows you to restore corrupted blocks from your backup sets, online. Thus, if you receive an error indicating that a given block is corrupted, RMAN can recover that block for you while the rest of the tablespace remains online.

RMAN in Oracle9i has a number of other new features outside the scope of this book. For a complete treatment on RMAN in Oracle9i, see *Oracle9i RMAN Backup and Recovery* by Robert Freeman (Oracle Press, 2002).

New Log Miner Features

Log Miner has several new features you can take advantage of in Oracle9i. First, you can instruct Log Miner to mine only committed transactions. Further, Log Miner can now translate DML statements associated with database clusters. Log Miner also supports translation of database DDL statements in Oracle9i. In addition, it supports new functionality to determine whether the catalog you are using is stale, and it allows you several different options regarding the dictionary you use to translate object information during the mining process. Finally, Log Miner can now skip REDO log corruption, providing an avenue for recovery of more transactions in the event of a major database failure.

Oracle9i *Data Guard*

Data Guard in Oracle9i replaces Oracle8i's standby database architecture. It offers several new features in Oracle9i, including the ability to configure the standby database architecture in a synchronous, no-data-loss mode. In synchronous no-data-loss mode, the primary server will not complete a commit until at least one of the remote standby servers has recorded the changes. This ensures that no data divergence occurs between the primary database and at least one of the standby servers at all times, at some performance cost. Oracle9i also allows you to manage many Data Guard configurations from OEM, making the administration of a Data Guard environment easier.

Finally, Oracle9iR2 introduces the concept of a logical standby database. The REDO logs from the primary database are archived to the standby site, where a process uses Log Miner to read the changes from the logs and then applies those changes to the standby database. The database can be open in read/write mode during this process.

Additionally, you can add more indexes on the standby database that are not present on the primary database.

TIP
Oracle9i Data Guard provides the ability to configure a standby database architecture in a synchronous, no-data-loss mode.

Real Application Clusters (RAC)

High Performance and high availability of information systems is a key requirement for day-to-day operations of the business. Since dependence on stored information has grown in the last couple of decades, large amounts of data is being accumulated and analyzed. There is an ever-increasing demand for high performance databases and at the same time, awareness and requirement for keeping such databases online all the time has increased. Global operations and e-business growth depend very much on the highly available stored data. With uneven and unpredictable load on the database systems, it became imperative for many business groups to search for high performance systems and suitable parallel systems to support complex and large database systems. Scalability is another important feature. As the business grows, data accumulation and data interaction increases. More and more users and applications begin to use the database systems. The database systems should be able to support the increased demand on the data usage without losing its performance and the scope of availability. Oracle9i introduced Real Application Clusters (RAC) to solve these issues. This section by no means covered all aspects of the RAC functioning. It merely highlighted some important concepts and inner workings of RAC. The scope of this book does not cover RAC specifically.

Parallel Databases

A Parallel Clustered Database is a complex application, which provides access to the same database (group of data tables, indexes and other objects) from any server in the cluster concurrently without compromising data integrity. Parallel databases typically contain multiple instances (nodes/servers) accessing the same physical storage or data concurrently. In terms of storage access type, parallel systems are implemented in two ways: a Shared-Nothing Model or a Shared-Disk Model.

In a **Shared-Nothing** model, also termed as Data-Partitioning Model, each system owns a portion of the database and each partition can only be read or modified by the owning system. Data partitioning enables each system to locally cache its portion of the database in processor memory without requiring cross-system communication to provide data access concurrency and coherency controls. IBM's database can operate this way.

In a **Shared-Disk model**, all the disks containing data are accessible by all nodes of the cluster. Disk sharing architecture requires suitable lock management techniques to control the update concurrency control. Each of the nodes in the cluster has direct access to all disks on which shared data is placed. Each node has a local database buffer cache. Oracle's RAC database operates this way.

With due emphasis on the high availability and high performance, Oracle has provided Oracle Parallel Server (OPS) for a long time. With Oracle9i, it drove into the next generation and re-built OPS as Real Application Clusters (RAC). RAC follows the shared-disk model, and thus has access to all the shared disks and has an extensive mechanism to coordinate the resources across the nodes. Shared disk technology has advanced rapidly over the past few years giving RAC added advantages. Storage Area Network (SAN) technology hides much of the complexities of hardware units, controllers, disk drives and interconnects from the servers, and provides just *storage volumes*. In the same way, a group of servers together in a cluster provide a single system image and computing resource. In another recent development, there has been increased interest in the Processing Area Network (PAN) as popularized by some of the new technology firms like Egenera (see http://www.egenera.com/pdf/system_data.pdf). BladeFrame computing provides hassle-free scalability in terms of adding extra nodes and management. All of these hardware advancements only strengthen an already compelling RAC story.

Architecture of Oracle RAC

At a very high level, RAC is multiple Oracle instances accessing a single Oracle database. The database is a single physical database stored on a shared storage system. Each of the instances resides on a separate host (also called node or server). All the nodes are clustered through a private interconnect and all nodes have access to the shared storage. All the nodes concurrently execute transactions against the same database. The cluster manager software, usually supplied by the cluster vendor, provides a single system image, controls node membership, and monitors the node status. Broadly, the major components include:

- Nodes/Servers

- High Speed Private Interconnect

- Cluster Manager or OSD (Operating System Dependent Layer)

- Shared Disk or Storage

- Cluster File System or Raw Devices

- Volume Manager

- Public Network

Cluster Interconnect

Parallel Processing relies on passing messages among multiple processors. Processors running parallel programs call for data and instructions, and then perform calculations. Each processor checks back periodically with the other nodes or a master node to plan its next move or to synchronize the delivery of results. These activities rely on message-passing software, such as industry-standard Message Passing Interface (MPI).

In Parallel databases, there is a great deal of message passing and data blocks, or pages, transferring to the **local cache** of another node. Much of the functionality and performance depends on the efficiency of the transport medium or methodology. It becomes very critical for the overall performance of the cluster and usage of the parallel application. As the parallel databases do not impose any constraints on the node to which users can connect and access, users have a choice to connect to any node in the cluster. Irrespective of the nature of the application, OLTP, or data warehousing databases, the movement of data blocks from one node to another using the interconnect is widely practiced. The role of the cluster interconnect to provide some kind of extended cache encompassing the cache from all the nodes is one of the most significant design features of the cluster. In general, the cluster interconnect is used for the following high-level functions:

- Health, status, and synchronization of messages

- Distributed lock manager (DLM) messages

- Accessing remote file systems

- Application-specific traffic

- Cluster alias routing

High performance, by distributing the computations across an array of nodes in the cluster, requires the cluster interconnect to provide a high data transfer rate and low latency communication between nodes. Also, the interconnect needs to be capable of detecting and isolating faults, and of using alternative paths. Some of the essential requirements for the interconnect are

- Low latency for short messages

- High speed and sustained data rates for large messages

- Low Host-CPU utilization per message

- Flow control, error control, and heartbeat continuity monitoring

- Host interfaces that execute control programs to interact directly with host processes ('OS bypass')

- Switch networks that scale well

Many of the cluster vendors have designed very competitive technology. Many of the interconnect products come close to the latency levels of a SMP (Symmetrical Multi-Processing) bus. Table 1-4 summarizes the various interconnect capabilities

The HP Memory Channel   Memory channel interconnect is a high-speed network interconnect that provides applications with a cluster wide address space. Applications map portions of this address space into their own virtual address space as 8 KB pages and then read from or write into this address space just like normal memory.

Myrinet   Myrinet is a cost-effective, high performance, packet communication and switching technology. It is widely used in Linux clusters. Myrinet software supports most of the common hosts and operating systems. The software is supplied by open source.

Scalable Interconnect (SCI)   SCI is the Sun's best performing cluster interconnect because of its high data rate and low latency. Applications that stress the interconnect will scale better using SCI compared to using our lower performing alternatives. Sun SCI implements Remote Shared Memory (RSM), a feature that bypasses the TCP/IP communication overhead of Solaris. This improves cluster performance.

Measurement	Typical SMP Bus	Memory Channel	Myrinet	SCI	Gigabit Ethernet
Latency (μs)	0.5	3	7 to 9	9	100
CPU overhead (μs)	< 1	< 1	< 1		
Messages per sec (millions)	> 10	> 2			
Hardware Bandwidth (MB/sec)	> 500	> 100	~250		~50

TABLE 1-4.   *Interconnect capabilities*

Veritas   Database Edition/Advanced Cluster (DBE/AC) communications consists of LLT (low latency transport) and GAB (Group Membership and Atomic Broadcast) services. LLT provides kernel-to-kernel communications and functions as a high performance for the IP stack. Use of LLT rather than IP reduces latency and overhead with IP stack.

HP HyperFabric Hyper Messaging Protocol (HMP)   HP Hyper-Fabric supports both standard TCP/UDP over IP and HP's proprietary Hyper Messaging Protocol. HyperFabric extends the scalability and reliability of TCP/UDP by providing transparent load balancing of connection traffic across multiple network interface cards. HMP coupled with OS bypass capability and the hardware support for protocol offload provides low latency and extremely low CPU utilization.

For building a high performance Oracle Real Application Cluster, selection of right interconnect is important. Care should be taken to select the appropriate technology suitable for your environment. Check with your vendor to get the up-to-date hardware that is available.

Internal Workings of Oracle RAC system

In 9i RAC, we no longer talk about DLM, PCM, non-PCM and Lock Monitor, etc. Most of the functionality is replaced or performed in the name of Global Cache Services. A lock is now treated as a "held resource." The background processes in the previous versions still exist, but serve different functions.

RAC Instances and Processes

RAC is a multi-instance database. Multiple instances access the same database concurrently. There is not much difference in terms of structure between a RAC instance and a stand-alone Oracle instance. Besides all the usual Oracle processes like PMON, SMON, LGWR, and DBWR, there are many special processes spawned to coordinate inter-instance communication and to facilitate resource sharing among nodes in a cluster. Because of the inter-instance buffer movement and the new set of blocks, called Past Image Blocks (to preserve data integrity), additional resources from the SGA are used.

- **LMON**   The Global Enqueue Service Monitor (LMON) monitors the entire cluster to manage global enqueues and resources. LMON manages instance and process expirations and the associated recovery for the Global Cache Service.

- **LMD**   The Global Enqueue Service Daemon (LMD) is the lock agent process that manages enqueue manager service requests for Global Cache Service enqueues to control access to global enqueues and resources. The LMD process also handles deadlock detection and remote enqueue requests.

- **LMSn**   These Global Cache Service Processes (LMSn) are processes for the Global Cache Service (GCS). RAC software provides for up to ten Global Cache Service processes. The number of LMSn varies depending on the amount of messaging traffic among nodes in the cluster.

  The LMSn processes are

  - The LMSn Handle blocking interrupts the remote instance for Global Cache Service resources

  - Manage resource requests and cross-instance call operations for shared resources

- Build a list of invalid lock elements and validate lock elements during recovery

- Handle global lock deadlock detection and monitor lock conversion timeouts

- **LCK process**   Manages global enqueue requests and cross-instance broadcasts.

- **DIAG**   The Diagnosability Daemon monitors the health of the instance. It captures data for instance process failures.

Global Cache Resources (GCS) and Global Enqueue Services (GES)

The key role is played by GCS and GES (which are basically RAC processes). GCS ensures a single system image of the data even though the data is accessed by multiple instances. The GCS and GES are integrated components of Real Application Clusters that coordinate simultaneous access to the shared database and to shared resources within the database and database cache. GES and GCS together maintain a Global Resource Directory (GRD) to record information about resources and enqueues. GRD remains in memory and is stored on all the instances. Each instance manages a portion of the directory. This distributed nature is a key point for fault tolerance of the RAC.

Coordination of concurrent tasks within a shared cache server is called synchronization. Synchronization uses the private interconnect and heavy message transfers. The following types of resources require synchronization: **Data Blocks and Enqueues.** GCS maintains the modes for blocks in the global role and is responsible for block transfers between the instances. LMS processes handle the GCS messages and do the bulk of the GCS processing.

An enqueue is a shared memory structure that serializes access to database resources. It can be local or global. Oracle uses enqueues in three modes: 1) Null (N) mode; 2) Share (S) mode; and 3) Exclusive (X) mode. Blocks are the primary structures for reading and writing into and out of buffers. It is often the most requested resource.

GES maintains or handles the synchronization of the dictionary cache, library cache, transaction locks, and DDL locks. In other words, GES manages enqueues other than data blocks. To synchronize access to the data dictionary cache, latches are used in exclusive mode and in single node cluster databases. Global enqueues are used in cluster database mode.

Cache Fusion and Resource Coordination

Because each node in Real Application Cluster has its own memory (cache) that is not shared with other nodes, RAC must coordinate the buffer caches of different nodes while minimizing additional disk I/O that could reduce performance. Cache Fusion is the technology that uses high speed interconnects to provide cache-to-cache transfers of data blocks between instances in a cluster. Cache Fusion functionality allows direct memory writes of dirty blocks to alleviate the need to **force a disk write** and re-read (or **ping**) the committed blocks. However, it is not to say that disk writes do not occur. Disk writes are still required for cache replacement and when a checkpoint occurs. Cache Fusion addresses the issues involved in concurrency between instances: Concurrent Reads on Multiple Nodes, Concurrent Reads and Writes on Different Nodes, and Concurrent Writes on Different Nodes.

Oracle only reads data blocks from disk if they are not already present in the buffer caches of any instance. Because data block writes are deferred, they often contain modifications from multiple transactions. The modified data blocks are written to disk only when a checkpoint occurs. Before we go further, let us understand some concepts introduced in 9i RAC.

Resource Modes and Roles

Because some data blocks can concurrently exist in multiple instances, there are two identifiers that help to coordinate. They are

■ **Resource mode**   The modes are null, shared, and exclusive. The block can be held in different modes depending on whether a resource holder intends to modify data or merely read them.

■ **Resource role**   The roles are locally and globally managed.

Global Resource Directory (GRD) is NOT a database. It is a collection of internal structures. It is used to find the current status of the data blocks. Whenever a block is transferred out of a local cache to another instance's cache, GRD is updated. The following information about a resource is available in GRD:

■ Data Block Identifiers (DBA)

■ Location of most current versions

■ Modes of the data blocks (N, S, X)

■ The roles of the blocks (local or global)

Past Image

To maintain the data integrity, a new concept of **Past Image** was introduced in the 9i Version of RAC. A past image (PI) of a block is kept in memory before the block is sent and an indication of whether or not it is a **dirty block**. In the event of failure, GCS can reconstruct the current version of the block by reading PI's. This PI is different from the CR block, which is needed for reconstructing read-consistent images. The CR version of a block represents a consistent snapshot of the data at a point in time.

As an example, Transaction-A of Instance-A has updated row-2 on block-5, and later another Transaction-B of Inst-B has updated row-6 on same block-5. Block-5 has been transferred from Inst-A to B. At this time, Past Image (PI) for block-5 is created on Inst-A.

SCN Processing

System Change Numbers (SCN) uniquely identify a committed transaction and the changes it makes. It is a logical timestamp that defines a committed version of a database at one point in time. Oracle assigns every committed transaction a unique SCN.

Since you have multiple instances that perform commits within RAC, the SCN changes need to be maintained within an instance, but at the same time, they must also be synchronized across all instances with a cluster. Therefore, SCN is handled by the Global Cache Service using Lamport SCN generation scheme, or by using a hardware clock or dedicated SCN server. SCNs are recorded in the redo log so that recovery operations can be synchronized in Oracle9i Real Application Clusters.

Is RAC "Unbreakable"?

Can it be brought down? Sure it can. Any bad design or choice will. There are many components involved in providing database service, besides the database itself. RAC may be up and running, but clients cannot reach it. There are intermediate network components involved between client machines and database servers. They may fail. Natural outages that destroy all of the hardware like fire, flood, and earthquake will make the cluster and database inoperable.

However, assuming that failures are localized or contained, RAC provides maximum protection and provides continuous database service. Even with the loss of many of the components, a RAC cluster can still function. But it calls for redundant design in terms of the all components involved. Design is the key word. Just setting up two or more nodes will not be enough; dual interconnects, dual paths to storage units, dual storage units, dual power supply, dual public network interface, etc. will create a robust Real Application Cluster. As an example, Table 1-5 shows the effect of individual component failures.

As long as one of the Oracle instances is available in the Cluster, client applications have data access and they can execute their applications without any problems.

Conclusion

This section by no means covered all aspects of the RAC functioning. It merely highlighted some important concepts and inner workings of RAC. Understanding special RAC requirements and implementation of global shared cache helps in proper planning of RAC and its appropriate usage.

Result	Component	Effect of Failure
OK	CPU panic/crash	Node failed, other node still active
OK	Memory crash	Node failed, other node still active
OK	Interconnect	With dual interconnects, OK
Down	Interconnect Switch	Nodes cannot communicate
OK	OS failure / freeze	Node Failed, other node still active
Down	Cluster Manager s/w	Cluster freezes, all nodes go down
OK	DB Instance Crash	Instance running on other node provides database service
OK	Control File (Corrupt / Lost)	Multiplexed control file will be used
OK	Redo log file	Multiplexed redo file
Down	Lost Data File	Requires media recovery
Down	Human Error	Depends on type of mistake
Down	Dropped Object	DB is available but applications stall
Down	DB software bug	DB may stall on all instances

TABLE 1-5. *The effect of individual component failures*

An entire book would be needed to cover RAC fully. The GV$ views are used much more to show statistics for the entire cluster, whereas the V$ views still show statistics from a single node. If you plan to use RAC, you must extend the V$ views and queries to the GV$ views for multiple nodes. This section is only an initial guide to help you see all of the components. The scope of this book does not cover RAC specifically.

TIPS
&
REVIEW

Tips Review

- Oracle9*i* provides additional space and memory requirements over previous versions of Oracle.

- If you can't figure out why your system isn't using the value in your init.ora file, you probably have an SPFILE overriding it.

- Resumable space allocation can be used to suspend/resume a session.

- Oracle-Managed Files (OMF) can be used to simplify database management.

- Dynamic memory management can be used to tune a database while the system is running, including altering the memory within the System Global Area (SGA).

- In Oracle9*i,* each tablespace can have a different block size, thus making block size selection a less critical selection before the database is created.

- The initialization parameter CURSOR_SHARING can be set to minimize issues with the shared pool.

- Oracle9*i* allows greater flexibility and provides better functionality for partitioning than previous versions of Oracle.

- You can use the DBMS_METADATA package to extract DDL from the database data dictionary.

- Free space management has been simplified with the introduction of Automatic Segment Space Management (ASSM).

- Oracle9*i* introduces some powerful data warehousing features, such as external tables and multitable inserts.

- Oracle9*i* introduces the MERGE command, also known as the upsert command because it updates the record if it's there and inserts the record if it's not there.

- You can use DBMS_XPLAN to display a common format of a query's execution plan.

- Oracle9*i* introduces new data/time datatypes to better handle time zones.

- You can use flashback query to fix user errors.

- Oracle9*i* Data Guard provides the ability to configure a standby database architecture in a synchronous, no-data-loss mode.

- RAC is the next generation is Relational Database Architecture. Get ready for it!

References

Oracle9i New Features, Robert Freeman, TUSC; Oracle Press, 2002.
Thanks to Robert Freeman for writing all but the RAC section of this chapter.
Thanks to Madhu Tumma of Credit Suisse First Boston for writing the RAC section.

CHAPTER
2

Basic Index Principles
(Beginner Developer
and Beginner DBA)

This chapter is for neither the experts nor those looking for fast answers. This is a chapter (maybe the only one) that looks at basic indexing theory. The toughest part of being a beginner is finding information that fills in the most basic gaps and visualization of Oracle's indexing capabilities. This chapter looks to serve that purpose. Although there is a considerable amount of material published at the intermediate and advanced level, the beginner's information is usually scarce, yet highly sought after.

Oracle offers a variety of indexing options. Knowing which option to use in a given situation can be crucial to an application's performance. A wrong choice may cause performance to come to a grinding halt or cause processes to be terminated because of deadlock situations. Making the correct choice can make you an instant hero, by taking processes that previously took hours or even days to run and providing the resources to finish these processes in minutes. This chapter discusses each of the indexing options and points out the benefits and limitations of each.

The topics covered in this chapter include the following:

- Basic index concepts
- Concatenated indexes
- The Oracle ROWID
- Suppressing indexes
- Selectivity
- The clustering factor
- The binary height
- Using histograms
- Fast full scans
- Skip-scans
- Types of indexes
- Fast index rebuilding

Basic Index Concepts

When accessing data from tables, Oracle has two options: to read every row in the table (also referred to as a full table scan), or to access a single row at a time by ROWID. When accessing less than 5 percent of the blocks of a table, you want to use an index. If the selected values are distributed across many blocks of the table, you may get better performance from a full table scan than from an index-based access of the rows.

With some of the new options available since Oracle8—like partitioning, parallel DML, improvements in parallel query, and larger I/O using the db_file_multiblock_read_count—the balance point between full table scans and index lookups is changing.

Indexes generally increase performance for SELECT, UPDATE, and DELETE statements (when few rows are accessed) and decrease performance for INSERT statements (because inserts to both the table and index must be performed). However, a DELETE statement deleting half of a table also needs to delete half of the rows for the index (very costly for this specific situation). In general, every index on a table slows INSERTs into the table by a factor of three; two indexes generally make the insert twice as slow as one index. (Yet, a two-part single index is not much worse than a single-part single index.)

If you update an indexed column in a table, it results in a key deletion and a key insertion in the index. An index on a table column makes the UPDATEs to that column slower by a factor of about three depending on the architecture and storage of data. An INSERT operation is also slower, because you need to insert the data record and the index record. You need to balance the index performance benefits of row retrieval against their negative effect on DML (INSERT, UPDATE, DELETE). Usually, you take the increased performance of the row retrieval by adding the index at the expense of slower DML operations on the indexed column.

To get a listing of all of the indexes on a table, query the DBA_INDEXES view, as shown in Listing 2-2. Note that you can retrieve the indexes for your schema only by accessing USER_INDEXES.

For example, suppose the indexes in Listing 2-1 have been created on the emp table provided as part of the Oracle demo tables.

```
create index emp_id1 on emp(empno, ename, deptno);
create index emp_id2 on emp (sal);
```

Listing 2-1: Creating indexes on the emp table

The query in Listing 2-2 shows the indexes on the emp table.

```
select     table_name, index_name
from       user_indexes
where      table_name = 'EMP' ;


TABLE_NAME                            INDEX_NAME
------------------------------------  ------------------------------
EMP                                   EMP_ID1
EMP                                   EMP_ID2
```

Listing 2-2: Retrieving index information

To get the specific columns that are indexed for a given table, access the USER_IND_COLUMNS view. This query is shown in Listing 2-3. Also note that DBAs can retrieve the columns that are indexed for all schemas by accessing DBA_IND_COLUMNS.

```
column index_name format a12
column column_name format a8
column table_name format a8
select     table_name, index_name, column_name, column_position
from       user_ind_columns
where      table_name = 'EMP'
order      by table_name, index_name, column_position;
```

Basic Index Concepts

TABLE_NA	INDEX_NAME	COLUMN_N	COLUMN_POSITION
EMP	EMP_ID1	EMPNO	1
EMP	EMP_ID1	ENAME	2
EMP	EMP_ID1	DEPTNO	3
EMP	EMP_ID2	SAL	1

Listing 2-3: Using the USER_IND_COLUMNS view to display the specific indexed columns for a given table

The emp table has two indexes. The first, EMP_ID1, is a concatenated index that indexes the empno, ename, and deptno columns. The second, EMP_ID2, is indexing only the sal column.

TIP
Query DBA_INDEXES and DBA_IND_COLUMNS to retrieve a list of the indexes on a given table. Use USER_INDEXES and USER_IND_COLUMNS to retrieve information for only your schema.

Concatenated Indexes

When a single index has multiple columns that are indexed, it is called a *concatenated* or *composite* index. Until Oracle9i's introduction of skip-scan index access, queries could use the index only under limited conditions.

Consider the example in Listing 2-4, where the emp table has a concatenated index key on empno, ename, and deptno. Note that empno is the first part, ename is the second part, and deptno is the third part. Prior to Oracle9i, you could not perform a range scan on the index key unless your WHERE clause specified a value for the leading column (empno). Oracle could choose to perform a fast full scan of the index in place of a full scan of the table.

```
select     job, empno
from       emp
where      ename = 'RICH';
```

Listing 2-4: Querying the emp table

The index key is not used because empno is not used in the WHERE clause, as you can see in Listing 2-5.

```
select     job, empno
from       emp
where      deptno = 30;
```

Listing 2-5: Querying the emp table – the index key is not used

The index key is not used because empno is not used in the WHERE clause, as shown in Listing 2-6.

```
select      job, empno
from        emp
where       empno = 7777;
```

Listing 2-6: Querying the emp table – a part of the index key is used

A part of the index key is used. The leading part, empno, is in the WHERE clause so Oracle performs a range scan of the index, as shown in Listing 2-7.

```
select      job, empno
from        emp
where       empno = 7777
and         empno = 'RICH';
```

Listing 2-7: Querying the emp table – a part of the index key is used

A part of the index key is used. The leading two parts are in the WHERE clause, as shown in Listing 2-8.

```
select      job, empno
from        emp
where       empno = 7777
and         ename = 'RICH'
and         deptno = 30;
```

Listing 2-8: Querying the emp table – the full index key is used

The full index key is used. All parts of the index key are used in the WHERE clause, and the number of rows is significantly reduced.

TIP
Prior to Oracle 9i, a concatenated index is used only if the leading edge of the index is being used.

The Oracle ROWID

Indexes provide Oracle with the ability to access a single row of data by supplying the ROWID of the individual row. The ROWID is a road map directly to the location of the individual row. You can also use and specify a column called rowid on any table if you would like to use it to check for duplicate values or some other reference to itself. But do this carefully because the rowid structure often changes from version to version. Index-organized tables (IOT) do not use physical rowids, so you cannot have a column of ROWIDs in an IOT. Also, if you reorganize the table (via export and import), any ROWID information stored in a table column or application is most likely made invalid.

The Oracle ROWID

TIP
Be careful when hard-coding Oracle's ROWID into specific code. The ROWID structure has changed from version to version, and it will probably change again in future releases. I recommend never to hard-code a ROWID.

Suppressing Indexes

Suppressing indexes is one of the most common mistakes of an inexperienced developer. Many traps within SQL will cause indexes not to be used. The following sections discuss some of the most common problems.

Using the NOT EQUAL Operators (<>, !=)

Indexes can be used only to find data that exists within a table. Whenever the NOT Equal operators are used in the WHERE clause, indexes on the columns being referenced cannot be used. Consider the following query on the CUSTOMERS table, which has an index on the CUST_RATING column. The statement in Listing 2-9 results in a full table scan to be performed even though there is an index on the CUST_RATING column. (A full table scan is usually desired because most records would *usually* be retrieved.)

```
select      cust_id, cust_name
from        customers
where       cust_rating <> 'aa';
```

Listing 2-9: Querying using a NOT EQUAL condition

Changing the statement to the one shown in Listing 2-10 would now use an index with the rule-based optimizer (using the index is a poor choice), but not the cost-based optimizer (much smarter).

```
select      cust_id, cust_name
from        customers
where       cust_rating < 'aa' or cust_rating > 'aa';
```

Listing 2-10: Querying using an OR condition

TIP
By replacing a NOT EQUAL operator with an OR condition, an index can be used to eliminate a full table scan, but only using rule-based optimization. Ensure that the result set retrieved is still less than 5 percent of the table volume for optimal performance.

Using IS NULL or IS NOT NULL

Using IS NULL or IS NOT NULL will also suppress index use because the value of NULL is undefined. No value in the database will equal a NULL value; not even NULL equals a NULL. The debate over NULL values in databases has gone on for many years. Some people strongly oppose their use, whereas others believe in the need to allow NULL values. NULL values pose several difficulties for SQL statements. Indexed columns that have rows containing a NULL value will not have an entry in the index. The statement shown in Listing 2-11 causes a full table scan to be performed, even though the sal column is indexed—unless the index is a bitmap index.

```
select      empno, ename, deptno
from        emp
where       sal is null;
```

Listing 2-11: Using a NULL value in a column

To disallow NULL values for all three of the columns, use NOT NULL when creating or altering the table. Note that if the table already contains data, you can set a column to NOT NULL only if it has a value for every row or if you use the DEFAULT clause of the ALTER TABLE command, as you can see in Listing 2-12.

```
alter table emp modify
(sal not null);
```

Listing 2-12: Disallowing a NULL value in a column

Note that an error will be returned if you attempt to insert a NULL value.

TIP
Creating a table specifying NOT NULL for a column will cause NULL values to be disallowed and eliminate the performance problems associated with using NULL values.

The table creation statement in Listing 2-13 provides a default value for the deptno column. When the column is not specified, the default value will be used.

```
create table employee
(empl_id number(8) not null, first_name varchar2(20) not null,
 last_name varchar2(20) not null, deptno number(4) default 10);

insert into employee(empl_id, first_name, last_name)
values (8100, 'REGINA', 'NIEMIEC');
1 row created.

select      *
from        employee;
```

Using IS NULL or
IS NOT NULL

```
   EMPL_ID FIRST_NAME           LAST_NAME               DEPTNO
---------- -------------------- -------------------- ----------
      8100 REGINA               NIEMIEC                      10

insert into employee
values (8200, 'RICH', 'NIEMIEC', NULL);

1 row created.

select     *
from       employee;

   EMPL_ID FIRST_NAME           LAST_NAME               DEPTNO
---------- -------------------- -------------------- ----------
      8100 REGINA               NIEMIEC                      10
      8200 RICH                 NIEMIEC
```

Listing 2-13: Creating a table creation with a default value for the deptno column

TIP
NULL values often cause indexes to be suppressed. Creating a table specifying NOT NULL and DEFAULT for an unspecified column can help avoid a potential performance issue.

Using Functions

Unless you are using function-based indexes, using functions on indexed columns in the WHERE clause of a SQL statement causes the optimizer to bypass indexes. Some of the most common functions are TRUNC, SUBSTR, TO_DATE, TO_CHAR, and INSTR. All of these functions cause the value of the column to be altered. Therefore, the indexes and the columns being referenced are not being used. The statement in Listing 2-14 causes a full table scan to be performed, even if there is an index on the hire_date column (as long as it isn't a function-based index).

```
select     empno, ename, deptno
from       emp
where      trunc(hiredate) = '01-MAY-81';
```

Listing 2-14: Using functions on indexed columns

Changing the statement to the one shown in Listing 2-15 allows for an index lookup.

```
select     empno, ename, deptno
from       emp
where      hiredate >= '01-MAY-81'
and        hiredate < (TO_DATE('01-MAY-81') + 0.99999);
```

Listing 2-15: Allowing for an index lookup

TIP
By altering the values being compared to the column, and not the columns themselves, the indexes become available. This is used to eliminate full table scans.

Comparing Mismatched Data Types

One of the more difficult performance issues to find is when there is a comparison of the wrong data types. Oracle does not complain about the types being incompatible—quite the opposite. Oracle implicitly converts the data in the VARCHAR2 column to match the numeric data type to which it is being compared. Consider the example in Listing 2-16, where account_number is a VARCHAR2.The following statement would cause a full table scan to be performed.

```
select    bank_name, address, city, state, zip
from      banks
where     account_number = 990354;
```

Listing 2-16: Querying with mismatched data types

Oracle internally changes the WHERE clause to be *to_number(account_number)=990354*, which suppresses the index. An EXPLAIN PLAN of this query shows only that the table was accessed using a "FULL SCAN" (usually to the bewilderment of the coder). To some DBAs and developers, this would appear to be a rare situation, but in many systems, numeric values are zero-padded and specified as VARCHAR2. The statement in Listing 2-16 should be rewritten as shown in Listing 2-17, to use the index on the account number by correctly using the single quote marks for the field.

```
select    bank_name, address, city, state, zip
from      banks
where     account_number = '990354';
```

Listing 2-17: Rewriting the query in Listing 2-16 to avoid mismatched data types

TIP
Comparing mismatched data types can cause Oracle to internally suppress an index. Even an EXPLAIN PLAN on the query will not lead you to understand why a full table scan is being performed. Only the knowledge of your data types can help you solve this problem.

Selectivity

Oracle offers several methods to determine the value of using an index, which depends on both the query and the data. One of the first ways is to determine the number of unique or distinct keys in the index. You can accomplish this task by analyzing the table or the index. Using the USER_INDEXES view, there is a column called distinct_keys. Comparing the number of distinct keys to the number of rows in the table, you can determine the selectivity of the index. The greater the selectivity, the better the index would be for returning small amounts of data.

TIP
The selectivity of an index is what helps the cost-based optimizer determine an execution path. The more selective the index is, the fewer the number of rows that will be returned for each distinct value. You can improve the selectivity by creating concatenated/composite indexes, but if the additional columns added to the index do not improve the selectivity greatly, then the cost of the additional columns may outweigh the gain.

The Clustering Factor

The clustering_factor column is in the USER_INDEXES view. This column indicates how organized the data is compared to the indexed columns. If the value of the clustering_factor column is close to the number of leaf blocks in the index, the data is well ordered in the table. If the value is close to the number of rows in the table, the data in the table is not well ordered.

For example, say the customer_id for the customers table was generated from a sequence generator and the customer_id was the primary key on the table. The index on customer_id would have a clustering factor very close to the number of leaf blocks. As the customers are added to the database, they are stored sequentially in the table the same way the sequence numbers are issued from the sequence generator. However, an index on the *customer_name* column would have a very high clustering factor because the arrangement of the customer names is random throughout the table.

If you index the customer_id column and then query the table by a range of customer numbers, the odds of getting a lot of blocks is high because each customer name might fall into a different block. If you query on a range of customer_ids, then many of the rows you'll retrieve will fall within the same block. So, if you think you're going to query a lot on customer_id, it would be great to load the table so that the rows fall into the table contiguously. If you're going to query the table by customer_name, then you might want to load the table in the order of customer names.

In a data warehouse, you may even want the same table replicated, but loaded in a different order. (Then the clustering factor would always be low.) In the data warehouse of the future (where space is even less expensive), you may even have a table for every column condition (perhaps ten of the same table loaded in ten different orders). Whereas corresponding indexes will help you retrieve the data faster in both cases, loading the data one way or the other could drastically lower the number of blocks that are retrieved.

However, there is a current downside to getting your rows in order when you load them: the problem with *hot* records. If you have a hot record (one that a lot of people want to change or read at the same time), then you don't want other often-requested records to be in the same hot block. So be careful; how you architect the system really depends on what you are trying to achieve.

The bottom line is that with a low clustering factor, the number of blocks that need to be read from the table can be dramatically lower. This, in turn, increases the possibility that those same data blocks would already be in memory (depending on the size of the cache). A high clustering factor increases the number of data blocks required to satisfy the query, making it less likely that the data is in memory.

TIP
You can use clustering of data within the table to improve the performance of statements that conduct range-scan-type operations. If you determine how the column is being used in the statements, indexing these column(s) may be a great benefit. The order in which you load the data determines how many blocks of data you'll have to retrieve.

The Binary Height

The *binary height* of an index plays a major role in the amount of I/O that needs to be performed to return the ROWID to the user process. Each level in the binary height adds an extra block that needs to be read, and because the blocks are not being read sequentially, they each require a separate I/O operation. In the following ilustration, we are retrieving the value "Him," an index with a binary height of 3, which is returning one row to the user, and would require four blocks to be read: three from the index and one from the table. As the binary height of an index increases, so will the amount of I/O needed to retrieve the data.

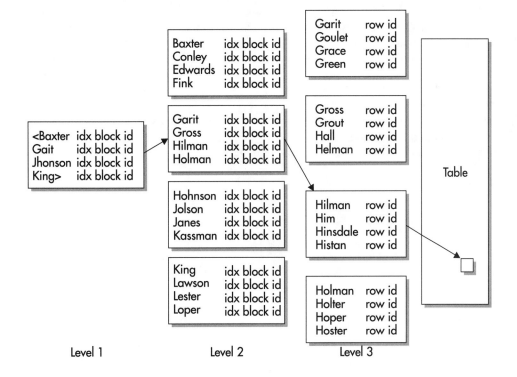

The Binary Height

After analyzing an index, you can query the b-level column of DBA_INDEXES to see its binary height, as shown in Listing 2-18.

```
EXECUTE DBMS_STATS.GATHER_INDEX_STATS ('SCOTT','EMP_ID1');

PL/SQL procedure successfully completed.

select      blevel, index_name
from        user_indexes
where       index_name = 'EMP_ID1';
    BLEVEL INDEX_NAME
---------- -----------------------------
         0 EMP_ID1
```

Listing 2-18: Analyzing an index

TIP

Analyzing the index or the table will provide the binary height of the index. Use the b-level column in the USER_INDEXES view to check the binary height of the indexes.

The binary height increases mainly due to the size of the table and the fact that the range of values in the indexed columns is very narrow. Having a large number of deleted rows in the index can also cause the height to increase. Updating the indexed column is similar to deleting because it adds to the number of deleted keys. Rebuilding the index may help to decrease the height.

TIP

If the number of deleted rows within an index approaches 20–25 percent, rebuild the indexes to help reduce the binary height and the amount of empty space that is being read during an I/O.

TIP
In general, the larger the database block size, the smaller the binary height of the index.

TIP
Each additional level in the b-level adds more performance costs during DML.

Using Histograms

The main reason for producing histograms is to help the optimizer plan properly if the data in a table is heavily skewed: for example, if one or two values make up a large percentage of a table. The creation of a *histogram* will let the cost-based optimizer know when using the index is appropriate, or when 80 percent of the table is going to be returned due to the value in the WHERE clause.

The use of histograms is not limited to indexes. Any column of a table can have a histogram built on it. Building the histograms on the indexed columns assists Oracle to determine the usefulness of an index in particular situations due to the data being skewed.

When creating histograms, a size is specified. This size relates to the number of buckets for the histogram. Each bucket contains information about the value of the column(s) and the number of rows. For example, say there is a table containing information about orders, and each order has a company code associated with it. If one company is responsible for 80 percent of the orders, the histogram may appear, as shown in Listing 2-19.

```
EXECUTE DBMS_STATS.GATHER_TABLE_STATS -
('scott','company', METHOD_OPT => 'FOR COLUMNS SIZE 10 company_code');

PL/SQL procedure successfully completed.
```

Listing 2-19: Creating a histogram

Using Histograms

This query creates a ten-bucket histogram on the COMPANY table, as shown in the following illustration.

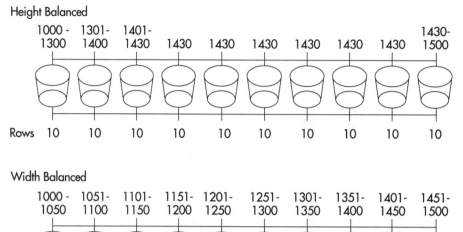

Height Balanced

1000 - 1300	1301- 1400	1401- 1430	1430	1430	1430	1430	1430	1430	1430- 1500
Rows 10	10	10	10	10	10	10	10	10	10

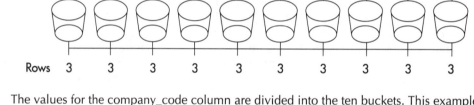

Width Balanced

1000 - 1050	1051- 1100	1101- 1150	1151- 1200	1201- 1250	1251- 1300	1301- 1350	1351- 1400	1401- 1450	1451- 1500
Rows 3	3	3	3	3	3	3	3	3	3

The values for the company_code column are divided into the ten buckets. This example shows that a large number (80 percent) of the company_code = 1430. Most of the width-balanced buckets contain only three rows; a single bucket contains 73 rows. In the height-balanced version of this distribution, each bucket has the same number of rows and most of the bucket endpoints are 1430, reflecting the skewed distribution of the data.

Oracle's histograms are height-balanced as opposed to width-balanced. Consequently, all of the buckets in the histogram contain the same number of rows. The starting and ending points for a bucket are determined by the balancing of rows contained in each bucket equally. The width-balanced histogram would specify the range values for each bucket and then count the number of rows within that range. Not an ideal option.

TIP

If the data in a table is skewed, histograms will provide the cost-based optimizer a balanced picture of the distribution (by balancing it into buckets). Using the histograms on columns that are not skewed will not provide an increase in performance.

TIP
By default, Oracle creates 75 buckets in a histogram. You can specify SIZE values ranging from 1 to 254.

Fast Full Scans

Fast full scans are an option that became available as of the release of version 7.3. This option allows Oracle to perform a full index scan operation. The fast full scan reads all of the leaf blocks in a b-tree index. The index is being read sequentially, so multiple blocks can be read at once. The DB_FILE_MULTIBLOCK_READ_COUNT parameter in the initialization file controls the number of blocks that can be read simultaneously.

The fast full scan can be used if all of the columns in the query for the table are in the index with the leading edge of the index not part of the WHERE condition. (You may need to specify the INDEX_FFS hint as detailed in Chapter 7.) In Listing 2-20, the emp table is used. It has a concatenated index on the columns empno, ename, and deptno.

```
select     empno, ename, deptno
from       emp
where      deptno = 30;
```

Listing 2-20: Querying the emp table

Because all of the columns in the SQL statement are in the index and the table has been analyzed, a fast full scan is available.

TIP
If the indexes are relatively small in comparison to the overall size of the table, the fast full scan may provide the performance burst necessary for the application. With concatenated indexes that contain most of the columns of a table, the index may be larger than the actual table, and the fast full scan could cause a degradation in performance.

TIP
Index fast full scans are commonly performed during joins in which only the indexed join key columns are queried.

Skip-Scans

As of Oracle9*i*, the index skip-scan feature enables the optimizer to use a concatenated index even if its leading column is not listed in the WHERE clause. Index skip-scans are faster than full scans of the index, requiring fewer reads to be performed. For example, the queries in Listing 2-21 show the difference between a full index scan and a skip-scan. See Chapter 6 to help you understand the execution plan or the statistics listed next.

```
create index skip1 on emp5(job,empno);

Index created.

select count(*)
from    emp5
where   empno=7900;

Elapsed: 00:00:03.13 (Result is a single row...not displayed)


Execution Plan

   0      SELECT STATEMENT Optimizer=CHOOSE (Cost=4 Card=1 Bytes=5)
   1   0    SORT (AGGREGATE)
   2   1      INDEX (FAST FULL SCAN) OF 'SKIP1' (NON-UNIQUE)

Statistics

6826  consistent gets
6819  physical reads

select /*+ index(emp5 skip1) */ count(*)
from    emp5
where   empno=7900;

Elapsed: 00:00:00.56

Execution Plan

   0      SELECT STATEMENT Optimizer=CHOOSE (Cost=6 Card=1 Bytes=5)
   1   0    SORT (AGGREGATE)
   2   1      INDEX (SKIP SCAN) OF 'SKIP1' (NON-UNIQUE)

Statistics

21  consistent gets
17  physical reads
```

Listing 2-21: Querying using a full index scan and a skip-scan

To influence the optimizer to choose a skip-scan, you may need to use a hint in the query as I just did here. Note that the hint influences the optimizer, but the optimizer might choose to ignore the hint based on other criteria. For example, if the table is very small, it may be faster to simply perform a full table scan.

TIP
For large tables with concatenated indexes, the index skip-scan feature can provide quick access even when the leading column of the index is not used in a limiting condition.

Types of Indexes

The following indexes are discussed in this section:

- B-tree indexes
- Bitmap indexes
- HASH indexes
- Index-organized tables
- Reverse key indexes
- Function-based indexes
- Partitioned indexes
- Local and global indexes

B-tree Indexes

B-tree indexes are the general-purpose indexes in Oracle. They are the default index types created when creating indexes. B-tree indexes can be single-column (simple) indexes or composite/concatenated (multicolumn) indexes. B-tree indexes can have up to 32 columns.

In the example in the following illustration, a b-tree index is located on the last_name column of the employee table. This index has a binary height of three; consequently, Oracle must go through two branch blocks to get to the leaf block containing the ROWID. Within each branch block, there are branch rows containing the block ID of the next block ID within the chain. (Level 2 in the illustration contains the block ID to go to in Level 3.)

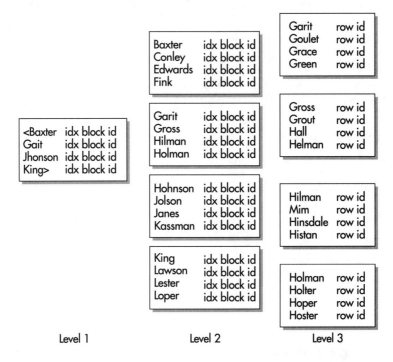

Level 1   Level 2   Level 3

 The leaf block contains the index values, the ROWID, and the data block address (DBA) for the next leaf block and the previous leaf block. Oracle then has the ability to transverse the binary tree in both directions. B-tree indexes contain the ROWIDs for every row in the table that has a value in the indexed column. Oracle does not index rows that contain NULL values in the indexed column. If the index is a concatenation of multiple columns and one of the columns contains a NULL value, the row will be in the index column containing the NULL value and will be left empty (treated as a NULL).

TIP
The values of the indexed columns are stored in an index. For this reason, you can build concatenated (composite) indexes that can be used to satisfy a query without accessing the table. This eliminates the need to go to the table to retrieve the data, reducing I/O.

Bitmap Indexes

In a *bitmap index,* Oracle builds a bitmap for each distinct key and then stores the ROWIDs associated with the key value as a bitmap. Bitmap indexes are ideal for a decision support system (DSS) and data warehouse. They provide fast access of very large tables using low- to medium-cardinality (number of distinct values) columns. Although bitmap indexes can have up to 30 columns, they are generally used for a small number of columns.

An example of where to use a bitmap index would be on a column called gender with two possible values: male and female. The cardinality would be only 2 (two unique values), and it would be a prime column for a bitmap index. The real power of the bitmap index is seen when a table contains multiple bitmap indexes. Then Oracle has the ability to merge the result sets from each of the bitmap indexes to quickly eliminate the unwanted data.

Listing 2-22 shows an example of creating a bitmap index.

```
create bitmap index dept_idx2_bm on dept (deptno);

Index created.
```

Listing 2-22: Creating a bitmap index

TIP

Use bitmap indexes for columns with a low cardinality. An example would be a column called sex with two possible values of male or female. (The cardinality is only 2.) Bitmaps are very fast for low-cardinality columns (few distinct values) because the size of the index is substantially smaller than a b-tree index. Because they are very small when they are a low-cardinality b-tree index, you can often retrieve over half of the rows in the table and still use a bitmap index.

TIP

Bitmap indexes usually outperform b-trees when loading tables (INSERT operations). Generally, bitmaps are three to four times faster than a b-tree index for low-cardinality columns (few distinct rows), but when new values account for over 70 percent of the inserts, b-trees are generally faster. When new records account for every record, b-trees are three times faster than bitmap indexes.

Bitmap Index Example

Consider a sample table called participant that contains surveys from individuals. The columns age_code, income_level, education_level, and marital_status have a separate bitmap index built into them. The following illustration displays the balance of the data in each histogram and the EXPLAIN PLAN output for a query accessing each of the bitmap indexes. The EXPLAIN PLAN output shows how the multiple bitmap indexes have been merged, creating a significant

Bitmap Indexes

performance gain. The result set from each bitmap index is combined with a single AND operation. The result is then converted into ROWIDs.

AGE_CODE	INCOME_LEVEL	EDUCATION_LEVEL	MARITAL_STATUS
18-22 A	10,000-14,000 AA	High School HS	Single S
23-27 B	14,001 - 18,000 BB	Bachelor BS	Married M
28-32 C	18,001 - 22,000 CC	Masters MS	Divorced D
33-37 D	22,001 - 26,000 DD	Doctorate PhD	Widowed W
...	...	...	...

```
Select ...
From Participant
Where Age_code = 'B'
  And Income_Level = 'DD'
  And Education_Level = 'HS'
  And Marital_Status = 'M'

SELECT STATEMENT Optimizer=CHOOSE
  SORT (AGGREGATE)
    BITMAP CONVERSION (RowID)
      BITMAP AND
        BITMAP INDEX (SINGLE VALUE) of 'PART_INCOME_LEVEL'
        BITMAP INDEX (SINGLE VALUE) of 'PART_AGE_CODE'
        BITMAP INDEX (SINGLE VALUE) of 'PART_EDUCATION_LEVEL'
        BITMAP INDEX (SINGLE VALUE) of 'PART_MARITAL_STATUS'
```

With multiple b-tree indexes, each index returns a range of ROWIDS that have to be compared with the range of ROWIDs produced by the other indexes. Each set needs to be compared, combined, and then compared with another set, until the final set of rows is determined. Because you store a unique column only once in a bitmap, there is a substantial space savings when the column is not very unique over b-tree indexes (as long as the cardinality is low).

TIP
Merging multiple bitmap indexes can lead to significant performance improvement when combined in a single query. Bitmap indexes also work better with fixed-length data types than they do with variable-length data types. Large block sizes improve the storage and read performance of bitmap indexes.

The query in Listing 2-23 displays index types. B-tree indexes are listed as NORMAL; bitmap indexes have an index_type value of BITMAP.

```
select index_name, index_type
from   user_indexes;
```

Listing 2-23: Displaying index types

TIP
To query a list of your bitmap indexes, query the index_type column in the USER_INDEXES view.

Bitmap indexes are not recommended for online transaction processing (OLTP) applications. B-tree indexes contain a ROWID with the indexed value, so Oracle has the ability to lock the index at the row level. Bitmap indexes are stored as compressed indexed values, which can contain a range of ROWIDs, so Oracle has to lock the entire range of the ROWIDs for a given value. This type of locking has the potential to cause deadlock situations with certain types of DML statements. SELECT statements are not affected by this locking problem.

Bitmap indexes have several restrictions, including the following:

- Bitmap indexes are not considered by the rule-based optimizer.

- Performing an ALTER TABLE statement and modifying a column that has a bitmap index built into it invalidates the index.

- Bitmap indexes do store the index key value in the index block; however, they cannot be used for any type of integrity checking.

- Bitmap indexes cannot be declared as unique.

TIP
Don't use bitmap indexes in heavy OLTP environments.

HASH Indexes

Using *HASH indexes* requires the use of HASH clusters. When a cluster or HASH cluster is created, a cluster key is defined. This key tells Oracle how to store the tables in the cluster. When data is stored, all the rows relating to the cluster key are stored in the same database blocks. With the data being stored in the same database blocks, using the HASH index, Oracle can access the data by performing one HASH function and one I/O—as opposed to accessing the data by using a b-tree index with a binary height of 4, where there would potentially need to be four I/Os performed to retrieve the data. The diagram in the following illustration shows an example of this.

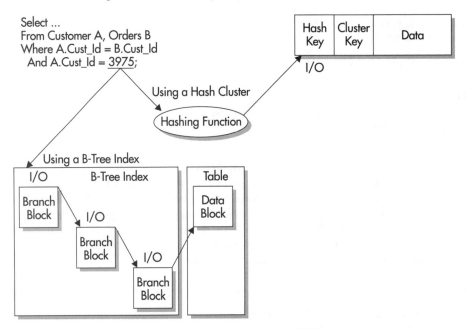

HASH indexes can potentially be the fastest way to access data in the database, but they do have drawbacks. The number of distinct values for the cluster key needs to be known before the HASH cluster can be created. This value needs to be specified at the time of creation. Underestimating the number of distinct values can cause collisions (two cluster key values with the same HASH value) within the cluster. These collisions are very costly. Collisions cause overflow buffers to be used to store the additional rows, thus causing additional I/O. If the number of distinct HASH values has been underestimated, the cluster will need to be re-created to alter the value. An `alter cluster` command cannot change the number of HASH keys.

HASH clusters have a tendency to waste space. If it is not possible to determine how much space is required to hold all of the rows for a given cluster key, space may be wasted. If it is not possible to allocate additional space within the cluster for future growth, then HASH clusters may not be the best option.

If the application often performs full table scans on the clustered table(s), HASH clusters may not be the appropriate option. Because of the amount of empty space within the cluster to allow for future growth, full table scans can be very resource-intensive.

 TIP
Be careful before implementing HASH clusters. The application should be reviewed fully to ensure that enough information is known about the tables and data before implementing this option. Generally, HASHing is best for static data with primarily sequential values.

TIP
Hash indexes are most useful when the limiting condition specifies an exact value rather than a range of values.

Index-Organized Tables

An index-organized table is stored in the order of the primary key, whereas a regular table is stored as an unorganized heap. An index-organized table alters the storage structure of a table to that of a b-tree index, sorted on the table's primary key. This unique type of table is treated like any other table. All DML and DDL statements are allowed. ROWIDs are not associated with the row of the table because of the structure of the table.

Index-organized tables provide faster key-based access to the data for statements involving exact match and range searches. UPDATE and DELETE statement performance may be improved because only the single structure needs to be modified. The amount of storage required is reduced because values of the key columns are not duplicated in the table and then again in an index. Index-organized tables can be partitioned, and you can index them using bitmap indexes.

Oracle also provides an even faster index-organized table where there is a row-overflow area. Based on parameters that you set, Oracle will store the extra (beyond the primary key and other nonkey columns that don't fit into your parameters) into an overflow area (heap) that connects to the index-organized table via a physical ROWID. The parameters you can set include the PCTTHRESHOLD, which is a percentage of each block. You can also set the parameter INCLUDING. It names a specific column, which is the last nonkey column in the CREATE TABLE that is allowed in the index-organized table; the rest go in the overflow area. The goal here, of course, is to ensure that the data in the overflow area is rarely needed or accessed. Obviously, if you need the overflow data, the access of it will be slow.

TIP
Consider using index-organized tables for tables that are always accessed using exact matches or range scans on the primary key.

TIP
You can create secondary indexes on index-organized tables.

Reverse Key Indexes

When sequential data is loaded, the index may encounter I/O-related bottlenecks. During the data loads, one part of the index and one part of the disk may be used much more heavily than any other part. To alleviate this problem, you should store your index tablespaces on disk architectures that permit the files to be physically striped across multiple disks.

Oracle provides reverse key indexes as another solution to this performance problem. When data is stored in a reverse key index, its values are reversed prior to being stored in the index. Thus, the values 1234, 1235, and 1236 are stored as 4321, 5321, and 6321. As a result, the index may update different index blocks for each inserted row.

You cannot reverse a bitmap index or an index-organized table.

TIP
If you have a limited number of disks and large concurrent sequential loads to perform, reverse key indexes may be a viable solution. For data loads (INSERT operations), reverse key indexes were between two-and-a-half to three times slower than b-tree indexes.

Function-Based Indexes

You can create *function-based indexes* on your tables. Without function-based indexes, any query that performs a function on a column cannot use that column's index. Thus, the query in Listing 2-24 cannot use an index on the JOB column.

```
select *
from    emp
where   UPPER(job) = 'MGR';
```

Listing 2-24: Querying on a column without a function-based index

The query in Listing 2-25 can use an index on the JOB column.

```
select * from emp
 where job = 'MGR';
```

Listing 2-25: Querying on a column using a function-based index

As of Oracle8i, you can create indexes that allow function-based queries to be supported by index accesses. Instead of creating an index on the column job, you can create an index on the column expression UPPER(job), as shown in Listing 2-26.

```
create index EMP$UPPER_JOB on
emp(UPPER(job));
```

Listing 2-26: Creating an index on a column expression

Although function-based indexes can be useful, be sure to consider the following questions when creating them:

- Can you restrict the functions that will be used on the column? If so, can you restrict all functions from being performed on the column?

- Do you have adequate storage space for the additional indexes?

- When you drop the table, you will be dropping more indexes (and therefore more extents) than before; how will that impact the time required to drop the table?

Function-based indexes are useful, but you should implement them sparingly. The more indexes you create on a table, the longer all INSERTs, UPDATEs, and DELETEs will take.

NOTE
For function-based indexes to be used by the optimizer, you must set the QUERY_REWRITE_ENABLED initialization parameter to TRUE. (Its default value is FALSE.)

To see the magnitude of the benefit of function-based indexes, consider the example in Listing 2-27, which includes a table that is a million rows.

```
select    count(*)
from      sample
where     ratio(balance,limit) >.5;

Elapse time: 20.1 minutes

create index ratio_idx1 on
sample (ratio(balance, limit));

select    count(*)
from      sample
where     ratio(balance,limit) >.5;

Elapse time: 7 seconds!!!
```

Listing 2-27: Processing benefit of a function-based index

Partitioned Indexes

A *partitioned index* is simply an index broken into multiple pieces. By breaking an index into multiple pieces, you are accessing much smaller pieces (faster), and you may separate the pieces onto different disk drives (eliminating I/O issues). Partitioned indexes were introduced in Oracle8. Both b-tree and bitmap indexes can be partitioned. HASH indexes cannot be partitioned. Partitioning can work several different ways. The tables are partitioned but the indexes are not partitioned; the table is not partitioned but the index is; or both the table and index are partitioned. Either way, the cost-based optimizer must be used. Partitioning adds many possibilities to help improve performance and increase maintainability.

Two types of partitioned indexes exist: local and global. Each type has two subsets, prefixed and nonprefixed. A table can have a number of combinations of the different types of indexes built on its columns. If bitmap indexes are used, they must be local indexes. The main reason to partition the indexes is to reduce the size of the index that needs to be read and the ability to place the partitions in separate tablespaces to help improve reliability and availability.

Oracle also supports parallel query and parallel DML when using partitioned tables and indexes. (See Chapter 11 for more information.) This adds the extra benefit of multiple processes helping to process the statement faster. Prior to Oracle9*i,* the maximum degree of parallelism is limited to the number of partitions.

Local (Commonly Used) Indexes

Local indexes are partitioned using the same partition key and same range boundaries as the table. Each partition of a local index contains keys and ROWIDs only from its corresponding table partition. Local indexes can be b-tree or bitmap indexes. If they are b-tree indexes, they can be unique or nonunique.

This type of index supports partition independence, meaning that individual partitions can be added, truncated, dropped, split, taken offline, etc., without dropping or rebuilding the indexes. Oracle maintains the local indexes automatically. Local index partitions can also be rebuilt individually while the rest of the partition goes unaffected.

Prefixed   *Prefixed indexes* contain keys from the partitioning key as the leading edge of the index. For example, let's take the participant table again. Say the table was created and range-partitioned using the survey_id and survey_date columns, and a local prefix index is created on the survey_id column. The partitions of the index are equipartitioned, meaning that the partitions of the index are created with the same range boundaries as those of the table.

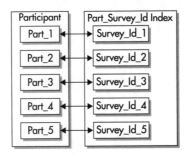

TIP
Local prefixed indexes allow Oracle to quickly prune unneeded partitions. This means that the partitions that do not contain any of the values appearing in the WHERE clause will not need to be accessed, thus improving the performance of the statement.

Nonprefixed   *Nonprefixed indexes* do not have the leading column of the partitioning key as the leading column of the index. Using the same participant table with the same partitioning key (survey_id and survey_date), an index on the survey_date would be a local nonprefixed index. A local nonprefixed index could be created on any column in the table, but each partition of the index will contain the keys only for the corresponding partition of the table.

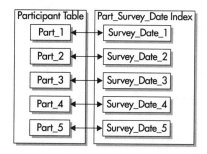

For a nonprefixed index to be unique, it must contain a subset of the partitioning key. In this example, we would need a combination of columns, including the survey_date and/or the survey_id columns. (As long as the survey_id column was not the leading edge of the index, it would be a prefixed index.)

TIP
For a nonprefixed index to be unique, it must contain a subset of the partitioning key.

Global Indexes

Global partitioned indexes contain keys from multiple table partitions in a single index partition. The partitioning key of a global partitioned index is different or specifies a different range of values. The creator of the global partitioned index is responsible for defining the ranges and values for the partitioning key. Global indexes can only be b-tree indexes. Global partitioned indexes are not maintained by Oracle. If a partition is truncated, added, split, dropped, etc., the indexes need to be rebuilt.

Prefixed   Normally, global prefixed indexes are not equipartitioned with the underlying table. Nothing prevents the index from being equipartitioned, but Oracle does not take advantage of the equipartitioning when generating query plans or executing partition maintenance operations. If the index is going to be equipartitioned, it should be created as a local index to allow Oracle to maintain the index and use it to help prune partitions that will not be needed.

TIP
If a global index is going to be equipartitioned, it should be created as a local index to allow Oracle to maintain the index and use it to help prune partitions that will not be needed.

Nonprefixed   Oracle does not support nonprefixed global indexes.

Partitioned Indexes

Fast Index Rebuilding

The REBUILD option of the ALTER INDEX statement is executed to quickly rebuild an index using the existing index instead of the table. Listing 2-28 shows the syntax.

```
alter index cust_idx1 rebuild parallel
tablespace cust_tblspc1
storage (pctincrease 0);

Index altered.
```

Listing 2-28: Using the rebuild option of the alter index statement

Modifications to the STORAGE clause can be made at this time, and the parallel option may also be used.

TIP
Use the REBUILD option of the ALTER INDEX statement for quickly rebuilding an index using the existing index instead of the table. You must have enough space to store both indexes during this operation.

TIP
You can use the REBUILD ONLINE option to allow DML operations on the table or partition during the index rebuild. You cannot specify REBUILD ONLINE for bitmap indexes or for indexes that enforce referential integrity constraints.

Tips Review

- Query dba_indexes and dba_ind_columns to retrieve a list of the indexes on a given table. A concatenated index will be used only if the leading edge of the index is being used.

- Be careful when hard-coding Oracle's ROWID into specific code.

- By replacing a NOT EQUAL operator with an OR condition, an index can be used to eliminate a full table scan.

- Creating a table specifying NOT NULL for a column will cause NULL values to be disallowed and eliminate the performance problems associated with using NULL values.

- By altering the values being compared to the column and not the columns themselves, the indexes become available. This is used to eliminate full table scans.

- Comparing mismatched data types can cause Oracle to internally suppress an index. Even an EXPLAIN PLAN on the query will not lead you to understand why a full table scan is being performed.

- The selectivity of an index is what helps the cost-based optimizer determine an execution path. The more selective it is, the fewer the number of rows returned. Improve the selectivity by creating concatenated/composite indexes.

- In general, the larger the database block size, the smaller the binary height of the index.

- Each additional level in the Blevel adds additional performance costs during DML.

- The clustering of data within the table can be used to improve the performance of statements that perform range-scan-type operations. By determining how the column is being used in the statements, indexing these column(s) may be a great benefit.

- Analyzing the index or the table provides the binary height of the index. Use the Blevel column in the USER_INDEXES view to check the binary height of the indexes.

- If the number of deleted rows within an index approaches 20–25 percent, rebuild the indexes to help reduce the binary height and the amount of empty space that is being read during an I/O.

- If the data in a table is skewed, histograms provide the cost-based optimizer a picture of the distribution. Using the histograms on columns that are not skewed will not provide an increase in performance, but will probably degrade it.

- By default, Oracle creates 75 buckets in a histogram. You can specify SIZE values ranging from 1 to 254.

- If the indexes are relatively small in comparison to the overall size of the table, then the fast full scan may provide the performance burst necessary for the application. With concatenated indexes that contain most of the columns of a table, the index may be larger than the actual table, and the fast full scan could cause degradation in performance.

- Index fast full scans are commonly performed during joins in which only the indexed join key columns are queried.

- For large tables with concatenated indexes, the index skip-scan feature can provide quick access even when the leading column of the index is not used in a limiting condition.

- The values of the indexed columns are stored in an index. For this reason, you can build concatenated (composite) indexes that can be used to satisfy a query without accessing the table. This eliminates the need to go to the table to retrieve the data, reducing I/O.

- Use bitmap indexes for columns with a low cardinality. An example is a column called sex, with two possible values of *male* or *female*. (The cardinality is only 2.)

- To query a list of your bitmap indexes, query the USER_INDEXES view.

- Merging multiple bitmap indexes can lead to significant performance improvement when combined in a single query. Bitmap indexes also work better with fixed-length data types than variable-length data types. Large block sizes improve the storage and read performance of bitmap indexes.

- Bitmap indexes usually outperform b-trees when loading tables (INSERT operations). Generally, bitmaps are three to four times faster than a b-tree index for low-cardinality (few distinct rows) columns. When new values account for over 70 percent of the inserts, b-trees are generally faster. When new records account for every record, b-trees are three times faster than bitmap indexes.

■ Don't use bitmap indexes in heavy OLTP environments; learn the restrictions associated with bitmap indexes.

■ Use caution before implementing HASH clusters. Review the application carefully to ensure that enough information is known about the tables and data before implementing this option. Generally speaking, HASHing is best for static data with primarily sequential values.

■ Hash indexes are most useful when the limiting condition specifies an exact value rather than a range of values.

■ Consider using index-organized tables for tables that are always accessed using exact matches or range scans on the primary key.

■ If you have a limited number of disks and large concurrent sequential loads to perform, reverse key indexes may be a viable solution.

■ For function-based indexes to be used by the optimizer, you must set the QUERY_REWRITE_ENABLED initialization parameter to TRUE. (Its default value is FALSE.)

■ Local prefixed indexes allow Oracle to quickly prune unneeded partitions. The partitions that do not contain any of the values appearing in the WHERE clause will not need to be accessed, thus improving the performance of the statement.

■ For a nonprefixed index to be unique, it must contain a subset of the partitioning key.

■ If a global index is going to be equipartitioned, it should be created as a local index to allow Oracle to maintain the index and use it to help prune partitions that will not be needed.

■ Use the REBUILD option of the ALTER INDEX statement for quickly rebuilding an index using the existing index instead of the table.

■ You can use the REBUILD ONLINE option to allow DML operations on the table or partition during the index rebuild. You cannot specify REBUILD ONLINE for bitmap indexes or for indexes that enforce referential integrity constraints.

References

Oracle Indexing; Greg Pucka, TUSC
Oracle7 Server Tuning; Oracle Corporation
Oracle8 Server Tuning; Oracle Corporation
Server Concepts; Oracle Corporation
Server Reference; Oracle Corporation
Oracle8 DBA Handbook; Kevin Loney
Tuning Tips: You will be Toast!; Rich Niemiec
Greg Pucka contributed the major portion of this chapter.
Kevin Loney contributed the major portion of the update for this chapter.

CHAPTER
3

Disk I/O and
Fragmentation (DBA)

U nbalanced disk I/O and UNDO management can hamper performance. This chapter investigates correctly locating and configuring some of the physical data files related to the Oracle database. The initialization parameters that relate to disk I/O are covered in Chapter 4 and also in Appendix A. This chapter focuses primarily on the physical files that make up the Oracle database and those tips and new features that can help you use your hardware most effectively. The chapter concludes with a list to help you plan your next system, or system upgrade, by posing questions designed to address common database administration issues.

The topics covered in this chapter include the following:

- Using disk arrays

- Distributing key data files across available hardware disks

- Using locally managed tablespaces

- Using table partitioning on large tables

- Using index partitioning

- Understanding fragmentation

- Eliminating fragmentation

- Using UNDO management

- Using rollback segments

- Using the simpler approach: undo tablespace

- Sorting in memory to reduce disk I/O

- Having multiple control files on different disks and controllers

- Using raw devices to improve I/O for write-intensive data

- Examining other disk I/O precautions and tips

- Considering issues in the planning stages

Using Disk Arrays

With the improvements in hardware and file systems and reduced cost in disk arrays, RAID has become essential in boosting I/O operations for Oracle databases. Special care must be taken, however, to both assure that the disk array configuration used enhances I/O while also providing appropriate protection against drive failure. Whether the RAID configuration is hardware or software based (I prefer hardware based), the configuration should be set up properly for best performance. The primary advantage of using disk arrays for Oracle database performance is that access to files is spread across multiple physical devices and controllers automatically. This greatly simplifies management of both small and large systems and can reduce the number of file systems across which you have to manage your data files.

A disk array is created by grouping several disks in such a way that the individual disks act as one logical disk. Therefore, during normal operation, a single logical device gets the benefit of multiple physical devices behind it. If a disk fails and all the data on the disk is destroyed, the group of disks can be structured so the data exists in more than one place. The system never goes down due to the failure of a single disk. Users continue to operate as if nothing has happened when there is a disk failure. The system alerts the system administrator that a specific disk has failed. The administrator pulls out the disk and slides in a new disk. The operating system automatically writes the missing information on the new disk. The system goes on without missing a beat.

Available RAID Levels

Most hardware companies offer disk arrays as their primary storage solution because of the benefits they provide to performance and availability. In addition, the RAID levels available have become pretty much standard regardless of the type of array you buy. The following list describes some of the more common options that you will want to consider:

- **RAID0** This level provides automatic disk striping. This means that the distribution of Oracle is automatically spread across multiple disks. The tablespace's corresponding data file pieces can be spread across and accessed from ten disks at the same time instead of one (a large savings in disk I/O).

- **RAID1** Automatic disk mirroring is available on most systems today. It's usually used for the operating system itself, but can be used with Oracle for higher availability.

- **RAID5** This level carries the parity on an extra disk, which allows for media recovery. Heavy read applications get the maximum advantage from this disk array distribution. It is a low-cost solution that is inefficient for write-intensive applications.

- **RAID 1+0** This level provides mirrored disks and striping. This incorporates the advantages of the first two RAID levels by providing the disk I/O benefit of RAID0 to the redundancy provided by RAID1. For high read/write environments such as OLAP, where sporadic access to data is the norm, this RAID level is recommended.

Many DBAs install systems with a RAID5 disk array to maximize use of available space on disk. Although RAID5 is a good choice for inexpensive redundancy, it is usually a poor choice for write-intensive performance. When a write request is made to a RAID5 array, a stripe of data must first be read from the array (usually 64–256KB), the new data is added to the stripe, a new parity block is calculated, and the data is written to disk. This process, regardless of the size of the write request, can limit throughput.

I recommend RAID5 only for mostly read or read-only file systems. I prefer to see RAID1+0 (striping with mirroring). RAID1+0 is faster because it does not have the same parity computation overhead as RAID5, and most RAID controllers will read from both sides of the mirror at the same time, effectively doubling your read throughput. Of course, with drive manufactures pushing 46GB hard disks these days, spreading out I/O is increasingly difficult.

Simplifying Setup and Maintenance

Using disk arrays makes Oracle data file setup and maintenance *much* easier for DBAs because manually balancing disks is not so arduous. While the automatic striping means that placement of database files is less crucial and more I/O efficient, it's still recommended that you manually balance disk I/O by properly setting up your file systems.

For example, consider setting up multiple logical devices instead of simply lumping them all together. This allows you to retain some control over where you place database files but gives you the benefits of the disk array for each of the file systems independently.

TIP
Never split a logical device in a disk array into two file systems. This eliminates your control over balancing I/O because you could mistakenly place two files that should be separated on the same physical devices without knowing it.

Is the Disk Array Made for a 24-Hour Shop?

Absolutely! The disk array using RAID means that media recovery relying or based on backups is less likely (higher availability). The operating system can take care of the recovery on its own most of the time, if a single disk goes bad. Usually, the operator need only replace the bad disk, and the information that is redundant in the array is automatically copied to disk. This affords the system less duplication in backup and recovery schemes.

Considering the Cost

To support disk arrays that mirror data, you need more (much more) disk storage along with faster and/or more processors. Although this can increase the price of your initial system, the benefits are usually well worth it. For these reasons, before making the decision to use disk arrays, think about how valuable it is to keep your system up and running. Also, keep in mind that most hardware companies offer disk arrays as standard solutions. Although it may be possible to configure a disk array to not use RAID, it is probably already part of the package.

Things to Remember

Remember the following tips:

- Use disk arrays to improve performance and protect your data against disk failure.

- Avoid creating a single logical device because this prevents you from properly balancing database files. One of the biggest mistakes I see sites making is setting up one and only one disk RAID, and then putting Oracle on it, with database, redo logs, and archives. They then expect to be able to fully recover if the raid architecture fails!

- Select the RAID level based on the availability your corporation needs to support compared to the costs of the additional hardware.

Distributing Key Data Files Across Available Hardware Disks

To operate the Oracle database efficiently, you must take special care to distribute key data files across available file systems. For example, heavily accessed tables should be located on file systems separate from corresponding indexes. In addition, online redo logs, control files, and archive logs should be stored separately from data files for recovery purposes.

The following files are of major concern:

- The SYSTEM tablespace

- The TEMPORARY tablespace

- The rollback segments or UNDO tablespace

- The online redo log files (try to put on your fastest disks)

- Key Oracle files located in the Oracle_Home directory

- Data files for heavily accessed tables

- Data files for heavily accessed indexes

- The operating system

Listing 3-1 illustrates file distribution across 11 file systems in a UNIX environment.

```
/: Operating System

/u01: Oracle software
/u02: Temporary Tablespace, Control File 1
/u03: Rollback Segments, Control File 2
/u04: Redo Logs, Archive Logs, Control File 4
/u05: System Tablespace
/u06: Data1, Control File 3
/u07: Redo Log Mirror, Index3
/u08: Data2
/u09: Index2
/u10: Data3
/u11: Index1
```

Listing 3-1: File distribution across 11 file systems

Storing Data and Index Files in Separate Locations

Tables that are joined (simultaneously accessed during a query) often should have their data and index separated. Listing 3-2 shows a table join and one possible solution for managing the data.

```
select  COL1, COL2 ....
from    CUST_HEADER, CUST_DETAIL
where   ...;

Disk1: CUST_HEADER Table
Disk5: CUST_HEADER Index
Disk8: CUST_DETAIL Table
Disk12: CUST_DETAIL Index
```

Listing 3-2: Table join and data management solution

Distributing Key Data

This solution allows the table join to be done while accessing four different disks and controllers. Separate data and index files onto different physical disks and controllers; consequently, when tables and indexes are accessed at the same time, they are not accessing the same physical disk. This could be expanded to involve a larger number of disks. Table and index partitioning help us accomplish this task more easily. As we'll see in "Avoiding Disk Contention by Using Partitions," table and index partitioning help us to accomplish this task more easily.

TIP
Separate key Oracle data files to ensure that disk contention is not a bottleneck. By separating tables and indexes of often-joined tables, you can ensure that even the worst of table joins do not result in disk contention.

Things to Remember
Remember the following tips:

- Distribute key data files (SYSTEM tablespace, TEMPORARY tablespace, rollback segments or UNDO segments, online redo logs files, the operating system disk, key Oracle files located in the ORACLE_HOME directory, data files for heavily accessed tables, and data files for heavily accessed indexes) across available hardware disks.

- Store data and index files in separate locations.

- For frequently joined tables, separate all data and index tablespaces so that none of the information from either table is located on the same disk.

- Store multiple copies of your control files on different disks and controllers.

Avoiding I/O Disk Contention
Disk contention occurs when multiple processes try to access the same physical disk simultaneously. Disk contention can be reduced, thereby increasing performance, by distributing the disk I/O more evenly over the available disks. Disk contention can also be reduced by decreasing disk I/O. To monitor disk contention, use the FILEIO Monitor to accomplish these tasks:

- Show how the actual database files are being hit by the users

- Move tables and indexes to spread hits equally across all disks

Use the FILEIO Monitor within Enterprise Manager to determine the I/O that is taking place on each database file. If the reads and writes are not distributed evenly between files, the tablespaces may need to be restructured for better performance. Figure 3-1 depicts a database that isn't distributed correctly because Disk1 is getting more hits by users. This is happening because the DBA didn't configure a TEMP tablespace, so sorting is done within the SYSTEM tablespace. An optimally balanced I/O distribution is shown in Figure 3-1 for comparison with the actual distribution.

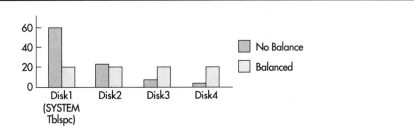

FIGURE 3-1. *File I/O Percentage of Hits Across All System Disks (Simple View)*

You can also determine file I/O problems by running the query shown in Listing 3-3.

```
set pagesize 100
col PHYRDS   format 999,999,999
col PHYWRTS  format 999,999,999
ttitle  "Disk Balancing Report"
col READTIM   format 999,999,999
col WRITETIM   format 999,999,999
col name format a40
spool fio1.out

select   name, phyrds, phywrts, readtim, writetim
from     v$filestat a, v$dbfile b
where    a.file# = b.file#
order    by readtim desc
/
spool off
```

Listing 3-3: Determining file I/O problems

The query output is shown in listing 3-4.

```
Fri Mar 24                                          page 1

                    Disk Balancing Report


NAME                      PHYRDS    PHYWRTS    READTIM    WRITETIM

/d01/psindex_1.dbf        48,310    51,798     200,564     903,199
/d02/psindex_02.dbf       34,520    40,224     117,925     611,121
/d03/psdata_01.dbf        35,189    36,904      97,474     401,290
/d04/rbs01.dbf             1,320    11,725       1,214      39,892
/d05/system01.dbf          1,454        10          10         956
```

Listing 3-4: Query output

A large difference in the number of physical writes and reads between disks shows which disk is being overburdened. In Listing 3-3, disks 1–3 are heavily used, while disks 4–5 are only lightly used. To get a better balance, you'll want to move the data files. Splitting data files across multiple disks or using partitions would also help move access to a table or an index to an additional disk.

TIP
Query v$filestat, joined with v$dbfile, to see how effectively data files have been balanced.

Moving Data Files to Balance File I/O

When you have a large imbalance if file I/O, you need to physically move data files to balance file I/O. To physically move a data file that is causing file contention, follow these steps:

1. Take the tablespace corresponding to the data file offline:

   ```
   ALTER TABLESPACE ORDERS OFFLINE;
   ```

2. Copy the data file to the new location on disk:

   ```
   $cp /disk1/orders1.dbf /disk2/orders1.dbf   (UNIX copy command)
   ```

3. Rename the data file to the new data file location for the tablespace:

   ```
   ALTER TABLESPACE ORDERS
   RENAME DATAFILE '/disk1/orders1.dbf' to '/disk2/orders1.dbf';
   ```

4. Bring the tablespace back online:

   ```
   ALTER TABLESPACE ORDERS ONLINE;
     Delete the old data file (when sure the moved data file can be accessed):

   $rm /disk1/orders1.dbf   (UNIX delete command)
   ```

TIP
Solve disk contention problems by moving data files to disks that are not as heavily accessed.

Things to Remember

Remember the following tips:

- Use the FileIO Monitor in Enterprise Manager (or v$filestat) to determine the I/O that is taking place on each database file.

- Restructure the tablespace if reads and writes are not distributed evenly between files.

Using Locally Managed Tablespaces

Prior to Oracle 8*i*, all tablespace extent information for segments was maintained by the Oracle data dictionary. As a result, any operations that occurred against segments in the database that related to extent allocation, such as extending or truncating a table, would incur operations against the data dictionary. This could become very expensive from the database management point of view because the data dictionary could become a bottleneck for these operations when many tables with many extents were involved.

With Oracle 8*i*, a new extent management option was provided called locally managed extents. With locally managed extents, these extent management operations were relocated to a bitmap block in the tablespace itself. This allows for improved performance because each tablespace in the database can now perform its own extent management instead of sharing a common location.

In addition to the improvements in where extents are managed, locally managed tablespaces use one of two options for how extents are allocated to segments that reside in the tablespace. These two options are autoallocate and uniform. In an autoallocate management scheme, Oracle uses an internal algorithm to increase extent sizes for segments as they grow. This method causes extents to vary in size to allow the segment to grow.

In uniform extent management, all extents in a tablespace are allocated with an equal size that is specified when the tablespace is created. This method is preferred because it reduces fragmentation of the tablespace and allows improved organization of segments by size. We discuss this further in the 'Eliminating Fragmentation" section later in the chapter.

Creating Tablespaces as Locally Managed

To create a tablespace as locally managed, use the extent management clause on the CREATE TABLESPACE statement to set the mode in which extents will be allocated:

```
CREATE TABLESPACE USER_256K_DAT datafile '/u01/user_256k_dat_01.dbf' SIZE
100M extent management local uniform size 256K;
```

Listing 3-5: Creating a tablespace

I recommend that when using uniform locally managed uniform tablespaces, you specify the extent size in the tablespace name. This allows you to more easily determine what the extent size for a segment is that resides in the tablespace and can make it easier to determine which tablespace a segment should be moved to when its size gets too large for the current tablespace.

If EXTENT_MANAGEMENT LOCAL is specified, you cannot specify the DEFAULT storage clause, which includes PCTINCREASE, INITIAL, NEXT, MINEXTENTS, MAXEXTENTS, FREELISTS, OPTIMAL, and BUFFER POOL. These parameters are ignored with respect to how extents are allocated, but they could cause confusion because other dictionary views such as dba_segments show the initial extent size to be what was defined in the segment storage clause.

In Oracle 9*i*R2, even the SYSTEM tablespace can be locally managed. If compatibility is 9.0 or higher, Oracle creates a locally managed tablespace by default, if the EXTENT_MANAGEMENT clause is not specified. Whether it is created as a uniform or autoallocated tablespace depends on the settings for MINEXTENT, INITIAL, NEXT, and PCTFREE.

Locally Managed Tablespaces

To get more information about the extent management of tablespaces in the database, use the query shown in Listing 3-6 (partial output displayed).

```
SELECT  tablespace_name, extent_management, allocation_type
  from  dba_tablespaces;


TABLESPACE_NAME        EXTENT_MAN ALLOCATIO
-----------------      ---------- ---------
SYSTEM                 DICTIONARY USER
TOOLS                  LOCAL      UNIFORM
TEMP                   LOCAL      UNIFORM
USERS                  LOCAL      UNIFORM
TS_SMALL_64K_DAT       LOCAL      UNIFORM
```

Listing 3-6: Getting more information about the extent management of tablespaces in the database

Migrating Dictionary-Managed Tablespaces to Locally Managed

It is possible to migrate dictionary-managed tablespaces to a locally managed method, but this is not recommended. The extent map is part of the segment header. At the tablespace level, you keep track of used and free extents. A list of extents for an object (extent map) is stored in the header block for each segment. This applies to dictionary and locally managed tablespaces. For dictionary-managed tablespaces, the tracking of used and free extents is done through the data dictionary tables uet$ and fet$. For locally managed tablespaces, bitmaps for managing free space are created in the datafile, but not in the file header.

The bitmaps go in their own blocks and are placed at the beginning of the file when a new datafile is created. Because the file already exists for migrated tablespaces, Oracle can't put these bitmap blocks at the front of the files, so they find room at the end of the file (space for the next free extent). For the migration to succeed, there must be enough free space left in the tablespace to create the bitmap blocks.

Whenever possible, rebuild dictionary-managed tablespaces to a locally managed uniform extent mode by using this method: export segments in the locally managed uniform tablespaces by dropping and re-creating the tablespace and then importing the segments back. Be sure to check your segment sizes before you perform this process. It might be more beneficial to split the single tablespace into several different tablespaces with differently sized extents to accommodate segments of vastly different sizes.

Also note that you can specify a TABLESPACE level export now. This exports all the tables in the tablespace, and their indexes (regardless of their tablespace) and all tables that have a partition located in the list of tablespaces.

Things to Remember

Remember the following tips:

- Create new tablespaces as locally managed tablespaces with a uniform extent size.

- Name tablespaces to include the size of the extent allocation to simplify the process of relocating segments.

■   Avoid migrating tablespaces to locally managed because it does not incorporate the
extent size management properties of these types of tablespaces.

NOTE
*(From a friend "down under"): "When I set up my databases now, I
create five locally managed tablespaces, one of type small, medium,
large, image, and index, with the blocks in each set to 16KB, 64KB,
1MB, 16MB, and 128KB. When it comes to putting tables in the
appropriate tablespace, it's easier to quickly work out whether
the tables are small, medium, or large, and then put them in the
appropriate tablespace. Makes it easier for developers. I don't really
know if this strategy is sound, but it really makes life a lot easier."*

Viewing File/Tablespace Information Using Enterprise Manger

You can also view tablespace and data file information by using Oracle's Enterprise Manager.
Chapter 5 covers this tool in depth, but a quick look is worth an additional mention here.

Performance Manager: Database Instance Information

Figure 3-2 shows how we can display file I/O information related to a given instance in the
Enterprise Manager utility provided by Oracle Corporation. The I/O-specific areas are located
in the Performance Manager section of the tool. A variety of additional options are available
within the tool, which are explored in Chapter 5.

You can access specific file I/O information or even system I/O, which includes information
about memory access, block writes, and physical reads, with Enterprise Manager. Although
Chapter 4 addresses issues related to initialization parameters and memory, remember that if
you allocate memory properly, physical disk I/O is also reduced.

Using indexes and tuning queries that cause large amounts of memory use can also decrease
physical disk reads. The lesson to learn is that major file I/O can't always be directly attributed to
disk balancing or object balancing. You must consider many factors.

Avoiding Disk Contention by Using Partitions

Some DBAs I know wouldn't consider partitioning a table unless it is at least 1GB in size, and
would use only composite partitioning if the table is at least 10GB in size. I usually partition
tables at 100MB. This number differs depending on environmental conditions.

Partitioning is probably the single best option available for increasing the performance related
to large tables. Partitioning is a way to increase efficiency by accessing smaller pieces of a table
or index instead of accessing the full table or index. This strategy can be particularly useful when
one or more users are accessing multiple parts of the same table. If these partitions (pieces) of the
table reside on different disks, the throughput is greatly increased.

Partitions can also be backed up and recovered independently of each other (even while
they are in use), eliminating potential disk I/O issues during backup times. Only when partitions
are properly implemented are the best performance-enhancing features of Oracle realized.

Locally Managed Tablespaces

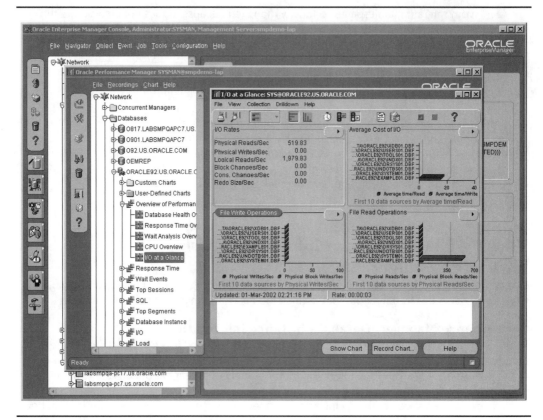

FIGURE 3-2. *Accessing File I/O Information about an Oracle Instance*

The best way to understand partitioning is to look at an example. Consider the one shown in Listing 3-7, where the dept table is partitioned into three partitions (pieces) using the deptno column.

```
create table dept
 (deptno        number(2),
  dept_name     varchar2(30))
  partition     by range(deptno)
(partition d1 values    less than (10) tablespace dept1,
 partition d2 values    less than (20) tablespace dept2,
 partition d3 values    less than (maxvalue) tablespace dept3);
```

Listing 3-7: Partitioning the dept table

In this example, I built three distinct partitions on the dept table. The key to getting better throughput is to ensure that each partition is placed on a different physical disk so that all three partitions can be accessed simultaneously. The tablespaces dept1, dept2, and dept3 must have physical files that are located on different physical disks.

Remember that the tablespace is the logical holder of information where the data file is the physical disk. You can have one tablespace that includes multiple data files, but a data file can relate to only a single tablespace. The key to partitioning to improve disk I/O is to ensure that the partitions that will be accessed simultaneously are located on different physical disks.

Data is entered into all three partitions of the table, as shown in Listing 3-8.

```
insert into dept values (1, 'ADMIN');
insert into dept values (7, 'MGMT');
insert into dept values (10, 'MANUF');
insert into dept values (15, 'ACCT');
insert into dept values (22, 'SALES');
COMMIT;
```

Listing 3-8: Entering data into all three table partitions

The dept table still looks like a single table when we select from it, as you can see in Listing 3-9.

```
select  *
from    dept;

DEPTNO   DEPT_NAME
1        ADMIN
7        MGMT
10       MANUF
15       ACCT
22       SALES
```

Listing 3-9: Viewing the dept table

We selected all records from all of the partitions in Listing 3-8. In the examples in Listing 3-10, we select individually from each partition; we select from a single partition and access only a *single* partition.

```
select  *
from    dept partition (d1);

DEPTNO   DEPT_NAME
1        ADMIN
7        MGMT

select  *
from    dept partition (d2);

DEPTNO   DEPT_NAME
10       MANUF
15       ACCT

select  *
from    dept partition (d3);
```

```
DEPTNO     DEPT_NAME
22         SALES

select  *
from    dept partition
where   deptno = 22;

DEPTNO     DEPT_NAME
22         SALES
```

Listing 3-10: Selecting from and accessing one partition (three examples)

Note that in Listing 3-10, we are eliminating the need to access the first or second partition (partition elimination). Partitioning indexes and using the parallel option along with partitions make partitioning even more powerful. Using RACs (Real Application Clusters) is even more powerful.

TIP
To minimize disk I/O on a single large table, break the table into multiple partitions that reside in tablespaces on different physical disks.

Getting More Information About Partitions

We can retrieve the information regarding partitions by accessing user_tables, dba_part_tables, and user_segments. Example queries to these three tables are displayed in Listings 3-11 through 3-13 with corresponding output for the examples in the previous section.

```
select  table_name, partitioned
from    dba_tables
where   table_name in ('DEPT','EMP');

TABLE_NAME     PAR
DEPT           YES
EMP            NO
```

Listing 3-11: Retrieving information about tables

In Listing 3-11, the par column indicates whether a table is partitioned.

```
select  owner, table_name, partition_count
from    dba_part_tables
where   table_name = 'DEPT';

OWNER      TABLE_NAME     PARTITION_COUNT
KEVIN      DEPT           3
```

Listing 3-12: Retrieving partition information

In Listings 3-12 and 3-13, there are three partitions on the dept table.

```
select   segment_name, partition_name, segment_type, tablespace_name
from     user_segments;


SEGMENT NAME    PARTITION NAME   SEGMENT TYPE        TABLESPACE NAME
EMP                              TABLE               USER_DATA
DEPT            D1               TABLE PARTITION     DEPT1
DEPT            D2               TABLE PARTITION     DEPT2
DEPT            D3               TABLE PARTITION     DEPT3
```

Listing 3-13: Retrieving table information

TIP

Tables can be easily partitioned into individual pieces to be accessed and/or manipulated; you can still access the entire table with a partitioned index or access the entire partitioned table with an index. Accessing the tables dba_tables, dba_part_table, and dba_segments provides additional information concerning tables that have been partitioned.

Other Types of Partitions

Several types of partitioning exist. The main ones are range, hash, composite, and list partitioning. There are also multiple index types associated with partitions. We've covered range partitioning in the previous section, but there is also multicolumn range partitioning as well.

Multicolumn Range Partitioning

Multicolumn range partitioning is the same as range partitioning except you use multiple columns to define the ranges. In Listing 3-14, we are breaking the data into quarters so that we can eliminate the quarters that we don't need when we view a single quarter, but also so that we can archive the data one quarter at a time without interfering with another quarter. We are also segmenting the data into multiple tablespaces as well so that better I/O is achieved.

```
create table cust_sales
(acct_no      number(5),
 cust_name    char(30),
 item_id      number(9),
 sale_day     integer not null,
 sale_mth     integer not null,
 sale_yr      integer not null)
partition by range (sale_yr, sale_mth, sale_day)
(partition cust_sales_q1 values less than (1998, 04, 01) tablespace users,
 partition cust_sales_q2 values less than (1998, 07, 01) tablespace users2,
 partition cust_sales_q3 values less than (1998, 10, 01) tablespace users,
```

Avoiding Disk Contention
by Using Partitions

```
partition cust_sales_q4 values less than (1999, 01, 01) tablespace users2,
partition cust_sales_qx values less than (maxvalue, maxvalue, maxvalue)
tablespace users2);
```

Listing 3-14: Breaking the data into quarters

TIP
You can also partition tables using multiple columns as the criteria.
You must specify maxvalue for all columns that are part of the
partition key.

Hash Partitioning

Hash partitioning is usually used when you are unsure where to put the breakpoints as you do in range partitioning. It breaks up data into the number of partitions specified based on the hash of the partition key specified. To get an even distribution, you should always specify a power of 2 (2, 4, 8, 16, etc.) as the number of hash partitions. Hash partitioning supports only local indexes. You can specify the names of the index and table partition names, and you can later add or reduce the number of partitions if you find you have too many or too few. Listing 3-15 shows a table with four hash partitions that is built on the partitioning key ACCT_NO and distributed across four tablespaces.

```
create table cust_sales_hash (
acct_no     number(5),
cust_name  char(30),
sale_day integer not null,
sale_mth  integer not null,
sale_yr     integer not null)
partition by hash (acct_no)
partitions 4
store in (users1, users2, users3, users4);
```

Listing 3-15: Creating a table with four partitions and data distributed across all four

TIP
When you don't know how to break up a table, but you know that it
needs to be partitioned and spread out, use hash partitioning.

Composite Partitioning

Sometimes a table is so large and accessed so frequently that you need a much better way to slice and dice it. Composite partitioning is the combination of using range and hash partitioning. You use range to allow partition elimination and then hash the partitions further. Composite partitioning supports local indexes and range-partitioned global indexes. Listing 3-16 shows an example of composite partitioning that could lead to incredible job security.

```
create table orders(
ordid number,
acct_no    number(5),
```

```
cust_name char(30),
orderdate date,
productid number)
 partition by range(orderdate)
 subpartition by hash(productid) subpartitions 8
   (partition q1 values less than  (to_date('01-APR-1998', 'dd-mon-yyyy')),
    partition q2 values less than  (to_date('01-JUL-1998', 'dd-mon-yyyy')),
    partition q3 values less than  (to_date('01-OCT-1998', 'dd-mon-yyyy')),
    partition q4 values less than(maxvalue));
```

Listing 3-16: Creating a table with composite partitioning

This example builds partitions based on the range of values listed for the ORDERDATE and puts them into partitions q1, q2, q3, and q4. It then subpartitions each of these into eight partitions based on a hash of the PRODUCTID. Also note that a query against USER_SEGMENTS shows only subpartitions numbered 5–36. The partitions of a composite-partitioned table are logical structures only as their data is stored in the segments of their subpartitions.

List Partitioning

Oracle9*i* added list partitioning for the DBA or developer who really knows their data well. List partitioning allows you to assign the individual column values associated with each of the partitions. Several restrictions on list partitioning are displayed after Listing 3-17.

```
create table dept_part
(deptno     number(2),
 dname      varchar2(14),
 loc        varchar2(13))
partition by list (dname)
(partition d1_east  values ('BOSTON', 'NEW YORK'),
partition d2_west  values ('SAN FRANCISCO', 'LOS ANGELES'),
partition d3_south values ('ATLANTA', 'DALLAS'),
partition d4_north values ('CHICAGO', 'DETROIT'));
```

Listing 3-17: Creating a table with list partitioning

List Partitioning Restrictions

List partitions have the following restrictions:

- You can specify only one partitioning key in the column list, and it cannot be a LOB column. If the partitioning key is an object type column, you can partition on only one attribute of the column type.

- Each partition value in the VALUES clause must be unique among all partitions of the table.

- You cannot list partition an index-organized table.

- The string comprising the list of values for each partition can be up to 4KB.

- The total number of partition values for all partitions cannot exceed 64KB-1.

- You cannot subpartition a list partition.

- MAXVALUE is not specified.

Partitionwise Joins

Oracle also allows two partitioned tables to be joined by only their partitions. Instead of joining many rows to many rows, you can now perform partition elimination on each table and then join the results. To join on partitions, the tables must be equipartitioned tables, which means the following:

- The tables are partitioned using the same partition key.

- The tables must be partitioned with the same partition break points.

Other Partitioning Options

This section covers some of the many options that can be used with partitioning. You can see that many of the options available for operations on tables are also available for partitions.

- **MODIFY PARTITION partition_name**   Modifies the real physical attributes of a table partition. You can specify any of the following as new physical attributes for the partition: LOGGING, ATTRIBUTE, PCTFREE, PCTUSED, INITRANS, MAXTRANS, and STORAGE.

- **RENAME PARTITION partition_name TO new_partition_name**   Renames table partition PARTITION_NAME to NEW_PARTITION_NAME.

- **MOVE PARTITION partition_name**   Moves table partition PARTITION_NAME to another segment. You can move partition data to another tablespace, recluster data to reduce fragmentation, or change a create-time physical attribute:

```
alter table dept move partition d3 tablespace dept4;
```

Listing 3-18: Moving a partition

In Listing 3-18, the d3 partition and all corresponding data is moved from the dept3 tablespace, where it originally resided, to the dept4 tablespace. Also note that if in the previous command, you add the NOLOGGING clause, it would set this partition to be a NOLOGGING partition. This means that any future DML performed on this partition is not logged in the redo, which is not good for recovery, making this partition unrecoverable by the redo application. To unset this attribute, you need another ALTER TABLE command. The NOLOGGING attribute also makes the local index UNUSABLE.

Table 3-1 shows the available partitioning options.

- **ADD PARTITION new_partition_name**   Adds a new partition new_partition_name to the high end of a partitioned table. You can specify any of the following as new physical attributes for the partition: LOGGING, PCTFREE, PCTUSED, INITRANS, MAXTRANS, and other storage attributes.

Maintenance Operation	Range	Hash	List	Composite
Add Partitions	X	X	X	X*
Coalesce Partitions		X		X**
Drop Partitions	X		X	X
Exchange Partitions	X	X	X	X*
Merge Partitions	X		X	X
Move Partitions	X	X	X	X**
Rename Partitions	X	X	X	X*
Split Partitions	X		X	X
Truncate Partitions	X	X	X	X*

* - applies also to subpartition
** - applies to subpartition only

TABLE 3-1. *Oracle available partitioning options*

- **VALUES LESS THAN (value_list)**   Specifies the upper bound for the new partition. The value_list is a comma-separated, ordered list of literal values corresponding to column_list. The value_list must collate greater than the partition bound for the highest existing partition in the table.

- **DROP PARTITION partition_name**   Removes partition partition_name, and the data in that partition, from a partitioned table:

```
alter table dept drop partition d3;
```
Listing 3-19: Dropping a partition

TIP
Dropping a table partition causes its local index (but not the other local partition indexes) to be dropped and a global index (one that exists on the entire table) to be unavailable. If you use global indexes, you will need to rebuild them if you drop partitions of a table.

- **TRUNCATE PARTITION partition_name**   Removes all rows from a partition in a table. Listing 3-20 shows the truncation of the d1 partition. When you perform a truncate, an index rebuild is not needed, unless you want to reduce the depth of the b-tree.

```
Alter table dept truncate partition d1;
Alter index dept_index rebuild partition d1;
```
Listing 3-20: Truncating a partition

Avoiding Disk Contention by Using Partitions

■ **SPLIT/MERGE PARTITION partition_name_old** Creates two new partitions, each with a new segment, new physical attributes, and new initial extents. The segment associated with the old partition is discarded. (The merge is the reverse of this.) Listing 3-21 shows *splitting* the d1 partition into a d1a partition and d1b partition at deptno=5.

```
Alter table dept split partition d1 at (5) into
  (partition d1a tablespace dept1,
   partition d1b tablespace dept2) ;
```

Listing 3-21: Splitting a partition

Note that if you want to rebuild the global indexes during this step, you add the UPDATE GLOBAL INDEXES clause to the end of the statement. Then, you don't have to rebuild the global indexes afterwards (shown after Listing 3-22).

```
SELECT segment_name, partition_name, segment_type
FROM   user_segments
WHERE  segment_name LIKE 'DEPT%';

   SEGMENT_NAME PARTITION_NAME SEGMENT_TYPE
   ------------ -------------- ----------------
   DEPT         D1A            TABLE PARTITION
   DEPT         D1B            TABLE PARTITION
   DEPT         D2             TABLE PARTITION


Alter index dept_index rebuild partition d1a;
Alter index dept_index rebuild partition d1b;
```

Listing 3-22: Rebuilding the global index

Listing 3-23 shows *merging* the d1a and d1b partition back into the partition named d1. Note that you must rebuild any global indexes and the local indexes for the altered partition after this operation if you don't include the UPDATE GLOBAL INDEXES clause.

```
Alter table dept merge partitions d1a, d1b
  into partition d1;

   SEGMENT_NAME PARTITION_NAME SEGMENT_TYPE
   ------------ -------------- ----------------
   DEPT         D1             TABLE PARTITION
   DEPT         D2             TABLE PARTITION

Alter index dept_index rebuild partition d1;
```

Listing 3-23: Merging partitions

■ **UNUSABLE LOCAL INDEXES** Marks all the local index partitions associated with partition_name as unusable.

- **REBUILD UNUSABLE LOCAL INDEXES** Rebuilds the unusable local index partitions associated with partition_name.

- **UNUSABLE** Marks the index or index partition(s) as unusable. An unusable index must be rebuilt, or dropped and re-created before it can be used. Whereas one partition is marked unusable, the other partitions of the index are still valid, and you can execute statements that require the index if the statements do not access the unusable partition. You can also split or rename the unusable partition before rebuilding it.

- **REBUILD PARTITION** Rebuilds one partition of an index. You can also use this option to move an index partition to another tablespace, or to change a create-time physical attribute.

Using Index Partitioning

Partitioned indexes have the same advantages as partitioned tables. Accessing smaller pieces instead of one index on the entire table increases performance when properly executed. There are local and global indexes, and prefixed or nonprefixed indexes. A local index has been partitioned; each piece is a local index. A global index is a nonpartitioned index, used before partitioning existed. A local index is an index for a single partition of a table. A local partitioned index is an index that is partitioned using the same partitioning key as the table on which it is created. This is also a prefixed index.

A global index is an index that does not use the same partitioning key as the partitioned table. A global index can be partitioned. A global index is a nonprefixed index. If you have a large partitioned table, and you need to access a column that is not part of the partitioning key, a global partitioned index on this column is the method I would choose if subpartitioning were not an option. If a partition of a table with a global index is dropped, the corresponding global index is invalidated. If a partition of a table with a local index is dropped, the local index is also dropped. You can also have a partitioned index on a nonpartitioned table.

Listing 3-24 is an example of a local partitioned index (the most common type). The index name is dept_index, and the index is on the deptno column of the dept table. The index is split into three pieces (d1, d2, and d3) that are located in three tablespaces (dept1, dept2, and dept3) that are striped differently from the location of the corresponding data. This ensures that accessing information from a partition of a table and its corresponding index partition results in accessing two physical disk drives instead of one—given that dept1 through dept3 are tablespaces that correspond to data files on different physical disks.

```
create index dept_index on dept (deptno)
  local
 (partition d1 tablespace dept2,
  partition d2 tablespace dept3,
  partition d3 tablespace dept1);

Index Created.
```

Listing 3-24: Creating a local partitioned index

Avoiding Disk Contention by Using Partitions

We can get the information regarding partitioned indexes by accessing dba_ind_partitions, as shown in Listing 3-25.

```
select      index_name, partition_name, tablespace_name
from        dba_ind_partitions
where       index_name = 'DEPT_INDEX'
order by  partition_name;


INDEX_NAME      PARTITION_NAME      TABLESPACE_NAME
DEPT_INDEX                  D1                  DEPT2
DEPT_INDEX                  D2                  DEPT3
DEPT_INDEX                  D3                  DEPT1
```

Listing 3-25: Accessing dba_ind_partitions

TIP
Indexes that are partitioned should also be prefixed; the partitioning key is the leading edge of the index.

Exporting Partitions

Partitions can be effortlessly exported. If the data in your table is segmented carefully, you can keep all new information in a single partition to export. This eliminates the need to export data from partitions that have not changed and have been previously exported. By using the export command and giving the owner.table.partition_name for the table to be exported, only the partition is exported.

```
exp user/pass file=tab.dmp tables=(owner.table.partition_name)
```

Listing 3-26: Exporting partitions

TIP
If data is partitioned correctly, all the new information falls into a single partition, enabling an export of a single partition of a large table during backups. This could save you time in your backup plan scenarios.

Eliminating Fragmentation

Fragmentation can hamper space management operations in the database, but it is a long-endured myth that overall, the number of extents in a segment *always* impacts performance against the database. It is an equally long-enduring myth that the number of extents *never* impacts performance. Bitmap indexes with many noncontiguous extents spanning multiple datafiles can be a big performance problem.

But generally, locally managed tablespaces have minimized most extent-related issues greatly. The need for reorganization is becoming a thing of the past, but when you need to reorganize the database, Oracle now has ways of doing it while the data is online or still available.

To avoid performance issues with extent management, you can do the following:

- Use locally managed uniform extent tablespaces.

- Use uniform extent sizes in dictionary-managed tablespaces, except the SYSTEM tablespace.

- Use extent sizes that are multiples of the database block size.

- Never set PCTINCREASE to anything other than zero in dictionary-managed tablespaces.

- Locate tables to tablespaces with an appropriate extent size.

- Avoid chaining by correctly setting PCTFREE (amount of space reserved in a block for updates).

- Rebuild or split tablespaces that contain large tables on a single disk.

- Avoid bitmap indexes that span multiple noncontiguous datafiles because they can cause performance problems when they have even a small amount of extents.

I recommend that you regularly monitor your database to find tables/indexes fragmented into multiple extents. In Oracle9*i*, for dictionary-managed tablespaces, you should try to keep the total number of extents being managed in a tablespace from exceeding 4096 (I have heard as low as 500) for performance reasons. The TEMP tablespace in particular can cause problems when the number of extents goes above 5000.

For locally managed tablespaces, I recommend that an individual segment not exceed 1024 extents. For segments that exceed these bounds, I recommend that you move them to tablespaces with larger extent sizes. By following these guidelines, you can reduce the impact of extent management operations on the system. The following queries shown in Listings 3-27 and 3-28 can help you find the extent counts for tablespaces and segments. (Substitute LOCAL or DICTIONARY in either of the queries for EXTENT_MANAGEMENT.)

```
select  a.tablespace_name, sum(extents)
from    dba_segments a, dba_tablespaces b
where   a.tablespace_name = b.tablespace_name
and     extent_management = 'DICTIONARY'
group   by a.tablespace_name;

TABLESPACE_NAME                    SUM(EXTENTS)
-------------------------------    ------------
SYSTEM                                     1915
TOOLS                                        96
UNDOTBS1                                     56
USERS                                         3
XDB                                         606
```

Listing 3-27: Retrieving information about dictionary-managed tablespaces

Avoiding Disk Contention by Using Partitions

```
select    segment_name, segment_type, extents, bytes, b.tablespace_name
from      dba_segments a, dba_tablespaces b
where     extent_management = 'LOCAL'
and       a.extents > 1024;


SEGMENT_NAME     SEGMENT_TYPE   EXTENTS   BYTES        TABLESPACE_NAME
ORDER            TABLE          2200      220000000    TOOLS
ORDER_IDX1       INDEX          1200      120000000    TOOLS
CUSTOMER         TABLE          7000       70000000    TOOLS
```

Listing 3-28: Retrieving information about locally managed tablespaces

TIP
Query DBA_SEGMENTS regularly to ensure that objects are not building up too many extents. Catching problems early is the key to avoiding performance issues later. Correctly locating objects in tablespaces with uniform extent sizes that are appropriate is the key.

Using the Correct Extent Size

When data is read from a table, it is either accessed by a ROWID operation via an index or by a full table scan. In most cases, access by ROWID is the preferred method. This is because the ROWID method allows the database to determine the exact block that a record resides in and therefore bypasses any extent allocation information in the segment. The short answer is that ROWID operations do not care how many extents are in the segment. Full tablescans, on the other hand, are performed using multiblock read operations in the database while the system scans through the extent map.

The extent map for a segment is stored in the segment header block, not the data dictionary. The data dictionary keeps track of which extents are allocated to which segment/object, but does not give any order to these extents. The extent map in the segment header block does give order to the extents and also provides information about whether these extents contain data. Database block sizes generally range from 4K to 32K.

Here's a simple example: A full table scan reads every block in the table up to the highwater mark. If each extent is the equivalent of 100-8KB data blocks (100 blocks each 8KB in size), in a single extent table, at most, 100 * 8KB of data can be handled with a single multiblock read. If there are 1000 extents, with 999 full extents, and one extent with only 40 blocks written, a full table scan reads ((999 * 100*8KB) + 40*8KB + overhead), or around 780MB. The maximum amount of data that can be read in a single I/O call is limited on each system. Two variables that determine the upper limit are SSTIOMAX and db_block_buffers/4. The SSTIOMAX limit is still around 1MB on most systems.

Creating a New Tablespace and Moving Data to It

If a table is getting very large, you can reduce the number of extents by creating a new tablespace and moving the data to the new location. In Listing 3-29, the customer table is fragmented into 100 extents of 1MB each, which can be found by querying the DBA_EXTENTS.

```
select   SEGMENT_NAME, BYTES
from     DBA_EXTENTS
where    SEGMENT_NAME = 'CUSTOMER';

SEGMENT_NAME              BYTES
CUSTOMER                  1048576
CUSTOMER                  1048576
CUSTOMER                  1048576
CUSTOMER                  1048576
..etc.
```

Listing 3-29: Querying DBA_EXTENTS

First, create a new customer table called customer1 into the new_10M_dat tablespace, as shown in Listing 3-30. (This tablespace has 10MB extents, which better accommodates its growth.)

```
CREATE TABLE CUSTOMER1
TABLESPACE NEW_10M_DAT
AS SELECT * FROM CUSTOMER;
```

Listing 3-30: Creating new customer table

After ensuring that the customer1 table was created, drop the original:

```
DROP TABLE CUSTOMER;
```

Listing 3-31: Dropping the table

NOTE
This doesn't work if the table contains foreign key references.

You can now rename your new table and build its corresponding indexes:

```
RENAME CUSTOMER1 TO CUSTOMER;
```

Listing 3-32: Renaming the table

You can also just do this in one easy step, as specified in the following code. Note, this does not set the NOLOGGING attribute on the table.

```
ALTER TABLE CUSTOMER MOVE TABLESPACE new_10M_dat NOLOGGING;
```

Listing 3-33: Altering the table

The new customer table now occupies only ten extents that are 10MB in size. If the customer table is growing even faster, you will want to move it to a tablespace with an even larger uniform extent size to accommodate this growth. Although you will still have to rebuild the indexes on the customer table (one of the drawbacks of this method), it does ensure that the table is never physically gone from the database until the new table is created. You can also use the COPY

Eliminating Fragmentation

command (since COPY is a DDL and not DML) to avoid the rollback segment use. You can also use the NOLOGGING option, but DDL does not generate much in the way of rollback anyway. A couple of examples follow.

```
create table orders_temp
as select * from orders
nologging;

Table created.
```

Listing 3-34: Creating a table with NOLOGGING

```
Create index ot_idx1 on orders_temp (order_no) nologging;

Index created.
```

Listing 3-35: Creating an index with NOLOGGING

TIP
Use the NOLOGGING option when rebuilding a problem table, but remember that it can impact your ability to recover the table in the event of a failure.

Exporting and then Reimporting the Table

You can also relocate the table by exporting, manually creating the table in the new tablespace, and then reimporting the table with the ignore=y option. Don't forget to include your indexes, grants, and constraints (set their import parameters to Y when you import), and make sure you create a large enough rollback segment for the import. This is also a good way of moving your indexes to tablespaces with a larger extent size by also using the indexfile that is created to modify their tablespace location. You can minimize the rollback area needed by setting COMMIT=Y (to commit during the table import), and you can set the buffer setting higher to increase the speed of the import. The following procedure, shown in Listing 3-36, handles the operation.

```
Export the CUSTOMER Table
Import the CUSTOMER table with indexfile=[file_name]
Modify indexfile file to create table in new location. (Optional: Modify
index locations also)
Drop the CUSTOMER Table

Create the table from the modified script.
Import the CUSTOMER Table (Ignore=y)
```

Listing 3-36: Exporting and reimporting the table

Do *not* use the (compress=y) when you export. This could be a method of reducing fragmentation, but although it could still be used, it often shouldn't. First of all, if you are still using dictionary-managed tablespaces, it ruins uniform extent allocation. Second, if you are using locally managed tablespaces, this just confuses matters because the object views in the database probably report the initial extent value as much larger than it actually is.

Using export/import might be faster than the method in the previous section, but could be a problem if something were to happen to the export file before you have a chance to do the import. Precreating the table in the new tablespace is a critical step, because the import normally wants to put the table back from where you exported it.

TIP

To speed up the actual import of the table, use the indexes=n option to not create the indexes at import time. Because you have the script file created for changing the table, you can run this after the import to re-create the indexes. Specify PARALLEL when creating the indexes if they are large.

Avoiding Chaining by Setting Percents Correctly

Chaining can occur when there isn't enough room in the data blocks to store changes. A chained record is one that exists in multiple blocks instead of a single block. Accessing multiple blocks for the same record can be costly in terms of performance. To see if you have chaining problems, run the utlchain.sql script that Oracle provides to create the chained_rows table. The utlchain.sql file is a file that comes with Oracle and is in the /rdbms/admin subdirectory of your ORACLE_HOME.

You should check for chaining on a weekly basis and fix any problems immediately. To generate the level of chaining in a table (customer in this example), run the query shown in Listing 3-37.

```
ANALYZE TABLE CUSTOMER
LIST CHAINED ROWS;
```

Listing 3-37: Generating the level of chaining in a table

Then, run the following query accessing the CHAINED_ROWS table to check the customer table for chaining, as shown in Listing 3-38.

```
select   HEAD_ROWID
from     CHAINED_ROWS
where    TABLE_NAME = 'CUSTOMER';
```

Listing 3-38: Checking the table for chaining

If no rows are returned, you don't have a chaining problem. If there is a chaining problem, then a select *count(*)* will tell you the number of chained rows. If you want to list the HEAD_ROWID, the query in Listing 3-38 will return the head_rowid for all chained rows. In V$SYSSTAT, *the table fetch continued row* is an indicator of chained rows as well.

To avoid chaining, correctly set PCTFREE (the amount of space reserved in a block for updates). This parameter is set when the table is created. The default value is set to 10 (10 percent free for updates), but this needs to be much higher in a table where there is a large frequency of update activity.

TIP
Find chaining problems by accessing the CHAINED_ROWS table.
Avoid chaining problems by correctly setting PCTFREE.

Rebuilding the Database

Although you should rarely need to do this, I would be remiss if I didn't include a general outline for that rare case. Each time you create or alter an object in the Oracle database, several internal tables are also updated and/or inserted into Oracle's internal data dictionary. As a result, your data dictionary is also at risk for fragmentation if you have a large number of objects and records associated with those objects.

You can resolve data dictionary fragmentation by rebuilding the database. However, be aware that this is a big step to take and can be very time-consuming (e.g., take up an entire weekend); therefore, it should be done only by an advanced DBA. It is not guaranteed to bring you any performance gains. As a result, it should be planned in advance and done only when absolutely necessary. To rebuild the database, an advanced DBA should complete the following steps:

1. Complete a full-database export.

2. Complete a full-image backup, which includes the following:

   ■ The database files

   ■ The control files

   ■ The online redo log files

   ■ The initialization parameters

3. Run a rebuild on the database by using the CREATE DATABASE command.

4. Make sure you have a large enough rollback segment and large enough temporary tablespace to handle importing the database and the creation of indexes.

5. Import the entire database.

Refer to the *DBA Administrators' Guide* for a more detailed approach.

Oracle Tuning Pack: Tablespace Viewer

The Tablespace Viewer (which is part of Tablespace Manager) is new in Enterprise Manager. The Tablespace Viewer (shown in Figure 3-3) provides a graphical view of all tablespaces, datafiles, segments, total data blocks, free data blocks, and percentage of free blocks available in the tablespace's current storage allocation. The tool provides the option of displaying all segments for a tablespace or all segments for a datafile. The Tablespace Viewer can be used to provide information for each segment, including average free space per block, chained rows, and other information that can be helpful in improving disk performance.

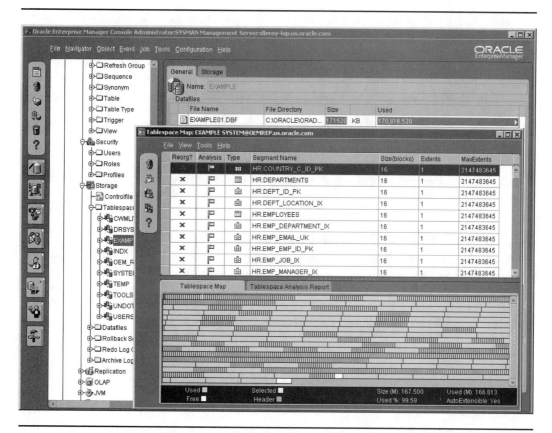

FIGURE 3-3. *Oracle Tuning Pack 2.0: Tablespace Viewer*

Eliminating Fragmentation

When a reorganization is necessary, the DBA can use a new feature called the Oracle Tablespace Manager Reorganization Wizard to automatically fix problem objects. The wizard in Oracle9*i* runs several SQL statements (ALTER TABLE, MOVE, and ALTER INDEX REBUILD statements) to fix fragmented or problematic objects. (Export and import is no longer used.) It checks for sufficient space prior to executing. The DBA can select a single segment, multiple segments, or the entire tablespace for defragmentation, including tables, indexes, and clusters. Segments can also be moved between tablespaces using the Tablespace Manager. See Chapter 5 for information regarding Enterprise Manager.

Things to Remember
Remember the following tips:

- Use the correct table and index extent sizes to avoid fragmentation within a tablespace.

- Create a new tablespace when necessary to move objects to another disk.

- When time is a factor, increase the size of the next extent to avoid getting large amounts of extents. Also note that having multiple extents is not the same as fragmentation. Fragmentation occurs when there are lots of little spaces that cannot be used or coalesced into a bigger free space. This occurs within tables when rows are deleted and in a tablespace when a segment is dropped or removed. Changing the next extent size so it is no longer uniform with the other extent sizes in the tablespace can actually contribute to fragmentation if the extent is later dropped.

- Avoid chaining by correctly setting PCTFREE and the database block size.

- Resolve data dictionary fragmentation by rebuilding the database.

- Use Oracle Enterprise Manager utilities to help you diagnose and correct fragmentation problems easier.

Using UNDO Management

If you want to speed up large numbers of INSERTs, UPDATEs, and DELETEs, increase the size of your log files (you can increase the time needed for media recovery) and make sure that they are on the fastest disk. Previously, you could also increase the LOG_CHECKPOINT_INTERVAL if it were set such that it would checkpoint prior to a log switch, but this parameter is being deprecated and currently defaults to zero (which indicates switching based on the redo log being full).

LOG_CHECKPOINT_INTERVAL is still a valid parameter, but its meaning changed in Oracle9i. Previously, it was the number of blocks that were written to the log before a checkpoint would be triggered. Now it indicates the number of redo log file blocks (OS block size) that can exist between an incremental checkpoint and the last block written to the redo log.

NOTE
An incremental checkpoint does not cause performance issues like a full checkpoint can.

Oracle relies on online redo log files to record changes to the database. Each time a transaction takes place in the database, an entry is added to the online redo log file (although this is not the only thing written to the redo logs). If you increase the size allocated for the log, you can increase performance. Uncommitted transactions generate redo entries, too. You can watch the logs spin during a large batch transaction. But keep the following characteristics in mind when you make modifications:

- A log file must be online and available while the database is up, or the database will halt (one of the few things that stops the database immediately).

- Online redo log files are recycled and offline redo log files are created automatically (if archiving is activated).

- Offline logs are the ones that have been closed for archiving or backup.

- The minimum is two online redo log files. Online redo log file multiplexing (additional copies) is recommended in the event that an online redo log file is lost. Mirroring the online redo logs improves the performance of archiving as well, because it allows the archive process to multiplex the reads across the two files.

- The number of initial log files and their size is determined when the database is created.

- Archive logging can be turned on and off by the ALTER DATABASE command, but the database has to be in MOUNT mode.

- Checkpoints are points when committed transactions in redo logs get written to the database.

Determining Whether Redo Log File Size Is a Problem

Two potential problems are possible that should be addressed. The first concerns batch jobs that do not have enough total redo space to complete or are so fast that the online redo logs wrap (all redo logs are used but not yet archived) before they have a chance to be archived to the offline redo logs. By listing the online redo logs with their last update date and time at the operating system level, you can determine how often they are switching.

You can also query V$LOG_HISTORY for the last 100 log switches. If you increase the size of the online redo logs, it may provide the space for large batch jobs doing large INSERT, UPDATE, and DELETE transactions. A better solution may be to increase the number of online redo logs so that the additional space is provided while also having a frequent log switch (smaller but more online redo logs), which gives a shorter time between offline redo logs that may be required for recovery.

The second concern is for very long-running jobs that are spending a large amount of time switching online redo logs. Long-running jobs are often much faster when the entire job fits into a single online redo log. For the online transaction processing (OLTP) type of environment, smaller online redo logs are usually better. My rule of thumb is for online redo logs to switch every half hour (not counting the long-running batch jobs that shorten this time). By monitoring the date and time of the online redo logs at the operating system level (or querying v$log_history), you can determine to increase the size or number of online redo logs to reach an optimum switching interval.

Listing 3-39 shows the time between log switches. It can be handy in determining whether you have a problem.

```
select b.recid,
       to_char(b.first_time,'dd-mon-yy hh:mi:ss') start_time, a.recid,
       to_char(a.first_time,'dd-mon-yy hh:mi:ss') end_time,
       round(((a.first_time-b.first_time)*24)*60,2) minutes
  from v$log_history a, v$log_history b
 where a.recid = b.recid+1
 order by a.first_time asc
/
```

Listing 3-39: Determining the time between log switches

Eliminating Fragmentation

Determining the Size of Your Log Files and Checkpoint Interval

You can determine the size of your online redo log files by checking the size at the operating system level or querying the V$LOG and V$LOGFILE tables. Then, you can add additional logs by using the ALTER DATABASE ADD LOGFILE command to create larger logs and then drop the smaller ones.

Keep in mind that the checkpoint interval forces a checkpoint based on the number of blocks specified for the CHECKPOINT_INTERVAL in the initialization file. So, if you increase the size of your online redo logs, make sure you also increase your checkpoint interval. Displaying information about redo logs is shown in the simplistic query in Listing 3-40.

```
select  a.member, a.group#, b.thread#, b.bytes, b.members, b.status
from    v$logfile a, v$log b
where   a.group# = b.group#;
```

MEMBER	GRP#	THRD#	BYTES	MEMBERS	STATUS
/disk1/log1a.ora	1	1	2048000	2	INACTIVE
/disk1/log2a.ora	2	1	2048000	2	CURRENT
/disk2/log1b.ora	1	1	2048000	2	INACTIVE
/disk2/log2b.ora	2	1	2048000	2	CURRENT

Listing 3-40: Displaying information about redo logs

This query output shows two groups of log files. Each group is mirrored, and has two log files in it. The data contained in the file /disk1/log1a.ora and the file /disk2/log1b.ora is exactly the same. (See multiplexing log files in the next section.)

Other Helpful Redo Log Commands

To multiplex online redo log files (create a mirrored copy), use the command shown in Listing 3-41.

```
alter database add logfile member '/disk2/log1b.ora' to group 1;
alter database add logfile member '/disk2/log2b.ora' to group 2;
```

Listing 3-41: Multiplexing online redo logs

TIP
Add larger log files and drop the smaller log files to increase the speed of large INSERT, UPDATE, and DELETE statements.

To drop an online redo log member, use this command:

```
alter database drop logfile member '/disk2/log2b.ora';
```

Listing 3-42: Dropping an online redo log member

To add a new online redo log group, use this command:

```
alter database add logfile member '/disk1/log3a.ora' size 10M;
```

Listing 3-43: Adding a new online redo log group

To drop an entire redo log group (all copies), use this command:

```
alter database drop logfile group 1;
```

Listing 3-44: Dropping an entire redo log group

To switch log files, use this command:

```
alter system switch logfile;
```

Listing 3-45: Switching log files

Things to Remember
Remember the following tips:

- Increase the size of your log files to increase the rate at which large INSERTS, DELETES, and UPDATES (DMLs) are processed.

- Put the redo logs on the fastest disk if you plan to write a lot of information. Try to use the outer edge of the disk (the fastest part) for the redo logs.

- Increase the size of online redo logs if log switches are occurring less than every half hour during normal business conditions (excluding infrequent large batch jobs).

- Increase the number of online redo logs if you are wrapping frequently during large batch jobs.

- Be aware that the initialization parameter LOG_CHECKPOINT_INTERVAL is measured in blocks, not bytes. If you accidentally put in the number of bytes that you want, your interval will be *way* too high because the interval is measured in blocks. This parameter will be reinterpreted and is defaulted to zero in Oracle9.

Additional Initialization Parameters
The following initialization parameters are also nice to know:

- **LOG_ARCHIVE_DEST_n**   This is the directory (*n* of them) location with archive prefix (arch). This is a location to write an additional copy(s) of archive logs (as redo logs are filled and are archived only in ARCHIVELOG mode). If you have the space, this is a nice safety net to save you if archiving errors occur. The destination may also be a remote database.

- **LOG_ARCHIVE_MIN_SUCCEED_DEST**   This is the minimum number of successful archives written for a redo log.

Eliminating Fragmentation

If transaction rates are so high that a single database writer can't keep up writing dirty blocks to disk, you may also need to set the DB_WRITER_PROCESSES parameter in the initialization file. If you can't use multiple processes (or if you don't have asynch I/O and want to emulate it), you can use DBWR_IO_SLAVES to distribute the load over multiple I/O slaves.

- **DB_WRITER_PROCESSES**   This is the number of database writers to write dirty blocks from the SGA to disk when one database writer isn't enough.

- **DBWR_IO_SLAVES**   If you can't use multiple processes (or if you don't have asynch I/O and want to emulate it), you can use DBWR_IO_SLAVES to distribute the load over multiple I/O slaves. (See Appendix A for more details on initialization parameters.)

Increasing Chances of Recovery: Committing After Each Batch

To increase your chances of recovering large batch processes, COMMIT after each batch process. Although this slows processing, it saves time if a recovery is necessary. A large batch process really depends on how large your system is, but a job that takes several hours should be broken into smaller jobs that can have frequent COMMITs so that the whole job doesn't need to be rerun in its entirety, in the event of a failure during the job.

Using Rollback Segments

Rollback segments hold the data snapshot (before image) during an update. If the initialization parameter is UNDO_MANAGEMENT=MANUAL, then rollback segments are used, as in previous versions of Oracle (covered in this section). If the initialization parameter is UNDO_MANAGEMENT=AUTO, then undo tablespace management is used (covered in the next section).

When a transaction is rolled back, a snapshot of the data is applied. When setting up your database using rollback segments, reserve multiple tablespaces for rollback segments so that users do not contend with each other in the same tablespace (which usually means the same physical disk), as shown in Listing 3-46.

```
Tablespace1/disk1:  rbseg1
Tablespace2/disk2:  rbseg2
Tablespace3/disk3:  rbseg3
Tablespace4/disk4:  rbseg4
Tablespace1/disk1:  rbseg5
Tablespace2/disk2:  rbseg6
Tablespace3/disk3:  rbseg7
Tablespace4/disk4:  rbseg8
```

Listing 3-46: Reserving multiple tablespaces for rollback segments

Avoiding Contention Among Rollback Segments

As a rule of thumb, you don't want more than one user using a rollback segment at once. Although a general recommendation for the number of rollback segments is based on four concurrent transactions per rollback segment, you should base the number of rollback segments on the needs of your system, not this guideline.

Monitoring Rollback Segment Waits and Contention

You can use Oracle's Enterprise Manager or the v$ views to check whether you have rollback segments that have grown to an excessive number of extents. Oracle's Enterprise Manager or the V$ views are also a good way to monitor rollback segment waits and contention. SQL statements like the one in Listing 3-47 can also be used to display rollback information.

```
select   a.name, b.extents, b.rssize, b.xacts, b.waits, b.gets,
         optsize, status
from     v$rollname a, v$rollstat b
where    a.usn = b.usn;


NAME     EXTENTS  RSSIZE    XACTS  WAITS  GETS  OPTSIZE    STATUS
SYSTEM         4  540672    1      0      51               ONLINE
RB1           2  10240000  0      0      427   10240000   ONLINE
RB2           2  10240000  1      0      425   10240000   ONLINE
RB3           2  10240000  1      0      422   10240000   ONLINE
RB4           2  10240000  0      0      421   10240000   ONLINE
```

Listing 3-47: Displaying rollback information

Examine the results to determine whether you need to add rollback segments. If the xacts (active transactions) are regularly above one for any of the rollback segments, increase the number of rollback segments to eliminate potential contention. If the wait is greater than zero, increase the number of rollback segments to eliminate contention.

Increasing Rollback Segments

If demand is high, you can increase the number of rollback segments by adding a rollback segment (you must also bring it online) named rb9 into the rollback2 tablespace, as shown in Listing 3-48.

```
Create rollback segment rb9
tablespace rollback2
storage (initial 1M next 2M);
```

Listing 3-48: Adding a rollback segment

Using Rollback Segments

TIP
*Try to keep the number of active users per rollback segment to one.
You can accomplish this task by monitoring the number of users per
rollback segment and adding rollback segments if needed. This keeps
waits and contention to a minimum.*

Isolating Large Transactions to Their Own Rollback Segments

When using rollback segments, keep in mind that batch processes may require one large
rollback segment. Use the SET TRANSACTION USE ROLLBACK SEGMENT ROLLBIG for large
transactions. You can't do this if you are using automatic undo mode. An example is displayed in
Listing 3-49. Also, note that you must precode the SET TRANSACTION with a COMMIT, even if
it is the first command for your session.

```
commit;
set transaction use rollback segment rb_big;
delete from big_table;
commit;
```

Listing 3-49: Using SET TRANSACTION

TIP
*Failure to use the SET TRANSACTION USE ROLLBACK SEGMENT
ROLLBIG command for a given UPDATE, INSERT, DELETE, or
BATCH program could cause the rollback segments to become
fragmented and become potentially too large for the corresponding
tablespace. The SET TRANSACTION command must be reissued after
a COMMIT or rollback process. If all the segments in the rollback
segment tablespace use the same extent sizes, you should not have
any fragmentation—lots of extents, yes, but the extents, once freed,
are reusable because they are all the same size.*

A rollback segment is dynamically extended as needed by a transaction up to the total
available space in the tablespace (transactions cannot span rollback segments) in which it
resides. The OPTIMAL storage option for a rollback segment dynamically shrinks extended
rollback segments to a specified size.

Although large transactions should be preceded with the SET TRANSACTION statement,
it is still a good idea to set the OPTIMAL option so that rollback segments are not accidentally
extended and not returned to their original size. Use the statement in Listing 3-50 to alter a
rollback segment to OPTIMAL.

```
alter rollback segment rb1
storage (optimal 15M);
```

Listing 3-50: Altering a rollback segment to OPTIMAL

Note that you may also use the OPTIMAL storage setting at rollback creation time.

You can also force a rollback segment to shrink to its optimal setting or a specified size using the commands in Listing 3-51.

```
alter rollback segment rb1 shrink;
alter rollback segment rb1 shrink to 15M;
```

Listing 3-51: Forcing a rollback segment to shrink to its optimal setting or a specified size

TIP
Do not depend on the OPTIMAL setting to constantly shrink rollback segments because this is a costly process in terms of performance. The OPTIMAL setting should be activated infrequently. Increase the setting for OPTIMAL if there are a lot of extends and shrinks. Also, note that you cannot shrink a rollback segment to less than the combined value of its first two extents.

TIP
Oracle recommends setting MINEXTENTS to 20 for rollback segments. This is mainly for read-consistency. If you query a table and someone is changing the data, your query cannot see these changes until they are committed. So, the rollback segments (or UNDO) are used to reconstruct the block to the state it was in when your query started. If the rollback information cannot be found in the rollback segments (or UNDO), the query aborts with an ORA-1555 error. If you have MINEXTENTS set to 2, when the rollback segment overwrites one of the extents, you lose about 50 percent of the stored UNDO data. If MINEXTENTS is set to 20, then you lose only 5 percent of the UNDO data when overwriting an extent with new UNDO information.

Using the Simpler Approach: Undo Tablespace

In 9*i*, Oracle offers a new approach for managing ROLLBACK or UNDO data in the database. This approach is the creation of undo tablespaces in the database, which greatly simplifies the management of these transactions. With rollback segments, undo blocks are overwritten by newer transactions as required. This leads to juggling by the DBA to ensure that large enough rollback segments are available for large transactions to avoid a Snapshot Too Old error and to ensure that enough rollback segments are available for the regular activity on the database to keep rollback header contention minimized.

The size of the undo area is fixed by setting the UNDO_TABLESPACE in the initialization file as well as setting the initialization parameter UNDO_MANAGEMENT=AUTO. If UNDO_MANAGEMENT is set to AUTO and the UNDO_TABLESPACE is not set, the SYSTEM tablespace is used, if there is no UNDO tablespace available. (Don't do this.)

With UNDO tablespaces, an initialization parameter called UNDO_RETENTION can also be used to specify the amount of time (in seconds) that undo information is retained in the tablespace after it is committed. This information can be rolled back in the event of user error. UNDO_RETENTION is not the same as FLASHBACK. UNDO_RETENTION simply tells the database how long the undo data should stick around. To actually use this undo data, you need to use the DBMS_FLASHBACK package, which can allow you to undo committed transactions—not just rollback active (uncommitted) transactions. Undo data for active transactions is always kept in the UNDO or ROLLBACK segments, in case the user decides to issue a ROLLBACK instead of a COMMIT.

For environments where nightly batch activity and daily OLAP activity is the norm, the dynamic changing of this parameter is a saving grace, because it is much easier than altering the transaction rollback segment or scripting out the offlining of all of the small rollback segments in the database. Be aware, though, that if the tablespace does not have enough room for all of the undo records, it reuses unexpired undo space as necessary. Fortunately, it is still easier to add space to the tablespace than to start resizing rollback segments for particular jobs.

Monitoring UNDO Space

The V$UNDOSTAT view can be used to monitor the use of undo space by current transactions in the instance. Each row in this view lists statistics collected in the instance for 10-minute intervals. Each row represents one snapshot of the statistics for undo space utilization, transaction volume, and query length, every 10 minutes for the last 24 hours.

Because rollback segments and undo tablespaces can be used in the same database, the V$ROLLSTAT view shows information on the undo segments in the undo tablespace when in automatic undo management mode. Information on the actual extents for the undo tablespace can be retrieved from the DBA_UNDO_EXTENTS view in the database.

Killing Problem Sessions

If the demand is at a temporary peak, you can stop a low priority problem session by using the system KILL command. But first, you must find the user who's running the job (often an INSERT, UPDATE, or DELETE statement) that is draining system resources or locking blocks of data. The following commands in Listing 3-52 help you find and KILL problematic users.

```
select  sid, serial#
from    v$session
where   username = 'BADUSER'


SID     SERIAL#
5       33
```

Listing 3-52: Querying to finding problematic users and query output

Use the following command to KILL the session:

```
alter system kill session '5,33';
```

Listing 3-53: KILLing a session

You can also use the code in Listing 3-54 to determine which rollback segment is processing each transaction (which may find a problem transaction), along with the corresponding user and SQL statement. (This query doesn't work for UNDO tablespaces.) The output has been slightly modified for readability.

```
select    a.name, b.xacts, c.sid, c.serial#, c.username, d.sql_text
from      v$rollname a, v$rollstat b, v$session c, v$sqltext d,
          v$transaction e
where     a.usn = b.usn
and       b.usn = e.xidusn
and       c.taddr = e.addr
and       c.sql_address = d.address
and       c.sql_hash_value = d.hash_value
order by a.name, c.sid, d.piece;


name    xacts   sid   serial#     username    sql_text
RB1     1       5     33          USER1       delete from test1;
RB2     1       7     41          USER9       update orders
                                              set items = 5
                                              where orderno = 555;
```

Listing 3-54: Determining which rollback segment is processing each transaction

This shows which users are currently using rollback segments. This query also shows how many users are using or waiting for the same rollback segment.

Things to Remember
Remember the following tips:

- Create enough rollback segments or use undo management.

- If you use undo management, make sure you have an undo tablespace.

- Reserve multiple tablespaces for rollback segments to balance I/O.

- Try to keep the number of active users per rollback segment to one. You can accomplish this goal by monitoring the number of users per rollback segment. This keeps waits and contention to a minimum.

- Isolate large transactions to their own rollback segment.

- In 9*i,* use Undo tablespaces to simplify your undo management.

Sorting in Memory to Reduce Disk I/O

Having the initialization parameters SORT_AREA_SIZE, HASH_AREA_SIZE, or the parameter PGA_AGGREGATE_TARGET set too small to accommodate sorts in memory can be a cause of fragmentation in the TEMP or even the SYSTEM tablespace (depending on how you set up your system). The fragmentation occurs because the temporary tablespace gets used for disk sorting

The Undo Tablespace

instead of in memory. When setting up your system, be aware that the temporary tablespace adheres to the following characteristics:

- It defaults to the TEMP or SYSTEM tablespace (depending on how you set things up) unless specified with ALTER USER or during the CREATE USER command. With Oracle9*i*, you can specify a DEFAULT TEMPORARY TABLESPACE for the database, and all users who do not have a temp tablespace specified default to this tablespace.

- It is used when memory is not large enough to process the entire data set.

The statements in Listing 3-55 generate temporary segments.

```
Create Index
select.... Order By
select.... Distinct
select.... Group By
select.... Union
select.... Intersect
select.... Minus
Unindexed Joins
Some Correlated Subqueries
```

Listing 3-55: Generating temporary segments

To lower your chances of fragmentation, configure the initialization parameters using SORT_AREA_SIZE, HASH_AREA_SIZE, or PGA_AGGREGATE_TARGET to eliminate disk sorts related to the previous SQL commands. (See Chapter 4 for more information on tuning the initialization parameters.) Also, make sure you create a separate tablespace for temporary sorting.

```
CREATE TEMPORARY TABLESPACE temp1

TEMPFILE 'temp01.dbf' SIZE 5M AUTOEXTEND ON;
```

Listing 3-56: Creating a tablespace for temporary sorting

Then, direct users to that temporary tablespace using the following statement:

```
ALTER USER username TEMPORARY TABLESPACE temp1;
```

Listing 3-57: Directing users to the temporary tablespace

Temporary tablespaces can also be locally managed. If you are on a version of the database that supports locally managed tablespaces, your temporary tablespaces should be locally managed to reduce disk contention during disk-sorting operations. Locally managed temporary tablespaces use tempfiles. *Tempfiles* carry some special characteristics that improve performance but can require some additional attention.

Locally managed temporary tablespaces have the following characteristics:

- Do not generate undo information and therefore do not require the disk impact of those operations.

- Do not carry the same dictionary extent overhead caused by dictionary-managed temporary tablespaces.

- Do not allocate the entire tempfile when created. This means that you may add a 2GB tempfile, but it will not show up as 2GB on disk until it is used.

- Are not maintained in the control file the same way other datafiles are. Therefore, utilities such as RMAN do not address them.

Having Multiple Control Files on Different Disks and Controllers

Control files store information regarding startup, shutdown, and archiving. Because your system is useless without at least one good control file, you should store three copies of the control files on separate disks and controllers (if possible). To view current control files, run the query shown in Listing 3-58.

```
select   name, value
from     v$parameter
where    name = 'control_files';


NAME               VALUE
control_files      /disk1/ora8/ctl1.ora,  /disk2/ora8/ctl2.ora,
                   /disk3/ora8/ctl3.ora
```

Listing 3-58: Querying to view the current control files

Using Raw Devices to Improve I/O for Write-Intensive Data

A raw device is an unmounted disk slice that Oracle can read and write without the overhead of UNIX I/O buffering. While raw devices may improve performance, they continue to be of degrading value as other options become prevalent. Most claims of substantial performance improvements resulting from using raw devices come from hardware sales representatives.

There is currently not widescale use of raw devices because there is little evidence regarding substantial performance gains achieved with raw devices. In my tests, raw devices have increased performance from 5–10 percent with an increased cost in maintenance. But for large data warehouses, raw devices can provide excellent performance and should definitely be explored. Oracle RACs no longer need raw devices in Oracle 9.2 if you are using clustered file systems.

Advantages of Using Raw Devices

There are several reasons you may choose to use raw devices (especially for a data warehouse):

- If I/O is the problem on your system *and* the CPU sits relatively idle.

- If asynchronous I/O is available on your platform.

■ If you have variable disk partitioning (able to slice the disk easily). Then, raw devices become a choice for write-intensive, sequentially accessed data and redo log files not included in backup procedures.

Drawbacks of Using Raw Devices

Although there are a number of advantages of using raw devices, there are some drawbacks:

■ Administration of raw devices is more costly. Many common operating system backup utilities provided by the hardware vendor cannot be used with raw devices.

■ If I/O is not the bottleneck, raw devices probably will not help much.

■ If variable disk partitioning is not available, you often allocate far more space than is needed for a given file, causing space to be wasted (very common).

■ If raw devices are used in a production environment, Oracle recommends that backup and recovery be thoroughly tested before employing the raw devices.

Examining Other Disk I/O Precautions and Tips

When looking at other disk I/O, be aware of the following precautions and tips:

■ Heavy batch processing may need much larger rollback, redo, and temp tablespace sizes.

■ Heavy DML (INSERT, UPDATE, and DELETE) processing may need much larger rollback, redo, and temporary tablespace sizes.

■ Heavy user access to large tables requires more CPU and memory, and larger temporary tablespace sizes.

■ Poorly tuned systems require more CPU and memory, and larger temporary tablespace sizes.

■ A greater number of well-balanced disks and controllers always increases performance (by reducing I/O contention).

■ An increase in the disk capacity can speed backup and recovery time by keeping a copy of the backup on disk instead of tape.

■ If you can afford it, EMC and/or solid state disks and solutions are still one of the absolute best ways to improve Oracle I/O performance.

Considering Issues in the Planning Stages

If you're planning a new system or an upgrade, here are some factors you'll want to consider:

■ What is the maximum possible disk capacity for the hardware?

■ Which disk sizes are available?

■ What will be the initial size of the database (including the number of users)?

■ What will be the future size of the database?

■ Will there be a RAID (striping) level for database files or OS?

■ Which recovery methods will be employed?

■ Which archiving methods will be used to store historical information?

■ How often will report output be kept on the system?

■ Which development space will be needed?

■ Which software will be installed, and how much space will it need to function efficiently?

■ Which system utilities will be installed, and how much space will they need to function efficiently?

■ Which type of mail system is going to be installed?

■ Which kinds of data transfer methods are going to be employed?

TIP
When you are in the system planning stage, ensure that you find out all of the information related to the current and future use of the system. Don't just think about the Oracle database needs—investigate the other software and applications that will have performance implications on your Oracle database.

Tips Review

■ Separate key Oracle data files to ensure that disk contention is not a bottleneck. By separating tables and indexes of often-joined tables, you can ensure that even the worst of table joins do not result in disk contention.

■ Query V$FILESTAT and V$DBFILE to see how effectively data files have been balanced.

■ Solve disk contention problems by moving data files to disks that are not as heavily accessed or moving tables to different tablespaces on different disks.

■ Use Enterprise Manager to quickly display information about tablespaces and data files that can be used for preventative maintenance. These utilities can also give you a general view of comparative overall system health if accessed regularly. See Chapter 5 for additional information.

■ To minimize disk I/O on a single large table, break the table into multiple partitions that reside on different physical disks.

■ Access DBA_TABLES, DBA_PART_TABLES, and DBA_SEGMENTS to provide additional information concerning tables that have been partitioned.

- Partition tables using multiple columns as the partitioning criteria.

- Dropping a table partition causes its local index (but not the other local partition indexes) to be dropped and a global index (one that exists on the entire table) to be unavailable. Don't use global indexes if it is a problem rebuilding them.

- If data is partitioned optimally, all the new information falls into a single partition, enabling an export of a single partition of every table during backups.

- Use NOLOGGING to improve performance when rebuilding a problem table.

- Find chaining problems by accessing the CHAINED_ROWS table. Avoid chaining problems by correctly setting PCTFREE.

- Add larger log files and drop the smaller log files to increase the speed of large INSERT, UPDATE, and DELETE statements.

- Try to keep the number of concurrent users per rollback segment to one. You can accomplish this task by monitoring the number of users per rollback segment and adding rollback segments if needed. This will keep waits and contention to a minimum.

- Failure to use the *set transaction use rollback segment <name>* command for a given UPDATE, INSERT, DELETE, or BATCH program could cause the rollback segments to become potentially too large for the corresponding tablespace when using MANUAL tablespace management.

- Using UNDO space management can help with the management of rollback. You do this by setting the initialization parameters UNDO_MANAGEMENT=AUTO and UNDO_TABLESPACE.

- You can use the DBMS_FLASHBACK package to rollback committed user transactions when an error has been made, whereas you use UNDO and rollback segments to store the before image (what the data was prior to a change) of uncommitted data.

- When you are in the system planning stage, ensure that you find out all of the information related to the current and future use of the system. Don't just think about the Oracle database needs; investigate the other software and applications that will affect your Oracle database's performance.

References

Many thanks to Bill Callahan, who completed the amazing update to this chapter!
TUSC DBA Guide, 1988-2002
DBA Reference Guide, Oracle Corporation

CHAPTER
4

Tuning the Database with Initialization Parameters (DBA)

TIPS & COVERED

The init.ora file determines many Oracle operating system environment attributes, such as memory allocated for data, resources allocated for I/O, and other crucial performance-related parameters. Each version of Oracle continues to add to the total number of init.ora parameters. Oracle 9*i* release 2 now has 797 (257 documented and 540 hidden) different init.ora parameters. As you might expect, an entire book could be written on how to set and tune each parameter; this book focuses on the key parameters that affect database performance.

The key to an optimized Oracle database is often the architecture of the system and the parameters that set the environment for the database. Setting four key init.ora parameters (SGA_MAX_SIZE, PGA_AGGREGATE_TARGET, DB_CACHE_SIZE, and SHARED_POOL_SIZE) can be the difference between subsecond queries and queries that take several minutes. This chapter focuses on the crucial init.ora parameters designed to achieve the greatest performance gain with the least effort, but it also lists the top 25 initialization parameters near the end of the chapter. The chapter concludes with a look at typical server configurations for various database sizes.

The topics covered in this chapter include the following:

- Identifying crucial init.ora parameters

- Changing the init.ora file without a restart

- Viewing the init.ora parameters with Enterprise Manager

- Increasing performance by tuning the DB_CACHE_SIZE

- Setting DB_BLOCK_SIZE to reflect the size of your data reads

Identifying Crucial init.ora Parameters

Tuning specific queries alone can lead to performance gains. However, the system will still be slow if you have incorrectly set the parameters for the initialization file because the initialization file plays such an integral role in the overall performance of an Oracle database. Although you can spend time setting all the init.ora parameters, you need to correctly set just four main parameters to realize significant performance gains:

- SGA_MAX_SIZE

- PGA_AGGREGATE_TARGET

- DB_CACHE_SIZE

- SHARED_POOL_SIZE

TIP
The key init.ora parameters in Oracle are SGA_MAX_SIZE, PGA_AGGREGATE_TARGET, DB_CACHE_SIZE, and SHARED_POOL_SIZE.

You can use the query shown in Listing 4-1 to find the current settings of the key init.ora parameters on your database.

```
Col name for a25
Col value for a50

select    name, value
from      v$parameter
where     name in ('sga_max_size', 'pga_aggregate_target',
                   'db_cache_size', 'shared_pool_size');
NAME                      VALUE
----------------------    --------------------
shared_pool_size          50331648
sga_max_size              135338868
db_cache_size             25165824
pga_aggregate_target      25165824
```

Listing 4-1: Finding the current settings of key init.ora parameters

Changing the init.ora File Without a Restart

With each version of Oracle, you can alter more and more parameters without needing to restart the database. This has greatly reduced the need for scheduled downtime to implement system-tuning changes. The following example shows changing the SHARED_POOL_SIZE to 128MB while the database is running:

```
SQL> ALTER SYSTEM SET SHARED_POOL_SIZE = 128M;
```

In addition to being able to dynamically change parameters, Oracle 9*i* provides for the use of an spfile to persistently store dynamic changes to the instance parameters. Prior to Oracle9*i*, any dynamic changes were lost when the database was restarted unless the parameters where added to the init.ora file manually. With Oracle 9*i*, dynamic changes can be stored in a server parameter (SP) file. The default order of precedence when an instance is started is to read parameter files in the following order:

- spfile<SID>.ora

- spfile.ora

- init<SID>.ora

Parameters can be dynamically modified at a systemwide or session-specific scope. In addition, parameters can be changed in memory only or persist across restarts via an spfile.

TIP
If you can't figure out why your system isn't using the value
in your init.ora file, you probably have an spfile overriding it.

Finally, in a Real Application Cluster environment, parameters can be changed for a single node or for all nodes in a cluster. Be careful about granting the ALTER SESSION privilege to users: knowledgeable developers can set individual parameters that positively affect their session

Changing the init.ora
Without Restarting

at the expense of others on the system. Listing 4-2 illustrates a list of init.ora parameters that can be set without shutting down and restarting the database.

There are two key fields in the V$PARAMETER view:

- **ISSES_MODIFIABLE** Indicates whether a user with the ALTER SESSION privilege can modify this init.ora parameter for his or her session.

- **ISSYS_MODIFIABLE** Indicates whether a user with the ALTER SYSTEM privilege can modify this particular parameter.

The query in Listing 4-2 displays a partial result of the init.ora parameters that can be modified with an ALTER SYSTEM or ALTER SESSION command.

```
select     name, value, isdefault, isses_modifiable, issys_modifiable
from       v$parameter
where      issys_modifiable <> 'FALSE'
or         isses_modifiable <> 'FALSE'
order by   name;
```

Listing 4-2: Retrieving a partial list of init.ora parameters

The result of the query is all of the init.ora parameters that can be modified.

NAME ISSYS_MOD	VALUE	ISDEFAULT	ISSES
aq_tm_processes IMMEDIATE	1	FALSE	FALSE
archive_lag_target IMMEDIATE	0	TRUE	FALSE
background_dump_dest IMMEDIATE	C:\oracle\admin\orcl9ir2\bdump	FALSE	FALSE
backup_tape_io_slaves DEFERRED	FALSE	TRUE	FALSE

TIP
Changing init.ora parameters dynamically is a powerful feature for both developers and DBAs. Consequently, a user with the ALTER SESSION privilege is capable of irresponsibly allocating 100MB+ for the SORT_AREA_SIZE for a given session, if it is not restricted.

Viewing the init.ora Parameters with Enterprise Manager

You can also use Enterprise Manager to view these settings on the Configuration screen under the Instance option. The section of Enterprise Manager displayed in Figure 4-1 shows the current settings

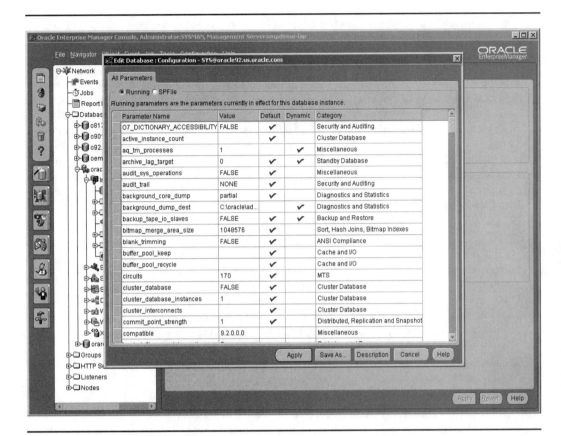

FIGURE 4-1. *Enterprise Manager—init.ora Parameters*

for the init.ora parameters and also shows whether the parameters can be modified (dynamic = ✓) without shutting down the database. Oracle Enterprise Manager is covered in detail in Chapter 5.

Increasing Performance by Tuning the DB_CACHE_SIZE

Long-time users of Oracle and readers of prior editions of this book will notice that some familiar parameters have not been mentioned. This is because parameters such as DB_BLOCK_BUFFERS have been deprecated. (A parameter _DB_BLOCK_BUFFERS is set behind the scenes for backward compatibility.) Although many of the familiar parameters from earlier versions of Oracle are still valid, using them disables many Oracle 9*i* features, including automatic cache memory management. This chapter focuses on the Oracle 9*i* parameters for tuning your system.

DB_CACHE_SIZE is the first parameter to look at in the init.ora because it's the most crucial parameter in Oracle. If the DB_CACHE_SIZE is set too low, Oracle won't have enough memory to operate efficiently and the system may run poorly, no matter what else you do to it. If DB_ CACHE_SIZE is too high, your system may begin to swap and may come to a halt.

DB_CACHE_SIZE makes up the area of the SGA that is used for storing and processing data in memory. As users request information, data is put into memory. If the DB_CACHE_SIZE parameter is set too low, then the least recently used data will be flushed from memory. If the flushed data is recalled with a query, it must be reread from disk (causing I/O and CPU resources to be used).

Retrieving data from memory can be over 10,000 times faster (based on the speed of memory and disk), but can also be about 100 times faster even when disk caching (memory on disk) and Oracle inefficiencies are taken into consideration. Therefore, the higher the percentage of time records found in memory (without being retrieved from disk), the faster the overall system performance (usually 100 times faster for well-tuned queries). Having enough memory allocated to store data in memory depends on whether enough memory is allocated to the DB_CACHE_SIZE.

TIP
Physical memory is generally substantially faster than retrieving it from disk, so make sure the SGA is large enough. One Oracle study showed Oracle memory access as averaging about 100 times faster than disk access. However, this takes into account disk caching advances, which you may not have on your system. The same study also showed an individual case where Oracle memory access was well over 10,000 times faster than disk (which was hard for me to believe), but it shows how important it is to measure this on your own unique system.

DB_CACHE_SIZE is the key parameter to tune the *data cache hit ratio*: the percentage of data block accesses that occur without requiring a physical read from disk. Although several situations can artificially inflate or deflate it, the data cache hit ratio is a key indicator of system efficiency. You can use the query in Listing 4-3 to view the data cache hit ratio.

```
column phys            format 999,999,999    heading 'Physical Reads'
column gets            format 999,999,999    heading ' DB Block Gets'
column con_gets        format 999,999,999    heading 'Consistent Gets'
column hitratio        format 999.99         heading ' Hit Ratio '
  select    sum(decode(name,'physical reads',value,0))phys,
            sum(decode(name,'db block gets',value,0)) gets,
            sum(decode(name,'consistent gets', value,0)) con_gets,
            (1 - (sum(decode(name,'physical reads',value,0)) /
            (sum(decode(name,'db block gets',value,0)) +
            sum(decode(name,'consistent gets',value,0))))) * 100 hitratio
from      v$sysstat;
Physical Reads  DB Block Gets Consistent Gets  Hit Ratio
--------------- --------------- --------------- -----------
      1,671          39,561          71,142       98.49
```

Listing 4-3: Viewing the data cache hit ratio

Although there are exceptions for unusual applications, a cache hit ratio of 95 percent or greater should be achievable for a well-tuned transactional application. Because such a large performance difference exists between disk and memory access, improving the data cache hit ratio from 90 to 95 percent nearly doubles system performance. Improving the cache hit ratio from 90 to 98 percent could yield nearly 500 percent improvement.

TIP
Poor joins and poor indexing can also yield very high hit ratios, so make sure your hit ratio isn't high for any reason other than because you have a well-tuned system. An unusually high hit ratio may indicate the introduction of code that is poorly indexed or includes join issues.

TIP
The best use of hit ratios is still to compare them over time, to help alert you if a substantial change occurs to a system on a given day. Some people deprecate the value of hit ratios, like tool vendors who don't see the value of tracking hit ratios over time because their tools are point-in-time or reactive-based tuning solutions. Hit ratios should never be your only tool, but they should definitely be one of many proactive tools in your arsenal.

Oracle continues to downplay the importance of hit ratios by reducing the discussions on hit ratio tuning. Oracle is beginning to focus on analyzing system performance in terms of work done (CPU or service time) vs. time spent waiting for work (wait time). Areas where hit ratios are still the primary tuning method are library cache and dictionary cache. See Chapter 14 on STATSPACK for more information on balancing the entire tuning arsenal, including hit ratios.

Using V$DB_CACHE_ADVICE in Tuning DB_CACHE_SIZE

V$DB_CACHE_ADVICE is a view introduced in Oracle 9*i* to assist in tuning DB_CACHE_SIZE. The view can be queried directly, and the data in the view is used by the Oracle kernel to make automatic cache management decisions. You use the Oracle 9.2 query shown in Listing 4-4 (note that 9.01 does not have the column size_factor) to view the effect of changing DB_CACHE_SIZE on the data cache hit ratio.

```
select name, size_for_estimate,
size_factor, estd_physical_read_factor
from v$db_cache_advice;

NAME                      SIZE_FOR_ESTIMATE SIZE_FACTOR ESTD_PHYSICAL_READ_FACTOR
------------------------- ----------------- ----------- -------------------------
DEFAULT                                   4       .1667                    1.8136
DEFAULT                                   8       .3333                    1.0169
DEFAULT                                  12          .5                    1.0085
DEFAULT                                  16       .6667                         1
```

DEFAULT	20	.8333	1
DEFAULT	24	1	1

Listing 4-4: Viewing the effect of changing DB_CACHE_SIZE on the data cache hit ratio

Reading these results, we see the following:

- The current cache size is 24MB (size_factor = 1).

- We can decrease the cache size to be 16MB and maintain the current cache hit ratio because the physical_read_factor = 1.

Although this view provides an estimate of how changing the cache size affects the cache hit ratio, you should test any changes to validate that the results are as forecasted. Oracle Enterprise Manager provides a graphical view of the data in V$DB_CACHE_ADVICE, as shown in Figure 4-2.

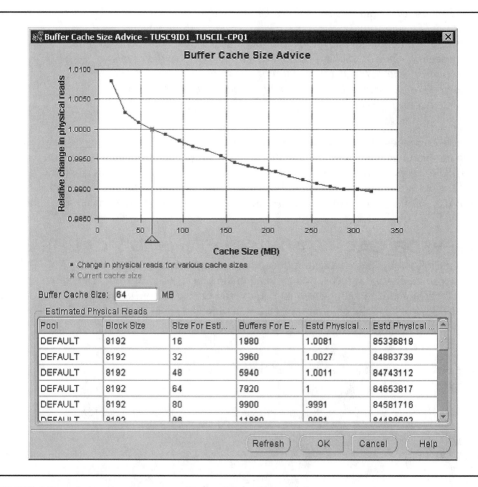

FIGURE 4-2. *Enterprise Manager—Buffer Cache Size Advice*

Keeping the Hit Ratio for the Data Cache above 95 Percent

The hit ratio for the data cache should generally be above 95 percent for transactional systems. However, the best use for a hit ratio is to study your system over time to see major changes that should warrant further investigation. Usually, if your hit ratio is below 95 percent, you may need to increase the number DB_CACHE_SIZE. In some instances, you can increase performance substantially by increasing the hit ratio from 95 to 98 percent—especially if the last 5 percent of the hits going to disk are the main lag on the system.

In Figure 4-3, notice how much of a performance problem is caused by setting the DB_CACHE_SIZE too low. Setting the DB_CACHE_SIZE at optimal (instead of setting it too low) results in a tremendous performance gain. Also note that setting it too high (200 percent of optimal) does not result in any additional gains in performance.

Monitoring the V$SQLAREA View to Find Slow Queries

Although hit ratios below 95 percent are usually a sign that your DB_CACHE_SIZE is set too low or that you have poor indexing, distortion of the hit ratio numbers is possible and needs to be taken into account while tuning. Hit ratio distortion and non-DB_CACHE_SIZE issues include the following:

- Recursive calls

- Missing or suppressed indexes

- Data sitting in memory

- Rollback segments

- Multiple logical reads

- Physical reads causing the system to use CPU

To avoid being misled, locate slow queries by monitoring the V$SQLAREA view. Once you isolate the queries that are causing performance hits, tune the queries or modify how the information is stored to solve the problem. Using Oracle's SQL Analyze, a DBA can generate the TopSQL for

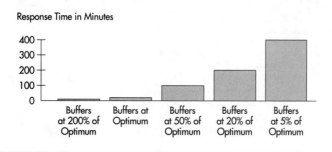

FIGURE 4-3. *Response Time—Memory-Intensive Report with Given SGA (Buffer) Settings*

his or her system. The TopSQL screen (Figure 4-4) displays a list of the worst SQL statements in the current cache based on disk reads per execution. The DBA can then "drag" the problem SQL from TopSQL into a tuning session to begin the process of analyzing and tuning the problem SQL. Chapter 5 discusses the benefits of Oracle's Enterprise Manager product in detail.

TIP
In Oracle9i, use the TopSQL monitor of Oracle's SQL Analyze to find problem queries.

Accuracy of Hit Ratios

If you are using hit ratios to measure performance, note the following two issues:

- Within Performance Manager, during peak times the number of disk reads is larger than the number of in-memory reads; thus, the negative hit ratio is being computed based on the deltas between physical reads and logical reads.

- STATSPACK in 8*i* did not include direct reads when calculating the hit ratios (fixed in 9*i*).

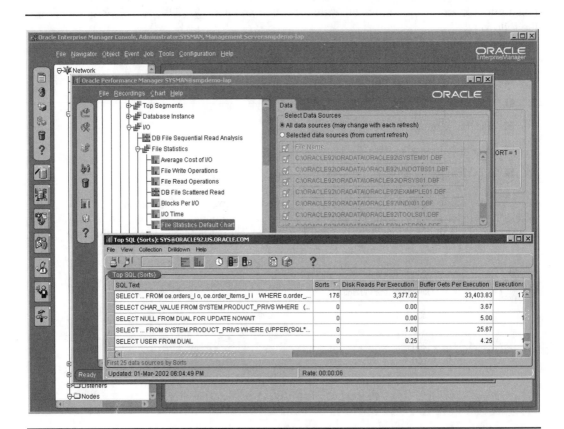

FIGURE 4-4. *Using Oracle's TopSQL of SQL Analyze to Find Problem Queries*

Poor Hit Ratios Occurring When an Index Is Suppressed

Consider the following query shown in Listing 4-5, where the customer table is indexed on the unique CUSTNO column. It is *not* optimal to have this index suppressed by using the NVL because it results in a poor hit ratio.

```
select      custno, name
from        customer
where       nvl(custno,0)  = 5789;
Tries (Logical Reads) = 105        Physical = 100
% hit ratio    =    (1   -     Physical/Tries) x 100
% hit ratio    =    (1 - 100/105) x 100%
% hit ratio    =    4.8%  (A very low/bad hit ratio)
```

Listing 4-5: Indexing the customer table

If you are looking at this in Enterprise Manager, an index is missing on a query that is being executed at the current time. Focus on the query that is causing this problem and fix the query. You can find the query by accessing the V$SQLAREA view, as shown in Chapter 5.

TIP
A low hit ratio for a query is an indication of a missing or suppressed index.

Getting High Ratios with Well-Indexed Queries

Consider the query in Listing 4-6, where the customer table is indexed on the unique custno column. In this situation, it is optimal to use the custno index because it results in an excellent hit ratio.

```
select      custno, name
from        customer
where       custno = 5789;
Tries (Logical Reads) = 105 Physical = 1
% hit ratio    =    (1   -     Physical/Tries) x 100
% hit ratio    =    (1 - 1/105) x 100%
% hit ratio    =    99%  (A very high/good hit ratio)
```

Listing 4-6: Indexing the customer table

If you are looking at this in Enterprise Manager, an index is usually on the query that is being executed.

Slow Queries Executing a Second Time, Resulting in Good Hit Ratios

When a full table scan is completed for the second time and the data is still in memory, you may see a good hit ratio even though the system is trying to run a slow query, as shown in Listing 4-7.

```
Tries (Logical Reads) = 105 Physical = 1
% hit ratio    =    (1   -     Physical/Tries) x 100
% hit ratio    =    (1 - 1/105) x 100%
% hit ratio    =    99%  (A very high/good hit ratio)
```

Listing 4-7: Running a slow query with data still in memory

Monitoring V$SQLAREA
View to Find Slow Queries

If you are looking at this in Enterprise Manager, it appears that an index is on the query being executed, when in fact, the data is in memory from the last time it was executed. The result is that you are hogging a lot of memory even though it appears that an indexed search is being done.

TIP
Slow queries show in V$SQLAREA view with poor hit ratios the first time they are executed. Make sure you tune them at that time. The second time they execute, they may not show a poor hit ratio.

Other Hit Ratio Distortions

There are several other hit distortions to consider:

- **Oracle Forms distortion**   Systems that use Oracle Forms (screens) a lot reuse information regularly. This reuse by some of the users of the system drives up the hit ratio. Other users on the system may not be experiencing hit ratios that are as good as the Forms users, yet the overall system hit ratio may look very good. The DBA must be aware that the Forms users can be helping the hit ratio to reach an artificially high level.

TIP
Oracle Forms applications usually have an unusually high hit ratio. If your site uses a lot of Oracle Forms, shoot for a higher hit ratio because the hit ratio will be artificially high.

- **Rollback segment distortion**   Because the header block of the rollback segment is usually cached, the activity to the rollback segment gives a falsely high hit ratio impact, when truly, there is no significant impact on the hit ratio.

TIP
Sites that use rollbacks to a greater extent by most users of the system should shoot for a higher hit ratio because the hit ratio could be artificially high from rollback use.

- **Index distortion**   An index range scan results in multiple logical reads on a very small number of blocks. Hit ratios as high as 86 percent can be recorded when none of the blocks are cached prior to the query executing. Make sure you monitor the hit ratio of individual poorly tuned queries, in addition to monitoring the big picture (overall hit ratio).

- **I/O distortion**   Physical reads that appear to be causing heavy disk I/O may actually be causing you to be CPU-bound. In tests, the same amount of CPU was used for 89 logical reads as was used to process 11 physical reads. The result was that the physical reads were costly because of *buffer management*. Fix the queries causing the disk I/O problems, and you will usually free up a lot of CPU as well. Performance degradation can spiral downward exponentially, but the good news is that when you begin to fix your system, it can often spiral upward exponentially. Probably the main reason some people love to tune is because it can be exhilarating.

Setting DB_BLOCK_SIZE to Reflect the Size of Your Data Reads

The DB_BLOCK_SIZE is the size of the default data block size when the database is created. With Oracle 9*i*, each tablespace can have a different block size, thus making block size selection a *less* critical selection before the database is created. That said, a separate cache memory allocation must be made for each different database block size. However, it is still very important to choose wisely. Although you can have different block size tablespaces, this is not truly a performance feature, because the nondefault buffer caches are not optimized for performance. So, you still want to put the bulk of your data in the default buffer cache.

You set the data block cache for the default block size using the DB_CACHE_SIZE init.ora parameter. Allocate cache for other database block sizes by using the DB_*n*K_CACHE_SIZE, where *n* is the block size in kilobytes. The larger the DB_BLOCK_SIZE, the more efficiently large amounts of data can be retrieved. A small DB_BLOCK_SIZE actually lets you retrieve single records faster and saves space in memory. In addition, a smaller block size can improve transactional concurrency and reduce log file generation rates. As a rule, a data warehouse should use the maximum block size available for your platform (either 16KB or 32KB), whereas a transaction processing system should use an 8KB block size. Rarely is a block size smaller than 8KB beneficial. If you have an extremely high transaction rate system or very limited system memory, you might consider a block size smaller than 8KB.

When conducting full table scans, which are limited to the maximum I/O of the box (usually 64KB—and as high as 1MB on many systems), you can increase the amount of data read into memory in a single I/O by increasing DB_BLOCK_SIZE to 8KB or 16KB, or by increasing the DB_FILE_MULTIBLOCK_READ_COUNT to be the (max I/O size)/DB_BLOCK_SIZE.

Environments that run a lot of single queries to retrieve data could use a smaller block size, but hot spots in those systems will still benefit from using a larger block size. Sites that need to read large amounts of data in a single I/O read should increase the DB_FILE_MULTIBLOCK_READ_COUNT. Setting the DB_FILE_MULTIBLOCK_READ_COUNT higher is especially important for data warehouses that retrieve lots of records. If the use of DB_FILE_MULTIBLOCK_READ_COUNT starts to cause many full table scans (because the optimizer now decides it can perform full table scans much faster and decides to do more of them), then set OPTIMIZER_INDEX_COST_ADJ between 1 and 10 (I usually use 10) to force index use more frequently.

TIP
Increasing the DB_FILE_MULTIBLOCK_READ_COUNT will allow more block reads in a single I/O, giving a benefit similar to a larger block size.

Setting SGA_MAX_SIZE to 25 Percent of the Size Allocated to Main Memory

The general rule is to start with an SGA_MAX_SIZE parameter at 25 percent of the size allocated to your main memory. A large number of users (300+) or a small amount of available memory may force you to make this 15–20 percent of physical memory. A small number of users (less than 100) or a large amount of physical memory may allow you to make this 30–50 percent of physical memory. If you set the SGA_MAX_SIZE less than 128MB, the _ksm_granule_size will be 4MB; if the SGA_MAX_SIZE is greater or equal to 128MB, the _ksm_granule_size will be 16MB.

This granule size determines the multiples for other initialization parameters. A granule size of 4MB means that certain initialization parameters will be rounded up to the nearest 4M. Therefore, if you set SGA_MAX_SIZE to 64M and DB_CACHE_SIZE to 9MB, the DB_CACHE_SIZE will be rounded to 12MB (because the granule size is 4MB). If you set SGA_MAX_SIZE to 200MB and DB_CACHE_SIZE to 9MB, the DB_CACHE_SIZE will be rounded to 16MB (because the granule size is 16MB).

TIP
The SGA_MAX_SIZE determines the granule size for other parameters. An SGA_MAX_SIZE < 128MB means a 4MB granule, whereas an SGA_MAX_SIZE >= 128MB means a 16MB granule size.

Tuning the SHARED_POOL_SIZE for Optimal Performance

Now that we have the memory available for the data set correctly (DB_CACHE_SIZE), we need to ensure that the query gets executed. If the query never makes it into memory, it can never request the data be put in memory; that's where the SHARED_POOL_SIZE comes in. SHARED_POOL_SIZE specifies the memory allocated in the SGA for data dictionary caching and shared SQL statements.

The data dictionary cache is very important because that's where the data dictionary components are buffered. Oracle references the data dictionary several times when a SQL statement is processed. Therefore, the more information (database and application schema and structure) that is stored in memory, the less information that will need to be retrieved from disk.

The data dictionary cache operates the same as the DB_CACHE_SIZE when caching information. For the best performance, it would be great if the entire Oracle data dictionary could be cached in memory. Unfortunately, this usually is not feasible. To deal with this problem, Oracle caches the execution plans for SQL statements, which reduces the number of times dictionary information must be accessed.

Using Stored Procedures for Optimal Use of the Shared SQL Area

Each time a SQL statement is executed, the statement is searched for in the shared SQL area and, if found, used for execution. This saves parsing time and improves overall performance. Therefore, to ensure optimal use of the shared SQL area, use stored procedures as much as possible. However, keep in mind the only time the SQL statement being executed can use a statement already in the shared SQL area is if the statements are identical (meaning they have the same content exactly, the same case, the same number of spaces, etc.). If the statements are not identical, the new statement will be parsed, executed, and placed in the shared SQL area. (Exceptions to this are possible when the initialization parameter CURSOR_SHARING has been set to SIMILAR or FORCE.)

In Listing 4-8, the statements are identical in execution, but the word "from" causes Oracle to treat the two statements as if they were different, thus *not* reusing the original cursor that was located in the shared SQL area.

```
SQL> select name, customer from customer_information;
SQL> select name, customer FROM customer_information;
```

Listing 4-8: Executing identical statements

TIP
PL/SQL must be written exactly the same to be reused. Case differences and any other differences will cause a reparse of the statement.

In Listing 4-9, we are using different values for ENAME, which is causing multiple statements to be parsed.

```
Begin
      SELECT ename  INTO   temp
      FROM   rich
      WHERE  ename = 'SMITH';
      SELECT ename  INTO   temp
      FROM   rich
      WHERE  ename = 'JONES';
end;
```

Listing 4-9: Using different values for ENAME

A query of V$SQLAREA (Listing 4-10) shows that two statements were parsed, even though they were very close to the same thing. Note, however, that PL/SQL converted each to uppercase *and* trimmed spaces *and* carriage returns (which is a benefit of using PL/SQL).

```
SELECT SQL_TEXT
FROM V$SQLAREA
WHERE SQL_TEXT LIKE 'SELECT ENAME%';
SQL_TEXT
-----------------------------------------------------
SELECT ENAME   FROM RICH  WHERE ENAME = 'JONES'
SELECT ENAME   FROM RICH  WHERE ENAME = 'SMITH'
```

Listing 4-10: Querying V$SQLAREA

In Listing 4-11, we see the problem with third-party applications that do not use bind variables (to keep the code "vanilla"). If the following is your output from V$SQLAREA, you may benefit from lowering the SHARED_POOL _SIZE, but CURSOR_SHARING is a better choice.

```
SQL_TEXT
-----------------------------------------------------
select empno from rich778 where empno =451572
select empno from rich778 where empno =451573
select empno from rich778 where empno =451574
select empno from rich778 where empno =451575
select empno from rich778 where empno =451576
etc…
```

Listing 4-11: Querying without bind variables

Tuning SHARED_POOL_SIZE
for Optimal Performance

Set CURSOR_SHARING = FORCE, and the query to V$SQLAREA will change, as shown in Listing 4-12.

```
SQL_TEXT
--------------------------------------------------
select empno from rich778 where empno =:SYS_B_0
```

Listing 4-12: Querying V$SQLAREA

Setting the SHARED_POOL_SIZE High Enough to Fully Use the DB_CACHE_SIZE

If the SHARED_POOL_SIZE is set too low, you will not get the full advantage of your DB_CACHE_SIZE. The queries that can be performed against the Oracle V$ views to determine the data dictionary cache hit ratio and the shared SQL statement are listed in the following section. These will help you determine if increasing the SHARED_POOL_SIZE will improve performance.

The SHARED_POOL_SIZE parameter is specified in bytes. The default value for the SHARED_POOL_SIZE parameter varies per system, but it is generally lower than necessary for large production applications.

Keeping the Data Dictionary Cache Hit Ratio at or above 95 Percent

The data dictionary cache is a key area to tune because the dictionary is accessed so frequently, especially by the internals of Oracle. At startup, the data dictionary cache contains no data. But as more data is read into cache, the likelihood of cache misses decreases. For this reason, monitoring the data dictionary cache should be done only after the system has been up for a while and stabilized. If the dictionary cache hit ratio is below 95 percent, you'll probably need to increase the size of the SHARED_POOL_SIZE parameter in the init.ora. However, keep in mind that this area is also the holder of the library cache.

Use the query in Listing 4-13 against the Oracle V$ view to determine the data dictionary cache hit ratio.

```
select    ((1 - (Sum(GetMisses) / (Sum(Gets) + Sum(GetMisses)))) * 100) "Hit Rate"
from      V$RowCache
where     Gets + GetMisses <> 0;

Hit Rate
91.747126
```

Listing 4-13: Determining the data dictionary cache hit ratio

TIP
Measure hit ratios for the row cache of the shared pool with the V$ROWCACHE view. A hit ratio of over 95 percent should be achieved. However, when the database is initially started, hit ratios will be around 85 percent.

Using Individual Row Cache Parameters to Diagnose Shared Pool Use   To diagnose a problem or overuse of the shared pool, use a modified query on the same table to see how each individual parameter makes up the row cache. The query in Listing 4-14 (a partial output listing) looks at the row cache in detail and places an asterisk (*) by those values that have a miss ratio greater than 10 percent.

```
column parameter         format a20              heading 'Data Dictionary Area'
column gets              format 999,999,999      heading 'Total|Requests'
column getmisses         format 999,999,999      heading 'Misses'
column modifications     format 999,999          heading 'Mods'
column flushes           format 999,999          heading 'Flushes'
column getmiss_ratio     format 9.99             heading 'Miss|Ratio'
set pagesize 50
ttitle 'Shared Pool Row Cache Usage'
select  parameter, gets, getmisses, modifications, flushes,
        (getmisses / decode(gets,0,1,gets)) getmiss_ratio,
        (case when (getmisses / decode(gets,0,1,gets)) > .1 then '*' else ' ' end) " "
from    v$rowcache
where   Gets + GetMisses <> 0;
Tue Aug 27                                                          page    1
                            Shared Pool Row Cache Usage
                          Total                               Miss
Data Dictionary Area      Requests         Misses    Mods  Flushes Ratio
--------------------      ------------   ------------ ------- ------- ----- -

dc_segments                    637            184        0        0   .29 *
dc_tablespaces                  18              3        0        0   .17 *
dc_users                       126             25        0        0   .20 *
dc_rollback_segments           235             21       31       30   .09
dc_objects                     728            167       55        0   .23 *
dc_global_oids                  16              6        0        0   .38 *
dc_object_ids                  672            164       55        0   .24 *
dc_sequences                     1              1        1        1  1.00 *
dc_usernames                   193             10        0        0   .05
dc_histogram_defs               24             24        0        0  1.00 *
dc_profiles                      1              1        0        0  1.00 *
dc_user_grants                  24             15        0        0   .63 *
```

Listing 4-14: Looking at row cache in detail

This query places an asterisk (*) next to any query that has misses greater than 10 percent. It does this by using the CASE expression to limit the miss ratio to the tenth digit, and then analyzes that digit for any value greater than zero (which would indicate a hit ratio of 10 percent or higher). Therefore, a .1 or higher returns an asterisk. The next section explains each column.

Identifying V$ROWCACHE View Contents   The following key columns appear in the V$ROWCACHE view:

- **parameter**   Identifies the specific data dictionary cache item (i.e., dc_ parameter)
- **count**   Shows the total number of entries in the cache
- **usage**   Shows the number of cache entries that contain valid data
- **fixed**   Shows the number of fixed entries in the cache

- **gets**   Shows the total number of requests for information

- **getmisses**   Shows the number of data requests resulting in cache misses

- **scans**   Shows the number of scan requests

- **scanmisses**   Shows the number of times a scan failed to find the data in the cache

- **scancompletes** (for subordinate cache type only)   Shows the number of times the list was scanned completely

- **modifications**   Shows the number of INSERTS, UPDATES, and DELETES

- **flushes**   Shows the number of times flushed to disk

Keeping the Library Cache Reload Ratio at Zero and the Hit Ratio above 95 Percent

For optimal performance, you'll want to keep the library cache reload ratio [sum(reloads)/sum(pins)] at zero and the library cache ratio above 95 percent. If the reload ratio is not zero, then there are statements that are being "aged out" that are later needed and brought back into memory. If the reload ratio is zero (0), that means items in the library cache were never aged or invalidated. If the reload ratio is above 1 percent, the SHARED_POOL_SIZE parameter should probably be increased. Likewise, if the library cache hit ratio comes in below 95 percent, the SHARED_POOL_SIZE parameter may need to be increased.

You can monitor the library cache in a couple of ways. The first method is to execute the STATSPACK report. (STATSPACK is covered in detail in Chapter 14.) The second is to use the V$LIBRARYCACHE view. The query in Listing 4-15 uses the V$LIBRARYCACHE view to examine the reload ratio in the library cache.

```
select    Sum(Pins) "Hits",
          Sum(Reloads) "Misses",
          ((Sum(Reloads) / Sum(Pins)) * 100)"Reload %"
from      V$LibraryCache;
Hits        Misses    Reload %
1969            50    0.253936
```

Listing 4-15: Using the V$LIBRARYCACHE view

The query in Listing 4-16 uses the V$LIBRARYCACHE view statement to examine the library cache's hit ratio in detail:

```
select    Sum(Pins) "Hits",
          Sum(Reloads) "Misses",
          Sum(Pins) / (Sum(Pins) + Sum(Reloads)) "Hit Ratio"
from      V$LibraryCache;
HITS        MISSES     HIT RATIO
1989             5     .99749248
```

Listing 4-16: Using the V$LIBRARYCACHE view statement

The previous hit ratio is excellent (over 99 percent) and does not require any increase in the SHARED_POOL_SIZE parameter.

Using Individual Library Cache Parameters to Diagnose Shared Pool Use   Using the modified query (Listing 4-17) on the same table, we can see how each individual parameter makes up the library cache. This may help diagnose a problem or overuse of the shared pool.

```
set numwidth 3
set space 2
set newpage 0
set pagesize 58
set linesize 80
set tab off
set echo off
ttitle 'Shared Pool Library Cache Usage'
column namespace     format a20             heading 'Entity'
column pins          format 999,999,999     heading 'Executions'
column pinhits       format 999,999,999     heading 'Hits'
column pinhitratio   format 9.99            heading 'Hit|Ratio'
column reloads       format 999,999         heading 'Reloads'
column reloadratio   format .9999           heading 'Reload|Ratio'
spool cache_lib.lis
select   namespace, pins, pinhits, pinhitratio, reloads, reloads
            /decode(pins,0,1,pins) reloadratio
from     v$librarycache;
```

```
Sun Mar 19                                              page    1
                    Shared Pool Library Cache Usage
                                          Hit                  Reload
Entity          Executions        Hits    Ratio    Reloads    Ratio
SQL AREA        1,276,366    1,275,672    1.00          2     .0000
TABLE/PROC        539,431      539,187    1.00          5     .0000
BODY                    0            0    1.00          0     .0000
TRIGGER                 0            0    1.00          0     .0000
INDEX                  21            0     .00          0     .0000
CLUSTER                15            5     .33          0     .0000
OBJECT                  0            0    1.00          0     .0000
PIPE                    0            0    1.00          0     .0000
JAVA SRCE               0            0    1.00          0     .0000
JAVA RES                0            0    1.00          0     .0000
JAVA DATA               0            0    1.00          0     .0000
11 rows selected.
```

Listing 4-17: Using individual library cache parameters

Use the following list to help interpret the contents of the V$LIBRARYCACHE view:

- **namespace**   Values SQL AREA, TABLE/PROCEDURE, BODY, and TRIGGER are the key types.

- **gets**   Shows the number of times a handle was requested for an item in library cache.

- **gethits** Shows the number of times a requested handle was already in cache.

- **gethitratio** Shows the ratio of gethits to gets (gethits/gets).

- **pins** Shows the number of times an item in library cache was executed.

- **pinhits** Shows the number of times an item was executed where that item was already in cache.

- **pinhitratio** Shows the ratio of pinhits to pins (pinhits/pins).

- **reloads** Shows the number of times an item had to be reloaded into cache because it aged out or was invalidated.

Keeping the Pin Hit Ratio for Library Cache Items Close to One

The pin hit ratio for all library cache items [sum(pinhits)/sum(pins)] should be close to one (1). A pin hit ratio of one means that every time the system executed something in library cache, it was already allocated and valid in cache. Although there will always be some misses due to the first time a request is made, misses can also be reduced by writing identical SQL statements.

Keeping the Miss Ratio Less Than 15 Percent

The miss ratio for data dictionary cache [sum(getmisses)/sum(gets)] should be less than 10 to 15 percent. A miss ratio of zero means that every time the system went into the data dictionary cache, it found what it was looking for and did not have to retrieve the information from disk. If the miss ratio [sum(getmisses)/sum(gets)] is greater than 10 to 15 percent, the init.ora SHARED_POOL_SIZE parameter should be increased.

TIP
Measure hit ratios for the library cache of the shared pool with the V$LIBRARYCACHE view. A hit ratio of over 95 percent should be achieved. However, when the database is initially started, hit ratios will be around 85 percent.

Using Available Memory to Determine if the SHARED_POOL_SIZE Is Set Correctly

The main thing people usually want to know is whether any memory is left in the shared pool. To find out how fast memory in the shared pool is being depleted (made noncontiguous) and also which percent is unused (and still contiguous), run the query in Listing 4-18 after starting the database and running production queries for a short period of time (after the first hour of the day).

```
col value for 999,999,999,999 heading "Shared Pool Size"
col bytes for 999,999,999,999 heading "Free Bytes"
select    to_number(v$parameter.value) value, v$sgastat.bytes,
          (v$sgastat.bytes/v$parameter.value)*100 "Percent Free"
from      v$sgastat, v$parameter
where     v$sgastat.name = 'free memory'
and v$parameter.name = 'shared_pool_size'
```

```
and v$sgastat.pool = 'shared pool';
Shared Pool Size        Free Bytes Percent Free
---------------- ---------------- ------------
      50,331,648       46,797,132   92.9775476
```

Listing 4-18: Determining how quickly memory in shared pool is being depleted

If plenty of contiguous free memory (greater than 2MB) is available after running most queries in your production system (you'll have to determine how long this takes), you don't need to increase the SHARED_POOL_SIZE parameter. I have never seen this parameter go all the way to zero. (Oracle saves a portion for emergency operations via the SHARED_POOL_RESERVED_SIZE parameter.) I have seen it go to 2GB (with a shared pool of only 100MB, which makes no sense and is a bug) when the shared pool started approaching zero. (But this is an indicator that the SHARED_POOL_RESERVED_SIZE is set too low.)

TIP
The V$SGASTAT view shows how fast the memory in the shared pool is being depleted. Remember that it is only a rough estimate. It shows you any memory that has never been used combined with any piece of memory that has been reused. Free memory will go up and down throughout the day based on how the pieces are fragmented.

TIP
The V$SGASTAT view is refreshed much better in Oracle8 than in Oracle7 and is an excellent source for monitoring the shared pool.

Using the X$KSMSP Table to Get a Detailed Look at the Shared Pool

The X$KSMSP table is a method of looking at the total breakdown for the shared pool. This table shows the amount of memory that is free, the amount that is freeable, and memory that is retained for large statements that won't fit into the current shared pool. Consider the query shown in Listing 4-19 for a more accurate picture of the shared pool. Refer to Chapter 13 for an in-depth look at this query and how it is adjusted as Oracle is started and as the system begins to need shared pool memory.

```
select    sum(ksmchsiz) Bytes, ksmchcls Status
from      x$ksmsp
group by  ksmchcls;
BYTES           STATUS
 50,000,000     R-free
         40     R-freea
888,326,956     free
    837,924     freeabl
 61,702,380     perm
    359,008     recr
```

Listing 4-19: Querying X$KSMSP

Tuning SHARED_POOL_SIZE for Optimal Performance

Oracle does not state what the values for status in the X$KSMSP table mean. I offer the following possible descriptions in Table 4-1, based on the behavior of these values as researched in Chapter 13. In Chapter 5, I also show how to graph these results in Enterprise Manager.

TIP
The general rule is to make the SHARED_POOL_SIZE parameter 50–150 percent of the size of your DB_CACHE_SIZE. In a system that makes use of a large amount of stored procedures but has limited physical memory, this parameter could make up as much as 150 percent of the size of DB_CACHE_SIZE. In a system that uses no stored procedures but has a large amount of physical memory to allocate to DB_CACHE_SIZE, this parameter may be 10–20 percent of the size of DB_CACHE_SIZE. I have worked on larger systems where the DB_CACHE_SIZE was set as high as 500MB. Note that in a shared server configuration (MTS), items from the PGA are allocated from the shared pool rather than the session process space.

Keep the following recommendations in mind:

■ If the dictionary cache hit ratio is low (below 95 percent), consider increasing SHARED_POOL_SIZE.

■ If the library cache reload ratio is high (> 1 percent), consider increasing SHARED_POOL_SIZE.

Waits Related to Initialization Parameters

Setting initialization parameters incorrectly often results in various types of performance issues that will show up as a general "waits" or "latch waits" in a STATSPACK report. Chapter 14 covers every type of wait and latch issue related to this. Tables 4-2 and 4-3 present wait and latch problems and potential fixes, in an attempt to peak your interest in reading Chapter 14.

Status	Possible Meaning
R-free	This is SHARED_POOL_RESERVED_SIZE (default 5 percent of SP).
R-freea	This is probably reserved memory that is freeable but not flushable.
free	This is the amount of contiguous free memory available.
freeabl	This is freeable, but not flushable, shared memory, currently in use.
perm	I have read that this is permanently allocated and nonfreeable memory; however, in testing this, it behaves as free memory not yet moved to the free area for use.
recr	This is allocated memory that is flushable when the shared pool is low on memory.

TABLE 4-1. *Possible values for status in the X$KSMSP table*

Wait Problem	Potential Fix
Free buffer	Increase the DB_CACHE_SIZE; shorten the checkpoint; tune the code.
Buffer busy	Segment header; add freelists or freelist groups.
Buffer busy	Data block; separate hot data; use reverse key indexes; smaller blocks. Data block; increase initrans and/or maxtrans.
Buffer busy	Undo header; add rollback segments or areas.
Buffer busy	Undo block; commit more; larger rollback segments or areas.
Latch free	Investigate the detail.
Log buffer space	Increase the log buffer; faster disks for the redo logs.
Scattered read	Indicates many full table scans; tune the code; cache small tables.
Sequential read	Indicates many index reads; tune the code (especially joins).

TABLE 4-2.   *Wait problems and potential fixes*

Some latch problems have often been bug-related in the past, so make sure you check Metalink for issues related to latches. Investigate any latches that have a hit ratio below 99 percent. Some of the more common latches on the problem list include the cache buffer chains, redo copy, library cache, and the cache buffer LRU chain.

Using Oracle Multiple Buffer Pools

There are pools for the allocation of memory that relate to the DB_CACHE_SIZE and SHARED_POOL_SIZE. Each of these parameters, which were all-inclusive of the memory they allocate, now has additional options for memory allocation within each memory pool. I will cover each separately.

Latch Problem	Potential Fix
Library cache	Use bind variables; adjust the shared_pool_size.
Shared pool	Use bind variables; adjust the shared_pool_size.
Row cache objects	Increase the shared pool.
Cache buffers chain	_DB_BLOCK_HASH_BUCKETS needs to be increased or prime.

TABLE 4-3.   *Latch problems and potential fixes*

Pools Related to DB_BLOCK_BUFFERS and Allocating Memory for Data

This section focuses on the Oracle pools that are used to store the actual data in memory. The init.ora parameters DB_CACHE_SIZE, DB_KEEP_CACHE_SIZE, and DB_RECYCLE_CACHE_SIZE are the determining factors for memory used to store data.

DB_CACHE_SIZE refers to the total size in bytes of the main buffer cache (or memory for data) in the SGA. Two additional buffer pools are DB_KEEP_CACHE_SIZE and DB_RECYCLE_CACHE_SIZE. These two pools serve the same purpose as the main buffer cache (DB_CACHE_SIZE), except that the algorithm to maintain the pool is different for all three available pools. Note that the BUFFER_POOL_KEEP and BUFFER_POOL_RECYCLE parameters have been deprecated and should no longer be used. Unlike BUFFER_POOL_KEEP and BUFFER_POOL_RECYCLE, the DB_KEEP_CACHE_SIZE and DB_RECYCLE_CACHE_SIZE parameters are not subtracted from the DB_CACHE_SIZE; they are allocated in addition to the DB_CACHE_SIZE.

The *main buffer cache* (defined by DB_CACHE_SIZE) maintains the Least Recently Used (LRU) list and flushes the oldest buffers in the list. Although all three pools use the LRU replacement policy, the goal for the main buffer cache is to fit most data being used in memory.

The *keep pool* (defined by DB_KEEP_CACHE_SIZE) is hopefully never flushed, and is intended for buffers that you want to be *pinned* indefinitely (buffers that are very important and need to stay in memory). Use the keep pool for small tables (that will all fit in this pool) that are frequently accessed and need to be in memory at all times.

The *recycle pool* (defined by DB_RECYCLE_CACHE_SIZE) is a pool in which you expect the data to be regularly flushed because too much data is being accessed to stay in memory. Use the recycle pool for large, less important data that is usually accessed only once in a while. (Usually inexperienced ad-hoc user tables are put here.)

The following examples give a quick overview of how information is allocated to the various buffer pools. Remember, if no pool is specified, the buffers in the main pool are used.

1. Create a table that will be stored in the keep pool upon being accessed:

   ```
   Create table state_list (state_abbrev varchar2(2), state_desc
   varchar2(25))
   Storage (buffer_pool keep);
   ```

2. Alter the table to the recycle pool:

   ```
   Alter table state_list storage (buffer_pool recycle);
   ```

3. Alter the table back to the keep pool:

   ```
   Alter table state_list storage (buffer_pool keep);
   ```

4. Find the disk and memory reads in the keep pool:

   ```
   select    physical_reads "Disk Reads",
             db_block_gets + consistent_gets "Memory Reads"
   from      v$buffer_pool_statistics
   where     name = 'KEEP';
   ```

NOTE
The previous query uses v$buffer_pool_statistics, which is created with catalog.sql.

Modifying the LRU Algorithm

This section is for experts. Skip this section if you've used Oracle for only a decade or less. You can use five undocumented initialization parameters (defaults are in parenthesis) to alter the LRU algorithm for greater efficiency when you have thoroughly studied and understood your system buffer usage.

- **_db_percent_hot_default (50)**   The percent of buffers in the hot region

- **_db_aging_touch_time (3)**   Seconds that must pass to increment touch count again

- **_db_aging_hot_criteria (2)**   Threshold to move a buffer to the MRU end of LRU chain

- **_db_aging_stay_count (0)**   Touch count reset to this when moved to MRU end

- **_db_aging_cool_count (1)**   Touch count reset to this when moved to LRU end

Setting the first parameter lower increases hanging on to older buffers, and setting it higher causes a flush sooner. Setting the second parameter lower gives a higher value to buffers that are executed a lot in a short period of time. Setting the third, fourth, and fifth parameters relates to how quickly to move things from the hot to cold end and how long they stay on each end.

Pools Related to SHARED_POOL_SIZE and Allocating Memory for Statements

This section focuses on the Oracle9*i* pools that are used to store the actual statements in memory. Unlike the pools related to the data, the LARGE_POOL_SIZE is allocated outside the memory allocated for SHARED_POOL_SIZE, but is part of the SGA.

The LARGE_POOL_SIZE is a pool of memory used for the same operations as the SHARED_POOL_SIZE is used to store memory. Oracle defines this as the size set aside for large allocations of the shared pool. I have found in testing that this memory (at the time of this writing) was allocated outside the SHARED_POOL_SIZE and taken from physical memory. You'll have to perform your own testing to determine where the allocations are coming from in your system and version of Oracle. The minimum setting is 300KB, but the setting must also be as big as the _LARGE_POOL_MIN_ALLOC, which is the minimum size of shared pool memory requested that will force an allocation in the LARGE_POOL_SIZE memory. Unlike the shared pool, the large pool does not have an LRU list. Oracle does not attempt to age memory out of the large pool.

You can view your pool settings by querying the V$PARAMETER view, as shown in Listing 4-20:

```
select    name, value, isdefault, isses_modifiable, issys_modifiable
from      v$parameter
where     name like '%pool%';
NAME                      Shared Pool ISDEFAULT ISSES ISSYS_MOD
------------------------  ----------- --------- ----- ---------
shared_pool_size          50331648    FALSE     FALSE IMMEDIATE
shared_pool_reserved_size 2516582     TRUE      FALSE FALSE
large_pool_size           8388608     FALSE     FALSE IMMEDIATE
java_pool_size            33554432    FALSE     FALSE FALSE
buffer_pool_keep                      TRUE      FALSE FALSE
buffer_pool_recycle                   TRUE      FALSE FALSE
global_context_pool_size              TRUE      FALSE FALSE
```

```
olap_page_pool_size          33554432     TRUE        TRUE   DEFERRED
8 rows selected.
```

Listing 4-20: Querying V$PARAMETER view

TIP
The additional buffer pools (memory for data) available in Oracle are initially set to zero.

Tuning the PGA_AGGREGATE_TARGET for Optimal Use of Memory

The PGA_AGGREGATE_TARGET specifies the total amount of session PGA memory that Oracle will attempt to allocate across all sessions. PGA_AGGREGATE_TARGET is new to Oracle9*i* and should be used in place of the *_SIZE parameters, such as SORT_AREA_SIZE. Also, in Oracle9*i*, the PGA_AGGREGATE_TARGET parameter does not automatically configure ALL *_SIZE parameters. For example, both LARGE_POOL_SIZE and JAVA_POOL_SIZE parameters are not affected by PGA_AGGREGATE_TARGET. The advantage of using PGA_AGGREGATE_TARGET is the ability to cap the total user session memory to minimize O/S paging.

When PGA_AGGREGATE_TARGET is set, WORKAREA_SIZE_POLICY must be set to AUTO. Like the V$DB_CACHE_ADVICE view, the V$PGA_TARGET_ADVICE (Oracle 9.2) and V$PGA_TARGET_ADVICE_HISTOGRAM views exist to assist in tuning the PGA_AGGREGATE_TARGET. Figures 4-5 and 4-6 graphically represent these views in Oracle Enterprise Manager.

The PGA_AGGREGATE_TARGET should be set to attempt to keep the ESTD_PGA_CACHE_HIT_PERCENTAGE greater than 95 percent. The query in Listing 4-21 returns the minimum value for the PGA_AGGREGATE_TARGET that is projected to yield a 95 percent or greater cache hit ratio.

```
SELECT  MIN(PGA_TARGET_FOR_ESTIMATE)
FROM    V$PGA_TARGET_ADVICE
WHERE   ESTD_PGA_CACHE_HIT_PERCENTAGE > 95;


MIN    (PGA_TARGET_FOR_ESTIMATE)
-----------------------------
              12582912
```

Listing 4-21: Determining the minimum value for PGA_AGGREGATE_TARGET

Modifying the Size of Your SGA to Avoid Paging and Swapping

Before you increase the size of your SGA, you must understand the effects on the physical memory of your system. If you increase parameters that use more memory than what is available on your system, serious degradation in performance may occur. When your system processes jobs, if it doesn't have enough memory, it will start paging or swapping to complete the active task.

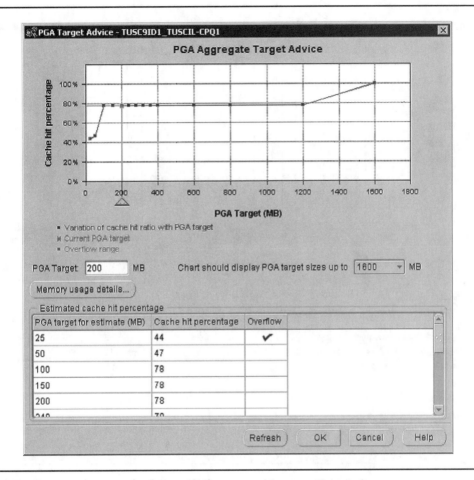

FIGURE 4-5. *Enterprise Manager—PGA Aggregate Target Advice*

When *paging* occurs, information that is not currently being used is moved from memory to disk. This allows memory to be used by a process that currently needs it. If paging happens a lot, the system will decrease in performance, causing processes to take longer to run.

When *swapping* occurs, an active process is moved from memory to disk temporarily so another active process that also desires memory can run. Swapping is based on system cycle time. If swapping happens a lot, your system is dead. Depending on the amount of memory available, an SGA that is too large can cause swapping.

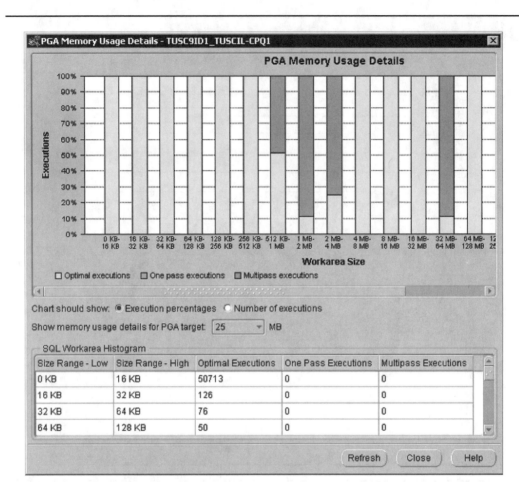

FIGURE 4-6. *Enterprise Manager—PGA Memory Usage Details*

Understanding the OPTIMIZER_MODE: Cost-Based vs. Rule-Based Optimization

The cost-based optimizer was built to make your tuning life easier by choosing better paths for your poorly written queries. Rule-based optimization was built on a set of rules about how Oracle processes statements. You should use cost-based optimization at all times because rule-based optimization is expected to eventually be eliminated and won't be available for use. Rule-based optimization is still available in Oracle9i, but now is the time to convert problem queries, created using rule-based optimization, to cost-based optimization, and to tune those queries for cost-based optimization. In Oracle, many features are available only when using the cost-based optimization. Oracle has stated that a rule-based optimizer will not be available in a future release. Because of the pending demise of the rule-based optimizer and the fact that not all new features are available if not using cost-based optimization, you shouldn't design applications to use the cost-based optimizer.

How Optimization Looks at the Data

Rule-based optimization is *Oracle-centric,* whereas cost-based optimization *is data-centric.* The optimizer mode under which the database operates is set via the init.ora parameter OPTIMIZER_MODE. The possible optimizer modes are as follows:

- **CHOOSE**   Uses cost-based optimization for all analyzed tables. This is a good mode for well-built and well-tuned systems (for advanced users).

- **RULE**   Always uses rule-based optimization. If you are still using this, you need to start using cost-based optimization, because rule-based optimization will be eliminated in Oracle10 (or so I am told).

- **FIRST_ROWS**   Gets the first row faster (generally forces index use). This is good for untuned systems that process lots of single transactions (for beginners).

- **FIRST_ROWS_(1 | 10 | 100 | 1000)**   Gets the first *n* rows faster. This is good for applications that routinely display partial results to users, such as paging data to a user in a web application.

- **ALL_ROWS**   Gets all rows faster (generally forces index suppression). This is good for untuned, high-volume batch systems (usually not used).

The default optimizer mode for Oracle9*i* is CHOOSE, but the optimizer will use rule-based optimization until the tables are analyzed (statistics are gathered for cost-based), even when the optimizer is set to CHOOSE. Also, cost-based optimization will be used even if the tables are not analyzed, if a hint is supplied.

TIP
Although an OPTIMIZER_MODE = CHOOSE will use cost-based optimization (when tables are analyzed), there is no OPTIMIZER_MODE called COST. This is a common misconception.

TIP
If you are not sure which optimizer mode to use, select CHOOSE and analyze all tables. By doing this, you will be using cost-based optimization. The cost-based optimizer is where the future of Oracle will be focused. As the data in a table changes, tables need to be reanalyzed regularly.

Creating Enough Dispatchers

When using the multithreaded servers, you need to watch for high busy rates for the existing dispatcher processes and increases in wait times for response queues of existing dispatcher processes.

If the wait time increases, as the application runs under normal use, you may wish to add more dispatcher processes, especially if the processes are busy more than 50 percent of the time.

Use the statement shown in Listing 4-22 to determine the busy rate.

```
select     Network,
           ((Sum(Busy) / (Sum(Busy) + Sum(Idle))) * 100) "% Busy Rate"
from       V$Dispatcher
group by Network;


NETWORK       % Busy Rate
TCP1                    0
TCP2                    0
```

Listing 4-22: Determining the busy rate

Use the statement in Listing 4-23 to check for responses to user processes that are waiting in a queue to be sent to the user.

```
select     Network Protocol,
           Decode (Sum(Totalq), 0, 'No Responses',
           Sum(Wait) / Sum(TotalQ) || ' hundredths of a second')
           "Average Wait Time Per Response"
from       V$Queue Q, V$Dispatcher D
where      Q.Type = 'DISPATCHER'
and        Q.Paddr = D.Paddr
group by Network;


PROTOCOL         Average Wait Time Per Response
TCP1             0 hundredths of a second
TCP2             1 hundredths of a second
```

Listing 4-23: Checking responses to user processes waiting in queue

Use the statement in Listing 4-24 to check the requests from user processes that are waiting in a queue to be sent to the user.

```
select     Decode (Sum(Totalq), 0, 'Number of Requests',
           Sum(Wait) / Sum(TotalQ) || 'hundredths of a second')
           "Average Wait Time Per Request"
from       V$Queue
where      Type = 'COMMON';


Average Wait Time Per Request
12 hundredths of a second
```

Listing 4-24: Checking requests from user processes waiting in queue

Open Cursors

If you don't have enough open cursors, you will receive errors to that effect. The key is to stay ahead of your system by increasing this init.ora parameter before you run out of open cursors. My recommendation is to use the operating system maximum as the setting for open cursors.

Twenty-Five Important Initialization Parameters

The following initialization parameters are what I consider to be the 25 most important parameters.

- **DB_CACHE_SIZE**   Initial memory allocated to data cache.

- **PGA_AGGREGATE_TARGET**   Soft memory cap for total of all users' PGA.

- **SHARED_POOL_SIZE**   Memory allocated for data dictionary, SQL, and PL/SQL.

- **SGA_MAX_SIZE**   Maximum memory to which the SGA can dynamically grow.

- **OPTIMIZER_MODE**   CHOOSE, RULE, FIRST_ROWS, FIRST_ROWS_*n*, or ALL_ROWS.

- **CURSOR_SHARING**   Converts literal SQL to SQL with bind variables, reducing parse overhead.

- **OPTIMIZER_INDEX_COST_ADJ**   Coarse adjustment between the cost of an index scan and the cost of a full table scan. Set between 1 and 10 to force index use more frequently.

- **QUERY_REWRITE_ENABLED**   Used to enable materialized view and function-based-index capabilities.

- **DB_FILE_MULTIBLOCK_READ_COUNT**   Used for full table scans to perform I/O more efficiently.

- **LOG_BUFFER**   Buffer for uncommitted transactions in memory.

- **DB_KEEP_CACHE_SIZE**   Memory allocated to keep pool.

- **DB_RECYCLE_CACHE_SIZE**   Memory allocated to recycle pool.

- **DBWR_IO_SLAVES** (also DB_WRITER_PROCESSES if you have async I/O)   Number of writers from SGA to disk for simulated async I/O.

- **LARGE_POOL_SIZE**   Total blocks in the large pool allocation for large PL/SQL.

- **STATISTICS_LEVEL (9.2)**   Used to enable advisory information and optionally keep additional O/S statistics to refine optimizer decisions.

- **HASH_JOIN_ENABLED**   Enables hash joining for fast table joins.

- **JAVA_POOL_SIZE**   Memory allocated to the JVM for Java stored procedures.

- **JAVA_MAX_SESSIONSPACE_SIZE**   Upper limit on memory that is used to keep track of user session state of Java classes.

- **MAX_SHARED_SERVERS**   Upper limit on shared servers when using shared servers.

- **PARALLEL_AUTOMATIC_TUNING**   Enables parallel query automatic tuning capabilities. It also helps to configure the default values for many other parameters.

NOTE
*The PARALLEL_AUTOMATIC_TUNING parameter is also used
by the database to automatically calculate the settings for
PARALLEL_ADAPTIVE_MULTI_USER, PARALLEL_MAX_SERVERS,
PROCESSES, SESSIONS, and TRANSACTIONS.*

- **WORKAREA_SIZE_POLICY**   Enables automatic PGA size management.
- **FAST_START_MTTR_TARGET**   Bounds time to complete a crash recovery.
- **LOG_CHECKPOINT_INTERVAL**   Checkpoint frequency (O/S blocks).

NOTE
*Prior to Oracle 8i, the parameters LOG_CHECKPOINT_INTERVAL and
LOG_CHECKPOINT_TIMEOUT were used to trigger a checkpoint, but
not anymore. The position in the redo log where recovery is to start is
referred to as the checkpoint position. All the data blocks referenced
in the redo log prior to that point are guaranteed to have already been
written to disk by DBWn. LOG_CHECKPOINT_INTERVAL is defined
as the "distance" between the checkpoint position and the end or tail
of the redo log. It can also be thought of as the "age" of the first entry in
the checkpoint queue. LOG_CHECKPOINT_INTERVAL is one of four
parameters that can be set to identify the checkpoint position. However,
the parameter resulting in the smallest number of redo blocks to recover
after an instance crash will be used to set the checkpoint position.*

- **OPEN_CURSORS**   Specifies the size of the private area used to hold user statements.
- **DB_BLOCK_SIZE**   Default block size for the database.

TIP
*Setting certain init.ora parameters correctly could be the difference
between a report taking two seconds and two hours. Try changes out
on a test system thoroughly before implementing those changes in a
production environment!*

Finding Undocumented init.ora Parameters

Querying the table X$KSPPI (shown in listing 4-25) returns the documented and undocumented
init.ora parameters. The query can be done only as user SYS, so be careful. See Chapter 13 for
a complete look at the X$ tables. My top 13 undocumented init.ora parameters are listed in
Appendix A. Appendix C provides a complete listing of the X$ tables as of this writing.

```
select KSPPINM, KSPPSTVL, KSPPSTDF
from   x$ksppi a, x$ksppcv b
```

```
where  a.indx=b.indx
order  by KSPPINM;
```

Listing 4-25: Querying X$KSPPI

The following is a brief description of the columns in the x$ksppi and x$ksppcv tables.

KSPPINM	Parameter name
KSPPITY	Parameter type
KSPPDESC	Parameter description
KSPPSTVL	Current value for the parameter
KSPPSTDF	Default value for the parameter

A partial output of the init.ora parameters is shown in Listing 4-26:

```
KSPPINM                              KSPPSTVL              KSPPSTDF
------------------------------       --------------------  ----------
...
_write_clones                        3                     TRUE
_yield_check_interval                100000                TRUE
active_instance_count                                      TRUE
aq_tm_processes                      1                     FALSE
archive_lag_target                   0                     TRUE
```

Listing 4-26: Partial output of init.ora parameters

TIP
Using undocumented initialization parameters can cause corruption. Never use these if you are not an expert! Ensure that you work with Oracle Support before setting these parameters.

Understanding the Typical Server

The key to mastering Oracle is understanding its dynamic nature. Oracle continues to have many attributes of earlier versions while also attacking the future of distributed database and object-oriented programming stored within the database. Experience from earlier versions of Oracle always benefits the DBA in future versions of Oracle. Some of the future changes that should be considered as you build your system are as follows:

- Oracle can be completely distributed and maintained at a single point. (A system with many databases and locations managed by one DBA will likely be the norm in the corporate future.)

- Database maintenance is becoming completely visual (all point-and-click maintenance as in Enterprise Manager). The V$ views are still your best access.

- Network throughput continues to be an issue that looks to be solved by technology (in the next two years).

- Internet and intranet access is pushing client/server back to browser/host types of setups with big security risks that are often overcome by the use of multiple databases.

- CPUs will continue to get faster, eliminating CPU as an issue. (I/O and correct design will continue to be the issues.)

- Object-oriented development will be crucial to rapid system development.

- Current database design theory is being rewritten to focus more on denormalization.

- Because of graphics, databases are becoming increasingly larger than they were in the past. Also, the fact that disk space is getting cheaper has made businesses more willing to keep data around longer.

Modeling a Typical Server

Table 4-4 contains rough estimates designed as setup guidelines. However, these are only *guidelines*: every system is different and must be tuned based on the system's demands. (CPU speed depends on the type of processor—RISC vs. Intel.)

Database Size	Up to 25GB	100–200GB	500–1000GB
Number of users	100	200	500
Number of CPUs	2 × 900 MHz	4 × 900 MHz	8+ × 900 MHz
System memory	2GB	4GB	16GB+
SGA_MAX_SIZE	512MB	1GB	2GB
PGA_AGGREGATE_TARGET	256MB	512MB	1GB
Total disk capacity	100GB	500–1000GB	1–3TB
Percentage of query	75 percent	75 percent	75 percent
Percentage of DML	25 percent	25 percent	25 percent
Percent batch	20 percent	20 percent	20 percent
Percent online	80 percent	80 percent	80 percent
Number of redo logs multiplexed?		6–10	6–12
Number of control files	4	4	4
Number of temporary tablespaces	1–4	1–4	2–5
Number of rollback segments (not needed if using UNDO)	4–10	8–20	10–25

TABLE 4-4. *Setup Guidelines*

Database Size	Up to 25GB	100–200GB	500–1000GB
Archiving used?	Yes	Yes	Yes
Buffer hit ratio	95 percent +	95 percent +	95 percent +
Dictionary hit ratio	95 percent +	95 percent +	95 percent +
Library hit ratio	95 percent +	95 percent +	95 percent +
Other system software (other than Oracle)	Minimum	Minimum	Minimum
Use raw devices?	No	No	No
Use parallel query?	Depends on queries	Depends on queries	Probably in many queries

TABLE 4-4.   *Setup Guidelines* (continued)

The following variables can cause diversion from the typical server:

- Heavy batch processing may need much larger rollback or UNDO, REDO, and TEMP tablespace sizes.

- Heavy DML processing may need much larger rollback or UNDO, REDO, and TEMP tablespace sizes.

- Heavy user access to large tables requires more CPU and memory, and larger TEMP tablespace sizes.

- Poorly tuned systems require more CPU and memory, and larger TEMP tablespace sizes.

- A greater number of disks and controllers always increase performance by reducing I/O.

- An increase in the disk capacity can speed backup and recovery time by going to disk and not tape.

TIPS & REVIEW

Tips Review

The key init.ora parameters in Oracle are SGA_MAX_SIZE, PGA_AGGREGATE_TARGET, DB_CACHE_SIZE, and SHARED_POOL_SIZE.

- If you can't figure out why your system isn't using the value in your init.ora file, you probably have an SPFILE overriding it.

- Changing init.ora parameters dynamically is a powerful feature, especially when you allocate memory on-the-fly to address performance issues.

- Physical memory is generally much faster than retrieving data from disk, so make sure the SGA is large enough to accommodate memory reads when it is effective to do so.

■ Poor joins and poor indexing also yield very high hit ratios, so make sure your hit ratio isn't high for a reason other than a well-tuned system. An unusually high hit ratio may indicate the introduction of code that is poorly indexed or includes join issues.

■ The best use of hit ratios is still to compare over time to help alert you of a substantial change to a system on a given day. Although some have deprecated hit ratios, they are usually tool vendors who don't see the value of tracking hit ratios over time because their tools are point-in-time or reactive-based tuning solutions. Hit ratios should never be your only tool, but they should definitely be one of many proactive tools in your arsenal.

■ In Oracle9i, use the TopSQL monitor of Oracle's SQL Analyze to find problem queries.

■ A low hit ratio for a query is an indication of a missing or suppressed index.

■ Slow queries show in V$SQLAREA view with poor hit ratios the first time they are executed. Make sure you tune them at that time. The second time they execute, they may not show a poor hit ratio.

■ Oracle Forms applications usually have an unusually high hit ratio. If your site uses a lot of Oracle Forms, shoot for a higher hit ratio because the hit ratio will be artificially high.

■ Sites in which most users of the system use rollbacks frequently should shoot for a higher hit ratio because the hit ratio could be artificially high from rollback use.

■ Increasing the DB_FILE_MULTIBLOCK_READ_COUNT allows more block reads in a single I/O, giving a benefit similar to a larger block size.

■ PL/SQL must be written *exactly* the same to be reused. Case differences and any other differences will cause a reparse of the statement.

■ Measure hit ratios for the row cache of the shared pool with the V$ROWCACHE view. A hit ratio of over 95 percent should be achieved. However, when the database is initially started, hit ratios will be around 85 percent.

■ Measure hit ratios for the library cache of the shared pool with the V$LIBRARYCACHE view. A hit ratio of over 95 percent should be achieved. However, when the database is initially started, hit ratios will be around 85 percent.

■ The V$SGASTAT view shows how fast the memory in the shared pool is being depleted. Remember that it is only a rough estimate. It shows you any memory that has never been used, combined with any piece of memory that has been reused. Free memory will go up and down throughout the day based on how the pieces are fragmented.

■ The general rule is to make the SHARED_POOL_SIZE parameter 50–150 percent of the size of your DB_CACHE_SIZE.

■ The additional buffer pools (memory for data) available in Oracle are initially set to zero.

■ Although an OPTIMIZER_MODE = CHOOSE will use cost-based optimization (when tables are analyzed), there is no OPTIMIZER_MODE called COST. This is a common misconception.

■ If you are not sure which optimizer mode to use, use CHOOSE and analyze all tables. By doing this, you will be using cost-based optimization. The cost-based optimizer is where the future of Oracle will be focused.

■ Use _CORRUPTED_ROLLBACK_SEGMENTS to get a database up that has corrupted rollback segments. Once up, drop and re-create the problem rollback segments. Use _ALLOW_RESETLOGS_CORRUPTION for the databases that were backed up (image copy) while the database was up. (See the *Oracle DBA Tips & Techniques* book by Sumit Sarin (Oracle Press, 2000) for more information.)

■ Setting certain init.ora parameters correctly could be the difference between a report taking two seconds and two hours. Try changes out on a test system thoroughly *before* implementing those changes in a production environment!

References

All about Oracle's Touch-Count Data Block Buffer Algorithm, Craig Shallahamer (excellent)
DBA Tuning; Now YOU are the Expert, Rich Niemiec; TUSC
Performance Tuning Guide, Oracle Corporation
Randy Swanson did the update for this chapter.

CHAPTER
5

Enterprise Manager
and Tuning Pack
(DBA and Developer)

This chapter provides a quick tour of Oracle Enterprise Manager 9.2 (OEM). The tour does not explore the entire product, nor teach you how to use all of the features. (That would take an entire book.) Rather, this chapter exposes you to some of the tools and tuning features that may be helpful in your tuning endeavors. Oracle Enterprise Manager is an excellent tuning tool for all levels of DBAs. The credit for this chapter must go to Valerie K. Kane and David LeRoy of Oracle, who tirelessly updated the previous chapter for not only the current release, but the next release of Enterprise Manager. I was quite fortunate that they ensured the timeliness of the information by pulling information from the future version of the product.

One way to ensure great performance for your system is to monitor it for potential performance issues before they become major problems. One of the vehicles that provides a GUI interface to tuning is Oracle Enterprise Manager and its related performance tuning add-on products. Oracle Enterprise Manager continues to change over time, but the core information has generally remained the same. The product becomes easier to implement in this version 9.2 with the addition of provided implementation scripts.

Oracle Enterprise Manager standard applications include a central management console and additional packs. The two packs discussed in this chapter are the Diagnostics pack and the Tuning pack. The Oracle Diagnostics pack includes Performance Overview, Top Sessions, TopSQL, Lock Monitor, Performance Manager, Advanced Events, Capacity Planner, and Trace Data Viewer. The Oracle Tuning pack includes SQL Analyze, Oracle Expert, Index Tuning Wizard, Tablespace Map, Reorg Wizard, and Outline Management. While space constraints prevent me from discussing all of these tools, I invite you to explore them on your own.

While the overall Oracle Enterprise Manager tool is most suited for work by the DBA, the SQL Analyze tool is suited for both the developer and the DBA who performs query tuning.

The following tips are covered in this chapter:

- Using the Enterprise Manager console to manage schema objects and storage

- Using Performance Overview to graphically view strategic tuning areas

- Using the graphical view of hit ratios for the buffer cache, library cache, rowcache, and memory sorts

- Creating your own custom charts in Performance Manager

- Using TopSQL to get the worst-performing queries on your system

- Using SQL Analyze to quickly view the EXPLAIN PLAN tree of a query

- Using SQL Analyze for a side-by-side comparison of SQL

- Using the Tuning Wizard within SQL Analyze

- Using the Tablespace Map

- Using Oracle Expert to generate a tuning report of suggested changes

- Using Oracle Expert to generate an implementation file for your tuning session to fix problem performance areas

The Enterprise Manager Console

The Enterprise Manager Console (Figure 5-1) provides integrated administration and improved display of management information through a two-pane, master/detail view of the DBA's global environment. The *master* left pane displays the navigator tree (navigator), while the *detail* right pane shows property sheets for objects selected within the navigator. In addition, all database administration has been entirely integrated into the console.

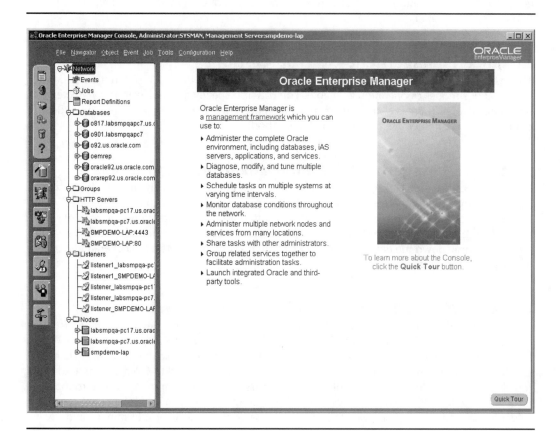

FIGURE 5-1. *Enterprise Manager Console*

The Instance Folder

You can use the Instance folder for a particular database to look at information about individual sessions, locks, resource plans, and the systemwide initialization parameters. Buttons on the left toolbar include an option to refresh the current database. A drop-down menu choice under Sessions includes the option to restrict or allows all sessions, usually used in conjunction with starting/stopping the database. The option to restrict sessions can be particularly helpful for database maintenance when it is important to disallow users from logging into the database.

Instance Management-The Status Screen

The Instance Manager status property sheet shows the output from the V$SGA view. It gives the general memory allocations to Oracle, showing the version of Oracle being used and the options that you have installed.

Instance Management–Startup Options

The Instance Manager startup options shown in Figure 5-2 allow the DBA to start the database in the various modes of operation available. You can also specify an initialization parameter within this screen. There is also a shutdown screen (not shown) that shows the standard shutdown options (Normal, Immediate, Transactional, and Abort).

Instance Management–The Initialization Parameters

This section of Instance Manager shows the init.ora parameters. You can view the initialization parameters by clicking the All Initialization Parameters button, as shown in Figure 5-2. Figure 5-3 shows the init.ora parameters after the button is clicked. It identifies the current setting for the parameter, as well as whether the parameter can be modified (dynamic=Yes) without shutting down the database. The Oracle initialization parameters are covered in detail in Chapter 4 and Appendix A.

Instance Management–Examine a Single Session

You can view all information related to a given user by looking at the Sessions screen, as shown in Figure 5-4. This screen can be particularly helpful in identifying an actual user known to be problematic. The session ID and serial number are displayed, enabling you to end the session or remove the user from the system. A section called In-Doubt Transactions (not shown) within the Distributed folder is used to issue a forced commit or forced rollback for a given session. While a single session is shown in the figure, you can select the Sessions folder to view all sessions on a single screen. All session IDs, usernames, terminals, and programs running are displayed on the screen.

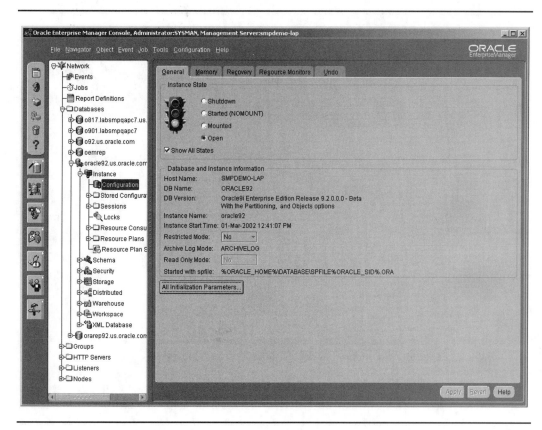

FIGURE 5-2. *Instance Management–The database status and startup options*

Instance Management
Memory Advisors

TIP
You can view all sessions by opening the Sessions folder. The detail also allows you to view Top Sessions.

Instance Management–Memory Advisors

Enterprise Manager also includes memory advisors that can help tune database memory structures. These advisors help you tune the buffer cache, shared pool, and PGA (Program Global Area). New in Oracle9i is the PGA_AGGREGATE_TARGET initialization parameter, which is described

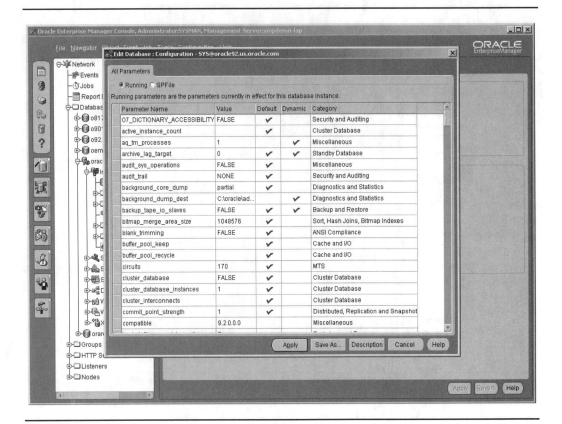

FIGURE 5-3. *Instance Management–The initialization parameters*

in Chapter 4. The PGA Aggregate Target Advice memory advisor (not shown) can be used to tune this parameter.

The Buffer Cache advisor (shown in Figure 5-5), for example, helps you determine an optimal size for the buffer cache by collecting statistics of your currently running system and presenting the estimated I/O savings for different cache sizes. Using the advisor, you can interpret the response of your system for the present buffer cache size, and you can set a new optimal size for your cache.

The Schema Folder

The Instance folder shows the information for a given instance, but the Schema folder goes one level deeper, showing an individual schema (within the database opened by a given instance)

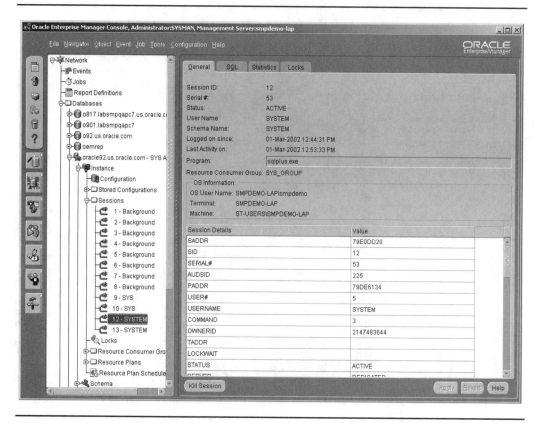

FIGURE 5-4. *Instance Management–Looking at a single session*

and the objects associated with that schema. This section does not show every screen available within the Schema folder. The choices that are available from the navigator include tables, clusters, functions, indexes, object types, package bodies, packages, procedures, synonyms, triggers, user-defined types, and views. One of the great aspects about coded objects, such as procedures and triggers, is that from the Schema folder, you can recompile the object with the click of a button. Multiple screens are associated with each choice.

Schema Management–Examine Specific Tables

In Figure 5-6, we drilled down into the table section for the SCOTT schema to view the DEPT table. All of the columns for the given table are displayed. The Storage tab shows storage information for the table (INITIAL, NEXT, PCTINCREASE, MINEXTENTS, MAXEXTENTS,

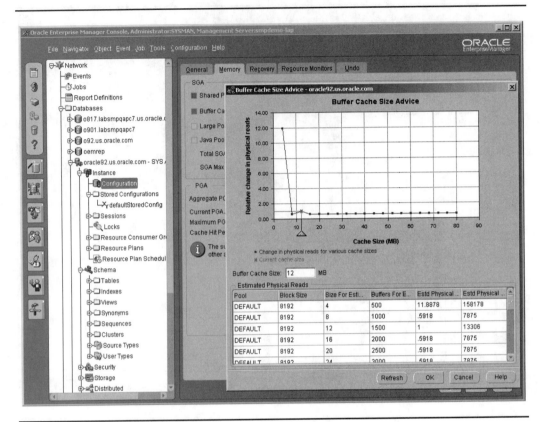

FIGURE 5-5. *The Buffer Cache advisor*

PCTFREE, and PCTUSED). The Constraints tab shows any constraints and has options for adding, removing, enabling, or disabling constraints. If you select the Tables folder, the number of rows and last analyzed date for all tables are displayed; this information shows up only if the table has been analyzed.

Using the Create Like button on the Console toolbar, you can create a DEPT2 table with the same column and storage information as the DEPT table. Simply select the DEPT table and click the Create Like button. The Create property sheet appears, containing the same specification as the DEPT table. You need only enter a new name.

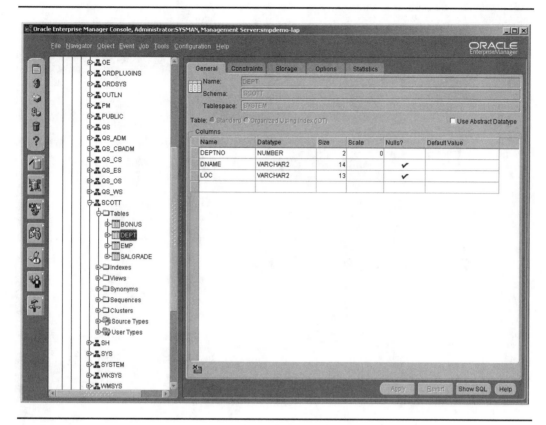

FIGURE 5-6. *Schema Management–Looking at specific tables*

You can also use the Show Object DDL option to generate the create statement for a table or other object. Right-clicking the DEPT table and choosing Show Object DDL from the shortcut menu produces the result shown in Figure 5-7.

Schema Management–Examine Specific Indexes

In Figure 5-8, we have drilled down one level deeper into the SCOTT schema, viewing the Indexes folder with all indexes owned by SCOTT. We find that there is a primary key called PK_DEPT on the DEPT table. We can view the general information about the index (a primary key constraint

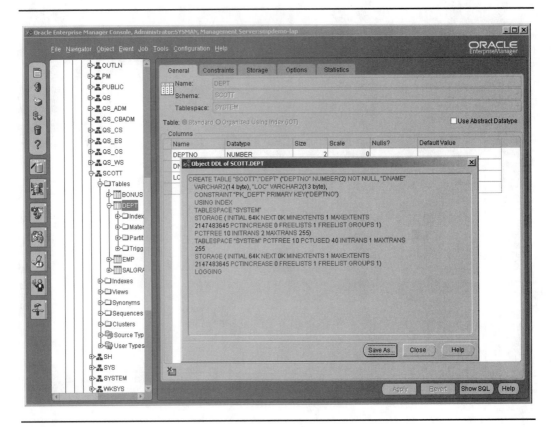

FIGURE 5-7. *Schema Management–Generating a DDL for an object*

in this example), such as the columns that are indexed. We can look at the storage information as we would the table definition by clicking the Storage tab.

TIP
Using the Schema folder within Enterprise Manager is a very quick way to look at tables and indexes when you are tuning your system.

Schema Management–Examine SYS Information

The more advanced DBAs may want to investigate Oracle's setup of the underlying tables that make up the database dictionary. In the example in Figure 5-9, the APPLY$_ERROR table was

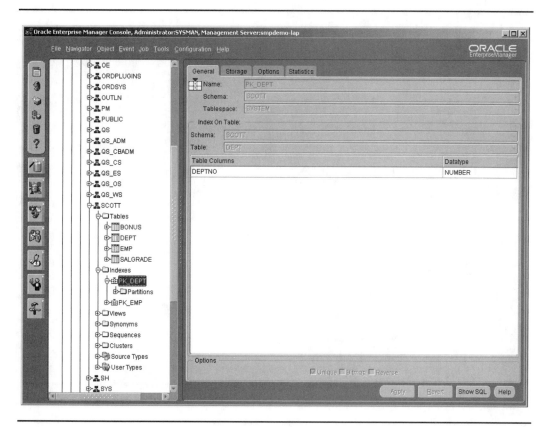

FIGURE 5-8. *Schema Management–Looking at indexes*

created with maxextents set to unlimited (actually, 2,147,483,645 extents). Depending on the number and size of certain objects within our database, the database may need to be configured so certain data dictionary clusters and tables are not fragmented.

CAUTION
Be careful! Modifying anything other than the storage parameters for the data dictionary objects in sql.bsq can cause database corruption and a desupported database.

TIP
Use Schema Manager to view information about the SYS schema and data dictionary tables that may be set up improperly for your size database.

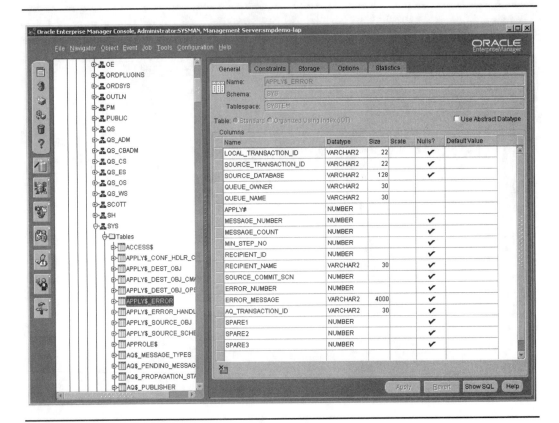

FIGURE 5-9. *Schema Management–Looking at specific SYS tables*

Schema Management–Examine Packages, Procedures, and Triggers

A new source of performance bottlenecks arrived with the advent of functions, packages, procedures, and triggers. At times, it is difficult to find the source code for a function, package, procedure, or trigger. With Enterprise Manager, the process is simplified by using the Schema folder in the console to select the code that is in question. You can cut and paste into SQL*Plus or use the Tuning pack to tune a problematic query found within a function or procedure. Using the Schema folder is a quick way to find the code that may need to be tuned within packages, procedures, and triggers. Figure 5-10 shows the code for the ADD_JOB_HISTORY procedure.

TIP
Use the Schema folder to quickly find code to tune that is related to packages, procedures, triggers, and functions for a given schema.

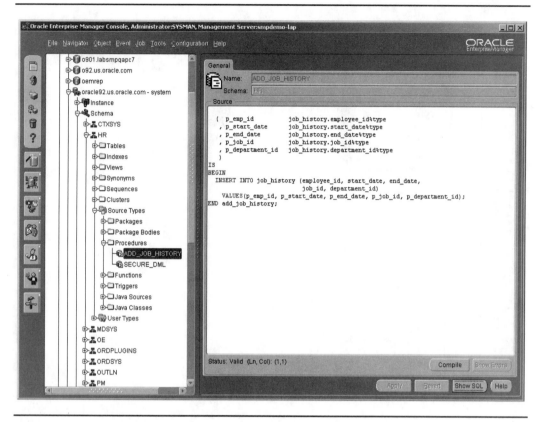

FIGURE 5-10. *Schema Management–Looking at a specific procedure*

The Security Folder

Use the Security folder for a quick way to look at security and limitations placed on individual users. The Users folder lists all Oracle users in a database. It includes tabs that allow you to display and change a user's password, tablespace quotas, system privileges, and roles that are assigned to the user. The Roles folder displays all roles that are available in the database. If you often grant a connect, resource, or DBA role to a user, this is a great way to see the result. The Profiles folder is the last folder under the Security folder in the navigator (Figure 5-11). It is one of the most helpful options for performance tuning. By assigning profiles to individual users, you can limit the user's ability to consume your entire system. The next section examines some of the available choices.

Security Management–Creating a Profile

In Figure 5-11, we've displayed the available profiles. Using profiles, a user can be limited by CPU per session, CPU per call, connect time, idle time, concurrent sessions, reads per session

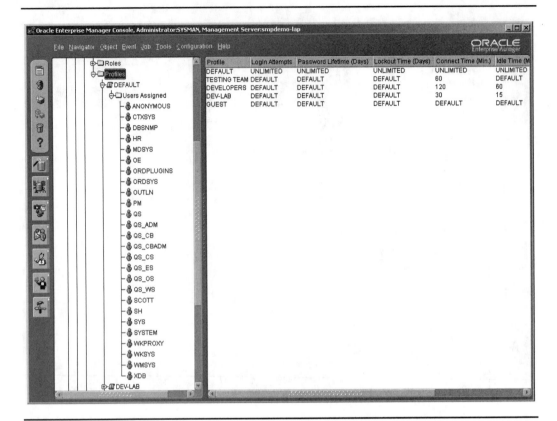

FIGURE 5-11. *Security Management–Profiles*

(helpful for ad-hoc query users), private SGA, and composite limit. The query used to create the LIMITED2 profile, displayed in Figure 5-12, can be viewed by clicking the View SQL button (which changes to the Hide SQL button when the SQL is visible).

TIP
Use profiles to limit ad-hoc query users and/or other users who are typically unpredictable or problematic in their use of system resources.

The Details Section

Listed below are descriptions for information that is listed in the details section when adding a new profile.

■ **CPU/Session**   The total amount of CPU time allowed in a session; the limit is expressed in seconds.

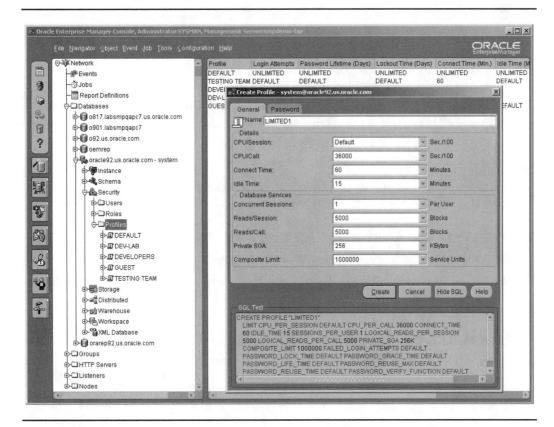

FIGURE 5-12.   *Security Management–Adding a new profile*

- **CPU/Call**   The maximum amount of CPU time allowed for a call (a parse, execute, or fetch); the limit is expressed in seconds.

- **Connect Time**   The maximum elapsed time allowed for a session; the limit is expressed in minutes.

- **Idle Time**   The maximum idle time allowed in a session; idle time is a continuous period of inactive time during a session; long-running queries and other operations are not subject to this limit; the limit is expressed in minutes.

The Database Services Section
Listed below are descriptions for information that is listed in the database services section.

- **Concurrent Sessions**   The maximum number of concurrent sessions allowed for a user.

- **Reads/Session**   The total number of data block reads allowed in a session; the limit includes blocks read from memory and disk.

Security Management
Create a Profile

- **Reads/Call**   The maximum number of data block reads allowed for a call (parse, execute, or fetch) to process a SQL statement.

- **Private SGA**   The maximum amount of private space a session can allocate in the shared pool of the System Global Area (SGA). This limit applies only for multithreaded server (MTS) architecture. The limit is expressed in kilobytes.

- **Composite Limit**   The total resource cost for a session; the resource cost for a session is the weighted sum of the CPU time used in the session, the connect time, the number of reads made in the session, and the amount of private SGA space allocated.

The Drop-Down List

You can enter a value in a field or choose from the drop-down list adjacent to the field. Click on the down arrow to display the list. The following options are available from the drop-down list:

- **Default**   Use the limit specified for this resource in the DEFAULT profile.

- **Unlimited**   The user's access to this resource is unlimited.

- **Values**   Select one of the existing values. The default values vary by field. If you have entered a value in the field, that value appears in the drop-down list.

The Storage Folder

The Storage folder is an excellent tool for monitoring and modifying tablespaces, datafiles, and rollback segments. This is also an extremely dangerous area in which to make changes. The changes that you make (such as taking a tablespace or datafile offline) can seriously affect users. This is not an area to play around in when connected to a production database. Figure 5-13 shows the datafiles section of the Storage folder. Information about each datafile is displayed, along with a helpful column showing the amount of space used in the datafile in a graphical format.

The Storage folder provides an easy way to quickly view the location of datafiles and rollback segments for potential disk balancing. It is an effective way to view the storage parameters for tablespaces and rollback segments. You can click a datafile in the object navigator, and select the autoextend tab to allow a datafile to grow dynamically, as space is needed. Remember that multiple datafiles can be part of a single tablespace, but a datafile cannot span multiple tablespaces.

TIP
Use the Storage folder to quickly find where database files and tablespaces are located, so you can strategically balance disk reads and writes.

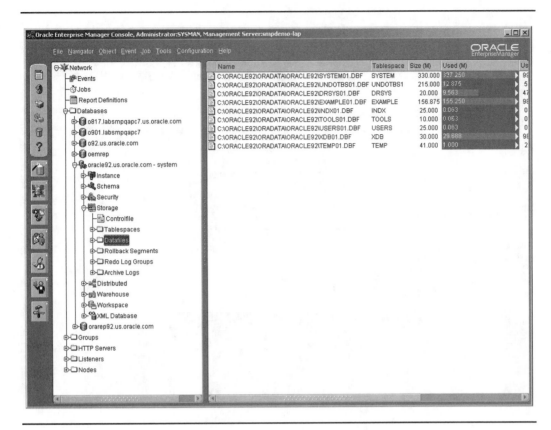

FIGURE 5-13. *Storage management*

The Oracle SQL Scratchpad and SQL*Plus Worksheet

Enterprise Manager includes SQL Scratchpad (Figure 5-14), which is particularly useful to developers and DBAs. SQL Scratchpad allows you to execute ad-hoc SQL, view the EXPLAIN PLAN, and display the query results in a tabular form. The results can be saved in HTML or a csv format. You can also save or load a list of your favorite SQL statements into the Scratchpad to be executed individually. SQL Scratchpad saves a history of the SQL you have executed and shows the execution time for each statement. Finally, it enables you to cancel long-running SQL statements.

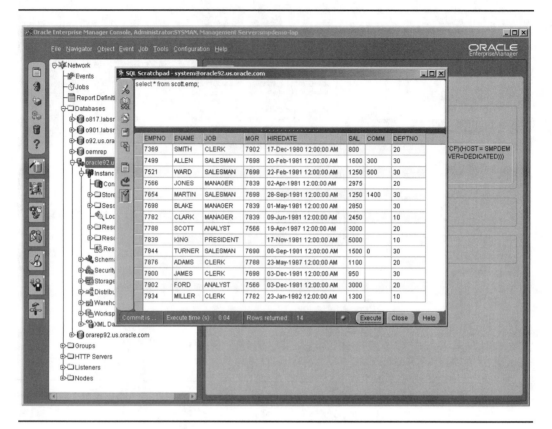

FIGURE 5-14. *SQL Scratchpad*

Enterprise Manager also includes SQL*Plus Worksheet, which can be used to connect to the database and run individual queries or SQL*Plus. It is a GUI SQL*Plus-like connection that shows your commands in the upper portion of the screen and the corresponding output in the lower portion of the screen, as shown in Figure 5-15.

TIP
Use SQL Scratchpad and Worksheet for quick windows to run SQL queries.

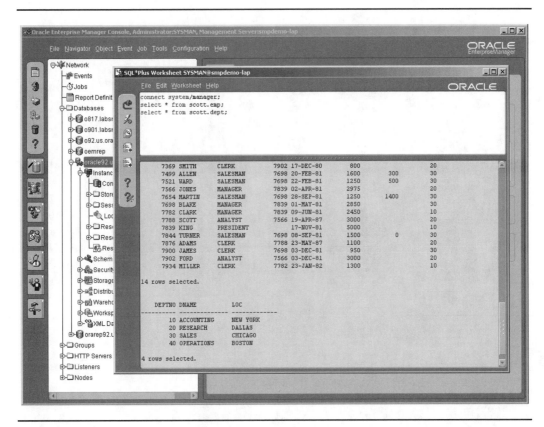

FIGURE 5-15. *SQL*Plus Worksheet*

Performance Manager

Enterprise Manager also includes Performance Manager, which can be used to monitor some of the crucial performance-related areas within the database. Many of the queries that are used to retrieve the information displayed in this section are queries to the V$ tables that Oracle has built. One of the best parts of Performance Manager is the Database Health Overview chart.

Performance Manager–The Database Health Overview Chart

The Database Heath Overview Chart (Figure 5-16) is the best of all worlds; it illustrates a large portion of performance-related information in a single chart. It is a snapshot of how the

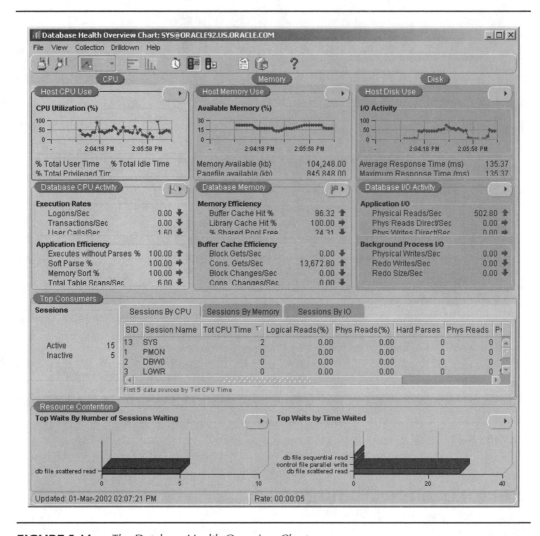

FIGURE 5-16. *The Database Health Overview Chart*

database "heart" is beating. You can access the Database Performance Overview Chart either directly from the console (under Tools | Application Management) or from within the Performance Manager application.

The Database Heath Overview Chart provides a consolidated view of key database and host performance metrics organized into three performance areas: CPU, Memory, and Disk. The top section shows the CPU, memory, and disk utilization for the host on which the database is running. The section below shows the CPU, memory, and disk metrics for the database. This organization makes it easy to see the relationship between host resources and database performance. The third section shows the top resource-consuming sessions, again organized by CPU, memory, or disk I/O. The last section shows the number and type of session waits.

From the Database Health Overview chart, you can also see if any metrics have triggered any alerts, shown as red (critical) or yellow (caution) flags. You can also drill down from any chart into more detailed information, historical values, or even advice on how to address the performance problem detected. This built-in diagnostics methodology is useful for both new and experienced DBAs.

In Figure 5-16, the data cache hit ratio is probably not a problem (96 percent), but at times, the physical writes are reasonably heavy compared to the reads and could cause a bottleneck of contention if the datafiles are not well balanced. The CPU spikes at times (in one case, to over 100 percent) but is still in the green (green flag). And despite other minor memory issues, the elements are pretty well balanced in this output. Drilling down into any of the sections provides additional information.

TIP

The Database Health Overview chart is probably the most helpful screen for system tuning within Enterprise Manager. It is a simple way to see the overall performance of your system on a single screen.

The Database Heath Overview Chart and other helpful charts are all part of Performance Manager. Using the navigator (as displayed in Figure 5-17), you can access the various areas of the Performance Manager.

TIP

Performance Manager includes many of the best performance queries to the V$ tables. It shows a graphical view of the output to many of these strategic areas. It is the fastest way to get a snapshot of your performance problems and areas for potential performance improvements.

Performance Manager–The Buffer Cache Hit Ratio

The buffer cache hit ratio can be calculated by accessing the V$SYSSTAT view, as discussed in Chapter 12. Performance Manager not only displays the hit ratio for the database buffers (memory allocated for users' data), but also graphically shows the output. Information can be stored in a repository (beyond the scope of this chapter) to trend your database as well. In Figure 5-18, the hit ratio displayed is very low at times and should be ideally closer to 95 percent on average.

The possible culprit in this case may be that a DB_CACHE_SIZE initialization parameter setting is too low or a poorly written query is executing an inordinate amount of physical reads (at the times that the hit ratio plunges). It could also be a development database or a data warehousing application that often references full table scans. A query of the V$SQLAREA or V$SQL view shows the queries causing the poor hit ratio. See Chapter 12, which discusses access to the V$ table, for information related to this topic.

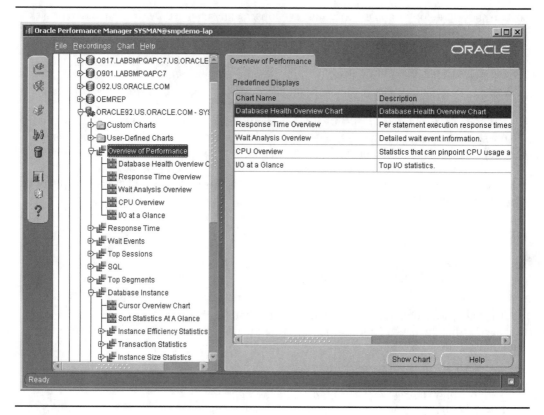

FIGURE 5-17. *Performance Manager*

TIP

Use the buffer cache hit percent to instantly view the ratio of memory reads to disk reads for your system. If the ratio is below 95 percent on average, it may be necessary to tune the DB_CACHE_SIZE parameter in the initialization file or to find and tune queries that are causing a large amount of disk reads. The Buffer Cache advisor may be used for a recommendation on the optimal buffer cache size. Data Warehouses and databases that often perform full table scans often have lower hit ratios. The best use of hit ratios is to monitor them for sudden changes from normal day-to-day values that could indicate a major problem has occurred.

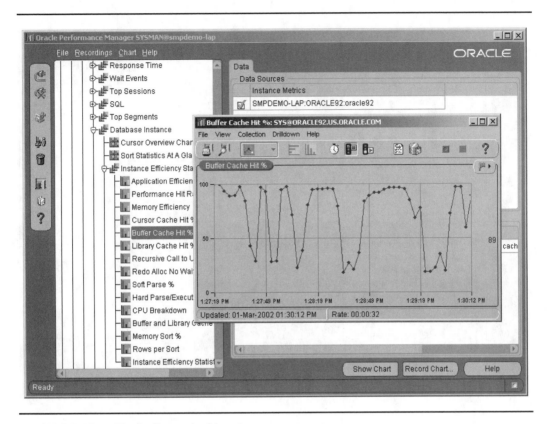

FIGURE 5-18. *The buffer cache hit ratio*

Performance Manager–The Library Cache Hit Ratio

The library cache hit ratio can be calculated by accessing the V$LIBRARYCACHE view, as
described in Chapter 12. Performance Manager not only displays the hit ratio for the library
cache (memory allocated for user statements such as SQL and PL/SQL), but also graphically
shows the output. In Figure 5-19, the hit ratio displayed is good (99.66 percent) most of the
time. If the hit ratio was below 95 percent, investigate the SHARED_POOL_SIZE initialization
parameter to determine if the setting could possibly be too low or pin (keep) some of the
often-used PL/SQL in memory using DBMS_SHARED_POOL.KEEP. A low library hit cache ratio
can also reflect a failure to make appropriate use of bind variables in the application, and instead
of executing large numbers of non-shareable SQL statements, each containing different lateral
rules. If so, the CURSOR_SHARING initialization parameter might help. See Chapter 4.

Performance Manager
The Library Cache Hit Ratio

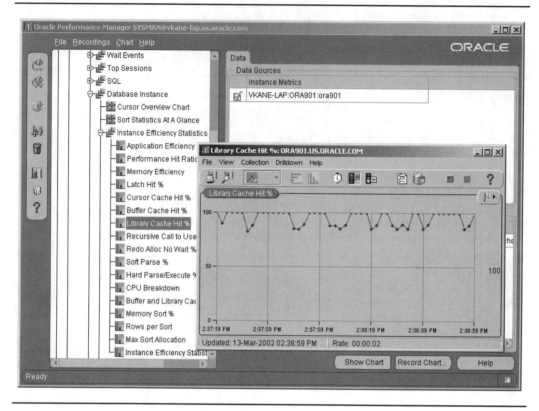

FIGURE 5-19. *The Library Cache Hit Ratio*

Performance Manager–The Data Dictionary Cache Hit Ratio

The data dictionary cache hit ratio can be calculated by accessing the V$ROWCACHE view, as seen in Chapter 12. Performance Manager not only displays the hit ratio for the data dictionary cache (the memory allocated for accessing Oracle's underlying tables), but also graphically shows the output. In Figure 5-20, the data dictionary cache hit ratio is displayed. The goal is to be 95 percent or higher on average after the system stabilizes, however, the use of public synonyms places a lower ceiling on the possible hit ratio. Investigate increasing the SHARED_POOL_SIZE initialization parameter when this hit ratio and the library hit ratio are both consistently too low.

TIP
Use the library cache and rowcache hit ratios for an instant view of the hit ratios related to the SHARED_POOL_SIZE init.ora parameter. Hit ratios that are consistently below 95 percent could indicate either a need to increase the SHARED_POOL_SIZE or it could indicate other problems with the shared pool.

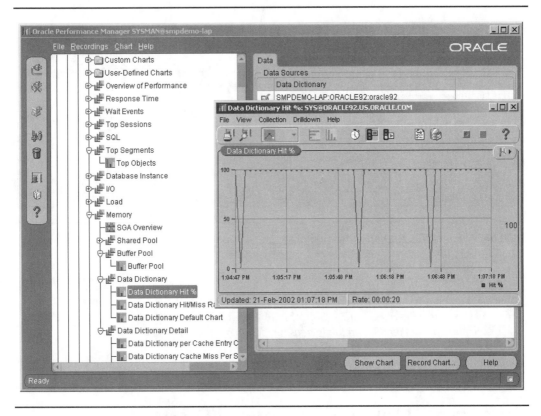

FIGURE 5-20.   *The data dictionary cache hit ratio*

Performance Manager–The SQL Area

The TopSQL chart is an excellent tool to analyze the worst statements that are in the SQL Area.
Figure 5-21 illustrates the TopSQL chart sorted by memory. Individual statements that identify
themselves as "memory hogs" can be identified here and tuned for better performance.

Performance Manager–The Memory Sort Hit Ratio

The memory sort hit ratio can be viewed by accessing the V$SYSSTAT view, discussed in
Chapter 12, or by viewing the Memory Sort % chart in Performance Manager which is displayed
in Figure 5-22. You can also use the Top Sessions or TopSQL views to isolate the sessions or SQL
in your database that are performing the most sorts to disk. If this hit ratio is below 99 percent, you
may want to increase the SORT_AREA_SIZE or PGA_AGGREGATE_TARGET initialization parameter
(depending on how you set up your sort areas), but be careful. This is a per-session parameter.
Additional parameters are added for sorting areas. See Chapter 4 and Appendix A for more
information.

Performance Manager
The Memory Sort Hit Ratio

SQL Text	Disk Reads Per Execution	Buffer Gets Per Execution	Executions	Disk Re
SELECT ... FROM oe.orders_l o, oe.order_items_l i WHERE o.order_...	3,427.72	33,512.39	110	37
SELECT ... FROM SYSTEM.PRODUCT_PRIVS WHERE (UPPER('SQL*...	1.00	25.67	3	
SELECT CHAR_VALUE FROM SYSTEM.PRODUCT_PRIVS WHERE (:..	0.00	3.67	3	
SELECT NULL FROM DUAL FOR UPDATE NOWAIT	0.00	5.00	12	
SELECT DECODE('A','A','1','2') FROM DUAL	0.00	3.00	12	
SELECT USER FROM DUAL	0.25	4.25	12	

First 25 data sources by Shareable Memory

Updated: 01-Mar-2002 05:59:06 PM   Rate: 00:00:06

FIGURE 5-21.   *TopSQL sorted by memory*

TIP
*If the memory sort hit ratio is below 99 percent, it may indicate a need
for an increase to the SORT_AREA_SIZE or PGA_AGGREGATE_TARGET
initialization parameter. Be careful: Increasing these parameters can also
cause problems if they are set too high. See Chapter 4 and Appendix A
for detailed information.*

Performance Manager–The System I/O Rate

Figure 5-23 shows the I/O At A Glance screen. This screen is useful if you have a system that
usually runs well and then receives a large spike in physical and/or buffer reads.

SQL Text	Sorts	Disk Reads Per Execution	Buffer Gets Per Execution	Executions
SELECT ... FROM oe.orders_l o, oe.order_items_l i WHERE o.order_...	176	3,377.02	33,403.83	17
SELECT CHAR_VALUE FROM SYSTEM.PRODUCT_PRIVS WHERE (...	0	0.00	3.67	
SELECT NULL FROM DUAL FOR UPDATE NOWAIT	0	0.00	5.00	1
SELECT ... FROM SYSTEM.PRODUCT_PRIVS WHERE (UPPER('SQL*...	0	1.00	25.67	
SELECT USER FROM DUAL	0	0.25	4.25	1

First 25 data sources by Sorts

Updated: 01-Mar-2002 06:04:49 PM   Rate: 00:00:06

FIGURE 5-22.   *The memory sort hit ratio TopSQL by sorts*

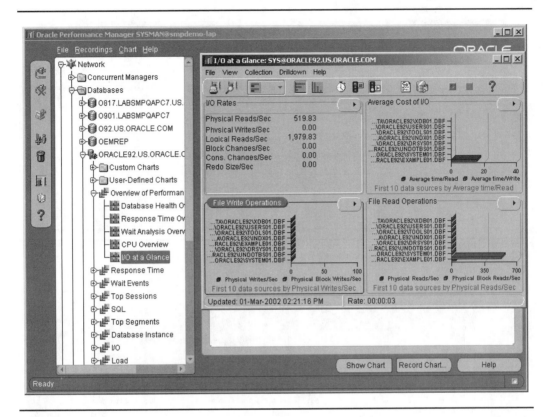

FIGURE 5-23. *The I/O at a Glance screen*

If an uncharacteristic spike occurs, you can use the Top Sessions view by I/O to find the sessions that are generating the most I/O (Figure 5-24). From the session details, you can drill down to the SQL statement and EXPLAIN PLAN to find table accesses that are potentially missing indexes. You can also query the V$SQLAREA for the username to find the query that is being executed.

Performance Manager–Database Instance Information

Figure 5-25 illustrates details for accessing information related to a given instance.

TIP
Performance Manager also has sections that pertain to preventive maintenance.

Performance Manager
Database Instance Information

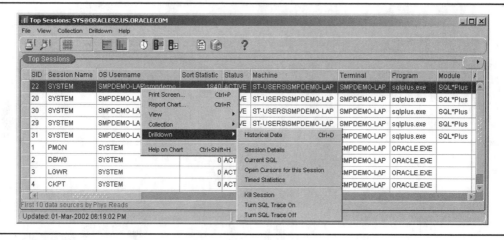

FIGURE 5-24. *The Top Sessions view by I/O with drill down to details*

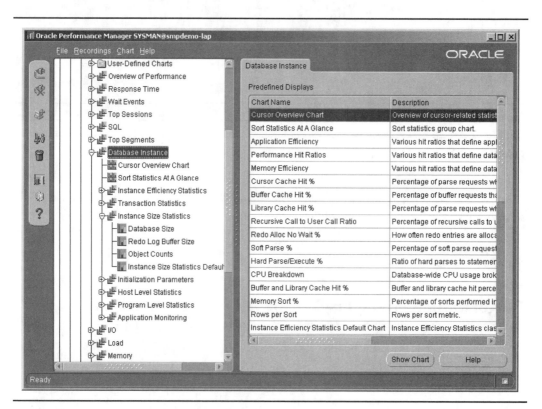

FIGURE 5-25. *Details for a database instance*

Performance Manager–Building Your Own Charts

Performance Manager also adds one extremely powerful tool, the option to build new charts or to modify current ones. The Chart pull-down menu offers both a New Chart option and a Modify Chart option.

Figure 5-26 shows a custom chart we built that accesses the X$BH table, charting the buffers used for data. (See Chapter 13 for more information regarding the X$ tables.) This chart shows the free buffers (never used), the available buffers (used but can be freed), and the buffers being used (currently in use).

You must set the display options (Figure 5-27) for the chart. The output is displayed in Figure 5-28.

Figure 5-29 shows a custom chart we built that accesses the X$KSMSP table charting the shared pool fragmentation. (See Chapter 13 for more information.)

The chart shows the memory chunks that are free, can be freed (recreateable chunks), in use (freeable chunks), and permanently retained. The output for the query in Figure 5-29 is displayed in Figure 5-30.

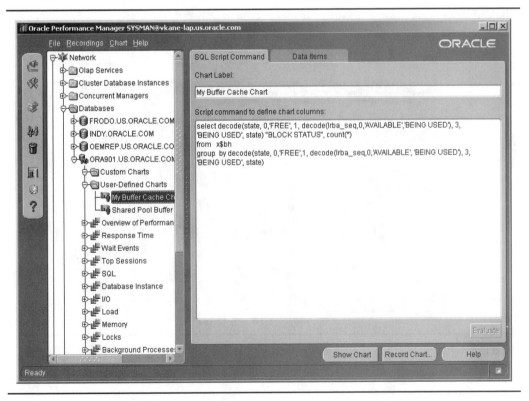

FIGURE 5-26. *Building a custom chart*

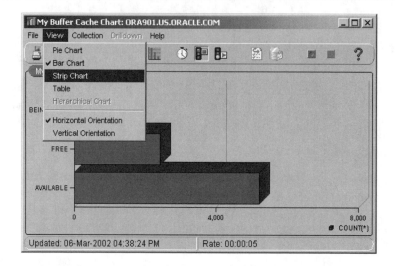

FIGURE 5-27. *Building a custom chart–Setting the display options*

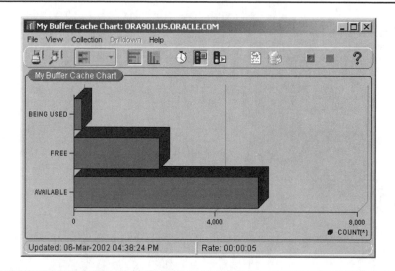

FIGURE 5-28. *Output of the custom chart for X$BH*

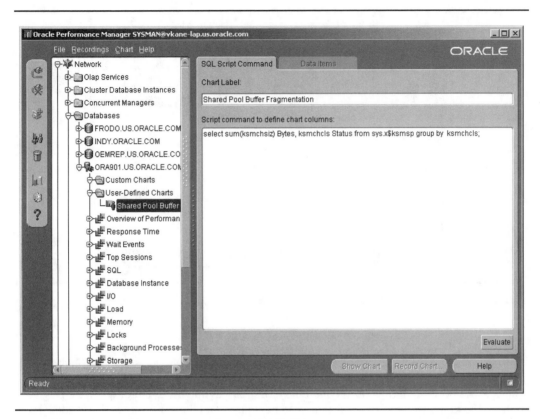

FIGURE 5-29. *Building a custom chart to X$KSMSP*

TIP
One of the most powerful features of Performance Manager is the ability to create your own charts. Queries that are contained in various parts of this book can be used to create custom charts. A couple of the queries from Chapter 13 accessing the X$ tables are displayed in this chapter as examples.

Performance Manager–Top Charts and Sessions

Enterprise Manager includes three types of "top" charts, or views: Top Sessions, TopSQL, and Top Objects. Each of these views displays the top sessions, SQL, or schema objects by

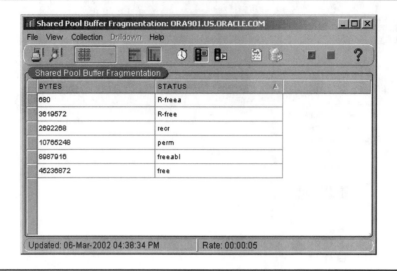

FIGURE 5-30. *Output of the custom chart to X$KSMSP*

consumption of a particular resource. For example, you can view the top sessions using the CPU or the tables generating the most physical reads. The Top Sessions view within Enterprise Manager is a powerful tool to quickly find the most troublesome users and/or queries on a given system. The tool is extremely versatile and can be used to find the "top" (or worst) session for a number of different performance criteria. A Top Sessions view is also included in the Database Health Overview chart. The Top Sessions chart can be customized using the Options dialog box displayed in Figure 5-31.

The Options dialog box can be used to sort the top sessions by largest resource used by using a number of filters. The "predefined" filter includes options for tracking top CPU, file I/O, memory, open cursors, and user transactions. The user filter can be used for tracking many statistics, including bytes sent/received from the client, CPU, logons, open cursors, recursive calls, connect time, logical (memory) reads, and SQL*Net round-trips. The cache and redo options show a variety of statspack statistics. The parallel server filter shows a variety of options that track parallel operations statistics. The SQL filter shows sorting statistics by session as well

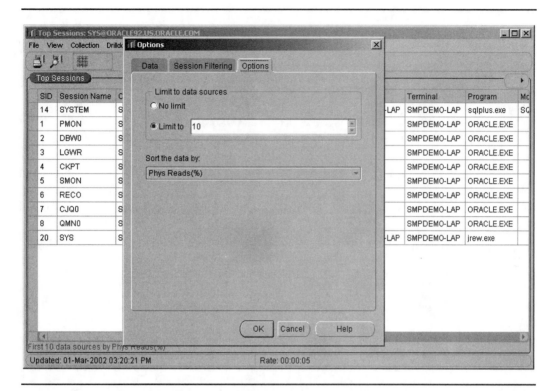

FIGURE 5-31. *The Top Sessions Options dialog box–The Options tab*

as physical and memory reads. The Other filter shows a variety of global and remote statistics, and the All filter shows the statistics for all of these categories. The Options tab (shown in Figure 5-31) allows the setting of a limited amount of top sessions or the ability to display all sessions. Figure 5-32 shows an example listing the top sessions.

If Top Sessions finds a problem user's session (perhaps an ad-hoc query user), you can then click on the top resource-consuming user (the top ones are shown in Figure 5-32) and use the

**Performance Manager
Top Charts and Sessions**

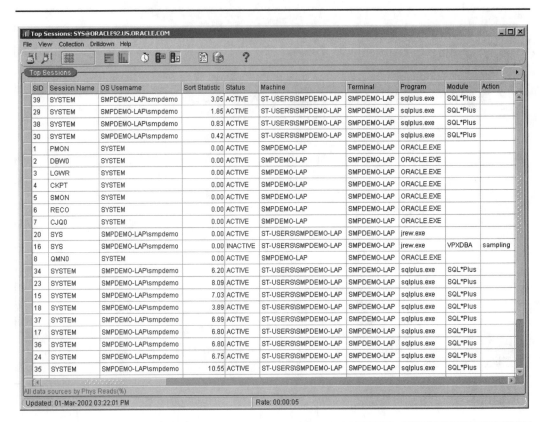

FIGURE 5-32. *The top sessions output*

Session pull-down menu to choose Kill. This kills the problem user's session. (See Figures 5-33 and 5-34.) In this example, an SQL*Plus user receives the message displayed in Figure 5-34.

TIP
Use the Top Session monitor to find the sessions that are using the most resources on your system. By investigating a problem session in more detail, you can free up resources for other processes.

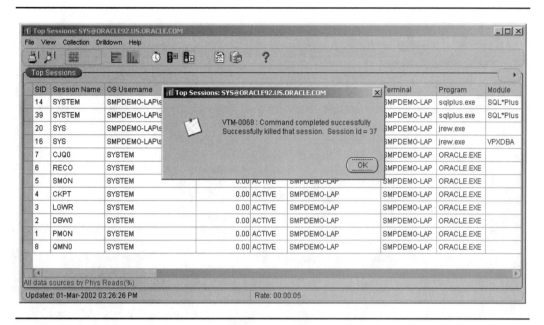

FIGURE 5-33. *The top session validates the kill session.*

TIP
When a user finds that he or she has executed a problem query and needs the DBA to end it, the Kill Session screen is an excellent tool for the DBA to use.

Oracle Tuning Pack–SQL Analyze

Using SQL Analyze, a DBA can also identify the topSQL for his or her system. The TopSQL screen, shown in Figure 5-35, displays a list of the worst SQL statements currently in the library cache based on disk reads per execution. The DBA can drag the problem SQL from TopSQL into a tuning session to begin the process of analyzing and tuning the problem SQL. Version 9.2 of this product allows the DBA to build a composite application workload over time and use this as a target for identifying high-impact SQL. This same composite workload can be subsequently used with Oracle Expert.

```
SQL*Plus Worksheet SYSMAN@smpdemo-lap                                    _ □ ×

File  Edit  Worksheet  Help                                         ORACLE
select * from scott.emp;



       EMPNO ENAME    JOB         MGR HIREDATE      SAL      COMM    DEPTNO
       ----- -----    ---         --- --------      ---      ----    ------
        7369 SMITH    CLERK      7902 17-DEC-80     800                  20
        7499 ALLEN    SALESMAN   7698 20-FEB-81    1600       300        30
        7521 WARD     SALESMAN   7698 22-FEB-81    1250       500        30
        7566 JONES    MANAGER    7839 02-APR-81    2975                  20
        7654 MARTIN   SALESMAN   7698 28-SEP-81    1250      1400        30
        7698 BLAKE    MANAGER    7839 01-MAY-81    2850                  30
        7782 CLARK    MANAGER    7839 09-JUN-81    2450                  10
        7788 SCOTT    ANALYST    7566 19-APR-87    3000                  20
        7839 KING     PRESIDENT       17-NOV-81    5000                  10
        7844 TURNER   SALESMAN   7698 08-SEP-81    1500         0        30
        7876 ADAMS    CLERK      7788 23-MAY-87    1100                  20
        7900 JAMES    CLERK      7698 03-DEC-81     950                  30
        7902 FORD     ANALYST    7566 03-DEC-81    3000                  20
        7934 MILLER   CLERK      7782 23-JAN-82    1300                  10

14 rows selected.

select * from scott.emp
       *
ERROR at line 1:
ORA-00028: your session has been killed
```

FIGURE 5-34.   *The ad-hoc user receives the bad news.*

TIP
By using SQL Analyze's TopSQL, you can generate statistics for the worst-performing queries on your system. The next step is to use the SQL Analyze tool to generate EXPLAIN PLANs and alternative SQL for the problem queries.

SQL Analyze–The EXPLAIN PLAN

The top SQL statement (shown in Figure 5-36), based on disk reads per execution, was dragged from the cache and the EXPLAIN PLAN was created using the Optimizer mode = "Choose."

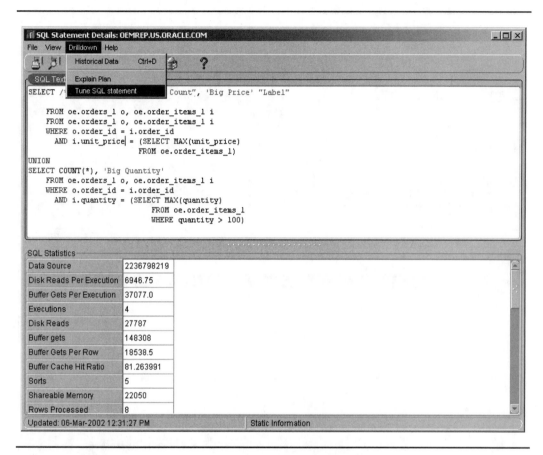

FIGURE 5-35. *Tuning Pack–The SQL Analyze TopSQL tuning tool*

A graphical plan was created for the options Cost and All Rows, as shown in Figure 5-37. The plan can be examined executing the Plan Walk feature, which describes each operation. See Chapter 6 for more information on reading and using the EXPLAIN PLAN tool.

TIP
Use SQL Analyze to quickly view the EXPLAIN PLAN tree of a query. When you drill down to an EXPLAIN PLAN from a performance chart, such as the Database Health Overview chart, you can view the EXPLAIN PLAN in a graphical format.

SQL Analyze
The EXPLAIN PLAN

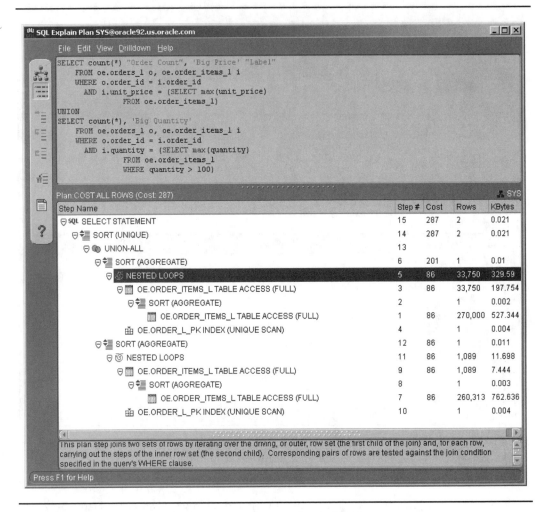

FIGURE 5-36. *Tuning Pack–The SQL Analyze EXPLAIN PLAN*

SQL Analyze–Execution Statistics

You can execute a statement from SQL Analyze to obtain execution statistics. You can also choose to execute the query multiple times to obtain running average statistics for the query. This is used to simulate the real-world environment where the query is often in memory. (See Figure 5-38.)

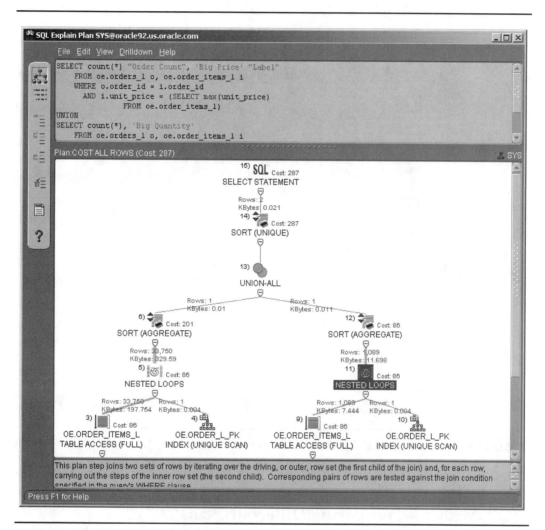

FIGURE 5-37.   *A graphical EXPLAIN PLAN*

TIP
Executing the statement in SQL Analyze will generate the query
statistics quicker than using Oracle's TRACE (discussed in Chapter 6).

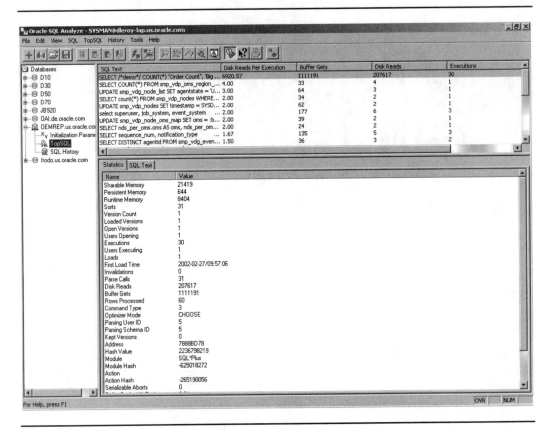

FIGURE 5-38. *Tuning Pack–SQL Analyze execution statistics*

SQL Analyze–Comparing Different Plans

A user can create a different plan for a problem statement and then use the SQL Analyze Comparison feature, which splits the screen to examine and walk each plan side-by-side (Figure 5-39). The comparison for this query shows whether using UNION or UNION ALL will be a better solution when the query is executed.

TIP
The SQL Analyze comparison feature allows a side-by-side comparison of SQL statements to help you find the best execution path. By using these what-if scenarios, you can find the best solution before actually executing the query.

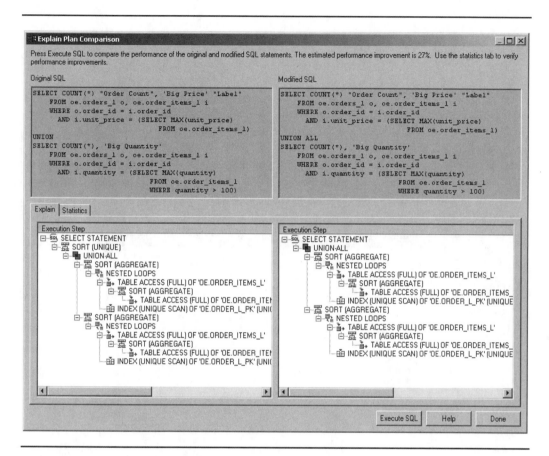

FIGURE 5-39.   *Tuning Pack–SQL Analyze Side-by-side before changes*

TIP

After you have found the query path that seems to be the correct one, make sure you execute it with statistics to ensure that it is the correct choice. The number given for the cost in the plan is not always an accurate reflection of how the query will perform.

SQL Analyze–The Tuning Wizard

Another excellent feature of the Tuning Pack is the SQL Analyze Tuning Wizard. This feature walks you through the SQL tuning process when evaluating a statement for potential performance

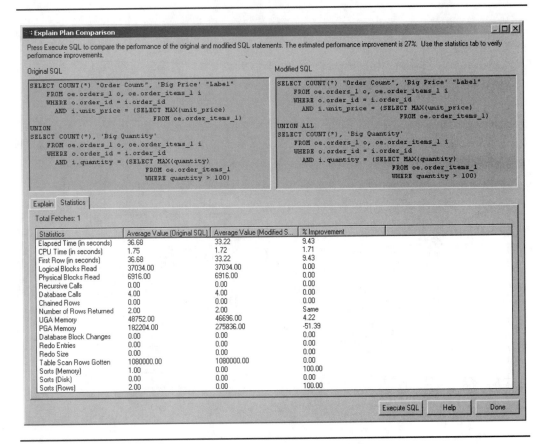

FIGURE 5-40. *Tuning Pack–SQL Analyze Side-by-side after changes*

impediments, such as finding faster access methods. In Figure 5-41, the Tuning Wizard has captured statistics for the objects used in the plan and evaluates the statement for alternative join optimization strategies. If the Tuning Wizard finds a candidate statement to fix, it creates alternative SQL to create a better plan if you decide to use the suggested strategy. In Figure 5-41, the suggestion is to replace UNION with UNION ALL.

TIP
The Tuning Wizard is a great tool for the beginner who is unfamiliar with how to tune problem SQL queries. The Tuning Wizard provides an alternative SQL query that could lead to better performance for a problem query that needs to be tuned.

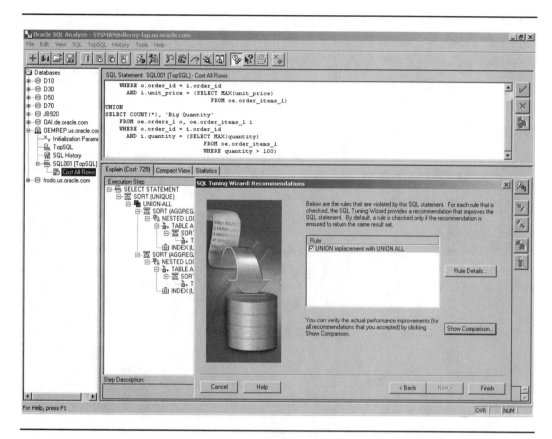

FIGURE 5-41. *Tuning Pack–The SQL Analyze Tuning Wizard*

The Tuning Wizard also provides statistics (Figure 5-42) about the performance gain from the original statement to the modified statement. It is a simple way to get an improved query, and it also illustrates the improvements made and the areas that they affect.

TIP
Optimizing the performance of a random query is not as important as optimizing the performance of queries in the area of your system that is causing a bottleneck. The Tuning Wizard itemizes where the performance gain will be, enabling you to focus on the entire area that is hurting your system most.

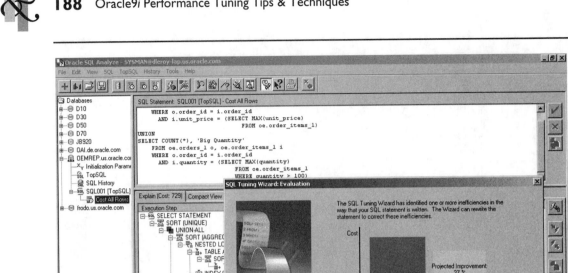

FIGURE 5-42. *Tuning Pack–The SQL Analyze Tuning Wizard statistics*

The Index Tuning Wizard

The Index Tuning Wizard (Figure 5-43) provides quick access to index tuning that is focused on high-impact SQL statements. The Wizard provides focused index tuning to improve table access for the top queries requiring tuning. Similarly, SQL Analyze provides index tuning focused on improving the performance of a specific SQL statement. It identifies the optimal index requirements for a high-impact SQL statement.

The Index Tuning Wizard allows you to test your index plans before you actually create the indexes. In the past, the main way to determine if an index would improve performance was to build the new index. The Index Tuning Wizard allows indexes to be tested with the Oracle Optimizer before they are built. The Index Tuning Wizard is part of the SQL Analyze application.

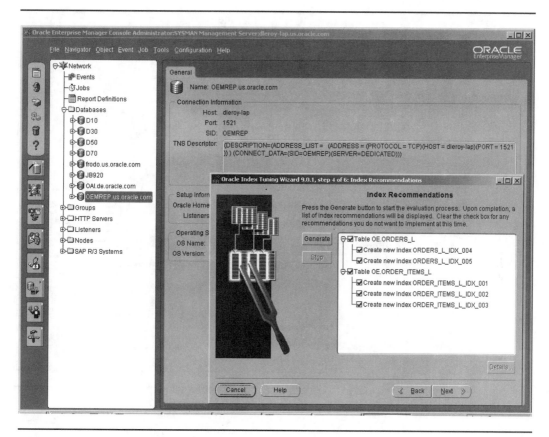

FIGURE 5-43.   *The Index Tuning Wizard*

It walks the user through the process of selecting a candidate index to test against a specific SQL statement. If the optimizer selects the new index for use by the query, the Wizard reports the change in "cost" of the query. This lets you iteratively test index plans and select the best index design before constructing the index.

Oracle Tuning Pack–Oracle Expert

Whereas SQL Analyze is focused on tuning individual SQL statements, Oracle Expert (version 1.6 in these examples) is focused on tuning from a more global perspective. (See Figure 5-44.) Oracle Expert automates overall database tuning in three areas: the top 25 instance parameters, indexes (add, drop, modify, and rebuild), and structures (sizing, placement, and OFA compliance). The

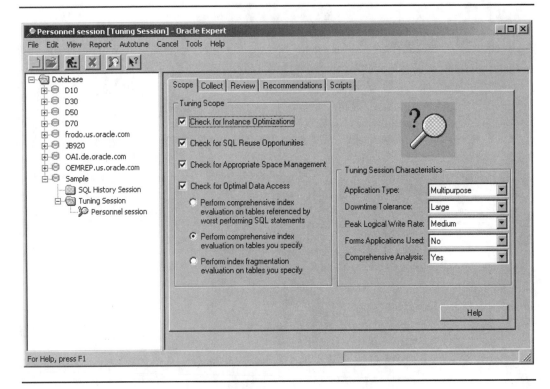

FIGURE 5-44. *Tuning Pack–An Oracle Expert tuning session*

DBA selects the scope for the tuning session, and sets up the data collection (which has Oracle Expert collect the data). The Oracle Expert engine analyzes the data and then provides tuning recommendations. Oracle Expert is built on a proprietary rule-based inference engine, which has over 1,000 tuning rules, one-third of which can be optionally customized by the user.

TIP
While SQL Analyze focuses on individual statements, Oracle Expert looks at the entire database system for areas requiring improvement.

Oracle Expert–Focusing on a Schema

A key part of setting the scope or focus of the tuning session is targeting a specific part of the database for index and structure tuning. Instance tuning will always be global, but index and structure tuning has to be focused on bottlenecks, because structure tuning is the basis for targeted optimization. The DBA should pick a particular schema or set of tables for targeted tuning. This way the engine (and DBA) is not overwhelmed with extraneous analysis. The user should pick the hot (often used) tables to tune first, and then move down the chain in subsequent tuning sessions. Note that in version 2.0, the product helps the DBA identify this table focus by providing the option of having the DBA identify the high-impact tables based on a workload analysis. In the example shown in Figure 5-45, the PERS schema has been selected for tuning, and we are using the existing dictionary statistics. Optionally, we could use Expert's own statistics or run ANALYZE for selected objects.

Oracle Expert–Setting Up the Rules for the Tuning Session

After our data is collected and reviewed for a schema, we can edit it if we want and customize some of the Oracle Expert rule values. This data editing and rule editing is an advanced feature. Figure 5-46 shows a rule edit screen for the DB_BLOCK_SIZE instance parameter. You can easily

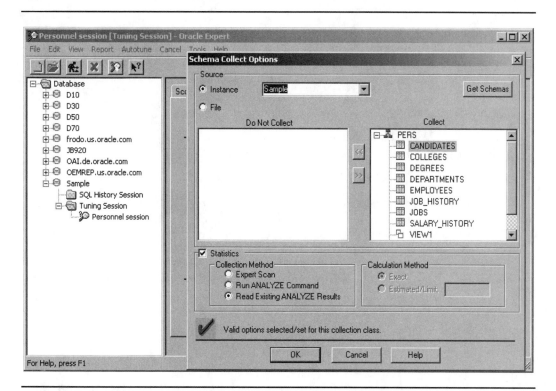

FIGURE 5-45. *Performance Pack–The Oracle Expert Schema Collect Options dialog box*

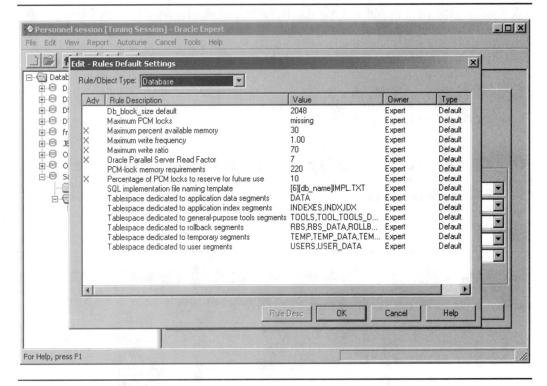

FIGURE 5-46. *Tuning Pack–Customizing Oracle Expert rule values*

receive access to the rule descriptions, and you can change the values and "instantiate" the new values at certain levels in the product. For example, if you change a rule that applies to table tuning, you can instantiate that new value for a specific table, or for all tables. Again, this is not an area that a beginner DBA would use.

TIP
Some expert-level tools allow the DBA to modify the Oracle Expert tool itself. The power of this tool becomes obvious for even the most knowledgeable DBAs.

Oracle Expert–Making Changes and Measuring the Impact

Figure 5-47 shows an example of data editing. The user targets a workload for collection (either from TRACing or from the SQL cache) and edits the workload SQL objects to affect the analysis.

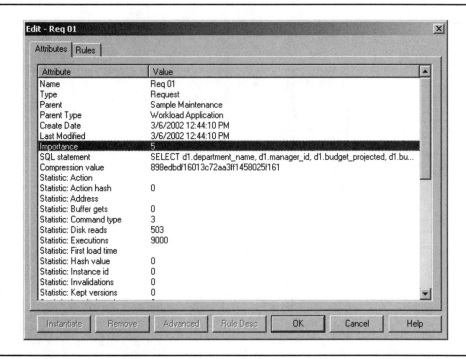

FIGURE 5-47. *Tuning Pack–Oracle Expert impact analysis*

In this example, an SQL object was collected and several variables can be changed, affecting this statement's impact during the Expert analysis: the frequency, the resources used, and the user-assigned importance rating. Or, the SQL statement itself can be edited. This helps model the impact of specific workloads on the assignment of database resources and decisions about dropping/modifying/adding indexes.

TIP
The advanced DBA can view the Oracle Expert impact analysis before and after query modifications, to view the effect that changes will potentially bring.

Oracle Expert–Examine the Recommendations
Figure 5-48 displays Oracle Expert's recommendation screen. It shows some index recommendations for one of our tables and some of our instance tuning recommendations. The DBA can scan them easily here and drill down into the details.

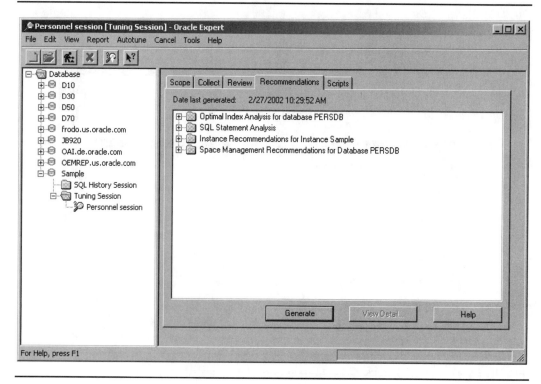

FIGURE 5-48. *Tuning Pack–Oracle Expert review recommendations*

In Figure 5-49, Oracle Expert is recommending two new indexes for the PERS' DEGREE table as well as noting that there is an existing unused index DEGREES_EMPLOYEE_ID_LP_IDX.

TIP
Oracle Expert provides a list of recommendations that can be clicked on to drill down into the detail before making the actual changes.

Oracle Expert–Drilling Down to Recommendation Detail

As you saw in Figure 5-49, we have drilled down into the recommendation detail screen for a specific index recommendation. This screen shows a brief summary, but an analysis report can also be generated to display further detail. This recommendation calls for a new, sorted index on three columns. The recommendation is based on three requests (select statements) from our workload, comprising predicate equality and inequality selects on these columns. Oracle Expert rates each valid SQL request and assigns a rank value to each. Based on the rank order,

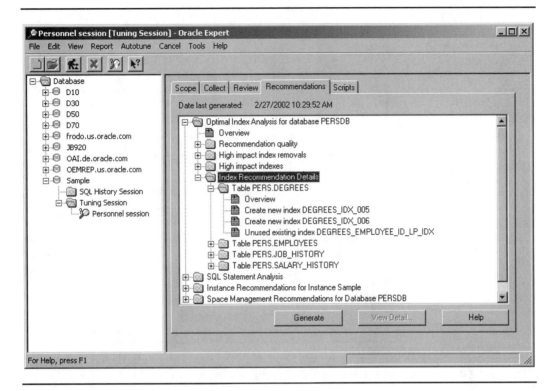

FIGURE 5-49.   *Tuning Pack–The Oracle Expert recommendation drilldown screen*

it assigns a weighted value to the requests and develops an importance rating for the index recommendation. Oracle Expert also analyzed DML workload for this table and computed a table volatility rating that is used to balance the weighted value of the ranked SQL requests. This is executed to determine the best index strategy for the table. This is an oversimplified description of the complex processes of Oracle Expert.

Oracle Expert–Recommended Systemwide Changes

You can drill down into areas that are recommended for systemwide performance issues. Figure 5-50 shows the recommendation detail for an instance tuning recommendation calling for an increase to several sorting parameters, including SORT_AREA_SIZE.

TIP
Oracle Expert not only provides recommendations for systemwide performance tuning, but it also describes why the change is recommended.

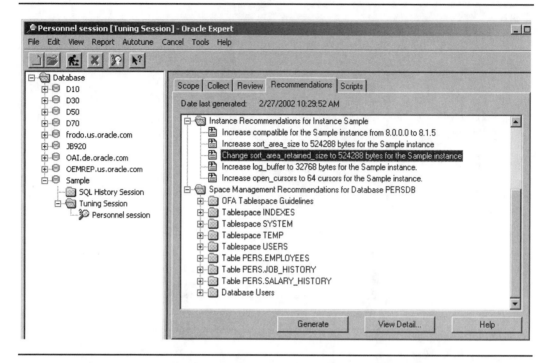

FIGURE 5-50. *Tuning Pack–The Oracle Expert systemwide recommendation drilldown screen*

Oracle Tuning Pack–The Tablespace Map

The Tablespace Map provides a graphical view of all tablespaces, datafiles, segments, total data blocks, free data blocks, and percentage of free blocks available in the tablespace current storage allocation. The tool provides the option of displaying all segments for a tablespace or all segments for a datafile. The Tablespace Map also provides additional information for each segment, including average free space per block, chained rows, and the last date that the object was analyzed.

When reorganization is necessary, you can use a new feature called the Oracle Reorg Wizard to automatically fix problem objects. The reorganization can be performed offline or online. You can select a single segment, multiple segments, or the entire tablespace for defragmentation, including tables, indexes, and clusters. You can also move segments between tablespaces using the Reorg Wizard.

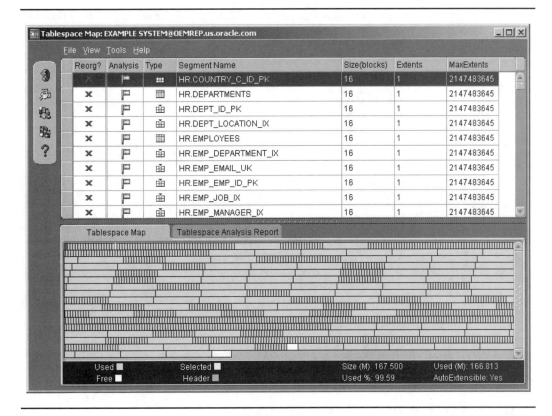

FIGURE 5-51. *Oracle Tuning Pack–The Tablespace Map*

The Oracle Expert Analysis Report

Oracle Expert generates a report providing additional detail on the Oracle Expert tuning section. The following is a portion of the Recommendation Summary (the full report was 36 pages) of the tuning analysis report *(tuning_report.txt)* generated by Oracle Expert for a tuning session. The report also generates a table of contents (not listed).

```
1  Recommendation Summary
   This section provides a summary of Oracle Expert's recommendations.
   Additional information can be found in the remainder of this report to
   explain Oracle Expert's reasoning for making each recommendation. These
```

```
recommendations were generated from an analysis performed on 04/26/2002
20:18:54.
  Optimal Index Analysis for database PERSDB
      o Overview
  Recommendation quality
      o Overview
      o Optimizer validation was disabled
  High impact index removals
      o Overview
    Table PERS.DEGREES
        o Unused existing index DEGREES_EMPLOYEE_ID_LP_IDX
    Table PERS.SALARY_HISTORY
        o Unused existing index SALARY_HISTORY_SALARY_A_GP_IDX
  High impact indexes
      o Overview
    Table PERS.EMPLOYEES
        o Create new index EMPLOYEES_IDX_001
        o Create new index EMPLOYEES_IDX_003
        o Create new index EMPLOYEES_IDX_004
    Table PERS.SALARY_HISTORY
        o Create new index SALARY_HISTORY_IDX_002
```

Oracle Expert also generates an implementation script with the actual SQL commands needed based on the tuning session. This script usually requires a bit of customization by the DBA, depending on which recommendations need to be implemented. This script can be very helpful when several index or structural changes must be made.

Business Impact Reporting

Oracle Enterprise Manager Release 9.2 provides tools that correlate performance of the E-Business enterprise with performance of the service levels across the most critical components of the Oracle Internet platform—host, database, web server, and applications. Through business impact reporting, specific customer problems in the areas of service-level monitoring, application health assessment, and administrative impact are solved.

Service-Level Reporting

Service-Level Monitoring is the measurement and reporting of the Oracle9i platform and Oracle applications' availability. It provides a mechanism for monitoring specific components that make up a service and that service's overall availability.

Application Health Assessment

Oracle Enterprise Manager's application heath assessment reports allow administrators to track both the health of their entire enterprise (e.g., obtain status of all targets contained in the repository with outstanding event alerts, job details, and basic target configuration) as well as system resource use. Figure 5-52 shows the Reporting home page for all systems being monitored.

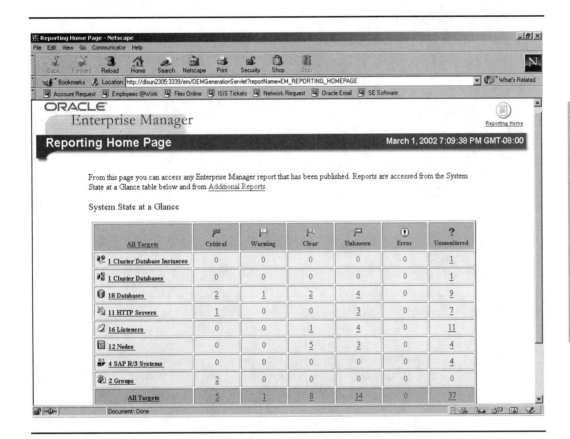

FIGURE 5-52.   *The Reporting home page*

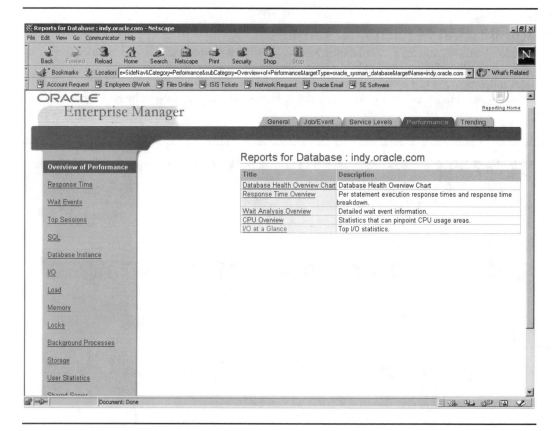

FIGURE 5-53. *Reports for a single database*

Figure 5-53 shows the HTML formatted reports available for each database.

Through performance and capacity planning reporting, Enterprise Manager allows businesses to see real-time vs. historical performance data. Figure 5-54 shows the Database Health Overview chart in real-time.

Figure 5-55 shows the drilldown detail for CPU usage. Both of these are HTML screens from the same report.

DBAs are able to manage databases and systems more effectively using this versatile tool. This comprehensive knowledge of system health and performance also enables businesses to plan and trend out for future growth. Enterprise Manager is the most powerful Oracle utility available. It's not just for beginners; the better you are, the better this tool is.

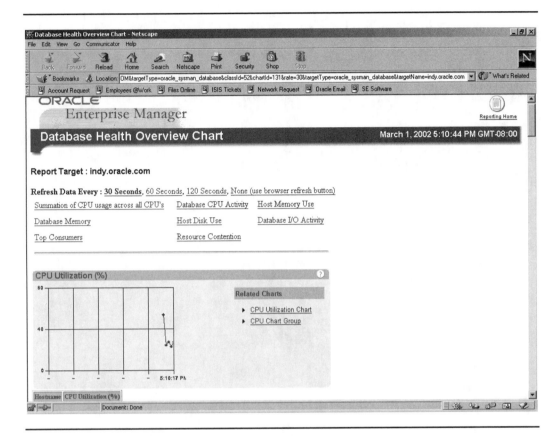

FIGURE 5-54. *Database health for a single database*

Tips Review

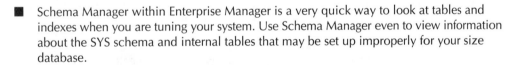

- Schema Manager within Enterprise Manager is a very quick way to look at tables and indexes when you are tuning your system. Use Schema Manager even to view information about the SYS schema and internal tables that may be set up improperly for your size database.

- Use Schema Manager to quickly find code to tune that is related to packages, procedures, and triggers for a given schema.

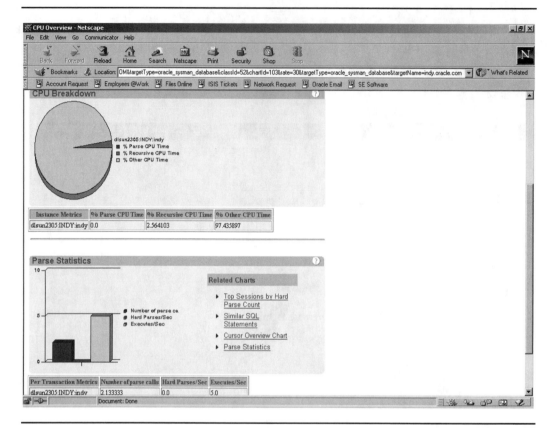

FIGURE 5-55. *Drill down to specific problems–CPU usage*

- Use profiles to limit ad-hoc query users and/or other users that are typically unpredictable or problematic in their use of system resources.

- Use Storage Manager to quickly find where database files and tablespaces are located so that you can strategically balance disk reads and writes.

- Performance Manager includes many of the best performance queries to the V$ tables. It shows a graphical view at the output to many of these strategic areas.

- Use the buffer cache hit ratio in Performance Manager to instantly see the ratio of memory reads to disk reads for your system. If the ratio is below 95 percent, tuning the DB_CACHE_SIZE parameter in the init.ora or finding queries that are causing a large amount of disk reads may be necessary. If the buffer cache hit ratio deviates appreciably higher or lower from normal values, you may also have an issue erupting.

■ Use the library cache and rowcache hit ratio charts in Performance Manager to instantly see the hit ratios that are related to the SHARED_POOL_SIZE init.ora parameter. Hit ratios that are below 95 percent indicate a need to increase the shared pool size, or could indicate other problems. See Chapter 12 for additional V$ information.

■ If the memory sort hit ratio is below 99 percent, it may indicate a need for an increase to the SORT_AREA_SIZE or PGA_AGGREGATE_TARGET parameter(s). But be careful: Increasing these can cause problems if it is set too high.

■ The Performance Manager Database Health Overview chart is probably the most helpful screen within Enterprise Manager. It is a simple way to see the overall performance of your system in a single screen.

■ One of the most powerful features of Performance Manager is the ability to create your own charts. Queries that are contained in various parts of this book can be used to create custom charts.

■ Use the Top Session monitor to find the sessions that are using the most resources on your system. By investigating a problem session in more detail, you can free up resources for other processes.

■ By using SQL Analyze's TopSQL, you can generate a list of the worst-performing queries on your system. The next step is to use the SQL Analyze tool to generate EXPLAIN PLANs and alternative SQL for the problem queries.

■ Use SQL Analyze to quickly view the EXPLAIN PLAN tree of a query in graphical or tabular format.

■ Executing a statement in SQL Analyze generates the query statistics a lot quicker than using Oracle's TRACE (detailed in Chapter 6).

■ The SQL Analyze comparison feature allows a side-by-side comparison of SQL statements to help you find the best execution path. By using these "what-if" scenarios, you can find the best solution without actually executing the query.

■ The Tuning Wizard within SQL Analyze is a great tool for the beginner who is unfamiliar with how to tune problem SQL queries. The Tuning Wizard provides an alternative SQL query that could lead to better performance for a problem query that needs to be tuned.

■ While SQL Analyze focuses on individual statements, Oracle Expert looks at the entire database system for areas requiring improvement. There are expert-level tools that even allow the DBA to modify the Oracle Expert tool itself.

■ Oracle Expert provides a list of recommendations that can be clicked on to drill down into the detail before making the actual changes.

■ Oracle Expert not only provides recommendations for systemwide performance tuning, but also describes why the change is recommended. You can also generate a tuning report and implementation file for your tuning session.

References

Oracle Enterprise Manager Reference Manual, Oracle Corporation

Tuning Pack 2.0, Oracle White Paper on technet.oracle.com

Many thanks to Valerie K. Kane and David LeRoy of Oracle, who contributed the majority of the figures and verbiage to this chapter. Many thanks to Ken Morse of Oracle, who contributed the majority of the figures and verbiage in the first tuning book on SQL Analyze, Oracle Expert, and Tuning Pack 2.0. Ken was a tremendous help to completing this chapter last time around. Lastly, thanks to Martin Pena for helping coordinate Oracle's part.

CHAPTER
6

Using EXPLAIN, TRACE, TKPROF, and STORED OUTLINES (Developer & DBA)

F inding and fixing problem queries has a lot to do with using the tools that are available. Different tools need to be used for different situations. The tools covered in this chapter are Oracle's provided utilities: TRACE, TKPROF, EXPLAIN PLAN, and STORED OUTLINES. The topics covered in this chapter include the following:

- Simple steps for using TRACE/TKPROF

- Sections of the TRACE output

- A more complex query traced, and what to look for to help performance

- Using EXPLAIN PLAN

- Reading EXPLAIN PLAN: top to bottom or bottom to top?

- Yet another EXPLAIN PLAN method: the parent/child tree structure method

- TRACing in developer tools

- Important columns in the PLAN_TABLE table

- TRACing for errors and the undocumented init.ora parameters

- Building and using STORED OUTLINES

The Oracle **TRACE** Utility

You use the Oracle TRACE utility to measure timing statistics for a given query, a batch process, and an entire system. It is a thorough method of finding where potential bottlenecks on the system reside. TRACE has the following functionality:

- TRACE runs the query and generates statistics about an Oracle query (or series of queries) that is executed.

- TRACE helps developers analyze every section of a query.

Generally, the Oracle TRACE utility records all database activity (particularly queries) in a *trace* file. The trace file is generated by Oracle TRACE, however, it is very hard to read and should be changed into a readable format using the TKPROF utility.

TIP
Although Oracle TRACE can be performed on Oracle9i, the TKPROF utility may not be included with the initial release of 9i on NT. Later releases should have it. Other ways of analyzing specific queries—EXPLAIN PLAN and AUTOTRACE— are discussed in the "Reading the EXPLAIN PLAN" section of this chapter.

Simple Steps for TRACE with a Simple Query

The steps for setting up and running Oracle's TRACE utility are listed here:

1. Set the following init.ora parameters:

```
TIMED_STATISTICS = TRUE
MAX_DUMP_FILE_SIZE = 20000 (operating system blocks)
USER_DUMP_DEST = /oracle/admin/ora9i/udump
```

The TIMED_STATISTICS parameter allows tracing to occur on the system. The USER_DUMP_DEST specifies the location for the files, and the MAX_DUMP_FILE_SIZE specifies the maximum file size in operating system blocks. This is the largest size that the file will grow to; any further data to be recorded will be ignored, will not be written to the trace file, and might be missed. All three of these parameters may also be set via an ALTER SYSTEM (for the entire system) command and take effect when the next user logs in, but will not affect those currently logged in to the system. You may also set the TIMED_STATISTICS and MAX_DUMP_FILE_SIZE at the session level using the ALTER SESSION (for an individual session) command.

2. Enable TRACE for a SQL*Plus session (this starts TRACing for an individual session):

```
alter session set SQL_TRACE true;
```

There are actually several different ways of starting and stopping trace sessions, which will be discussed later in this chapter.

3. Run the query to be TRACEd:

```
select      table_name, owner, initial_extent, uniqueness
from        ind2
where       owner || '' = 'SCOTT' ; --Note: An index on "OWNER" is
suppressed
```

4. Disable TRACE for the SQL*Plus session:

```
alter session set SQL_TRACE false;
```

You do not actually have to stop the trace to examine the trace file, but it is a good idea.

5. You can also enable TRACE for all sessions by setting the SQL_TRACE parameter in the init.ora. You must shut down and restart the database for this to take effect. This is *not* suggested!

```
SQL_TRACE = TRUE
```

After running TRACE, your output filename will look something like the following:

```
ora_19554.trc
```

> **TIP**
> *Setting TIMED_STATISTICS = TRUE in the init.ora will begin TRACing upon the user's command. But be careful; setting SQL_TRACE = TRUE in the init.ora will cause the entire system and all queries to be traced and could cause performance degradations.*

Finding the generated trace file may be the trickiest part of this whole process. The generated file should be named for the process ID of the TRACE session and will include that number in the filename. Looking for the date and time of the file makes it easy to find if you are the only one tracing something. In the previous example, 19544 is the process ID of the session being traced. The trace filenames may vary between ora% and ora_% depending on the operating system on which the trace was performed, and the file should appear in the location specified by the USER_DUMP_DEST init.ora parameter. Another way of finding the file is to put a marker inside (such as issuing a query like SELECT 'Rich1' FROM DUAL;), and then use a file search utility like grep or Windows search to find the text.

You can use the query in Listing 6-1, running from the same session, to obtain the number included in the trace filename (assuming you can see the v$ views).

```
select spid, s.sid,s.serial#, p.username, p.program
from    v$process p, v$session s
where   p.addr = s.paddr
and     s.sid = (select sid from v$mystat where rownum=1);
```

Listing 6-1: Obtaining the number included in the TRACE file name

Run TKPROF to put the TRACE file into readable format:

```
tkprof ora_19554.trc rich2.prf explain=system/manager
```

The TKPROF utility translates the TRACE file generated by the SQL TRACE facility to a readable format. You can run TKPROF against a TRACE file that you have previously created, or you can run it while the program that is creating the TRACE file is still running. Table 6-1 lists options for TKPROF.

The syntax for TKPROF is as follows:

Vaiable	Definition
tkprof tracefile output_file [sort = parameters] [print=number] [explain=username/password] TRACEfile	This is the name of the TRACE file containing the statistics by SQL_TRACE.
Output_file	This is the name of the file where TKPROF writes its output.
SORT = parameters	This is the order in which to display the statements in the output. There are about 20 different options for sorting the output—you can even combine options.
PRINT = number	This is the number of statements to include in the output. If this statement is not included, TKPROF will list all statements in the output.

TABLE 6-1. *Command-line Options*

Vaiable	Definition
EXPLAIN = username/password	Run the EXPLAIN PLAN on the user's SQL statements in the TRACE file. This option creates a plan_table of its own, so the user will need to have privileges to create the table and space in which to create it. When TKPROF is finished, this table is dropped.
INSERT = filename	This option creates a script to create a table and store the TRACE file statistics for each SQL statement traced.
RECORD = filename	This option produces a file of all the user's SQL statements.
SYS = YES|NO	This option allows the user to request that the recursive SQL statements (issued by the SYS user) not be displayed in the output. The default is YES. Recursive SQL usually includes internal calls and any table maintenance, such as adding an extent to a table during an insert.
SORT = parameters	A tremendous number of sorting options are available. My favorites are FCHCPU (CPU time of fetch); FCHDSK (disk reads for fetch); FCHCU and FCHQRY (memory reads for fetch); FCHROW (number of rows fetched); EXEDSK (disk reads during execute); EXECU and EXEQRY (memory reads during execute); EXEROW (rows processed during execute); EXECPU (execute CPU time); PRSCPU (parse CPU); and PRSCNT (times parsed).

TABLE 6-1. *Command-line Options* (continued)

The following are some quick examples using these options.
Run TKPROF and list only the top five CPU (fetch + execute + parse) results:

```
tkprof ora_19554 rich2 explain=system/manager sort=(FCHCPU,EXECPU,PRSCPU) print=5
```

Run TKPROF and omit all recursive statements:

```
tkprof ora_19554 rich2 explain=system/manager sys=no
```

Run TKPROF and create a file that will create a table and insert records from the trace:

```
tkprof ora_19554.trc rich2.prf explain=system/manager insert=sqlinsert1.ins
```

Listing 6-2 shows the output of insert1.in.

```
alter session set sql_trace true ;
select count(*) from emp ;
alter session set sql_trace false ;
```

Listing 6-2: Output of insert1.ins

Run TKPROF and create a file that shows your trace session:

```
tkprof ora_19554.trc rich2.prf explain=system/manager record=record1.sql
```

Simple Steps for TRACE with a Simple Query

Listing 6-3 shows the partial output of record1.sql.

```
REM  Edit and/or remove the following  CREATE TABLE
REM  statement as your needs dictate.
CREATE TABLE  tkprof_table
(date_of_insert                        DATE
,cursor_num                            NUMBER
,depth                                 NUMBER
,user_id                               NUMBER
,parse_cnt                             NUMBER
...etc...
,sql_statement                         LONG );
INSERT INTO tkprof_table VALUES
(SYSDATE, 1, 0, 5, 0, 0, 0, 0, 0, 0, 0 , 1, 0, 0, 0, 0, 0, 1, 0
, 0, 0, 0, 0, 0, 0, 0, 4294877296 , 'alter session set sql_trace true');
INSERT INTO tkprof_table VALUES
(SYSDATE, 1, 0, 5, 1, 450648, 471000, 0, 46, 2, 1 , 1, 0, 0, 0, 0, 0, 0, 0
, 2, 10015, 10000, 0, 685, 4, 1, 50000, 'select count(*) from emp');
INSERT INTO tkprof_table VALUES
(SYSDATE, 1, 0, 5, 1, 0, 0, 0, 0, 0, 1 , 1, 0, 0, 0, 0, 0, 0, 0
, 0, 0, 0, 0, 0, 0, 0, 7481000, 'alter session set sql_trace false');
```

Listing 6-3: Partial output of record1.sql

TIP
The TKPROF utility puts a TRACEd output into a readable format. Without running TKPROF, it would be difficult to read the output of a TRACE. By specifying explain = username/password (above), we are able to get the EXPLAIN execution path, in addition to the execution statistics of the query.

TIP
To use multiple sort parameters, you can just repeat the sort = parameter on the command line, as tkprof source_file out_file sort = parm1 sort = parm2.

```
select    TABLE_NAME, OWNER, INITIAL_EXTENT, UNIQUENESS
from      IND2
where     OWNER = 'SCOTT';
```

	count	cpu	elapsed	disk	query	current	rows
Parse:	1	1	2	0	0	0	
Execute:	1	0	0	0	0	2	0
Fetch:	2	69	113	142	430	0	36

Here is the execution plan (no index used):

```
TABLE ACCESS (FULL) OF 'IND2'
```

The output above shows 142 disk reads (physical reads) and 430 total reads (query + current). The number of memory reads is the total reads less the disk reads, or 288 memory reads (430 – 142). Having such a high number of disk reads compared to physical reads is certainly a potential problem unless you are running a data warehouse or queries that often do need full table scans. The execution path shows a full table scan confirming that we may have a potential problem.

TIP
A traced query with a large number of physical reads usually indicates a missing index. The disk column indicates the physical reads (usually when an index is not used), and the query column added to the current column is the total number of block reads. A query with a large number of query reads and a low number of disk reads indicates the use of an index, but if it is overly high, it could indicate a bad index or bad join order of tables. A query with a large number of current reads usually indicates a large DML (UPDATE, INSERT, DELETE) query.

Listing 6-4 shows what happens when we rerun the query (after restarting the system) to be traced, now using an index on the OWNER table.

```
select     table_name, owner, initial_extent, uniqueness
from       ind2
where      owner = 'SCOTT' ;   (The index on "OWNER" is not suppressed)
```

Listing 6-4: Rerunning the query

Listing 6-5 shows the output of the file rich2.prf.

```
select     table_name, owner, initial_extent, uniqueness
from       ind2
where      owner = 'SCOTT' ;
```

	count	cpu	elapsed	disk	query	current	rows
Parse:	2	0	0	0	0		
Execute:	2	0	0	0	0	0	0
Fetch:	4		66	0	148	0	72

Listing 6-5: Output of rich2.prf

The following shows the Execution plan (index used):

```
TABLE ACCESS (BY ROWID) OF 'IND2'
  INDEX (RANGE SCAN) OF 'IND2_1' (NON-UNIQUE)
```

TIP
A traced query output with only memory reads (query-consistent reads) indicates that an index is being used.

The Sections of a TRACE Output

The TRACE utility has multiple sections, including the SQL statements, statistics, information, and EXPLAIN PLAN. Each of these sections is discussed in the following sections.

The SQL Statement

The first section of a TKPROF statement is the SQL statement. This statement will be exactly the same as the statement that was executed. If there were any hints or comments in the statement, they would be retained in this output. This can be helpful when you are reviewing the output from multiple sessions. If you find a statement that is causing problems, you can search for the exact statement. Remember, some of the statements from Oracle Forms are generated dynamically, so parts of the query (particularly WHERE clause predicates) may be displayed as bind variables (:1) and not actual text.

The Statistics Section

This section contains all the statistics for this SQL statement and all the recursive SQL statements generated to satisfy this statement. This section has eight columns, the first being the type of call to the database. There are three types of calls: Parse, Execute, and Fetch. Each call type generates a separate line of statistics. The other seven columns are the statistics for each type of call. Table 6-2 below summarizes this.

Column	Definition
Count	The number of times this type of call was made.
Cpu	The total CPU time for all of the calls of this type for this statement. If the TIMED_STATISTICS parameter in the init.ora is not set to TRUE, this statistic and the elapsed statistic will be 0.
Elapsed	The total elapsed time for this call.
Disk	The total number of data blocks retrieved from disk to satisfy this call. This is the number of physical reads.
Query	The total number of data buffers retrieved from memory for this type of call. SELECT statements usually retrieve buffers in this mode. This is the number of consistent gets.
Current	The total number of data buffers retrieved from memory for this type of call. Update, insert, or delete usually access buffers in this mode, although SELECT statements may use a small number of buffers in this mode also. This is the number of db block gets.
Rows	The total number of rows processed by this statement. The rows processed for SELECT statements will appear in the row of Fetch statistics. Inserts, updates, and deletes will appear in the Execute row.

TABLE 6-2. *Statistics section*

Information Section

The information section contains information about the number of missed library cache from parse and execute calls. If the number of misses is high, there may be a problem with the size of the shared pool. You should check the hit ratio and the reload rate of the library cache.

There is also information about the current optimizer mode setting. This section shows the username of the last user to parse this statement.

The Source Row Operation Section

The source row information section is a new section in TKPROF output, and it lists the number of rows cross-referenced with the operation that used the rows. The output looks something like that shown in Listing 6-6.

```
Rows      Row Source Operation
-------   --------------------------------------------------------
      1   TABLE ACCESS FULL DUAL
```

Listing 6-6: Source row information

> **TIP**
> *Note that the trace file is a point-in-time picture of what happened on the system at a given moment. In contrast, the explain plan (detailed next) is generated when the TKPROF listing is analyzed, which could be some time later. The row source operation listing is generated as part of the trace file and can be used to see if the database objects have changed since the trace was performed.*

The EXPLAIN PLAN

I find this section of the TKPROF to be the most useful. The first column of this section is the number of rows processed by each line of the execution plan. Here, you will be able to see how bad a statement is. If the total number of rows in the fetch statistics is low compared to the number of rows being processed by each line of the EXPLAIN PLAN, you may want to review the statement.

It is also possible that only one line of the execution plan is processing a large number of rows compared to the rest of the statement. This can be caused by full table scans or the use of a bad index.

A More Complex TKPROF Output

Listing 6-7 illustrates a TRACEd query with a slightly higher complexity.

```
select    Item_Item_Id, InitCap(Item_Description)
from      Item
where     Item_Classification = 1
and       Item_Item_Id Between 1000000 And 2700000
```

```
and         Item_Item_Id Not In (Select Invitem_Item_Id
from        Inventory_Item
where       Invitem_Location_Id = '405')

call      count      cpu elapsed      disk   query   current   rows
Parse     1     0.00         0.00         0       0     0  0
Execute         1    0.00         0.00        0       0    0  0
Fetch     27   20.87        21.24         0    4408      0399
Totals    29   20.87        21.24         0    4408      0399

Misses in library cache during parse: 0
Optimizer hint: CHOOSE

Parsing user id: 106    (C12462)
RowsExecution Plan
0           SELECT STATEMENT    OPTIMIZER HINT: CHOOSE
572           FILTER
598             TABLE ACCESS (BY ROWID) OF 'ITEM'
599               INDEX (RANGE SCAN) OF 'ITEM_PK' (UNIQUE)
278790      INDEX (RANGE SCAN) OF 'INVITEM_PK' (UNIQUE)
```

Listing 6-7: Higher complexity TRACEdquery

Table 6-3 lists some of the problems to look for in the TKPROF output.

Problems	Solutions
The parsing numbers are high.	The SHARED_POOL_SIZE may need to be increased.
The disk reads are very high.	Indexes are not being used or may not exist.
The "query" and/or "current" (memory reads) are very high.	Indexes may be on columns with low cardinality (columns where an individual value generally makes up a large percentage of the table; like a y/n field). Removing/suppressing the index or using histograms or a bitmap index may increase performance. A poor join order of tables or bad order in a concatenated index may also cause this.
The Parse elapse time is high.	There may be a problem with the number of open cursors.
The number of rows processed by a row in the EXPLAIN PLAN is high compared to the other rows.	This could be a sign of an index with a poor distribution of distinct keys (unique values for a column). This could also be a sign of a poorly written statement.
The number of Misses in the library cache during Parse is greater than 1.	This indicates that the statement had to be reloaded. You may need to increase the SHARED_POOL_SIZE in the init.ora or do a better job of sharing SQL.

TABLE 6-3.   *Problems to look for in the TKPROF output.*

Digging into the TKPROF Output

When we compare the TKPROF output to the actual object's physical characteristics, we start to see how Oracle is really working. Consider a CUSTOMER table with over 100,000 records contained in over 1000 blocks. By querying DBA_TABLES and DBA_EXTENTS, we can see the blocks that are both allocated (1536) and being used (1382), as shown in Listing 6-8.

```
select sum(blocks)
from dba_segments
where segment_name = 'CUSTOMER';

SUM(BLOCKS)
-----------
      1536

select blocks, empty_blocks
from dba_tables
where table_name = 'CUSTOMER';

    BLOCKS EMPTY_BLOCKS
---------- ------------
      1382          153
```

Listing 6-8: FInding blocks allocated and blocks being used

If we look at the TKPROF output of a query that counts all records in the CUSTOMER table (shown in Listing 6-9), we see that it performs a full table scan because this is the first access after a startup. Also note that the number of blocks accessed (mostly physical disk access) is slightly higher than the total number of blocks in the table (seen in the previous queries). All but 4 of the 1387 query blocks read are disk reads. (Disk reads are a subset of the query, which are the sum of disk and memory reads in consistent mode.)

```
SELECT COUNT(*)
FROM CUSTOMER;
```

call	count	cpu	elapsed	disk	query	current	rows
Parse	1	3505.04	3700.00	0	0	0	0
Execute	1	0.00	0.00	0	0	0	0
Fetch	2	1101.59	18130.00	1383	1387	15	1
total	4	4606.63	21830.00	1383	1387	15	1

```
Misses in library cache during parse: 1
Optimizer goal: CHOOSE
Parsing user id: 5
```

```
Rows     Row Source Operation
-------  -------------------------------------------------------
      1  SORT AGGREGATE
 114688    TABLE ACCESS FULL CUSTOMER
```

Listing 6-9: Count of al the records in the CUSTOMER table

If we run this query a second time (shown in Listing 6-10), a big change occurs. If we look at the TKPROF output of a query that counts all records in the CUSTOMER table this time, we see that it still performs a full table scan, but now there are many fewer disk reads because most of the blocks needed are already cached in memory. Most of the 1387 query blocks read are memory reads. (Only 121 are disk reads.)

```
SELECT COUNT(*)
FROM   CUSTOMER

call      count      cpu    elapsed       disk      query    current       rows
-------  ------  -------  ---------  ---------  ---------  ---------  ---------
Parse         1     0.00       0.00          0          0          0          0
Execute       1     0.00       0.00          0          0          0          0
Fetch         2   901.29    2710.00        121       1387         15          1
-------  ------  -------  ---------  ---------  ---------  ---------  ---------
total         4   901.29    2710.00        121       1387         15          1

Misses in library cache during parse: 0
Optimizer goal: CHOOSE
Parsing user id: 5

Rows     Row Source Operation
-------  -------------------------------------------------------
      1  SORT AGGREGATE
 114688    TABLE ACCESS FULL CUSTOMER
```

Listing 6-10: Count of all the records in the CUSTOMER table (blocks cached in memory)

TIP
Full table scans are one of the first things directed by Oracle to be pushed out of memory (become least recently used as soon as you run them) because they are so inefficient, usually using a lot of memory.

 ## Using EXPLAIN PLAN Alone

The EXPLAIN PLAN command allows developers to view the query execution plan that the Oracle optimizer will use to execute a SQL statement. This command is very helpful in improving performance of SQL statements, because it does not actually execute the SQL statement—it only outlines the plan to use and inserts this execution plan in an Oracle table. Prior to using the EXPLAIN PLAN command, a file called utlxplan.sql (located in the same directory as catalog.sql, which is usually located in the ORACLE_HOME/rdbms/admin directory) must be executed under the Oracle account that will be executing the EXPLAIN PLAN command.

The script creates a table called PLAN_TABLE that the EXPLAIN PLAN command uses to insert the query execution plan in the form of records. This table can then be queried and viewed to determine if the SQL statement needs to be modified to force a different execution plan. Oracle supplies queries to use against the plan table too: utlxpls.sql and utlxplp.sql. (Either will work, but utlxplp.sql is geared toward parallel queries.) An EXPLAIN PLAN example is shown next (executed in SQL*Plus).

Q. Why use EXPLAIN without TRACE?

A. The statement is *not* executed; it only shows what will happen if the statement is executed.

Q. When do you use EXPLAIN without TRACE?

A. When the query will take exceptionally long to run.

The following illustration demonstrates the procedures for running TRACE vs. EXPLAIN:

TRACE	EXPLAIN PLAN
It takes four *hours* to trace a query that takes four hours to run.	It takes less than a *minute* to EXPLAIN PLAN a query that takes four hours to run.
Set up Init.ora Parameters	Create PLAN_TABLE table
Create PLAN_TABLE table	Explain Query
Run Query	PLAN_TABLE is populated
Statement is executed PLAN_TABLE is populated	Query PLAN_TABLE
Run TKPROF	Output shows EXPLAIN PLAN
Output shows disk and memory reads in addition to EXPLAIN PLAN output	

Using EXPLAIN PLAN Alone

Q. How do I use EXPLAIN by itself?

1. Find the script; it is usually in the ORACLE_HOME/rdbms/admin:

```
"utlxplan.sql"
```

2. Execute the script utlxplan.sql in SQLPLUS:

```
@utlxplan
```

This creates the PLAN_TABLE for the user executing the script. You can create your own PLAN_TABLE, but use Oracle's syntax—*or else!*

3a. Run EXPLAIN PLAN for the query to be optimized:

```
explain plan for
select      CUSTOMER_NUMBER
from        CUSTOMER
where       CUSTOMER_NUMBER = 111;
Explained.
```

3b. Run EXPLAIN PLAN for the query to be optimized (using a tag for the statement):

```
explain plan
set statement_id = 'CUSTOMER' for
select      CUSTOMER_NUMBER
from        CUSTOMER
where       CUSTOMER_NUMBER = 111;
```

TIP
Use the SET STATEMENT_ID = 'your_identifier' when the PLAN_TABLE will be populated by many different developers. I rarely use the SET STATEMENT_ID statement. Instead, I EXPLAIN a query, look at the output, and then delete from the PLAN_TABLE table. I continue to do this (making changes to the query) until I see an execution plan that I think will be favorable. I then run the query to see if the performance has improved. If multiple developers/DBAs are using the same PLAN_TABLE, the SET STATEMENT_ID will be essential to identifying a statement.

4. Select the output from the PLAN_TABLE:

```
select      operation, options, object_name, id, parent_id
from        plan_table
where       statement_id = 'CUSTOMER';
```

Operation	Options	Object Name	ID	Parent
select statement			0	
Table Access	By ROWID	Customer	1	
Index	Range Scan	CUST_IDX	2	1

TIP
Use EXPLAIN instead of TRACE so you don't have to wait for the query to run. EXPLAIN shows the path of a query without actually running the query. Use TRACE only for multiquery batch jobs to find out which of the many queries in the batch job are slow.

TIP
You can use the utlxpls.sql and utlxplp.sql queries provided by Oracle to query the PLAN_TABLE without having to write your own query and without having to format the output.

An Additional EXPLAIN Example for a Simple Query

1. Run the query with the EXPLAIN syntax embedded prior to the query:

```
explain plan
set statement_id = 'query 1' for
select    customer_number, name
from      customer
where     customer_number = '111';
```

2. Retrieve the output of EXPLAIN by querying the PLAN_TABLE.

   To retrieve the information for viewing, a SQL statement must be executed. Two scripts provided in the Oracle documentation are displayed in Steps 2 and 3, along with the results of each based on the previous EXPLAIN PLAN command. Note that this example varies from the last example. The customer_number column is an indexed number field, which in the second example is suppressed (by forcing a to_char) because of a data type mismatch. ('111' is in quotes.) In the first example, I treated the customer_number column correctly as a number field. (111 is not in quotes.)

```
select    operation, options, object_name, id, parent_id
from      plan_table
where     statement_id = 'query 1'
order by  id;
```

Operation	Options	Object Name	ID	Parent ID
select Statement			0	
Table Access	Full	Customer_Information	1	0

3. Retrieve a more intuitive and easy to read output of EXPLAIN:

```
select    lpad(' ', 2*(level-1)) || operation || ' ' || options || ' ' ||
          object_name || ' ' || decode(id, 0, 'Cost = ' || position) "Query Plan"
from      plan_table
start     with id = 0
and       statement_id = 'query 1'
connect by prior id = parent_id
and       statement_id = 'query 1';
```

Output:

```
Query Plan
select statement      Cost=220
    Table Access Full Customer
```

EXPLAIN PLAN—Read It Top to Bottom or Bottom to Top?

Whether you should read from top to bottom or bottom to top depends on how you write the query that retrieves the information from the PLAN_TABLE table. That is probably why many people disagree about which way to read the result (all methods may be correct). Listing 6-11 shows the order of execution based on the query that retrieves the information. In this example, the output is read top to bottom with one caveat: you must read it from the innermost to the outermost. This listing shows a method that should clear up any questions.

The SQL statement should be placed after the FOR clause of the EXPLAIN PLAN statement.

```
delete     from plan_table;
explain plan
set        statement_id = 'SQL1' for
select     to_char(sysdate, 'MM/DD/YY HH:MI AM'), to_char((trunc((sysdate -4 -1),
           'day') +1), 'DD-MON-YY')
from       bk, ee
where      bk_shift_date >= to_char((trunc(( sysdate - 4 - 1), 'day') + 1), 'DD-
           MON-YY')
and        bk_shift_date <= to_char((sysdate - 4), 'DD-MON-YY')
and        bk_empno = ee_empno(+)
and        substr(ee_hierarchy_code, 1, 3) in ('PNA', 'PNB', 'PNC', 'PND', 'PNE',
           'PNF')
order by   ee_job_group, bk_empno, bk_shift_date
/
select     LPad(' ', 2*(Level-1)) || Level || '.' || Nvl(Position,0) || ' ' ||
           Operation || ' ' || Options || ' ' || Object_Name || ' ' || Object_Type
           || ' ' || Decode(id, 0, Statement_Id ||' Cost = ' || Position) || cost
           || ' ' || Object_Node "Query Plan"
from       plan_table
start      with id = 0 And statement_id = 'SQL1'
connect by prior id = parent_id
and        statement_id = 'SQL1'
/
 Query Plan
1.0 SELECT STATEMENT     SQL1  Cost =
    2.1 SORT ORDER BY (7th)
        3.1 FILTER (6th)
            4.1 NESTED LOOPS OUTER (5th)
                5.1 TABLE ACCESS BY ROWID BK (2nd)
                    6.1 INDEX RANGE SCAN I_BK_06 NON-UNIQUE (1st)
                5.2 TABLE ACCESS BY ROWID EE (4th)
                    6.1 INDEX UNIQUE SCAN I_EE_01 UNIQUE (3rd)
```

Listing 6-11: Order of execution besed on the query retrieving the information

Reading the EXPLAIN PLAN

Using the previous EXPLAIN PLAN, I will elucidate the steps. The numbers in the left column in Table 6-4 identify each step. They are listed in the order in which they are executed.

TIP
Whether the EXPLAIN PLAN is read from top to bottom or from bottom to top depends entirely on the query used to select information from the PLAN_TABLE. Both methods of reading the query may be correct, given that the query selecting the information is correctly structured.

Setting AUTOTRACE On

There is also an easier method for generating an EXPLAIN PLAN and statistics about the performance of a query with SQL*Plus. The main difference between AUTOTRACE and EXPLAIN PLAN is that AUTOTRACE actually executes the query (in the way TRACE does) and automatically queries the plan table, whereas EXPLAIN PLAN does neither. The AUTOTRACE command (available in SQLPLUS 3.3 and later) generates similar information, as shown in Listing 6-12. To use AUTOTRACE, the user must possess the PLUSTRACE role (by running plustrce.sql, which is usually located in the ORACLE_HOME/sqlplus/admin directory).

Step	Action
6.1	This is the index range scan of I_BK_06. This is the first step. This index is on the BK_SHIFT_DATE column. This step performs a scan of this index to produce a list of ROWIDs that fall between the two dates.
5.1	This retrieves the rows from the BK table.
6.1	This scans the I_EE_01 index. This index is on the EE_EMPNO column. Using the BK_EMPNO retrieved from the previous step, this index is scanned to retrieve the ROWIDs to produce a list of the EE_EMPNOs that match the BK_EMPNOs.
5.2	This retrieves the rows from the EE table.
4.1	This is a nested loop. The two lists are joined, producing one list.
3.1	This is a filter. The rest of the conditions of the WHERE clause are applied.
2.1	This is SORT_ORDER_BY. The remaining rows are sorted according to the ORDER BY clause.
1.0	This tells which type of statement it is.

TABLE 6-4. *Reading the EXPLAIN PLAN*

```
SET AUTOTRACE ON
select     count(name)
from       emp7
where      name = 'branches';
```

Listing 6-12: Setting AUTOTRACE on

Output:

```
Count(Name)

100

Query Plan
   0        SELECT STATEMENT Optimizer=CHOOS
   1    0    SORT (AGGREGATE
   2    1     INDEX (RANGE SCAN) OF 'EMP7_I1' (NON-UNIQUE)

Statistics
          0  recursive calls
          0  db block gets
          1  consistent gets
          1  physical reads
          0  redo size
        223  bytes sent via SQL*Net to client
        274  bytes recd via SQL*Net from client
          2  SQL*Net roundtrips to/from client
          1  sorts (memory)
          0  sorts (disk)
          1  rows processed
```

TIP
The AUTOTRACE option provides an EXPLAIN PLAN and statistics for a query. The AUTOTRACE provides many of the TRACE and TKPROF statistics such as disk reads (physical reads) and total reads (consistent reads + db block gets).

TIP
If the error "Unable to verify plan table format or existence" occurs when enabling AUTOTRACE, you must create a plan table using utlxplan.sql.

TIP
AUTOTRACE may fail when querying system views because the user may not have permission to view underlying objects.

Table 6-5 shows other AUTOTRACE Options.

Option	Function
SET AUTOT ON	Short way of turning on AUTOTRACE
SET AUTOT ON EXP	Shows only the explain plan
SET AUTOTRACE ON STAT	Shows only the statistics
SET AUTOT TRACE	Does not show the output of the query

TABLE 6-5. *AUTOTRACE options*

EXPLAIN PLAN When Using Partitions

Table partitions yield different outputs for their EXPLAIN PLANs (as shown in Listing 6-13). In this listing, we create a partitioned table in three parts with a partitioned index. Broadly speaking, partitions are tables stored in multiple places in the database. For more information on partitioning tables, refer to Chapter 3.

```
create table dept1
     (deptno      number(2),
      dept_name       varchar2(30))
      partition by range(deptno)
      (partition d1 values      less than (10),
       partition d2 values      less than (20),
       partition d3 values      less than (maxvalue));

insert into dept1 values (1, 'DEPT 1');
insert into dept1 values (7, 'DEPT 7');
insert into dept1 values (10, 'DEPT 10');
insert into dept1 values (15, 'DEPT 15');
insert into dept1 values (22, 'DEPT 22');

create index dept_index
     on dept1 (deptno)
     local
     (partition d1,
      partition  d2 ,
      partition  d3 );
```

Listing 6-13: EXPLAIN PLANS of table partitions

We now generate an EXPLAIN PLAN that forces a full table scan to access the first two partitions, as shown in Listing 6-14.

```
explain plan for
select      dept_name
from        dept1
```

```
where       deptno || '' = 1
or          deptno || '' = 15;
```

Listing 6-14: Forcing a full table scan

When selecting from the plan table, you must select the additional columns partition_start (starting partition) and partition_stop (ending partition). For a full table scan, all partitions will be accessed:

```
select      operation, options, id, object_name, partition_start,
            partition_stop
from        plan_table;
```

Output (for the full table scan):

Operation	Options	Id	Object Name	Partition Start	Partition Stop
SELECT STATEMENT					
PARTITION	CONCATENATED	1		1	3
TABLE ACCESS	FULL	2	DEPT1	1	3

The previous example shows that a full table scan on the DEPT1 table is performed. All three partitions are scanned. The starting partition is 1 and the ending partition is 3.

Next, an EXPLAIN PLAN is generated in Listing 6-15 for an index range scan of partition 2 only:

```
explain plan for select dept_name
from        dept1
where       deptno   = 15;
Explained.
```

Listing 6-15: EXPLAIN PLAN for an index range scan of partition 2 only

We now generate an EXPLAIN PLAN for an index range scan accessing only the second partition, as in Listing 6-16.

```
select      operation, options, id, object_name, partition_start,
            partition_stop
from        plan_table;
```

Listing 6-16: EXPLAIN PLAN for an index range scan accessing only the second partition

Output (for the index range scan):

Operation	Options	Id	Object Name	Partition Start	Partition Stop
SELECT STATEMENT					
TABLE ACCESS	BY LOCAL INDEX ROWID	1	DEPT1	2	2
TABLE ACCESS	RANGE SCAN	2	DEPTIDX	2	2

This output shows that the only partition of the table OR index that is accessed is the second partition. This is because the value for deptno = 15 is within the second partition of the DEPT1 table. The DEPTNO column is also indexed, and this value is also within the second partition of the index.

TIP
Partitions can also be viewed by the EXPLAIN PLAN by accessing the columns PARTITION_START and PARTITION_STOP in the PLAN_TABLE table.

Finding High Disk and/or Memory Reads Without Using TRACE

Is there another method for retrieving problem disk and memory read information without tracing everything? Yes! By using V$SQLAREA, you can find the problem queries on your system. Listing 6-17 shows how to find the problem queries. In this query, we are searching for queries where the disk reads are greater than 10,000 (missing or suppressed index potentials). If your system is much larger, you may need to set this number higher.

```
select      disk_reads, sql_text
from        v$sqlarea
where       disk_reads > 10000
order by    disk_reads desc;


DISK_READS       SQL_TEXT
    12987        select     order#,columns,types from orders
                 where      substr(orderid,1,2)=:1
    11131        select     custid, city from customer
                 where      city = 'CHICAGO'
```

Listing 6-17: Finding problem queries

This output suggests that there are two problem queries causing heavy disk reads. The first has the index on ORDERID suppressed by the SUBSTR function; the second shows that there may be a missing index on CITY.

In the query in Listing 6-18, we are searching for queries where the memory reads are greater than 200,000 (overindexed query potentials). If your system is much larger, you may need to set this number higher.

```
select     buffer_gets, sql_text
from       v$sqlarea
where      buffer_gets > 200000
order by   buffer_gets desc;
BUFFER_GETS     SQL_TEXT
    300219      select order#,cust_no, from orders
                where division = '1'
```

Listing 6-18: Searching for queries with overindexed query potentials

The output suggests that one problem query is causing heavy memory reads. The index on DIVISION appears to have a low cardinality (few unique divisions) and should be suppressed for this statement to improve the performance.

TIP
Accessing the V$SQLAREA table can give statistics that are often found when tracing a query. See Chapter 12 for additional information on accessing the V$SQLAREA table.

Reading the EXPLAIN PLAN

Yet Another EXPLAIN PLAN Output Method: Building the Tree Structure

Although many people find the earlier EXPLAIN PLAN methods sufficient, others require a more theoretical approach that ties to the parent/child relationships of a query and the corresponding tree structure. For some people, this makes using EXPLAIN easier to visualize, and it is included here for that audience.

1. The following is the query to be EXPLAINed:

```
explain plan
set statement_id = 'SQL2' for
select    cust_no ,cust_address ,cust_last_name, cust_first_name ,cust_mid_init
from      customer
where     cust_phone = '3035551234';
```

2. This is the query used for this approach:

```
select    LPAD(' ',2*(LEVEL-1))||operation "OPERATION", options "OPTIONS",
          DECODE(TO_CHAR(id),'0','COST = ' || NVL(TO_CHAR(position),'n/a'),
          object_name) "OBJECT NAME", id ||'-'|| NVL(parent_id, 0)||'-'||
          NVL(position, 0) "ORDER", SUBSTR(optimizer,1,6) "OPT"
from plan_table
start     with id = 0
and   statement_id = 'SQL2'
connect by prior id = parent_id
and       statement_id = 'SQL2';
```

3. Here is the output for this approach:

OPERATION	OPTIONS	OBJECT NAME	ORDER	OPT
SELECT STATEMENT		COST = n/a	0-0-0	RULE
TABLE ACCESS	BY ROWID	CUSTOMER	1-0-1	
INDEX	RANGE SCAN	IX_CUST_PHONE	2-1-1	

Note that two new columns are introduced:

- **ORDER** This column contains the ID, the parent ID, and the position of the step in the execution plan. The ID identifies the step but does not imply the order of execution. The parent ID identifies the parent step of the step. The position indicates the order in which children steps are executed that have the same parent ID.

- **OPT** This column contains the current mode of the optimizer.

4. The execution tree is constructed.

Based on the execution plan in the illustration, an execution tree can be constructed to get a better feel for how Oracle is going to process the statement. To construct the tree, simply start with Step 1, find all other steps whose parent step is 1, and draw them in. Repeat this procedure until all the steps are accounted for. The execution tree for the execution plan for the query in this example is displayed here.

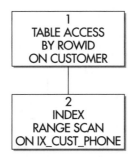

5. The execution plan is interpreted.

To understand how Oracle is going to process a statement, you must understand in what sequence Oracle is going to process the steps and what Oracle is doing in each step.

The sequence is determined by the parent/child relationship of the steps. Basically, the child step is always performed first, at least once, and feeds the parent steps from there. When a parent has multiple children, children steps are performed in the order of the step position, which is the third number displayed in the ORDER column of the execution plan. When the execution tree is constructed, if the lower-position children for a parent are arranged left to right, the execution tree reads left to right, bottom to top.

Another Example Using the Tree Approach

1. The following is the query to be EXPLAINed:

```
select     a.cust_last_name, a.cust_first_name, a.cust_mid_init, b.order_desc,
           b.order_create_dt
from       customer a, order_hdr b
where      cust_phone = :host1
and        b.cust_no = a.cust_no
and        b.order_status = 'OPEN';
```

2. Here is the execution plan:

OPERATION	OPTIONS	OBJECT NAME	ORDER	OPTRULE
SELECT STATEMENT		COST = n/a	0-0-0	
NESTED LOOPS			1-0-1	
TABLE ACCESS	BY ROWID	ORDER_HDR	2-1-1	
INDEX	RANGE SCAN	IX_ORDER_STATUS	3-2-1	
TABLE ACCESS	BY ROWID	CUSTOMER	4-1-2	
INDEX	UNIQUE SCAN	PK_CUSTOMER	5-4-1	

Another Example Using the Tree Approach

3. The following illustration shows the execution tree.

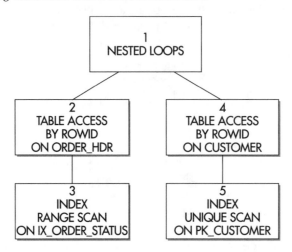

4. The execution plan sequence is determined for the query.

This statement has five steps. Child Step 3 is executed first. Because it is a range scan, it returns 0, 1, or many ROWIDs to Step 2. For each ROWID returned, Step 2 accesses the order table by ROWID, gets the requested data, and returns the data to Step 1. For each row of data received from Step 2, Step 1 sends the CUST_NO to Step 5. Step 5 uses the customer number to perform a unique scan to get the ROWID. The ROWID is then returned from Step 5 to Step 4. If no ROWID is found, Step 4 tells Step 1 to eliminate that particular row. If a ROWID is found, Step 4 accesses the table by ROWID and retrieves the data. Once it gets the data, if the phone number is correct, it returns the data to Step 1, where it is merged with the result from Steps 2 and 3 for that row and returned to the user. If the phone number is incorrect, Step 4 returns no row and Step 1 throws out the row.

5. The performance is reviewed.

Is this a good table access order? In most order-entry systems where there are lots of customers and many open orders at a given time, why would you want to spin through all open orders first, get the data for each one, go to the CUSTOMER table for each of those, and then throw out all but the one open order for the customer with the right phone number? To correct this situation, we want to first go to the customer table based on phone number because most of the rows will be filtered out in the first step, thus improving performance. How do we do this? Consider the changes made next.

6a. Performance changes occur (the driving table is changed):

```
select      a.cust_last_name, a.cust_first_name, a.cust_mid_init, b.order_desc,
            b.order_create_dt
from        order_hdr b, customer a
where       cust_phone = :host1
and         b.cust_no = a.cust_no
and         b.order_status = 'OPEN';
```

6b. The *new* execution plan is determined:

OPERATION	OPTIONS	OBJECT NAME	ORDER	OPT
SELECT STATEMENT		COST = n/a	0-0-0	RULE
NESTED LOOPS			1-0-1	
TABLE ACCESS	BY ROWID	CUSTOMER	2-1-1	
INDEX	RANGE SCAN	IX_CUST_PHONE	3-2-1	
TABLE ACCESS	BY ROWID	ORDER_HDR	4-1-2	
AND-EQUAL			5-4-1	
INDEX	RANGE SCAN	IX_ORDER_CUST	6-5-1	
INDEX	RANGE SCAN	IX_ORDER_STATUS	7-5-2	

6c. The performance of the semituned query is reviewed.

Why did the table order change? In rule-based optimization, when faced with multiple tables to join and identical access paths to enter into each (in this case, each table starts with an index range scan on a single-column index), the table lowest in the FROM clause gets accessed first. So by switching the FROM clause around, the execution plan changed. In cost-based optimization, it may have figured this out in the first place based on table and index statistics. If not, hints could have been used to achieve the same result.

Is this a good table access order? The table order is good because the CUSTOMER half of the query is executed first and will probably return only one row to the ORDER half of the query.

Is the AND-EQUAL optimal? In this case, no. Why churn through 1000 ROWIDs in the ORDER_STATUS index and all the ROWIDs in the CUST_NO index and keep only the ones that match? What we should do is either pick the most unique index of the two and use it, or create a composite index on CUST_NO and ORDER status. Changing the driving table was the right thing to do. Now, we must stop Oracle from using the order status index to completely tune the query.

7a. The *tuned* query is shown next (the index on ORDER_STATUS is suppressed):

```
select    a.cust_last_name, a.cust_first_name, a.cust_mid_init, b.order_desc,
          b.order_create_dt
from      order_hdr b, customer a
where     cust_phone = :host1
and       b.cust_no = a.cust_no
and       b.order_status || '' = 'OPEN';
```

7b. The *tuned* execution plan is shown next:

OPERATION	OPTIONS	OBJECT NAME	ORDER	OPTRULE
SELECT STATEMENT		COST = n/a	0-0-0	
NESTED LOOPS			1-0-1	
TABLE ACCESS	BY ROWID	CUSTOMER		2-1-1
INDEX	UNIQUE SCAN	PK_CUSTOMER		3-2-1
TABLE ACCESS	BY ROWID	ORDER_HDR	4-1-2	
INDEX	RANGE SCAN	IX_ORDER_STATUS		5-4-1

To determine how Oracle is going to process a SQL statement, you must generate and interpret an execution plan for the statement. With access to the tools that can generate execution plans for SQL, along with a rudimentary understanding of the information that is in an execution plan and the knowledge of how to construct an execution tree, a developer or DBA can begin exploring the vast variety of EXPLAIN PLANs that the diverse SQL code produces and learn fairly quickly how to tune and develop quality SQL.

Tracing/EXPLAINing Problem Queries in Developer Products

Although you can issue the ALTER SESSION SET SQL_TRACE TRUE; command on the SQL*Plus command line to TRACE SQL statements, this is tough when it comes to using developer products. One drawback to this option is that you are not able to trace a form or report; you need to cut the code out of the form or report and run it from SQL*Plus. This process can be very time-consuming if you do not know which statements you need to trace.

There is another way to produce a trace of the execution of a form. If you are using an earlier version of Oracle Forms, such as Forms 3.0, you can include an *-s* on the command line; when using Forms (versions 4–6), you can include statistics = yes on the command line. This way, you are able to trace individual forms. Later versions of Oracle Forms and Oracle Reports allow tracing from inside a form or report. Please refer to the Forms and/or Reports documentation for an explanation of how to use these options. Oracle Applications often has a menu item to do this as well.

TIP
You can also use TRACE within the Developer/2000 products. You simply need to set statistics = yes on the command line for forms, or you may embed the tracing within an actual trigger to turn tracing on and off.

Important Columns in the PLAN_TABLE Table

The descriptions for some of the more important columns available in the PLAN_TABLE table are as follows:

- **STATEMENT_ID** The value of the option STATEMENT_ID parameter specified in the EXPLAIN PLAN statement.

- **TIMESTAMP** The date and time when the EXPLAIN PLAN statement was issued.

- **REMARKS** Any comment (of up to 80 bytes) you wish to associate with each step of the EXPLAIN PLAN. If you need to add or change a remark on any row of the PLAN_TABLE table, use the UPDATE statement to modify the rows of the PLAN_TABLE table.

- **OPERATION** The name of the internal operation performed in this step. See Appendix A of *Oracle Server Tuning* for information on the contents of this column. In the first row generated for a statement, the column contains one of four values: DELETE, INSERT, SELECT, or UPDATE, depending on the type of the statement.

- **OPTIONS** A variation on the operation described in the OPERATION column. See Appendix A of *Oracle Server Tuning* for information on the contents of this column.

TIP
The OPERATION and OPTIONS columns of the PLAN_TABLE are the most important columns for tuning a query. The OPERATION column shows the actual operation performed (including type of join), and the OPTIONS column tells you when there is a full table scan being performed (that may need an index).

- **OBJECT_NODE**   The name of the database link used to reference the object (a table name or view name). For local queries using the parallel query option, this column describes the order in which output from operations is consumed.

- **OBJECT_OWNER**   The name of the user who owns the schema containing the table or index.

- **OBJECT_NAME**   The name of the table or index.

- **OBJECT_INSTANCE**   A number corresponding to the ordinal position of the object as it appears in the original statement. The numbering proceeds from left to right, outer to inner, with respect to the original statement text. Note that view expansion results in unpredictable numbers.

- **OBJECT_TYPE**   A modifier that provides descriptive information about the object, for example, NON-UNIQUE for indexes.

- **OPTIMIZER**   The current mode of the optimizer.

- **SEARCH_COLUMNS**   Not currently used.

- **ID**   A number assigned to each step in the execution plan.

TIP
The ID column shows the order in which a statement is processed. One of the basic rules of tuning a SQL statement is to change the query such that the ID of the order in which steps in the query execute is changed. Changing the order in which steps execute in a query will usually change the performance of a query either positively or negatively. Using HINTS (see Chapter 7) will force a query to execute in a different statement order and will usually make a query faster or slower.

- **PARENT_ID**   The ID of the next execution step that operates on the output of the ID step.

TIP
The PARENT_ID column is very important because it shows the dependencies of two steps in an EXPLAIN PLAN. If a section of the EXPLAIN PLAN has a PARENT_ID, it implies that this statement must run prior the PARENT_ID that is specified.

Important Columns in the PLAN_TABLE Table

- **POSITION**   The order of processing for steps that all have the same PARENT_ID.

- **OTHER**   Other information that is specific to the execution step that a user may find useful.

- **OTHER_TAG**   The contents of the OTHER column.

- **COST**   The cost of the operation as *estimated* by the optimizer's cost-based approach. For statements that use the rule-based approach, this column is NULL. Cost is not determined for table access operations. The value of this column does not have any particular unit of measurement; it is merely a weight value used to compare costs of execution plans.

- **CARDINALITY**   The cost-based approach's *estimate* of the number of rows accessed by the operation.

- **BYTES**   The cost-based approach's *estimate* of the number of bytes accessed by the operation.

TIP
The BYTES column is extremely important when evaluating how to tune a query. When an index is used and the number of bytes is great, it implies that doing a full table scan would perhaps be more efficient (i.e., reading the index and data is more costly than just reading the data in a full table scan). Also, the number of bytes helps us to determine which table should be accessed first in the query (driving table), because one table may limit the number of bytes needed from another. See Chapter 9 for tips on choosing the driving table.

TIP
Remember that both the COST and BYTES values in a query are estimates; it is quite possible for a version of a query with a higher estimated cost or bytes to run faster than another with a lower value.

Helpful Oracle-Supplied Packages
You can also TRACE the sessions of other users by using their session information within the DBMS_SYSTEM package. First, you must get the user's information from the v$SESSION. You then pass that information to the procedure to begin tracing (Listing 6-19).

```
select     sid, serial#
from       v$session
where      username = 'SCOTT';
```

Listing 6-19: Passing user information to the procedure to begin tracing

Output:

```
SID      SERIAL#
  9        190
1 row selected.
```

Begin tracing the username by using the following package as SYS(the SID and SERIAL# for the user's session must be entered):

```
execute dbms_system.set_sql_trace_in_session(9,190,TRUE);
PL/SQL procedure successfully completed.
```

TIP
It is also possible to enable TRACE by calling the procedure
DBMS_ORACLE_TRACE_USER.SET_ORACLE_TRACE.

You can also initiate TRACE for the session that you are using the DBMS_SESSION package. This package is particularly helpful for tracing queries within stored procedures, as well as for use within PL/SQL code.

```
execute DBMS_SESSION.SET_SQL_TRACE (TRUE);
PL/SQL procedure successfully completed.
```

INIT.ORA Parameters for Undocumented TRACE

One area that the experts can investigate is the X$KSPPI table. A brief listing for undocumented TRACE parameters in init.ora is shown in Listing 6-20. Note that Oracle does not support use of undocumented features of the product.

```
SQL> run
  1  select     ksppinm "Parameter Name", ksppstvl "Value",ksppstdf "Default"
  2  from       x$ksppi x, x$ksppcv y
  3  where      x.indx = y.indx
  4* and ksppinm like '/_%trace%' escape '/'
```

Parameter Name	Value	Default
_trace_files_public	FALSE	TRUE
_ksi_trace		TRUE
_trace_processes	ALL	TRUE
_trace_archive	FALSE	TRUE
_trace_events		TRUE
_trace_buffers	ALL:256	TRUE
_trace_flush_processes	ALL	TRUE
_trace_file_size	65536	TRUE
_trace_options	text,multiple	TRUE
_dlmtrace		TRUE
_db_block_trace_protect	FALSE	TRUE

```
_trace_buffer_flushes          FALSE                        TRUE
_trace_multi_block_reads       FALSE                        TRUE
_trace_cr_buffer_creates       FALSE                        TRUE
_trace_buffer_gets             FALSE                        TRUE
_dump_MTTR_to_trace            FALSE                        TRUE
_kkfi_trace                    FALSE                        TRUE
_px_trace                      none                         TRUE
_oracle_trace_events                                        TRUE
_oracle_trace_facility_version                              TRUE
_smm_trace                     0                            TRUE

21 rows selected
```

Listing 6-20: Undocumented TRACE parameters in init.ora

TIP
The X$KSPPI table can be accessed only by the SYS user. See Chapter 13 for tips on accessing the x$ tables and using some of these parameters. Do not use any undocumented parameters without consulting Oracle Corporation. Also, the layout and column names of these views have been known to change between Oracle releases.

Tracing Errors Within Oracle for More Information

This section explains the use of one of the undocumented features of TRACE. Before using undocumented init.ora parameters, please contact Oracle Corporation. To TRACE errors for a session, you can alter and monitor the session (shown next) or set an event in the init.ora. (See Chapter 13 for more information.) Sessions can be traced for errors by running the query shown next (used to TRACE a 4031 error). These queries build a TRACE file in your _trace_archive_dest (found in x$ksppi) that contains a dump of the full error text.

Use the following command:

```
alter session set events='4031 trace name errorstack level 4';
```

TIP
Tracing queries can help performance, but using the TRACE facility built within the undocumented TRACE init.ora parameters (discussed previously) can give great insight into solving errors within Oracle.

Tracing by Enabling Events

Trace sessions can also be initiated by using this command:

```
Alter session set events '10046 trace name context forever, level 1'
```

The value of the level ('1' in the previous command) can be '1' (regular trace), '4' (trace bind variables), '8' (trace wait states), or '12' (regular trace, plus bind variables and wait states). Information about bind variables and wait states can then appear in the trace file, but will be ignored by TKPROF when formatting the report. Output in the trace file for the previous command could look like that shown in Listing 6-21:

```
SELECT SYSDATE   FROM DUAL  WHERE SYSDATE IN ( :b1  )
END OF STMT
PARSE #4:c=0,e=0,p=0,cr=0,cu=0,mis=0,r=0,dep=1,og=4,tim=0
BINDS #4:
 bind 0: dty=12 mxl=07(07) mal=00 scl=00 pre=00 oacflg=03 oacfl2=1 size=8
offset=0
   bfp=0ddcc774 bln=07 avl=07 flg=05
   value="11/19/2000 19:25:47"
WAIT #1: nam='SQL*Net message to client' ela= 0 p1=1413697536 p2=1 p3=0
```

Listing 6-21: Output in the TRACE file

To turn event tracing off, use the following command:

```
Alter session set events '10046 trace name context off'
```

Using Stored Outlines

Up until recently, the chief use for execution plans was to determine what Oracle was doing with queries at run time as a tuning tool. A fairly new facility called STORED OUTLINES allows a query to use a predetermined execution plan every time that query is run, no matter where the query is run from. People sometimes speak of the STORED OUTLINES as storing an execution plan, but this is not really what happens. Instead, Oracle stores a series of *hints*—instructions to the database to execute a query in a precise way—to duplicate the execution plan as saved during a recording session.

Oracle can replicate execution plans for queries using stored outlines through a process similar to using the EXPLAIN PLAN functionality in SQL*PLUS. First, you set up the stored outline session by telling Oracle to save outlines for queries you are about to run using the ALTER SESSION command. Next, you execute the query for which you want the outline stored. (This is usually done on a session-only basis so as not to affect other users—more on this later.) Finally, if the execution plan is acceptable, it can be saved to the database and used by everyone everywhere. The following sections describe each of these steps in greater detail.

TIP
Oracle Corporation likes to refer to STORED OUTLINES as PLAN STABILITY. For further information on using STORED OUTLINES, see the Oracle documentation on Plan Stability.

Setting Up STORED OUTLINES

Unfortunately, as with most of the spectacular new features that Oracle provides, the setup process for using STORED OUTLINES is complex. Many user *and* session privileges absolutely must be set up properly before outlines can be stored, or stored ones can be used. Otherwise, they won't work, but Oracle won't tell you explicitly why.

The following privileges are required to use STORED OUTLINES:

- CREATE ANY OUTLINE
- EXECUTE_CATALOG (to use the DBMS_OUTLN package)
- PLUSTRACE (to use AUTOTRACE, if applicable)

Beyond permissions, STORED OUTLINES further require use of both the cost-based optimizer and several specific session parameters (environment settings). These settings broadly include those ending with _ENABLED:

- QUERY_REWRITE _ENABLED = TRUE
- STAR_TRANSFORMATION_ENABLED = TRUE
- OPTIMIZER_FEATURES_ENABLE = TRUE
- USE_STORED_OUTLINES = TRUE (to use existing STORED OUTLINES)
- CREATE_STORED_OUTLINES = TRUE (to create or edit STORED OUTLINES)
- USE_PRIVATE_OUTLINES = TRUE (to use private outlines, current session only)

How OUTLINES Are Stored

Like most other features, Oracle stores OUTLINES in internal database tables whose contents are available through the usual distribution of system views (USER_*, ALL_*, and DBA_*). Of course, only the DBA privileged few can see the DBA views, while the ALL_* views display information about objects the user can see (but may not own), and the USER_* views show information about those objects the current user actually owns. For brevity, we will consider the USER_* views. The views chiefly used by STORED OUTLINES are these:

- USER_OUTLINES
- USER_OUTLINE_HINTS

The contents of USER_OUTLINES look something like the following:

```
NAME                            CATEGORY                        USED
------------------------------- ------------------------------- ---------
TIMESTAMP VERSION
--------- -----------------------------------------------------------
SQL_TEXT
-----------------------------------------------------------------------
SIGNATURE
--------------------------------
SYS_OUTLINE_020213193254787     DEFAULT                         UNUSED
13-FEB-02 9.0.1.2.0
select id
from s_emp
where id = 1
```

A small listing from the USER_OUTLINE_HINTS table (multiple rows would probably be displayed) looks like Listing 6-22.

```
NAME                                 NODE      STAGE    JOIN_POS
----------------------------  -
---------  ----------  ----------              HINT--------
----------------------------------------------------------------------SYS_O
UTLINE_020213193254787
  SYS_OUTLINE_020213193254787        1          3          0
ORDERED
  SYS_OUTLINE_020213193254787        1          3          0
NO_FACT(S_EMP)
```

Listing 6-22: Sample listing from the USER_HINT table

You should create the outline tables in your own schema (which is a good idea). If you don't, the outlines will be stored in the SYSTEM tablespace (which is almost always a mistake). The outline tables can be created in the current schema by running the DBMS_OUTLN_EDIT .CREATE_EDIT_TABLES procedure with the following command:

```
exec dbms_outln_edit.create_edit_tables
```

Creating and Using Stored Outlines

There are two kinds of stored outlines: *private,* which are session-specific, and *public,* which can affect the entire database. Which kind is being used is controlled by the USE_PRIVATE_ OUTLINES session parameter setting: private if parameter is set to TRUE. Generally, it's best to use private outlines until an optimal execution plan is generated. Private OUTLINES can be saved publicly using the CREATE OR REPLACE PRIVATE OUTLINE command; public outlines can be created from private ones using the CREATE OR REPLACE OUTLINE ... FROM PRIVATE ... command. This process is called *editing* and is used to copy an existing private outline to a public one. When in place, Oracle uses the stored outlines automatically and invisibly to the user executing the command.

TIP
Oracle applies STORED OUTLINES to query execution on a per-query basis. To be used on a given query, the query must match its stored equivalent perfectly. The slightest variation will cause Oracle to decide that the queries are different and the outline is not to be used. The rules are like the cursor-sharing that Oracle uses to parse queries with the shared pool.

Although outlines can be edited using SQL*PLUS to update them, this isn't really recommended because it's difficult. An easier and better way to update them is to use the outline editor provided with Oracle Enterprise Manager. For more information on Oracle Enterprise Manager, see Chapter 5.

Using Stored Outlines

Outlines can initially be created in a couple of different ways. Setting the CREATE STORED_OUTLINES session parameter to TRUE (if everything is set up correctly, of course) causes an outline (with a cryptic SYS-prefixed name for each generated outline) to be generated for *every* query executed, similar to using TRACE to monitor an entire session. A more precise (and controllable) way is to create an outline for a specific query using the CREATE OUTLINE command, as follows (Listing 6-23):

```
create or replace outline pb_outline on
  select e.last_name, e.salary
    from s_emp e
where userid = 'lngao';
```

Listing 6-23: Creating an outline for a specific query using CREATE OUTLINE

In this example, pb_outline is the outline created. This method has the big advantage of giving you control over what's happening *and* the ability to give the outline a usable name.

Oracle provides some helpful packages that you can use to work with STORED OUTLINES. The DBMS_OUTLN and DBMS_OUTLN_EDIT may be investigated for additional possibilities when using stored outlines. Unlike most Oracle packages, these don't belong to the SYS user, and although they can be described in SQL*PLUS, their source code is not available from the USER_SOURCE view (unlike most packages, where at least the headers are visible). The tables underlying the views cannot be directly maintained either. (They are system tables.)

Dropping Stored Outlines

How do you get rid of stored outlines when you don't want them anymore? Use the DROP_UNUSED procedure in the DBMS_OUTLN package. The following command shows how to drop all unused outlines:

```
execute dbms_outln.drop_unused
```

To remove outlines that *have* been used, first apply the DBMS_OUTLN.CLEAR_USED procedure, which accepts an outline name (available from the USER_OUTLINES view) and can be run only against one outline at a time. A short PL/SQL program could be written to clear outlines en masse.

To determine whether an outline is actually being used, examine the USED column in USER_OUTLINES. You can also query the OUTLINE_CATEGORY column in the V$SQL view to see things that are still in the cache, as shown in Listing 6-24.

```
SELECT  OUTLINE_CATEGORY, OUTLINE_SID
FROM    V$SQL
WHERE   SQL_TEXT = 'portion of query%'
```

Listing 6-24: Query using OUTLINE_CATEGORY

Stored Outlines Example

This chapter closes with a short demonstration of using STORED OUTLINES. The first code section (Listing 6-25) is the code; the second is the spooled result when it was run (Listing 6-26).

```
--table s_emp contains the following structure
--and contains a unique index on userid
/*
SQL> desc s_emp;

 Name                    Null?    Type
 -----------------------------------------
 ID                      NOT NULL NUMBER(7)
 LAST_NAME               NOT NULL VARCHAR2(25)
 FIRST_NAME                       VARCHAR2(25)
 USERID                           VARCHAR2(8)
 START_DATE                       DATE
 COMMENTS                         VARCHAR2(255)
 MANAGER_ID                       NUMBER(7)
 TITLE                            VARCHAR2(25)
 DEPT_ID                          NUMBER(7)
 SALARY                           NUMBER(11,2)
 COMMISSION_PCT                   NUMBER(4,2)
*/

analyze table s_emp compute statistics;

alter session set query_rewrite_enabled      = true;
alter session set use_stored_outlines        = true;
alter session set star_transformation_enabled = true;

--first create the public outline without a hint (user the index on userid)
create or replace outline pb_outline on
select e.last_name,
       e.salary
  from s_emp e
 where userid = 'lngao';

--create storage tables for private outlines
--OL$, OL$HINTS and OL$NODES
exec dbms_outln_edit.create_edit_tables;

create private outline pr_outline from pb_outline;

--edit the ol$hints table
--use a full table scan rather than the index just to see if this works
update ol$hints
   set hint_text = 'FULL(E)'
 where hint# = 6;

commit;

--resynch stored outline definition
--alter system flush shared_pool;   --or
create private outline pr_outline from private pr_outline;  --this is probably a
better option
```

Using Stored Outlines

```
--to test the new private outline
alter session set use_private_outlines = true;

set autotrace on;

select e.last_name,
       e.salary
  from s_emp e
 where userid = 'lngao';

set autotrace off;

--make your changes permanent
create or replace outline pb_outline from private pr_outline;

--use the new public outline
alter session set use_private_outlines = false;
```

Listing 6-25: Using STORED OUTLINES

When run, the previous code produced the output in Listing 6-26.

```
SQL> @outlines
DOC>SQL> desc s_emp;
DOC>
DOC> Name               Null?      Type
DOC> -------------------------------------------
DOC> ID                 NOT NULL NUMBER(7)
DOC> LAST_NAME                   NOT NULL VARCHAR2(25)
DOC> FIRST_NAME                  VARCHAR2(25)
DOC> USERID                      VARCHAR2(8)
DOC> START_DATE                  DATE
DOC> COMMENTS                    VARCHAR2(255)
DOC> MANAGER_ID                  NUMBER(7)
DOC> TITLE                       VARCHAR2(25)
DOC> DEPT_ID                     NUMBER(7)
DOC> SALARY                      NUMBER(11,2)
DOC> COMMISSION_PCT              NUMBER(4,2)
DOC>*/

Table analyzed.
Session altered.
Session altered.
Session altered.
Outline created.
Table created.
Outline created.
1 row updated.
Commit complete.
Session altered.
```

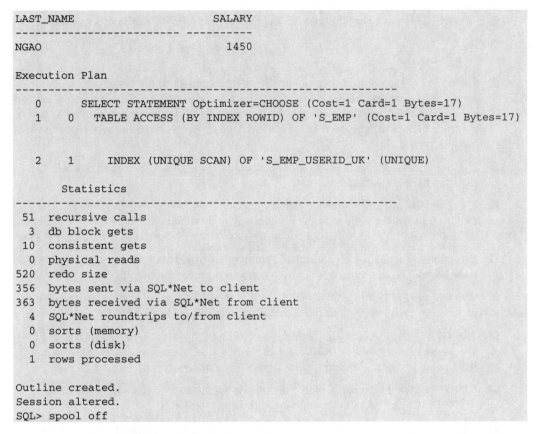

```
LAST_NAME                          SALARY
------------------------  ----------
NGAO                                 1450


Execution Plan
----------------------------------------------------------
   0      SELECT STATEMENT Optimizer=CHOOSE (Cost=1 Card=1 Bytes=17)
   1   0    TABLE ACCESS (BY INDEX ROWID) OF 'S_EMP' (Cost=1 Card=1 Bytes=17)


   2   1      INDEX (UNIQUE SCAN) OF 'S_EMP_USERID_UK' (UNIQUE)


        Statistics
----------------------------------------------------------
   51  recursive calls
    3  db block gets
   10  consistent gets
    0  physical reads
  520  redo size
  356  bytes sent via SQL*Net to client
  363  bytes received via SQL*Net from client
    4  SQL*Net roundtrips to/from client
    0  sorts (memory)
    0  sorts (disk)
    1  rows processed

Outline created.
Session altered.
SQL> spool off
```

Listing 6-26: Spooled output of Listing 6-25

TIPS & REVIEW

Tips Review

- Although Oracle TRACE can be performed on Oracle 9*i,* the TKPROF utility may not be included with the initial release of 9*i* on NT.

- Setting SQL_TRACE = TRUE in the init.ora causes the entire system and all queries to be TRACEd, and could cause performance degradations.

- The TKPROF utility puts TRACEd output into a readable format. Without running TKPROF, it would be difficult to read the output of a TRACE. By specifying explain = username/password, we are able to get the EXPLAIN execution path in addition to the execution statistics of the query.

- To use multiple sort parameters, just repeat the sort = parameter on the command line, as tkprof source_file out_file sort = parm1 sort = parm2 .

- Specifying explain = username/password in TKPROF returns the EXPLAIN execution path in addition to the execution statistics of the query.

- A TRACEd query with a large number of physical reads usually indicates a missing index.

- A TRACEd query output with only memory reads usually indicates that an index is being used.

- The trace file is a point-in-time picture of what happened on the system at a given moment. In contrast, the explain plan is generated when the TKPROF listing is analyzed, which could be some time later. The row source operation listing is generated as part of the trace file and can be used to see if the database objects have changed since the trace was performed.

- If multiple developers/DBAs are using the same PLAN_TABLE, SET STATEMENT_ID is essential to identifying a statement.

- Use EXPLAIN instead of TRACE so that you don't have to wait for the query to run. EXPLAIN shows the path of a query without actually running the query. Use TRACE only for multiquery batch jobs to find out which of the many queries in the batch job is slow.

- You can use the utlxpls.sql and utlxplp.sql queries provided by Oracle to query the plan table without having to write your own query and format the output.

- Whether the EXPLAIN PLAN is read from top to bottom or from bottom to top depends entirely on the query used to select information from the PLAN_TABLE.

- The AUTOTRACE option also provides an EXPLAIN PLAN for a query. AUTOTRACE also provides many of the TRACE and TKPROF statistics, such as disk reads (physical reads) and memory reads (consistent reads + db block gets).

- If the error "Unable to verify plan table format or existence" occurs when enabling AUTOTRACE, a plan table must be created using utlxplan.sql.

- AUTOTRACE may fail when querying system views because the user may not have permission to view underlying objects.

- Partitions can also be viewed by the EXPLAIN PLAN by accessing the columns PARTITION_START and PARTITION_STOP in the PLAN_TABLE table.

- Accessing the V$SQLAREA table can give statistics that are often found when tracing a query.

- You can also use TRACE within the Developer/2000 products. You simply need to set statistics = yes on the command line for Oracle Forms.

- The OPERATION and OPTIONS columns of the PLAN_TABLE are the most important columns for tuning a query. The OPERATION column shows the actual operation performed (including type of join), and the OPTIONS column tells you when there is a full table scan being performed that may need an index.

- The ID column shows the order in which a statement is processed. One of the primary rules of tuning a SQL statement is to change the query such that the ID of the order in which the steps in the query execute is changed. Changing the order in which steps execute in a query usually changes the performance of a query, either positively or negatively.

- The PARENT_ID column is very important because it shows the dependencies of two steps in an EXPLAIN PLAN. If a section of the EXPLAIN PLAN has a PARENT_ID, it implies that this statement *must* run prior to the PARENT_ID that is specified.

- The BYTES column is extremely important when evaluating how to tune a query. When an index is used and the number of BYTES is great, it implies that perhaps doing a full table scan would be more efficient (i.e., reading the index and data is more costly than just reading the data in a full table scan). Also, the number of bytes helps us to determine which table should be accessed first in the query, because one table may limit the number of bytes needed from another.

- Both the COST and BYTES values in a query are estimates; it is quite possible for a version of a query with a higher estimated cost or bytes to actually run faster than another with a lower value.

- It is also possible to enable TRACE by calling the procedure DBMS_ORACLE_TRACE_USER.SET_ORACLE_TRACE.

- The x$ksppi table can be accessed only by the SYS user. See Chapter 13 for tips on accessing the x$ tables and using some of these parameters. Do not use *any* undocumented parameters without consulting Oracle Corporation. Note that the layout and column names of these views have been known to change between releases of Oracle.

- TRACing queries can help performance, but using the TRACE facility built into the undocumented TRACE init.ora parameters can give great insight to (and better information for) solving errors within Oracle.

- Oracle Corporation likes to refer to STORED OUTLINES as PLAN STABILITY.

- Oracle applies STORED OUTLINES to query executions on a per-query basis. To be applied, a query must match its stored equivalent perfectly. The slightest variation could cause Oracle to decide that the queries are different and the outline should not be used. The rules are like those Oracle uses to parse queries when running them in the database.

References

Many thanks to Mark Riedel for upgrading this chapter to Oracle9*i*, and to Jake Van der Vort, Dave Hathway, Greg Pucka, and Roger Behm for contributions to this chapter.

CHAPTER
7

Basic Hint Syntax
(Developer and DBA)

Although the optimizer is incredibly accurate at choosing the correct optimization path and use of indexes for thousands of queries on your system, it is not perfect. Oracle provides hints that you can specify for a given query so the optimizer is overridden, hopefully achieving better performance for a given query. This chapter focuses on the basic syntax and use of hints. Chapters 8 and 9 have more complex examples, using various hints covered in this chapter.

The most helpful hints that you use for your system may not be the same ones that I have found to be best, because of the diversity of every system. Common to most systems is the use of the FULL, INDEX, and ORDERED hints. A system with the parallel option probably uses the PARALLEL hint most often. The following tips are covered in this chapter:

- The top hints used, the available hints and groupings, and specifying multiple hints

- When using an alias, you must use the alias, not the table in the hint

- The CHOOSE hint to force cost-based optimization

- The RULE hint to force rule-based optimization

- The FIRST_ROWS hint to generally force the use of indexes

- The ALL_ROWS hint to generally force a full table scan

- Using the FULL hint to force a full table scan

- The INDEX hint to force the use of an index

- The NO_INDEX hint is used to disallow a specified index from being used

- The INDEX_JOIN hint allows the merging of indexes on a single table

- The INDEX_ASC hint to use and index in ascending order

- The INDEX_DESC hint to use and index in descending order

- The AND_EQUAL hint is used to access multiple b-tree indexes

- The INDEX_COMBINE hint is used to access multiple bitmap indexes

- Forcing fast full scans with the INDEX_FFS

- The ORDERED hint for specifying the driving order of tables

- The LEADING hint specifies only the first driving table

- The ORDERED_PREDICATES hint forces predicate order

- The NO_EXPAND hint helps to eliminate OR expansion

- Forcing the use of the ROWID

- Queries involving multiple locations and the DRIVING_SITE hint

- The USE_MERGE hint to change how tables are joined internally

- Forcing the subquery to process earlier with PUSH_SUBQ

- The parallel query option and using PARALLEL and NOPARALLEL

- Using APPEND and NOAPPEND with parallel options

- Caching and pinning a table into memory with the CACHE hint

- A table specified as CACHE, but you prevent the caching with NOCACHE

- Forcing clustering with the CLUSTER hint

- Forcing cluster hashing with the HASH hint

- Override the CURSOR_SHARING setting with the CURSOR_SHARING_EXACT hint

Top Hints Used

I conducted an informal survey at TUSC to see which top three hints both DBAs and developers use in their day-to-day tuning. The results were not surprising to me, but if you've never used hints, this list will help you figure out where to start. Here is the list of TUSC's top ten, in order of use:

1. INDEX
2. ORDERED
3. PARALLEL
4. FIRST_ROWS
5. RULE
6. FULL
7. LEADING
8. USE_NL
9. APPEND
10. USE_HASH

The top three in this list are also the top three that I've used the most since hints were introduced. I've frequently used all ten of these in my tuning, so they are a great place to start. Also, remember something that Eyal Aronoff says: "They are hints, not commands." A hint is a suggestion for the optimizer, not a command; it doesn't always get used.

Using Hints Sparingly

Hints fall into two primary categories: usage directives and compiler directives. Usage directives are those that can be set at the init.ora level in addition to the statement level (i.e., CHOOSE, RULE, FIRST_ROWS, ALL_ROWS). If you have an OLTP (On-Line Transaction Processing) database, setting the optimizer (at the init.ora level) from CHOOSE to FIRST_ROWS immediately focuses the optimizer on returning the first few rows faster (best response time). It does this in a variety of ways, but one major way is that it generally performs joins in a nested loop fashion. If you have a data warehouse database, setting the optimizer (at the init.ora level) from CHOOSE to

ALL_ROWS immediately focuses the optimizer on returning all rows faster (best throughput). It also moves the optimizer toward doing more merge joins and hash joins instead of nested loops. In both database cases (OLTP and data warehouse), the goal is to solve performance issues systemwide instead of needing to tune individual queries.

When there are queries inside a data warehouse that behave more like OLTP or vice versa, you may need to use hints for those specific statements. As you begin to use hints, you will find yourself tuning the same problem over and over. This is the symptom of a larger problem of a missing index or poorly fragmented table (storage issue). Tuning the symptoms (using compiler directives in the short term) will determine your pattern in the long term. You will then hopefully be able to use a usage directive to fix the problem systemwide. Use hints with this in mind, and you'll use them only rarely.

Fixing the Design First

In a three-table join, depending on the column order of the index on the intersection table, the query usually accesses the tables in a particular order. By correctly indexing the intersection table and the joined columns of the other tables, you will eliminate many of your performance problems before they happen. If you are using an ORDERED or LEADING hint over and over for joins, review the indexes on the joined tables to help you change how the optimizer is looking at the problem. Rewriting SQL statements so they correctly use indexes will also solve many of your problems, eliminating the need for a hint. Putting a function on an indexed column may suppress the index and cause the tables to drive differently. Always use hints when you have exhausted the other avenues for tuning a query. If you find that you are using the same hint for the same problem over and over, you almost certainly have a problem that can be fixed systemwide instead. Always try to unlock the system problem inside each query-level issue. This will also help you avoid the pain caused by hints working differently when you upgrade to a new version.

Available Hints and Groupings

The available hints vary according to the version of the database installed. While this chapter focuses on the hints that are used frequently, many of the hints that are not covered in detail someone may give great performance gains forBullet1 with a particular system.

Hints are separated into different categories in the following sections based on which type of operation is being modified by the hint. Each hint is discussed in detail, including syntax and example(s).

Changing the Execution Path

The hints modify the execution path when an optimizer processes a particular statement. The init.ora parameter OPTIMIZER_MODE can be used to modify all statements in the database to follow a specific execution path, but a hint to a different execution path overrides anything that is specified in the init.ora. However, cost-based optimization will not be used if tables have not been analyzed. Hints that change the execution path include the following:

ALL_ROWS*	CHOOSE*
FIRST_ROWS(n)*	RULE*

*Covered in this chapter

Using Access Method Hints

The hints that are grouped into access methods allow the coder to vary the way the actual query is accessed. This group of hints is most frequently used, especially the INDEX hint. It provides direction about whether and how indexes are used, and how the corresponding indexes will be merged to get the final answer. The access method hints are listed next:

AND_EQUAL*	CLUSTER*	FULL*
HASH*	INDEX*	INDEX_ASC*
INDEX_COMBINE*	INDEX_DESC*	INDEX_FFS*
INDEX_JOIN*	NO_INDEX*	ROWID*

Covered in this chapter

Using Query Transformation Hints

Query transformation hints are especially helpful in a data warehouse where you are familiar with using fact and dimension tables. The FACT hint can force a given table to be the FACT or driving table for a query. The NO_FACT hint does the opposite. The STAR hint is used to efficiently access the FACT table when joining multiple tables. The query transformation hints are listed here:

FACT	MERGE	NO_EXPAND
NO_FACT	NO_MERGE	NOREWRITE**
REWRITE**	STAR	STAR_TRANSFORMATION
USE_CONCAT		

**Covered in detail in Chapter 8*

Using Join Operation Hints

The join operations grouping shows how joined tables merge data together. A join operation, such as USE_MERGE or USE_HASH, may be best for retrieving all rows for a query (throughput), while USE_NL may be best for retrieving the first row (response time).

DRIVING_SITE*	HASH_AJ	HASH_SJ
LEADING*	MERGE_AJ	MERGE_SJ
NL_AJ	NL_SJ	ORDERED*
PUSH_SUBQ*	USE_HASH*	USE_MERGE*
USE_NL		

Covered in detail in this chapter

Using Parallel Execution

The parallel execution grouping applies to databases using the parallel option. These hints override the table specification for the degree of parallelism.

NOPARALLEL*	NOPARALLEL_INDEX	PARALLEL*
PARALLEL_INDEX	PQ_DISTRIBUTE	

Covered in detail in this chapter

Using Other Hints

The APPEND and NOAPPEND hints can be used without the parallel option, but they are frequently used with it. The cache grouping pertains to the hints that will put items as most recently used (CACHE) or least recently used (NOCACHE).

APPEND*	CACHE*	CURSOR_SHARING_EXACT
NOAPPEND*	NO_UNNEST	NO_PUSH_PRED
NOCACHE*	ORDERED_PREDICATES*	PUSH_PRED
NOCACHE*	ORDERED_PREDICATES*	PUSH_PRED
UNNEST		

Covered in detail in this chapter

Specifying a Hint

If you incorrectly specify a hint in any way, it becomes a comment and is ignored. Be very careful to get the hint syntax *exactly* correct. The best way to ensure that a hint has been correctly specified is to run an explain plan, or set AUTOTRACE to ON in SQL*Plus to see if the hint was used. Some hints are overridden by Oracle despite the fact that a hint's purpose is primarily to override decisions made by the Oracle Optimizer. The following shows basic hint syntax (in this example, it is for a FULL hint):

Syntax

```
select     /*+ FULL(table) */ column1,…
```

The *(table)* in the previous syntax is the table name on which to perform a full table scan.

Example

```
select     /*+ FULL(emp) */ empno, ename, deptno
from       emp
where      deptno = 1;
```

In this example, if there were an index on the deptno column, a full table scan would be performed. The hint is not required to be uppercase.

Example (Incorrect hint syntax)

```
select      /* FULL(emp) */ empno, ename, deptno
from        emp
where       deptno = 1;
```

In this query, if there were an index on the deptno column, the index would be used because the hint is missing the plus sign (+).

TIP
*Incorrect hint syntax leads to the hint being interpreted as a comment.
If an additional hint is specified correctly, it will be used.*

Specifying Multiple Hints

You can use more than one hint at a time, although this may cause some or all of the hints to be ignored. The basic syntax is to separate hints with spaces.

Syntax

```
select      /*+ FULL(table) CACHE(table)*/ column1,…
```

The *(table)* in this syntax is the table name on which to perform the full scan and cache.

Example

```
select      /*+ FULL(emp) CACHE(emp)*/ empno, ename, deptno
from        emp
where       deptno = 1;
```

TIP
*Multiple hints are separated with a space. Specifying multiple hints
that conflict which each other causes the query to use none of the
conflicting hints.*

Using an Alias

When you use aliases on a given table that you want to use in a hint, you must specify the alias and not the table name in the hint. If you specify the table name in the hint when an alias is used, the hint is not used.

Syntax

```
select      /*+ FULL(table) */ column1,…
```

The *(table)* in this syntax has to be replaced with the alias in the following example because the query uses an alias. If an alias is used, the alias must be used in the hint or the hint will not work.

Example

```
select      /*+ FULL(A) */ empno, ename, deptno
from        emp A
where       deptno = 1;
```

TIP
If an alias is used, the alias must be used in the hint or the hint will not work.

Using Hints

The hints discussed here are available as of Oracle9i. Consult Oracle documentation for more information on these or other hints.

Using the CHOOSE Hint

When you think of cost-based optimization, you may think the hint for cost-based optimization is COST. It is not! The hint for cost-based optimization is CHOOSE. The CHOOSE hint causes the optimizer to choose the optimal plan for a given query. If CHOOSE is specified in the OPTIMIZER_MODE init.ora parameter, it causes cost-based optimization for the entire database unless overridden for a given query. You can also set the OPTIMIZER_MODE parameter at the session level (which is great for testing different optimizer modes). If tables in a query have not been analyzed (using the DBMS_STATS package or ANALYZE), rule-based optimization will still be used. If one of the tables in a multitable join has been analyzed, cost-based optimization will be used for the entire query, and Oracle makes its best guess for the nonanalyzed tables. In general, all tables in a join should be analyzed before you use cost-based optimization for the join. The syntax for the CHOOSE hint is as follows:

Syntax

```
select      /*+ CHOOSE */ column1, …
```

Example

```
select      /*+ CHOOSE */ empno, ename, deptno
from        emp
where       deptno = 1;
```

TIP
The CHOOSE hint uses cost-based optimization for the entire query unless all of the tables in the query have not been analyzed. If one table of a multitable join query has been analyzed, cost-based optimization will be used for all tables. Generally, you should choose an index if one is available on the nonanalyzed tables. It will use rule-based optimization if none of the tables have been analyzed. The CHOOSE hint may be set as the default for the entire database by setting OPTIMIZER_MODE=CHOOSE in the init.ora file; query-level hints will override the default setting for a given query.

Using the RULE Hint

Every hint that is issued causes the use of the cost-based optimizer except the RULE hint. The RULE hint causes the optimizer to use rule-based optimization. This means that the distribution of data in the table or indexes is not considered. Instead, the optimizer executes the query based on Oracle's predefined set of rules, such as using the ROWID or unique indexes before other options, which govern how a query executes. The RULE hint also causes the statement to avoid using any other hints except the DRIVING_SITE and ORDERED hints, which are used despite rule-based optimization.

Syntax

```
select     /*+ RULE */ column1, …
```

Example

```
select     /*+ RULE */ empno, ename, deptno
from       emp
where      deptno = 1;
```

If an index exists on the deptno column, it would be used for this statement even if the index were a poor choice for the query.

TIP
The RULE hint forces Oracle to use predefined rules (such as using ROWID and UNIQUE indexes) over using the statistics about the data. The RULE hint may be set as the default for the entire database by setting OPTIMIZER_MODE=RULE in the init.ora file; some query-level hints will override the default for a given query. I predict that the rule-based optimizer will finally disappear in the Oracle11 database.

Using the FIRST_ROWS Hint

The FIRST_ROWS (response time) hint directs a query to optimize on the basis of retrieving the first row the fastest. This is especially helpful when users of the system are using Oracle Forms to retrieve a single record on their screen. This would be a poor choice for a batch-intensive environment where a lot of rows are generally retrieved by a query. The FIRST_ROWS hint generally forces the use of indexes, which under normal circumstances may not have been used. The FIRST_ROWS hint is used, even when statistics are not gathered when using cost-based optimization.

The FIRST_ROWS hint is ignored in UPDATE and DELETE statements, because all rows of the query must be updated or deleted. It is also ignored when any grouping statement is used (GROUP BY, DISTINCT, INTERSECT, MINUS, UNION), because all of the rows for the grouping have to be retrieved for the grouping to occur. The statement may also choose to avoid a sort when there is an ORDER BY in the statement, if an index scan can do the actual sort. The optimizer may also choose NESTED LOOPS over a SORT MERGE when an index scan is available and the index is on the inner table. The inner table shortens the result set that is joined back to the outside table in the query; specifying access paths overrides this hint.

You may also specify the number of rows (as in the second example that follows) that you want FIRST_ROWS to optimize getting. (The default is one.) Note that this amount is set in powers of 10 up to 1000. The new method of using FIRST_ROWS *(n)* is based totally on costs, and it is sensitive to the value of *n*. With small values of *n*, the cost-based optimizer (CBO) tends to generate plans that consist of nested loop joins with index lookups. With large values of *n*, the CBO tends to generate plans that consist of hash joins and full table scans (behaves more like ALL_ROWS).

Syntax

```
select      /*+ FIRST_ROWS(n) */ column1, …
```

Example

```
select      /*+ FIRST_ROWS */ empno, ename, deptno
from        emp
where       deptno = 1;
```

Example

```
select      /*+ FIRST_ROWS(10) */ empno, ename, deptno
from        emp
where       deptno = 1;
```

TIP
The FIRST_ROWS hint causes the optimizer to choose a path that retrieves the first row (or a specified number of rows) of a query fastest, at the cost of retrieving multiple rows more slowly. The FIRST_ROWS hint may be set as the default for the entire database by setting OPTIMIZER_MODE= FIRST_ROWS in the init.ora file; query-level hints will override the default setting for a given query.

Using the ALL_ROWS Hint

The ALL_ROWS hint directs a query to optimize a query on the basis of retrieving all of the rows the fastest (best throughput). This is especially helpful when users of the system are in a heavy batch report environment and running reports that retrieve a lot of rows. This would be a poor choice for a heavy Oracle Forms environment where users are trying to view a single record on a screen. The ALL_ROWS hint may suppress the use of indexes that would have been used under normal circumstances. Specifying access path hints overrides the use of this hint.

Syntax

```
select      /*+ ALL_ROWS */ column1, ...
```

Example

```
select      /*+ ALL_ROWS */ empno, ename, deptno
from        emp
where       deptno = 1;
```

TIP
The ALL_ROWS hint causes the optimizer to choose a path that will retrieve all the rows of a query fastest, at the cost of retrieving one single row more slowly. The ALL_ROWS hint may be set as the default for the entire database by setting OPTIMIZER_MODE= ALL_ROWS in the init.ora file; query-level hints will override the default setting for a given query.

Using the FULL Hint

The FULL hint directs a query to override the optimizer and perform a full table scan on the specified table in the hint. The FULL hint has different functionality based on the query that you are tuning. You can use it to force a full table scan when a large portion of the table is being queried. The cost of retrieving the index and the rows may be larger than just retrieving the entire table. The full hint may also cause an unexpected result. Causing a full table scan may cause tables to be accessed in a different order, because a different driving table is used. This may lead to better performance, making you think that the full table scan was the key benefit, when changing the order of the driving table was the real cause of the increased performance. The syntax for the FULL hint is as follows:

Syntax

```
select      /*+ FULL(table) */ column1,...
```

The *(table)* is the table name on which to perform the full scan. If an alias is used, it must be used in the hint or it will not work.

Example

```
select      /*+ FULL(emp) */ empno, ename, deptno
from        emp
where       deptno = 1;
```

The FULL hint in the previous example would be particularly helpful if the only department in the company were one (1). Going to an index on deptno and the EMP table would be slower than simply performing a full table scan on the EMP table.

The FULL hint is also a necessary part of using some of the other hints. The CACHE hint can cause a table to be cached only when the full table is accessed. Some of the hints in the parallel grouping also necessitate the use of a full table scan. Each of these hints is discussed later in this chapter.

TIP
The FULL hint performs a full table scan on the table that is specified, and not all tables in the query. The FULL hint may also lead to better performance, which is attributable to causing a change in the driving table of the query and not the actual full table scan.

Using the INDEX Hint

The INDEX hint is frequently used to force one or more indexes to be executed for a given query. Oracle generally chooses the correct index or indexes with the optimizer, but when the optimizer chooses the wrong index or no index at all, this hint is excellent. You may also use multiple indexes with this hint, and Oracle will choose one or more of the indexes specified based on the best plan. If you specify only one index, the optimizer considers only one index.

Syntax

```
select      /*+ INDEX (table index1, index2…) */ column1, …
```

Example

```
select      /*+ INDEX (emp deptno_idx) */ empno, ename, deptno
from        emp
where       deptno = 1;
```

In this example, the deptno_idx index on the emp table will be used.

Example

```
select      /*+ INDEX (emp deptno_idx, empno_idx) */ empno, ename, deptno
from        emp
where       deptno = 1
and         empno = 7750;
```

In the second example, Oracle may use the deptno_idx index, the empno_idx index, or a merge of both of them. We have placed this decision in the optimizer's hands to decipher the best choice. It would have been best to specify the index only on the empno column (empno_idx) if this were the most restrictive statement (usually much more restrictive than the department).

TIP
The INDEX hint causes the optimizer to choose the index specified in the hint. Multiple indexes for a single table can be specified, but it is usually better to specify only the most restrictive index on a given query (avoiding the merging of the result of each index). If multiple indexes are specified, Oracle chooses which (one or more) to use, so be careful, or your hint could potentially be overridden.

Example

```
select     /*+ INDEX */ empno, ename, deptno
from       emp
where      deptno = 1
and        empno = 7750;
```

In this example, no index is specified. Oracle now weighs all of the possible indexes that are available and chooses one or more to be used. Because we have not specified a particular index, but we have specified the INDEX hint, the optimizer will not do a full table scan.

TIP
Without a specified index, the INDEX hint will not consider a full table scan, even though no indexes have been specified. The optimizer will choose the best index or indexes for the query.

Using the NO_INDEX Hint

The NO_INDEX hint disallows the optimizer from using a specified index. This is a great hint for tuning queries with multiple indexes. While you may not know which of the multiple indexes to drive the query with, you might know which ones you don't want the optimizer to use. You may also want to disallow an index for many queries prior to dropping an index that you don't think is necessary.

Syntax

```
select     /*+ NO_INDEX (table index1, index2…) */ column1, …
```

Example

```
select     /*+ NO_INDEX (emp deptno_idx) */ ename, deptno
from       emp
where      deptno = 1;
```

In this example, the deptno_idx index on the emp table will not be used. If the NO_INDEX hint is used and no index is specified, a full table scan will be performed. If the NO_INDEX and a conflicting hint (such as INDEX) are specified for the same index, then both hints are ignored (as in the following example).

Example

```
select     /*+ NO_INDEX (emp deptno_idx) INDEX (emp deptno_idx) */ ename, deptno
from       emp
where      deptno = 1;
```

TIP
The NO_INDEX hint must be in the tuning expert's toolkit. You use it to keep the optimizer from considering an index so that you can evaluate the need for the index prior to dropping it or so that you can evaluate other indexes. Be careful not to conflict with other index hints.

Using the INDEX_JOIN Hint

The INDEX_JOIN hint merges separate indexes from a single table together so that only the indexes need to be accessed. This saves a trip back to the table. It can be used only with the cost-based optimizer.

Syntax

```
select     /*+ INDEX_JOIN (table index1, index2…) */ column1, …
```

Example

```
select     /*+ index_join(test2 year_idx state_idx) */ state, year
from       test2
where      year = '1972'
and        state = MA
```

In this query, the optimizer will merge the year_idx and state_idx indexes and will not need to access the test2 table. All information is contained in these two indexes when they are merged together. For a more detailed example, see Chapter 8.

TIP
The INDEX_JOIN hint not only allows you to access only indexes on a table, which is a scan of fewer total blocks, but it is also five times faster than using an index and scanning the table by ROWID.

Using the AND_EQUAL Hint

The AND_EQUAL hint is used to specify multiple indexes where you want the optimizer to use all indexes that you specify. For bitmap indexes, use the INDEX_COMBINE hint instead of this one. This index differs from the preceding INDEX_JOIN hint in that the merged indexes that are specified then access the table. With the INDEX_JOIN hint, only the indexes are accessed. This hint will not work if the WHERE clause accesses a primary key (PK). If the WHERE clause accesses the PK, then only the PK is needed.

Syntax

```
select     /*+ AND_EQUAL (table index1, index2...) */ column1, ...
```

Example

```
select     /*+ AND_EQUAL (emp deptno_idx, empno_idx) */ empno, ename, deptno
from       emp
where      deptno = 1
and        empno = 7750;
```

In this example, Oracle uses a merge of both the deptno_idx index and the empno_idx index. If you find that you use this hint often, you might want to drop the single indexes for a single concatenated one.

TIP
The AND_EQUAL hint causes the optimizer to merge multiple indexes for a single table instead of choosing which one is better (as in the INDEX hint).

Using the INDEX_COMBINE Hint

The INDEX_COMBINE hint is used to specify multiple BITMAP indexes when you want the optimizer to use all indexes that you specify. You can also use the INDEX_COMBINE hint to specify single indexes. (This is preferred over using the INDEX hint for bitmaps.) For b-tree indexes, use the AND_EQUAL hint instead of this one.

Syntax

```
select     /*+ INDEX_COMBINE (table index1, index2...) */ column1, ...
```

Example

```
select     /*+ INDEX_COMBINE (emp deptno_bidx, mgr_bidx) */ empno, ename, deptno
from       emp
where      deptno = 1
and        mgr = 7698;
```

Hints–INDEX_COMBINE

In this example, Oracle uses a merge of both the deptno_idx index and the empno_idx bitmap indexes.

TIP
The INDEX_COMBINE hint causes the optimizer to merge multiple bitmap indexes for a single table instead of choosing which one is better (as with the INDEX hint).

Using the INDEX_ASC Hint

The INDEX_ASC hint currently performs exactly the same function as the INDEX hint. Because indexes are already scanned in ascending order, this does nothing more than the current INDEX hint. So what is it good for? Oracle does not guarantee that indexes will be scanned in ascending order in the future, but this hint will guarantee that an index will be scanned in ascending order.

Syntax

```
select      /*+ INDEX_ASC (table index1, index2…) */ column1, …
```

Example

```
select      /*+ INDEX_ASC (emp deptno_idx) */ empno, ename, deptno
from        emp
where       deptno = 1;
```

In this example, the deptno_idx index on the emp table will be used.

TIP
The INDEX_ASC hint does exactly what the INDEX hint does because indexes are already scanned in ascending order. It is used to guarantee this to be true, because Oracle may change this default in the future. In Oracle9i, descending indexes are actually sorted in descending order, which was not true in Oracle8i. Oracle treats descending indexes as function-based indexes. The columns marked DESC are sorted in descending order.

Using the INDEX_DESC Hint

The INDEX_DESC hint causes indexes to be scanned in descending order (of their indexed value or order), which is the opposite of the INDEX and INDEX_ASC hints. This hint is overridden when the query has multiple tables, because the index needs to be used in the normal ascending order to be joined to the other table in the query.

Syntax

```
select      /*+ INDEX_DESC (table index1, index2…) */ column1, …
```

Example

```
select      /*+ INDEX_DESC (emp deptno_idx) */ empno, ename, deptno
from        emp
where       deptno = 1;
```

TIP
*The INDEX_DESC hint processes an index in descending order of
how it was built. This hint will not be used if more than one table
exists in the query.*

Using the INDEX_FFS Hint

The INDEX_FFS hint indicates that a fast full scan of the index should be performed. This hint
accesses only the index and not the corresponding table. It will be used only if all of the information
that the query needs to retrieve is in the index. This hint can provide great performance gains,
especially when the table has a large number of columns.

Syntax

```
select      /*+ INDEX_FFS (table index) */ column1, …
```

Example

```
select      /*+ INDEX_FFS (emp deptno_idx) */ deptno, empno
from        emp
where       deptno = 1;
```

The INDEX_FFS hint will be used only if the deptno_idx index contains both the deptno and
empno columns as part of it.

TIP
*The INDEX_FFS processes only the index and does not take the result
and access the table. All columns that are used and retrieved by the
query must be contained in the index.*

Using the ORDERED Hint

The ORDERED hint causes tables to be accessed in a particular order, based on the order of the
tables in the FROM clause of the query, which is often referred to as the driving order for a query.
Generally, the optimizer chooses the driving table in queries; however, using the ORDERED hint
causes the first table in the FROM clause to be the driver. The ORDERED hint also guarantees the
driving order. When the ORDERED hint is not used, Oracle may internally switch the driving
table when compared to how tables are listed in the FROM clause. (The EXPLAIN PLAN can
show how tables are accessed.) This hint provides so many complex possibilities that much of
the next chapter is focused on this subject. (Please see Chapter 8 for more information regarding

Hints–ORDERED

tuning joins.) This chapter briefly covers the ORDERED hint, mainly for syntactical purposes. Contrary to the documentation, it can be used for cost- or rule-based optimization.

Syntax

```
select    /*+ ORDERED */ column1, …
```

Example

```
select    /*+ ORDERED */ empno, ename, dept.deptno
from      emp, dept
where     emp.deptno = dept.deptno
and       dept.deptno = 1
and       emp.empno = 7747;
```

If both tables (emp and dept) have been analyzed (using the cost-based optimizer), and there are no indexes on either table, and we are in Oracle9*i*, the emp table is accessed first and the dept table is accessed second. A lot of possible variations (covered in Chapters 8 and 9) cause this to work differently.

Example

```
select    /*+ ORDERED */ emp.empno, ename, deptno, itemno
from      emp, dept, orders
where     emp.deptno = dept.deptno
and       emp.empno = orders.empno
and       dept.deptno = 1
and       emp.empno = 7747
and       orders.ordno = 45;
```

If all three tables (emp, dept, and orders) have been analyzed (using cost-based optimization), and there are no indexes on any of the tables, and we are in Oracle9*i*, the emp table would be accessed first and then joined to the dept table, which would be accessed second. The result would be joined with the orders table, which is accessed last. A lot of possible variations (covered in Chapter 8) cause this to work differently.

TIP
The ORDERED hint is one of the most powerful hints available.
It processes the tables of the query in the chronological order in
which they are listed in the FROM clause. Many variations cause
this to work differently: the version of Oracle, the existence of indexes
on the tables, and which tables have been analyzed. However, when
a multitable join is slow and you don't know what to do, the ORDERED
hint should be one of the first hints you try!

Using the LEADING Hint

As the complexity of queries increases, it becomes more difficult to figure out the order of all of the tables using the ORDERED hint. You can often figure out which table should be accessed first (driving table), but you may not know which table to access after that one. The LEADING hint allows you to specify one table to drive the query; the optimizer figures out which table to use after that. If you specify more than one table with this hint, it is ignored. The ORDERED hint overrides the LEADING hint.

Syntax

```
select      /*+ LEADING (table1) */ column1, …
```

Example

```
select      /*+ LEADING(DEPT) */ emp.empno, ename, dept.deptno, itemno
from        emp, dept, orders
where       emp.deptno = dept.deptno
and         emp.empno = orders.empno
and         dept.deptno = 1
and         emp.empno = 7747
and         orders.ordno = 45;
```

If all three tables (emp, dept, and orders) have been analyzed (using cost-based optimization), and there are no indexes on any of the tables, and we are in Oracle9*i*, the DEPT table would be accessed first (driving the query). The optimizer would figure out the rest (probably accessing the intersection table EMP next).

TIP
The LEADING hint works similarly to the ORDERED hint. The LEADING hint is used to specify a single table to drive a query with while allowing the optimizer to figure out the rest.

Using the ORDERED_PREDICATES Hint

The ORDERED_PREDICATES hint is used to rectify issues with the optimizer, changing the order of conditions in the WHERE clause (the predicates). If there are indexes on a predicate, they are evaluated first; other than that, the hint causes the optimizer to evaluate the query from top to bottom.

Syntax

```
select      /*+ ORDERED_PREDICATES */ column1, …
```

Hints— ORDERED_PREDICATES

Example

```
select      /*+ ORDERED_PREDICATES */ empno, job
from        emp
where       deptno = 1
and         empno = 7747
and         ename = 'SYS';
```

If you do not specify the ORDERED_PREDICATES hint, the optimizer evaluates things in the order specified in the WHERE clause other than subqueries (which will go first). There are other exceptions as well based on using user-defined functions and type methods. In the previous example, the query is performed from top to bottom (given that there aren't predicates used as index keys). If there are no indexes on deptno, empno, or ename, then *deptno = 1* is evaluated first, *empno = 7777* is evaluated second, and *ename = 'SYS'* is evaluated last.

TIP
The ORDERED_PREDICATES hint is used to ensure that conditions get evaluated in the desired order.

Using the ROWID Hint

The ROWID hint causes Oracle to use the ROWID (when possible) to go to the exact physical location (block address) to retrieve the requested information.

Syntax

```
select      /*+ ROWID (table) */ column1, …
```

Consider an emp table with the following records:

EMPNO	ENAME	HERO
1000	RICH	REGINA
1000	RICH	REGINA
1000	RICH	REGINA
2000	JOE	LORI
2000	JOE	LORI
3000	BRAD	KRISTEN

The following example demonstrates how using the ROWID hint in a query finds duplicate values: in this case, duplicate empno values.

```
select      /*+ ROWID (a) */ empno, count(*)
from   emp a
where rowid not in
(select      max(rowid)
from emp b
where       a.empno = b.empno)
group by  empno;
```

Output

```
EMPNO    COUNT(*)
1000     2
2000     1
```

The previous query must hint the alias (the alias is a for the emp table) to use the hint. This query finds duplicate empno's in the emp table. It does an AGGREGATE merge max(), and the ROWID hint in this scenario is actually not used (despite the correct syntax) because of the max() function performed. The real goal here is to give you a query to find duplicates and the syntax for the ROWID hint. It is not recommended that you reference actual ROWIDs.

TIP
The ROWID hint processes queries using the ROWID, if possible, based on how the queries are written.

Using the NO_EXPAND Hint

The NO_EXPAND hint is used to keep the optimizer from going off the deep end when it is evaluating IN-lists that are combined with an OR. It disallows the optimizer from using OR expansion. Without the NO_EXPAND hint, the optimizer creates an explain plan a mile long.

Syntax

```
select      /*+ NO_EXPAND */ column1, ...
```

Example

```
select /*+ FIRST_ROWS NO_EXPAND */  col1, col2...
from    members
where  (memb_key between 205127 and 205226
or      memb_key between 205228 and 205327
or      memb_key between 205330 and 205429
or      memb_key between 205431 and 205530);
```

Chapter 8 includes an expanded example (no pun intended) that shows that using the NO_EXPAND hint made this query almost 50 times faster than without the hint.

Example (Using Oracle9*i* Sample Schema Tables)

```
select /*+ FIRST_ROWS NO_EXPAND */  product_id, translated_name
from    oe.product_descriptions
where  language_id = 'US'
and    (product_id between 2187 and 2193
or      product_id between 2326 and 2330
or      product_id between 3176 and 3177
or      product_id between 3245 and 3249);
```

TIP
The NO_EXPAND hint prevents the optimizer from using OR expansion and is used where the query will become substantially more complex as a result of the expansion.

Using the DRIVING_SITE Hint

The DRIVING_SITE hint is identical to the ORDERED hint, except this hint is for processing data by driving it from a particular database. The table specified in the hint will be the driving site that will be used to process the actual join. This hint can be used with either cost- or rule-based optimization.

Syntax

```
select      /*+ DRIVING_SITE (table) */ column1, …
```

Example

```
select      /*+ DRIVING_SITE (deptremote) */ empno, ename, deptremote.deptno
from        emp, dept@oratusc deptremote
where       emp.deptno = deptremote.deptno
and         deptremote.deptno = 10
and         empno = 7747;
```

Oracle would normally retrieve the rows from the remote site and join them at the local site if this hint were not specified. Because the *empno = 7747* limits the query greatly, we would rather pass the small number of rows from the emp table to the remote site instead of pulling an entire dept table department back to our local site to process.

Limiting the rows that are retrieved from a remote site can also be achieved by creating a view locally for the remote table. The local view should have the WHERE clause that will be used so that the view will limit the rows returned from the remote database before they are sent back to the local database. I have personally tuned queries from hours to seconds using this method.

The location specification is not specified in the hint (just the table name). However, if an alias were used, the alias would have to be used instead of the table name in the hint.

TIP
The DRIVING_SITE hint is extremely powerful because it will potentially limit the amount of information that will be processed over your network. The table specified with the DRIVING_SITE hint will be the location for the join to be processed. Using views for remote tables can also lead to better performance by limiting the number of rows passed from the remote site before the records are sent to the local site.

Using the USE_MERGE Hint

The USE_MERGE hint is generally used to achieve the best throughput for a given query. Assume you are joining two tables together. The row set returned from each table is sorted and then merged (known as a sort-merged join) to form the final result set. Because each row is sorted and then merged together, this action is fastest in retrieving all rows from a given query. If you wanted the first row faster instead, USE_NL would be the hint to use, as this illustration shows.

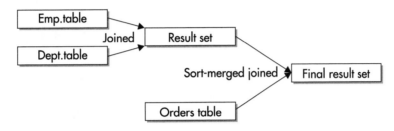

Syntax

```
select     /*+ USE_MERGE (table) */ column1, …
```

Example

```
select     /*+ USE_MERGE(orders) */ emp.empno, ename, dept.deptno, itemno
from       emp, dept, orders
where      emp.deptno = dept.deptno
and        emp.empno = orders.empno
and        dept.deptno = 1
and        emp.empno = 7747
and        orders.ordno = 45;
```

The USE_MERGE hint in this query causes the orders table to be joined in a sort-merge join to the resulting row source resulting from the join of the emp and dept tables. The rows are sorted and then merged together to find the final result. See Chapter 9 for a more detailed discussion of joins.

TIP
In a three or more table join, the USE_MERGE hint causes the table(s)
specified in the hint to be sort-merge joined with the resulting row set
from a join of the other tables in the join.

Using the USE_NL Hint

The USE_NL (use nested loops) hint is usually the fastest way to return a single row (response time); thus, it is consequently slower at returning all the rows. This hint causes a statement to be processed using nested loops, which takes the first matching row from one table based on the

Hints—USE_NL

result from another table. This is the opposite of a merge join, which retrieves rows that match the conditions from each table and then merges them together—this usually takes a lot longer to get the first row.

Syntax

```
select      /*+ USE_NL (table index1, index2…) */ column1, …
```

Example

```
select      /*+ ORDERED USE_NL(dept) */ empno, ename, dept.deptno
from        emp, dept
where       emp.deptno = dept.deptno
and         dept.deptno = 1
and         emp.empno = 7747;
```

The USE_NL hint causes Oracle to take the resulting rows returned from the emp table and process them with the matching rows from the dept table (the specified nested loop table). The first row that matches from the dept table can be returned to the user immediately (as in an Oracle Form), as opposed to waiting until all matching rows are found. The ORDERED hint guarantees that the emp table is processed first.

TIP
The USE_NL hint usually provides the best response time (the first row comes back faster) for smaller result sets, whereas the USE_MERGE hint usually provides the best throughput when the USE_HASH hint can't be used.

Using the USE_HASH Hint

The USE_HASH hint is usually the fastest way to join many rows together from multiple tables if you have the memory for this operation. USE_HASH is similar to the nested loops where one result of one table is looped through the result from the joined table. The difference here is that the second table (the one being looped through) is put into memory. You must have a large enough HASH_AREA_SIZE or PGA_AGGREGATE_TARGET (see Chapter 4) for this to work properly; otherwise, the operation will occur on disk.

Syntax

```
select      /*+ USE_HASH (table1) */ column1, …
```

Example

```
select      /*+ USE_HASH (dept) */ empno, ename, dept.deptno
from        emp, dept
where       emp.deptno = dept.deptno
and         emp.empno = 7747;
```

The USE_HASH hint causes Oracle to take the resulting rows returned from the EMP table and process them with the matching rows from the DEPT table (the specified hash table), which are hashed into memory. The first row that matches from the dept table can be returned to the user immediately, as opposed to waiting until all matching rows are found. Sometimes the optimizer will override this hint. In the previous query, if we added the condition *and dept.deptno=1*, the optimizer would override the USE_HASH hint and do the more efficient nested loops join (because the DEPT table has been narrowed down by this condition).

TIP
*The USE_HASH hint usually provides the best response time
for larger result sets.*

Using the PUSH_SUBQ Hint

The PUSH_SUBQ hint can lead to dramatic performance gains (an increase of over 100 times in performance) when used in the appropriate situation. The best situation in which to use this hint is when the subquery will return a relatively small number of rows (quickly); those rows can then be used to substantially limit the rows in the outer query. PUSH_SUBQ causes the subquery to be evaluated at the earliest possible time. This hint cannot be used when the query uses a merge join and cannot be used with remote tables. Moving the subquery to be part of the main query (when possible) can lead to the same gains when the tables are driven in the correct order (accessing the former subquery table first).

Syntax

```
select      /*+ PUSH_SUBQ */ column1, …
```

Example

```
select      /*+ PUSH_SUBQ */ emp.empno, emp.ename, itemno
from        emp, orders
where       emp.empno = orders.empno
and         emp.deptno =
(select     deptno
from        dept
where       loc = 'BELMONT');
```

This query processes the subquery to be used by the outer query at its earliest possible time.

TIP
*The PUSH_SUBQ hint can improve performance greatly when the
subquery will return only a few rows very fast, and those rows can be
used to limit the rows returned in the outer query.*

Using the PARALLEL Hint

The PARALLEL hint causes full table scan queries to break a query into pieces (the degree of parallelism) and process each piece with a different operating system process. Parallel DML can be used only when you install the Partitioning Option with your database. The *Degree of Parallelism* is applied to each operation of a SQL statement. A query that requires a sort operation causes the number of processes used to be double the degree specified. The operation that does the breaking up and putting back together of the pieces also requires a process. Therefore, if the degree you set for a query is 4, it may use four processes for the query plus four more processes for the sorting, plus one more process for the breaking up and putting together of the four pieces. The total used with a degree of 4 is actually 4 + 4 + 1, or nine (9) total processes.

The PARALLEL hint allows you to specify the desired number of concurrent servers that can be used for a parallel operation. In Oracle9*i*, the hint can be applied to the INSERT, UPDATE, and DELETE portions of a statement (you have to commit immediately after if you use this) as well as to the table scan partition (parallel scanning of partitions). Once again, you must have the partitioning option installed for this to work. You should create tables with the parallel clause where you plan to use this option. See Chapter 11 for a detailed look at all of the requirements and rules associated with this powerful option.

Syntax

```
/*+ PARALLEL (table, DEGREE, INSTANCES) */
```

The degree is the number of pieces into which the query is broken. The instances (the second number specified after the degree) are the number of instances that are used.

Example

```
select     /*+ PARALLEL (order_line_items) */ invoice_number, invoice_date
from       order_line_items
order by   invoice_date;
```

This statement does not specify a degree of parallelism. The *Default Degree of Parallelism* is dictated by the table definition when the table was created.

Example

```
select     /*+ PARALLEL (order_line_items, 4) */  invoice_number, invoice_date
from       order_line_items
order by   invoice_date;
```

This statement specifies a degree of parallelism of four. As per the previous discussion, as many as nine query servers may be allocated or created to satisfy this query.

Example

```
select     /*+ PARALLEL (oli, 4) */ invoice_number, invoice_date
from       order_line_items oli
order by   invoice_date;
```

In this example, an alias is used and now must be used in the hint instead of using the table name.

TIP
Using the PARALLEL hint will enable the use of parallel operations. If the degree is not specified with the hint, the default degree specified during the table creation will be used.

Using the NOPARALLEL Hint

If a table is created with a parallel degree set, the table will use that degree for all full table scan queries. However, you may also "turn off" the use of parallel operations in any one given query on a table that has been specified to use parallel operations using the NOPARALLEL hint. The NOPARALLEL hint is a query with a degree of one (1).

Syntax

```
select     /*+ NOPARALLEL (table) */
```

Example

```
select     /*+ NOPARALLEL (oli) */ invoice_number, invoice_date
from       order_line_items oli
order by   invoice_date;
```

TIP
Using the NOPARALLEL hint disables parallel operations in a statement that would otherwise use parallel processing due to a parallel object definition.

Using the APPEND Hint

The APPEND hint is a great hint to use if you have space to burn. The APPEND hint does not check to see if there is space within currently used blocks for inserts, but instead appends the data into new blocks. You might potentially waste space, but you will gain speed in return. If you never delete rows from a table, you should definitely use the APPEND hint.

If parallel loading is used with SQL*Loader, you must use the APPEND option for SQL*Loader. Also, if an INSERT is parallelized using the PARALLEL hint, APPEND will be used by default. You can use the NOAPPEND hint (next section) to override this behavior.

Syntax

```
insert /*+ APPEND */ …
```

Hints–APPEND

Example

```
insert /*+ APPEND */
into     emp (empno, deptno)
values   (7747, 10);
```

TIP
*The APPEND hint inserts values into a table without checking the free
space in the currently used blocks, but instead appends the data into
new blocks.*

Using the NOAPPEND Hint

The NOAPPEND hint is used to override the default for the PARALLEL inserts (the default, of
course, is APPEND). The NOAPPEND hint is the opposite of the APPEND hint and checks for
free space within current blocks before using new ones.

Syntax

```
insert     /*+ NOAPPEND */ …
```

Example

```
insert     /*+ PARALLEL(emp) NOAPPEND */
into     emp (empno, deptno)
values   (7747, 10);
```

TIP
*The NOAPPEND hint overrides a PARALLEL hint, which normally
uses the APPEND hint by default.*

Using the CACHE Hint

The CACHE hint causes a full table scan to be cached (pinned) into memory, so future users
accessing the same table find it in memory instead of going to disk. This creates one potentially
large problem. If the table is very large, it is taking up an enormous amount of memory (SGA -
DB_CACHE_SIZE space for data in particular). For small lookup tables, however, this is an excellent
option to use. Tables can be created with the CACHE option to be cached the first time they are
accessed.

Syntax

```
select     /*+ CACHE(table) */ column1, …
```

Example

```
select      /*+ FULL(dept) CACHE(dept) */ deptno, loc
from        dept;
```

The entire dept table is now cached in memory and is marked as a most recently used (MRU) object.

TIP
The CACHE hint should be used with small lookup tables that are often accessed by users. This ensures that the table remains in memory.

Using the NOCACHE Hint

The NOCACHE hint causes a table that is specified to be CACHED at the database level to *not* get cached when you access it.

Syntax

```
select      /*+ NOCACHE(table) */ column1, …
```

Example

```
alter       table dept cache;

select      deptno, loc
from        dept;
```

In this example, the table is cached because the table was altered to use this option.

Example

```
alter       table dept cache;

select      /*+ NOCACHE(dept) */ deptno, loc
from        dept;
```

In this example, the table is not cached despite the ALTER statement and is put on the least recently used (LRU) list.

TIP
The NOCACHE hint should be used to prevent caching a table specified with the CACHE option—basically, when you want to access the table but you don't want to cache it.

Using the CLUSTER Hint

The CLUSTER hint is used only for clusters. A cluster is usually created when tables are joined so often that it is faster to create an object containing information about the joined tables that are accessed most often. A cluster is identical to denormalizing a table or group of tables. The CLUSTER hint forces the use of the cluster. If hashing is used for the cluster (see the next section and Chapter 2 for more information), the HASH hint should be considered. I have not had much luck with using clusters and gaining performance.

Syntax

```
select    /*+ CLUSTER (table) */ column1, …
```

TIP
The CLUSTER hint forces the use of a cluster. It is good to have clusters if the joined tables are frequently accessed but not frequently modified.

Using the HASH Hint

Hash indexes require the use of hash clusters. When a cluster or hash cluster is created, a cluster key is defined. The cluster key tells Oracle how to identify the rows stored in the cluster and where to store the rows in the cluster. When data is stored, all of the rows relating to the cluster key are stored in the same database blocks. With the data being stored in the same database blocks, using the hash index, Oracle can access the data by performing one hash function and one I/O—as opposed to accessing the data by using a b-tree index. Hash indexes can potentially be the fastest way to access data in the database, but they do have drawbacks. (See Chapter 2 for more information.) Note that you can even create a hash cluster that contains a single table.

Syntax

```
select    /*+ HASH(table) */ column1, …
```

Example

```
select    /*+ HASH(emp) */ empno, dept.deptno
from      emp, dept
where     emp.deptno = dept.deptno
where     empno = 7747;
```

In this query, Oracle uses the hash key to find the information in the emp table. (Note that you must create a hash cluster prior to using this.)

TIP
Be careful implementing hash clusters. The application should be reviewed fully to ensure that enough information is known about the tables and data before implementing this option. Generally speaking, hashing is best for static data with primarily sequential values. I have not had a lot of luck with these.

Using the **CURSOR_SHARING_EXACT** Hint

The CURSOR_SHARING_EXACT hint is used to ensure that statements are not modified so that they can be reused. This hint can be used to correct any minor issues when you don't want to use cursor sharing that erupts when your initialization CURSOR_SHARING parameter is set to either FORCE or SIMILAR.

Syntax

```
select      /*+ CURSOR_SHARING_EXACT */ column1, …
```

Example

```
select      /*+ CURSOR_SHARING_EXACT */ empno, ename
from        emp
where       empno = 123;
```

In this example, Oracle will not be able to reuse a current statement in the shared pool unless it is exactly like this one is. It will not try to create a bind variable. Chapter 4 contains additional examples related to cursor sharing.

TIP
The CURSOR_SHARING_EXACT hint overrides the init.ora setting of CURSOR_SHARING to either FORCE or SIMILAR.

Problems with Hints

Often, we find that a hint won't behave like we want it to. Sometimes the optimizer overrides the hint, but usually people have a problem related to one of the following:

- The hint syntax is incorrect.
- The table(s) is not analyzed.
- There is a conflict with another hint.
- You are not in cost mode.

- The hint requires an initialization parameter to be set for it to work.
- There is an alias for a table and you've hinted the table.
- The hint requires a different version than you have.
- You don't understand the correct application for the hint.
- You haven't slept lately; it is because of many of the aforementioned reasons.
- There is a software bug.

Hints at a Glance

The following table describes each hint discussed in this chapter.

Hint	Use
CHOOSE	Forces cost-based optimization
RULE	Forces rule-based optimization
FIRST_ROWS	Generally forces the use of indexes
ALL_ROWS	Generally forces a full table scan
FULL	Forces a full table scan
INDEX	Forces the use of an index
NO_INDEX	Disallows a specified index from being used
INDEX_JOIN	Allows the merging of indexes on a single table
INDEX_ASC	Uses an index ordered in ascending order
INDEX_DESC	Uses an index ordered in descending order
AND_EQUAL	Accesses multiple b-tree indexes
INDEX_COMBINE	Accesses multiple bitmap indexes
INDEX_FFS	Forces fast full scans
ORDERED	Specifies the driving order of tables
LEADING	Specifies only the first driving table
ORDERED_PREDICATES	Forces predicate order
NO_EXPAND	Helps eliminate OR expansion
ROWID	Goes to the exact physical location (block address) to retrieve the requested information
STAR	Forces a star query plan
DRIVING_SITE	Processes data by driving it from a particular database
USE_MERGE	Changes how tables are joined internally

Hint	Use
PUSH_SUBQ	Forces the subquery to process earlier
PARALLEL	Causes full table scan queries to break query into pieces and process each piece with a different process
NO_PARALLEL	Turns off use of parallel operations in any one given query for a table that is specified to use parallel operations
APPEND	Appends data into new blocks
NOAPPEND	Checks for free space within current blocks before using new ones
CACHE	Causes a full table scan to be pinned into memory
NOCACHE	Causes a table that is specified to be cached at database level to not get cached when you access it
CLUSTER	Forces clustering
HASH	Forces cluster hashing
CURSOR_SHARING_EXACT	Overrides the CURSOR_SHARING setting

Tips Review

- Incorrect hint syntax leads to the hint being interpreted as a comment.

- Multiple hints are separated with a space between each. At times, specifying multiple hints can cause the query to use none of the hints.

- If an alias is used, the alias must be used in the hint or it will not work.

- The CHOOSE hint uses cost-based optimization for the entire query unless all of the tables in the query have not been analyzed.

- The RULE hint forces Oracle to use predefined rules (such as using ROWID and UNIQUE indexes) over using the statistics about the data. The RULE hint may set in the initialization file for the entire database, but some query-level hints override it on a given query.

- The FIRST_ROWS hint causes the optimizer to choose a path that retrieves the first row of a query fastest, at the cost of retrieving multiple rows more slowly.

- The ALL_ROWS hint causes the optimizer to choose a path that retrieves all rows of a query fastest, at the cost of retrieving one single row more slowly.

- The FULL hint performs a full table scan on the table that is specified (not all tables in the query).

- The INDEX hint causes the optimizer to choose the index specified in the hint.

- The INDEX_JOIN hint allows you to access and merge together only indexes on a table, which is a scan of fewer total blocks and often faster scanning of the table by ROWID.

- The NO_INDEX hint is used to disallow the optimizer from using the specified index.

- The AND_EQUAL hint causes the optimizer to merge multiple b-tree indexes for a single table instead of choosing which one is better (as in the INDEX hint).

- The INDEX_COMBINE hint causes the optimizer to merge multiple bitmap indexes for a single table instead of choosing which one is better (as in the INDEX hint).

- The INDEX_ASC hint does exactly what the INDEX hint does because indexes are already scanned in ascending order. It is used to guarantee this to be true, because Oracle may change this default in the future.

- The INDEX_DESC hint processes an index in descending order of how it was built. This hint will not be used if more than one table exists in the query.

- The INDEX_FFS hint processes only the index and does not take the result and access the table. All columns that are used and retrieved by the query must be contained in the index.

- The ROWID hint processes a query using the ROWID, if it is possible, based on how the query is written.

- The ORDERED hint is one of the most powerful hints provided. It processes the tables of the query in the order that they are listed in the FROM clause. (The first table in the FROM is processed first.) There are, however, many variations that cause this to work differently.

- The LEADING hint is used to specify a single table to drive a query with while allowing the optimizer to figure out the rest of the query. The ORDERED hint overrides LEADING.

- The NO_EXPAND hint prevents the optimizer from using OR expansion.

- The DRIVING_SITE hint is extremely powerful, as it will potentially limit the amount of information to be processed over your network. The table specified with the DRIVING_SITE hint will be the location for the join to be processed.

- Using views for remote tables can also lead to better performance by limiting the number of rows passed from the remote site before the records are sent to the local site.

- The NO_EXPAND hint prevents the optimizer from using OR expansion.

- The DRIVING_SITE hint is extremely powerful, as it will intentially limit the amount of information to be processed over your network. The table specified with the DRIVING_SITE hint will be the location for the join to processed.

- Using views for remote tables can also lead to better perfomance by limiting the number of rows passed from the remote site before the records are sent to the local site.

- In a three or more table join, the USE_MERGE hint causes the table(s) specified in the hint to merge the resulting row set from a join to the other tables in the join.

- The USE_NL hint usually provides the best response time (first row comes back faster), whereas the USE_MERGE hint usually provides the best throughput.

- The PUSH_SUBQ hint can improve performance greatly when the subquery returns only a few rows very fast and those rows can be used to limit the rows returned in the outer query.

- The PARALLEL hint enables the use of parallel operations. If the degree is not specified with the hint, the default degree specified during the table creation is used.

- The NOPARALLEL hint disables parallel operations in a statement that would otherwise use parallel processing due to a parallel object definition.

- The APPEND hint inserts values into a table without checking the free space in the currently used blocks, but instead appending the data into new blocks.

- The CACHE hint should be used with small lookup tables that are often accessed by users. This ensures that the table remains in memory.

- The NOCACHE hint should be used to prevent caching a table specified with the CACHE option—basically, when you want to access the table but you don't want to cache it.

- The CLUSTER hint forces the use of a cluster scan to access the table(s). It is good to have clusters if the joined tables are frequently accessed but not frequently modified.

- Caution should be taken before implementing hash clusters. You should review the application fully to ensure that enough information is known about the tables and data before you implement this option. Generally speaking, hashing is best for static data with primarily sequential values.

- The CURSOR_SHARING_EXACT hint overrides the init.ora setting of CURSOR_SHARING to either FORCE or SIMILAR.

References

Oracle7 Server Tuning, Oracle Corporation
Oracle8 Server Tuning, Oracle Corporation
Oracle8 Tuning, Oracle Corporation
Performance Tuning Guide Version 7.0, Oracle Corporation
Oracle8 DBA Handbook, Kevin Loney
Tuning Tips: You Will Be Toast! Rich Niemiec
Oracle9i Performance Tuning Guide, Oracle Corporation
Oracle9i Database Performance Guide and Reference, Oracle Corporation

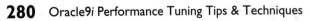

> **NOTE**
> *Oracle9i introduced the Sample Schema (see the Oracle9i Sample Schemas Release 1 (9.0.1) manual, Part Number A90129-01), which is a collection of schemas and objects (filled with data) that can be created either through the Database Configuration Assistant tool, or by running a script. These schemas were designed to replace the SCOTT schema, which simply cannot keep up with all the new technology being introduced. There are five main schemas: HR – Human Resources, which most closely resembles SCOTT; OE – Order Entry, which has an object-type subschema; SH – Sales History, which is a data warehousing schema; PM – Product Management, which demonstrates audio-visual datatypes and other special datatypes; and the QS schema, which contains several queue tables.*
>
> *The scripts to create these tables have been shipped with the database since Oracle9i 9.0.1. They make the creation of examples so much easier because you no longer have to create and populate the tables. However, you may have to drop some constraints and indexes to get a particular example to work. (Thanks to Janet Stern for this note.)*

CHAPTER
8

Query Tuning
(Developer and
Beginner DBA)

T his chapter focuses on specific queries you may encounter and provides some general information for tuning them. Examples of query tuning are spread throughout this book, along with instructions to make them more effective based on your system's architecture. This chapter focuses on some of the most common queries that can be tuned on *most* systems. A query can display various behaviors depending on the architecture of the system, the distribution of data in the tables, the specific version of Oracle, and a variety of other exceptions to the rules.

This chapter uses strictly cost-based examples for timings (except where noted). No other queries were performed at the time of the tests in this chapter. Many hints are used throughout this chapter. For a detailed look at hints and their syntax and structure, please refer to Chapter 7. Multiple table queries are the focus of Chapter 9 and are not covered here.

Please note that this chapter is not all-inclusive. The other queries discussed throughout the book must also be investigated when trying to increase performance for a given query. Some of the most dramatic examples include using Oracle's parallel features (Chapter 11), using partitioned tables and indexes (Chapter 3), and using PL/SQL (Chapter 10). Note the benefits of EXPLAINing and TRACing queries (Chapter 6).

The topics covered in this chapter include the following:

- Querying the V$SQLAREA and V$SQL

- Determining when to use an index

- Forgetting the index

- Creating an index

- Checking the index on a table

- Indexing properly

- Fixing a bad index

- Indexing the SELECT and WHERE

- Using the fast full scan

- Making queries "magically" faster

- Caching a table in memory

- Using multiple indexes (use the most selective)

- Using the index merge

- Handling suppressed indexes

- Using function-based indexes

- Understanding the "curious" OR

- Using the EXISTS function

Querying V$SQLAREA and V$SQL

V$SQLAREA and V$SQL are great views you can query to find the worst performing SQL statements that need optimization. The value in the DISK_READS column signifies the volume of disk reads that are being performed on the system. This value combined with the executions (DISK_READS/ executions) returns the SQL statements that have the most disk hits per statement execution. Any statement that makes the top of this list is most likely a problem query that needs to be tuned. Statspack also lists the resource-intensive queries; see Chapter 14 for detailed information.

Selecting from the V$SQLAREA View to Find the Top Queries

You can use the query shown in Listing 8-1 to fix the top resource intensive queries existing in your database; this query alone is worth the price of this book if you haven't heard of V$sqlarea yet.

```
select      b.username username, a.disk_reads reads,
            a.executions exec, a.disk_reads /decode
            (a.executions, 0, 1,a.executions) rds_exec_ratio,
            a.sql_text Statement
from        V$sqlarea a, dba_users b
where       a.parsing_user_id = b.user_id
and         a.disk_reads > 100000
order       by a.disk_reads desc;
```

USERNAME	READS	EXEC	RDS EXEC RATIO	STATEMENT
ADHOC1	7281934	1	7281934	select custno, ordno from cust, orders
ADHOC5	4230044	4	1057511	select ordno from orders where trunc(ordno) = 721305
ADHOC1	801716	2	400858	select custno, ordno from cust where nvl(custno,0) = '314159'

Listing 8-1: Finding the resource intensive queries in the database

You can replace the DISK_READS column in the preceding statement with the BUFFER_GETS column to provide information on SQL statements requiring the most memory.

TIP
Query V$sqlarea to find your problem queries that need to be tuned.

Selecting from the V$SQL View to Find the Top Queries

Oracle9*i* has an additional view to access the SQL statements that have been parsed. Querying V$sql allows you to see the shared SQL area statements individually versus grouped together (as V$sqlarea does). Listing 8-2 shows a faster query to get the top statements from V$sql. (This query can also access V$sqlarea by changing only the table name.)

```
select * from
  (select address,
    rank() over ( order by buffer_gets desc ) as rank_bufgets,
    to_char(100 * ratio_to_report(buffer_gets) over (), '999.99') pct_bufgets
from    V$sql )
where   rank_bufgets < 11
/

ADDRESS   RANK_BUFGETS  PCT_BUF
--------  ------------  -------
131B7914             1    66.36
131ADA6C             2    24.57
131BC16C             3     1.97
13359B54             4      .98
1329ED20             5      .71
132C7374             5      .71
12E966B4             7      .52
131A3CDC             8      .48
131947C4             9      .48
1335BE14            10      .48
1335CE44            10      .48
```

Listing 8-2: Finding the resource intensive queries

You can alternatively select SQL_TEXT instead of ADDRESS if you want to see the SQL, as shown in Listing 8-3.

```
select * from
  (select sql_text,
    rank() over ( order by buffer_gets desc ) as rank_bufgets,
    to_char(100 * ratio_to_report(buffer_gets) over (), '999.99') pct_bufgets
from    V$sql )
where   rank_bufgets < 11
/
```

Listing 8-3: Using SQL_TEXT

TIP
You can also query V$SQL to find your problem queries that need to be tuned.

Determining When to Use an Index

In Oracle version 5, many DBAs called the indexing rule the 80/20 Rule; you needed to use an index if less than 20 percent of the rows were being returned by a query. In version 7, this number was reduced to about 7 percent on average, and in version 8, the number is closer to 4 percent. Figure 8-1 shows when an index should generally be used (in V5 and V6 for rule-based optimization and in V7 and V8 for cost-based optimization). However, the distribution of data, whether parallel query or partitioning, can be used, and other factors need to be considered as well. Chapter 9 details how to make this graph for your own queries. If the table has less than 1000 records (small tables), then the graph is also different. For small tables, Oracle's V7 and V8 cost-based optimizer generally uses the index when only less than 1 percent of the table is queried.

This graph shows you Oracle's progress. The less you access, the more likely you will use an index. Because of the many variables with Oracle9*i*, the graph could continue to go down as the trend is showing from V5–V8, or it could go up slightly depending on how you architect the database. Oracle9*i* makes you the creator of where the graph goes based on how the data and indexes are architected and accessed.

TIP
When a small number of rows ("small" is version dependent) are to be returned based on a condition in a query, you generally want to use an index on that condition (column), given that the small number of rows also return a small number of individual blocks (usually the case).

Forgetting the Index

Although it seems obvious that columns, which are generally restrictive, require indexes, it is not always common knowledge. Chapter 2 covered basic index principles and structure; this section focuses on query-related issues surrounding indexes.

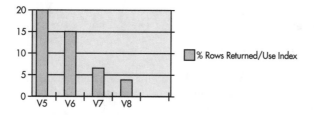

FIGURE 8-1. *The percentage of rows retrieved when an index should be used with data distributed equally in each block*

NOTE
I once went to a job where the users were suffering from incredibly poor performance. When I asked for a list of tables and indexes, they said they had a list of tables but hadn't figured out what indexes were or whether they should use them. I was asked if I thought I could help their performance. I initially thought this was my dream tuning job! But then I realized I had been training experts too long and had forgotten that not everyone is as far along in their performance education.

Even if you have built indexes correctly for most columns needing them, you may miss a crucial column here and there. If you forget to put an index on a restrictive column, the speed of those queries will not be optimized. Consider Listing 8-4, in which the percentage of rows returned by any given CUST_ID is less than 1 percent. Under these circumstances, an index on the CUST_ID column should normally be implemented. This query does *not* have an index on CUST_ID.

```
select  count(*)
from    sales2
where   cust_id = 22340;

  COUNT(*)
----------
     25750

Elapsed: 00:04:47.00 (4 minutes, 47 seconds)

Execution Plan
-----------------------------------------------------------
   0      SELECT STATEMENT Optimizer=CHOOSE
   1   0    SORT (AGGREGATE)
   2   1      TABLE ACCESS (FULL) OF 'SALES2'

121,923 consistent gets (memory reads)
121,904 physical reads (disk reads)
5,000 times slower than using an index (we'll see this in a moment)
```

Listing 8-4: Querying with no index

The query is not only extremely slow, but it also uses a tremendous amount of memory, disk I/O, and CPU. This results in an impatient user and a frustrating wait for other users due to the lack of system resources. (Sound familiar?)

Creating an Index

To accelerate the query in Listing 8-4, you could build an index on the CUST_ID column, as shown in Listing 8-5. The STORAGE clause must be based on the size of the table and the column. The table is over 25 million rows. (The space for the index is about 461MB.) You could also perform an alter session set SORT_AREA_SIZE = 500000000 (if you have the O/S memory needed; or use PGA_AGGREGATE_TARGET), and the index creation would be much faster. The STORAGE clause must be based on the size of the table and the column. The table is over 25 million rows.

```
create index sales2_idx1 on sales2(cust_id)
tablespace rich
storage (initial 400M next 10M pctincrease 0);
Index Created.
```

Listing 8-5: Creating an index

Checking the Index on a Table

Before creating indexes, check for current indexes that exist on that table to ensure there will not be conflicts. Once you have created the index, verify that it exists by querying the DBA_IND_COLUMNS view, as shown in Listing 8-6.

```
select    table_name, index_name, column_name, column_position
from      dba_ind_columns
where     table_name = 'SALES2'
and       table_owner = 'SH'
order     by index_name, column_position;


TABLE NAME         INDEX NAME      COLUMN NAME    COLUMN POSITION
SALES2             SALES2_IDX1     CUST_ID                      1
```

Listing 8-6: Querying DBA_IND_COLUMNS to find indexes for a table

The TABLE_NAME is the table that is being indexed, the INDEX_NAME is the name of the index, the COLUMN_NAME is the column being indexed, and the COLUMN_POSITION is the order of the columns in a multipart index. Because our index involved only one column, the COLUMN_POSITION is 1. (CUST_ID is the first and only column in the index.) In the "Indexing the SELECT and WHERE" section later in this chapter, you will see how a multipart index appears.

Indexing Properly

Rerun the same query that has the CUST_ID properly indexed, as shown in Listing 8-7. The query is dramatically faster; more importantly, it no longer "floods" the system with a tremendous amount of data to the SGA (low number of memory reads) and subsequently reduces the physical reads.

```
select count(*)
from    sales2
where   cust_id = 22340;

  COUNT(*)
----------
     25750


Elapsed: 00:00:00.06 (0.06 seconds)

Execution Plan
-----------------------------------------------------------
   0       SELECT STATEMENT Optimizer=CHOOSE
```

Selecting from V$SQL View to Find Top Queries

```
     1     0    SORT (AGGREGATE)
     2     1       INDEX (RANGE SCAN) OF 'SALES_IDX' (NON-UNIQUE)

89 consistent gets (memory reads)
64 physical reads (disk reads)
```

Listing 8-7: Querying with CUST_ID using the index

TIP
You'll have a lot of slow queries if you don't index columns that are restrictive (return a small percentage of the table). Building indexes on restrictive columns is the first step toward better system performance.

Fixing a Bad Index

In the PRODUCT table there is also a COMPANY_NO column. Because this company's expansion has not occurred, all rows in the table have a COMPANY_NO = 1. What if you are a beginner who has heard that indexes are good, and you have decided to index the COMPANY_NO column?

The cost-based optimizer analyzes the index as bad and suppresses it internally. The table *must* be reanalyzed after the index is created for the cost-based optimizer to make the informed choice. As shown in Listing 8-8, the index created on COMPANY is correctly suppressed by Oracle internally (because it would access the entire table and index).

```
select     product_id, qty
from       product
where      company_no = 1;

Elapsed time: 405 seconds (all records are retrieved via a full table scan)

OPERATION              OPTIONS       OBJECT NAME
SELECT STATEMENT
TABLE ACCESS             FULL           PRODUCT

49,825 consistent gets (memory reads)
41,562 physical reads (disk reads)
```

Listing 8-8: Querying with Oracle internally suppressing the index

You can override the suppression and force the use of the index (bad choice), as shown in Listing 8-9.

```
select    /*+ index(product company_idx1) */ product_id, qty
from      product
where     company_no = 1;

Elapsed time: 725 seconds  (all records retrieved using the index on company_no)
```

```
OPERATION              OPTIONS          OBJECT NAME

SELECT STATEMENT
TABLE ACCESS           BY ROWID         PRODUCT
     INDEX             RANGE SCAN       COMPANY_IDX1

4,626,725 consistent gets (memory reads)
80,513 physical reads (disk reads)
```

Listing 8-9: Overriding an index suppression and forcing the use of the index

You can also suppress indexes yourself that you deem to be poor by using the FULL hint (Listing 8-10).

```
select    /*+ FULL(PRODUCT) */ product_id, qty
from      product
where     company_no = 1;

Elapsed time: 405 seconds (all records are retrieved via a full table scan)

OPERATION              OPTIONS          OBJECT NAME
SELECT STATEMENT
TABLE ACCESS           FULL             PRODUCT

49,825 consistent gets (memory reads)
41,562 physical reads (disk reads)
```

Listing 8-10: Using the FULL hint to suppress indexes

TIP
Bad indexes (indexing the wrong columns) can cause as much trouble as forgetting to use indexes on the correct columns. Although Oracle's cost-based optimizer generally suppresses poor indexes, problems can still develop when a bad index is used at the same time as a good index.

WARNING
Some people's first reaction when they find a query that uses a poor index is to drop the index. However, you should first suppress the index and then investigate the impact of the index on other queries. Unless your query was the only one being performed against the given table, changing/dropping an index might be a detrimental solution. The next section investigates indexing columns that are both in the SELECT and WHERE clauses of the query.

Indexing the SELECT and WHERE

You now know that dropping an index can hurt a query's performance. Consider the query in Listing 8-11—a million-row employee table from the famous SCOTT.EMP table—that the index was created to help. This query does not have indexes.

```
select ename
from    employees
where   deptno = 10;


Elapsed time: 55 seconds (a full table scan is performed)


OPERATION              OPTIONS        OBJECT NAME
SELECT STATEMENT
TABLE ACCESS           FULL           EMPLOYEES
```

Listing 8-11: Querying the employees table without using indexes

First, you place an index on the DEPT_NO column to try to improve performance, as Listing 8-12 shows.

```
Create index dept_idx1 on employees (dept_no)
Tablespace test1
Storage (initial 20M next 5M pctincrease 0);


select    emp_name
from      employees
where     dept_no = 10;


Elapsed time: 70 seconds (the index on dept_no is used but made things worse)


OPERATION              OPTIONS          OBJECT NAME
SELECT STATEMENT
TABLE ACCESS           BY INDEX ROWID   EMPLOYEES
     INDEX             RANGE SCAN       DEPT_IDX1
```

Listing 8-12: Using the index on the DEPT_NO column

This situation is now worse. In this query, only the EMP_NAME is selected. If this query is crucial on the system, you should choose to index both the SELECT and the WHERE columns. By doing this, a concatenated index is created, as Listing 8-13 shows.

```
Drop index dept_idx1;


Create index emp_idx1 on employees (dept_no, emp_name)
Tablespace test1
Storage (initial 20M next 5M pctincrease 0);
```

Listing 8-13: Creating a concatenated index on employees

The query in Listing 8-14 is now tremendously faster.

```
select     emp_name
from       employees
where      dept_no = 10;


Elapsed time: Less than 1 second (the index on dept_no AND emp_name is used)


OPERATION                  OPTIONS      OBJECT NAME
SELECT STATEMENT
INDEX                      RANGE SCAN   EMP_IDX1
```

Listing 8-14: Querying with a concatenated index is much faster

The table itself did not have to be accessed to increase the query's speed. Indexing both the column in the SELECT clause and the column in the WHERE clause allows the query to access only the index.

TIP
For crucial queries on your system, consider concatenated indexes on the columns contained in both the SELECT and the WHERE clauses so that only the index is accessed.

Using the Fast Full Scan

The previous section demonstrated that if you index both the SELECT and the WHERE, the query is much faster. Oracle does not guarantee that only the index will be used under these circumstances. However, the INDEX_FFS hint guarantees that only the index will be used under these circumstances. This hint is a fast full scan of the index, which accesses only the index and not the corresponding table. Using the query from the previous section with the index on EMP_NAME and DEPT_NO yields the following (Listing 8-15).

```
select     /*+ index_ffs(employees emp_idx1) */ emp_name
from       employees
where      dept_no = 10;


Elapsed time: Less than 1 second (only the index is accessed)


OPERATION                  OPTIONS      OBJECT NAME
SELECT STATEMENT
INDEX                      RANGE SCAN EMP_IDX1
```

Listing 8-15: Querying with the index on EMP_NAME and DEPT_NO

The query is now guaranteed to access only the index. Also note, however, that sometimes your queries will scan the *entire* index, which is often not as good, so be careful.

TIP
*The INDEX_FFS (available since Oracle8) will process only the index
and will not access the table. All columns that are used and retrieved
by the query must be contained in the index.*

Making Queries "Magically" Faster

Consider the following query from the last example, in which you added a hint called RICHS_
SECRET_HINT. Some people believe this hint (buried deep in the X$ tables) is the hidden secret
to tuning. First, the query is run and no index is used, as shown in Listing 8-16.

```
select     emp_name, job
from       employees
where      dept_no = 10
and        emp_name = 'ADAMS';


Elapsed time: 50 seconds (one record is retrieved in this query)


OPERATION              OPTIONS       OBJECT NAME
SELECT STATEMENT
TABLE ACCESS           FULL          EMPLOYEES
```

Listing 8-16: Running the query with no index

No index can be used on this query. A full table scan is performed.
You now add Rich's secret hint to the query, as shown in Listing 8-17.

```
select    /*+ richs_secret_hint */ emp_name, job
from       employees
where      dept_no = 10
and        emp_name = 'ADAMS';


Elapsed time: 3 seconds (one record is retrieved in this query)


OPERATION              OPTIONS       OBJECT NAME
SELECT STATEMENT
TABLE ACCESS           FULL          EMPLOYEES
```

Listing 8-17: Using Rich's secret hint the query is "magically" faster

The hint worked and the query is "magically" faster, although a full table scan was still performed.
Actually, the data is now stored in memory, and querying the data from memory is much faster
than going to disk for the data—so much for the magic!

TIP
*When a query is run multiple times in succession, it becomes faster
because you have cached the data in memory (although full table scans
are aged out of memory quicker than indexed scans). Sometimes,
people are tricked into believing that they have made a query faster,
when they are actually accessing data stored in memory.*

Caching a Table in Memory

Although it is disappointing that no secret hint exists for tuning, we can use this knowledge to our advantage. In the last section, the query ran faster the second time because it was cached in memory. What if the most-often-used tables were cached in memory? Well, the first problem is that if we cannot cache every table in memory, we must focus on the smaller and more-often-used tables to be cached. We can also use multiple buffer pools, as discussed in Chapter 4. The query in Listing 8-18 is an unindexed customer table to return one of the rows.

```
select      cust_no, name
from        customer
where       cust_no = 1;


Elapsed time: 5 seconds (one record is retrieved in this query without an index)


OPERATION             OPTIONS       OBJECT NAME
SELECT STATEMENT
TABLE ACCESS          FULL          CUSTOMER
```

Listing 8-18: Querying an unindexed customer table

The database is then stopped and restarted so as to not influence the timing statistics. The table is altered to cache the records:

```
Alter table customer cache;
Table altered.
```

Then you query the unindexed but now cached customer table to return one of the rows, as shown in Listing 8-19.

```
select      cust_no, name
from        customer
where       cust_no = 1;


Elapsed time: 5 seconds (one record is retrieved in this query without an index)


OPERATION             OPTIONS       OBJECT NAME
SELECT STATEMENT
TABLE ACCESS          FULL          CUSTOMER
```

Listing 8-19: Querying the unindexed but cached customer table

Still 5 seconds? The table has been altered to be cached, but the data is not in memory yet. Every subsequent query will now be faster. You query the unindexed (but now cached) customer table to return one of the rows, as Listing 8-20 shows.

```
select      cust_no, name
from        customer
where       cust_no = 1;


Elapsed time: 1 second (one record is retrieved in this query without an index)
```

OPERATION	OPTIONS	OBJECT NAME
SELECT STATEMENT		
TABLE ACCESS	FULL	CUSTOMER

Listing 8-20: Querying the unindexed but cached customer table

The query is faster because the table is cached in memory; in fact, all queries to this table are now fast regardless of the condition used. A cached table is "pinned" into memory and will be placed at the most-recently-used end of the cache; it will be pushed out of memory only after other full table scans to tables that are not cached are pushed out. Running a query multiple times places the data in memory so that subsequent queries are faster—only caching a table ensures that the data is not pushed out of memory later.

WARNING
Caching an often-used but relatively small table into memory ensures that the data is not pushed out of memory by other data. But be careful—cached tables can alter the execution path normally chosen by the optimizer, leading to an unexpected execution order for the query. (It can affect the driving table in nested loop joins.)

Using Multiple Indexes (Use the Most Selective)

Having multiple indexes on a table can cause problems when you execute a query in which the choices include using more than one of the indexes. The optimizer almost always chooses correctly. Consider an example in which the percentage of rows returned by any given PRODUCT_ID is less than 1 percent where the data is equally distributed between the blocks. Under these circumstances, you place an index on the PRODUCT_ID column. The query in Listing 8-21 has a single index on PRODUCT_ID.

```
select     product_id, qty
from       product
where      company_no = 1
and        product_id = 167;

Elapsed time: 1 second (one record is retrieved; the index on product_id is used)
```

OPERATION	OPTIONS	OBJECT NAME
SELECT STATEMENT		
TABLE ACCESS	BY ROWID	PRODUCT
INDEX	RANGE SCAN	PROD_IDX1

```
107 consistent gets (memory reads)
1 physical reads (disk reads)
```

Listing 8-21: Querying with a single index on PRODUCT_ID

Now you create an additional index on the company column. In Listing 8-22, all of the records have a COMPANY = 1, an extremely poor index. You rerun the query with both indexes (one on PRODUCT_ID and one on COMPANY) existing on the table.

```
select      product_id, qty
from        product
where       company_no = 1
and         product_id = 167;


Elapsed time: 725 seconds (one record is returned; a full table scan is performed)


OPERATION              OPTIONS         OBJECT NAME
SELECT STATEMENT
TABLE ACCESS           FULL            PRODUCT


4,626,725 consistent gets (memory reads)
80,513 physical reads (disk reads)
```

Listing 8-22: Querying using single indexes on PRODUCT_ID and COMPANY_NO

Oracle has chosen not to use either of the two indexes (perhaps because of a multiblock initialization parameter; your results will vary based on your architecture), and the query performed a full table scan. Depending on the statistical data stored and the version of Oracle used, I have seen this same query use the right index, the wrong index, no index at all, or a merge of both indexes. The solution is to rewrite the query to force the use of the correct index, which is the most restrictive, as shown in Listing 8-23. Or better yet, fix the real initialization parameter issue.

```
select      /*+ index(product prod_idx1) */ product_id, qty
from        product
where       company_no = 1
and         product_id = 167;


Elapsed time: 1 second (one record is retrieved)


OPERATION              OPTIONS         OBJECT NAME
SELECT STATEMENT
TABLE ACCESS           BY ROWID        PRODUCT
      INDEX            RANGE SCAN      PROD_IDX1


107 consistent gets (memory reads)
1 physical reads (disk reads)
```

Listing 8-23: Forcing the use of the index on PRODUCT_ID

TIP
When multiple indexes on a single table are used within a query, use the most restrictive index when you need to override an optimizer choice. Although Oracle's cost-based optimizer generally forces the use of the most restrictive index, variations occur based on the version of Oracle used, the structure of the query, and the initialization parameters used. Fix the larger issue if you see this as a trend.

TIP
Bitmap indexes usually behave differently because they are usually much smaller. See Chapter 2 for more information on the differences.

Using the Index Merge

The index merge allows you to merge two separate indexes and use the result of the indexes instead of going to the table from one of the indexes. Consider Listing 8-24. The following statistics are based on 1,000,000 records. The table is 210MB.

```
create    index year_idx on test2 (year);

create    index state_idx on test2 (state);

select    /*+ rule index(test2) */ state, year
from      test2
where     year = '1972'
and       state = 'MA'

SELECT STATEMENT Optimizer=HINT: RULE
   TABLE ACCESS (BY INDEX ROWID) OF 'TEST2'
      INDEX (RANGE SCAN) OF 'STATE_IDX' (NON-UNIQUE)

Elapsed time: 23.50 seconds

select    /*+ index_join(test2 year_idx state_idx) */
          state, year
from      test2
where     year = '1972'
and       state = 'MA'

SELECT STATEMENT Optimizer=CHOOSE
   VIEW OF 'index$_join$_001'
      HASH JOIN
         INDEX (RANGE SCAN) OF 'YEAR_IDX' (NON-UNIQUE)
         INDEX (RANGE SCAN) OF 'STATE_IDX' (NON-UNIQUE)
Elapsed time: 4.76 seconds
```

Listing 8-24: Using the index merge is much faster

The first query in Listing 8-24 tests the speed of using just one of the indexes and then goes back to the table. (Under certain scenarios, Oracle tunes this with an AND-EQUAL.) You then use the INDEX_JOIN hint to force the merge of two separate indexes and use the result of the indexes instead of going back to the table. When the indexes are both small compared to the size of the table, performance may improve.

Handling Suppressed Indexes

If you build the perfect system with all of the correctly indexed columns, you are still not guaranteed successful system performance. Along with the prevalence in business of the bright-eyed ad-hoc query user comes a variety of tuning challenges. One of the most common is the suppression of perfectly good indexes. Any modification of the column side of a WHERE clause results in the suppression of that index (unless function-based indexes are used). Alternative methods for writing the same query do not modify the column that is indexed. Listings 8-25–8-28 show some examples, which are often fixed by the optimizer internally.

```
select      product_id, qty
from        product
where       product_id+12 = 166;


Elapsed time: 405 second


OPERATION                OPTIONS          OBJECT NAME
SELECT STATEMENT
TABLE ACCESS             FULL             PRODUCT
```

Listing 8-25: Performing a math function on the column

```
select      product_id, qty
from        product
where       product_id = 154;


Elapsed time: 1 second


OPERATION                OPTIONS          OBJECT NAME
SELECT STATEMENT
TABLE ACCESS             BY ROWID         PRODUCT
      INDEX              RANGE SCAN       PROD_IDX1
```

Listing 8-26: Performing the math function on the other side of the clause

```
select      product_id, qty
from        product
where       substr(product_id,1,1) = 1;


Elapsed time: 405 second

OPERATION                OPTIONS          OBJECT NAME
SELECT STATEMENT
TABLE ACCESS             FULL             PRODUCT
```

Selecting from V$SQL View to Find Top Queries

Listing 8-27: Performing a function on the column

```
select     product_id, qty
from       product
where      product_id like '1%';


Elapsed time: 1 second


OPERATION                  OPTIONS           OBJECT NAME
SELECT STATEMENT
TABLE ACCESS               BY ROWID          PRODUCT
      INDEX                RANGE SCAN        PROD_IDX1
```

Listing 8-28: Rewriting the function so the column is not altered

TIP
Any modification to the column side of the query results in the suppression of the index unless a function-based index is used.

Using Function-Based Indexes

As seen in the previous section, one of the biggest problems with indexes is that developers and ad-hoc users often suppress them. Luckily, you can combat this problem by using function-based indexes. They allow you to create an index based on a function or expression. The value of the function or expression is specified by the person creating the index and is stored in the index. Function-based indexes can involve multiple columns, arithmetic expressions, or can be a PL/SQL function or C callout. The following example shows a function-based index.

```
CREATE INDEX emp_idx ON emp (UPPER(ename));
```

An index has been created on the ENAME column when the UPPER function is used on this column. Listing 8-29 queries the EMP table using the function-based index.

```
select ename, job, deptno
from    emp
where   upper(ename) = 'ELLISON';
```

Listing 8-29: Querying the EMP table using a function-based index

The function-based index (EMP_IDX) can be used for the previous query. For large tables where the condition retrieves a small amount of records, the query yields substantial performance gains over a full table scan. See Chapter 2 for additional details and examples.

You must set the following initialization parameters to use function-based indexes. (The optimization mode must be cost-based as well.)

```
query_rewrite_enabled = true


query_rewrite_integrity = trusted
```

TIP
When you use function-based indexes to create indexes on functions often used on selective columns in the WHERE clause, you may experience dramatic performance gains.

Understanding the "Curious" OR

The cost-based optimizer often has problems when you use the OR clause. Think of the OR as multiple queries that are then merged. Consider the example in Listing 8-30, in which a single primary key is on COL1, COL2, and COL3. Prior to Oracle9*i*, Oracle performed this query in the following way:

```
select *
from    table_test
where   pk_col1 = 'A'
and     pk_col2 in ('B','C')
and     pk_col3 = 'D';


2       Table Access By Rowid TABLE_TEST
1       Index Range Scan TAB_PK

pk_col2 and pk_col3 were not used for the index access
```

Listing 8-30: Querying with only part of the primary key

Since Oracle9*i*, Oracle has improved this query (internally performs OR-expansion), and the result now uses the full primary key and concatenates the result together (Listing 8-31). This method is much faster than using only part of the primary key (as in Listing 8-30), even though the previous query looks better because there are fewer lines in the explain plan. Don't be tricked: fewer lines in the explain plan doesn't mean a more efficient query.

```
5    Concatenation
2    Table Access By Rowid TAB
1    Index Unique Scan TAB_PK
4    Table Access By Rowid TAB
3    Index Unique Scan TAB_PK
```

Listing 8-31: Querying with the full primary key and concantenating the result

To get this desired result prior to 9*i*, you had to break up the query, as shown in Listing 8-32.

```
SELECT *
from    table_test
WHERE   (pk_col1 = 'A'
AND      pk_col2 = 'B'
AND      pk_col3 = 'D')
OR       (pk_col1 = 'A'
AND      pk_col2 = 'C'
AND      pk_col3 = 'D');
```

Selecting from V$SQL View to Find Top Queries

```
5   Concatenation
2   Table Access By Rowid TAB
1   Index Unique Scan TAB_PK
4   Table Access By Rowid TAB
3   Index Unique Scan TAB_PK
```

Listing 8-32: Breaking up the query; the full primary key is used

> **TIP**
> *Oracle has improved the way it performs the OR clause. The NO_EXPAND hint can still be helpful because it prevents the optimizer from using OR expansion, as described in Chapter 7.*

Using the EXISTS Function

Another helpful tip to remember is to use the EXISTS function instead of the IN function in most circumstances. The EXISTS function checks to find a single matching row to return the result in a subquery. Because the IN function retrieves and checks all rows, it is slower. Oracle has also improved the optimizer so that it often performs this optimization for you as well. Consider the example in Listing 8-33, in which the IN function leads to very poor performance. This query is faster only if the ITEMS table is extremely small.

```
select    product_id, qty
from      product
where     product_id = 167
and       item_no in
   (select   item_no
    from     items);


Elapsed time: 25 minutes (The items table is 10 million rows)

OPERATION                 OPTIONS          OBJECT NAME
SELECT STATEMENT
NESTED LOOPS
   TABLE ACCESS           BY ROWID         PRODUCT
      INDEX               RANGE SCAN       PROD_IDX1
      SORT
         TABLE ACCESS     FULL             ITEMS
```

Listing 8-33: Querying with the IN function

In Listing 8-33, the entire ITEMS table is retrieved.

This query is faster when the condition PRODUCT_ID = 167 is used; this predicate substantially limits the outside query, as shown in Listing 8-34.

```
select    product_id, qty
from      product a
where     product_id = 167
and       exists
```

```
(select    'x'
 from      items b
 where     b.item_no = a.item_no);

Elapsed time: 2 seconds (The items table query search is limited to 3 rows)

OPERATION                OPTIONS           OBJECT NAME
SELECT STATEMENT
FILTER
    TABLE ACCESS         BY ROWID          PRODUCT
        INDEX            RANGE SCAN        PROD_IDX1
    INDEX                RANGE SCAN        ITEM_IDX1
```

Listing 8-34: Using the EXISTS and limiting the outside query

In this query, only the records retrieved in the outer query (from the PRODUCT table) are checked against the ITEMS table. This query can be substantially faster than the first query if the ITEM_NO in the ITEMS table is indexed or if the ITEMS table is very large, yet the items are limited by the condition PRODUCT_ID = 167 in the outer query.

TIP
Using the nested subquery with an EXISTS may make queries dramatically faster, depending on the data being retrieved from each part of the query. Oracle9i has a much-improved optimizer that often performs some semblance of this transformation for you.

Tips Review

- Query V$SQLAREA and V$SQL to find problem queries that need to be tuned.

- When a small number of rows ("small" is version dependent) are to be returned based on a condition in a query, you generally want to use an index on that condition (column), given that the rows are not skewed within the individual blocks.

- You will have a lot of poor queries if you are missing indexes on columns that are generally restrictive. Building indexes on restrictive columns is the first step toward better system performance.

- Bad indexes (indexing the wrong columns) can cause as much trouble as forgetting to use indexes on the correct columns. Although Oracle's cost-based optimizer generally suppresses poor indexes, problems can still develop when a bad index is used at the same time as a good index.

- For crucial queries on your system, consider concatenated indexes on the columns contained in both the SELECT and the WHERE clauses.

- The INDEX_FFS processes *only* the index and does not take the result and access the table. All columns that are used and retrieved by the query *must* be contained in the index. This is a much better way to guarantee that the index will be used.

■ When a query is run multiple times in succession, it becomes faster because you have now cached the data in memory. Sometimes people are tricked into believing that they have made a query faster, when they are actually accessing data stored in memory.

■ Caching an often-used but relatively small table into memory ensures that the data is not pushed out of memory by other data. Also, be careful—cached tables can alter the execution path normally chosen by the optimizer, leading to an unexpected execution order for the query. (It can affect the driving table in nested loop joins.)

■ When multiple indexes on a single table are used within a query, use the most restrictive index. Although Oracle's cost-based optimizer generally forces the use of the most restrictive index, variations occur based on the version of Oracle used and the structure of the query.

■ Any modification to the column side of the query results in the suppression of the index unless a function-based index is created. Function-based indexes can dramatically improve performance when you use them on selective columns in the WHERE clause.

■ Oracle's optimizer now performs OR-expansion, which improves the performance of certain queries that ran poorly in prior versions.

References

DBA Tips or a Job Is a Terrible Thing to Waste, Deb Dudek; TUSC
DBA Tuning Tips: Now YOU are the Expert, Rich Niemiec; TUSC
Query Optimization in Oracle9i, An Oracle Whitepaper; Oracle
Thanks to Connor McDonald for his feedback on V$SQLAREA.

CHAPTER
9

Table Joins and Other
Advanced Tuning

This chapter was the most painful to write because the complexities of Oracle come to light here. The driving table or the first table accessed in a query is an important aspect of superior performance. If you have designated the wrong table as the driving table in a query, this choice can make the difference between hours and seconds. Usually, the cost-based optimizer chooses the correct table, but your indexing on tables affects how this works. If you need to change the driving table using a hint, this symptom often indicates an indexing plan that still needs work. When you have to tune multiple tables using hints, it gets progressively harder to tune increasing numbers of tables. With only two or three tables, it's easy enough to use an ORDERED hint (guaranteeing the order of the tables) and then try variations of the order of the tables until the fastest outcome is achieved. However, in a ten-table join, there are 3,628,800 possible combinations, which makes trying all combinations slightly time-consuming. Using a LEADING hint simplifies this chore, but it is still far more daunting than building the correct indexing scheme in the first place.

One of the greatest challenges of this book was trying to put driving tables into a useful format for readers. The optimizer's complexity and all the potential paths for joining and optimizing a query can be mind-boggling. Suppressing a single index in a query can affect the driving table, how Oracle joins tables in a query, and how Oracle uses or suppresses other indexes. This chapter focuses on helping you make better decisions when choosing a driving table. Although I have a good understanding of how Oracle performs these complexities, putting that understanding into words was the challenging task for the first half of this chapter. The challenge for the second half was relating performance tuning to mathematical equations and Gaussian distributions.

The topics covered in this chapter include the following:

- Join methods

- Table join initialization parameters

- Comparing the primary join methods

- A two-table join: equal-sized tables (cost-based)

- A two-table INDEXED join: equal-sized tables (cost-based)

- Forcing a specific join method

- Eliminating join records (candidate rows) in multitable joins

- A two-table join between a large and small table

- Three table joins: not as much fun (cost-based)

- Bitmap join indexes

- Third-party product tuning

- Tuning distributed queries

- When you have everything tuned

- Miscellaneous tuning snippets

- Tuning using simple mathematical techniques

- More mathematical techniques: apply control theory

Join Methods

Since the days of Oracle6, the optimizer has used four different ways to join row sources together: the NESTED LOOPS join, the SORT-MERGE join, and the CLUSTER join. (There is also the favorite of the ad-hoc query user, the CARTESIAN join.) In Oracle7.3, the HASH join was introduced, and in Oracle8*i*, the INDEX join was introduced, making for a total of five primary join methods. Each has a unique set of features and limitations. Before you attack a potential join issue, you need to know the following:

- Which table will drive the query and when will each table be accessed given the path that is chosen for the query? What are the alternate driving paths?

- What are the Oracle join possibilities (described in this section)? Remember, each join possibility for Oracle can yield different results depending on the join order, the selectivity of indexes, and the available memory for sorting and/or hashing.

- Which indexes are available and what is the selectivity of the indexes? The selectivity of an index can not only cause the optimizer to use or suppress an index, but it can also change the way the query drives and may determine the use or suppression of other indexes in the query.

- Which hints provide alternate paths and which hints suppress or force an index to be used? These hints change the driving order of the tables, and they change how Oracle performs the join and which indexes it uses or suppresses.

- Which version of Oracle are you using? Your choices vary depending on the version and release of Oracle you are using. The optimizer also works differently depending on the version.

NESTED LOOPS Joins

Suppose somebody gave you a telephone book and a list of 20 names to look up, and asked you to write down each person's name and corresponding telephone number. You would probably go down the list of names, looking up each one in the telephone book one at a time. This task would be pretty easy because the telephone book is alphabetized by name. Moreover, somebody looking over your shoulder could begin calling the first few numbers you write down while you are still looking up the rest. This scene describes a NESTED LOOPS join.

In a NESTED LOOPS join, Oracle reads the first row from the first row source and then checks the second row source for matches. All matches are then placed in the result set and Oracle goes on to the next row from the first row source. This continues until all rows in the first row source have been processed. The first row source is often called the outer or *driving* table, whereas the second row source is called the *inner* table. Using a NESTED LOOPS join is one of the fastest methods of receiving the first records back from a join.

NESTED LOOPS joins are ideal when the driving row source (the records you are looking for) is small and the joined columns of the inner row source are uniquely indexed or have a highly selective non-unique index. NESTED LOOPS joins have an advantage over other join methods in that they can quickly retrieve the first few rows of the result set without having to wait for the entire result set to be determined. This situation is ideal for query screens where an end user can read the first few records retrieved while the rest are being fetched. NESTED LOOPS joins are also flexible in that any two-row sources can always be joined by NESTED LOOPS—regardless of join condition and schema definition.

However, NESTED LOOPS joins can be very inefficient if the inner row source (second table accessed) does not have an index on the joined columns or if the index is not highly selective. If the driving row source (the records retrieved from the driving table) is quite large, other join methods may be more efficient.

Figure 9-1 illustrates the method of executing the query shown in Listing 9-1.

```
select      /*+ ordered */ ename, dept.deptno
from        dept, emp
where       dept.deptno = emp.deptno
```

SORT-MERGE Joins

Suppose two salespeople attend a conference and they each collect over 100 business cards from potential new customers. They now each have a pile of cards in random order, and they want to see how many cards are duplicated in both piles. The salespeople alphabetize their piles, and then

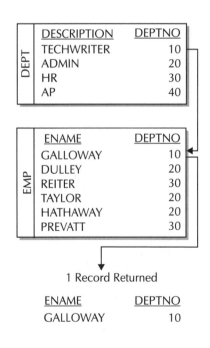

NESTED LOOPS Join

The loop would continue until each of the DEPTNOs in the DEPT table have been checked against those in the EMP table. The subsequent loop results are (for DEPTNO's 20, 30, and 40):

The second loop:
3 Records Returned

ENAME	DEPTNO
DULLEY	20
TAYLOR	20
HATHAWAY	20

The third loop:
2 Records Returned

ENAME	DEPTNO
REITER	30
PREVATT	30

The fourth loop:
No Records Returned

FIGURE 9-1. *Query for NESTED LOOPS Join figure*

they call off names one at a time. Because both piles of cards have been sorted, it becomes much easier to find the names that appear in both piles. This example describes a SORT-MERGE join.

In a SORT-MERGE join, Oracle sorts the first row source by its join columns, sorts the second row source by its join columns, and then merges the sorted row sources together. As matches are found, they are put into the result set.

SORT-MERGE joins can be effective when lack of data selectivity or useful indexes render a NESTED LOOPS join inefficient, or when both of the row sources are quite large (greater than 5 percent of the records). However, SORT-MERGE joins can be used only for equijoins (WHERE D.deptno = E.deptno, as opposed to WHERE D.deptno >= E.deptno). SORT-MERGE joins require temporary segments for sorting (if SORT_AREA_SIZE is set too small). This can lead to extra memory utilization and/or extra disk I/O in the temporary tablespace.

Figure 9-2 illustrates the method of executing the query shown in Listing 9-2.

```
select      /*+ ordered */ ename, dept.deptno
from        emp, dept
where       dept.deptno = emp.deptno
```

CLUSTER Joins

A CLUSTER join is really just a special case of the NESTED LOOPS join. If the two row sources being joined are actually tables that are part of a cluster, and if the join is an equijoin between the cluster keys of the two tables, then Oracle can use a CLUSTER join. In this case, Oracle reads each row from the first row source and finds all matches in the second row source by using the CLUSTER index.

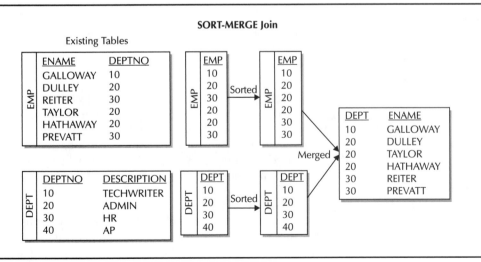

FIGURE 9-2. *Query for SORT-MERGE Join figure*

CLUSTER joins are extremely efficient because the joining rows in the two row sources will actually be located in the same physical data block. However, clusters carry certain caveats of their own, and you cannot have a CLUSTER join without a cluster. Therefore, CLUSTER joins are not very commonly used.

HASH Joins

HASH joins are the usual choice of the Oracle optimizer when the memory is set up to accommodate them. In a HASH join, Oracle accesses one table (usually the smaller of the joined results) and builds a hash table on the join key in memory. It then scans the other table in the join (usually the larger one) and probes the hash table for matches to it. Oracle uses a HASH join only if the database initialization parameter HASH_JOIN_ENABLED is set to TRUE and the parameter PGA_AGGREGATE_TARGET is set to a large enough value. (_HASH_AREA_SIZE is available for backward compatibility, whereas in pre-Oracle9i you would use HASH_AREA_SIZE.) This is similar to a NESTED LOOPS join—Oracle first builds a hash table to facilitate the operation. When using an ORDERED hint, the first table in the FROM clause is the table used to build the hash table.

HASH joins can be effective when the lack of a useful index renders NESTED LOOPS joins inefficient. The HASH join might be faster than a SORT-MERGE join; in this case, because only one row source needs to be sorted, and could possibly be faster than a NESTED LOOPS join because probing a hash table in memory can be faster than traversing a b-tree index. As with SORT-MERGE joins and CLUSTER joins, HASH joins work only on equijoins. As with SORT-MERGE joins, HASH joins use memory resources and can drive up I/O in the temporary tablespace if the sort memory is not sufficient (which can cause this join method to be extremely slow). Finally, HASH joins are available only when cost-based optimization is used.

Figure 9-3 illustrates the method of executing the query shown in Listing 9-3.

```
select    /*+ ordered */ ename, dept.deptno
from      emp, dept
where     dept.deptno = emp.deptno
```

Index Joins

Prior to Oracle8i, you always had to access the table unless the index contained all of the information required. As of Oracle8i, if a set of indexes exists that contains all of the information required by the query, then the optimizer can choose to generate a sequence of HASH joins between the indexes. Each of the indexes are accessed using a range scan or fast full scan, depending on the conditions available in the WHERE clause. This method is extremely efficient when a table has a large number of columns, but you want to access only a limited number of those columns. The more limiting the conditions in the WHERE clause, the faster the execution. The optimizer evaluates this as an option when looking for the optimal path of execution.

You must create indexes on the appropriate columns (those that will satisfy the entire query) to ensure that the optimizer has the INDEX join as an available choice. This task usually involves adding indexes on columns that may not be indexed or on columns that were not indexed together previously. The advantage of INDEX joins over fast full scans is that fast full scans have a *single* index satisfying the entire query. INDEX joins have multiple indexes satisfying the entire query.

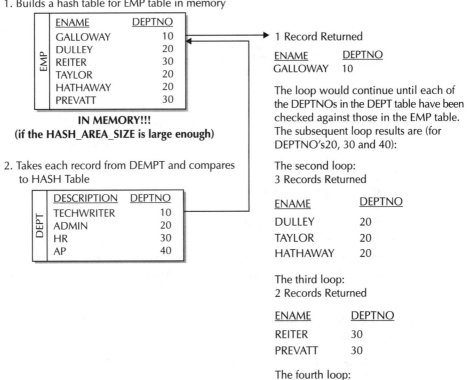

HASH Join

1. Builds a hash table for EMP table in memory

ENAME	DEPTNO
GALLOWAY	10
DULLEY	20
REITER	30
TAYLOR	20
HATHAWAY	20
PREVATT	30

IN MEMORY!!!
(if the HASH_AREA_SIZE is large enough)

2. Takes each record from DEMPT and compares to HASH Table

DESCRIPTION	DEPTNO
TECHWRITER	10
ADMIN	20
HR	30
AP	40

1 Record Returned

ENAME	DEPTNO
GALLOWAY	10

The loop would continue until each of the DEPTNOs in the DEPT table have been checked against those in the EMP table. The subsequent loop results are (for DEPTNO's20, 30 and 40):

The second loop:
3 Records Returned

ENAME	DEPTNO
DULLEY	20
TAYLOR	20
HATHAWAY	20

The third loop:
2 Records Returned

ENAME	DEPTNO
REITER	30
PREVATT	30

The fourth loop:
No Records Returned

Index Joins

FIGURE 9-3. *Query for HASH Join figure*

Two indexes (one on ENAME and one on DEPTNO) have been created prior to the execution of the corresponding query in Listing 9-4. Note that the query does not need to access the table! Figure 9-4 shows this index merge in a graphic format.

```
select   ENAME, DEPTNO
from     EMP
where    DEPTNO = 20
and      ENAME = 'DULLY';
```

Listing 9-4: Query to merge two indexes

INDEX-MERGE Join

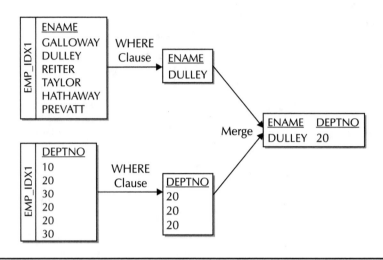

FIGURE 9-4. *An INDEX MERGE Join of EMP_IDX1 and EMP_IDX2*

The statistics in Listing 9-5 are based on 1 million records. The table is 210MB. Indexes were created on doby, state, and dobmsy.

```
create    index doby on test2  ( doby );
create    index state on test2   ( state );
create    index dobmsy on test2  (state, doby );
```

Listing 9-5: Creating indexes

Neither doby nor state individually are very limiting; consequently, the first indication is to execute a full table scan, as shown in Listing 9-6.

```
select    /*+ FULL(test2) */  state, doby
from      test2
where     doby = '1972'
and       state = MA
SELECT STATEMENT Optimizer=CHOOSE
   TABLE ACCESS (FULL) OF 'TEST2'
Elapse time: 12.6 seconds
```

Listing 9-6: Full table scan since neither index is selective enough

Using a single index on doby is slower than the full table scan, as shown in Listing 9-7.

```
select    /*+ rule index(test2 doby) */ state, doby
from      test2
where     doby = '1972'
```

```
and         state = MA
SELECT STATEMENT Optimizer=HINT: RULE
   TABLE ACCESS (BY INDEX ROWID) OF 'TEST2'
      INDEX (RANGE SCAN) OF 'DOBY' (NON-UNIQUE)

Elapsed time: 13:45 seconds
```

Listing 9-7: Using a single index instead of a full table scan

Using a single index on state is also slower than a full table scan, as shown in Listing 9-8.

```
select      /*+ rule index(test2 state) */ state, doby
from        test2
where       doby = '1972'
and         state = MA
SELECT STATEMENT Optimizer=HINT: RULE
   TABLE ACCESS (BY INDEX ROWID) OF 'TEST2'
      INDEX (RANGE SCAN) OF 'STATE' (NON-UNIQUE)

Elapsed time: 23.50 seconds
```

Listing 9-8: Using a single index on state

However, using an index join of doby and state is quicker than a full table scan because the table does not need to be accessed, as in Listing 9-9.

```
select      /*+ index_join(test2 doby state) */ state, doby
from        test2
where       doby = '1972'
and         state = MA
SELECT STATEMENT Optimizer=CHOOSE
   VIEW OF 'index$_join$_001'
      HASH JOIN
         INDEX (RANGE SCAN) OF 'DOBY' (NON-UNIQUE)
         INDEX (RANGE SCAN) OF 'STATE' (NON-UNIQUE)

Elapsed time: 4.76 seconds
```

Listing 9-9: Using an index join of doby and state is much faster

However, the INDEX_FFS (if a single index on all needed columns exists) is still the most efficient method (Listing 9-10).

```
select      /*+ index_ffs(test2 dobmsy) */ state, doby
from        test2
where       doby = '1972'
and         state = MA
SELECT STATEMENT Optimizer=CHOOSE
   INDEX (FAST FULL SCAN) OF 'DOBMSY' (NON-UNIQUE)

Elapsed time: 3.6 seconds
```

Listing 9-10: Using the INDEX_FFS hint to scan the index only

Index Joins

Although fast full scan is the most efficient option in this case, the index join accommodates more situations.

Table Join Initialization Parameters

Performance of SORT-MERGE joins and HASH joins is strongly affected by certain initialization parameters. Join performance can be crippled if certain parameters are not set properly.

SORT-MERGE Join Parameters

The initialization parameter DB_FILE_MULTIBLOCK_READ_COUNT specifies how many blocks Oracle should read at a time from disk when performing a sequential read such as a full table scan. Because SORT-MERGE joins often involve full table scans, setting this parameter will reduce overhead when scanning large tables.

The initialization parameter PGA_AGGREGATE_TARGET (or SORT_AREA_SIZE) specifies how much memory can be used for sorting, and this has a strong impact on performance of all sorts. Because SORT-MERGE joins require sorting of both row sources, allocated memory for sorting can greatly impact SORT-MERGE join performance. If an entire sort cannot be completed in the amount of memory specified by this parameter, then a temporary segment in the temporary tablespace is allocated. In this case, the sort is performed in memory one part at a time, and partial results are stored on disk in the temporary segment. If memory allocated for sorting is set very small, then excessive disk I/O is required to perform even the smallest of sorts. If it is set too high, then the operating system may run out of physical memory and resort to swapping.

HASH Join Parameters

The three parameters HASH_JOIN_ENABLED, PGA_AGGREGATE_TARGET (HASH_AREA_SIZE is available for backward compatibility), and _HASH_MULTIBLOCK_IO_COUNT (use undocumented initialization parameters only after consulting with Oracle Support) control HASH join behavior. Unlike most other initialization parameters, these three can also be dynamically altered with the alter session command.

The initialization parameter HASH_JOIN_ENABLED dictates whether the optimizer should consider using HASH joins. If you do not want HASH joins to be used, set this parameter to FALSE.

The initialization parameter PGA_AGGREGATE_TARGET (or HASH_AREA_SIZE) specifies memory that can be used to build a hash table for a HASH join. If this parameter is set too small, then partial hash tables need to be stored in temporary segments. If this parameter is set too big, then physical memory may be exhausted.

The initialization parameter _HASH_MULTIBLOCK_IO_COUNT specifies how many blocks should be read at a time when building the hash table, somewhat similar to DB_FILE_MULTIBLOCK_READ_COUNT for SORT-MERGE joins.

Comparing the Primary Join Methods

Table 9-1 gives a quick view of the primary join types.

Category	NESTED LOOPS Join	SORT-MERGE Join	HASH Join
Optimizer hint	USE_NL.	USE_MERGE.	USE_HASH.
When you can use it	Any join.	Equijoins only.	Equijoins only.
Resource concerns	CPU, disk I/O.	Memory, temporary segments.	Memory, temporary segments.
Features	Efficient with highly selective indexes and restrictive searches. Used to return the first row of a result quickly.	Better than NESTED LOOPS when an index is missing or the search criteria is not very selective. Can work with limited memory.	Better than NESTED LOOPS when an index is missing or the search criteria is not very selective. It is usually faster than a SORT-MERGE.
Drawbacks	Very inefficient when indexes are missing or if index criteria are not limiting.	Requires a sort on both tables. It is built for best optimal throughput and does not return the first row until all rows are found.	Can require a large amount of memory for the hash table to be built. Does not return the first rows quickly. Can be extremely slow if it must do the operation on disk.

TABLE 9-1. *Primary Join Methods*

A Two-Table Join: Equal-Sized Tables (Cost-Based)

Consider the following tables (they have been analyzed) that will be used for this example:

```
SMALL1    10000 rows    No Indexes
SMALL2    10000 rows    No Indexes
```

This section of examples is important as we look at how the cost-based optimizer works, with all conditions being equal in a join (same size tables/no indexes).

Example 1

Neither table has an index, and there aren't any other noteworthy conditions on the tables. Oracle uses a HASH join if the initialization parameters have been set up to allow a HASH join; otherwise, it uses a SORT-MERGE join. The first table accessed will be SMALL1, which is important for a HASH join but irrelevant for a SORT-MERGE join. A HASH join typically chooses the smaller

HASH Join Parameters

result set to access first to build the hash table. In this example, both tables are equal, so the first one in the FROM clause is used, as shown in Listing 9-11.

```
select    small1.col1, small2.col1
from      small1, small2
where     small1.col1 = small2.col1;
```

Listing 9-11: A simple join of two small tables

Join Method: HASH-Join   The SMALL1 table is accessed first and used to build a hash table. Oracle accesses the SMALL1 table and builds a hash table on the join key (COL1) in memory. It then scans SMALL2 and probes the hash table for matches to SMALL2.

Join Method: SORT-MERGE Join (if hash initialization parameters are not set up)
Although SMALL1 would normally be the driving table (because it is first in the FROM clause and we are in cost-based optimization), a SORT-MERGE join forces the sorting of each of the tables before they are merged together (because there are no indexes). A full table scan is needed on both tables and the order in the FROM clause has no impact, as in Listing 9-12.

```
select    small1.col1, small2.col1
from      small2, small1
where     small1.col1 = small2.col1;
```

Listing 9-12: Reverse the order of the tables in the FROM clause

Join Method: HASH-Join   The SMALL2 table is accessed first and used to build a hash table. Oracle accesses the SMALL2 table and builds a hash table on the join key (COL1) in memory. It then scans SMALL1 and probes the hash table for matches to SMALL1.

Join Method: SORT-MERGE Join (if hash initialization parameters are not set up)
Although SMALL2 would normally be the driving table (because it is first in the FROM clause and we are in cost-based optimization), a SORT-MERGE join forces the sorting of each of the tables before they are merged together (because there are no indexes). A full table scan is needed on both tables, and the order in the FROM clause has no impact.

Example 1 Outcomes
If you have set up the initialization parameters for hashing, Oracle builds a hash table from the join values of the *first* table, then probes that table for values from the second table. If you have not set up the initialization parameters for hashing, the *first* table in the FROM clause in cost-based optimization is the driving table. However, in a SORT-MERGE join, this has no impact because each table must be sorted and then merged together. Also note that the order of tables cannot be guaranteed when all conditions are *not* equal (when you have tables of different sizes or with different indexes) because the optimizer chooses the order unless you specify the ORDERED hint.

Lastly, if neither table was analyzed in example 1, Oracle resorts to previous version behavior by accessing the last table in the FROM clause and using a SORT-MERGE join (yes, even in Oracle9i). This is noted here so you will realize this behavior may indicate that you haven't analyzed your tables.

Example 2
Neither table has an index, and you will use the ORDERED hint, as in Listing 9-13.

```
select     /*+ ORDERED */ small1.col1, small2.col1
from       small1, small2
where      small1.col1 = small2.col1;
```

Listing 9-13: Use an ORDERED hint to ensure table access order

Join Method: HASH-Join   The SMALL1 table is accessed first and used to build a hash table. Oracle accesses the SMALL1 table and builds a hash table on the join key (COL1) in memory. It then scans SMALL2 and probes the hash table for matches to SMALL2.

Join Method: SORT-MERGE Join (if hash initialization parameters are not set up)
Although SMALL1 would normally be the driving table (because it is first in the FROM clause and we are in cost-based optimization), a SORT-MERGE join forces the sorting of each of the tables before they are merged together (because there are no indexes). A full table scan is needed on both tables, and the order in the FROM clause has no impact (Listing 9-14).

```
select     /*+ ORDERED */ small1.col1, small2.col1
from       small2, small1
where      small1.col1 = small2.col1;
```

Listing 9-14: Reversing the table order with the ORDERED hint

Join Method: HASH-Join   The SMALL2 table is accessed first and used to build a hash table. Oracle accesses the SMALL2 table and builds a hash table on the join key (COL1) in memory. It then scans SMALL1 and probes the hash table for matches to SMALL1.

Join Method: SORT-MERGE Join (if hash initialization parameters are not set up)
Although SMALL2 would normally be the driving table (because it is first in the FROM clause and we are in cost-based optimization), a SORT-MERGE join forces the sorting of each of the tables before they are merged together (because there are no indexes). A full table scan is needed on both tables, and the order in the FROM clause has no impact.

Example 2 Outcomes

If hash initialization parameters are set up, Oracle builds a hash table from the join values of the *first* table listed, then probes that hash table for values from the *second* table listed. If hash initialization parameters are not set up, the *first* table in the FROM clause in cost-based optimization is the driving table when an ORDERED hint is used; but in a SORT-MERGE join, this has no impact because each table must be sorted and then merged together.

TIP
Using cost-based optimization, the first table in the FROM clause is the driving table when the ORDERED hint is used. This overrides the optimizer from choosing the driving table. If a SORT-MERGE join is used, then the order of the tables has no impact because neither will drive the query. Knowing which table is generally the driving table when using an ORDERED hint in small joins can help you solve larger table join issues and also help you find indexing problems.

HASH Join Parameters

TIP
When hash initialization parameters are set up, the optimizer uses HASH joins in lieu of SORT-MERGE joins. With HASH joins, the first table is used to build a hash table (in memory if available), and the second table in the FROM clause then probes for corresponding hash table matches. The first table in the FROM clause (using the ORDERED hint) is the first table accessed in a HASH join.

A Two-Table INDEXED Join: Equal-Sized Tables (Cost-Based)

To get a better understanding of the driving table and how Oracle processes a query, it is instructive to have an example where all conditions are equal in both tables. Although the queries in this section look strange because we are trying to keep all conditions equal, they are helpful in understanding the way joins work. Consider the following tables (they have been analyzed) that will be used for this example:

```
SMALL1      10000 rows    Index on COL1
SMALL2      10000 rows    Index on COL1
```

NOTE
This section of examples is important as we look at how the cost-based optimizer works using indexes. Although the query in this section wouldn't normally be written, it shows how the driving table works with a two-table join, all conditions being equal. In other words, it is only for instructional purposes.

Example I
Both tables have an index on the COL1 column, as in Listing 9-15.

```
select      small1.col1, small2.col1
from        small1, small2
where       small1.col1 = small2.col1
and         small1.col1 = 77
and         small2.col1 = 77;
```

Listing 9-15: Simple join with common predicates

EXPLAIN PLAN output:

```
SELECT STATEMENT Optimizer=CHOOSE
   NESTED LOOPS (Cost=2 Card=3 Bytes=90)  (small1 result checks small2 matches)
      INDEX (RANGE SCAN) OF 'SMALL1_IDX'  (This is first/gets first row to check)
      INDEX (RANGE SCAN) OF 'SMALL2_IDX'  (This is second/checks for matches)
```

Join Method: NESTED LOOPS Join   The SMALL1 table (first table in the FROM clause) is the driving table of the query. Oracle retrieves the records from the index on SMALL1 and then takes each record and checks for matches in the SMALL2 index. A NESTED LOOPS join will be faster when the source rows from the SMALL1 table are a small set and there is a reasonably selective index on the SMALL2 joining column (Listing 9-16).

```
select    small1.col1, small2.col1
from      small2, small1
where     small1.col1 = small2.col1
and       small1.col1 = 77
and       small2.col1 = 77;
```

Listing 9-16: Reverse the order of the tables in the FROM clause

EXPLAIN PLAN output:

```
SELECT STATEMENT Optimizer=CHOOSE
  NESTED LOOPS (Cost=2 Card=3 Bytes=90)   (small2 result checks small1 matches)
    INDEX (RANGE SCAN) OF 'SMALL2_IDX'   (This is first/gets first row to check)
    INDEX (RANGE SCAN) OF 'SMALL1_IDX'   (This is second/checks for matches)
```

Join Method: NESTED LOOPS Join   The SMALL2 table (first table in the FROM clause) is the driving table of the query. Oracle retrieves the records from the index on SMALL2 and then takes each record and checks for matches in the SMALL1 index. A NESTED LOOPS join will be faster when the source rows from the SMALL2 table are a small set and there is a reasonably selective index on the SMALL1 joining column.

Example 1 Outcomes

All conditions being equal, the *first* table in the FROM clause in cost-based optimization is the driving table. The index is used on the join condition for the second table. In Example 1, Oracle used a NESTED LOOPS join to join the queries, but a HASH join or MERGE join was also possible depending on the number of records in the table and index.

Example 2

Both tables have an index on the COL1 column and we use the ORDERED hint (Listing 9-17).

```
select    /*+ ORDERED */ small1.col1, small2.col1
from      small1, small2
where     small1.col1 = small2.col1
and       small1.col1 = 77
and       small2.col1 = 77;
```

Listing 9-17: Force the order of table access with the ORDERED hint

EXPLAIN PLAN output:

```
SELECT STATEMENT Optimizer=CHOOSE
  NESTED LOOPS   (Each result from small1 is checked for matches in small2)
```

HASH Join Parameters

```
INDEX (RANGE SCAN) OF 'SMALL1_IDX'  (This is first/gets first row to check)
INDEX (RANGE SCAN) OF 'SMALL2_IDX'  (This is second/checks for matches)
```

Join Method: NESTED LOOPS Join   The SMALL1 table (first table in the FROM clause) is the driving table of the query. Oracle retrieves the records from the index on SMALL1 and then takes each record and checks for matches in the SMALL2 index. A NESTED LOOPS join will be faster when the source rows from the SMALL1 table are a small set and there is a reasonably selective index on the SMALL2 joining column (Listing 9-18).

```
select   /*+ ORDERED */ small1.col1, small2.col1
from     small2, small1
where    small1.col1 = small2.col1
and      small1.col1 = 77
and      small2.col1 = 77;
```

Listing 9-18: Reverse the order of the tables in the FROM

EXPLAIN PLAN output:

```
SELECT STATEMENT Optimizer=CHOOSE
  NESTED LOOPS  (Each result from small2 is checked for matches in small1)
    INDEX (RANGE SCAN) OF 'SMALL2_IDX'  (This is first/gets first row to check)
    INDEX (RANGE SCAN) OF 'SMALL1_IDX'  (This is second/checks for matches)
```

Join Method: NESTED LOOPS Join   The SMALL2 table (first table in the FROM clause) is the driving table of the query. Oracle retrieves the records from the index on SMALL2 and then takes each record and checks for matches in the SMALL1 index. A NESTED LOOPS join will be faster when the source rows from the SMALL2 table are a small set and there is a reasonably selective index on the SMALL1 joining column.

Example 2 Outcomes

All conditions being equal, the *first* table in the FROM clause in cost-based optimization using a NESTED LOOPS join is the driving table with or without the ORDERED hint. Only the ORDERED hint guarantees the order in which the tables will be accessed. The index is used on the join condition for the second table.

TIP
Using cost-based optimization and a NESTED LOOPS join as the means of joining, the first table in the FROM clause is the driving table (all other conditions being equal), but only the ORDERED hint guarantees this. In NESTED LOOPS joins, choosing a driving table that is the smaller result set (not always the smaller table) makes fewer loops through the other result set (from the nondriving table) and usually results in the best performance.

Forcing a Specific Join Method

When choosing an execution plan for a query involving joins, the Oracle optimizer considers all possible join methods and table orders. The optimizer does its best to evaluate the merits of each option and to choose the optimal execution plan, but sometimes the optimizer does not choose the best solution because of poor indexing strategies.

In these situations, you can use the USE_NL, USE_MERGE, and USE_HASH hints to request a specific join method, and you can use the ORDERED hint to request a specific join order. The optimizer does its best to observe the wishes of these hints, but if you ask for something impossible (such as a SORT-MERGE join on an antijoin), the hint will be ignored.

NOTE
There is no hint to request a CLUSTER join.

When tuning SQL that uses joins, you should run benchmark comparisons between different join methods and table execution order. For example, if a report joins two tables that form a master-detail relationship and the proper primary-key and foreign-key indexes are in place, the optimizer will probably choose to use a NESTED LOOPS join. However, if you know that this particular report joins all of the master records to all of the detail records, you might think it's faster to use a SORT-MERGE join or HASH join instead. Run a benchmark to ensure that you have the best solution.

Listing 9-19 shows an example query and its TKPROF output, Listing 9-20 shows the same query with a USE_MERGE hint, and Listing 9-21 shows it with a USE_HASH hint. In this example, the indexes were built so that a full table scan must be executed on the PURCHASE_ORDER_LINES table. (Using an index would have been the better choice but not as instructional.) You can see that in this situation the HASH join cut CPU time by almost 40 percent and logical I/Os by about 98 percent. The goal is not to demonstrate how to tune this type of query, but how to use different types on joining.

```
select       /*+ USE_NL (a b) */
             b.business_unit,b.po_number,b.vendor_type,a.line_number,
             a.line_amount,a.line_status,a.description
from         purchase_order_lines a, purchase_orders b
where        b.business_unit = a.business_unit
and          b.po_number = a.po_number
order by     b.business_unit,b.po_number,a.line_number
```

Listing 9-19: Forcing a NESTED LOOPS join

TKPROF output:

call	count	cpu	elapsed	disk	query	current	rows
Parse	1	0.01	0.01	0	0	0	0
Execute	1	0.04	0.12	0	0	1	0

```
Fetch      73370     23.47    23.55     2071    298667    2089     73369
total      73372     23.52    23.68     2071    298667    2090     73369


Rows       Execution Plan
0          SELECT STATEMENT    GOAL: CHOOSE
73369        SORT (ORDER BY)
73369        NESTED LOOPS
73726          TABLE ACCESS   GOAL: ANALYZED (FULL) OF 'PURCHASE_ORDER_LINES'
73369          TABLE ACCESS   GOAL: ANALYZED (BY ROWID) OF 'PURCHASE_ORDERS'
73726            INDEX   GOAL: ANALYZED (UNIQUE SCAN) OF 'PURCHASE_ORDERS_PK'
(UNIQUE)
```

The PURCHASE_ORDER_LINES table is the driving table. Each record (one at a time) is taken from the PURCHASE_ORDER_LINES table, and for each one, you loop through for matches in the PURCHASE_ORDER table. This is slow because the driving table list is large. (PURCHASE_ORDER_ LINES has a large number of rows.)

```
select     /*+ USE_MERGE (a b) */
           a.business_unit,a.po_number,a.vendor_type,b.line_number,
           b.line_amount,b.line_status,b.description
from       purchase_orders a,purchase_order_lines b
where      b.business_unit = a.business_unit
and        b.po_number = a.po_number
order by   a.business_unit,a.po_number,b.line_number
```

Listing 9-20: Forcing a SORT-MERGE join

TKPROF output:

call	count	cpu	elapsed	disk	query	current	rows
Parse	1	0.01	0.01	0	0	0	0
Execute	1	0.02	0.15	0	0	2	0
Fetch	73370	17.49	19.57	3772	4165	3798	73369
total	73372	17.52	19.73	3772	4165	3800	73369

```
Rows       Execution Plan
0          SELECT STATEMENT    GOAL: CHOOSE
73369        SORT (ORDER BY)
73369        MERGE JOIN
886            SORT (JOIN)
886              TABLE ACCESS   GOAL: ANALYZED (FULL) OF 'PURCHASE_ORDERS'
73726          SORT (JOIN)
73726            TABLE ACCESS   GOAL: ANALYZED (FULL) OF 'PURCHASE_ORDER_LINES'
```

For the SORT-MERGE case, Oracle sorts both tables and then merges the result. This method is still not an efficient way to perform the query.

```
select     /*+ USE_HASH (a b) */
           a.business_unit,a.po_number,a.vendor_type,b.line_number,
           b.line_amount,b.line_status,b.description
```

```
from        purchase_orders a,purchase_order_lines b
where       b.business_unit = a.business_unit
and         b.po_number = a.po_number
order by    a.business_unit,a.po_number,b.line_number
```

Listing 9-21: Forcing a HASH join

TKPROF output:

call	count	cpu	elapsed	disk	query	current	rows
Parse	1	0.00	0.00	0	0	0	0
Execute	1	0.05	0.13	0	0	1	0
Fetch	73370	14.88	14.95	2071	4165	2093	73369
total	73372	14.93	15.08	2071	4165	2094	73369

```
Rows       Execution Plan
0          SELECT STATEMENT    GOAL: CHOOSE
73369        SORT (ORDER BY)
137807         HASH JOIN
886              TABLE ACCESS   GOAL: ANALYZED (FULL) OF 'PURCHASE_ORDERS'
73726            TABLE ACCESS   GOAL: ANALYZED (FULL) OF  'PURCHASE_ORDER_LINES'
```

The HASH join has proved to be the most efficient because it puts the PURCHASE_ORDERS table into a hash table, then scans to retrieve the corresponding records from PURCHASE_ORDER_LINES. If you cannot get the correct order of access, you can use the SWAP_JOIN_INPUTS hint as well.

Oracle chose to do a NESTED LOOPS method of joining the tables, but this method was not the most efficient way of joining in this case. Using the USE_HASH hint, you can cut CPU time by almost 40 percent and logical I/Os by about 98 percent. Although the CPU reduction is impressive, the reduction in logical I/Os (memory reads) is saving SGA memory for other users. Sometimes when you are retrieving a large amount of data, access using a full table scan is the most efficient method.

TIP
To change the method that Oracle uses to join multiple tables, use the USE_MERGE, USE_NL, and USE_HASH hints. Multiple tables may need to be specified for the hint to work, and the driving order will usually be from first to last in the FROM clause.

Eliminating Join Records (Candidate Rows) in Multitable Joins

Suppose you have a list of 1000 residents of your town along with each resident's street address, and you are asked to prepare an *alphabetized* list of residents who have the newspaper delivered to their home. (Only 50 get the newspaper.) You could first alphabetize the list of 1000 names (all residents in the town), and then look up each street address in the list of 50 residents who get the newspaper. (Sort the 1000 and then find the 50.) A faster method would be to look up each

HASH Join Parameters

street address of those who get the newspaper first, and then get the names of the residents at that street and do the alphabetization last. (Find the 50 who get the newspaper from the list of 1000, and then sort the 50 matches.) Either way, you will need to look at the 1000 street addresses. However, these lookups will eliminate many names from the list, and the sorting will be faster when you have a list of only 50 to sort.

You can apply the same concept when writing SQL joining tables together. The Oracle optimizer is pretty smart about choosing the most efficient order in which to perform tasks, but how a query is written can constrain the options available to the optimizer.

The query in Listing 9-22 leaves the optimizer no choice but to read all of Acme's invoice lines (the large table/the intersection table), when in fact, only the unpaid invoices (the small table) are of interest.

```
select     v.vendor_num, i.invoice_num, sum (l.amount)
from       vendors v, invoices i, invoice_lines l
where      v.vendor_name = 'ACME'
and        l.vendor_num = v.vendor_num
and        i.vendor_num = l.vendor_num
and        i.invoice_num = l.invoice_num
and        i.paid = 'N'
group by   v.vendor_num, i.invoice_num
order by   i.invoice_num
```

Listing 9-22: INVOICE_LINES as the intersection table

You could rewrite this query as shown in Listing 9-23.

```
select     v.vendor_num, i.invoice_num, sum (l.amount)
from       vendors v, invoices i, invoice_lines l
where      v.vendor_name = 'ACME'
and        i.vendor_num = v.vendor_num
and        i.paid = 'N'
and        l.vendor_num = i.vendor_num
and        l.invoice_num = i.invoice_num
group by   v.vendor_num, i.invoice_num
order by   i.invoice_num
```

Listing 9-23: INVOICES as the intersection table

In the rewritten query in Listing 9-23, the optimizer eliminates all of the paid invoices (the new intersection table) before joining to the INVOICE_LINES table. If most of the invoices in the database have already been paid, then the rewritten query will be significantly faster. (The schema design in this example is dubious, and is used only for illustrative purposes.)

TIP
In a three-table join, the driving table is the intersection table or the table that has a join condition to each of the other two tables in the join. Try to use the most limiting table as the driving table (or intersection table) so that your result set from the join of the first two tables is small when you join it to the third table.

A Two-Table Join Between a Large and Small Table

Consider the following tables that will be used for this example:

```
PRODUCT           70 thousand rows      Index on PRODUCT_ID
PRODUCT_LINES   4 million rows        Index on PRODUCT_ID
```

This section uses only cost-based optimization on Oracle8. This is an important section of examples because it looks at a situation often encountered. It involves a two-table join between a small (business small) and a large table. The subsequent conditions (beyond the join itself) are on the column that we are joining. At times, the index on this column in the subsequent condition is suppressed. Unfortunately, this situation leads to seven possible situations, based on various conditions. This section covers three of the main situations, and the results are summarized at the end.

Example I

Neither table can use an index (they are suppressed), and there are no other conditions (Listing 9-24).

```
select    product.name, product_lines.qty
from      product, product_lines
where     product.product_id || ''  = product_lines.product_id || '';
```

Listing 9-24: Two table join; Indexes can't be used

EXPLAIN PLAN output:

```
SELECT STATEMENT Optimizer=CHOOSE
  HASH JOIN
    TABLE ACCESS FULL OF 'PRODUCT'
    TABLE ACCESS FULL OF 'PRODUCT_LINES'
```

```
select    product.name, product_lines.qty
from      product_lines, product
where     product.product_id || ''  = product_lines.product_id || '' ;
```

Listing 9-25: Reversing the order of the tables in the FROM clause

EXPLAIN PLAN output:

```
SELECT STATEMENT Optimizer=CHOOSE
  HASH JOIN
    TABLE ACCESS FULL OF 'PRODUCT'
    TABLE ACCESS FULL OF 'PRODUCT_LINES'
```

Example I Outcome

All conditions being equal, the *first* table in the FROM clause in cost-based optimization is the driving table. However, because these tables are different sizes, Oracle chooses the smaller table

HASH Join Parameters

to be the driving table regardless of the order in the FROM clause. The product table is used to build a hash table on the join key (PRODUCT_ID), and then the PRODUCT_LINES table is scanned, probing the hash table for join key matches.

TIP
Using cost-based optimization, when a large and small table are joined, the smaller table is used to build a hash table in memory on the join key. The larger table is scanned and then probes the hash table for matches to the join key. Also note that if there is not enough memory for the hash, the operation can become extremely slow because the hash table may be split into multiple partitions that could be paged to disk. If the ORDERED hint is specified, then the first table in the FROM clause will be the driving table and it will be the one used to build the hash table.

Example 2
A subsequent clause allows the large table to use the PRODUCT_ID index (Listing 9-26).

```
select     product.name, product_lines.qty
from       product, product_lines
where      product.product_id = product_lines.product_id
and        product_lines.product_id = 4488;
```

Listing 9-26: Adding a subsequent clause (additional predicate)

EXPLAIN PLAN output:

```
SELECT STATEMENT Optimizer=CHOOSE
  MERGE JOIN
    TABLE ACCESS BY INDEX ROWID PRODUCT
      INDEX RANGE SCAN PRODUCT_ID1
    BUFFER SORT
      TABLE ACCESS BY INDEX ROWID PRODUCT_LINES
        INDEX RANGE SCAN PRODUCT1
```

```
select     product.name, product_lines.qty
from       product_lines, product
where      product.product_id = product_lines.product_id
and        product_lines.product_id = 4488;
```

Listing 9-27: Reversing the order of the tables in the FROM clause

EXPLAIN PLAN output:

```
SELECT STATEMENT Optimizer=CHOOSE
  MERGE JOIN
    TABLE ACCESS BY INDEX ROWID PRODUCT
      INDEX RANGE SCAN PRODUCT_ID1
```

```
    BUFFER SORT
        TABLE ACCESS BY INDEX ROWID PRODUCT_LINES
            INDEX RANGE SCAN PRODUCT1
```

Example 2 Outcomes

When a subsequent condition on PRODUCT_ID on the large table exists, the larger table is always
the driving table regardless of the order in the FROM clause. The order of the tables in the FROM
clause will not alter the order in which Oracle performs this join unless an ORDERED hint is used.
In example 2, a SORT-MERGE join is executed.

TIP
*Using cost-based optimization, when a large and small table are
joined, the larger table is the driving table if an index can be used
on the large table. If the ORDERED hint is specified, then the first
table in the FROM clause will be the driving table.*

Example 3

A subsequent clause allows the small table to use the PRODUCT_ID index. The large table will
still drive the query after getting this condition (on PRODUCT_ID) passed to it by the join. Oracle
is smart enough to figure out that PRODUCT_ID exists in both tables and it is more efficient to
limit the PRODUCT_LINES table. In the "Three-Table Joins: Not as Much Fun (Cost-Based)" section
of this chapter, Oracle's excellent internal processing to improve queries will become more evident.

```
select      product.name, product_lines.qty
from        product, product_lines
where       product.product_id = product_lines.product_id
and         product.product_id = 4488;
```

Listing 9-28: Adding a subsequent clause (additional predicate)

EXPLAIN PLAN output:

```
SELECT STATEMENT Optimizer=CHOOSE
    MERGE JOIN
        TABLE ACCESS BY INDEX ROWID PRODUCT
            INDEX RANGE SCAN PRODUCT_ID1
        BUFFER SORT
            TABLE ACCESS BY INDEX ROWID PRODUCT_LINES
                INDEX RANGE SCAN PRODUCT1
```

```
select      product.name, product_lines.qty
from        product_lines, product
where       product.product_id = product_lines.product_id
and         product.product_id = 4488;
```

Listing 9-29: Reversing the table order

HASH Join Parameters

EXPLAIN PLAN output:

```
SELECT STATEMENT Optimizer=CHOOSE
  MERGE JOIN
    TABLE ACCESS BY INDEX ROWID PRODUCT
      INDEX RANGE SCAN PRODUCT_ID1
    BUFFER SORT
      TABLE ACCESS BY INDEX ROWID PRODUCT_LINES
        INDEX RANGE SCAN PRODUCT1
```

Example 3 Outcomes
When a subsequent condition on PRODUCT_ID on the small table exists, the larger table gets this condition passed to it via the join and is *still* the driving table. The order of the tables in the FROM clause will not alter the procedure unless an ORDERED hint is used.

Summary
The examples in this section demonstrate the value of some of the optimizer's behavior. It almost always chooses how to drive a query correctly, but sometimes it must be corrected for a given query. It chooses the right path in most situations.

Three-Table Joins: Not as Much Fun (Cost-Based)

In a three-table join, Oracle joins two of the tables and joins the result with the third table.

When the query in Listing 9-30 is executed, the EMP, DEPT, and ORDERS tables will be joined together, as illustrated in Figure 9-5.

```
select    /*+ ORDERED +/ ENAME, DEPT.DEPTNO, ITEMNO
from      EMP, DEPT, ORDERS
where     emp.deptno = dept.deptno
and       emp.empno = orders.empno
```

Listing 9-30: A three table join

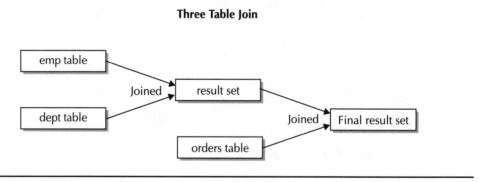

FIGURE 9-5. *A Three-Table Join*

Which table is the driving table in a query? People often give different answers depending on the query that accesses the PLAN_TABLE. Listing 9-31 shows a query that has only one possible way to be accessed (the subqueries must be accessed first) and a query to the PLAN_TABLE that will be used for the remainder of this chapter. This listing is provided to ensure that you understand how to read the output effectively.

```
explain plan for
 select    name
 from      customer
 where     cust_no =
  (select  cust_no
   from    product_lines
   where   qty = 1
   and     product_id =
    (select  product_id
     from    product
     where   product.product_id = 807
     and     description = 'test'));
```

Listing 9-31: A query to guarantee table access order

Listing 9-32 is quick and simple EXPLAIN PLAN query (given the PLAN_TABLE is empty).

```
select    lpad(' ',2*level)||operation oper, options, object_name
from      plan_table
connect   by prior id = parent_id
start     with id = 1
order by  id;
```

Listing 9-32: The EXPLAIN PLAN query

Listing 9-33 shows an abbreviated EXPLAIN PLAN output. (See Chapter 6 for additional EXPLAIN PLAN information.)

OPER	OPTIONS	OBJECT_NAME
TABLE ACCESS	BY INDEX ROWID	CUSTOMER
INDEX	RANGE SCAN	CUST1
TABLE ACCESS	BY INDEX ROWID	PRODUCT_LINES
INDEX	RANGE SCAN	PRODUCT_ID1
TABLE ACCESS	BY INDEX ROWID	PRODUCT
INDEX	RANGE SCAN	PRODUCT1

Listing 9-33: EXPLAIN PLAN Output

The order of access is PRODUCT, PRODUCT_LINES, and CUSTOMER. The innermost subquery (to the product table) must execute first so that it can return the PRODUCT_ID to be used in the PRODUCT_LINES table (accessed second), which returns the CUST_NO that the CUSTOMER table (accessed third) needs.

HASH Join Parameters

TIP
*To ensure that you are reading your EXPLAIN PLAN correctly, run a
query in which you are sure of the driving table (with nested subqueries).*

One exception to the previous subquery is shown in Listing 9-34.

```
explain plan for
 select    name
 from      customer
 where     cust_no =
  (select  cust_no
   from     product_lines
   where    product_lines.product_id = 807
   and      qty = 1
   and      product_id =
    (select   product_id
     from      product
     where     product.product_id = 807
     and       description = 'test'));
```

Listing 9-34: The optimizer passes the subquery condition outward

EXPLAIN PLAN output:

OPER	OPTIONS	OBJECT_NAME
TABLE ACCESS	BY INDEX ROWID	CUSTOMER
INDEX	RANGE SCAN	CUST1
FILTER		
TABLE ACCESS	BY INDEX ROWID	PRODUCT_LINES
INDEX	RANGE SCAN	PRODUCT_ID1
TABLE ACCESS	BY INDEX ROWID	PRODUCT
INDEX	RANGE SCAN	PRODUCT1

The expected order of table access is based on the order in the FROM clause: PRODUCT,
PRODUCT_LINES, and CUSTOMER. The actual order of access is PRODUCT_LINES, PRODUCT,
and CUSTOMER. The PRODUCT_LINES query takes the PRODUCT_ID from the subquery to the
PRODUCT table and executes first.

Bitmap Join Indexes

Oracle changes the boundaries of relational database design and implementation with the
addition of new indexing features. The bitmap join index allows you to build a single index
across the joined columns of two tables. The ROWIDs from one table are stored along with the
other table. Both of these features are incredible performance gold mines, which was also the
case of the function-based index, and they are as powerful as the designer, developer, or DBA
who implements them. This section focuses on the bitmap join index.

Bitmap Indexes

To fully appreciate where a bitmap join index is helpful, it is important to understand a bitmap index. Bitmap indexes are most helpful in a data warehouse environment because they are generally great (fast) when you are only SELECTing data. A bitmap index is smaller than a b-tree index because it stores only the ROWID and a series of bits. In a bitmap index, if a bit is set, it means that a row in the corresponding ROWID (also stored) contains a key value. For example, consider the EMP table with two new columns, gender and marital status:

Empno	Gender (M/F)	Married (Y/N)
1001	F	Y
1002	F	Y
1003	F	N
1004	M	N
1005	M	Y

The bitmaps stored may be the following (the actual storage depends on the algorithm used internally):

Empno=	Gender=F	Married=Y
1001	1	1
1002	1	1
1003	1	0
1004	0	0
1005	0	1

As you can tell from the previous example, it would be easy to find all of the females by searching for the gender bit set to a '1' in the example. You can similarly find all of those married or even quickly find a combination of gender and marital status.

You should use b-tree indexes when columns are unique or near unique; you should at least consider bitmap indexes in all other cases. Although you generally would *not* use a b-tree index when retrieving 40 percent of the rows in a table, using a bitmap index usually makes this task faster than doing a full table scan. This is seemingly in violation of the 80/20 or 95/5 rules, which are generally to use an index when retrieving 5–20 percent or less of the data and to do a full table scan when retrieving more. Bitmap indexes are smaller and work differently than b-tree indexes. You can use bitmap indexes even when retrieving large percentages (20–80 percent) of a table. You can also use bitmaps to retrieve conditions based on NULLs (because NULLs are also indexed), and can be used for not equal conditions for the same reason. The best way to find out is to test!

Bitmap Index Caveats

Bitmap indexes do not perform well in a heavy DML (UPDATE, INSERT, DELETE) environment and generally are not used in certain areas of an OLTP environment. There is a heavy cost if you are doing a lot of DML, so be very careful with this. Also, be careful if you are still using the rule-based optimization; bitmap indexes are *not* considered by the rule-based optimizer. Using NOT NULL constraints and fixed-length columns help bitmaps use less storage, so a good designer is once again worth his or her weight in gold. Use the INDEX_COMBINE hint instead of the INDEX or AND_EQUAL hints for bitmap indexes. Like b-tree indexes, bitmap indexes should be rebuilt (alter index...rebuild) if there is a lot of DML (UPDATE, INSERT, DELETE) activity.

Bitmap Join Index

In a typical business relational database, you are often joining the same two or three tables over and over. The bitmap join index can give you substantial gains when properly applied to many of these circumstances. In a bitmap join index, the ROWIDs from one table are stored along with the indexed column from the joined table. The bitmap join index in Oracle9i is a lot like building a single index across two tables. You must build a primary key or unique constraint on one of the tables. When you are looking for information from just the columns in the index or a count, then you will be able to access the single join index. Let's look at a very simplistic example to learn how to use it. Then we'll look at how you can apply it to multiple columns and multiple tables.

Example I

Let's create two sample tables to use from our friendly EMP and DEPT tables, as shown in Listing 9-35.

```
create table emp1
as select * from scott.emp;

create table dept1
as select * from scott.dept;
```

Listing 9-35: Creating EMP and DEPT tables

You must then add a unique constraint (or have a primary key) to the DEPT1 table to use this type of index. You can then create the bitmap index on the EMP1 table that includes the columns of both tables (Listing 9-36).

```
alter table dept1
add constraint dept_constr1 unique (deptno);

create bitmap index empdept_idx
 on emp1(dept1.deptno)
 from emp1, dept1
 where emp1.deptno = dept1.deptno;
```

Listing 9-36: Adding the constraint and creating a bitmap index

You are now storing the ROWID to the DEPT1 table in the bitmap index that maps to the DEPTNO column in the EMP1 table. To test how well this works, you can perform a simple count(*) of the intersection rows between the two tables (you would usually have additional limiting conditions), forcing the use of the bitmap index with an INDEX hint (Listing 9-37).

```
select /*+ index(emp1 empdept_idx) */ count(*)
from    emp1, dept1
where   emp1.deptno = dept1.deptno;
```

Listing 9-37: Forcing the bitmap join index

```
COUNT(*)
---------------
       14
Elapsed: 00:00:00.67
Execution Plan
-----------------------------------------------------------
    0        SELECT STATEMENT Optimizer=CHOOSE
    1   0      SORT (AGGREGATE)
    2   1        BITMAP CONVERSION (COUNT)
    3   2          BITMAP INDEX (FULL SCAN) OF 'EMPDEPT_IDX'
```

You can see from the AUTOTRACE output (using SET AUTOTRACE ON while in SQL*Plus) that the bitmap index was used. Although this simplistic example shows how to count an index (instead of the table) and uses some benefits of the bitmap join index, the next section explores better uses by manipulating columns outside the join in the index.

Best Uses for the Bitmap Join Index

Example 1 showed a basic use of the bitmap join index focusing on just the joined columns. The next three sections show targeted areas where you may find the best use of the bitmap join index.

Bitmap Join Indexes on Columns Other Than the Join

Consider this example where EMP1 and DEPT1 tables are once again joined on the DEPTNO column. In this example, you want to index the LOC column instead of the join column. This allows you to select the location column from the DEPT1 table by directly accessing only the index and the EMP1 table. Remember, the join condition must be on the primary key or unique column. The example in Listing 9-38 assumes that the unique constraint on dept1.deptno from the previous example in Listing 9-36 exists.

```
Create bitmap index emp_dept_location
on     emp1 (dept1.loc)
from   emp1, dept1
where  emp1.deptno = dept1.deptno;
```

Listing 9-38: Creating the bitmap join index

The query in Listing 9-39 can now use the bitmap join index appropriately.

```
select emp1.empno, emp1.ename, dept1.loc
from    emp1, dept1
where   emp1.deptno = dept1.deptno;
```

Listing 9-39: The bitmap join index is used

Bitmap Join Indexes on Multiple Columns

Consider an example where you want an index on multiple columns. The syntax is still the same, but now you include multiple columns in the index. The example in Listing 9-40 assumes that the unique constraint on dept1.deptno from the previous example in Listing 9-36 exists.

```
Create bitmap index emp_dept_location_deptname
on     emp1 (dept1.loc, dept1.dname)
from   emp1, dept1
where  emp1.deptno = dept1.deptno;
```

Listing 9-40: Creating the bitmap join index

The query in Listing 9-41 would now be able to use the bitmap join index appropriately.

```
select emp1.empno, emp1.ename, dept1.loc, dept1.dname
from   emp1, dept1
where  emp1.deptno = dept1.deptno;
```

Listing 9-41: The bitmap join index can now be used

Bitmap Join Indexes on Multiple Tables

As you become more familiar with using the bitmap join index, you will be able to solve complex business problems that involve multiple tables. The following example shows how to apply the bitmap join index to multiple tables. The syntax is still the same, but it has now been expanded to include multiple columns in the index and multiple tables being joined for the index. The example in Listing 9-42 assumes that the unique constraint on dept1.deptno from the previous example in Listing 9-36 exists and additionally on sales1.empno (creation not shown).

```
Create bitmap index emp_dept_location_ms
on     emp1 (dept1.loc, sales1.marital_status)
from   emp1, dept1, sales1
where  emp1.deptno = dept1.deptno
and    emp1.empno = sales1.empno;
```

Listing 9-42: Creating the bitmap join index

The query in Listing 9-43 would now be able to use the bitmap join index appropriately.

```
select emp1.empno, emp1.ename, dept1.loc, sales1.marital_status
from   emp1, dept1, sales1
where  emp1.deptno = dept1.deptno;
and    emp1.empno = sales1.empno;
```

Listing 9-43: The bitmap join index is used

Bitmap Join Index Caveats

Because the result of the join is stored, only one table can be updated concurrently by different transactions, and parallel DML is supported only on the fact table. Parallel DML on the dimension table marks the index unusable. No table can appear twice in the join, and you can't create a bitmap join index on an index-organized table (IOT) or a temporary table.

Another Nice Use for the Join Index

A nice tuning trick when you are counting rows is to try to count the index instead of the table. Consider the following large table example used for counting. These tables each contain roughly 2 million rows each so that you can see the impact that is possible on a larger scale. The new tables, EMP5 and EMP6, each have 2 million rows with empno indexes on them (Listing 9-44).

```
alter table emp5
add constraint emp5_constr unique (empno);select count(*)
from emp5, emp6
where emp5.empno=emp6.empno;
```

Listing 9-44: Adding the constraint and running a join without the bitmap index

```
  COUNT(*)
------------------
   2005007
Elapsed: 00:01:07.18

Execution Plan
----------------------------------------------------------
   0        SELECT STATEMENT Optimizer=CHOOSE
   1    0   SORT (AGGREGATE)
   2    1    NESTED LOOPS
   3    2     TABLE ACCESS (FULL) OF 'EMP6'
   4    2     INDEX (RANGE SCAN) OF 'EMP5I_EMPNO' (NON-UNIQUE)

Statistics
----------------------------------------------------------
6026820  consistent gets
7760  physical reads
```

There is an index on the EMP5 table, but there is no correlation or index back to the EMP6 table because the index on EMP6 has only empno as the second part of a concatenated index. The result is a relatively slow query. If you make empno the only part or the leading part of the concatenated index, you will solve this problem. Instead, use the new Oracle9*i* bitmap join index, as shown in Listing 9-45.

```
create bitmap index emp5_j6
 on emp6(emp5.empno)
 from emp5,emp6
 where emp5.empno=emp6.empno;
Index created.

Elapsed: 00:02:29.91

select /*+ index(emp6 emp5_j6) */ count(*)
from emp5, emp6
where emp5.empno=emp6.empno;
```

Listing 9-45: Creating and using the bitmap join index

```
  COUNT(*)
-------------------
  2005007
Elapsed: 00:00:00.87


Execution Plan
-----------------------------------------------------------
   0       SELECT STATEMENT Optimizer=CHOOSE
   1    0     SORT (AGGREGATE)
   2    1       BITMAP CONVERSION (COUNT)
   3    2         BITMAP INDEX (FULL SCAN) OF 'EMP5_J6'


Statistics
-----------------------------------------------------------
970   consistent gets
967   physical reads
```

Performing a count of the bitmap join index makes this very fast. I chose this example for a reason. The real problem with the original slow query was not that it took a minute to execute, but that it performed over 6 million memory block reads and over 7 thousand disk block reads. You may not receive any wait events, but you have a poorly written query that will cause problems when you begin to have volumes of users on the system. Take a step up to expert level by finding queries with large memory and disk reads and do proactive tuning so you don't get to wait states and need to reactively tune things. Using a bitmap join index is one way to improve performance.

Third-Party Product Tuning

Sometimes, you are at the mercy of a third-party product. Although you cannot modify the code, you can often modify the use of indexes. The following three examples are from a financials third-party product.

Example 1

This query was taking 22 minutes to run. By providing a hint to a more efficient index, the query execution time was reduced to 15 seconds.

Listing 9-46 shows the query before the hint is added.

```
update PS_COMBO_DATA_TBL
set     EFFDT_FROM = TO_DATE ('1990-01-01', 'YYYY-MM-DD'),
        EFFDT_TO = TO_DATE ('2099-01-01', 'YYYY-MM-DD')
where   SETID = 'RRD'
and     PROCESS_GROUP = 'GROUP1'
and     COMBINATION = 'ACCT/NOLOC'
and     VALID_CODE = 'V'
and     EFFDT_OPEN = 'Y'
and     EXISTS
  (select    'X'
   from      PS_JRNL_LN
   where     BUSINESS_UNIT = '00003'
   and       PROCESS_INSTANCE = 0000085176
   and       JRNL_LINE_STATUS = '3'
```

```
and        ACCOUNT = PS_COMBO_DATA_TBL.ACCOUNT
and        PRODUCT = PS_COMBO_DATA_TBL.PRODUCT )
```

Listing 9-46: Query before adding the hint

Listing 9-47 shows the query after the hint is added.

```
update PS_COMBO_DATA_TBL
set    EFFDT_FROM = TO_DATE ('1990-01-01', 'YYYY-MM-DD'),
       EFFDT_TO = TO_DATE ('2099-01-01', 'YYYY-MM-DD')
where  SETID = 'RRD'
and    PROCESS_GROUP = 'GROUP1'
and    COMBINATION = 'ACCT/NOLOC'
and    VALID_CODE = 'V'
and    EFFDT_OPEN = 'Y'
and    EXISTS
 (select   /*+ INDEX(PS_JRNL_LN PSGJRNL_LN) */  'X'
  from     PS_JRNL_LN
  where    BUSINESS_UNIT = '00003'
  and      PROCESS_INSTANCE = 0000085176
  and      JRNL_LINE_STATUS = '3'
  and      ACCOUNT = PS_COMBO_DATA_TBL.ACCOUNT
  and      PRODUCT = PS_COMBO_DATA_TBL.PRODUCT )
```

Listing 9-47: Query after adding the INDEX hint

Example 2

The query in Listing 9-48 was taking 33 minutes to run. By creating a concatenated index on the PS_GROUP_CONTROL table (columns: DEPOSIT_BU, DEPOSIT_ID, PAYMENT_SEQ_NUM), the query execution time was reduced to 30 seconds (Listing 9-48).

```
select    C.BUSINESS_UNIT, C.CUST_ID,  C.ITEM,
          C.ENTRY_TYPE, C.ENTRY_REASON, C.ENTRY_AMT,
          C.ENTRY_CURRENCY, C.ENTRY_AMT_BASE,
          C.CURRENCY_CD, C.POSTED_FLAG, D.PAYMENT_SEQ_NUM
from      PS_PENDING_ITEM C,
          PS_GROUP_CONTROL D
where     D.DEPOSIT_BU = :1
and       D.DEPOSIT_ID = :2
and       D.PAYMENT_SEQ_NUM = :3
and       D.GROUP_BU = C.GROUP_BU
and       D.GROUP_ID = C.GROUP_ID
order by  D.PAYMENT_SEQ_NUM
```

Listing 9-48: Index on PS_GROUP_CONTROL helped performance

EXPLAIN PLAN before index is added:

```
Execution Plan
RULE SELECT STATEMENT
```

```
    SORT ORDER BY
      NESTED LOOPS
        ANALYZED TABLE ACCESS FULL PS_GROUP_CONTROL
        ANALYZED TABLE ACCESS BY ROWID PS_PENDING_ITEM
          ANALYZED INDEX RANGE SCAN PS_PENDING_ITEM
```

EXPLAIN PLAN after index is added:

```
Execution Plan
RULE SELECT STATEMENT
      SORT ORDER BY
        NESTED LOOPS
          ANALYZED TABLE ACCESS BY ROWID PS_GROUP_CONTROL
            INDEX RANGE SCAN PSAGROUP_CONTROL
          ANALYZED TABLE ACCESS BY ROWID PS_PENDING_ITEM
            ANALYZED INDEX RANGE SCAN PS_PENDING_ITEM
```

Example 3

The query in Listing 9-49 was taking 20 minutes to run and was reduced to 30 seconds. You create a concatenated unique index on the PS_CUST_OPTION table (columns: CUST_ID, EFFDT) instead of the current index, which is only on CUST_ID. This forces Oracle to use a concatenated unique index rather than a single-column index, as shown in Listing 9-49.

```
INSERT INTO PS_PP_CUST_TMP  (PROCESS_INSTANCE,
 DEPOSIT_BU, DEPOSIT_ID, PAYMENT_SEQ_NUM, CUST_ID,
 PAYMENT_AMT, PAYMENT_DT, PP_METHOD, SETID,
 SUBCUST_QUAL1, SUBCUST_QUAL2, PP_HOLD, PP_MET_SW,
 PAYMENT_CURRENCY)
select    DISTINCT P.PROCESS_INSTANCE, P.DEPOSIT_BU,
          P.DEPOSIT_ID, P.PAYMENT_SEQ_NUM, C.CUST_ID,
          P.PAYMENT_AMT,   P.PAYMENT_DT, O.PP_METHOD,
          O.SETID, C.SUBCUST_QUAL1, C.SUBCUST_QUAL2,
          O.PP_HOLD, 'N', P.PAYMENT_CURRENCY
from      PS_CUST_OPTION O, PS_CUSTOMER C, PS_ITEM I,
          PS_SET_CNTRL_REC S, PS_PAYMENT_ID_ITEM X,
          PS_PP_PAYMENT_TMP P
where     P.PROCESS_INSTANCE = 85298
and       S.SETCNTRLVALUE = I.BUSINESS_UNIT
and       I.CUST_ID = C.CUST_ID
and       I.ITEM_STATUS = 'O'
and       (X.REF_VALUE = I.DOCUMENT
or        SUBSTR (X.REF_VALUE, 3, 7)
          = SUBSTR (I.DOCUMENT, 4, 7))
and       S.RECNAME = 'CUSTOMER'
and       S.SETID = C.SETID
and       O.SETID = C.REMIT_FROM_SETID
and       O.CUST_ID = C.REMIT_FROM_CUST_ID
and       O.EFFDT =
      (select    MAX (X.EFFDT)
       from       PS_CUST_OPTION X
```

```
      where      X.SETID = O.SETID
      and        X.CUST_ID = O.CUST_ID
      and        X.EFF_STATUS = 'A'
      and        X.EFFDT <= P.PAYMENT_DT)
and        O.PP_METHOD <> ' '
and        P.DEPOSIT_BU = X.DEPOSIT_BU
and        P.DEPOSIT_ID = X.DEPOSIT_ID
and        P.PAYMENT_SEQ_NUM = X.PAYMENT_SEQ_NUM
and        X.REF_QUALIFIER_CODE = 'D';
```

Listing 9-49: Unique concatenated index on PS_CUST_OPTION helped performance

EXPLAIN PLAN before index added:

```
Execution Plan
RULE INSERT STATEMENT
     SORT UNIQUE
       NESTED LOOPS
         NESTED LOOPS
           NESTED LOOPS
             NESTED LOOPS
               NESTED LOOPS
                 ANALYZED TABLE ACCESS BY ROWID PS_PP_PAYMENT_TMP
                   ANALYZED INDEX RANGE SCAN PSAPP_PAYMENT_TMP
                 ANALYZED INDEX RANGE SCAN PSAPAYMENT_ID_ITEM
               ANALYZED INDEX RANGE SCAN PSDSET_CNTRL_REC
             ANALYZED INDEX RANGE SCAN PSEITEM
           ANALYZED TABLE ACCESS BY ROWID PS_CUSTOMER
           ANALYZED INDEX UNIQUE SCAN PS_CUSTOMER
         ANALYZED TABLE ACCESS BY ROWID PS_CUST_OPTION
         ANALYZED INDEX RANGE SCAN PSACUST_OPTION
       SORT AGGREGATE
       ANALYZED TABLE ACCESS BY ROWID PS_CUST_OPTION
         ANALYZED INDEX RANGE SCAN PSACUST_OPTION
```

EXPLAIN PLAN after index added:

```
Execution Plan
RULE INSERT STATEMENT
     SORT UNIQUE
       NESTED LOOPS
         NESTED LOOPS
           NESTED LOOPS
             NESTED LOOPS
               NESTED LOOPS
                 ANALYZED TABLE ACCESS BY ROWID PS_PP_PAYMENT_TMP
                   ANALYZED INDEX RANGE SCAN PSAPP_PAYMENT_TMP
                 ANALYZED INDEX RANGE SCAN PSAPAYMENT_ID_ITEM
               ANALYZED INDEX RANGE SCAN PSDSET_CNTRL_REC
             ANALYZED INDEX RANGE SCAN PSEITEM
```

Bitmap Indexes

```
        ANALYZED TABLE ACCESS BY ROWID PS_CUSTOMER
          ANALYZED INDEX UNIQUE SCAN PS_CUSTOMER
      ANALYZED TABLE ACCESS BY ROWID PS_CUST_OPTION
        ANALYZED INDEX RANGE SCAN PS_CUST_OPTION
    SORT AGGREGATE
      ANALYZED TABLE ACCESS BY ROWID PS_CUST_OPTION
        ANALYZED INDEX RANGE SCAN PS_CUST_OPTION
```

TIP
You may not be able to modify actual code for some third-party products, but you can often add, force, or suppress indexes to improve the performance.

Tuning Distributed Queries

When improperly written, distributed queries can sometimes be disastrous and lead to poor performance. In particular, a NESTED LOOPS join between two row sources on separate nodes of a distributed database can be very slow because Oracle moves all the data to the local machine (depending on how the query is written). Listing 9-50 shows a simple distributed query and its execution plan. This query is slow because for each row retrieved from the CUSTOMERS table, a separate query is dispatched to the remote node to retrieve records from the bookings table. This results in many small network packets moving between the two nodes of the database, and the network latency and overhead degrade performance.

```
select    customer_id, customer_name, class_code
from      customers cust
where     exists
(select   1
 from     bookings@book bkg
 where    bkg.customer_id = cust.customer_id
 and      bkg.status = 'OPEN' )
order by  customer_name;
```

TKPROF output:

call	count	cpu	elapsed	disk	query	current	rows
Parse	1	0.00	0.01	0	0	0	0
Execute	1	0.00	0.00	0	0	0	0
Fetch	156	0.41	11.85	0	476	2	155
total	158	0.41	11.86	0	476	2	155

```
Rows    Execution Plan
0       SELECT STATEMENT    GOAL: CHOOSE
155       SORT (ORDER BY)
467         FILTER
467           TABLE ACCESS    GOAL: ANALYZED (FULL) OF 'CUSTOMERS'
0               REMOTE [BOOK.WORLD]
```

```
SELECT "CUSTOMER_ID","STATUS" FROM "BOOKINGS" BKG WHERE
     "STATUS"='open' AND "CUSTOMER_ID"=:1
```

Listing 9-50: Inefficient distributed query

The query in Listing 9-50 can be rewritten in a form that causes less network traffic. In Listing 9-51, one query is sent to the remote node to determine all customers with open bookings. The output is the same but performance is greatly improved. Both versions of the query use roughly the same CPU time and logical I/Os on the local node, but the elapsed time is about 97 percent better in Listing 9-51. This gain is attributable to reduced network overhead.

```
select     customer_id, customer_name, class_code
from       customers
where      customer_id in
(select    customer_id
 from      bookings@book
 where     status = 'OPEN' )
order by   customer_name;
```

TKPROF output:

call	count	cpu	elapsed	disk	query	current	rows
Parse	1	0.00	0.01	0	0	0	0
Execute	1	0.00	0.00	0	0	0	0
Fetch	156	0.07	0.27	0	467	0	155
total	158	0.07	0.28	0	467	0	155

```
Rows    Execution Plan
0       SELECT STATEMENT    GOAL: CHOOSE
155       SORT (ORDER BY)
155        NESTED LOOPS
156         VIEW
1000         SORT (UNIQUE)
1000          REMOTE [BOOK.WORLD]
                  SELECT "CUSTOMER_ID","STATUS" FROM "BOOKINGS" BOOKINGS WHERE
                      "STATUS"='open'
155         TABLE ACCESS    GOAL: ANALYZED (BY ROWID) OF 'CUSTOMERS'
156          INDEX    GOAL: ANALYZED (UNIQUE SCAN) OF 'SYS_C002109'
                  (UNIQUE)
```

Listing 9-51: Tuned distributed query

When distributed queries cannot be avoided, use IN clauses, set operators such as UNION and MINUS, and use everything else you can to reduce the network traffic between nodes of the database. Using views that limit the records in a table can also improve performance by reducing what is sent from the remote client to the local client. With Oracle8, you can use the DRIVING_SITE hint to control which node of the distributed database drives the distributed query. In Oracle7, the driving site is always the local node where the query originated.

Bitmap Indexes

> **TIP**
> *When distributed queries cannot be avoided, use IN clauses, set*
> *operators such as UNION and MINUS, and use everything else you*
> *can to reduce the network traffic between nodes of the database.*
> *Queries written in a manner that causes looping between distributed*
> *nodes (distributed databases) can be extremely slow.*

When You Have Everything Tuned

If you successfully tune all of *your* queries, then you can start working on those that go to the
data dictionary views. The example in Listing 9-52 shows that even Oracle's own views have
some highly complex joining schemes.

```
select     *
from       dba_ind_columns
where      table_name = 'PRODUCT_LINES';
```

Execution plan output:

```
Execution Plan
----------------------------------------------------------
   0      SELECT STATEMENT Optimizer=CHOOSE
   1    0   NESTED LOOPS
   2    1     NESTED LOOPS
   3    2       NESTED LOOPS (OUTER)
   4    3         NESTED LOOPS
   5    4           NESTED LOOPS
   6    5             NESTED LOOPS
   7    6               NESTED LOOPS
   8    7                 TABLE ACCESS (FULL) OF 'IND$'
   9    7                 TABLE ACCESS (BY INDEX ROWID) OF 'OBJ$'
  10    9                   INDEX (UNIQUE SCAN) OF 'I_OBJ1' (UNIQUE)
  11    6                 TABLE ACCESS (CLUSTER) OF 'USER$'
  12   11                   INDEX (UNIQUE SCAN) OF 'I_USER#' (NON-UNIQUE)
  13    5               TABLE ACCESS (BY INDEX ROWID) OF 'ICOL$'
  14   13                 INDEX (RANGE SCAN) OF 'I_ICOL1' (NON-UNIQUE)
  15    4             TABLE ACCESS (CLUSTER) OF 'COL$'
  16    3           TABLE ACCESS (CLUSTER) OF 'ATTRCOL$'
  17    2         TABLE ACCESS (BY INDEX ROWID) OF 'OBJ$'
  18   17           INDEX (UNIQUE SCAN) OF 'I_OBJ1' (UNIQUE)
  19    1       TABLE ACCESS (CLUSTER) OF 'USER$'
  20   19         INDEX (UNIQUE SCAN) OF 'I_USER#' (NON-UNIQUE)
```

Listing 9-52: Example query to data dictionary views

Miscellaneous Tuning Snippets

The issues covered in this section will help the advanced DBA: we'll look briefly at RAC and Linux; we'll explore the Snapshot Too Old developer coding issue along with external tables; and we'll set the event to dump every wait and explore what's really going on by performing block dumps.

Real Application Clusters (RAC)

Full coverage of Oracle9*i* RAC is outside the scope of this book. Therefore, this section simply provides a brief overview. For more information, refer to the online documentation and Metalink notes.

How do you scale the hardware that runs this database so that when you need more CPU power or want to service additional users you have it? Welcome to the world of Oracle9*i* Real Application Clusters! RACs allow you to share *one* database while having *multiple* System Global Areas (SGAs) on multiple pieces of hardware. Using Oracle's *Cache Fusion,* which is a process where you can move data from one SGA to another (saving costly disk I/O) when needed (via a high-speed fiber interconnect), you get the most scalable Oracle to date. It employs a Global Cache Service, which maintains the block mode for blocks in the global role. It is responsible for block transfers between instances. The Global Cache Service employs various background processes such as the Global Cache Service Processes (LMSn) and Global Services Daemon (GSD).

Also, with Cache Fusion in Oracle9*i*, the disk ping protocol has been eliminated (a major benefit over OPS). Cache Fusion changes the use of PCM locks in Oracle and relates locks to the shipping of blocks through the system via IPC. The main ideas are to separate the modes of locks from roles assigned to lock holders, and to maintain knowledge about versions of past images of blocks throughout the system.

Imagine a single database running on an eight-machine cluster (eight machines hooked up by Cache Fusion to the same database) with 256GB of memory on each instance. It's available now from Compaq (Tru64 UNIX); that's 2T of physical memory making 1.7+ TB (terabytes) of combined SGA impossible to imagine, along with 256 CPUs and 10T file systems. Sun and HP provide similar truly super computers. But remember, an Oracle9*i* RAC can be a cluster of two Linux boxes as well. I'm still anxiously awaiting the 16 exabytes (e-cubed?) of addressable memory (theoretically possible in 64 bit, but physically not available yet).

Oracle9*i* RAC provides scalability, availability, and reliability by supplying automatic parallelism across nodes in the RAC cluster, sharing block images through a high-speed interconnect (using Cache Fusion), and allowing for automatic failover to nonfailed nodes in the RAC cluster. Oracle9*i* RAC overcomes limits of shared-nothing databases used by other database vendors such as IBM and Microsoft, by using the shared-disk model and allowing internode block transfer via memory instead of using forced-disk write technology. Because RAC automatically handles node failure, no downtime is required like it is for data rebuild or repartition in shared-nothing configurations.

RAC allows the DBA true transparent scalability. To increase the number of servers in almost all other architectures, changes were required or in many cases, performance would actually get worse. With RAC, current benchmarks show 80–95 percent scalability. This automatic, transparent scaling is due almost entirely to the RAC's Cache Fusion and the unique parallel architecture of the RAC implementation on Oracle9*i*. Each node in the RAC has its own SGA, which pulls in data based on user requests. With Cache Fusion, Oracle checks other node SGAs to see whether data exists in memory (on some node) prior to going to disk to find the data. Cache Fusion is implemented through the high-speed cluster interconnect that runs between the servers. Different types of interconnect exist for different types of hardware, but the interconnect should generally always be 1GB or faster.

If the RAC cluster uses a SAN or other network storage device, this is known as a Shared System Disk (root) system. A RAC system must use a cluster file system, in which any server can read or write to any disk in the shared disk subsystem. This allows any instance access to all datafiles, control files, and redo and rollback areas. The ability to access all disks allows for instance recovery after an instance failure has occurred. The work of the failed instance is automatically absorbed by all surviving nodes until the failed instance is brought back online, at which time, it is fully synchronized and restored to service automatically. Some vendors provide a cluster file system that allows nonraw devices. (Tru64 was the first to provide this functionality.) A RAC cluster provides for automatic shared execution of Oracle applications. Consequently, for any Oracle instance application, all queries and other processing are automatically shared among all of the servers in the RAC cluster. The sharing of application processing to all servers in the RAC cluster leads to automatic load balancing across all cluster members.

Oracle RAC displays great disaster tolerance. If a single or multiple nodes fail, the load is redistributed between all of the remaining nodes. If the database is globally distributed, then a disaster to a single site will not affect other sites.

Red Hat is Red Hot: Linux Is Making a Move

It was bad enough when we discovered that the anti-UNIX web site funded by Microsoft was being run on a copy of FreeBSD UNIX. It was even more evidence explaining why the market is shifting to UNIX when the anti-UNIX web site went offline the next day after switching from FreeBSD UNIX to Windows 2000. Linux didn't really hit the enterprise until Red Hat included clustering capabilities in its Advanced Server enterprise edition.

In May 2002, Red Hat Inc. introduced its latest Linux release designed for use in enterprise environments: Red Hat Linux Advanced Server V2.1. The Red Hat Linux Advanced Server product significantly extends the capabilities provided by the earlier Red Hat Linux High Availability Server products. Red Hat Linux Advanced Server V2.1 is based on the Red Hat Linux V7.2 and Red Hat Linux Professional V7.2 products. It has been designed explicitly for the enterprise computing market to deliver superior application support, performance, availability, and scalability.

The biggest advantage of Advanced Server is the inclusion of a fully featured high availability clustering capability called Cluster Manager. This functionality provides continued application operation in the event of server shutdown or failure. Additionally, the IP Load Balancing (Piranha) network feature provided in the earlier Red Hat Linux High Availability Server product was retained and enhanced. Advanced Server is based on Linux Kernel 2.4.9 and also includes numerous other performance and scalability enhancements. These include support for features such as Asynchronous I/O, increased SMP granularity (particularly in the SCSI I/O subsystem, permitting increased I/O throughput), and SMP Scheduler enhancements (support process-CPU affinity which improves CPU cache hit rate).

The simplest Cluster Manager configuration comprises a pair of servers and an external SCSI or Fibre Channel storage array. Both servers are connected to the external storage array and access its disks directly. The Cluster Manager software is used to control access to storage partitions so that only one server can access a particular partition at a time. This restriction is required because standard applications do not support concurrent access to their data files from multiple systems. Each server then operates in the same manner as if it were a single standalone system, running applications and accessing data on its allocated storage partitions.

Using multiple servers in this fashion is often referred to as *scale-out computing,* that is, adding compute power to a configuration with additional systems; *scale-up computing,* on the other hand, refers to supporting larger numbers of processors in an SMP system. In addition to their connections to the shared storage array, the two servers are also connected to each other using a network or serial interface so that they can communicate with each other. In the event that one of the servers shuts down or fails, the other server detects the event and automatically starts to run the applications that were previously running on the failed server.

The migration of the application from the failed server to the remaining server is called *failover.* Because both servers are connected to the external shared storage, the operational server can access the failed server's disk partitions and its applications can continue to operate normally. If necessary, the remaining server also takes over the IP address of the failed server so that network operations can continue without interruption.

It is worth briefly contrasting Cluster Manager clusters with Oracle RAC clusters. As described earlier, Cluster Manager clusters are suitable for the wide range of applications that have been designed to run on a single server system. Cluster Manager permits these applications to be deployed, unmodified, in a high availability environment. Oracle RAC is one of the few UNIX/Linux applications on the market today that supports concurrent read/write access to a single database from multiple servers. This complex technology is suitable for single-instance database applications that are too large to be handled by a single server. Using Oracle RAC, it is possible to add servers (more than two servers are supported) and increase the transaction rate against a single database.

TIP
RAC provides availability, scalability, and recoverability that will drive the future of computing. Linux is the next operating system wave that you will find Oracle increasingly running on.

External Tables

External tables allow you to access data that is not inside the database. Relational databases took off in the 1980s because of the ability to access data through relational tables. This was the first move away from mainframes and legacy systems that stored information in flat files or some facsimile of that. Oracle9*i* will be the next paradigm in relational database technology. External tables extend the relational model beyond the database. Now we have a means by which to access all of the legacy data. We have a way to access all of that information dumped into flat files (perhaps, via third-party products).

One of the most costly parts of the extract, transform, load (ETL) process used for data warehousing and business intelligence is loading data into temporary tables so that it can be used with other tables already in the database. Although external tables were introduced primarily to assist in the ETL process, Pandora's box cannot be closed. I have seen a plethora of uses for external tables and I believe it's just the beginning. If Java and XML were minor aspects integrated into the relational model, the use of external tables brings the entire machine into the database and forever changes the rules of engagement.

The simple example in Listing 9-53 shows you exactly how to use external tables. First, you need a flat file of data to access for the examples. You do this by simply spooling some data from our familiar friend, the EMP table.

```
spool emp4.dat
set head off
set verify off
set feedback off
set pages 0
select empno||','||ename ||','|| job||','||deptno||','
from    scott.emp;
spool off
```

Output of the emp4.dat file:

```
7369,SMITH,CLERK,20,
7499,ALLEN,SALESMAN,30,
7521,WARD,SALESMAN,30,
7566,JONES,MANAGER,20,
7654,MARTIN,SALESMAN,30,
```

Listing 9-53: Using external tables

Then you need to create a directory from within SQL*Plus so that Oracle knows where to find your external tables.

```
SQL> create directory rich_new as '/u01/home/oracle/rich';
Directory created.
```

You then create the actual table definition that will reference the flat file that resides externally. Note that even if you successfully create the table, access to the external table may not necessarily result in a successful query. If the data is not stored in the column definition of your table, you will get an error when you select the actual data. An example of the create table command is shown in Listing 9-54.

```
create table emp_external4
(empno char(4), ename char(10), job char(9), deptno char(2))
organization external
(type oracle_loader
 default directory rich_new
 access parameters
 (records delimited by newline
  fields terminated by ','
  (empno , ename, job, deptno ))
 location ('emp4.dat'))
reject limit unlimited;
Table created.

SQL> desc emp_external4
Name                              Null?    Type
-----------------------------     -------- --------------
```

```
EMPNO                                      CHAR(4)
ENAME                                      CHAR(10)
JOB                                        CHAR(9)
DEPTNO                                     CHAR(2)

select  *
from    emp_external4;

EMPNO           ENAME           JOB             DEPTNO
--------        --------------  ------------    --------------
7369            SMITH           CLERK           20
7499            ALLEN           SALESMAN        30
7521            WARD            SALESMAN        30
...
```

Listing 9-54: Using the `create table` command

There is currently no support for DML (`insert`, `update`, `delete`) commands, but you can always do this outside the database because the data is in a flat file. Using shell scripting as shown in Listing 9-55, you can certainly replicate those commands. Although you can't create an index currently, external tables are pleasantly and surprisingly fast.

```
SQL> insert into emp_external4 …
            *
ERROR at line 1:
ORA-30657: operation not supported on external organized table
SQL> create index emp_ei on emp_external4(deptno)
                        *
ERROR at line 1:
ORA-30657: operation not supported on external organized table
```

Listing 9-55: Shell scripting

To count records, you can either use the UNIX command or do it within the database. Either way, you have a means to work with data that is in flat files that are not within the database. Listing 9-56 is the wc (word count) command with the -l, which indicates to count the lines. This is a simple UNIX command for counting records in a flat file. I created a file with 200,020 rows for the next more intensive test.

```
$ wc -l emp4.dat
  200020  200020 4400400 emp4.dat
$ ls -l emp4.dat
-rwxr-xr-x   1 oracle   oinstall 4400400 Aug  9 06:31 emp4.dat
```

Listing 9-56: Using the `wc` command

You can also count the records in the flat file using SQL, since you've now built an external table. The command shown in Listing 9-57 takes less than 1 second to return its result.

```
select count(*)
from    emp_external4;
  COUNT(*)
```

```
------------------
    200020
Elapsed: 00:00:00.63
```

Listing 9-57: Counting records in the flat file using SQL

Once you know you can count records in less than 1 second, you press on to look for specific information. Can you count selective pieces of data that fast? Yes. The code in Listing 9-58 looks for specific employee numbers (empno) from the flat file, which is now referenced via an external table. The result is returned to once again in less than 1 second.

```
select count(*)
from    emp_external4
where   empno=7900;


COUNT(*)
     20
Elapsed: 00:00:00.82
```

Listing 9-58: Looking for specific employee numbers from the flat file

Once you know you can scan through 200,000 records in less than 1 second (on a single processor machine in my case), you want to see how fast you can scan through millions of records. The example in Listing 9-59 builds a second table and joins it with the first so you can test scanning through 4 million rows. The result is less than 3 seconds to scan through this massive amount of data using only modest hardware.

```
create table emp_external5
(empno char(4), ename char(10), job char(9), deptno      char(2))
organization external
  ...
location ('emp5.dat'));
```

Listing 9-59: Building a second table and joining it with the first

Now you join the two 200-thousand-row tables to create a join that merges the 20 rows in the first result set with the 20 rows of the second table, as in Listing 9-60. This results in a join accessing 4 million rows with a result set of 400 rows. The result is an answer in less than 3 seconds.

```
select a.empno, b.job, a.job
from    emp_external4 a, emp_external5 b
where   a.empno = b.empno
and     a.empno = 7900
and     b.empno = 7900;
400 rows selected.

Elapsed: 00:00:02.46
```

Listing 9-60: Joining tables and merging result sets

Listing 9-61 shows the execution plan for the previous join.

```
Execution Plan
---------------------------------------------------------------
   0        SELECT STATEMENT Optimizer=CHOOSE
   1    0   MERGE JOIN
   2    1     SORT (JOIN)
   3    2       EXTERNAL TABLE ACCESS (FULL) OF 'EMP_EXTERNAL5'
   4    1     SORT (JOIN)
   5    4       EXTERNAL TABLE ACCESS (FULL) OF 'EMP_EXTERNAL4'
```

Listing 9-61: Execution plan for Listing 9-60

You can also use hints with external tables, and you can join external tables with regular tables. You can parallelize the operation, and you can even insert the data from the external table directly into the database at any time. The possibilities are endless. External tables are not just a serious advantage of using Oracle9*i*; they are one of the largest enhancements to relational technology perhaps in the past decade. They give you the window into the data that is *not* in your database. They allow you to access those legacy systems that have data stored in a multitude of flat files. They provide you the path to consolidate those legacy systems by moving step by step into the future.

Consider the quick use for an external table to read the alert file shown in Listing 9-62. The original script for this was written by Dave Moore and passed to me by Howard Horowitz. The following is an alteration of those scripts.

```
SQL> Create directory BDUMP as 'f:\ora9i2\admin\ora9i2\bdump';
Directory created.

SQL> Create table alert_log (text varchar2(200))
Organization EXTERNAL
(Type oracle_loader
Default directory BDUMP
Access parameters
(Records delimited by newline
Badfile 'rich1.bad'
Logfile 'rich1.log')
Location ('alert_ora9i2.log'))
Reject limit unlimited;
Table created.

select *
from    alert_log
where   rownum < 4;

TEXT
----------------------------------------------------------------
Mon May 20 22:05:03 2002
alter database rename global_name to ora9i2.world
Completed: alter database rename global_name to ora9i2.world
```

Listing 9-62: Using an external table to read the alert file

External Tables

WARNING
External tables are one of the best Oracle inventions in many versions. Your innovative mind will drive you to new heights using external tables. But be careful: data residing outside the database is not subject to the same Oracle backups and security as data inside the database.

Snapshot Too Old: Developer Coding Issue

Oracle holds rollback information in case of the need to rollback a transaction, and also to keep a read-consistent version of data. Long-running queries may need the read-consistent versions of the data in the rollback segments because they may not be the same System Change Number (SCN) as the ones currently in memory. (They may have been changed since the start of the query.) If the rollback segment holding the original data is overwritten, the user receives the dreaded Snapshot Too Old error. With advances in Oracle9*i*, this error would be rare indeed (using automatic undo management), but there is another, more frequent occurrence in the later versions of Oracle.

In their infinite wisdom, developers find wonderful ways to update information that they are querying within the same piece of code causing this problem. They are the ones both querying and updating, and causing the Snapshot Too Old error to occur. One flawed developer method is known as the Fetch Across Commit. In this method, the developer selects a large number of rows from a table into a cursor. Then, the developer fetches the rows to use for an update to the table, committing after a select number (say every 1000 records) based on a counter. What happens is that the cursor needs a read-consistent image of the table, yet the developer is committing 1000 records within the same code to the table. The result is a Snapshot Too Old error.

NOTE
See an excellent paper by Dave Wotton (listed in the references) on understanding Snapshot Too Old for a detailed explanation of this esoteric problem.

TIP
In addition to the more typical reasons, when developers modify the data as it is being selected, fetching across commits, the Snapshot Too Old error can occur. To fix this problem, close and reopen the cursor causing the issue.

Set Event to Dump Every Wait

In Chapter 14, you learned that STATSPACK is probably the best tuning tool Oracle offers. It is excellent for showing everything in a single report for you to analyze. But what if you have a burning issue and you directly need to dump exactly what the system is doing so you can see every wait on the system? If the compilation of all waits in the V$ views is not enough to solve problems and you need to see the waits real time, the answer is the very dangerous Set Event 10046 at the system level. (You can also do this at the session level.)

This event dumps every single wait that occurs so you can search through and see exactly what's causing the problem. You should use this strategy only as a last resort, and you should rarely use it. You need a lot of disk space to use it when you have a lot of waits.

When you're ready to dump the problem, here's how to turn it on:

```
Alter system set events '10046 trace name context forever, level 12';
```

Listing 9-63 shows what you'll get (in your USER_DUMP_DEST).

```
Dump file f:\ora9i2\admin\ora9i2\udump\ora9i2_ora_240.trc
Mon Feb 17 00:31:47 2003
...etc...
PARSING IN CURSOR #1 len=69 dep=0 uid=49 oct=42 lid=49 tim=189871918082
hv=3799341816 ad='12954910'
Alter session set events '10046 trace name context forever, level 12'
END OF STMT
EXEC #1:c=10014,e=51216,p=0,cr=0,cu=0,mis=1,r=0,dep=0,og=4,tim=189871484620
WAIT #1: nam='SQL*Net message to client' ela= 64 p1=1111838976 p2=1 p3=0
*** 2003-02-17 00:32:00.000
WAIT #1: nam='SQL*Net message from client' ela= 12734591 p1=1111838976 p2=1 p3=0
=====================
PARSE ERROR #1:len=55 dep=0 uid=49 oct=42 lid=49 tim=189884741177 err=1756
Alter session set events '10046 trace name context off
WAIT #1: nam='SQL*Net break/reset to client' ela= 255 p1=1111838976 p2=1 p3=0
WAIT #1: nam='SQL*Net break/reset to client' ela= 258 p1=1111838976 p2=0 p3=0
WAIT #1: nam='SQL*Net message to client' ela= 13 p1=1111838976 p2=1 p3=0
*** 2003-02-17 00:32:16.000
WAIT #1: nam='SQL*Net message from client' ela= 16306602 p1=1111838976 p2=1 p3=0
=====================
PARSING IN CURSOR #1 len=55 dep=0 uid=49 oct=42 lid=49 tim=189901104969
hv=1730465789 ad='129530c8'
Alter session set events '10046 trace name context off'
END OF STMT
```

Listing 9-63: USER_DUMP_DEST content

Although this output shows some irrelevant waits that came up when you quickly turn this on and off, when you have a real problem, the waits will be clear. You will be looking for a section with something like Listing 9-64, which shows a latch free issue. (See Chapter 14 for how to resolve this issue.) When you don't know what you're waiting for, this gives you a slightly more "at the street" level understanding of exactly what's going on than the V$ views.

```
WAIT #2: nam='latch free' ela= 0 p1=-2147423252 p2=105 p3=0
WAIT #2: nam='latch free' ela= 0 p1=-2147423252 p2=105 p3=1
WAIT #2: nam='latch free' ela= 0 p1=-1088472332 p2=106 p3=0
WAIT #2: nam='latch free' ela= 0 p1=-2147423252 p2=105 p3=0
WAIT #2: nam='latch free' ela= 0 p1=-2147423252 p2=105 p3=1
WAIT #2: nam='latch free' ela= 1 p1=-2147423252 p2=105 p3=2
WAIT #2: nam='latch free' ela= 0 p1=-2147423252 p2=105 p3=0
WAIT #2: nam='latch free' ela= 1 p1=-2147423252 p2=105 p3=1
```

Set Event to Dump Every Wait

```
WAIT #2: nam='latch free' ela= 0 p1=-2147423252 p2=105 p3=0
WAIT #2: nam='latch free' ela= 0 p1=-2147423252 p2=105 p3=1
```

Listing 9-64: Latch free issue

When you have a nice dump of the problem, here's how you turn it off:

```
Alter system set events '10046 trace name context off';
```

> **WARNING**
> *Using the event 10046 at the system level can give a real-time dump of waits. Be careful because you can quickly use a lot of space on a very busy system. Only an expert who has the help of Oracle Support should use this method.*

Block Dumps: The Last Word (Extremely Advanced Only)

If nothing has been advanced enough for you so far, this section will be worth the price of the book and should keep you busy for the next decade tuning your system to perfection (if you'd like). Oracle often has perplexing new features: either I can't seem to get them working, or there's simply a bug in the program that I am unaware of. How do you find out if a problem is yours or Oracle's? Dump the blocks one at a time.

Consider the following intense example. Find the table/index block information that you want to dump, as in Listing 9-65.

```
SELECT FILE_ID, BLOCK_ID, BLOCKS FROM DBA_EXTENTS
WHERE SEGMENT_NAME = 'EMP'
AND OWNER = 'SCOTT';

   FILE_ID        BLOCK_ID          BLOCKS
---------- --------------- ------------
         1           50465               3
```

Listing 9-65: Finding the table/index block information to dump

Dump the table/index block information, as in Listing 9-66.

```
ALTER SYSTEM DUMP DATAFILE 5 BLOCK 50465
/
ALTER SYSTEM DUMP DATAFILE 5 BLOCK 50466
/
ALTER SYSTEM DUMP DATAFILE 5 BLOCK 50467
/
```

Listing 9-66: Dumping the table/index block information

You could also issue the following command to dump the range of blocks:

```
ALTER SYSTEM DUMP DATAFILE 5 BLOCK MIN 50465 BLOCK MAX 50467;
```

The ALTER SYSTEM command, above, selects and then dumps the data blocks for the EMP table owned by SCOTT to the USER_DUMP_DEST. The information that is dumped is very cryptic, but it can be helpful for tuning purposes.

The dump in Listing 9-67 compares two different bitmap join indexes. One is on the DEPTNO column where the tables are also being joined by DEPTNO. The other is on the LOCATION column where the table is being joined by DEPTNO. By comparing index information, you can see that the LOCATION column was included in the stored part of the index, even though the query was going back to the table to retrieve the location column in the query. The problem was an Oracle bug that you would discover only by performing this dump (partially shown in Listing 9-67: only the first record is displayed for each).

```
DUMP OF BITMAP JOIN INDEX ON location JOINING deptno ON EMP1/DEPT1
row#0[3912] flag: -----, lock: 0
col 0; len 7; (7): 43 48 49 43 41 47 4f
col 1; len 6; (6): 00 40 f3 31 00 00
col 2; len 6; (6): 00 40 f3 31 00 0f
col 3; len 3; (3): c9 36 0a
...
----- end of leaf block dump -----
End dump data blocks tsn: 0 file#:
DUMP OF BITMAP JOIN INDEX ON deptno JOINING deptno ON EMP1/dept1 TABLE ***
row#0[3917] flag: -----, lock: 0
col 0; len 2; (2): c1 0b
col 1; len 6; (6): 00 40 f3 31 00 00
col 2; len 6; (6): 00 40 f3 31 00 0f
col 3; len 3; (3): c9 40 21
...
----- end of leaf block dump -----
End dump data blocks tsn: 0 file#:
```

Listing 9-67: Dump

The best use for dumping blocks is to see how Oracle really works. Get ready for a long night if you plan to use this tip; I spent a weekend playing with this the first time I used it.

TIP
Dumping data blocks can be a valuable tool to understand how Oracle works and to investigate problem tuning areas. Only a tuning expert should use block dumps, and even an expert should use the help of Oracle Support.

Tuning Using Simple Mathematical Techniques

This section discusses some simple but effective mathematical techniques you can use to significantly improve the performance of some Oracle SQL-based systems. These techniques can leverage the effectiveness of Oracle performance diagnostic tools and uncover hidden performance problems that can be overlooked by other methods. Using these techniques also helps you make performance predictions at higher loads.

> **NOTE**
> *This section was provided by Joe A. Holmes. I am extremely grateful for his contribution because I believe it ties all the chapters of this book together.*

The methodology called Simple Mathematical Techniques involves isolating and testing the SQL process in question under ideal conditions, graphing the results of rows processed versus time, deriving equations using simple methods (without regression), predicting performance, and interpreting and applying performance patterns directly to tuning SQL code.

Traditional Mathematical Analysis

First of all, do not be intimidated by this section. You *will* be able to understand this, and the information provided will help you predict response times for your queries as the tables grow.

Traditional mathematical methods are very useful for analyzing performance. These may include graphing performance metrics on an *x-y* coordinate axis to obtain a picture of what a process is really doing, and applying Least Squares Regression or Polynomial Interpolation to derive equations for predicting performance at higher loads. Computer science academics and specialists use these techniques extensively for performance analysis, which is laden with problems. First, textbook notation and explanations are often very complex and difficult to understand. Most math textbooks I have encountered regarding approximation and interpolation, for example, are steeped in theory rather than providing clear and practical examples.

Second, little or no information is available on how to apply this kind of analysis directly to tuning SQL code. This is probably because SQL analysis requires more specific interpretations to be useful rather than something more broad or general.

Seven-Step Methodology

The following are seven steps in the methodology. Note that deriving performance equations and interpreting patterns are discussed in more detail in the sections that follow.

■ **Step 1:** Isolate the SQL code in question.

The SQL code in question is isolated from surrounding system code and placed in a SQL*PLUS or PL/SQL script that can be run independently to duplicate the production process.

■ **Step 2:** Run tests under ideal conditions.

In this context, "ideal" is defined as one SQL process running on a dedicated machine with hardware processing power fixed and executed under high-volume data.

■ **Step 3:** Graph performance observations on an *x-y* coordinate axis.

From tests, the number of rows processed (*x*) versus time (*y*) for each SQL statement within a process is graphed on an *x-y* coordinate axis. We refer to this as a *row-time metric.* Ideally, the optimizer is for the most part more mechanical and less random, creating a more clearly defined and predictable trendline. The basic line shape can provide clues to the cause of underlying performance problems.

■ **Step 4:** Use simple equation determination.

Once points are plotted on a graph, you assume that what appears straight is a linear function and what appears curved upwards is a quadratic function. (Other shapes may appear, but they are beyond the scope of this section.) From these observations, you can use either a simple two-point linear or three-point quadratic method to determine the equations. You can perform both methods easily by hand or with a basic calculator. You can also use spreadsheets like Microsoft Excel with graphing and trendline (regression) capabilities. Each separate SQL statement is graphed and analyzed individually.

■ **Step 5:** Predict performance.

You can use derived equations to predict performance at much higher loads than are practical to test. Because the accuracy of the predictions may decrease as the predicted load increases, it is suggested that you make only ballpark predictions.

It may be advantageous to calculate two performance lines: the first as a lower bound if the performance line is truly linear, and the second as an upper bound if the performance line might turn out to be a quadratic curve. The predicated value would therefore lie somewhere in between. Later, you may want to try a test to see how close your prediction was to the actual time. Also be aware that it is not as important whether a slow-running process is predicted to take 20 or 24 hours, but rather, whether it can be improved to, say, 1 hour.

■ **Step 6:** Interpret performance patterns and experiment.

The shape of the performance lines and the nature of the equations can provide clues about the cause of underlying performance problems and support (or sometimes contradict) the interpretations of diagnostic tools. You can conduct experiments on SQL code based on pattern clues and the correction applied to production code. You can graph tests of an improved process again and compare the results with the original process.

■ **Step 7:** Keep a record of results to build expertise.

To build up your expertise at using both these mathematical methods and your interpretation of Oracle diagnostic tools, keep a record of before and after performance graphs, the true cause of performance problems, and the effective solutions you found. Graphs provide hard evidence of performance problems that you can present in a clear visual form to management and end users.

Deriving Performance Equations

The following discusses two simple methods for equation determination based on simplified versions of Newton's Divided Difference Interpolating Polynomial. You can use these methods if you assume that what appears as a straight line is linear and what appears as upward sloping is quadratic.

Simple Linear Equation Determination

The following is a simple two-point method for determining a linear best-performance line equation:

$y = a_0 + a_1x$ (This is the final equation to use for linear queries.)
y = the number of rows in the table
x = the time to process the query
a_1 = the slope of the line (Calculate this with two query tests.)
a_0 = the y-intercept of the line (Calculate this with two query tests.)

Seven-Step Methodology

Figure 9-6 shows points from an ideal test that appears linear. You visually select two points (x_1, y_1) and (x_2, y_2) that define a straight line of minimum slope, where:

slope: $a_1 = (y_2 - y_1)/(x_2 - x_1)$
y-intercept: $a_0 = y_1 - a_1 x_1$

A Simple Example   These equations look great, but let's look at a real-life query (Listing 9-68). You must time the query based on two different table sizes to get an equation for the line.

```
select ename, deptno
from    emp
where   deptno = 10;
```

Listing 9-68: Using a basic query to the EMP table

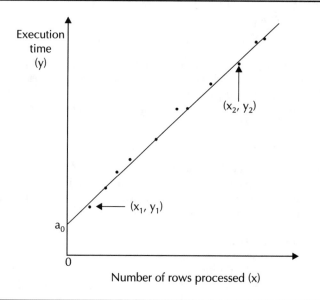

FIGURE 9-6.   *Linear Best-Performance Line*

For a very small system, consider the response for two tests:

When 1000 records were in the EMP table, this query took 2 seconds.
When 2000 records were in the EMP table, this query took 3 seconds.

Therefore, you know that:

y_1 = 2 (seconds)
x_1 = 1000 (records)
y_2 = 3 (seconds)
x_2 = 2000 (records)

■ **Step 1:** Find the slope of the line.

$a_1 = (y_2 - y_1)/(x_2 - x_1)$
$a_1 = (3 - 2)/(2000 - 1000)$
$a_1 = 0.001$ (The slope of the line is 0.001.)

■ **Step 2:** Get the y-intercept.

$a_0 = y_1 - a_1x_1$
$a_0 = 2 - (0.001)(1000)$
$a_0 = 2 - 1$
$a_0 = 1$ (The y-intercept is 1.)

■ **Step 3:** Now you can calculate response for any size EMP table.

You now have everything you need for this query, so you can figure out how long this query will take as the number of rows in the EMP table increases.
What will the response time be for 3000 rows?

$y = a_0 + a_1x$ (The response time is y and x is the number of rows in the table.)
$y = 1 + (0.001)(3000)$
$y = 1 + 3$
$y = 4$ seconds (The response time for this query in a 3000-row EMP table will be 4 seconds.)

What will the response time be for 100,000 rows?

$y = a_0 + a_1x$
$y = 1 + (0.001)(100,000)$
$y = 101$ seconds (The response time for a 100,000-row EMP table will be 1 minute and 41 seconds.)

Seven-Step Methodology

Simple Quadratic Equation Determination

Unfortunately, many queries don't behave linearly. Consequently, the previous section doesn't always help you. But never fear—a simple method for curved lines is next. Once again, do not be intimidated by this section. You *will* be able to understand this, and with this information, you will be able to predict query scaling (predict any response time for an increased number of rows). The following is a simple three-point method for determining a quadratic best-performance equation. This is the equation that you will use:

$y = a_0 + a_1x + a_2x^2$ (This is the final equation to use for nonlinear queries.)
y = response time for a query
x = number of rows
a_0, a_1, a_2 = constants derived based on the curve the query creates

Figure 9-7 shows points from an ideal test.

You visually select three points, $(0, y_0)$, (x_1, y_1), and (x_2, y_2) that appear to be of minimum slope on a quadratic-like curve. The midpoint between $x0$ and x_1 is x_a, and the midpoint between x_1 and x_2 is x_b, such that:

$x_a = (x_1 + 0)/2$ and $x_b = (x_2 + x_1)/2$

When joined, $(0, y_0)$ and (x_1, y_1) form a secant with slope S_a, and (x_1, y_1) and (x_2, y_2) form a secant with slope S_b. The x midpoints (x_a, y_a) and (x_b, y_b) lie on the desired curve with tangents

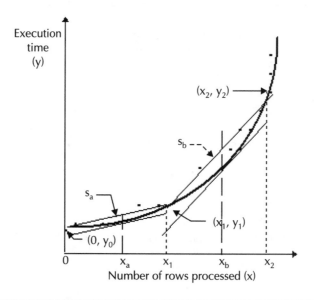

FIGURE 9-7. *Quadratic Best-Performance Curve*

having slopes S_a and S_b, respectively. From the derivative of a quadratic equation, which gives the slope of the curve at the midpoints, we have:

$$S_a = (y_1 - y_0)/(x_1 - 0) = a_1 + 2a_2x_a$$
S_a = slope of the lower part of the curve
$$S_b = (y_2 - y_1)/(x_2 - x_1) = a_1 + 2a_2x_b$$
S_b = slope of the upper part of the curve

Using Gauss elimination, you solve for the a_i coefficients, such that:

$$a_2 = (S_b - S_a)/[2(x_b - x_a)] = (S_b - S_a)/x_2$$
$$a_1 = S_a - 2a_2x_a = S_a - a_2x_1$$
$$a_0 = y_0$$

You'll have to use these three equations to get a_0, a_1, and a_2 and then you can use the final equation. These will be the constants in the equation that will give you the response time of a query as you vary the number of rows in the table.

NOTE
This method will not work in all cases. If any a_i coefficients are negative, the equation may dip below the X axis and something else must be used. Often, the origin or $a_0 = y_0 = 0$ works best with this method.

A Simple Example   All of these equations look great, but let's look at a real-life query (Listing 9-69). You must time the query based on two different table sizes to get an equation for the line. The ORDERS table has an index on ORDNO, but it is suppressed by the NVL function (causing the nonlinear response time). The real solution to this problem is to eliminate NULLs in the ORDERS table and remove the NVL function from the query. However, this example is for instructional purposes to generate a quadratic equation.

```
select    ordno, total
from      orders
where     nvl(ordno,0) = 7777;
```

Listing 9-69: Query the ORDERS table suppressing the index

For your system, consider the response of this query for two tests:

- When there were 100 records in the ORDERS table, this query took 5 seconds.

- When there were 2000 records in the ORDERS table, this query took 1000 seconds.

You want to know how bad this query will be when you have 10,000 rows in the ORDERS table. Therefore, you know that:

y_1 = 5 (seconds)
x_1 = 100 (records)
y_2 = 1000 (seconds)
x_2 = 2000 (records)
y_0 = 1 (second – estimate); this is the y-intercept

You could calculate y_0 by using two points near the lower part of the curve (near 100 rows using the linear equations from the previous section), but because the lower part of the curve is small (5 seconds for 100 rows), you can guesstimate this to be 1 second. (You should calculate it.)

- **Step 1:** Calculate S_a and S_b.

    $S_a = (y_1 - y_0)/(x_1 - 0)$
    $S_a = (5 - 1)/(100 - 0)$
    $S_a = 0.04$ (The slope of the lower part of the curve is almost horizontal.)
    $S_b = (y_2 - y_1)/(x_2 - x_1)$
    $S_b = (1000 - 5)/(2000 - 100)$
    $S_b = 0.52$ (The slope of the upper part of the curve is much higher than the lower part.)

- **Step 2:** Calculate a_0, a_1, and a_2.

    $a_2 = (S_b - S_a)/x_2$
    $a_2 = (0.52 - 0.04)/2000$
    $a_2 = 0.00024$
    $a_1 = S_a - a_2 x_1$
    $a_1 = 0.04 - (0.00024)(100)$
    $a_1 = 0.016$
    $a_0 = y_0$
    $a_0 = 1$ (The y-intercept is 1.)

- **Step 3:** Create the equation to use as the table grows.

    $y = a_0 + a_1 x + a_2 x_2$
    $y = 1 + (0.016)x + (0.00024)x^2$ (This is your equation to calculate future responses.)

- **Step 4:** Calculate the *expected* response for 10,000 rows.

    $y = 1 + (0.016)x + (0.00024)x^2$
    $y = 1 + (0.016)(10,000) + (0.00024)(10,000^2)$
    $y = 24,161$ (The query will take 24,161 seconds or just under 7 hours; you have a problem.)

You'll have to fix the NVL problem soon so the users don't have to wait 7 hours. But in reality, you have calculated only a couple of points, and this should be extended out further to get a better future estimate of performance.

TIP
Spreadsheets like Microsoft Excel are very useful tools for graphing performance metrics and automatically deriving trendline equations. For example, to create a graph using Excel, list the observed (x,y) data in cells. Highlight the cells and select Chart Wizard | XY (Scatter) | Chart Sub-type. Select a Line subtype and click Next | Next | Finish to create the graph. To derive a trendline equation, click the graph line once and select Chart | Add Trendline. On the Type tab, select Linear, Polynomial Order=2 (for quadratic) or other model type. To show the trendline equation, on the Options tab, select Display Equation On Chart. Then click OK to complete the graph. The solution equation can be programmed back into the spreadsheet and used to predict values at higher volumes.

Pattern Interpretation

Graphical performance patterns provide clues to underlying SQL problems and solutions, as seen in Figure 9-8. The ultimate goal in using these methods is to convert a steep linear or quadratic best-performance line to one that is both shallow and linear by optimizing the SQL process. This may involve experiments with indexes, temp tables, optimizer hint commands, or other methods of Oracle SQL performance tuning.

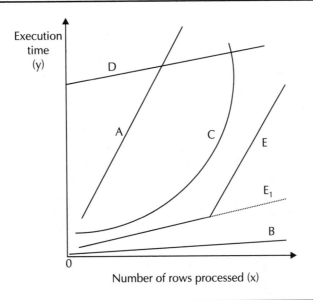

FIGURE 9-8. *Examples of Performance Patterns*

With pattern interpretation, it is important to perform your own application-specific SQL experiments to develop expertise at using these methods. Table 9-2 shows more specific interpretations—based on my personal experience—that provide a general idea of how you can apply what you observe directly to tuning SQL code. Assuming the scale is correct, pattern interpretation often provides a more accurate picture of what is actually happening to a process and may support or even contradict what a diagnostic tool tells you.

General Linear and Quadratic Interpretations

A shallow linear performance line usually indicates a relatively efficient process compared to something much steeper or curved. The slope a_1 indicates the rate y increases for a given x. Scale is important because a shallow line on one scale can look steep on another, and vice versa. A large a_0 coefficient always indicates an inefficient process.

An upward-sloping (concave) quadratic curve almost always indicates a problem with the process because as more rows are added, the time to process each additional row increases.

Pattern in Figure 9-8	Possible Problem	Possible Solution
A	Missing index on a query SELECTing values.	Create an index. Fix a suppressed index.
A	Overindexed table suffering during DML statements.	Delete some of the indexes or index fewer columns (or smaller columns) for the current indexes.
B	No problem.	Don't touch it!
C	Missing index on a query SELECTing values.	Create an index. Fix a suppressed index.
C	Overindexed table suffering during an INSERT.	Delete some of the indexes or index fewer columns (or smaller columns) for the current indexes.
D	Doing a full tablescan or using the ALL_ROWS hint when you shouldn't be.	Try to do an indexed search. Try using the FIRST_ROWS hint to force the use of indexes.
E	The query was fine until some other limitation (such as disk I/O or memory) was encountered.	Find out which ceiling you hit caused this problem. Increasing the SGA may solve the problem, but this could be many things.
E_1	If the limitation in line E is corrected, processing should continue along a straight line.	Further tuning may improve the process to line B.

TABLE 9-2.   *Graphical representations of various tuning situations*

Coefficient a_2 affects the bowing of the curve. If it is very small, the equation may be more linear. However, even a very slight bowing may be an indicator of something more insidious under much higher volumes.

In rare cases, a quadratic curve might appear downward sloping (convex), indicating a process where as more rows are added, the time to process each additional one decreases (i.e., economies of scale). This is desirable and may occur at a threshold, where a full tablescan is more efficient than using an index.

Indexing

Missing indexes commonly cause poor SQL performance. In Figure 9-8, line *A* or *C* could result from a missing index, depending on code complexity and data volume. Proper indexing improves performance to line *B*. Overindexing can be as bad as missing indexes. Line *A* or *C* could be a process that is forced to use an index, whereas a full tablescan would improve the process to *B*. Inserting into an indexed table is always slower than into an index-free table. Line *A* or *C* could be from an INSERT into a heavily indexed table versus line *B* with no indexing.

Indexing Example   Listing 9-70 illustrates what can happen with indexing analysis. Suppose you have two tables, TABLE_A and TABLE_B, and there is a one-to-many relationship between them using KEY_FIELD. There does not have to be a join between the two tables.

```
TABLE_A
KEY_FIELD       NUMBER
TOTAL           NUMBER


TABLE_B
KEY_FIELD       NUMBER
AMOUNT          NUMBER
```

Listing 9-70: Two tables used for the example

You want to perform the following update within a KEY_FIELD:

```
table_a.total = table_a.total + sum(table_b.amount)
```

The SQL statement shown in Listing 9-71 will do this. Note that the EXISTS subquery must be used to prevent the NULLing out of any table_a.total fields, where table_a.key_field does not match total_b.key_field.

```
update    table_a ta  set ta.total =
(select    ta.total + sum(tb.amount)
 from      table_b tb
 where     tb.key_field = ta.key_field
 group by  ta.total)
where    exists
(select    null
 from      table_b tb2
 where     tb2.key_field = ta.key_field);
```

Listing 9-71: Query to be investigated

If there is a unique index on table_a.key_field and a nonunique index on table_b.key_field, then the performance will be similar to line *B* in Figure 9-8. However, if there is no index on table_b.key_field or the cost-based optimizer decides to shut it off, a line will be generated similar to *A* or *C*. The reason is that the EXISTS subquery heavily depends on indexing.

I have seen cases where the number of rows in TABLE_A was small (< 2000) but the cost-based optimizer shut off the index on TABLE_B and reported a small EXPLAIN PLAN cost. This was regardless of the number of rows in TABLE_B (which was up to 800,000 rows). Actual tests showed a steep performance line that contradicted the EXPLAIN PLAN cost. This is an example of uncovering a problem that may have been overlooked by a diagnostic tool.

When the optimizer (cost-based) finds a query to retrieve less than 5–6 percent (based on the average distribution) of the data in a table, the optimizer generally drives the query with an index if one exists. Figure 9-9 shows how Oracle has evolved through the past years prior to Oracle9i.

Optimizer Execution Plan

You can graph performance patterns to leverage available diagnostic tools. For example, you analyzed a slow and complex SQL statement that used views, and ran high-volume data under the Oracle cost-based optimizer. Results showed a very high performance line identical to D in Figure 9-8. The Oracle EXPLAIN PLAN also showed an inefficient execution plan. Once an effective optimizer hint command was found (i.e., FIRST_ROWS) and added directly to the SQL statements that defined the views, performance improved dramatically to line *B*.

Multiple Table Joins

Complex multiple-table join statements often run poorly regardless of the conventional tuning used and may be similar to lines *A* or *C* in Figure 9-8. From past experience, rather than trying to tune only the statement with conventional techniques, a more effective solution is to decompose it into a series of simple SQL statements using temporary tables. The final result would be the same but at a much faster speed, represented by a composite line at *B*.

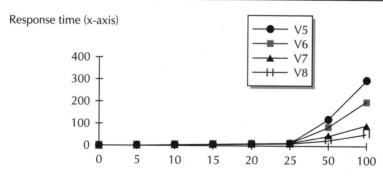

FIGURE 9-9. *Optimum Percentage of Rows for Index for a Given Version of Oracle*

Jackknifing

Jackknifing is a pattern where a performance line starts off shallow but then veers steeply upward at a certain threshold point, similar to *E* in Figure 9-8. Two linear equations may define the behavior; its cause could be anything from disk I/O or memory limitations to a switch in the optimizer execution plan due to changing data volumes. Possible solutions are to increase the system's limitations, run fresh optimizer statistics, use the rule-based optimizer, or break the statement into selection ranges. Proper tuning might either straighten out the line to $E_{\prime}$ or improve it further to line *B*.

Riding the Quadratic Curve

Often, a poorly performing SQL process is designed and tested on low-volume data, but in production under higher volumes, its true and degrading quadratic nature is revealed, as shown by curve *A* in Figure 9-10. In this example, a process was created and tested up to $x_{\prime}$. Performance was believed to be close to line *B*, but once in production and when the volume was increased to x_{3}, the line really turned out to be curve *A*.

If a proper tuning solution cannot be found, a quadratic process of unknown cause can still be improved by breaking the original statement into lower-volume selection ranges and riding the shallow part of the quadratic curve. Suppose in Figure 9-10, you break the process into three selection ranges: [from 0 to x_{0}] that rides the lower part of curve *A*, [from x_{1} to x_{2}] that rides the lower part of curve $A_{\prime}$, and [from x_{2} to x_{3}] that rides the lower part of curve A_{2}. The overall result is something closer to line *B* [from 0 to x_{3}] with y_{3}' a lot less time than the original y_{3}. Although this technique may not be the best solution, it could still solve the problem.

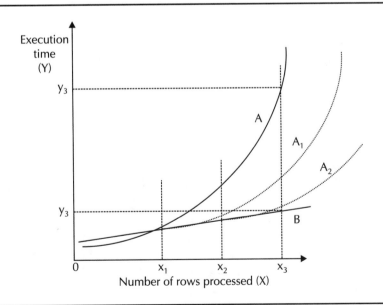

FIGURE 9-10. *Example of Riding the Quadratic Curve*

Breaking up the process using an SQL loop and commit mechanism can sometimes buy better overall performance for processes like updates and deletes that use rollback segments, than running everything all at once.

Volatility Effects

Running under ideal conditions and graphing the results makes it much easier to analyze the effects of outside traffic and its resulting volatility. For example, line *A* in Figure 9-11 is from an inefficient linear process run under ideal conditions. Suppose a controlled amount of traffic from another process is then run at the same time. It could be a large query, insert, update, or backup, etc. This second test moves line *A* by 100 percent to A_1. In other words, the process with added traffic on the system is twice as slow.

Now suppose you optimize the original process. Under an ideal test of the new process, the best performance line shifts down to *B*. If you were to predict what would happen if you applied the same controlled traffic to the new process, you might predict a 100 percent shift to B_1. However, since the slopes between *A* and *B* differ (with *A* being much steeper than *B*), the 100 percent time increase from *B* to B_1 would be much less than from *A* to A_1. In fact, an actual traffic test on line *B* might prove to be much less than even the predicted 100 percent due to the overall efficiency of the line *B* process. In general, more efficient SQL processes are less susceptible to added traffic effects than less efficient processes.

Mathematical Techniques Conclusions

Simple Mathematical Techniques is an effective Oracle SQL performance analysis and tuning methodology that involves running tests under ideal conditions, graphing performance observations,

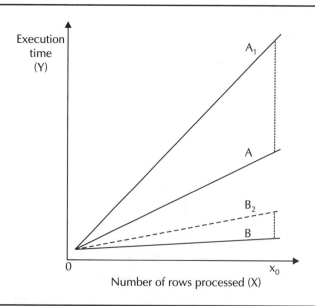

FIGURE 9-11. *Example of volatility effects*

and using simple linear and quadratic equation determination for predicting performance at higher loads. It also includes the interpretation of performance patterns that can be applied directly to tuning SQL code.

The methodology acts as a catalyst by combining the use of some traditional mathematical analysis with Oracle diagnostic tools to aid in their interpretation and to leverage their effectiveness. It can also help you identify hidden problems that may be overlooked by other diagnostic methods by providing a broad picture of performance. The technique can also help you overcome performance-tuning barriers such as inexperience with Oracle, lack of hard evidence, or difficulties with diagnostic tool interpretation that may prevent effective performance tuning. You can also analyze volatility effects from outside traffic. Graphs provide a visual picture of performance for presentation to management and end users. And you can use spreadsheets such as Microsoft Excel with these techniques for quick and easy performance analysis.

TIP

If you want an Oracle symphony as great as Beethoven's, you must learn and know how to apply mathematical techniques to your tuning efforts. You don't have to learn everything that you learned in college calculus; merely apply the simple equations in this chapter to tie everything in this book together. Thank you Joe Holmes for doing the math for us!

More Mathematical Techniques: Apply Control Theory

This section discusses another more complex mathematical technique that compares performance tuning to the Kalman filter and Gaussian distributions. Although you can often see performance trends when you are tuning, this section looks to unlock the patterns in a more advanced manner yet. This section uses a different approach to predict query performance that is usually used in control theory. The idea is based on linear prediction methods, in particular, the one known as the Kalman approach. Maurizio Bonomi of Italy provided this section. I am thankful for this forward-thinking contribution.

This method of applying control theory involves concepts such as *state* and *output* of a linear system, describing a generic dynamic system with a couple of equations in the following general form:

$$\begin{cases} x(k+1) = Ax(k) + v_1(k) \\ y(k) = Hx(k) + v_2(k) \end{cases}$$

where

- $x(k)$ is the *state*: a vector with, in general, n components

- $y(k)$ is the *output*: a vector with, in general, p components

- $v_1(k), v_2(k)$ are independent noises described as White Gaussian Noises (WGN); they are known

- A, H are deterministic matrices; they are known

Why is the concept of *state* in a system so important? The state contains the evolution of the system—its history. It's clear that you can have global information only if you know where the system "has been in time." This is then completed by all the other parameters. The previous equations can be used to solve the following problem: estimate query performance in time, taking into account the optimizer's different choices, the computer's workload choices, or other kinds of situations.

Note that we will consider a scalar system, even though a more generic representation could be considered using particular values in the matrices. Query performance strongly depends on the choices the optimizer makes and on the computer's workload, so it's useful to consider these parameters in the model. We are not in an ideal case but in a more realistic work situation.

Imagine a system affected by noise, where this noise is the uncertainty caused by the possible variation of the parameters in time. The general scheme can be thought of as:

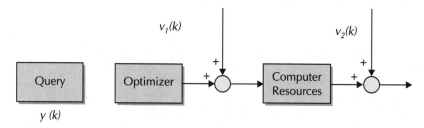

The output represents the query execution and also the time spent for it. The meaning of the three blocks indicated (Query, Optimizer and Computer Resources) is as follows:

- **Query**   SQL statement to analyze; includes the parser block for syntax and semantic analysis.

- **Optimizer**   SQL processing engine to generate the optimal plan for the row source generator.

- **Computer resources**   Set of resources used to produce the results; includes the row source generator and SQL execution.

Clearly, the heart of the argument is the optimizer, so important phases like parsing and execution are contained in other parts of the system and not explicitly shown (but considered). Now let's consider these variables:

- $x(k)$ is the state of the system. It represents the cost of the best execution plan calculated by the optimizer; this should be the best way to retrieve data from the tables.

- $y(k)$ is the output of the system. It corresponds to the time to execute the query (as soon as possible is desired).

- $v_1(k)$ is the noise that "dirties" the optimizer's performance.

- $v_2(k)$ is the noise that "dirties" the computer resources (performance).

The optimizer's performance should generate the best execution plan, but this is not always the case. There are some fundamental reasons for the lack of performance of the optimizer. Incorrect optimizer settings can change how the optimizer processes queries (using OPTIMIZER_MODE in the initialization file). If poor statistics are collected about a table, there could be a problem related to database management that causes poor performance. Growth of the tables on which we retrieve data could skew data unexpectedly.

Computer performance can vary from day to day and, more generally, over time. We have several workload situations through the normal working time and, further, we have to take into account that the applications on the database can increase in the following months/years. We can have a situation in which a query is executed when the CPUs and RAM memory are occupied by other applications. In another case, many applications (previously not anticipated to be running) can engage the resources in an unpredictable way or all at once.

Now the question is how to describe these noise sources with an efficient statistical method. The proposed answer is Gaussian distribution.

Now take a look at this hypothesis. The Gaussian probability distribution with mean μ and standard deviation σ is a Gaussian function of the form:

$$P(x) = \frac{1}{\sigma\sqrt{2\pi}} e^{-(x-\mu)^2/2\sigma^2}$$

$P(x)dx$ gives the probability that a variable with a Gaussian distribution takes on a value in the range $[x, x+dx]$. Note that this distribution is also known as Normal distribution.

Figure 9-12 illustrates the graph of the Gaussian distribution, where we have put $\mu = 0$ arbitrarily. Notice that the peak of the distribution is centered about $x = \mu$.

To understand the choice of this distribution for our parameters, it's important to comprehend the meaning of mean and standard deviation. The *mean* determines the position of the graph. When it changes, the diagram moves along the X axis, on the left where μ decreases and on the right where μ increases. The *standard deviation* determines the width of the distribution. When it varies, it affects the overall distribution. For example, when it decreases, the distribution becomes more narrow, increasing the peak.

It's possible to propose that the choices made by the optimizer, along with the rhythm of growth of tables or computer performance, have the kind of distribution that could be interpreted as follows: the range of highest probability of occurrence is concentrated around the expected value (mean); notice that 68.3 percent of the entire area is in this interval.

Furthermore, Gaussian distribution has many convenient properties, so random variables with unknown distributions are often assumed to be Gaussian, especially in physics. Although this assumption can be dangerous, it is often accurate due to a surprising result known as the *Central Limit Theorem*: the mean of any set of variables with any distribution having a finite mean and variance tends to the Gaussian distribution.

Mathematical Techniques Conclusions

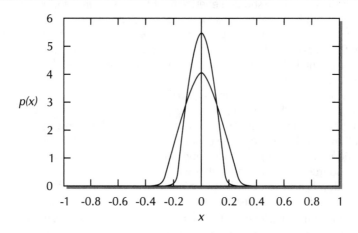

FIGURE 9-12. *A Gaussian distribution is considered*

The Kalman filter is a very powerful system used to estimate query performance. It is essentially a set of mathematical equations that implement a predictor-corrector-type estimator that is *optimal* in the sense that it minimizes the estimated error covariance when some presumed conditions are met. In general, it supports estimations of past, present, and even future states, and it can do so even when the precise nature of the modeled system is unknown.

The filter is often used in control theory. Since it was introduced, it has been the subject of extensive research and application, probably because of advances in digital computing that made its use practical. I don't know if it's ever been used in problems regarding databases or query performance. My intention is to try to estimate query performance, and this concept, as you'll see, can be used to evaluate indexes and other interesting aspects.

Database design involves many possible choices and problems: you have to correctly facilitate both a logical, physical implementation of the database (tablespaces, initialization parameters, memory allocation, and so on) and correctly select the hardware on which the system runs. Often, people consider only the design aspect, leaving the other aspects to the power of processors or to the amount of RAM memory to solve.

Remember, any program runs on a physical structure (hardware), and its performance heavily depends on that foundation.

We gave you the mathematical representation of the filter in a general form. Let's consider a scalar system, governed by the linear stochastic difference equations:

$$\begin{cases} x(k+1) = x(k) + v_1(k) \\ y(k) = \lambda x(k) + v_2(k) \end{cases}$$

What about the matrices A, H? The general $n \times n$ matrix A relates the state at the previous time step $k-1$ to the state at the current step k, in the absence of either a driving function or process noise. In our system, we can assume that in the absence of these noise factors, the optimizer always generates the same execution plan, so we have the constant value *1* (one).

The general $n \times l$ matrix H in the second equation (measurement equation) relates the states to the measurement $y(k)$. Here we consider a scalar parameter λ, with constant value.

What does λ represent? It relates the state, the cost generated by the optimizer, to the measurement (output), the time to execute our query. We can think of a proportionality relationship, because it's logical to assume that if the cost calculated increases, the time to execute the query increases. The geometric interpretation is a tangent and the physics interpretation is a time:

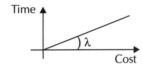

We have:

$$\lambda = \frac{\Delta y(k)}{\Delta x(k)} = \frac{Time[seconds]}{Cost[dimensionless\_value]} \quad \Rightarrow \quad dimension \quad is \quad [seconds]$$

We have a constant value, with dimension [*seconds*], that relates the optimal cost generated by the optimizer and the time to execute the query.

The system must be calibrated with some measurement "on the field" to determine this value. The random variables $v_1(k)$, $v_2(k)$ represent the process and measurement noise, respectively. They are assumed to be independent (of each other), white noise and with normal probability distributions:

$$v_1(k) \sim N(0,Q)$$
$$v_2(k) \sim N(0,R)$$

In practice, the process noise covariance Q and the measurement noise covariance R matrices might change in time; however, here we assume they are constant.

The process noise is the one that dirties the optimizer's performance, so the process is the optimizer (its behavior). On the other hand, the measurement noise is the one that dirties the computer performance, so the process is the execution of our query on the hardware platform. Let's look more at the filter.

We consider $\bar{x}_k \in \Re^n$ as our *a priori* estimate at step k given knowledge of the process prior to step k, and $x_k \in \Re^n$ to be our *a posteriori* state estimate at step k given measurement y_k. We can define *a priori* and *a posteriori* estimate errors as

$$\bar{e}_k \equiv x_k - \bar{x}_k$$
$$e_k \equiv x_k - x_k$$

The *a priori* estimate error covariance is then

$$P_k = E[e_k e_k^T]$$

and the *a posteriori* estimate error covariance is

$$P_k = E[e_k e_k^T]$$

Notice that E is the expected value.

The goal is to find an equation that computes an *a posteriori* state estimate x_k as a linear combination of an *a priori* estimate x_k^- and a weighted difference between an actual measurement y_k and a measurement prediction Hx_k^-, as shown in the following equation:

$$x_k = x_k^- + K(y_k - Hx_k^-)$$

The difference $K(y_k - Hx_k^-)$ is known as the *measurement innovation,* and it reflects the discrepancy between the predicted measurement Hx_k^- and the actual measurement y_k; if zero, we are in complete agreement.

The general $n \times m$ matrix K is chosen to be the *gain* that minimizes the *a posteriori* error covariance. One form of the resulting K that minimizes it is

$$K_k = P_k^- H^T (HP_k^- H^T + R)^{-1} = \frac{P_k^- H^T}{HP_k^- H^T + R}$$

Looking at the equations in this section, you can see that it is possible to consider, or not to consider, the variables. It's possible to assume your system can be affected by one or more noise sources, considering a different structure each time. That's the real power of this method, because you are able to consider different situations with different weights, taking into account only what you consider important in your system. The basic idea is to estimate the query performance, and this concept, as we'll see, can be used as an evaluation index of other very interesting aspects. It's clear that according to the choices made, different evaluation indexes are more appropriate for distinct situations.

For example, the optimizer generates the best execution plan in every situation, but the execution is slow due to problems with computer resources. In the model, we'll have $v_1(k) = 0$ and $v_2(k)$ with an appropriate description (according to the situation). Then, we can have an indication about the correct choice of hardware.

There are several possible situations: We will consider some examples. If $v_1(k) = 0$, the optimizer always generates the best execution plan. The equations are

$$\begin{cases} x(k+1) = x(k) \\ y(k) = \lambda x(k) + v_2(k) \end{cases}$$

The first equation says that the state of the system is constant and the output is affected by an additive noise with a Gaussian distribution. The solution of the Kalman filter exists: the prediction is the mean value on all data, taking into account as additional information, the mean value of the initial state. (This improves the estimation.) We have an indication about hardware.

If $v_2(k)=0$, we have no problems with computer performance. The execution is always the best possible. We have problems with the optimizer. The equations are

$$\begin{cases} x(k+1)= x(k)+v_1(k) \\ y(k)= \lambda x(k) \end{cases}$$

In this situation, we can consider a subset of situations, according to the kind of noise. For example, we can consider the probability of a poor statistic collection from the data dictionary, the probability of a different optimizer approach and goal, or both. The probability distribution is, for each variable, a Gaussian distribution. Therefore, if we consider the third condition, we can sum the single effects having a global noise with a Gaussian distribution itself (which can be proved by the classical statistical method). The solution of the Kalman filter exists in the general form and can show an evaluation index for the lack of performance. We can have the general situation, governed by the equations:

$$\begin{cases} x(k+1)= x(k)+v_1(k) \\ y(k)= \lambda x(k)+v_2(k) \end{cases}$$

It's possible to consider all the situations demonstrated. The solution of the Kalman filter exists and can indicate the global effect. You could use this as an evaluation index to estimate the behavior for your system in the more general condition. Note that you can take into account the kind of variable you need for a particular situation: the probability distribution must be Gaussian, but in the situations where that's not the case, it is possible to use the Central Limit Theorem to describe it as a Gaussian distribution. (In general, this represents a very good approximation.) The filter can be implemented using the Matlab package. Other software packages can also do this.

Summary
Here is a summary of steps that you will use for this process:

- **Step 1:** Know your goal, what you want to investigate. There are two basic targets:

  - **Global information:** The situation where you need information about the whole system, taking into account possible problems on the hardware platform and possible trouble in the database.

  - **Partial information:** The condition where you need information about a specific part of the system, considering only the portion you think will probably cause a number of problems. For example, you know your budget is low and the hardware platform is insufficient due to poor resources (number of CPUs, number of disks, amount of memory, and so on).

Mathematical Techniques Conclusions

■ **Step 2:** Take some "measurements" on the system to determine the λ parameter, to have or estimate the possible statistical distribution and all the associated parameters (covariance matrices) Q, R, to give the initial state x_0 and the initial error covariance P_0 (we consider 0 as initial time). That's all the Kalman filter needs: you must start the engine and it needs fuel!

■ **Step 3:** The Kalman filter starts to run; we have:

Kalman filter time update equations:

$$\hat{x}_k^- = A\hat{x}_{k-1}$$
$$P_k^- = AP_{k-1}A^T + Q$$

Kalman filter measurement update equations:

$$K_k = P_k^- H^T (HP_k^- H^T + R)^{-1}$$
$$\hat{X}_k = \hat{X}_k^- + K_k(y_k - H\hat{x}_k^-)$$
$$P_k = (I - K_k H)P_k^-$$

Kalman filter cycle: The time update equations project the current state estimate and the covariance estimate ahead of time. The measurement update equations adjust the projected estimate by an actual measurement at the time. The first task during the measurement update is to compute the Kalman gain K_k. The next step is to actually measure the process to obtain y_k and then to generate an *a posteriori* state estimate by incorporating the measurement. The final step is to obtain an *a posteriori* error covariance estimate.

■ **Step 4:** After each time and measurement update pair, the process is repeated with the previous *a posteriori* estimates used to project or predict the new *a priori* estimates. You can see the recursive nature of the Kalman filter, where the current estimate is conditioned on all the past measurements.

■ **Step 5:** A graph can be obtained using all the results given by the filter, so it is possible to provide an interpretation to the problem. The graph may indicate what's wrong or point to poor choices made and can show how these problems will affect the system. You could build a small repository to keep the results and the conclusions to compare different situations.

Example 1

Consider a generic query. You don't have any problem with the optimizer. You are sure it always generates the best execution plan. However, the execution time grows due to poor computer resources; that is, you have fixed a number of CPUs and an amount of memory that seems to be insufficient when many different applications (not necessarily on the database) engage the resources. You want to show a problem on the hardware platform.

Consider the computer workload with a Gaussian distribution.

- The parameters are

  $Q = 1e^{-5}$ You could certainly let $Q = 0$, but assuming a small but nonzero value gives you more flexibility in tuning the filter.

  $R = (0.001)^2$

  $\lambda = 0.3$

  initial state (cost) $x_0 = 10$

  initial error covariance $P_0 = 1$: this choice is arbitrary, but it's not critical because you could choose any value $P_0 \neq 0$ and the filter eventually converges.

- The execution time (measurement) is a vector

  y=[1,1.4,1.9,2.6,3.3,4.2,6.1,8,9.7,12.4]

Using the Matlab package and source code (downloaded from the Web) that implement the Kalman filter, you can obtain the graph in Figure 9-13.

The filter gives a good execution time estimate, showing the problem related to the hardware platform. In this case, it could be appropriate to evaluate a different configuration to have enough resources to run all the applications.

Example 2

Consider a generic query.

Let's say you have a problem with both the optimizer and computer resources. You have enough processors but not enough memory. Consider the statistical distribution for the memory usage as a Gaussian distribution (depends on the number of applications that engage the resource). Furthermore, the execution plan shows a possible problem on the query itself. You want to investigate this combination.

- The parameters are

  $Q = 0.1$

  $R = 0.01$

  $\lambda = 0.45$

  initial state (cost) $x_0 = 80$

  initial error covariance $P_0 = 1$: this choice is arbitrary, but it's not critical because you could choose any value $P_0 \neq 0$ and the filter will eventually converge.

- The execution time (measurement) is a vector

  y=[10.4,12.3,13.5,15.6,17.1,19.3,21,23.7,25.8,28.2]

**Mathematical Techniques
Conclusions**

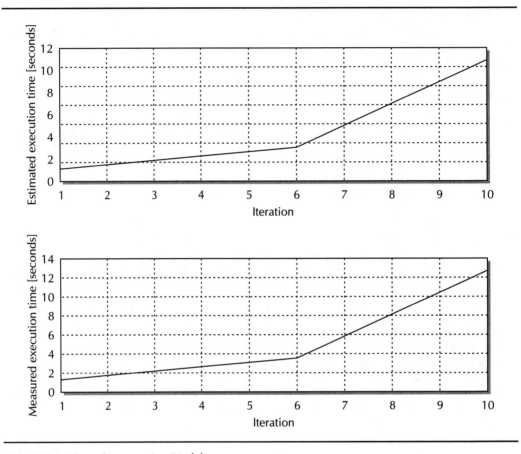

FIGURE 9-13. *Output using Matlab*

Using the Matlab package and source code (downloaded from the Web) that implements the Kalman filter, you can obtain the graph in Figure 9-14.

TIP
The future of performance tuning will link in mathematical techniques including control theory as has been done with both mechanical and electrical engineering. The Kalman filter is an attempt to blaze this new trail to help simplify performance tuning and take it into the future.

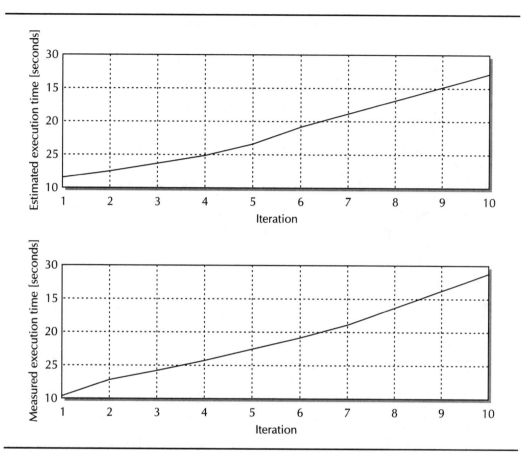

FIGURE 9-14.   *Output using Matlab*

Tips Review

- The optimizer often uses HASH joins in lieu of SORT-MERGE joins if the correct initialization parameters are set. With HASH joins, the driving table is used to be a hash table; on the join key, the other table is scanned and the result probes the hash table for matches. If there is not enough memory, the hash table could be split into multiple partitions and it may also be swapped to disk. Be careful: HASH joins can be slow when memory is low or the tables are poorly indexed.

- Using cost-based optimization, the first table in the FROM clause is the driving table when all other conditions are equal. If the ORDERED hint is used, then the first table in the FROM clause is also the driving table.

- Using cost-based optimization and NESTED LOOPS joins as the means of joining, the first table in the FROM clause is the driving table (all other conditions being equal), but only the ORDERED hint guarantees this. In NESTED LOOPS joins, choosing a driving table that is the smaller result set (not always the smaller table) means making less loops to the other result set (from the nondriving table) and usually results in the best performance.

- The columns that are retrieved can change which indexes Oracle uses and also changes the way Oracle joins the tables in the query.

- To change the way Oracle joins multiple tables, use the USE_MERGE, USE_NL, and USE_HASH hints.

- In a three-table join, the driving table is the intersection table or the table that has a join condition to each of the other two tables in the join. Try to use the most limiting table as the driving table (or intersection table) so that your result set from the join of the first two tables is small when you join it to the third table. Also, ensure that all join conditions on all tables are indexed!

- To ensure that you are reading your EXPLAIN PLAN correctly, run a query for which you are sure of the driving table (with nested subqueries).

- You may not be able to modify actual code for some third-party products, but you can often add, force, or suppress indexes to improve the performance.

- When distributed queries cannot be avoided, use IN clauses, set operators such as UNION and MINUS, and do whatever else you can to reduce the network traffic between nodes of the database. Queries written in a manner that cause looping between distributed nodes (distributed databases) can be extremely slow.

- If you want an Oracle symphony as great as Beethoven's, you must learn and know how to apply mathematical techniques to your tuning efforts. You don't have to learn everything you learned in college calculus; merely apply the simple equations in this chapter to tie everything in this book together.

- If you've read and understood this entire chapter, you're probably among the top tuning professionals and you will see the heights and joys that I've seen with tuning Oracle.

References

Tuning Joins: Roger Schrag, Database Specialists.

Holmes, J. A., "Leveraging Oracle Performance Tuning Tools Using Simple Mathematical Techniques," *SELECT Magazine*, Vol. 5, No. 4, July 1998, IOUG-A, pp. 36–42.

Holmes, J. A., "Seven Deadly SQL Traps and How to Avoid Them," *SELECT Magazine*, Vol. 6, No 4, July 1999, IOUG-A, pp. 22–26.

Holmes, J. A., "Amazing SQL*Plus Tricks," *SELECT Magazine*, Vol. 7, No. 4, July 2000, IOUG-A, pp. 26–33.

Aronoff, E., K. Loney, & N. Sonawalla, *"Advanced Oracle Tuning and Administration,"* Oracle Press, Osborne/McGraw-Hill, 1997.

Chapra, S., & R. Canale, *Numerical Methods for Engineers; with Programming and Software Applications,* Third Edition, McGraw-Hill Book Co., 1998.

Holmes, J. A., "SQL Performance Analysis and Tuning Using Simple Mathematical Techniques," *The Carleton Journal of Computer Science*, No. 2, 1998, Carleton University Press Inc., Ottawa, ON, pp. 9–14.

Jain, R., *The Art of Computer Systems Performance Analysis: Techniques for Experimental Design, Measurement, Simulation and Modeling,* John Wiley & Sons, Inc., 1991.

Understanding "Snapshot Too Old," Dave Wotton; http://home.clara.net/dwotton/dba/snapshot.htm.

The tips and techniques section of www.ioug.org.

Oracle9*i* Documentation. Oracle Corporation.

Oracle9*i* Web Development, Bradley Brown, October 2001.

Oracle Professional, February 2002, Dave Moore.

Managing Oracle9*i* Real Application Clusters: An Oracle White Paper, March 2001.

Oracle9i RAC—Cache Fusion delivers Scalability: An Oracle White Paper, May 2001.

Building Highly Available Database Servers using RAC: An Oracle White Paper, May 2001.

Real Application Cluster Documentation Set: technet.oracle.com.

Oracle9*i* New Features: TUSC Presentation, Rich Niemiec, September 2001.

Delivering High Availability Solutions with Red Hat Linux Advanced Server 2.1; Red Hat, 2002.

Advantages of Oracle9*i* Real Application Clusters: Mike Ault, TUSC, 2002.

Oracle9*i* Performance Tips and Techniques: Rich Niemiec, August, 2002.

Oracle9*i* new features: Randy Swanson, www.tusc.com.

Special thanks to Maurizio Bonomi, Joe Holmes, Roger Schrag, Joe Trezzo, Sean McGuire, Judy Corley, Greg Pucka, Jake Van der Vort, Randy Swanson, Bob Taylor, and Mark Greenhalgh for contributions to this chapter.

CHAPTER
10

Using PL/SQL to Enhance Performance (Developer and DBA)

Once you have all of the great queries to monitor your system, you need to automate them. PL/SQL gives you the ability to do so while also providing some great packages and procedures that you can use for tuning. The PL/SQL engine processes all PL/SQL requests and passes the statements on to Oracle for execution. When PL/SQL is passed to Oracle, it is placed in Oracle's System Global Area (SGA), more particularly in the shared pool. In Oracle, PL/SQL source code can be stored in the database in the form of procedures, functions, packages, and triggers.

Once these objects are stored in the database in compiled format, they can be executed from any Oracle tool by any user who has been granted EXECUTE privilege on that object. Upon execution, the p-code (executable code) is loaded into the SGA shared pool and executed by Oracle. A PL/SQL object remains in the SGA shared pool until the object is aged out with a Least Recently Used (LRU) algorithm. Therefore, if any process calls the object, it does not have to be reloaded into the SGA shared pool as long as it has not been aged out.

Consequently, Oracle looks in the SGA shared pool (which is very efficient) for the object prior to going to disk (which is not as efficient) to load the object. How well the SQL within the PL/SQL is tuned is probably the biggest driving factor of performance, yet there are also other tuning considerations that are covered in this chapter. The first portion of this chapter is dedicated to understanding and being able to locate the PL/SQL.

The topics covered in this chapter include the following:

- Using DBMS_APPLICATION_INFO for real-time monitoring

- Using log timing information in a database table

- Reducing PL/SQL program unit iterations and iteration time

- Using ROWID for iterative processing

- Standardizing on data types, IF statement order, and PLS_INTEGER

- Reducing the calls to SYSDATE

- Reducing the use of the MOD function

- Pinning objects in the Shared Pool

- Identifying PL/SQL objects that need to be pinned

- Using and modifying DBMS_SHARED_POOL.SIZES

- Getting detailed object information from DBA_OBJECT_SIZE

- Finding invalid objects

- Finding disabled triggers

- Finding and tuning the SQL when objects are used

- Using the time component when working with DATE data types

- Tuning and testing PL/SQL

- Examining the implications of PL/SQL object location

- Using rollback segments to open large cursors

- Using temporary database tables for increased performance

- Integrating a user tracking mechanism to pinpoint execution location

- Limiting the use of dynamic SQL

- Looking at some examples for beginners

Using DBMS_APPLICATION_INFO for Real-Time Monitoring

The DBMS_APPLICATION_INFO package provides a powerful mechanism for communicating point-in-time information about the execution in an environment. Listing 10-1 shows an example that enables a long-running PL/SQL program unit to provide information on the progress of the routine every 1000 records. The PL/SQL code segment updates the application information with the number of records processed and the elapsed time every 1000 records.

```
DECLARE
    CURSOR cur_employee IS
        SELECT employee_id, salary, ROWID
        FROM    s_employee_test;
    lv_new_salary_num NUMBER;
    lv_count_num       PLS_INTEGER := 0;
    lv_start_time_num PLS_INTEGER;
BEGIN
    lv_start_time_num := DBMS_UTILITY.GET_TIME;
    FOR cur_employee_rec IN cur_employee LOOP
        lv_count_num := lv_count_num + 1;
        -- Determination of salary increase
        lv_new_salary_num := cur_employee_rec.salary;
        UPDATE s_employee_test
        SET     salary      = lv_new_salary_num
        WHERE   rowid = cur_employee_rec.ROWID;
        IF MOD(lv_count_num, 1000) = 0 THEN
            DBMS_APPLICATION_INFO.SET_MODULE('Records Processed: ' ||
                lv_count_num, 'Elapsed: ' || (DBMS_UTILITY.GET_TIME -
                lv_start_time_num)/100 || ' sec');
        END IF;
    END LOOP;
    COMMIT;
        DBMS_APPLICATION_INFO.SET_MODULE('Records Processed: ' ||
            lv_count_num, 'Elapsed: ' || (DBMS_UTILITY.GET_TIME -
            lv_start_time_num)/100 || ' sec');
END;
/
```

Listing 10-1: Updating all employees' salary

To monitor the progress, the V$SESSION view can be queried, as shown in Listing 10-2.

```
SELECT username, sid, serial#, module, action
FROM   v$session
WHERE  username = 'PLSQL_USER';
```

Listing 10-2: Querying the V$SESSION view

Listing 10-3 is the output from the V$SESSION view, when queried three different times. The last time is when the PL/SQL program unit was completed.

```
USERNAME    SID SERIAL# MODULE                     ACTION
---------- --- ------- -------------------------- ------------------
PLSQL_USER   7       4 SQL*Plus
PLSQL_USER  10      10 Records Processed: 1000    Elapsed: 0.71 sec
USERNAME    SID SERIAL# MODULE                     ACTION
---------- --- ------- -------------------------- ------------------
PLSQL_USER   7       4 SQL*Plus
PLSQL_USER  10      10 Records Processed: 10000   Elapsed: 4.19 sec
USERNAME    SID SERIAL# MODULE                     ACTION
---------- --- ------- -------------------------- ------------------
PLSQL_USER   7       4 SQL*Plus
PLSQL_USER  10      10 Records Processed: 25000   Elapsed: 9.89 sec
```

Listing 10-3: V$SESSION view output

Your response time depends on how fast your system is and how well it is architectured. The two records are being returned in Listing 10-3 because both the execution of the PL/SQL program unit to update employees' salary and the SQL statement to monitor the progress via the V$SESSION view are executed under the PLSQL_USER schema in two different SQL*Plus sessions. Listing 10-3 illustrates a valuable technique to deploy in an environment and provides a real-time monitoring mechanism. It becomes easier to accurately determine how long a program has been running and to estimate how long a program has to complete.

If DBAs do not want users querying V$SESSION view information for all users, they can create a view on the V$SESSION view to limit the retrieval to only the executing users' session information. This task can be accomplished by executing the commands in Listing 10-4 under the SYS user. This syntax creates the new view. (The new view name used was session_log, but any name could have been used.)

```
CREATE VIEW session_log AS
SELECT *
FROM   v$session
WHERE  username = USERNAME;
```

Listing 10-4: V$SESSION view limiting user information retrieval

The syntax in Listing 10-5 creates a public synonym.

```
CREATE PUBLIC SYNONYM session_log FOR session_log;
```

Listing 10-5: Creating a public synonym

The following syntax grants SELECT permission to all users:

```
GRANT SELECT ON session_log TO PUBLIC;
```

Listing 10-6: Granting SELECT permission to all users

Once the session_log view is set up, as shown in the preceding statements, the V$SESSION view query in Listing 10-4 can be changed to SELECT from the session_log view, as in Listing 10-7, to limit the output to only the user executing the query.

```
SELECT username, sid, serial#, module, action
FROM    session_log;
```

Listing 10-7: Limiting output to user executing the query

TIP
Use the Oracle-supplied DBMS_APPLICATION_INFO package to log point-in-time information to the V$SESSION view to enable monitoring of long-running processes.

Using Log Timing Information in a Database Table

Monitoring performance is an ongoing process. Many variables in an environment can change and affect performance over time; therefore, performance should be monitored continuously. Some of the variables include user growth, data growth, reporting growth, application modification/ enhancement deployment, and additional load on the system from other applications. With this in mind, an Oracle system must be regularly monitored to ensure performance remains at, or above, an acceptable level.

One method of monitoring the system performance is to create a mechanism for logging timing statistics for certain aspects of an application. Batch programs are good candidates for this monitoring procedure. The monitoring procedure can be accomplished by inserting timing statistics into a database table. Listing 10-8 provides the database table logging method by creating a database table and then integrating INSERT statements for the timing of the process into the table.

The important information to log in the database table is the program identifier (some unique method of identifying the program), the date and time the program is executed, and the elapsed time of the execution. One column has been added for this application, namely, the number of records updated. This additional column is important for this application to monitor the growth of employee records being processed. When creating a timing log table for your application, add columns to store additional important processing information that may affect your timing results. Therefore, the table in Listing 10-8 can be created to log the timing information.

```
CREATE TABLE process_timing_log
    (program_name       VARCHAR2(30),
     execution_date     DATE,
     records_processed  NUMBER,
     elapsed_time_sec   NUMBER);
```

Listing 10-8: Creating process_timing_log table

Once the table is created, PL/SQL program units can be enhanced to log the timing information into the process_timing_log table, as illustrated in Listing 10-9.

```
CREATE OR REPLACE PROCEDURE update_salary AS
    CURSOR cur_employee IS
        SELECT employee_id, salary, ROWID
        FROM   s_employee_test;
    lv_new_salary_num NUMBER;
    lv_count_num        PLS_INTEGER := 0;
    lv_start_time_num PLS_INTEGER;
    lv_total_time_num NUMBER;
BEGIN
    lv_start_time_num := DBMS_UTILITY.GET_TIME;
    FOR cur_employee_rec IN cur_employee LOOP
        lv_count_num := lv_count_num + 1;
        -- Determination of salary increase
        lv_new_salary_num := cur_employee_rec.salary;
        UPDATE s_employee_test
        SET    salary      = lv_new_salary_num
        WHERE  rowid = cur_employee_rec.ROWID;
    END LOOP;
    lv_total_time_num := (DBMS_UTILITY.GET_TIME -
        lv_start_time_num)/100;
    INSERT INTO process_timing_log
        (program_name, execution_date, records_processed,
        elapsed_time_sec)
    VALUES
        ('UPDATE_SALARY', SYSDATE, lv_count_num,
        lv_total_time_num);
    COMMIT;
END update_salary;
/
```

Listing 10-9: Populating the process_timing_log table

As shown in Listing 10-9, the timer is started at the beginning of the program unit and then stopped at the end of the program unit. The difference between the start and ending timer is logged into the process_timing_log for each execution of the update_salary program. If the update_salary program unit is executed three times, as shown in Listing 10-10, then three timing records are inserted into the process_timing_log table.

```
EXECUTE update_salary
EXECUTE update_salary
EXECUTE update_salary
```

Listing 10-10: Executing update_salary three times

Another method is to use the DBMS_PROFILER package to get timing statistics per line of PL/SQL code. See Metalink article 104377.1, "Performance of New PL/SQL Features," for more information.

Listing 10-11 retrieves the information from the process_timing_log table.

```
SELECT    program_name,
          TO_CHAR(execution_date,'MM/DD/YYYY HH24:MI:SS') execution_time,
          records_processed, elapsed_time_sec
FROM      process_timing_log
ORDER BY 1,2;


PROGRAM_NAME    EXECUTION_TIME        RECORDS_PROCESSED ELAPSED_TIME_SEC
------------    ------------------    ----------------- ----------------
UPDATE_SALARY   07/02/2002 19:43:57              25252             8.89
UPDATE_SALARY   07/02/2002 19:44:07              25252             9.11
UPDATE_SALARY   07/02/2002 19:44:15              25252             8.62
```

Listing 10-11: Retrieving information from process_timing_log

This output shows one possible result. There is a difference in the elapsed time for the same program execution. If the difference increases over time, this may indicate a need to analyze the program unit further or the application to determine what caused the execution time increase. With logging mechanisms in place, the elapsed time can be monitored at any time because the timing information is being logged to a database table.

In Listing 10-11, the time logged is per program unit. If the program is complex and executed for an extended period of time, it may be desirable to change the logging of timing statistics from once in the program. The INSERT into the process_timing_log table could be performed after a certain number of iterations or to log timing for certain functionality in a program unit.

TIP

Log (INSERT) execution timing information into a database table for long-running PL/SQL program units to integrate a proactive performance-monitoring mechanism into your system. The database table can be reviewed at any time to determine if performance has decreased over time.

TIP
System load in terms of number of active sessions can have a large impact on the performance of program execution; therefore, it would be helpful to modify the database table logging method to include a column for the number of active sessions. This column can be filled by adding one additional query to the program unit being executed to retrieve the count from the V$SESSION view.

Reducing PL/SQL Program Unit Iterations and Iteration Time

Any PL/SQL program unit involving looping logic is a strong candidate for performance improvements. Potential improvements for these types of programs can be accomplished two ways. The first is to reduce the number of iterations by restructuring the logic to accomplish the same functional result. The second is to reduce the time per iteration. Either reduction often improves performance dramatically.

To bring this point into perspective, think of the following scenario: We need to process 9000 employee records in a PL/SQL routine, and to process each employee takes 2 seconds. This equates to 18000 seconds, which equates to 5 hours. If the processing per employee is reduced to 1 second, the time to process the 9000 employees is reduced by 9000 seconds or 2.5 hours—quite a difference!

Listing 10-12 shows a minor restructuring of a PL/SQL program unit to illustrate reducing per-loop processing and overall processing. The program unit processes a loop 1,000,000 times. Each iteration adds to the incremental counter used to display a message each 100,000 iterations and adds to the total counter used to check for loop exiting. To view DBMS_OUTPUT, make sure you issue the SET SERVEROUTPUT ON command first.

```
CREATE OR REPLACE PACKAGE stop_watch AS
   pv_start_time_num      PLS_INTEGER;
   pv_stop_time_num       PLS_INTEGER;
   pv_last_stop_time_num PLS_INTEGER;
-- This procedure creates a starting point for the timer routine and
-- is usually called once at the beginning of the PL/SQL program unit.
PROCEDURE start_timer;

This procedure retrieves a point in time and subtracts the current
-- time from the start time to determine the elapsed time. The
-- interval elapsed time is logged and displayed. This procedure is
-- usually called repetitively for each iteration or a specified
-- number of iterations.
PROCEDURE stop_timer;
END stop_watch;
/
Package created.

CREATE OR REPLACE PACKAGE BODY stop_watch AS
```

```
PROCEDURE start_timer AS
BEGIN
   pv_start_time_num     := DBMS_UTILITY.GET_TIME;
   pv_last_stop_time_num := pv_start_time_num;
END start_timer;
PROCEDURE stop_timer AS
BEGIN
   pv_stop_time_num := DBMS_UTILITY.GET_TIME;
   DBMS_OUTPUT.PUT_LINE('Total Time Elapsed: ' ||
      TO_CHAR((pv_stop_time_num - pv_start_time_num)/100,
      '999,999.99') || ' sec   Interval Time: ' ||
      TO_CHAR((pv_stop_time_num - pv_last_stop_time_num)/100,
      '99,999.99') || ' sec');
   pv_last_stop_time_num := pv_stop_time_num;
END stop_timer;
END;
/

Package body created.

SET SERVEROUTPUT ON

DECLARE
   lv_counter_num       PLS_INTEGER := 0;
   lv_total_counter_num PLS_INTEGER := 0;
BEGIN
   stop_watch.start_timer;
   LOOP
      lv_counter_num       := lv_counter_num + 1;
      lv_total_counter_num := lv_total_counter_num + 1;
      IF lv_counter_num >= 100000 THEN
         DBMS_OUTPUT.PUT_LINE('Processed 100,000 Records. ' ||
            'Total Processed ' || lv_total_counter_num);
         lv_counter_num := 0;
         EXIT WHEN lv_total_counter_num >= 1000000;
      END IF;
   END LOOP;
   stop_watch.stop_timer;
END;
/

Processed 100,000 Records. Total Processed 100000
Processed 100,000 Records. Total Processed 200000
Processed 100,000 Records. Total Processed 300000
Processed 100,000 Records. Total Processed 400000
Processed 100,000 Records. Total Processed 500000
Processed 100,000 Records. Total Processed 600000
Processed 100,000 Records. Total Processed 700000
Processed 100,000 Records. Total Processed 800000
Processed 100,000 Records. Total Processed 900000
```

Reducing Iterations and Iteraion time

```
Processed 100,000 Records. Total Processed 1000000
Total Time Elapsed:            .71 sec    Interval Time:        .71 sec

PL/SQL procedure successfully completed.
```

Listing 10-12: Minor restructuring of a PL/SQL program unit

By changing the program to add to the lv_total_counter_num variable only each time the incremental counter reaches 100000, the overall execution time is reduced, as shown in Listing 10-13.

```
DECLARE
    lv_counter_num        PLS_INTEGER := 0;
    lv_total_counter_num PLS_INTEGER := 0;
BEGIN
    stop_watch.start_timer;
    LOOP
        lv_counter_num        := lv_counter_num + 1;
        IF lv_counter_num >= 100000 THEN
            DBMS_OUTPUT.PUT_LINE('Processed 100,000 Records. Total ' ||
                'Processed ' || lv_total_counter_num);
            lv_total_counter_num := lv_total_counter_num +
                lv_counter_num;
            lv_counter_num := 0;
            EXIT WHEN lv_total_counter_num >= 1000000;
        END IF;
    END LOOP;
    stop_watch.stop_timer;
END;
/
```

Listing 10-13: Reducing overall execution time

The DBMS_OUTPUT.PUT_LINE output for the record-processed numbers was not included in Listing 10-13. Listing 10-14 illustrates the performance difference by changing the iteration logic to reduce the timing per iteration. The example is basic and shows a 34 percent increase on 1,000,000 iterations. Based on the restructuring and the iterations, this improvement can make a big difference.

```
Total Time Elapsed:            .47 sec    Interval Time:        .47 sec
PL/SQL procedure successfully completed.
```

Listing 10-14: Result of reducing the timing per iteration

TIP
When a PL/SQL program unit involves extensive looping or recursion, concentrate on reducing the execution time per iteration. This adds up fast, and it is easy to do the math to determine the overall improvement potential. The looping or recursion should also be reviewed for restructuring to reduce the number of iterations, while keeping the functionality. With the extreme flexibility of PL/SQL and SQL, typically, you can accomplish the same result in a variety of ways. If a PL/SQL program unit is not performing optimally, sometimes you have to rewrite the logic another way.

Using ROWID for Iterative Processing

The ROWID variable can help improve PL/SQL programs that retrieve records from the database, perform manipulation on the column values, and then complete with an UPDATE to the retrieved record. When retrieving each record, the ROWID can be added to the selected column list. When updating each record, the ROWID can be used in the predicate clause. The ROWID is the fastest access path to a record in a table, even faster than a unique index reference.

The performance improvement of using the ROWID is illustrated in Listing 10-15. The example retrieves each of the 25,000 employee records, calculates a new salary for each employee, and then updates the employees' salary. The actual salary calculation is not shown. The first PL/SQL code segment shows the timing results with the UPDATE using the employee_id column, which has a unique index on the column.

```
DECLARE
   CURSOR cur_employee IS
      SELECT employee_id, salary
      FROM   s_employee_test;
   lv_new_salary_num NUMBER;
BEGIN
   stop_watch.start_timer;
   FOR cur_employee_rec IN cur_employee LOOP
      -- Determination of salary increase
      lv_new_salary_num := cur_employee_rec.salary;
      UPDATE s_employee_test
      SET    salary       = lv_new_salary_num
      WHERE  employee_id = cur_employee_rec.employee_id;
   END LOOP;
   COMMIT;
   stop_watch.stop_timer;
END;
/
```

Listing 10-15: Timing results with UPDATE using the employee_id column

Listing 10-16 shows the timing of two executions of Listing 10-15.

```
Total Time Elapsed:          9.35 sec   Interval Time:       9.35 sec
PL/SQL procedure successfully completed.


Total Time Elapsed:          9.15 sec   Interval Time:       9.15 sec
PL/SQL procedure successfully completed.
```

Listing 10-16: Timing of two executions

The same functionality is maintained while changing the UPDATE to perform the UPDATE based on the ROWID. This involves adding the ROWID in the SELECT statement and changing the UPDATE predicate clause, as shown in Listing 10-17.

```
DECLARE
   CURSOR cur_employee IS
      SELECT employee_id, salary, ROWID
      FROM   s_employee_test;
   lv_new_salary_num NUMBER;
BEGIN
   stop_watch.start_timer;
   FOR cur_employee_rec IN cur_employee LOOP
      -- Determination of salary increase
      lv_new_salary_num := cur_employee_rec.salary;
      UPDATE s_employee_test
      SET    salary = lv_new_salary_num
      WHERE  rowid  = cur_employee_rec.ROWID;
   END LOOP;
   COMMIT;
   stop_watch.stop_timer;
END;
/
```

Listing 10-17: Performing UPDATE based on ROWID

Listing 10-18 shows the timing of two executions of Listing 10-17.

```
Total Time Elapsed:          8.76 sec   Interval Time:       8.76 sec
PL/SQL procedure successfully completed.


Total Time Elapsed:          8.96 sec   Interval Time:       8.96 sec
PL/SQL procedure successfully completed.
```

Listing 10-18: Timings of two executions

As evidenced from the timings, the execution occurs faster by using the ROWID. The first PL/SQL code segment UPDATE statement retrieves the result by using the index on employee_id to get the ROWID, and then goes to the table to search by ROWID; in contrast, the second

PL/SQL code segment UPDATE statement goes directly to the table to search by ROWID, thus eliminating the index search. The performance improvement would increase when more records are involved and when the index use is not referring to a unique index.

TIP
Use the ROWID variable to enhance performance when SELECTing a record in a PL/SQL program unit when the record needs to be manipulated in the same PL/SQL program unit.

Standardizing on Data Types, IF Statement Order, and PLS_INTEGER

You can introduce several minor programming modifications into your standard PL/SQL development that can improve performance. Three of these techniques are outlined in this section.

- Ensuring the same data types in comparison operations
- Ordering IF conditions based on the frequency of the condition
- Using the PLS-INTEGER PL/SQL data type for integer operations

Ensuring the Same Data Types in Comparison Operations

When variables or constant values are compared, they should have the same data type definition. If the comparison does not involve the same data types, then Oracle implicitly converts one of the values, thus introducing undesired overhead. Any time values are compared in a condition, the values should be the same data type. This standard should be used when developing PL/SQL program units and is good programming form.

Listing 10-19 illustrates the cost of comparing different data types, namely a numeric data type to a character value in the IF statement.

```
CREATE OR REPLACE PROCEDURE test_if (p_condition_num NUMBER) AS
   lv_temp_num          NUMBER := 0;
   lv_temp_cond_num     NUMBER := p_condition_num;
BEGIN
   stop_watch.start_timer;
   FOR lv_count_num IN 1..100000 LOOP
      IF lv_temp_cond_num = '1' THEN
         lv_temp_num := lv_temp_num + 1;
      ELSIF lv_temp_cond_num = '2' THEN
         lv_temp_num := lv_temp_num + 1;
      ELSIF lv_temp_cond_num = '3' THEN
         lv_temp_num := lv_temp_num + 1;
      ELSIF lv_temp_cond_num = '4' THEN
         lv_temp_num := lv_temp_num + 1;
      ELSIF lv_temp_cond_num = '5' THEN
         lv_temp_num := lv_temp_num + 1;
```

```
        ELSIF lv_temp_cond_num = '6' THEN
            lv_temp_num := lv_temp_num + 1;
        ELSIF lv_temp_cond_num = '7' THEN
            lv_temp_num := lv_temp_num + 1;
        ELSE
            lv_temp_num := lv_temp_num + 1;
        END IF;
    END LOOP;
    stop_watch.stop_timer;
END;
/
```

Listing 10-19: Comparing different data types

Listing 10-20 shows the execution of the test_if procedure.

```
EXECUTE test_if(8)
```

Listing 10-20: Executing test_if

The output in Listing 10-21 is the execution result of the test_if procedure.

```
Total Time Elapsed:           .56 sec   Interval Time:          .56 sec
PL/SQL procedure successfully completed.
```

Listing 10-21: Execution result of test_if

Unnecessary overhead is introduced with the different data types. If the procedure is changed to the same data type comparisons, the execution in Listing 10-22 is much faster:

```
CREATE OR REPLACE PROCEDURE test_if (p_condition_num NUMBER) AS
    lv_temp_num         NUMBER := 0;
    lv_temp_cond_num    NUMBER := p_condition_num;
BEGIN
    stop_watch.start_timer;
    FOR lv_count_num IN 1..100000 LOOP
        IF lv_temp_cond_num = 1 THEN
            lv_temp_num := lv_temp_num + 1;
        ELSIF lv_temp_cond_num = 2 THEN
            lv_temp_num := lv_temp_num + 1;
        ELSIF lv_temp_cond_num = 3 THEN
            lv_temp_num := lv_temp_num + 1;
        ELSIF lv_temp_cond_num = 4 THEN
            lv_temp_num := lv_temp_num + 1;
        ELSIF lv_temp_cond_num = 5 THEN
            lv_temp_num := lv_temp_num + 1;
        ELSIF lv_temp_cond_num = 6 THEN
            lv_temp_num := lv_temp_num + 1;
        ELSIF lv_temp_cond_num = 7 THEN
```

```
        lv_temp_num := lv_temp_num + 1;
    ELSE
        lv_temp_num := lv_temp_num + 1;
    END IF;
  END LOOP;
  stop_watch.stop_timer;
END;
/
```

Listing 10-22: Changing the procedure to the same data type comparisons

Listing 10-23 illustrates the execution of the new test_if procedure.

```
EXECUTE test_if(8)

Total Time Elapsed:        .43 sec    Interval Time:        .43 sec
PL/SQL procedure successfully completed.
```

Listing 10-23: Executing new test_if procedure

As shown in Listing 10-23, the execution is 23 percent faster. The improvement increases as the frequency of execution increases.

TIP
Ensure that all conditional comparisons compare the same data types. Additionally, it helps to ensure that the data types within the numeric family are comparing the same subtype. Therefore, in Listing 10-20, the comparison in the IF statement to a 1, 2, 3, and so forth, is comparing a NUMBER to a PLS_INTEGER. There is still some internal Oracle conversion overhead taking place. To eliminate this overhead, the 1, 2, 3... should be changed to 1.0, 2.0, 3.0.... When this change is made to Listing 10-20, the timing was reduced to 26 seconds.

Ordering IF Conditions Based on the Frequency of the Condition

The natural programming method when developing IF statements with multiple conditions is to order the conditional checks based on some sequential order. This order is typically alphabetical or numerically sequenced to create a more readable segment of code, but usually is not the most optimal. Especially when using the ELSIF condition several times in an IF statement, the most frequently met condition should appear first, followed by the next frequent match, and so forth.

In the previous section, the execution of the procedure was always carried out by passing an 8, which meant every loop had to check all eight conditional operations of the IF logic to satisfy the condition. If we pass a 1, which is equivalent to saying the first condition satisfies all IF executions, we get a more optimized result, as shown in Listing 10-24.

```
EXECUTE test_if(1)

Total Time Elapsed:          .14 sec   Interval Time:      .14 sec
PL/SQL procedure successfully completed.
```

Listing 10-24: Passing a 1 for more optimized results

The output in Listing 10-24 illustrates a performance improvement with the most efficient ordering of IF conditions. Therefore, take the extra step of analyzing IF condition ordering before coding the conditions to ensure maximum efficiency.

TIP
Ensure that the string of PL/SQL IF conditions appears in the order of most frequently satisfied, not a sequential order based numerically or alphanumerically.

Using the PLS_INTEGER PL/SQL Data Type for Integer Operations

The typical standard for declaring a numeric data type is to use the data type of NUMBER. In PL/SQL release 2.2, Oracle introduced the PLS_INTEGER data type. This data type can be used in place of any numeric family data type declaration, as long as the content of the variable is an integer and remains within the bounds of –2147483647 and +2147483647. Therefore, most counters and operations with integers can use this data type. The PLS_INTEGER involves fewer internal instructions to process, thus increasing performance when using this numeric data type. The more references to this variable, the more improvement realized.

This improvement is illustrated in Listing 10-25. The code segment is the same example as in Listings 10-22 and 10-24, with the data type declarations being changed to PLS_INTEGER from NUMBER.

```
CREATE OR REPLACE PROCEDURE test_if (p_condition_num PLS_INTEGER) AS
   lv_temp_num          PLS_INTEGER := 0;
   lv_temp_cond_num     PLS_INTEGER := p_condition_num;
BEGIN
   stop_watch.start_timer;
   FOR lv_count_num IN 1..100000 LOOP
      IF lv_temp_cond_num = 1 THEN
         lv_temp_num := lv_temp_num + 1;
      ELSIF lv_temp_cond_num = 2 THEN
         lv_temp_num := lv_temp_num + 1;
      ELSIF lv_temp_cond_num = 3 THEN
         lv_temp_num := lv_temp_num + 1;
```

```
      ELSIF lv_temp_cond_num = 4 THEN
          lv_temp_num := lv_temp_num + 1;
      ELSIF lv_temp_cond_num = 5 THEN
          lv_temp_num := lv_temp_num + 1;
      ELSIF lv_temp_cond_num = 6 THEN
          lv_temp_num := lv_temp_num + 1;
      ELSIF lv_temp_cond_num = 7 THEN
          lv_temp_num := lv_temp_num + 1;
      ELSE
          lv_temp_num := lv_temp_num + 1;
      END IF;
    END LOOP;
    stop_watch.stop_timer;
END;
/
```

Listing 10-25: Using PLS_INTEGER

The following illustrates the execution of the test_if procedure:

```
EXECUTE test_if(1)
```

Listing 10-26: Executing test_if

The performance improvement in Listing 10-27 is evident based on the results of the execution:

```
Total Time Elapsed:          .14 sec    Interval Time:          .14 sec
PL/SQL procedure successfully completed.
```

Listing 10-27: Results of executing test_if

TIP
Use the PLS_INTEGER when processing integers to improve performance.

TIP
If a number with precision is assigned to a PLS_INTEGER variable, the value is rounded to a whole number as if the ROUND function were performed on the number.

Reducing the Calls to SYSDATE

Using the SYSDATE variable is a convenient method of retrieving the current date and time. Calls to SYSDATE involve some overhead; therefore, if this variable is needed to log the date of certain processing, the call to this variable should be made once at the start of the program versus each iteration. This technique of calling SYSDATE once at the start of the program assumes the date logging is desired when the program started.

The reduction of SYSDATE calls is illustrated in Listing 10-29. The example loops through 10,000 iterations, calling SYSDATE (only the date portion of the variable because the TRUNC function is used to truncate the time portion) every iteration.

```
DECLARE
    lv_current_date     DATE;
BEGIN
    stop_watch.start_timer;
    FOR lv_count_num IN 1..10000 LOOP
        lv_current_date := TRUNC(SYSDATE);
    END LOOP;
    stop_watch.stop_timer;
END;
/
```

Listing 10-28: Calling SYSDATE every iteration

Listing 10-29 shows the timing of two executions of Listing 10-28.

```
Total Time Elapsed:          .10 sec   Interval Time:        .10 sec
PL/SQL procedure successfully completed.


Total Time Elapsed:          .08 sec   Interval Time:        .08 sec
PL/SQL procedure successfully completed.
```

Listing 10-29: Timing two executions of Listing 10-28

Listing 10-30 is modified to retrieve the SYSDATE only once, at the beginning of the program, and set to another variable each iteration.

```
DECLARE
    lv_current_date     DATE := TRUNC(SYSDATE);
    lv_final_date       DATE;
BEGIN
    stop_watch.start_timer;
    FOR lv_count_num IN 1..10000 LOOP
        lv_final_date := lv_current_date;
    END LOOP;
    stop_watch.stop_timer;
END;
/
```

Listing 10-30: Modified call to SYSDATE

Listing 10-31 shows the timing of two executions of Listing 10-30.

```
Total Time Elapsed:          .00 sec   Interval Time:        .00 sec
PL/SQL procedure successfully completed.
```

```
Total Time Elapsed:          .01 sec    Interval Time:        .01 sec
PL/SQL procedure successfully completed.
```

Listing 10-31: Timings of two executions of Listing 10-30

As evident in Listing 10-31, overhead is associated with the SYSDATE call, and the number of calls to SYSDATE should be reduced, if possible. The example for SYSDATE was executed under Oracle 7.3.2. When the same two PL/SQL code segments were executed under Oracle 8.1.5 and Oracle 9.2.0, the timings were quite different than what might be expected. The following table shows the execution timing differences between Oracle versions of Listings 10-26 and 10-27.

PL/SQL Code Segment	Oracle 7.3.2 Timing	Oracle 8.1.5 Timing	Oracle 9.2.0 Timing
SYSDATE call inside loop	4.80 sec/3.31 sec	2.98 sec/2.97 sec	.10 sec/.10 sec
SYSDATE call before loop	.06 sec/.06 sec	.01 sec/.01 sec	.00 sec/.00 sec

As mentioned in the introduction of this chapter, differences exist between Oracle versions, hardware platforms, and operating systems, which can cause different timing results than the ones shown in this book. Therefore, always create a test environment where you can accurately and consistently monitor timings to ensure that performance enhancements introduced in the test environment will be realized in production.

TIP
Attempt to limit the calls to SYSDATE in iterative or recursive loops because overhead is associated with this variable. Set a PL/SQL DATE variable to SYSDATE in the declaration and reference the PL/SQL variable to eliminate the overhead.

Reducing the Use of the MOD Function

Certain PL/SQL functions are more costly to use than others. MOD is one function that is better to be performed with additional PL/SQL logic to improve the overall performance. This is illustrated in Listing 10-32. This is a useful function but, if executed in an IF statement as illustrated in the following example, additional overhead is introduced. For more information on MOD, see Chapter 6.

```
BEGIN
   stop_watch.start_timer;
   FOR lv_count_num IN 1..10000 LOOP
      IF MOD(lv_count_num, 1000) = 0 THEN
         DBMS_OUTPUT.PUT_LINE('Hit 1000; Total: ' || lv_count_num);
      END IF;
   END LOOP;
   stop_watch.stop_timer;
END;
/
```

Listing 10-32: Using MOD

Listing 10-33 shows the timing of two executions of Listing 10-32. (The DBMS_OUTPUT .PUT_LINE output is displayed only once.)

```
Hit 1000; Total: 1000
Hit 1000; Total: 2000
Hit 1000; Total: 3000
Hit 1000; Total: 4000
Hit 1000; Total: 5000
Hit 1000; Total: 6000
Hit 1000; Total: 7000
Hit 1000; Total: 8000
Hit 1000; Total: 9000
Hit 1000; Total: 10000
Total Time Elapsed:         .04 sec    Interval Time:         .04 sec
PL/SQL procedure successfully completed.


Total Time Elapsed:         .04 sec    Interval Time:         .04 sec
```

Listing 10-33: Timing of two executions of Listing 10-32

Listing 10-33 is modified to eliminate the MOD function use and perform the same check with additional PL/SQL logic, as illustrated in Listing 10-34.

```
DECLARE
   lv_count_inc_num PLS_INTEGER := 0;
BEGIN
   stop_watch.start_timer;
   FOR lv_count_num IN 1..10000 LOOP
      lv_count_inc_num := lv_count_inc_num + 1;
      IF lv_count_inc_num = 1000 THEN
         DBMS_OUTPUT.PUT_LINE('Hit 1000; Total: ' || lv_count_num);
         lv_count_inc_num := 0;
      END IF;
   END LOOP;
   stop_watch.stop_timer;
END;
/

Hit 1000; Total: 1000
Hit 1000; Total: 2000
Hit 1000; Total: 3000
Hit 1000; Total: 4000
Hit 1000; Total: 5000
Hit 1000; Total: 6000
Hit 1000; Total: 7000
Hit 1000; Total: 8000
Hit 1000; Total: 9000
Hit 1000; Total: 10000
Total Time Elapsed:         .01 sec    Interval Time:         .01 sec
```

```
PL/SQL procedure successfully completed.

Total Time Elapsed:        .00 sec    Interval Time:        .00 sec
```

Listing 10-34: Eliminating MOD and performing same check with additional PL/SQL logic

As shown in Listings 10-33 and 10-34, the MOD function adds overhead and is better performed with PL/SQL IF statements. Listing 10-32 was executed under Oracle 7.3.2. When the same two PL/SQL code segments were executed under Oracle 8.1.5 and Oracle 9.2.0, the timings were quite different than what might be expected. Table 10-2 shows the timing differences between versions of Listings 10-33 and 10-34.

PL/SQL Code Segment	Oracle 7.3.2 Timing	Oracle 8.1.5 Timing	Oracle 9.2.0 Timing
MOD utilized	.58 sec/.43 sec	.09 sec/.09 sec	.04 sec/.04 sec
MOD simulated	.11 sec/.05 sec	.02 sec/.02 sec	.01 sec/.01 sec

TIP
The MOD function is one function that is faster to perform with additional PL/SQL logic. While this is minor, it is a standard technique to introduce into your PL/SQL standard programming techniques.

Pinning Objects in the Shared Pool

The SHARED_POOL_SIZE sets the amount of shared pool allocated in the SGA. (See Chapter 4 and Appendix A for a detailed look at SHARED_POOL_SIZE and closely related shared pool parameters.) The shared pool stores all SQL statements and PL/SQL blocks executed under the Oracle database. Based on the method in which Oracle manages the SGA shared pool, as far as aging, the SGA shared pool can become fragmented.

In addition, because Oracle does not age any objects that are currently being processed by a session, there is the possibility that you can get an Oracle error indicating that the SGA shared pool does not have enough memory for a new object. The exact error message you receive is "ORA-4031: unable to allocate *XXX* bytes of shared memory" (where *XXX* is the number of bytes it is attempting to allocate). If this error is ever received, it means that your SGA shared pool should be increased in size as soon as possible.

The method prior to Oracle9 was to modify the initialization parameter SHARED_POOL_SIZE and then shut down and start up the database. The quick but costly method of eliminating this error until the next database shutdown was to flush the SGA shared pool. This was accomplished with the command in Listing 10-500 (allowed only if ALTER SYSTEM privilege is assigned to a user):

```
alter system flush shared_pool;
```

Listing 10-35: Flushing the SGA shared pool

In Oracle9, you can modify the SHARED_POOL_SIZE without shutting down the database as long as you don't exceed the SGA_MAX_SIZE. This eliminates the need to perform tasks that you had to do in previous versions. You still want to pin the large objects into the shared pool when the database has started and make sure that the shared pool is large enough for all of these statements to be cached.

TIP
In Oracle9, the SHARED_POOL_SIZE may be modified while the database is up, as long as you don't exceed the SGA_MAX_SIZE. See Chapter 4 for additional information about setting initialization parameters.

Pinning (Caching) PL/SQL Object Statements into Memory

If you cannot maintain a sufficient SHARED_POOL_SIZE to keep all statements in memory, it may be prudent to keep the most important objects cached (pinned) in memory. Listing 10-36 shows how to pin PL/SQL object statements (the procedure PROCESS_DATE is pinned) in memory using the DBMS_SHARED_POOL.KEEP procedure.

```
begin
dbms_shared_pool.keep('process_date','p');
end;

or

L 10-37

execute dbms_shared_pool.keep ('SYS.STANDARD');
```

Listing 10-36: Using DBMS_SHARED_POOL.KEEP to pin PROCESS_DATE in memory

By pinning an object in memory, the object is not aged out or flushed until the next database shutdown.

TIP
Use the DBMS_SHARED_POOL.KEEP procedure to pin PL/SQL objects into the shared pool.

NOTE
To use this procedure, you must first run the DBMSPOOL.SQL script. The PRVTPOOL.PLB script is automatically executed after DBMSPOOL.SQL runs. These scripts are not run by CATPROC.SQL.

Pinning All Packages

To pin all packages in the system, execute the code in Listing 10-37 (from Oracle's Metalink).

```
declare
own varchar2(100);
nam varchar2(100);
cursor pkgs is
    select      owner, object_name
    from        dba_objects
    where       object_type = 'PACKAGE';
begin
    open pkgs;
    loop
        fetch pkgs into own, nam;
        exit when pkgs%notfound;
        dbms_shared_pool.keep(own || '.' || nam, 'P');
    end loop;
end;
/
```

Listing 10-37: Pinning all packages in the system

A more targeted approach, pinning only packages that needed to be reloaded, would be better than pinning *all* packages, especially because most DBA interfaces since Oracle8*i* involve PL/SQL packages. However, the fact that the table is deleted with each startup might cause problems, because pinned packages shouldn't need to be reloaded every day. At the very least, you should check to make sure you are not trying to pin invalid packages.

Common problem packages that are shipped with Oracle (and should be kept) include STANDARD, DBMS_STANDARD, and DIUTIL.

TIP
Use the DBMS_SHARED_POOL.KEEP procedure combined in PL/SQL to pin all packages when the database is started (if memory/shared pool permits) and avoid all errors involving loading packages in the future.

Identifying PL/SQL Objects that Need to Be Pinned

Fragmentation that causes several small pieces to be available in the shared pool, and not enough large contiguous pieces, is a common occurrence in the shared pool. The key to eliminating shared pool errors (as noted in the previous section) is to understand which of the objects is large enough to cause problems when you attempt to load them. Once you know the problem PL/SQL, you can then pin this code when the database has started (and the shared pool is completely contiguous). This ensures that your large packages are already in the shared pool when they are called, instead of searching for a large contiguous piece of the shared pool (which may not be there later as the system is used).

You can query the V$DB_OBJECT_CACHE view to determine PL/SQL that is both large and currently not marked "kept." These are objects that may cause problems (due to their size and need for a large amount of contiguous memory) if they need to be reloaded later. This shows only the current statements in the cache. Listing 10-38 searches for those objects requiring greater than 100KB.

```
select     name, sharable_mem
from       v$db_object_cache
where      sharable_mem > 100000
and        type in ('PACKAGE', 'PACKAGE BODY', 'FUNCTION', 'PROCEDURE')
and        kept = 'NO';
```

Listing 10-38: Searching for objects requiring more than 100KB

TIP
Query the V$DB_OBJECT_CACHE table to find objects that are not pinned and are also large enough to potentially cause problems.

Using and Modifying DBMS_SHARED_POOL.SIZES

An alternative and very precise indication of shared pool allocation can be viewed through the DBMS_SHARED_POOL.SIZES package procedure. This call accepts a MINIMUM SIZE parameter and displays all cursors and objects within the shared pool of a size greater than that provided. The actual statement issued to retrieve this information is shown in Listing 10-39.

```
select     to_char(sharable_mem / 1000 ,'999999') sz, decode
           (kept_versions,0,' ',rpad('yes(' || to_char(kept_versions)
           || ')' ,6)) keeped, rawtohex(address) || ',' || to_char
           (hash_value)  name, substr(sql_text,1,354) extra, 1 iscursor
from       v$sqlarea
where      sharable_mem > &min_ksize * 1000
union
select     to_char(sharable_mem / 1000 ,'999999') sz, decode(kept,'yes',
           'yes   ','') keeped, owner || '.' || name || lpad(' ',29 -
           (length(owner) + length(name) ) ) || '(' || type || ')'
           name, null  extra, 0 iscursor
from       v$db_object_cache v
where      sharable_mem > &min_ksize * 1000
order by   1 desc;
```

Listing 10-39: Calling DBMS_SHARED_POOL.SIZES

This query can be placed into a procedure package of your own construction, to display a formatted view of cursors and objects within the shared pool.

Finding Large Objects

You can use the DBMS_SHARED_POOL.SIZES package procedure (*DBMS_SHARED_POOL* is the package and *sizes* is the procedure within the package) to view the objects using shareable memory higher than a threshold that you set. Execute this package as displayed in Listing 10-40 for a threshold of 100KB (the output follows):

```
Set serveroutput on size 5000;

begin
dbms_shared_pool.sizes(100);
end;

SIZE(K) KEPT    NAME
------- ------
-----------------------------------------------------------------
377             SYS.STANDARD                    (PACKAGE)
312             SYS.DBMS_STATS_INTERNAL         (PACKAGE)
287             SYS.DBMS_STATS                  (PACKAGE BODY)
266             XDB.XDB$BOOTSTRAP               (PACKAGE BODY)
255             RMAN.DBMS_RCVMAN                (PACKAGE BODY)
226             ODM.ODM_ABN_MODEL               (PACKAGE BODY)
222             SYS.DBMS_REPCAT_UTL             (PACKAGE BODY)
219             SYS.DBMS_RCVMAN                 (PACKAGE BODY)
215             MDSYS.MD                        (PACKAGE)
207             OLAPSYS.DBMS_ODM                (PACKAGE BODY)
186             SYS.DBMS_REPCAT                 (PACKAGE)
177             SYS.LT                          (PACKAGE)
175             SYS.WM_DDL_UTIL                 (PACKAGE BODY)
172             SYS.LTADM                       (PACKAGE BODY)
171             CTXSYS.DRIG                     (PACKAGE)
170             RMAN.DBMS_RCVMAN                (PACKAGE)
167             SYS.DBMS_REPCAT_SNA_UTL         (PACKAGE BODY)
166             SYS.DBMS_RCVMAN                 (PACKAGE)
166             SYS.DIANA                       (PACKAGE)
163             SYS.LT                          (PACKAGE BODY)
161             MDSYS.SDO_GEOM                  (PACKAGE)
154             SYS.DBMS_BACKUP_RESTORE         (PACKAGE)
153             SYS.LTDTRG                      (PACKAGE BODY)
150             SYS.DBMS_REPCAT_DECL            (PACKAGE)
149             WKSYS.WKDS_ADM                  (PACKAGE BODY)
144             SYS.DBMS_REPCAT_UTL             (PACKAGE)
144             WKSYS.WK_CRW                    (PACKAGE BODY)
134             SYS.DBMS_SYS_SQL                (PACKAGE)
133             SYS.DBMS_SQL                    (PACKAGE)
124             MDSYS.SDO_LRS                   (PACKAGE)
```

```
119        RMAN.DBMS_RCVCAT              (PACKAGE BODY)
118        XDB.XDB$BOOTSTRAP            (PACKAGE)
117        SYS.DBMS_METADATA_INT       (PACKAGE BODY)
109        SYS.DBMS_REPCAT_UTL4        (PACKAGE BODY)
108        MDSYS.SDO_LRS               (PACKAGE BODY)
104        OLAPSYS.OLAPFACTVIEW        (PACKAGE BODY)
104        SYS.DBMS_REPCAT_UTL3        (PACKAGE BODY)
103        SYS.DBMS_REPCAT_MAS         (PACKAGE BODY)
103        SYS.DBMS_REPCAT_RPC         (PACKAGE)
```

Listing 10-40: DBMS_SHARED_POOL.SIZES and output

TIP
Use the DBMS_SHARED_POOL.SIZES package procedure to find specific information about an object.

Getting Detailed Object Information from DBA_OBJECT_SIZE

Query the DBA_OBJECT_SIZE view to show the memory used by a particular object that includes much more detailed information concerning the object, as shown in Listing 10-41.

```
Compute sum of source_size on report
Compute sum of parsed_size on report
Compute sum of code_size on report
Break on report
select     *
from       dba_object_size
where      name = 'RDBA_GENERATE_STATISTICS';
```

OWNER	NAME	TYPE	SOURCE_SIZE	PARSED_SIZE	CODE_SIZE
RDBA	RDBA_GENERATE_STATISTICS	PACKAGE	5023	4309	3593
RDBA	RDBA_GENERATE_STATISTICS	PACKAGE BODY	85595	0	111755
SUM			90618	4309	115348

Listing 10-41: Querying Query the DBA_OBJECT_SIZE view and output

Getting Contiguous Space Currently in the Shared Pool

Why does the shared pool return errors when an object is loaded? A large enough piece of the shared pool is not available to fit the piece of code. You saw in the last section how to find the size of the code that you have. You also saw in *Pinning Objects in the Shared Pool* how to pin pieces of code into the shared pool. Now you must look at the query that tells you which code, that has made it into the shared pool, is either very large and should be pinned or should be investigated and shortened if possible.

The following query in Listing 10-42 accesses an X$ table (see Chapter 15); you must be the SYS user to access these tables:

```
select     ksmchsiz, ksmchcom
from       x$ksmsp
where      ksmchsiz > 10000
and        ksmchcom like '%PL/SQL%';
```

Listing 10-42: Accessing an X$ table

This query shows that the packages that have been accessed are very large and should be pinned when the database has started. If the last line of this query is eliminated, it also shows the large pieces of free memory (KSMCHCOM = "free memory" and KSMCHCOM = "permanent memory") that are still available (unfragmented) for future large pieces of code to be loaded. See Chapter 13 for more details on the x$ tables and example output.

TIP
Query x$ksmsp to find all large pieces of PL/SQL that have appeared in the shared pool. These are candidates to be pinned when the database has started.

Finding Invalid Objects

Developers often change a small section of PL/SQL code that fails to compile upon execution, forcing an application failure. A simple query, reviewed daily, will help you spot these failures before the end user does (Listing 10-43).

```
col        "Owner" format a12
col        "Object" format a20
col        "OType" format a12
col        "Change DTE" format a20
select     substr(owner,1,12) "Owner", substr(object_name,1,20)
           "Object", object_type "OType", to_char(last_ddl_time,
           'DD-MON-YYYY HH24:MI:SS') "Change Date"
from       dba_objects
where      status <> 'VALID'
order by   1, 2;
```

Listing 10-43: Finding invalid objects

Listing 10-43 displays any objects that are INVALID, meaning they were never compiled successfully, or changes in dependent objects have caused them to become INVALID. If we had a procedure PROCESS_DATE, for example, found to be INVALID, we could manually recompile this procedure with the following command:

```
alter procedure PROCESS_DATE compile;
```

Listing 10-44: Manually recompiling PROCESS_DATE

Once this command is executed and the PROCESS_DATE passes the recompile, the procedure would be changed by Oracle automatically from INVALID to VALID. Another manual method that exists is to call the DBMS_UTILITY.COMPILE_SCHEMA package procedure as outlined in Listing 10-45 to recompile all stored procedures, functions, and packages for a given schema:

```
begin
dbms_utility.compile_schema('USERA');
end;
```

Listing 10-45: Calling DBMS_UTILITY.COMPILE_SCHEMA

To find the state of all PL/SQL objects for your schema, execute the code in Listing 10-46:

```
column    object_name  format a20
column    last_ddl_time heading 'last ddl time'
select    object_type, object_name, status, created, last_ddl_time
from      user_objects
where     object_type in ('PROCEDURE', 'FUNCTION', 'PACKAGE',
          'PACKAGE BODY', 'TRIGGER');


OBJECT_TYPE          OBJECT_NAME          STATUS  CREATED   last ddl
-----------------    --------------------  ------- --------- ---------
PACKAGE              DBMS_REPCAT_AUTH     VALID   12-MAY-02 12-MAY-02
PACKAGE BODY         DBMS_REPCAT_AUTH     VALID   12-MAY-02 12-MAY-02
TRIGGER              DEF$_PROPAGATOR_TRIG VALID   12-MAY-02 12-MAY-02
PROCEDURE            ORA$_SYS_REP_AUTH    VALID   12-MAY-02 12-MAY-02
TRIGGER              REPCATLOGTRIG        VALID   12-MAY-02 12-MAY-02
```

Listing 10-46: Finding the state of all PL/SQL objects for the schema

TIP
Query DBA_OBJECTS (for systemwide objects) or USER_OBJECT (for only your schema) to find the state of objects and avoid errors and reloading by the user. You can recompile individual objects or an entire schema with DBMS_UTILITY.COMPILE_SCHEMA.

Finding Disabled Triggers

In some respects, a disabled trigger is far more dangerous than an invalid object because it doesn't fail—it just doesn't *execute*! This can have severe consequences for applications, and consequently, business processes, that depend on business logic stored within procedural code. Listing 10-47 identifies disabled triggers.

```
col       "Owner/Table" format a30
col       "Trigger Name" format a25
col       "Event" format a15
col       "Owner" format a10
select    substr(owner,12) "Owner", trigger_name "Trigger Name",
          trigger_type "Type", triggering_event "Event",
```

```
            table_owner||'.'||table_name "Owner/Table"
from        dba_triggers
where       status <> 'ENABLED'
order by    owner, trigger_name;
```

Listing 10-47: Identifying disabled triggers

If you run the query in Listing 10-47 as checking only SYS and certain columns, you will get the disabled triggers shown in Listing 10-48 that Oracle builds.

```
Select      trigger_name "Trigger Name",STATUS,
            trigger_type "Type", triggering_event "Event"
from        dba_triggers
where       status <> 'ENABLED'
and         owner = 'SYS'
order by    owner, trigger_name;


Trigger Name                 STATUS    Type               Event
---------------------------  --------  -----------------  ----------------
AURORA$SERVER$SHUTDOWN        DISABLED  BEFORE EVENT       SHUTDOWN
AURORA$SERVER$STARTUP         DISABLED  AFTER EVENT        STARTUP
NO_VM_CREATE                  DISABLED  BEFORE EVENT       CREATE
NO_VM_DROP                    DISABLED  BEFORE EVENT       DROP
SYS_LOGOFF                    DISABLED  BEFORE EVENT       LOGOFF
SYS_LOGON                     DISABLED  AFTER EVENT        LOGON
```

Listing 10-48: Disabled triggers Oracle builds

To find all triggers for your schema, execute the code shown in Listing 10-49.

```
column      trigger_name      format a15
column      trigger_type      format a15
column      triggering_event  format a15
column      table_name        format a15
column      trigger_body      format a25
select      trigger_name, trigger_type, triggering_event,
            table_name, status, trigger_body
from        user_triggers;

TRIGGER_NAME TRIGGER_TYPE       TRIGGERING_EVENT TABLE_NAME STATUS   TRIGGER_BODY
UPDATE_TOTAL AFTER STATEMENT    INSERT OR UPDATE ORDER_MAIN ENABLED  begin
                                OR DELETE                            update
total_orders
                                                                     set
order_total = 10;
                                                                     end;
```

Listing 10-49: Finding all the triggers for the schema

TIP
*Query DBA_TRIGGERS (for systemwide objects) or USER_TRIGGERS
(for only your schema) to find the state of triggers and avoid errors
with disabled triggers. Disabled triggers can have fatal results for an
application: they don't fail, they just don't execute.*

Using PL/SQL Tables for Fast Reference Table Lookups

Programs that are designed to process data coming into a system usually incorporate numerous
reference table lookups to properly validate and/or code the incoming data. When the reference
tables are searched, using a unique key that is a numerical data type, the query performance
against the reference tables can be drastically increased by loading the reference tables into
PL/SQL tables. Consider an incoming data set that contains a single numerical column that must
be translated to a coded string using a reference table. Listing 10-50 is a program to handle this
task using the classic approach of repeated searches against the reference table:

```
declare
New_Code varchar2(10);
cursor C1 (The_Code IN number) is
   select      ref_string
   from        Ref_Table
   where       ref_num = The_Code;
   cursor CMain is
     select    *
     from      incoming_data;
begin
   -- Open a cursor to the incoming data.
   for In_Data in CMain loop
     begin
        -- Calculate the reference string from the
        -- reference data.
        open C1(In_Data.coded_value);
        fetch C1 into New_Code;
        if C1%notfound then
          close C1;
          raise NO_DATA_FOUND;
        end if;
        close C1;
        -- processing logic...
        -- Commit each record as it is processed.
        commit;
     exception
        when NO_DATA_FOUND then
           -- Appropriate steps...
        when OTHERS then
           -- Appropriate steps...
```

```
      end;
    end loop;
end;
```

Listing 10-50: Using repeated searches against the reference table

While this program may appear to be written efficiently, it is in fact hampered by the repeated queries against the reference table. Even though Oracle may have the entire reference table in memory, due to pinning or prior queries, a certain amount of overhead is still involved with processing the queries.

A more efficient technique is to load the entire reference table into a PL/SQL table. The numerical column (against which the searches are performed) is loaded as the array index. When a lookup against the reference data is required, the PL/SQL table is used instead of the actual reference table—the code in the incoming data that must be translated is used as the array index of the PL/SQL table. The inherent nature of working with PL/SQL tables is that if an INVALID array index is used (meaning the code in the incoming data does not match any value in the reference table), the NO_DATA_FOUND exception will be raised. Listing 10-51 shows the same processing program as shown in Listing 10-50, rewritten using a PL/SQL table to store the reference data:

```
declare
  type Ref_Dat_Array is table of varchar2(10)
  index by binary_integer;
  Ref_Dat  Ref_Dat_Array;
  New_Code varchar2(10);
  cursor C1 is
    select *
    from Ref_Table;
  cursor CMain is
    select *
    from incoming_data;
begin
  -- First, load the reference array
  -- with data from the reference table.
  for C1_Rec in C1 loop
    Ref_Dat(C1_Rec.Ref_Num) := C1_Rec.Ref_String;
  end loop;
  -- Open a cursor to the incoming data.
  for In_Data in CMain loop
    begin
      -- Calculate the reference string from the
      -- reference data.
      New_Code := Ref_Dat(In_Data.coded_value);
      -- processing logic...
      -- Commit each record as it is processed.
      commit;
    exception
      when NO_DATA_FOUND then
        -- Appropriate steps...
      when OTHERS then
        -- Appropriate steps...
```

Using PL/SQL Tables for Fast Lookups

```
    end;
  end loop;
end;
```

Listing 10-51: Using a PL/SQL table to store reference data

The result should be a drastic increase in processing speed due to the reduced overhead in working with the PL/SQL tables in comparison to the actual database table.

TIP
Load reference tables into PL/SQL tables for faster lookups. This takes advantage of the performance of array indexes in PL/SQL.

Finding and Tuning SQL When Objects Are Used

At times, the hardest part of tuning stored objects is finding the actual code that is stored in the database. This section looks at queries that retrieve SQL that can be tuned. In this section, we query views that retrieve information about the actual source code that exists behind the stored objects.

Listing 10-52 retrieves the code for a procedure you created called PROCESS_DATE.

```
column     text   format a80
select     text
from       user_source
where      name = 'PROCESS_DATE'
order by   line;
```

Listing 10-52: Retrieving the code for PROCESS_DATE

This query works for querying a procedure, trigger, or function. For packages, change the last line to ORDER BY type, line, as shown in Listing 10-53.

```
TEXT
procedure process_date is
  test_num number;
 begin
 test_num := 10;
 if test_num = 10 then
  update order_main
  set       process_date = sysdate
  where    order_num = 12345;
 end if;
 end;
```

Listing 10-53: Querying a package using ORDER BY

To retrieve the code for the familiar DBMS_RULE package, use the code in Listing 10-54

```
column    text format a80
select    text
from      dba_source
where     name  = 'DBMS_RULE'
and       type  = 'PACKAGE'
order by  line;

TEXT
----------------------------------------------------------------------------
---
PACKAGE dbms_rule AUTHID CURRENT_USER AS
  PROCEDURE evaluate(
        rule_set_name          IN       varchar2,
        evaluation_context     IN       varchar2,
        event_context          IN       sys.re$nv_list := NULL,
        table_values           IN       sys.re$table_value_list := NULL,
        variable_values        IN       sys.re$variable_value_list := NULL,
        stop_on_first_hit      IN       boolean := FALSE,
        simple_rules_only      IN       boolean := FALSE,
        true_rules             OUT      sys.re$rule_hit_list,
        maybe_rules            OUT      sys.re$rule_hit_list);

  PROCEDURE evaluate(
        rule_set_name          IN       varchar2,
        evaluation_context     IN       varchar2,
        event_context          IN       sys.re$nv_list := NULL,
        table_values           IN       sys.re$table_value_list := NULL,
        column_values          IN       sys.re$column_value_list,
        variable_values        IN       sys.re$variable_value_list := NULL,
        attribute_values       IN       sys.re$attribute_value_list,
        stop_on_first_hit      IN       boolean := FALSE,
        simple_rules_only      IN       boolean := FALSE,
        true_rules             OUT      sys.re$rule_hit_list,
        maybe_rules            OUT      sys.re$rule_hit_list);
END dbms_rule;

27 rows selected.
```

Listing 10-54: Retrieving the code for DBMS_RULE

To attempt to retrieve the package body for the DBMS_JOB package, use the code in Listing 10-55.

```
column    text   format a80
select    text
from      dba_source
```

Finding and Tuning SQL

```
where      name  = 'DBMS_JOB'
and        type  = 'PACKAGE BODY'
order by   line;


TEXT
PACKAGE BODY dbms_job wrapped
0
abcd
abcd
...
:2 a0 6b d a0 ac :3 a0 6b b2
ee :2 a0 7e b4 2e ac e5 d0
b2 e9 93 a0 7e 51 b4 2e
:2 a0 6b 7e 51 b4 2e 6e a5
57 b7 19 3c b0 46 :2 a0 6b
ac :2 a0 b2 ee ac e5 d0 b2
e9 :2 a0 6b :3 a0 6e :4 a0 :5 4d a5
57 :2 a0 a5 57 b7 :3 a0 7e 51
```

Listing 10-55: Attempting to retrieve the package body for DBMS_JOB

In Listing 10-55, the package was wrapped (protected) using the WRAP command, and the output is unreadable. If you find yourself tuning the code, you need sleep.

To retrieve the package body for the DBMS_OUTPUT package, use the code in Listing 10-56.

```
column     text   format a80
select     text
from       user_source
where      name  = 'DBMS_OUTPUT'
and        type  = 'PACKAGE BODY'
order by   line;


TEXT
package body dbms_output as
  enabled            boolean := FALSE;
  buf_size           binary_integer;
  tmpbuf             varchar2(500)  := '';
  putidx             binary_integer := 1;
  amtleft            binary_integer := 0;
  getidx             binary_integer := 2;
  getpos             binary_integer := 1;
  get_in_progress    boolean := TRUE;
  type char_arr is table of varchar2(512) index by binary_integer;
  buf  char_arr;
  idxlimit    binary_integer;
procedure enable (buffer_size in integer default 20000) is
    lstatus integer;
```

Listing 10-56: Retrieving the package body for DBMS_OUTPUT

In Listing 10-56, the package is wrapped and is not viewable.

To retrieve the source code for a trigger, use the code in Listing 10-57.

```
column    trigger_name        format a15
column    trigger_type        format a15
column    triggering_event    format a15
column    table_name          format a15
column    trigger_body        format a25
select    trigger_name, trigger_type, triggering_event, table_name, trigger_body
from      user_triggers;

TRIGGER_NAME TRIGGER_TYPE     TRIGGERING_EVEN   TABLE_NAME   TRIGGER_BODY
UPDATE_TOTAL AFTER STATEMENT  INSERT OR UPDATE  ORDER_MAIN   begin
                             OR DELETE                        update order_main
                                                              set order_total = 10;
                                                            end;
```

Listing 10-57: Retrieving the source code for a trigger

To find the dependencies for PL/SQL objects, use the code in Listing 10-58.

```
column    name                format a20
column    referenced_owner    format a15 heading R_OWNER
column    referenced_name     format a15 heading R_NAME
column    referenced_type     format a12 heading R_TYPE
select    name, type, referenced_owner, referenced_name,referenced_type
from      user_dependencies
order by  type, name;

NAME             TYPE         R_OWNER     R_NAME       R_TYPE
INSERT_RECORD    PROCEDURE    USERA       ORDER_MAIN   TABLE
INSERT_RECORD    PROCEDURE    SYS         STANDARD     PACKAGE
PROCESS_DATE     PROCEDURE    SYS         STANDARD     PACKAGE
PROCESS_DATE     PROCEDURE    USERA       ORDER_MAIN   TABLE
```

Listing 10-58: Finding dependencies for PL/SQL objects

TIP
*Finding the source code behind PL/SQL package procedures involves
querying the USER_SOURCE and DBA_SOURCE views. Finding the
source code behind a trigger involves querying the USER_TRIGGERS
and DBA_TRIGGERS views. Find dependencies by querying the
USER_DEPENDENCIES and the DBA_DEPENDENCIES views.*

Using the Time Component When Working with DATE Data Types

When working with the Oracle DATE data type, it is more accurate to think of it as a TIME data type because the DATE data type always stores a complete temporal value, down to the second. It is impossible to insert a date value only into either a PL/SQL variable or database column that is defined as a DATE. If you don't keep this behavior in mind during the design of an application, the finished product may exhibit undesirable side effects. One of the most common side effects of improper date management within an application is when reports, which filter the data by a date value, return different results across multiple executions.

When a column or variable of this type (DATE) is initialized with a value, any missing component (if any) will be automatically supplied by Oracle. If the initialization value contains the date component, only then will Oracle supply the time component, and vice versa. This begs the question: How can you tell which component, if any, is missing during the initialization? Quite simply, both components are automatically present only when a date variable is initialized from another date variable. The system variable SYSDATE is one such date variable. Thus, whenever a column or variable is initialized from SYSDATE, it will contain a value representing the date and time when the initialization occurred.

If it is January 10, 1998 at 3:25:22 A.M., and you execute the following command:

```
Date_Var_1 date := SYSDATE;
```

Listing 10-59: Executing SYSDATE

the value contained in the variable Date_Var_1 will be

```
10-JAN-1998 03:25:22.
```

Listing 10-60: SYSDATE output

It is also possible to initialize a date variable using a text string. For example:

```
Date_Var_2 date := '10-JAN-98';
```

Listing 10-61: Initializing a date variable using a text string

The value contained in the variable Date_Var_1 will be

```
10-JAN-98 00:00:00
```

Listing 10-62: Output of Listing 10-61

Listing 10-63 is a simple PL/SQL block that will allow you to see this for yourself.

```
DECLARE
  date_var_2 DATE;
BEGIN
  date_var_2 := '10-JAN-98';
  DBMS_OUTPUT.PUT_LINE('Selected date is '|| to_char(date_var_2, 'DD-MON-YYYY HH24:MI:SS'));
END;
/
```

Listing 10-63: PL/SQL block initializing a date variable using a text string

TIP
A DATE data type always stores a complete temporal value, down to the second. It is impossible to insert a date value into only either a PL/SQL variable or database column that is defined as a DATE.

At this point, it should be clear that Date_Var_1 and Date_Var_2 are not equal. Even if they both contain a date component of 10-JAN-98, their time components differ by almost three-and-a-half hours. Herein lies the problem with a program that does not anticipate the time component that is inherent with date values. Consider an application that uses the SYSDATE variable to initialize the accounting date of records inserted into a database table. If a PL/SQL processing program (or a simple SQL SELECT statement, for that matter) does not take the time component of the records into account, then records will be missed during processing.

Knowing that the date values in a table contain time values other than 12:00 midnight, the statements in Listing 10-64 would miss records.

The problem: The time is not the same and these statements all miss records.

```
select    *
from      table
where     date_column = SYSDATE;
select    *
from      table
where     date_column = trunc(SYSDATE);
select    *
from      table
where     date_column = '10-JAN-98';
select    *
from      table
where     date_column between '01-JAN-98' and '10-JAN-98';
```

Listing 10-64: Missing records

The solution: Truncate the time on both sides of the WHERE clause.

One way to prevent this problem is to negate the difference in time components on both sides of the conditional test, as shown in Listing 10-65.

```
select    *
from      table
where     trunc(date_column) = trunc(SYSDATE);
select    *
from      table
where     trunc(date_column) = '10-JAN-98';
select    *
from      table
where     trunc(date_column) between '01-JAN-98' and '10-JAN-98';
```

Listing 10-65: Negating the difference in time components

Tuned solution: The time is truncated on the noncolumn side of the WHERE clause.

This technique has the undesirable effect of suppressing any indexes that might otherwise improve query performance—the TRUNC function on the column_name suppresses the index on the column. The desired technique would be to adjust the filter conditions to include all possible times within a given date. Also note in Listing 10-66 that .000011574 of one day is 1 second.

```
select    *
from      table
where     date_column between trunc(SYSDATE) and
          trunc(SYSDATE + 1) - .000011574;

select    *
from      table
where     date_column between to_date('10-JAN-98') and
          to_date('11-JAN-98') - .000011574;

select    *
from      table
where     date_column between to_date('01-JAN-98') and
          to_date('11-JAN-98') - .000011574;
```

Listing 10-66: Adjusting filter conditions to include all possible times within given date

TIP
The Oracle DATE has both date and time included in it. Avoid suppressing indexes when trying to match dates. The key is to never modify the column side in the WHERE clause. Do all modifications on the noncolumn side. As you saw in Chapter 2, you can add a function-based index to overcome this issue.

Tuning and Testing PL/SQL

You can also use PL/SQL to time your PL/SQL and ensure that it is performing to your standards. Listing 10-67 is a simple example of how you can write a script that allows you to test and tune your procedures (a procedure called get_customer in this example) directly from SQL*Plus (or PL/SQL within SQL*Plus).

```
set serveroutput on
declare
cust_name char(100);
begin
dbms_output.put_line('Start Time:
    '||to_char(sysdate,'hh24:mi:ss'));
    get_customer(11111,cust_name);
    dbms_output.put_line('Complete Time:
```

```
   '||to_char(sysdate,'hh24:mi:ss'));
   dbms_output.put_line(cust_name);
end;
```

Listing 10-67: Testing and tuning a procedure using PL/SQL

TIP
Use PL/SQL to display the start and end time for your PL/SQL.
Basically, don't forget to use PL/SQL to tune your PL/SQL. Use things
like the package DBMS_PROFILER to get timing statistics per line of
PL/SQL code.

Examining the Implications of PL/SQL Object Location

At TUSC, we generally recommend storing the PL/SQL objects on the server side, for many of the obvious reasons. The server is usually much more powerful and objects are reused much more often (especially when pinned into the shared pool). The security methods employed are also more straightforward. Sending the PL/SQL objects to be processed on the client side can be dependent on the power of the client and can reduce the number of round-trips from client to server. But, when written correctly, the calls may be limited back to the server. (See the next section for an example.)

There is certainly a continuing debate on this issue, but with the evolving thin client, the server will probably be the only place to store the PL/SQL. Figure 10-1 diagrams how PL/SQL is executed when stored on the server side. Some additional reasons for storing code on the server are as follows:

- Performance is improved because the code is already compiled code (p-code).

- Objects can be pinned in the Oracle SGA.

- Transaction-level security is enabled at the database level.

- There is less redundant code and fewer version control issues.

- There is an ability to query source online because it is stored in the data dictionary.

- It is easier to determine impact analysis because it is stored in the data dictionary.

- Less memory is used because only one copy of the code is in memory.

- If packages are used, then the entire package is loaded upon initially being referenced.

TIP
Where to store the PL/SQL code is an ongoing debate. Generally, the
server side is the preferred place to store the code and may become
the only choice as thin clients become more prevalent.

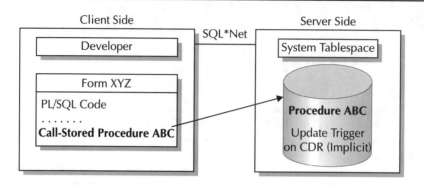

FIGURE 10-1. *Executing an Object on the Server Side*

Using Rollback Segments to Open Large Cursors

This section is intended for developers and DBAs not using Oracle's automatic undo management. Any skilled PL/SQL developer should be familiar with the need to properly size and use rollback segments when attempting large INSERTS/UPDATES/DELETES to the database. If a rollback segment of the appropriate size is not explicitly set prior to the performance of a large data manipulation operation, the operation may fail. The error code usually returned is "ORA-01562: failed to extend rollback segment."

The reason for the failure is that transactions that do not explicitly set the rollback segment have one randomly assigned by Oracle. If this randomly assigned rollback segment is insufficiently sized to hold the entire transaction, the operation will fail. Errors of this type can be eliminated by anticipating the amount of data that will be changed, choosing an appropriately sized rollback segment (the DBA_ROLLBACK_SEGS view is helpful in this regard), and setting this rollback segment just prior to the DML statement. Listing 10-68 demonstrates the proper set of statements:

```
commit;
set transaction use rollback segment rbs1;
update big_table
set column_1 = column_1 * 0.234;
commit;
```

Listing 10-68: Setting a rollback segment

It is a little known fact that Oracle uses rollback segments during the usage of cursors, even if DML statements are not being issued from within the cursor loop. The rollback segments are being used as a type of work area as a cursor loop is being executed. Thus, it is quite possible that a cursor loop will fail if a rollback segment of insufficient size is used to read the cursor. The failure does not occur immediately—only after numerous iterations of the cursor loop have been performed.

Because the error message that is returned is the same as what would be returned when a single DML statement fails, many developers are fooled into thinking that the error lies elsewhere in their code. Valiant efforts are made to properly manage transaction sizes *within* the cursor loops, but to no avail. To successfully open a large cursor, it is imperative that a large rollback segment be set just prior to the opening of the cursor, as shown in Listing 10-69.

```
commit;
set transaction use rollback segment rbs_big;
for C1_Rec in C1 loop
-- your processing logic goes here ...
end loop;
```

Listing 10-69: Setting a large rollback segment

If large amounts of data are being manipulated within the cursor loop, the code should be setting rollback segments within the cursor loop as well. This prevents the DML statements from using the same rollback segment that is being used to ensure that the large cursor can be read.

TIP
If you are not using automatic undo management (see Chapter 3 for more information), then you may need to specify a large enough rollback segment when opening a large cursor.

Using Active Transaction Management to Process Large Quantities of Data

When coding procedures that will process large quantities of data, remember to take into account the size of the rollback segments. The rollback segments are the weak link in a program that performs mass data manipulation. A procedure that performs a single COMMIT statement at the end just won't do if it is to be used to process millions of rows of data. It could be argued that a single transaction could be used to process mass quantities of data, provided the rollback segments were large enough. There are two flaws in this logic: (1) rarely is it feasible to devote gigabytes of valuable drive space to serve as rollback space; and (2) should a hardware or software error occur, then the entire data set would have to be reprocessed. Thus, active transaction management is always the desired technique when processing large quantities of data; it yields efficient use of drive space (devoted to rollback segments) and provides for automatic recovery in the event of hardware/software failures.

Active transaction management is a coding technique that consists of three components: setting transactions for cursor and DML statements, performing intermittent database COMMITs, and using a table column as a processing flag to indicate which records have been processed. Consider the database procedure in Listing 10-60:

```
declare
  counter number;
  cursor C1 is
    select    rowid,column_1,column_2,column_3
```

```
    from       big_table
    where      process_time is NULL;
begin
  Counter := 0;
  commit;
  set transaction use rollback segment rbs_big;
  for C1_Rec in C1 loop
    -- Commit every 1000 records processed.
    if (Counter = 0) or (Counter >= 1000)
      then
        commit;
        set transaction use rollback segment rbs_medium;
        Counter := 0;
      else
        Counter := Counter + 1;
    end if;
    Processing logic...
    update big_table
    set process_time = sysdate
    where rowid = C1_Rec.rowid;
  end loop;
  commit;
end;
```

Listing 10-70: A database procedure

The SET TRANSACTION statements ensure that an appropriately sized rollback segment is used for both cursor reading and DML statements. The database COMMIT for every 1000 records processed performs two functions: prevents the DML statements from exceeding the capacity of the rollback segment, and divides the records being processed into discrete units so that, in the event of hardware/software failure, you don't lose the work you've done. Finally, the process_time column serves as the processing flag that allows the procedure to identify records that have not yet been processed.

TIP
Specify the correct size rollback segment for transactional processing. Limiting the amount of data manipulated between COMMITs is a key to avoiding rollback segment errors.

Using Temporary Database Tables for Increased Performance

PL/SQL tables are great for specific cases, especially when repeated iterations are involved and the amount of data is relatively small; the memory cost (per session) can add up fast if not used properly. When a temporary storage area is needed to house large volumes of records for a short period of time, the method of creating, indexing, and querying a temporary database table should be viewed as a viable and useful option. I have seen far too many developers abandon the common method of temporary database tables after the introduction and expansion of PL/SQL tables; remember, using PL/SQL tables is not the preferred method in all cases.

Oracle writes undo data for temporary tables to facilitate transaction recovery, rollback to savepoints, read consistency, and reclaim space. Thus, transactions in temporary tables will generate redo because we need to log the changes made to the rollback or undo segments. The redo generated should be less than the redo generated for DML on permanent tables.

Integrating a User Tracking Mechanism to Pinpoint Execution Location

Oracle-developed applications continue to become increasingly more complicated from a development standpoint, with all the products available and being used, as well as the location flexibility of PL/SQL program unit source code. When users express their displeasure over performance or inform the DBA that they are stuck, it is important to know what the users were executing at that point in time and the location in the source code of the actual processing logic.

The Oracle-supplied DBMS_APPLICATION_INFO package provides a mechanism for logging the location of processing logic execution. Developers can integrate calls to this package to log the current location of the process executing. A standard can be deployed to call the DBMS_APPLICATION_INFO.SET_MODULE procedure to identify the product the user is currently executing. (For example, this can be accomplished in a startup trigger of Oracle Forms by logging the fact the user is in Forms and including the Form name, and upon exiting the Form, by making these values NULL.)

In procedures or functions, the DBMS_APPLICATION_INFO.SET_MODULE procedure can be called to identify the procedure name and, optionally, the time—down to the second—of when the user running the procedure has "officially" entered the procedure. Upon exiting the procedures or functions, the same procedure can be called to set these values to NULL.

Limiting the Use of Dynamic SQL

Oracle provides the Oracle-supplied package DBMS_SQL, enabling the creation of dynamic SQL and PL/SQL commands. This is an extremely powerful feature, but also dangerous if not used appropriately. When designing and developing Oracle applications, one of the hardest decisions to make is where to draw the line on building in dynamic capabilities and flexibility. Developing dynamic and flexible applications is extremely helpful from a functional perspective. However, the more dynamic and flexible an application, the more potential for performance degradation.

A completely accurate and functional application is considered a failure if it does not perform at acceptable levels. Users will reject an application if they have to wait to do their job. I am not advocating the elimination of dynamic or flexible applications, but a balance must exist. Build flexibility into applications when necessary, not just to make every application module more flexible for the future, just in case business rules may change. Build flexibility into applications only when you are sure the flexibility is needed and the performance impact will be negligible.

The DBMS_SQL package provides the dynamic and flexible means in PL/SQL program units. Use this package when needed, but do not abuse it, unless you want to set yourself up for failure.

TIP
If you integrate the DBMS_SQL package into a PL/SQL program unit to create SQL statements dynamically for a production application, remember that optimizing the generated SQL statements will be difficult.

TIP
Oracle 8.1 introduces a more efficient implementation of executing dynamic SQL and PL/SQL statements with the EXECUTE IMMEDIATE PL/SQL command.

Looking at Some Examples for Beginners

Because you may be a beginner at PL/SQL, I am also including an example of a piece of PL/SQL code, procedure, function, package, and trigger. I feel it is important that you have a feel for what these objects look like and how they differ, especially if you haven't seen some of them before. This section is intentionally placed at the end only as a short reference section to give you a feel for how each piece of code looks. The goal is not to teach you how to write PL/SQL. (Please refer to Joe Trezzo's book, *Procedures, Functions, Packages and Triggers,* for that.)

Both procedures and functions can take parameters and can be called from PL/SQL. However, procedures typically perform an action. The parameters used in procedures can be in(put), out(put), and/or in(put)/out(put) parameters, whereas functions typically compute a value and the parameters can be only in(put) parameters. As a matter of fact, you can't even specify the "direction" of the parameters. Functions permit the passing of only one return value. Functions are "selectable," so you can create your own user-defined functions that return information. As of Oracle version 7.2, developers can create user-defined functions that can be used to process through a standard SQL-type function.

Functions can also be used when creating indexes so the index key is sorted in a fashion that matches your queries.

Creating PL/SQL Code

Listing 10-71 shows how to create PL/SQL code.

```
declare
   acct_balance      NUMBER(11,2);
   acct              CONSTANT NUMBER(4)  := 3;
   debit_amt         CONSTANT NUMBER(5,2) := 500.00;
begin
  select  bal into acct_balance
  from    accounts
  where   account_id = acct
  for     update of bal;
    if acct_balance >= debit_amt THEN
    update       accounts
    set   bal = bal - debit_amt
    where        account_id = acct;
```

```
      else
      insert into temp values
            (acct, acct_balance, 'Insufficient funds');
                  -- insert account, current balance, and message
      end if;
  commit;
end;
```

Listing 10-71: Creating PL/SQL Code

Creating a Procedure
Listing 10-72 shows how to create a procedure.

```
create or replace procedure
    get_cust (in_cust_no in char, out_cust_name out char,
    out_cust_addr1 out char, out_cust_addr2 out char,
    out_cust_city out char, out_cust_st out char,
    out_cust_zip out char, out_cust_poc out char) IS
begin
  select   name, addr1, addr2, city, st, zip, poc
  into      out_cust_name, out_cust_addr1, out_cust_addr2,
            out_cust_city, out_cust_st, out_cust_zip,
            out_cust_poc
  from      customer cust, address addr
  where     cust.cust_no = addr.cust_no
  and       addr.primary_flag = 'Y'
  and       cust.cust_no = in_cust_no;
end       get_cust;
```

Listing 10-72: Creating a procedure

Executing the Procedure from PL/SQL
Listing 10-73 shows how to execute a PL/SQL procedure.

```
get_cust (12345, name, addr1, addr2, city, st, zip, poc);
```

Listing 10-73: Executing a PL/SQL procedure

Creating a Function
Listing 10-74 shows how to create a function.

```
create or replace function  get_cust_name (in_cust_no number)
return char
IS
  out_cust_name cust.cust_last_name%type;
begin
```

Creating a Function

```
 select   cust_last_name
 into     out_cust_name
 from     cust
 where    customer_id = in_cust_no;
 return   out_cust_name;
end get_cust_name;
```

Listing 10-74: Creating a function

Executing the get_cust_name Function from SQL

Listing 10-75 shows how to execute the GET_CUST_NAME function.

```
select   get_cust_name(12345)
from     dual;
```

Listing 10-75: Executing GET_CUST_NAME

Creating a Package

Listing 10-76 shows how to create a packge.

```
Create or replace package emp_actions IS   -- package specification

   procedure hire_employee
        (empno NUMBER, ename CHAR, ...);
   procedure retired_employee (emp_id NUMBER);
end emp_actions;
/

Create or replace package body emp_actions IS   -- package body

   procedure hire_employee
        (empno NUMBER, ename CHAR, ...)
is
   begin
      insert into emp VALUES (empno, ename, ...);
   end hire_employee;
   procedure fire_employee (emp_id NUMBER) IS
   begin
      delete from emp WHERE empno = emp_id;
   end fire_employee;
end emp_actions;
/
```

Listing 10-76: Creating a Package

Using PL/SQL in a Database Trigger

Listing 10-77 shows how to use PL/SQL in a database trigger.

```
create trigger audit_sal
   after update of sal ON emp
   for each row
begin
   insert into emp_audit VALUES( ...)
end;
```

Listing 10-77: Using PL/SQL in a database trigger

Tips Review

- For PL/SQL to be reused in memory or to be stored within a procedure, function, or trigger, it must be written exactly the same every time it's executed.

- Use bind variables instead of constants to avoid fragmenting the shared pool. Setting the CURSOR_SHARING initialization parameter (see Chapter 4) can mitigate this problem.

- Access the V$SQLAREA view to find case (upper and lower) issues or to find a particular object that is problematic.

- The shared pool can be modified dynamically while the database is up in Oracle9.

- Use the DBMS_SHARED_POOL.KEEP procedure to pin PL/SQL objects.

- Query the V$DB_OBJECT_CACHE view to find objects that are not pinned and that are also large enough to potentially cause problems.

- Use the DBMS_SHARED_POOL.SIZES package procedure to find specific information about an object.

- Query DBA_OBJECTS (for systemwide objects) *or* USER_OBJECT (only for your schema) to find the state of objects and avoid errors and reloading by the user.

- Query DBA_TRIGGERS (for systemwide objects) *or* USER_TRIGGERS (only for your schema) to find the state of triggers and avoid errors with disabled triggers. Disabled triggers can have fatal results for an application: they don't fail, they just don't execute.

- Load reference tables into PL/SQL tables for faster lookups.

- Finding the source code behind PL/SQL objects involves querying the USER_SOURCE, DBA_SOURCE, USER_TRIGGERS, and DBA_TRIGGERS views. Find dependencies by querying the USER_DEPENDENCIES and the DBA_DEPENDENCIES views.

- The Oracle DATE has both date and time included in it. Avoid suppressing indexes when trying to match dates. The key is to never modify the column side in the WHERE clause. Do all modifications on the noncolumn side.

- Use PL/SQL to display the start and end time for your PL/SQL.

- Generally, the server side is the preferred place to store PL/SQL.

- Do not reference form fields within the body of a trigger or program unit.

- Specify the correct sized rollback segment within the PL/SQL for large cursors.

References

PL/SQL Tips and Techniques, Oracle Press, Joe Trezzo
Procedures, Functions, Packages and Triggers, Joe Trezzo
SQL Language Reference Manual, Oracle Corporation
Application Developer's Guide, Oracle Corporation
Frank Naude's underground Oracle web page
"OOPs–Objected Oriented PL/SQL," *Select Magazine,* April 1996, Bradley Brown
Oracle PL/SQL Programming, Oracle Press, Scott Urman
Oracle DBA Handbook, Oracle Press, Kevin Loney
Oracle PL/SQL Programming, O'Reilly & Associates, Steven Feuerstein
Using SQL to Examine Stored Code, Integrator, February 1996, Steven Feuerstein

Many thanks to Joe Trezzo, Bob Taylor, Jake Van der Vort, and Dave Ventura of TUSC for contributions to this chapter. Bob Taylor did the Oracle9 update to the chapter. Thanks Bob!

CHAPTER
11

Using Parallel Features to Improve Performance (DBA)

P arallel query technology was first introduced with Oracle release 7.1. The Parallel Query Option (PQO), which in Oracle9i is called the Parallel Executions Option (PEO), makes query operations and DML statements parallel, generating potentially significant performance benefits. Enhancements have been added to the PEO for each release of the RDBMS kernel. In Oracle9i, most operations can be parallelized, including queries, DML, and DDL operations. As of Oracle9i, intrapartition parallelism, parallelism for data replication and recovery, and data loading are supported; multiple parallel query server processes can even execute against the same partition.

The topics covered in this chapter include the following:

- Basic concepts of parallel operations

- Parallel DML and DDL statements and operations

- Parallel DML statements and operations since Oracle9i

- Parallelism and partitions

- Inter- and intraoperation parallelization

- Creating table and index examples using parallel operations

- Parallel DML statements and examples

- Monitoring parallel operations via the V$ views

- Using EXPLAIN PLAN and AUTOTRACE on parallel operations

- Tuning parallel execution and the Oracle9i initialization parameters

- Parallel loading

- Performance comparisons and monitoring parallel operations

- Other parallel notes

Basic Concepts of Parallel Operations

Using parallel operations enables multiple processes (and potentially processors) to work together simultaneously to resolve a single SQL statement. This feature improves data-intensive operations, is dynamic (the execution path is determined at run time), and (when wisely implemented) makes use of all of your processors and disk drives. There are some overhead costs and administrative requirements, but the PEO can improve the performance of many operations.

Consider a full tablescan. Rather than have a single process execute the tablescan, Oracle can create multiple processes to scan the table in parallel. The number of processes used to perform the scan is called the *degree of parallelism* (DOP). The degree can be set in a hint at table creation time or as a hint in the query. Figure 11-1 shows a full tablescan of the EMP table broken into four separate parallel query server processes. (The degree of parallelism is 4.) A fifth process, the query coordinator, is created to coordinate the four parallel query server processes.

TIP
Parallel processes commonly involve disk accesses. If the data is not distributed across multiple disks, using the PEO may lead to an I/O bottleneck.

If the rows returned by the full tablescan shown in Figure 11-1 also need to be sorted, the resulting operation will look like Figure 11-2 instead. Oracle may use one process to coordinate the query, four processes to run the query, and four processes to sort the query. The total is now nine processes, although the degree of parallelism is still 4. If you had nine processors (CPUs), your machine could use all nine processors for the operation (depending on the setup of your system and other operations that are being performed at the same time). If you have fewer than nine processors available, you may encounter some CPU bottleneck issues as Oracle manages the query.

Because the query coordination parts of the operation take resources, fast-running queries are not usually enhanced (and may be degraded) with the use of parallel operations.

TIP
Using parallel operations on very small tables or very fast queries can also degrade performance because the query coordination may also cost performance resources. You should evaluate whether the parallel cost exceeds the nonparallelized cost.

Both queries (Figure 11-1 and Figure 11-2) require access to the physical disks to retrieve data, which is then brought into the SGA. Balancing data on those disks based on how the query is "broken up" makes a large I/O difference.

TIP
When the parallel degree is set to N, it is possible to use (2*N) + 1 total processes for the parallel operation. Although parallel operations deal with processes and not processors, when a large number of processors are available, Oracle usually uses the additional processors to run parallel queries, usually enhancing the performance of the query.

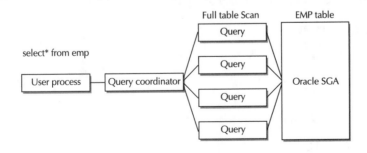

FIGURE 11-1.   *A Simple Full Tablescan with Parallel Execution (disk access not shown)*

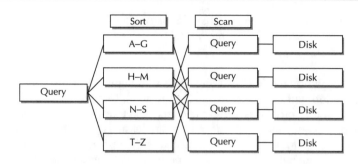

FIGURE 11-2. *A Simple Full Tablescan Requiring a Sort with Parallel Execution (SGA not shown)*

Parallel DML and DDL Statements and Operations

Oracle supports parallelization of both DDL and DML operations. Oracle can parallelize the following operations on tables and indexes:

- SELECT
- UPDATE, INSERT, DELETE
- MERGE
- CREATE TABLE AS
- CREATE INDEX
- REBUILD INDEX
- MOVE/SPLIT/COALESCE PARTITION
- ENABLE CONSTRAINT

The following operations can also be parallelized within a statement:

- SELECT DISTINCT
- GROUP BY
- ORDER BY
- NOT IN
- UNION and UNION ALL
- CUBE and ROLLUP
- Aggregate functions such as SUM and MAX

- NESTED LOOPS joins

- SORT/MERGE joins

- Star transformations

TIP
As of Oracle8i, parallel DML statements are allowed. This
functionality applies to partitioned tables and indexes.

Oracle uses the cost-based optimizer to determine whether to parallelize a statement and to
determine the degree of parallelism applied. Note that if the table being queried is partitioned,
Oracle8*i* can use only one parallel query server process per partition.

Parallel DML Statements and Operations Since Oracle9*i*

In Oracle9*i*, most operations can be parallelized, including queries, DML, and DDL operations.
As of Oracle9*i*, intrapartition parallelism is supported; multiple parallel query server processes
can execute against the same partition.

The degree of parallelism may be limited based on a number of factors. Although the partitioning
strategy does not play as significant a role for parallelism in Oracle9*i*, you should still be aware of
other limiting factors:

- The number of processors available on the server.

- You still have to have the partition option enabled, and UPDATE, DELETE, and MERGE
  are parallelized only for partitioned tables.

- The number of parallel query server processes allowed for the instance, set via the
  PARALLEL_MAX_SERVERS initialization parameter.

- The parallel degree limit supported for your user profile, if you use the Database
  Resource Manager.

- The number of parallel query server processes used by other users in the instance.

- The setting for the PARALLEL_ADAPTIVE_MULTI_USER parameter, which may limit
  your parallelism in order to support other users.

- The setting for the PARALLEL_AUTOMATIC_TUNING parameter, which, when enabled,
  sets the PARALLEL_ADAPTIVE_MULTI_USER to TRUE.

It is important to monitor your parallel operations in multiuser environments to guarantee
they are allocated the resources that you planned for them to use. The Database Resource
Manager can help allocate resources.

Parallel DML Statements
and Operations

Parallelism and Partitions

Oracle's partitioning feature can have a significant impact on parallel operations in Oracle8i. *Partitions* are logical divisions of table data and indexes, and partitions of the same table or index can reside in multiple tablespaces. Given this architecture, the following important distinctions exist with Oracle8i parallel operations on partitions:

■ There is no parallelism within a partition.

■ Operations are performed in parallel on partitioned objects *only* when more than one partition is accessed.

In Oracle8i, if a table is partitioned into 12 logical divisions and a query executed against the table will access only 6 of those partitions (because the dimension of the data dictates the partition in which the data is stored), a maximum of 6 parallel server processes will be allocated to satisfy the query.

NOTE
As of Oracle9i, these restrictions are no longer in effect.

Inter- and Intraoperation Parallelization

Due to the distribution of data, the processor allocated to each parallel server process, and the speed of devices servicing the parallel server data request, each parallel query server process may complete at different times. As each server process completes, it passes its result set to the next lower operation in the statement hierarchy. Any single parallel server process may handle or service statement operation requests from any other parallel execution server at the next higher level in the statement hierarchy.

TIP
Any server process allocated for a statement may handle any request from a process within the same statement. Therefore, if some processes are faster than others, the ones that are faster can consume the rows produced by the child set of parallel execution processes as soon as they are available with the ones that are slower (but only at the next higher statement hierarchy level).

The optimizer evaluates a statement and determines how many parallel query server processes to use during its execution. This intraoperation parallelization is different from interoperation parallelization. *Intraoperation parallelization* is dividing a single task within a SQL statement, such as reading a table, among parallel execution servers. When multiple parts of a SQL statement are performed in parallel, the results from one set of parallel execution servers are passed to another set of parallel execution servers. This is known as *interoperation parallelization*.

The degree of parallelism is applied to each operation of a SQL statement that can be parallelized, including the sort operation of data required by an ORDER BY clause. As shown previously in Figure 11-2, a query with a degree of parallelism of 4 may acquire up to nine processes.

Examples of Using Inter- and Intraoperations (PARALLEL and NOPARALLEL Hints)

You can parallelize SQL statements via a SQL hint or by the object-level options declared for the table or index. Listing 11-1 illustrates a statement hint.

```
select      /*+ parallel (ORDER_LINE_ITEMS) */
            Invoice_Number, Invoice_Date
from        ORDER_LINE_ITEMS
order by    Invoice_Date;
```

Listing 11-1: Using the Statement Hint

The preceding statement does *not* specify a degree of parallelism. The default degree of parallelism dictated by the table definition or the initialization parameters will be used. When you create a table, you can specify the degree of parallelism to use for the table, as shown in Listing 11-2.

```
create table ORDER_LINE_ITEMS
            (Invoice_Number   NUMBER(12) not null,
             Invoice_Date     DATE not null)
parallel 4;
```

Listing 11-2: Specifying the Degree of Parallelism

When you execute queries against the ORDER_LINE_ITEMS table without specifying a degree of parallelism for the query, Oracle uses 4 as the default degree. To override the default, specify the new value within the PARALLEL hint, as shown in Listing 11-3.

```
select      /*+ parallel (ORDER_LINE_ITEMS, 6) */
            Invoice_Number, Invoice_Date
from        ORDER_LINE_ITEMS
order by    Invoice_Date;
```

Listing 11-3: Specifying the New Value Within the PARALLEL Hint

Listing 11-3 specifies a degree of parallelism of 6. As many as 13 parallel execution servers may be allocated or created to satisfy this query.

To simplify the hint syntax, use table aliases, as shown in Listing 11-4. If you assign an alias to a table, you must use the alias, not the table name, in the hint.

```
select      /*+ parallel (oli, 4) */
            Invoice_Number, Invoice_Date
from        ORDER_LINE_ITEMS oli
order by    Invoice_Date;
```

Listing 11-4: Using Table Aliases

Examples of Inter- and Intraoperations

TIP
Using the PARALLEL hint enables the use of parallel operations. If you use the PARALLEL hint but do not specify the degree of parallelism with the hint or set it at the table level, the query still executes in parallel, but the DOP is calculated from the initialization parameters CPU_COUNT and PARALLEL_THREADS_PER_CPU.

You can also "turn off" the use of parallel operations in a given query on a table that has been specified to use parallel operations. The ORDER_LINE_ITEMS table has a default degree of parallelism of 4, but the query in Listing 11-5 overrides that setting via the NOPARALLEL hint.

```
select     /*+ noparallel (oli) */
           Invoice_Number, Invoice_Date
from       ORDER_LINE_ITEMS oli
order by   Invoice_Date;
```

Listing 11-5: Overriding the Degree of Parallelism Setting via the NOPARALLEL Hint

TIP
The use of the NOPARALLEL hint disables parallel operations in a statement that would otherwise use parallel processing due to a parallel object definition.

To change the default degree of parallelism for a table, use the PARALLEL clause of the `alter table` command, as shown in Listing 11-6.

```
alter table order_line_items
parallel (parallel 4);
```

Listing 11-6: Using the PARALLEL clause

To disable parallel operations for a table, use the NOPARALLEL clause of the `alter table` command, as shown in Listing 11-7.

```
alter table order_line_items
noparallel;
```

Listing 11-7: Using the NOPARALLEL clause

The coordinator process evaluates the following in determining whether to parallelize the statement:

- Hints contained in the SQL statement
- Session values set via the alter session force parallel command
- Table/index defined as parallel as well as table/index statistics

You are advised to specify an explicit degree of parallelism in either the SQL statement itself or in the table definition. You can rely on default degrees of parallelism for many operations, but for performance management of time-sensitive operations, you should specify the degree of parallelism using a hint.

TIP
Specify the degree of parallelism using a hint instead of relying on the
table definition to ensure that all operations are tuned for the given query.

Creating Table and Index Examples Using Parallel Operations

To further illustrate the application of parallel operations in SQL statements, consider the implementations of parallel operations for table and index creation shown in Listings 11-8 and 11-9.

```
create table ORDER_LINE_ITEMS
tablespace tbsp1
storage (initial 75m next 75m pctincrease 0)
parallel (parallel 4)
as
select      /*+ parallel (OLD_ORDER_LINE_ITEMS,4) */ *
from        OLD_ORDER_LINE_ITEMS;
```

Listing 11-8: Using parallel operations for table creation

```
create index ORDER_KEY on ORDER_LINE_ITEMS (Order_Id, Item_Id)
tablespace idx1
storage (initial 10m next 1m pctincrease 0)
parallel (parallel 5) NOLOGGING;
```

Listing 11-9: Using parallel operations for index creation

The CREATE INDEX statement creates the ORDER_KEY index using parallel sort operations. The CREATE TABLE statement creates a new table ORDER_LINE_ITEMS with a degree of parallelism of 4 by selecting from an existing OLD_ORDER_LINE_ITEMS table using a parallel operation. In Listing 11-8, two separate operations within the CREATE TABLE command are taking advantage of parallelism: the query of the OLD_ORDER_LINE_ITEMS table is parallelized, and the insert into ORDER_LINE_ITEMS is parallelized.

NOTE
Although parallel queries increase the performance of operations that
modify data, the redo log entries are written serially and could cause a
bottleneck. By using the NOLOGGING option introduced in Oracle8,
you can avoid this bottleneck during the table and index creations.

Examples of Inter- and Intraoperations

Because the writes to the redo log files are serial, redo log writes may effectively eliminate the parallelism you have defined for your statements. Using NOLOGGING forces the bulk operations to avoid logging, but individual INSERT commands will still be written to the redo log files. If you use the NOLOGGING option, you must have a way to recover your data other than via the archived redo log files.

TIP
*Use NOLOGGING to remove the I/O bottleneck caused by serial
writes to the redo logs.*

Up to this point, we have ignored the physical location of the data queried in the example SELECT statements. If a full scanned table's data is all contained on a single disk, you may succeed only in creating a huge I/O bottleneck on the disk. An underlying principle of the performance gains that you can achieve using parallel operations is that the data is stored on different devices, all capable of being addressed independently of one another.

Not only that, but using the PEO may make your system perform *worse*. If your system has processing power to spare but has an I/O bottleneck, using PEO will generate more I/O requests faster, creating a larger queue for the I/O system to manage. If you already have an I/O bottleneck, creating more processes against that same bottleneck will not improve your performance. You need to redesign your data distribution across your available I/O devices.

TIP
*Make sure your data is properly distributed, or the parallel query
server processes may add to existing I/O bottleneck problems.*

Returning to the `create index` statement shown in Listing 11-9, consider the following tips:

- Index creation will use temporary tablespace if there is not enough memory available to perform the sort in memory (SORT_AREA_SIZE). Construct the temporary tablespace in such a way that the physical data files are striped across at least as many disks as the degree of parallelism of the CREATE INDEX statement.

- When adding/enabling a primary or unique key for a table, you cannot create the associated index in parallel. Instead, create the index in parallel first and then use ALTER TABLE to add/enable the constraint and specify the USING INDEX clause. For this to work, the index must have the same name as the constraint.

Real-World Example of Distributing Data for Effective Parallel Operations

Returning to the CREATE TABLE statement example, the following conditions/sequence of events might be pursued if this were an initial data load of a small but growing data warehouse:

1. A tablespace (TBSP1) is created comprising four data files, each 100MB in size, on separate disks.

2. The CREATE TABLE statement is then executed specifying MINEXTENTS 4, creating four extent allocations of 75MB each (and thus on four separate disks/devices) because extents cannot span datafiles.

3. The table storage definition is subsequently changed to a NEXT allocation of 25MB for subsequent, smaller data loads/population.

4. The temporary tablespace definition in this instance uses at least four data files to physically comprise the tablespace.

This method illustrates that careful planning and management of table and temporary tablespace construction can provide the underlying physical data distribution necessary to extract the most performance from parallel DDL operations.

TIP
Effective parallel operations depend greatly on how the data is physically located. Avoid introducing I/O bottlenecks into your database.

As of Oracle9*i*, you can use the Oracle-Managed File (OMF) feature to create datafiles for your tablespaces. If you use this feature, all of the OMF datafiles created will be placed in the directory specified via the DB_CREATE_FILE_DEST initialization parameter. To avoid creating I/O conflicts, you should point that parameter to a logical volume spanning multiple disks. You can move OMF datafiles after they have been created, following the standard procedures for moving datafiles and renaming them internally via the ALTER DATABASE or ALTER TABLESPACE commands.

Parallel DML Statements and Examples

The Oracle8 RDBMS introduced the capability to perform DML operations in parallel. Parallel DML support must be enabled within a SQL session to perform a parallelized DML statement operation. The following conditions apply to parallel DML:

- You cannot enable a parallel DML session without first completing your transaction. You must first perform a commit or rollback.

- The session must be enabled via the command alter session enable parallel dml.

- You cannot access a table modified by parallel DML until the parallel transaction has ended (via commit or rollback).

NOTE
Parallel DML mode does not affect parallel DDL or parallel queries.

The following statements prevent parallel DML:

- SELECT for UPDATE

- LOCK TABLE
- EXPLAIN PLAN

NOTE
Statement failure does not disable parallel DML within your session.

 ## Parallel DML Restrictions

Consider the following restrictions when using parallel DML.

- UPDATE, MERGE, and DELETE operations cannot be parallelized on nonpartitioned tables.

- After a table has been modified by a parallel DML command, no DML operation or query can access the same table again within the same transaction. You need to execute a commit or rollback command between such transactions.

- If the ROW_LOCKING initialization parameter is set to INTENT, inserts, updates, and deletes are not parallelized. (Its default value is ALWAYS.)

- If a table has triggers on it, parallel DML operations are not supported. Likewise, tables involved in replication cannot be the subject of parallel DML operations.

- Deletes on tables having a foreign key with DELETE CASCADE will not be parallelized; nor will deletes on tables having deferred constraints or self-referencing foreign keys if the primary keys are involved in the DML.

- Parallel DML is not supported on object or LOB columns but can be performed on other columns of the same table.

- DML against clustered tables cannot be parallelized.

- Any INSERT/UPDATE/MERGE/DELETE statement referencing a remote object will not be parallelized.

- Prior to Oracle9i, recovery from a system failure during parallel DML was performed serially, but in Oracle9i, Oracle can parallelize both the rolling forward stage and the rolling back stage of transaction recovery.

TIP
Parallel DML is limited to specific types of tables, and sometimes only certain columns within them. You must manage your tables to properly enable parallel DML operations.

 ## Parallel DML Statement Examples

Listings 11-10 and 11-11 illustrate the use of parallel DML statements. In Listing 11-10, a new transaction is created for the session and parallel DML is enabled.

```
commit;
alter session enable parallel dml;
```

Listing 11-10: Using parallel DML statements

In Listing 11-11, a table named COSTS (a partitioned table from the Oracle sample schema) is updated, with a degree of parallelism of 4, and the table is then queried.

```
update       /*+ PARALLEL (costs, 4) */ COSTS
set          Unit_Price = Unit_Price * 1.15
where        Prod_Id > 40000;
27041 rows updated.

select       COUNT(*)
from         COSTS;
select COUNT(*) from COSTS
*
ERROR at line 1:
ORA-12838: cannot read/modify an object after modifying it in parallel

commit;
Commit complete.
```

Listing 11-11: Using parallel DML statements

The query failed because the parallel transaction had not been committed on this table. But if you do the same select, but for a different table, you will not get this error.

TIP
You must issue a commit or rollback after using parallel DML statements. Otherwise, you will receive an error doing a SELECT statement on the same table that follows a parallel DML statement on that table.

Listing 11-12 shows a parallel DDL statement. Note that in this example, two different sections are parallelized: the query, with a degree of 6, and the population of the table, with a degree of 4.

```
create table COST_SUMMARY
parallel 4
as    select /*+ PARALLEL (COSTS, 6) */
            Prod_Id, Time_Id, SUM(Unit_Cost) Cost
from   COSTS
group  by Prod_Id, Time_Id;
```

Listing 11-12: Using a parallel DDL statement

Parallel DML Statement Examples

Instead of using the CREATE TABLE AS SELECT syntax, you could have created the table first and then parallelized an INSERT, as shown in Listing 11-13. The APPEND hint fills only new blocks and is used here only for the purpose of showing you the syntax for it.

```
insert    /*+ APPEND PARALLEL (COST_SUMMARY,4) */
into      COST_SUMMARY (Prod_Id, Time_Id, Cost)
select    /*+ PARALLEL (COSTS, 6) */
          Prod_Id, Time_Id, SUM(Unit_Cost) Cost
from      COSTS
group by Prod_Id, Time_Id;

27041 rows created.
```

Listing 11-13: Parallelizing an insert

TIP
You can use the PARALLEL hint in multiple sections of an INSERT AS SELECT. Inserting with a degree of parallelism of 4 requires MAXTRANS on a table to be set to at least 4 and also requires four rollback segments large enough to handle each transaction. (The set transaction use rollback segment command does not work with parallel.)

NOTE
Rollback segment resources should not be a problem if you are using Automatic Undo Management.

Monitoring Parallel Operations via the V$ Views

The V$ dynamic performance views are always a great place for instance monitoring and evaluating the current performance of the database; parallel operations are no exception. The key performance views for monitoring parallel execution at a system level are V$PQ_TQSTAT and V$PQ_SYSSTAT. In general, V$ views beginning with *V$PQ* have been superceded by similar views beginning with *V$PX*, so the V$PQ_* views may be obsolete in a future release. In the following sections, you will see examples of the most commonly used V$ views for monitoring parallel operations.

V$PQ_TQSTAT

Detailed statistics on all parallel server processes and the producer/consumer relationship between them are presented in the V$pq_tqstat view. Additional information is presented on the number of rows and bytes addressed by each server process. V$PQ_TQSTAT is best used by the DBA tuning long-running queries that require very specific tuning and evaluation of data distribution between server processes. Listing 11-14 shows an example of the data available from V$pq_tqstat. This view is good for locating uneven distribution of work between parallel execution servers.

```
select      DFO_Number, TQ_ID, Server_Type,
            Num_Rows, Bytes, Waits, Process
from        V$PQ_TQSTAT;


DFO_NUMBER TQ_ID SERVER_TYPE NUM_ROWS    BYTES WAITS TIMEOUTS PROCE
---------- ----- ----------- -------- ------- ----- -------- -----
         1     0 Consumer       14315  123660    14        0 P000
         2     0 Producer       23657  232290     7        0 P003
         2     0 Producer       12323   90923     7        0 P002
         2     0 Producer       12321   92300     7        0 P001
         2     0 Consumer      190535 2234322    48        2 QC
```

Listing 11-14: Using V$pq_tqstat to locate uneven distribution of work between parallel execution servers

In this example, the results for two parallel operations can be seen. The first parallel operation involved only one parallel execution server. The second parallel operation involved three parallel execution servers (P001, P002, and P003) and a coordinator process, QC. For the second parallel operation (DFO_Number = 2), you can see that process P003 did more work than any other process. More testing is required to determine if a problem exists. Also note that the last record in the output in Listing 11-14 is for a query coordinator process. It has a higher-than-average number of waits because it needs to communicate with all the other query server processes.

V$PQ_SYSSTAT

V$pq_sysstat provides parallel statistics for all parallelized statement operations within the instance. V$pq_sysstat is ideal for evaluating the number of servers executing currently high-water mark levels, and the frequency of startup and shutdown of parallel servers, as shown in Listing 11-15.

```
select      Statistic, Value
from        V$PQ_SYSSTAT;


STATISTIC                 VALUE
------------------------- -------
Servers Busy                 12
Servers Idle                  0
Servers Highwater            12
Server Sessions              39
Servers Started              13
Servers Shutdown              7
Servers Cleaned Up            0
Queries Initiated             5
DML Initiated                 3
DDL Initiated                 0
DFO Trees                     5
Local Msgs Sent           91261
```

V$PQ_SYSSTAT

```
Distr Msgs Sent          0
Local Msgs Recv'd    91259
Distr Msgs Recv'd        0
```

Listing 11-15: Using V$pq_sysstat

TIP
To easily determine if parallel DML is being used, query the DML initiated statistic before and after executing a parallel DML statement.

Listing 11-16 illustrates the statistics found on a freshly started instance. These statistics illustrate parallel servers executing during the UPDATE statement in the Parallel DML Statement Examples section earlier in this chapter where there was a degree of parallelism of 4.

```
select      Statistic, Value
from        V$PQ_SYSSTAT;

STATISTIC                  VALUE
--------------------    -------
Servers Busy                  4
Servers Idle                  0
Servers Highwater             4
Server Sessions               4
Servers Started               0
Servers Shutdown              0
Servers Cleaned Up            0
Queries Initiated             0
DML Initiated                 1
DDL Initiated                 0
DFO Trees                     1
Local Msgs Sent               8
Distr Msgs Sent               0
Local Msgs Recv'd            12
Distr Msgs Recv'd             0
```

Listing 11-16: Viewing the statistics found on a freshly started instance

As you can see, four parallel execution servers were used and no new processes were started. Next, query V$pq_sysstat after an INSERT operation specifying a parallel degree of 4. The subsequent execution of the INSERT statement produces the statistics shown in Listing 11-17 from the V$pq_sysstat view.

```
STATISTIC                  VALUE
--------------------    -------
Servers Busy                  4
Servers Idle                  0
Servers Highwater             8
```

```
Server Sessions           16
Servers Started            4
Servers Shutdown           4
Servers Cleaned Up         0
Queries Initiated          0
DML Initiated              2
DDL Initiated              0
DFO Trees                  3
Local Msgs Sent          108
Distr Msgs Sent            0
Local Msgs Recv'd        122
Distr Msgs Recv'd          0
```

Listing 11-17: Viewing statistics from V$pq_sysstat after an INSERT

Query V$pq_sysstat after a SELECT on a table defined with a hint specifying a parallel degree of 5. Listing 11-18 illustrates V$pq_sysstat output following the query. Note the values for Servers Busy and Servers Highwater.

```
select      Statistic, Value
from        V$PQ_SYSSTAT;

STATISTIC                 VALUE
--------------------      -------
Servers Busy               5
Servers Idle               0
Servers Highwater          8
Server Sessions           20
Servers Started            5
Servers Shutdown           4
Servers Cleaned Up         0
Queries Initiated          1
DML Initiated              2
DDL Initiated              0
DFO Trees                  4
Local Msgs Sent          117
Distr Msgs Sent            0
Local Msgs Recv'd        136
Distr Msgs Recv'd          0
```

Listing 11-18: Viewing V$pq_sysstat after a SELECT

In this case, the hint has overridden the default degree of parallelism defined for the table, using five parallel query server processes.

V$PQ_SYSSTAT

TIP
If the number of servers started consistently increases, consider increasing the PARALLEL_MIN_SERVERS initialization parameter. However, if a parallel execution server is started through the PARALLEL_MIN_SERVERS parameter, it does not exit until the database shuts down, the parallel process aborts, or the process is killed. This can lead to process memory fragmentation, so increase this number only when you are sure it is needed.

TIP
A PARALLEL hint overrides the degree of parallelism defined for a table when determining the degree of parallelism for an operation.

V$PQ_SESSTAT

To provide the current session statistics, query the V$PQ_SESSTAT view. Use this view to see the number of queries executed within the current session, as well as the number of DML operations parallelized. Listing 11-19 shows sample output of a simple query from this view.

```
select Statistic, Last_Query, Session_Total
from   V$PQ_SESSTAT;

STATISTIC                 LAST_QUERY   SESSION_TOTAL
-----------------------   ----------   -------------
Queries Parallelized               0               1
DML Parallelized                   1               2
DDL Parallelized                   0               0
DFO Trees                          1               3
Server Threads                     6               0
Allocation Height                  6               0
Allocation Width                   0               0
Local Msgs Sent                   27             171
Distr Msgs Sent                    0               0
Local Msgs Recv'd                 27             167
Distr Msgs Recv'd                  0               0
```

Listing 11-19: Querying V$pq_sesstat

The output shown in V$PQ_SESSTAT refers only to the current session, so it is most useful when performing diagnostics during testing or problem resolution processes. Note that V$PX_SESSTAT has a similar name but a completely different set of columns. V$PX_SESSTAT joins session information from V$PX_SESSION with the V$SESSTAT table. V$PQ_SESSTAT will likely be obsolete in a future release. V$PX_SESSION can also give information on the process requested degree (req_degree) as compared to the actual degree (degree) that ended up being used. A listing of V$ views related to parallel operations is given in the Other Parallel Notes section at the end of this chapter.

Listing 11-20 shows a simple example of querying V$PX_SESSTAT. In this example, if you tried to execute a parallel query where the specified degree of parallelism (12) is greater than PARALLEL_MAX_SERVERS (10), you might see the following:

```
select  DISTINCT Req_Degree, Degree
from    V$PX_SESSTAT;

REQ_DEGREE                          DEGREE
------------------- -------------------
                12                      10
```

Listing 11-20: Querying V$px_sesstat

The V$PX_SESSTAT view is populated only while a parallel operation is executing; as soon as the parallel operation finishes, the contents of this view are cleared. You can also view the contents of the V$PX_SESSTAT view through OEM by accessing the Parallel Query Sessions chart of Oracle Performance Manager.

Using **EXPLAIN PLAN** and **AUTOTRACE** on Parallel Operations

You can use the explain plan command to see tuned parallel statements. When you create a PLAN_TABLE for your database (via the utlxplan.sql script in the /rdbms/admin subdirectory under the Oracle software home directory), Oracle includes columns that allow you to see how parallelism affects the query's execution path. The information about the parallelization of the query is found in the Object_Node, Other_Tag, and Other columns in PLAN_TABLE.

TIP

New columns may be added to the PLAN_TABLE with each new release of Oracle. You should drop and re-create your PLAN_TABLE following each upgrade of the Oracle kernel. If you upgrade an existing database to a new version of Oracle, you should drop your old PLAN_TABLE and reexecute the utlxplan.sql script to see all of the new PLAN_TABLE columns.

The Object_Node column provides information about the query server processes involved. The Other_Tag column describes the function of the Other column's entries. The Other column contains a derived SQL statement—either for a remote query or for parallel query operations. Table 11-1 shows the possible values for Other_Tag and their associated Other values.

When an operation is parallelized, it may be partitioned to multiple query server processes based on ranges of ROWID values; the ranges are based on contiguous blocks of data in the table. You can use the Other_Tag column to verify the parallelism within different operations of the query, and you can see the parallelized query in the Other column. For example, the query in Listing 11-21 forces a MERGE JOIN to occur between the COMPANY and SALES tables; because

Value	Description
PARALLEL_COMBINED_WITH_CHILD	The parent of this operation performs the parent and child operations together; Other is NULL.
PARALLEL_COMBINED_WITH_PARENT	The child of this operation performs the parent and child operations together; Other is NULL.
PARALLEL_TO_PARALLEL	The SQL in the Other column is executed in parallel, and results are returned to a second set of query server processes.
PARALLEL_TO_SERIAL	The SQL in the Other column is executed in parallel, and the results are returned to a serial process (usually the query coordinator).
PARALLEL_FROM_SERIAL	The SQL operation consumes data from a serial operation and outputs it in parallel; Other is NULL.
SERIAL	The SQL statement is executed serially (the default); the Other column is NULL.
SERIAL_FROM_REMOTE	The SQL in the Other column is executed at a remote site.
SERIAL_TO_PARALLEL	The SQL in the Other column is partitioned to multiple query server processes.

TABLE 11-1. *Possible Values for PLAN_TABLE.Other_Tag for PEO*

a MERGE JOIN involves full tablescans and sorts, multiple operations can be parallelized. You can use the Other_Tag column to show the relationships between the parallel operations.

```
select /*+ FULL(company) FULL(sales) USE_MERGE(company sales)*/
       COMPANY.Name, Sales.Sales_Total
  from COMPANY, SALES
 where COMPANY.Company_ID = SALES.Company_ID
   and SALES.Period_ID = 3;
```

Listing 11-21: Forcing a MERGE JOIN

Listing 11-22 shows the EXPLAIN PLAN for the MERGE JOIN query.

```
MERGE JOIN
  SORT JOIN
    TABLE ACCESS FULL COMPANY
  SORT JOIN
    TABLE ACCESS FULL SALES
```

Listing 11-22: EXPLAIN PLAN for the MERGE JOIN query

As shown in the plan, Oracle performs a full tablescan (TABLE ACCESS FULL) on each table, sorts the results (using the SORT JOIN operations), and merges the result sets. The query of PLAN_TABLE in Listing 11-23 shows the Other_Tag for each operation. The query shown in Listing 11-24 generates the EXPLAIN PLAN listings.

```
select  LPAD(' ',2*Level)||Operation||' '||Options
              ||' '||Object_Name   Q_Plan, Other_Tag
from PLAN_TABLE
where Statement_ID = 'TEST'
connect by prior ID = Parent_ID and Statement_ID = 'TEST'
start with ID=1;
```

Listing 11-23: Showing the Other_Tag for each operation

Listing 11-24 shows the result of the query in Listing 11-23 for the MERGE JOIN example.

```
Q_PLAN                               OTHER_TAG
-------------------------------     ---------------------------
MERGE JOIN                          PARALLEL_TO_SERIAL
   SORT JOIN                        PARALLEL_COMBINED_WITH_PARENT
     TABLE ACCESS FULL COMPANY      PARALLEL_TO_PARALLEL
   SORT JOIN                        PARALLEL_COMBINED_WITH_PARENT
     TABLE ACCESS FULL SALES        PARALLEL_TO_PARALLEL
```

Listing 11-24: Results of MERGE JOIN query

From Listing 11-24, you can see (by their Other_Tag values of PARALLEL_TO_PARALLEL) that each of the TABLE ACCESS FULL operations is parallelized, and provides data to a parallel sorting operation. Each of the TABLE ACCESS FULL operations' records in PLAN_TABLE will have the parallel query text in their Other column values. The Other column values for the TABLE ACCESS FULL operations will show that the table will be scanned based on ranges of ROWID values. The SORT JOIN operations, which are PARALLEL_COMBINED_WITH_PARENT (their "parent" operation is the MERGE JOIN) will have NULL values for their Other column values. The MERGE JOIN operation, which is PARALLEL_TO_SERIAL (the merge is performed in parallel; output is provided to the serial query coordinator process), will have an Other column value that shows how the merge occurs.

The Object_Node column values display information about the query server processes involved in performing an operation. Listing 11-25 shows the Object_Node and Other columns for the TABLE ACCESS FULL of COMPANY operation performed for the MERGE JOIN query shown in Listing 11-24.

```
set long 1000
select Object_Node, Other
  from PLAN_TABLE
 where Operation||' '||Options = 'TABLE ACCESS FULL'
   and Object_Name = 'COMPANY';

OBJECT_NODE OTHER
```

EXPLAIN PLAN and AUTOTRACE

```
-----------  -----------------------------------------------
:Q15000      SELECT /*+ ROWID(A1) */ A1."COMPANY_ID" C0,
                    A1."NAME" C1
             FROM "COMPANY" A1
             WHERE ROWID BETWEEN :1 AND :2
```

Listing 11-25: Object_Node and Other columns

As shown in this listing, the Object_Node column references a parallel query server process. (Q15000 is an internal identifier Oracle assigned to the process for this example.) The Other column shows that the COMPANY table is queried for ranges of ROWID values. Each of the query server processes performing the full tablescan performs the query, shown in Listing 11-25, for a different range of ROWIDs. The SORT JOIN and MERGE JOIN operations sort and merge (in parallel) the results of the tablescans.

TIP

When using the explain plan command for a parallelized query, you cannot rely on querying just the operations-related columns to see the parallelized operations within the explain plan. At a minimum, you should query the Other_Tag column to see which operations are performed in parallel. If an operation is not performed in parallel and you think it should be, you may need to add hints to the query, set a degree of parallelism for the tables, or check the size of the query server pool to make sure query server processes are available for use by the query. Also, there are Consumer Group limitations, and settings for PARALLEL_ADAPTIVE_USER and PARALLEL_MIN_PERCENT. These could also prevent parallelism from occurring.

Oracle provides a second script, utlxplp.sql, also located in the /rdbms/admin subdirectory under the Oracle software home directory. The utlxplp.sql script queries the PLAN_TABLE, with emphasis on the parallel query data within the table. You must create the PLAN_TABLE (via the utlxplan.sql script) and populate it (via the explain plan command) prior to running the utlxplp.sql script.

TIP

When using explain plan for parallel operations, use the utlxplp.sql script to view the PLAN_TABLE.

Using set autotrace on

You can have the explain plan automatically generated for every transaction you execute within SQL*Plus. The set autotrace on command will cause each query, after being executed, to display both its execution path and high-level trace information about the processing involved in resolving the query.

To use the set autotrace on command, you must have first created the PLAN_TABLE table within your account. When using the set autotrace on command, you do not set a Statement_ID and you do not have to manage the records within the PLAN_TABLE. To disable the autotrace feature, use the set autotrace off command.

If you use the set autotrace on command, you will not see the explain plan for your queries until *after* they complete, unless you specify TRACEONLY. The explain plan command shows the execution paths without running the queries first. Therefore, if the performance of a query is unknown, use the explain plan command before running it. If you are fairly certain that the performance of a query is acceptable, use set autotrace on to verify its execution path.

Listing 11-26 shows the effect of the set autotrace on command. When a MERGE JOIN query is executed, the data is returned from the query, followed by the explain plan. The explain plan is in two parts; the first part shows the operations involved, and the second part shows the parallel-related actions. Listing 11-26 shows the first part of the autotrace output.

```
set autotrace on

rem
rem for this example, disable hash joins
rem to force merge joins to occur.
rem
alter session set hash_join_enabled=FALSE;
rem
select
 /*+ FULL(company) FULL(sales) USE_MERGE(company sales)*/
      COMPANY.Name, Sales.Sales_Total
 from COMPANY, SALES
where COMPANY.Company_ID = SALES.Company_ID
  and SALES.Period_ID = 3;

<records returned here>

Execution Plan
-------------------------------------------------------------
   0      SELECT STATEMENT Optimizer=CHOOSE (Cost=10 Card=1 Bytes=59)
   1    0   MERGE JOIN* (Cost=10 Card=1 Bytes=59)                        :Q17002
   2    1     SORT* (JOIN)                                               :Q17002
   3    2       TABLE ACCESS* (FULL) OF 'COMPANY' (Cost=1 Card=1 Bytes=20) :Q17000
   4    1     SORT* (JOIN)                                               :Q17002
   5    4       TABLE ACCESS* (FULL) OF 'SALES' (Cost=1 Card=1 Bytes=39)  :Q17001
```

Listing 11-26: Effect of the `set autotrace on` command

The AUTOTRACE output shows the ID column of each row, along with the operations and the objects on which they act. The information at the far right (:*Q17002* and so on) identifies the parallel query servers used during the query.

The second portion of the AUTOTRACE output for the MERGE JOIN example uses the step ID values to describe the parallelism of the execution path's operations, as shown in Listing 11-27.

```
 1 PARALLEL_TO_SERIAL            SELECT /*+ ORDERED NO_EXPAND USE_MERGE(A2) *
                                 / A1.C1,A2.C1,A2.C2 FROM :Q17000 A1,:Q17001
                                 A2 WHERE A1.C0=A2.C0
 2 PARALLEL_COMBINED_WITH_PARENT
 3 PARALLEL_TO_PARALLEL          SELECT /*+ ROWID(A1) */ A1."COMPANY_ID" C0,A
                                 1."NAME" C1 FROM "COMPANY" A1 WHERE ROWID BE
                                 TWEEN :1 AND :2
```

EXPLAIN PLAN and AUTOTRACE

```
4 PARALLEL_COMBINED_WITH_PARENT
5 PARALLEL_TO_PARALLEL          SELECT /*+ ROWID(A1) */ A1."COMPANY_ID" C0,A
                                1."SALES_TOTAL" C1,A1."PERIOD_ID" C2 FROM "S
                                ALES" A1 WHERE ROWID BETWEEN :1 AND :2 AND A
                                1."PERIOD_ID"=3
```

Listing 11-27: Using step ID values to describe execution path operations parallelism

The first column in this listing is the step's ID value, which allows you to find the operation it refers to (from the first portion of the AUTOTRACE output). The second value is the Other_Tag value for the step. The third column is the Other value for the step, showing the parallelized SQL. Also note that just setting `autotrace` on will also list statistics at the end.

Tuning Parallel Execution and the Oracle9*i* Initialization Parameters

Parameters related to physical memory are generally set much higher in a database that uses parallel operations than in a nonparallel environment. The settings shown in Table 11-2 are general parameter settings, but your settings must be based on your unique business environment. Also note that OPTIMIZER_PERCENT_PARALLEL is obsolete in Oracle9*i*.

Initialization Parameter	Meaning	Suggested Values
COMPATIBLE	Setting this parameter to the release level of the instance allows you to take advantage of all of the functionality built into the RDBMS engine. Oracle recommends backing up the database *before* changing this parameter!	Generally set to the default value for the database version. Standby databases must use a consistent setting for both the primary and standby.
*DB_BLOCK_SIZE	Sets the database block size for the database.	In general, use the largest supported size for data warehousing and smaller sizes for OLTP. In Oracle9*i*, you can create caches and tablespaces with differing database block sizes.

TABLE 11-2. *Oracle9i Parallel Initialization Parameters*

Initialization Parameter	Meaning	Suggested Values
*DB_CACHE_SIZE (This was DB_BLOCK_BUFFERS times DB_BLOCK_SIZE in previous versions of Oracle.)	To support a larger number of processes performing parallel queries and DML operations, increase the memory available.	Increase to support parallel operations.
*DB_FILE_MULTIBLOCK_READ_COUNT	Determines how many blocks are read at once during a full table scan. Improves the performance of parallel operations using table scans.	OS-dependent.
*DISK_ASYNCH_IO	Supports asynchronous writes to the operating system, reducing a potential I/O bottleneck.	Whether DISK_ASYNCH_IO should be set to TRUE depends on whether the OS supports asynchronous I/O, and how stable it is on that platform.
*DML_LOCKS	Sets the maximum number of DML locks acquired for the database. The default value assumes an average of four tables referenced per transaction.	Default value is 4*TRANSACTIONS. Increase to support parallel DML.
*ENQUEUE_RESOURCES	Specifies the number of distinct database structures that can be locked concurrently within the database. If parallel DML is used, increase beyond the default value.	Default value is derived from SESSIONS. An enqueue resource is a memory structure that stores the lock ID, information about locks held against the object, and locks requested. So, the setting of ENQUEUE_RESOURCES minus the number of enqueues taken up by the background processes is the total number of other locks you can have active concurrently on your system.
*FAST_START_PARALLEL_ROLLBACK	Sets the maximum number of processes that can exist for performing parallel rollback during recovery following a system crash.	Default value is LOW, limiting the number of processes to 2*CPU_COUNT. Set to HIGH to increase the limit to 4*CPU_COUNT.

TABLE 11-2. *Oracle9i Parallel Initialization Parameters* (continued)

Tuning Parallel Execution & Oracle9i initparams

Initialization Parameter	Meaning	Suggested Values
*HASH_AREA_SIZE	Specifies the maximum amount of memory, in bytes, to use for hash joins.	Increase if hash joins are frequently used by parallel queries. Increase this parameter only if you do not have a larger than average SORT_AREA_SIZE, because the default value is derived from SORT_AREA_SIZE. You can and should use PGA_AGGREGASIZE instead.
LARGE_POOL	The large pool allocation heap is used by parallel execution for message buffers. Parallel execution allocates buffers out of the large pool only when PARALLEL_AUTOMATIC_TUNING is set to TRUE.	Default value should be OK, but if you increase the value of PARALLEL_EXECUTION_MESSAGE_SIZE, you should set this parameter to a higher value.
*LOG_BUFFER	Increase to support the transaction volume generated by parallel DML.	Default value is 524288, set to 512KB minimum. Increase if parallel DML is used extensively.
PARALLEL_ADAPTIVE_MULTI_USER	Reduces the degree of parallelism based on number of active parallel users.	Set this to FALSE and control parallel resources with the Database Resource Manager instead, if needed.
PARALLEL_AUTOMATIC_TUNING	When set to TRUE, Oracle sets values for the initialization parameters related to parallel operations.	TRUE. For those new to setting parallel parameters in a database, setting this parameter to TRUE would prove useful. Also, if set to TRUE, the parallel query servers can use the LARGE_POOL instead of the SHARED_POOL, which would improve performance of the overall system.

TABLE 11-2. *Oracle9i Parallel Initialization Parameters* (continued)

Initialization Parameter	Meaning	Suggested Values
PARALLEL_BROADCAST_ENABLED	Allows the optimizer to send a small table result set to each of the parallel servers handling pieces of the large table in a hash and merge join scenario.	TRUE/FALSE, default value is FALSE. Setting this parameter to TRUE may improve the performance of a join between a very large and a very small table.
PARALLEL_EXECUTION_MESSAGE_SIZE	Specifies the size of messages for all parallel operations. Larger values than the default will require a larger shared pool size.	Operating system-dependent; values range from 2148–65535. Setting this parameter to a larger value than the default leads to better throughput for parallel operations, but uses more memory, which may cause performance problems for nonparallel operations or applications.
PARALLEL_MAX_SERVERS	Maximum number of parallel query server processes allowed to exist simultaneously.	Default value is derived from the values of CPU_COUNT, PARALLEL_AUTOMATIC_TUNING, and PARALLEL_ADAPTIVE_MULTI_USER. Oracle recommends to start at 16 × CPUs or set to 2 × DOP × (concurrent users). *Set this parameter!*
PARALLEL_MIN_PERCENT	If this percentage of the degree of parallelism (number of servers) required by the query is not available, statement will terminate with an error (ORA-12827). This is effective when a serial execution of the statement is undesired.	Default value is 0, range of values is 0–100. If 0, parallel operations will always execute in parallel. If 100, operations execute in parallel only if all servers can be acquired.

TABLE 11-2. *Oracle9i Parallel Initialization Parameters* (continued)

Tuning Parallel Execution & Oracle9i initparams

Initialization Parameter	Meaning	Suggested Values
PARALLEL_MIN_SERVERS	Minimum number of servers created when instance originates. As servers idle out or terminate, the number of servers never falls below this number.	0–O/S limit. Realistically, start with 10–24. Consider changing if V$ views show heavy use of parallel queries. *Set this parameter!*
PARALLEL_THREADS_PER_CPU	Specifies the default degree of parallelism for the instance, based on the number of parallel execution processes a CPU can support during parallel operations.	Any nonzero number; default is OS-dependent. This "number times CPUs" is the number of threads used in parallel operations.
PGA_AGGREGATE_TARGET	Enables the automatic sizing of SQL working areas used by memory-intensive SQL operators such as a sort and hash join.	A useful parameter to help control paging, because you set the PGA target to the total memory on your system that is available to the Oracle instance and subtract the SGA. It is used for sorting operations as well as others as discussed in Chapter 4.
RECOVERY_PARALLELISM	Number of recovery processes that will be devoted to instance or media recovery.	A value between 2 and PARALLEL_MAX_SERVERS. A value of 0 or 1 indicates that serial recovery will be performed.
*ROLLBACK_SEGMENTS	Names the rollback segments for the instance.	Increase the number of rollback segments if parallel DML is extensively used. Using UNDO Management may be a better idea. See Chapter 3 for more info.
ROW_LOCKING	Specifies whether row locks are acquired during UPDATE operations.	Set to ALWAYS if using parallel DML. Using the value INTENT will inhibit parallel DML.
*SHARED_POOL_SIZE	Size of Oracle shared pool. Portion of shared pool is used for query server communication.	Increase existing parameter value by 5–10 percent for heavy, concurrent PQ use, but this is needed only if you are setting Parallel Automatic Tuning to FALSE.

TABLE 11-2. *Oracle9i Parallel Initialization Parameters* (continued)

Initialization Parameter	Meaning	Suggested Values
*SORT_AREA_RETAINED_ SIZE	Set equal to SORT_AREA_SIZE. Amount of sort space retained on a per-user basis. Parallel query server processes will be allocated and retain sort space.	Default value, as derived from SORT_AREA_SIZE setting, but this is needed only if you are setting Parallel Automatic Tuning to FALSE.
*SORT_AREA_SIZE	Per-user maximum allocation of sort space. Each parallel query server process uses this amount of sort space as well. Set this value = SORT_AREA_ RETAINED_SIZE because sort space will most often increase to this maximum. Be careful of physical memory limits!	64KB–1MB; limited by physical memory; using PGA_Aggregate_target is better.
*TAPE_ASYNCH_IO	Supports asynchronous writes to the operating system, reducing a potential I/O bottleneck.	This parameter affects writes only to serial devices. This is useful for parallel backup operations or for use with RMAN, but not important for parallel query or DML. The default is TRUE.
*TRANSACTIONS	Specifies the number of concurrent transactions, which will increase if parallel DML is extensively used.	Default value is derived from SESSIONS setting. Increase to support parallel DML.

*Has an indirect effect on parallel options

TABLE 11-2. *Oracle9i Parallel Initialization Parameters* (continued)

TIP
Be sure your environment is properly configured to support the increase in processes and transactions generated by parallel operations.

The parameters in the initialization file define and shape the environment used by parallel operations. You enable parallel operations for your commands by using a PARALLEL hint on a SQL statement or using the PARALLEL clause during a create/alter table command. When you are considering adjusting any initialization parameter, fully investigate the *Oracle 9i Database Administrator's Guide* or the appropriate server installation guide for your system *prior* to experimenting with an Oracle database.

Parallel Loading

To use Parallel Data Loading, start multiple SQL*Loader sessions using the PARALLEL keyword. Each session is an independent session requiring its own control file. Listing 11-28 shows three separate Direct Path loads, all using the PARALLEL=TRUE parameter on the command line:

```
sqlldr USERID=SCOTT/PASS CONTROL=P1.CTL DIRECT=TRUE PARALLEL=TRUE
sqlldr USERID=SCOTT/PASS CONTROL=P2.CTL DIRECT=TRUE PARALLEL=TRUE
sqlldr USERID=SCOTT/PASS CONTROL=P3.CTL DIRECT=TRUE PARALLEL=TRUE
```

Listing 11-28: Using PARALLEL=TRUE parameter

Each session creates its own log, bad, and discard files (p1.log, p1.bad, etc.) by default. You can have multiple sessions loading data into different tables, but the APPEND option is still required. APPEND is very fast because it fills only unused blocks. The SQL*Loader REPLACE, TRUNCATE, and INSERT options are not allowed for Parallel Data Loading. If you need to delete the data using SQL commands, you must manually delete the data.

TIP
*If you use Parallel Data Loading, indexes are not maintained by the SQL*Loader session, unless you are loading a single table partition. Before starting a parallel loading process, you must drop all indexes on the table and disable all of its PRIMARY KEY and UNIQUE constraints. After the parallel loads complete, you need to re-create or rebuild the table's indexes. Inserting data using APPEND and UNRECOVERABLE is the fastest way to insert data into a table without an index. External tables may provide faster extract, transform, load (ETL) operations yet.*

In Parallel Data Loading, each load process creates temporary segments for loading the data; the temporary segments are later merged with the table. If a Parallel Data Load process fails before the load completes, the temporary segments will not have been merged with the table. If the temporary segments have not been merged with the table being loaded, no data from the load will have been committed to the table.

You can use the SQL*Loader FILE parameter to direct each data loading session to a different datafile. By directing each loading session to its own database datafile, you can balance the I/O load of the loading processes. Data loading is very I/O-intensive and must be distributed across multiple disks for parallel loading to achieve significant performance improvements over serial loading.

TIP
Use the FILE parameter to direct the writes generated by parallel data loads.

After a Parallel Data Load, each session may attempt to reenable the table's constraints. As long as at least one load session is still under way, attempting to reenable the constraints will fail. The final loading session to complete should attempt to reenable the constraints, and should succeed. You should check the status of your constraints after the load completes. If the table being loaded has PRIMARY KEY and UNIQUE constraints, you should first re-create or rebuild the associated indexes in parallel and then manually enable the constraints.

TIP
The PARALLEL option for data loading improves performance of loads, but can also cause space to be wasted when not properly used.

Performance Comparisons and Monitoring Parallel Operations

To show the performance difference between a nonparallel operation and a parallel operation, the following tests were performed:

1. Started the database with 12 parallel server processes and checked the background processes that were created.

2. Ran a query without PARALLEL and checked the speed.

3. Ran a query with PARALLEL that required sorting with a degree of 6.

4. Checked the output of V$PQ_SYSSTAT and V$PQ_SESSTAT.

Listing 11-29 shows the `ps -ef` output (`ps -ef` is a UNIX or Linux O/S command) for 12 parallel servers running. We started the database with the parameter PARALLEL_MIN_SERVERS = 12. The name of the database is fdr1.

```
#ps -ef
oracle  2764     1  0 17:08:30    ?    0:00 ora_pmon_fdr1
oracle  2766     1  0 17:08:34    ?    0:00 ora_lgwr_fdr1
oracle  2768     1  0 17:08:38    ?    0:00 ora_reco_fdr1
oracle  2770     1  0 17:08:42    ?    0:00 ora_d000_fdr1
oracle  2769     1  0 17:08:40    ?    0:00 ora_s000_fdr1
oracle  2767     1  0 17:08:36    ?    0:00 ora_smon_fdr1
oracle  2771     1  4 17:08:44    ?    0:33 ora_p000_fdr1
oracle  2772     1  5 17:08:46    ?    0:42 ora_p001_fdr1
oracle  2773     1  4 17:08:48    ?    0:33 ora_p002_fdr1
oracle  2774     1  4 17:08:50    ?    0:32 ora_p003_fdr1
oracle  2775     1  5 17:08:52    ?    0:40 ora_p004_fdr1
oracle  2776     1 14 17:08:54    ?    1:26 ora_p005_fdr1
```

```
oracle  2819  2802 13 17:12:39    ?    1:44 ora_p006_fdrl
oracle  2820  2802  1 17:12:41    ?    0:05 ora_p007_fdrl
oracle  2821  2802  0 17:12:43    ?    0:01 ora_p008_fdrl
oracle  2822  2802  0 17:12:45    ?    0:01 ora_p009_fdrl
oracle  2825  2802  2 17:12:47    ?    0:11 ora_p010_fdrl
oracle  2826  2802 10 17:12:49    ?    1:18 ora_p011_fdrl
```

Listing 11-29: `ps -ef` output for 12 parallel servers

Next, run the query *without* using parallel execution servers. Listing 11-30 shows a partial result set. (You can time this in a variety of ways, as shown in Chapter 6, or just by selecting sysdate from dual.)

```
select     Job_Sub_Code job, SUM(Amount_Cost), SUM(Amount_Credit),
           SUM(Amount_Debit)
from       JOB_ORDER_LINE_ITEMS
group by   Job_Sub_Code;

JOB SUM(AMOUNT_COST) SUM(AMOUNT_CREDIT) SUM(AMOUNT_DEBIT)
--- --------------- ------------------ -----------------
02  9834013.62       20611471.9          0
04  38670782.7       43440986.1          0
05  1252599.77       7139753.85          0
07     8899.66               0           0
12  1689729.94       3355174.16          0
14   103089.64       3287384.45          0
```

Listing 11-30: Running a query without using parallel execution servers

For this test, the elapsed time was 2 minutes, 30 seconds.
Next, run the query using PARALLEL, as shown in Listing 11-31.

```
select     /*+ PARALLEL (JOB_ORDER_LINE_ITEMS,6) */
           Job_Sub_Code, SUM(Amount_Cost), SUM(Amount_Credit),
           SUM(Amount_Debit)
from       JOB_ORDER_LINE_ITEMS
group by   Job_Sub_Code;
```

Listing 11-31: Running a query using parallel execution servers

For this test, the elapsed time was just over 1 minute. The query completes over twice as fast, with a degree of 6.

TIP

Increasing the degree of a parallel operation does not always decrease the time of execution. It depends on the complete setup of the system you have. The degree specifies only the number of parallel execution servers that should be used for the operation. The number of parallel execution servers used depends on the parameter settings and the Database Resource Manager settings.

Listing 11-32 shows the V$ view data when executing the preceding query using PARALLEL with a degree of 12.

```
select      Statistic, Value
from        V$PQ_SYSSTAT;


STATISTIC                  VALUE
--------------------       -----
Servers Busy                  12
Servers Idle                   0
Servers Highwater             12
Server Sessions               39
Servers Started               13
Servers Shutdown               7
Servers Cleaned Up             0
Queries Initiated              5
DML Initiated                  0
DDL Initiated                  0
DFO Trees                      5
Local Msgs Sent            91261
Distr Msgs Sent                0
Local Msgs Recv'd          91259
Distr Msgs Recv'd              0


select      *
from        V$PQ_SESSTAT;


STATISTIC                  LAST_QUERY  SESSION_TOTAL
--------------------       ----------  -------------
Queries Parallelized                1              4
DML Parallelized                    0              0
DDL Parallelized                    0              0
DFO Trees                           1              4
Server Threads                     12              0
Allocation Height                   6              0
Allocation Width                    1              0
Local Msgs Sent                 20934          83722
Distr Msgs Sent                     0              0
Local Msgs Recv'd               20934          83722
Distr Msgs Recv'd                   0              0
```

Listing 11-32: V$ view data when executing a query using PARALLEL with a degree of 12

Performance Comparisons & Parallel Operations

Other Parallel Notes

Planning (or reengineering) the physical location of data files is key to successful parallel data access. Determine an appropriate degree of parallelism for each parallelized SQL statement and parallelize the creation of your physical design. Don't let the initialization parameters dictate how the degree of parallelism is determined. Remember, you're usually trying to optimize a small number of slow queries, not every table access. Experiment with conservative parameters; use parallel operations for table or index creations and hint the degree of parallelism you identify as optimal. Use proper syntax for the parallel hints or they will be ignored. Other V$ views that may be helpful to you include V$px_session (session performing parallel operations), V$px_sesstat (statistics for sessions performing parallel operations), V$px_process (parallel processes), V$px_process_sysstat (statistics for parallel execution servers), V$sesstat (user session statistics), V$filestat (file I/O statistics), V$parameter (init.ora parameters), and V$pq_tqstat (workload statistics for parallel execution servers).

The parallel features offered in Oracle are incredibly powerful tools when used in a targeted fashion—most databases can be tuned to place indexes in the right quantity and location to deliver acceptable performance. Use parallel operations for those statements that cannot be written any other way but to scan an entire table or address a partitioned large table/index. Parallelized operations are powerful tools for managing data warehouses or performing periodic maintenance activities. The database environment must be configured to take full advantage of the benefits parallelism offers.

Tips Review

- Parallel processes commonly involve disk accesses. If the data is not distributed across multiple disks, using parallel operations may lead to an I/O bottleneck.

- When the parallel degree is set to *N*, it is possible to use (2*N) + 1 total processes for the parallel operation. Although parallel operations deal with processes and *not* processors, when a large number of processors are available, Oracle usually uses the additional processors to run parallel queries, usually enhancing the performance of the query.

- Using parallel operations on very small tables or very fast queries can also degrade performance because the query coordination also uses performance resources. You should evaluate whether the parallel cost exceeds the nonparallelized cost.

- As of Oracle9*i*, parallelized INSERT does not require a partitioned table.

- As of Oracle9*i*, intrapartition parallelism restrictions are no longer in effect.

- Using the PARALLEL hint enables the use of parallel operations. If the degree is not specified with the hint, the default degree during the table creation is used, or the degree is calculated from various initialization parameters.

- The use of the NOPARALLEL hint disables parallel operations in a statement that would otherwise use parallel processing due to a parallel object definition.

- Specify the degree of parallelism using a hint instead of relying on the table definition to ensure that all operations are tuned for the given query.

■   Effective parallel operations depend greatly on how the data is physically located. Avoid introducing I/O bottlenecks into your database.

■   To use parallel DML, you must first enable a parallel DML session.

■   Statement failure does not disable parallel DML within your session.

■   Parallel DML is limited to specific types of tables—and sometimes only certain columns within them. You must manage your tables to properly enable parallel DML operations.

■   You *must* issue a commit or rollback after using parallel DML statements. Otherwise, you will receive an error doing a SELECT statement on the same table that follows a parallel DML statement on that table.

■   The PARALLEL hint may be used in multiple sections of an INSERT...AS SELECT.

■   If the number of servers started consistently increases, you may consider increasing the PARALLEL_MIN_SERVERS initialization parameter. However, if a parallel execution server is started through the PARALLEL_MIN_SERVERS parameter, it does not exit until the database shuts down, the parallel process aborts, or the process is killed. This can lead to process memory fragmentation, so increase this only when you are sure it's needed.

■   A PARALLEL hint overrides the parallel object definition when it comes to which degree of parallelism the operation will use. The degree of parallelism specified in the hint is applied to all statement operations that can be parallelized, when possible.

■   New columns may be added to the PLAN_TABLE with each new release of Oracle. You should drop and re-create your PLAN_TABLE following each upgrade of the Oracle kernel. If you upgrade an existing database to a new version of Oracle, you should drop your old PLAN_TABLE and reexecute the utlxplan.sql script to see all of the new PLAN_TABLE columns.

■   When using the explain plan command for a parallelized query, you cannot rely on querying just the operations-related columns to see the parallelized operations within the explain plan. At a minimum, you should query the Other_Tag column to see which operations are performed in parallel. If an operation is not performed in parallel and you think it should be, you may need to add hints to the query, set a degree of parallelism for the tables, or check other factors that limit parallel resources.

■   You can use the utlxplp.sql script to query the parallel-related columns from PLAN_ TABLE following an EXPLAIN PLAN.

■   Be sure your environment is properly configured to support the increase in processes and transactions generated by parallel operations.

■   If you use Parallel Data Loading, indexes are not maintained by the SQL*Loader session. Before starting a parallel loading process, you must drop all indexes on the table and disable all of its PRIMARY KEY and UNIQUE constraints. After the loads complete, you can re-create the table's indexes.

■   Use the FILE parameter to direct the writes generated by parallel data loads.

- The PARALLEL option for data loading improves performance of loads, but can also cause space to be wasted when not properly used.

- The degree of a parallel operation does not always decrease the time of execution. It depends on the complete setup of the system you have. The degree specifies only the number of parallel execution servers that *should* be used for the operation. The number of parallel execution servers used depends on the parameter settings and the Database Resource Manager settings.

References

Oracle Parallel Query; Jake Van der Vort, TUSC
Oracle8 Server Tuning; Oracle Corporation
Oracle8*i Server Concepts*; Oracle Corporation
Oracle8i, Oracle9i Server Reference; Oracle Corporation
Oracle9i Server Concepts; Oracle Corporation
Oracle9i Data Warehousing Guide; Oracle Corporation
Oracle8 Advanced Tuning & Administration, Eyal Aronoff, Kevin Loney,
and Noorali Sonawalla (Oracle Press)
Thanks to R&R Donnelley and Sons, A.T. Kearney, Inc., and the TUSC DBA*Tech Team.
Jake Van der Vort contributed the major portion of the original chapter.
Kevin Loney did the update to Oracle9*i.*

CHAPTER
12

The V$ Views
(Developer & DBA)

S enior DBAs often tell junior DBAs that back in version 6, when they were the junior DBA, they used to know every V$ view by heart. In version 6, there were only 23 V$ views and the DBAs from the old days had it pretty easy. In Oracle9*i*, there are now 259 V$ views and almost 400 X$ tables; the challenge is just beginning.

Almost every great tuning or DBA product has one aspect in common. Most of them access the V$ view information to get the insightful information that is retrieved about the database, individual queries, or an individual user. Accessing the V$ views has become quite prevalent due to the numerous presentations by Joe Trezzo and other V$ gurus. If you currently don't look at the V$ views, you don't know what you're missing. The V$ views are unfiltered and unbiased looks into the heart of the Oracle database. They are the link to moving from the average to the expert DBA.

Chapter 13 more extensively explores the X$ tables, which are the underlying part of the V$ views. Appendixes B and C provide information about the V$ views and also the creation scripts from the X$ tables. Unfortunately, I can't show every great V$ script due to space limitations. Please check our web site (www.tusc.com) for the latest V$ scripts available.

Topics covered in this chapter include the following:

- Creating V$ views and granting access to them

- Getting a listing of all V$ views

- Getting a listing of the X$ scripts that make up the V$ views

- Examining the underlying objects that make up the DBA_ views

- Querying V$DATABASE to get database creation time and archiving information

- Querying V$LICENSE to view licensing limits and warning settings

- Accessing V$OPTIONS to view all options that have been installed

- Querying V$SGA to allocate basic memory for Oracle

- Querying V$SGASTAT to allocate detailed memory for Oracle

- Finding init.ora settings in V$PARAMETER

- Determining hit ratio for data (V$SYSSTAT)

- Determining hit ratio for the data dictionary (V$ROWCACHE)

- Determining hit ratio for the shared SQL and PL/SQL (V$LIBRARYCACHE)

- Deciding which objects need to be pinned and whether there is contiguous free memory (V$DB_OBJECT_CACHE)

- Finding the problem queries accessing V$SQLAREA, V$SQLTEXT, V$SESSION, and V$SESS_IO

- Finding out what users are doing and which resources they are using

- Identifying locking problems and killing the corresponding session

- Finding users with multiple sessions

- Balancing I/O using the views V$DATAFILE, V$FILESTAT, and DBA_DATA_FILES

- Checking to see if freelists is sufficient
- Checking for roles and privileges
- Using a table grouping the V$ views by category to match the poster

V$ View Creation and Access

The V$ views are created by the catalog.sql script. As of Oracle9*i*, there are approximately 259 V$ views. The actual number varies by the version and platform. Here is the number of each from Oracle6 to Oracle9.2:

Version	V$ Views	X$ Tables
6	23	(?)
7.1	72	126
8.0	132	200
8.1	185	271
9.0	227	352
9.2	259	394

They are all created with the prefix of *v_$*. Two of the views are created by the catldr.sql script, which is used for SQL*Loader direct load statistical information. The underlying view definitions (technically, these views are never created; their definitions are hard coded into the binary) for each V$ view can be seen in the V$ view named V$FIXED_VIEW_DEFINITION. The views are created by selecting from one or more X$ tables. A view is created for each *v_$* view to allow users to access the view. Users cannot access the actual *v$* views (they actually access the v_$ views; the v$ objects are only visible to SYS) and, therefore, this method provides access to these views via a view on a view. The view name changes the prefix of each view to *V$*. Lastly, a public synonym is created on each view because the SYS user owns the tables. Listing 12-1 shows an example of a V$ view creation in the catalog.sql script.

```
create or replace view gv_$datafile as
select *
from   gv$datafile;

create or replace public synonym gv$datafile for gv_$datafile;
```

Listing 12-1: Creating a V$ view in the catalog.sql script

The complete sequence of events is detailed in the following steps:

1. The GV$ view definitions are created from the X$ tables when the database is created:

   ```
   create  or replace view gv$fixed_table as
   select  inst_id,kqftanam, kqftaobj, 'TABLE', indx
   from    X$kqfta
   union all
   ```

```
select  inst_id,kqfvinam, kqfviobj, 'VIEW', 65537
from    X$kqfvi
union all
select  inst_id,kqfdtnam, kqfdtobj, 'TABLE', 65537
from    X$kqfdt;
```

2. The version-specific catalog script is executed:

```
SQL> @catalog
```

3. A v_$ view is created from the V$ view:

```
create or replace view v_$fixed_table
as
select *
from    v$fixed_table;
```

4. A new V$ synonym is created on the v_$ view:

```
create or replace public synonym v$fixed_table for v_$fixed_table;
```

TIP
The V$ views that are accessed by SYSTEM are actually synonyms that point to the v_$ views that are views of the original V$ views based on the X$ tables. (Better read that one again!)

The only operation that can be performed on these views is a SELECT. To provide access to the V$ views, you must grant access to the underlying v_$ view.

You cannot grant access to the V$ views (even as the SYS user):

```
connect    sys/change_on_install as sysdba

Grant select on v$fixed_table to richn;
ORA-02030: can only select from fixed tables/views.
```

Although the error message (following the previous code) for attempting to grant access to V$FIXED_TABLE is erroneous, the grant will not be allowed. You may, however, grant access to the underlying v_$ view that is behind the V$ view.

To connect to the SYS superuser, use the following:

```
Connect sys/change_on_install as sysdba
Connected.
```

To grant access to an underlying view to the desired user, use the following:

```
grant select on v_$fixed_table to richn;
Grant succeeded.
```

To connect as the desired user, use this:

```
conn  richn/tusc
Connected.
```

Access the V$FIXED_TABLE view via the synonym V$FIXED_TABLE created for V_$FIXED_TABLE with the following:

```
select count(*)
from   v$fixed_table;
COUNT(*)
--------
     912
```

You still *can't* access the v_$fixed_table even though that was the grant made:

```
select count(*)
from   v_$fixed_table;
ORA-00942: table or view does not exist.
```

You *can* access the v_$fixed_view if you preface it with SYS:

```
conn   richn/tusc
select count(*)
from   SYS.v_$fixed_table;
COUNT(*)
--------
     912
```

To avoid confusion, it is better to give access to the v_$ tables and notify the DBA that he or she has access to the V$ views. Using this method, you may give access to the V$ view information without giving out the password for the SYS or SYSTEM accounts. The key is granting SELECT access to the original SYS-owned v_$ view.

TIP
When other DBAs need access to the V$ view information, but not the SYS or SYSTEM passwords, grant the user access to the v_$ views. The user may then access the V$ views that have public synonyms to the v_$ views. However, scripts should always be written to query the SYS.V_$ views directly, to avoid the performance cost of de-referencing the public synonym.

WARNING
You should grant non-DBA users privileges to the V$ views only as needed, and use caution. Remember, performance costs come with querying the V$ views and the larger your environment, the greater those costs.

Obtaining a Count and Listing of All V$ Views

To get a count of all V$ views for a given version of Oracle, query the V$FIXED_TABLE view. The number of V$ views continues to change even within the same version. The examples that follow display the V$ view queries for Oracle9*i*. The frontier in the world of the V$ views continues to expand with each version of Oracle.

Query to get a count of V$ views, as shown in Listing 12-2.

```
select count(*)
from    v$fixed_table
where   name like 'V%';

COUNT(*)
--------
259
```

Listing 12-2: Getting a count of V$ views

The number of V$ views has increased substantially from Oracle8 to Oracle9*i* (132 to 259). Many of the V$ views continue to be undocumented. The methods of exploring information are continually growing in Oracle because the number of views continues to expand. In Oracle8, the GV$ views were introduced. The GV$ (global V$) views are the same as the V$ views with an additional column for the instance ID (very important for RAC).

Get a list of GV$ views, as in Listing 12-3 (partial listing; complete list in Appendix B).

```
select    name
from      v$fixed_table
where     name like 'GV%'
order by name;
NAME
----------------------------------
GV$ACCESS
GV$ACTIVE_INSTANCES
GV$ACTIVE_SESS_POOL_MTH
GV$AQ1
GV$ARCHIVE
GV$ARCHIVED_LOG
GV$ARCHIVE_DEST
GV$ARCHIVE_DEST_STATUS
GV$ARCHIVE_GAP
GV$ARCHIVE_PROCESSES
GV$AW_CALC
...
```

Listing 12-3: Partial listing of GV$ views

TIP
Query V$FIXED_TABLE to obtain a listing of all GV$ and V$ views in the database. The GV$ views are the exact same as the V$ views, except the instance ID contains an identifier.

Finding the X$ Tables Used to Create the V$ Views

To understand where the V$ view information comes from, query the underlying X$ tables. (See Chapter 13 for X$ table information.) At times, it may be advantageous to query the underlying X$ tables because the V$ views are often the join of several X$ tables. The X$ tables are very cryptic because they are similar to the underlying table constructs of the Oracle Data Dictionary. Oracle creates V$ views in the SGA to allow users to examine the information stored in the X$ tables in a more readable format. In fact, when SELECTs are performed against the V$ views, the SELECTs are actually retrieving information out of the SGA—and more specifically, out of the X$ tables.

With the knowledge of the V$ view underlying a given SELECT statement, you have the capability to create customized views; simply copy the existing V$ view underlying the SELECT statement and modify it or create a new customized SELECT on the X$ tables. This technique allows more selective and more optimized queries. Listing 12-4 is used to access the underlying query to the X$ tables. To get a listing of the X$ tables that make up the V$ views, you must access the V$FIXED_TABLE_DEFINITION view (output formatted for readability).

```
select    *
from      v$fixed_view_definition
where     view_name = 'GV$FIXED_TABLE';
```

Output:

```
VIEW_NAME          VIEW_DEFINITION
--------------     -----------------------------------------------------------

GV$FIXED_TABLE     select  inst_id,kqftanam, kqftaobj, 'TABLE', indx
                   from    X$kqfta
                   union all
                   select  inst_id,kqfvinam, kqfviobj, 'VIEW', 65537
                   from    x$kqfvi
                   union all
                   select  inst_id,kqfdtnam, kqfdtobj, 'TABLE', 65537
                   from    x$kqfdt
```

Listing 12-4: Accessing the underlying query to the X$ tables

TIP
Access the V$FIXED_VIEW_DEFINITION view to get all of the information of the underlying X$ tables that make up a V$ view.

Also note that as of Oracle8, there are indexes on the underlying X$ tables to provide faster execution of queries performed on the V$ views. You can view the index information on the underlying X$ tables through the V$INDEXED_FIXED_COLUMN view. (See Chapter 13 for more information.)

Finding the Underlying Objects That Make Up the DBA_ views

Some people think the DBA_ views also come from the X$ tables and/or the V$ views. They actually come from Oracle's underlying database tables (although some access the X$ tables as well). To look at the objects that make up the DBA_ views, access DBA_VIEWS, as in Listing 12-5.

> **NOTE**
> *You may need to set long 2000000 to see all of this output.*

```
select text
from   dba_views
where  view_name='DBA_IND_PARTITIONS';

TEXT
--------------------------------------------------------------------------------
select u.name, io.name, 'NO', io.subname, 0,  ip.hiboundval,ip.hiboundlen,ip.part#,
       decode(bitand(ip.flags, 1), 1, 'UNUSABLE', 'USABLE'), ts.name,
       ip.pctfree$,ip.initrans, ip.maxtrans, s.iniexts * ts.blocksize,
       decode(bitand(ts.flags, 3), 1, to_number(NULL),  s.extsize * ts.blocksize),
       s.minexts, s.maxexts, decode(bitand(ts.flags,3),1, to_number(NULL),s.extpct),
       decode(bitand(ts.flags, 32), 32, to_number(NULL),
          decode(s.lists, 0, 1, s.lists)),
       decode(bitand(ts.flags, 32), 32, to_number(NULL),
          decode(s.groups, 0, 1, s.groups)),
       decode(mod(trunc(ip.flags / 4), 2), 0, 'YES', 'NO'),
       decode(bitand(ip.flags, 1024), 0, 'DISABLED', 1024, 'ENABLED', null),
       ip.blevel, ip.leafcnt, ip.distkey, ip.lblkkey, ip.dblkkey,
       ip.clufac, ip.rowcnt, ip.samplesize, ip.analyzetime,
       decode(s.cachehint, 0, 'DEFAULT', 1, 'KEEP', 2, 'RECYCLE', NULL),
       decode(bitand(ip.flags, 8), 0, 'NO', 'YES'), ip.pctthres$,
       decode(bitand(ip.flags, 16), 0, 'NO', 'YES'),'',''
from   obj$ io, indpart$ ip, ts$ ts, sys.seg$ s, user$ u
where  io.obj# = ip.obj# and ts.ts# = ip.ts# and ip.file#=s.file# and
       ip.block#=s.block# and ip.ts#=s.ts# and io.owner# = u.user#
     union all
select u.name, io.name, 'YES', io.subname, icp.subpartcnt,
       icp.hiboundval, icp.hiboundlen, icp.part#, 'N/A', ts.name,
       icp.defpctfree, icp.definitrans, icp.defmaxtrans,
       icp.definiexts, icp.defextsize, icp.defminexts, icp.defmaxexts,
       icp.defextpct, icp.deflists, icp.defgroups,
       decode(icp.deflogging, 0, 'NONE', 1, 'YES', 2, 'NO', 'UNKNOWN'),
       'N/A', icp.blevel, icp.leafcnt, icp.distkey, icp.lblkkey, icp.dblkkey,
       icp.clufac, icp.rowcnt, icp.samplesize, icp.analyzetime,
       decode(icp.defbufpool, 0, 'DEFAULT', 1, 'KEEP', 2, 'RECYCLE', NULL),
       decode(bitand(icp.flags, 8), 0, 'NO', 'YES'), TO_NUMBER(NULL),
       decode(bitand(icp.flags, 16), 0, 'NO', 'YES'),'',''
from   obj$ io, indcompart$ icp, ts$ ts, user$ u
where  io.obj# = icp.obj# and icp.defts# = ts.ts# (+) and u.user# = io.owner#
     union all
```

```
select u.name, io.name, 'NO', io.subname, 0,
       ip.hiboundval, ip.hiboundlen, ip.part#,
       decode(bitand(ip.flags, 1), 1, 'UNUSABLE',
               decode(bitand(ip.flags, 4096), 4096, 'INPROGRS', 'USABLE')),
       null, ip.pctfree$, ip.initrans, ip.maxtrans,
       0, 0, 0, 0, 0, 0, 0,
       decode(mod(trunc(ip.flags / 4), 2), 0, 'YES', 'NO'),
       decode(bitand(ip.flags, 1024), 0, 'DISABLED', 1024, 'ENABLED', null),
       ip.blevel, ip.leafcnt, ip.distkey, ip.lblkkey, ip.dblkkey,
       ip.clufac, ip.rowcnt, ip.samplesize, ip.analyzetime,
       'DEFAULT',
       decode(bitand(ip.flags, 8), 0, 'NO', 'YES'), ip.pctthres$,
       decode(bitand(ip.flags, 16), 0, 'NO', 'YES'),
       decode(i.type#,
               9, decode(bitand(ip.flags, 8192), 8192, 'FAILED', 'VALID'),
               ''),
       ipp.parameters
from   obj$ io, indpart$ ip,  user$ u, ind$ i, indpart_param$ ipp
where  io.obj# = ip.obj# and io.owner# = u.user# and
       ip.bo# = i.obj# and ip.obj# = ipp.obj#
```

Listing 12-5: Objects that make up the DBA_ views

Never modify the underlying objects; many DBAs have corrupted their database in this manner. Do *not* do the following in Listing 12-6, but note that it is possible:

```
Connect sys/change_on_install as sysdba
Connected.

DELETE FROM OBJAUTH$;  -- Don't do this! If you commit this, your database is over!
13923 rows deleted.

Rollback;
Rollback complete.
```

Listing 12-6: Objects that should never be modified

TIP
The DBA_ views are not derived from the X$ tables or V$ views. The fact that you can delete rows from obj$ is a great reason to never be the SYS superuser.

Using Helpful V$ Scripts

The rest of this chapter is dedicated to scripts that are very helpful in analyzing different areas of the Oracle database. Many of these scripts are dynamic and provide valuable insight into areas of the database that may need to be analyzed to determine resource contention at a point in time. Typically, the result is that the DBA performs some operation to immediately eliminate the contention by tuning a query or increasing an init.ora parameter to reduce the resource contention in the future. Revoking access to a given ad-hoc query user, or restricting his or her system resource use with profiles, could be an emergency option as well. The next three sections include scripts that retrieve the following:

- Basic database information
- Basic licensing information
- Database options installed in your database

Basic Database Information

Getting the basic information about your instance is usually as easy as logging in to SQL*Plus, because all of the information shows in the banner at that time. If you would like to see the full banner header, you can access the V$VERSION view to display the banner. Listing 12-7 shows a quick way to see the version you are using as well as other information.

```
SQL> select * from v$version;

BANNER
----------------------------------------------------------------
Oracle9i Enterprise Edition Release 9.2.0.1.0 - Production
PL/SQL Release 9.2.0.1.0 - Production
CORE    9.2.0.1.0        Production
TNS for 32-bit Windows: Version 9.2.0.1.0 - Production
NLSRTL Version 9.2.0.1.0 - Production
```

Listing 12-7: Viewing version information

Accessing V$DATABASE gives you basic information concerning the database. The most important information in the output is to ensure that you are in the desired ARCHIVELOG mode. The output also gives you the exact date when the database was created, as you can see in Listing 12-8.

```
select name, created, log_mode
from    v$database;

NAME      CREATED      LOG_MODE
--------- ---------    ---------------
ORA9I2    20-MAY-02    ARCHIVELOG
```

Listing 12-8: Basic information about the database

TIP
Query the V$VERSION and V$DATABASE to view basic database information such as the version, to find out when your database was created, and to find out basic archiving information.

Basic Licensing Information

The V$LICENSE view allows a DBA to monitor the system activity in terms of overall database numbers at any time. It provides a DBA with a log of the maximum number of concurrent sessions at any time, which allows a company to ensure they are licensed properly. The current number of sessions is displayed along with the session warning level and session maximum level.

A session warning level of 0 indicates that the init.ora session warning parameter was not set; therefore, no warning message displays. A session maximum level of 0 indicates that the init.ora session maximum parameter was not set; therefore, there is no limit on the number of sessions.

The script should be executed periodically to provide a DBA with the actual number of sessions on the system throughout the day and to ensure proper licensing. Setting the init.ora parameter LICENSE_MAX_SESSIONS = 110 limits the sessions to 110. Setting the init.ora parameter LICENSE_SESSIONS_WARNING = 100 gives every user past the one-hundredth a warning message so they will (hopefully) notify the DBA that the system is closing in on a problem. The LICENSE_MAX_USERS init.ora parameter is used to set the number of named users that can be created in the database. In Listing 12-9, there is no limit and the value is set to 0.

```
select *
from    v$license;


SESS_MAX    SESS_WARNING    SESS_CURRENT    SESS_HIGHWATER    USERS_MAX
--------    ------------    ------------    --------------    ---------
     110             100              44               105            0
```

Listing 12-9: Querying V$LICENSE for license thresholds

TIP
Query the V$LICENSE view to see the maximum sessions that you are allowed. You can also set warnings when you get close to the maximum.

Database Options Installed in Your Database

The script in Listing 12-10 describes what options are installed on your database and are available for use. If you have purchased a product that does not show up in this list, you may have incorrectly installed it. Query the V$OPTION view to check for installed products or log on to SQL*Plus to see the products that are installed.

```
select *
from    v$option;
```

To get the following output, you need to order by PARAMETER.

Output:

```
PARAMETER                               VALUE
--------------------------------------  --------
Advanced replication                    TRUE
Application Role                        TRUE
Bit-mapped indexes                      TRUE
Block Media Recovery                    TRUE
Change Data Capture                     TRUE
Coalesce Index                          TRUE
Connection multiplexing                 TRUE
Connection pooling                      TRUE
Database queuing                        TRUE
```

```
Database resource manager          TRUE
Duplexed backups                   TRUE
Enterprise User Security           TRUE
Export transportable tablespaces   TRUE
Fast-Start Fault Recovery          TRUE
File Mapping                       TRUE
Fine-grained Auditing              TRUE
Fine-grained access control        TRUE
Heap segment compression           TRUE
Incremental backup and recovery    TRUE
Instead-of triggers                TRUE
Java                               TRUE
Join index                         TRUE
Managed Standby                    TRUE
Materialized view rewrite          TRUE
Materialized view warehouse refresh TRUE
OLAP                               TRUE
OLAP Window Functions              TRUE
Objects                            TRUE
Online Index Build                 TRUE
Online Redefinition                TRUE
Oracle Data Guard                  TRUE
Oracle Data Mining                 TRUE
Oracle Label Security              FALSE
Parallel backup and recovery       TRUE
Parallel execution                 TRUE
Parallel load                      TRUE
Partitioning                       TRUE
Plan Stability                     TRUE
Point-in-time tablespace recovery  TRUE
Proxy authentication/authorization TRUE
Real Application Clusters          FALSE
Sample Scan                        TRUE
Spatial                            TRUE
Streams                            TRUE
Transparent Application Failover   TRUE
Trial Recovery                     TRUE
Very Large Memory                  TRUE
Visual Information Retrieval       TRUE

48 rows selected.
```

Listing 12-10: Querying V$OPTION to see options installed

The previous database has the Partitioning option, but it does not have Real Application Clusters (RAC) installed.

TIP
Query the V$OPTION view to retrieve the Oracle options you have installed. The V$VERSION view will give the versions of the base options that are installed.

Summary of Memory Allocated (V$SGA)

V$SGA gives the summary information for the System Global Area (SGA) memory structures of your system, as shown in Listing 12-11. The "Database Buffers" is the number of bytes allocated to memory for data. It comes from the init.ora parameter DB_CACHE_SIZE. The "Redo Buffers" comes primarily from the value of the init.ora parameter LOG_BUFFER, which is used to buffer changed records and flushed to the redo logs whenever a COMMIT is issued.

```
select *
from   v$sga;

NAME                                VALUE
------------------------------- ----------------
Database Buffers                    2,667,577,344
Fixed Size                                734,080
Redo Buffers                            1,335,296
Variable Size                         352,321,536
```

Listing 12-11: Summary information for the SGA

This output indicates a relatively large SGA with a buffer cache that includes DB_CACHE_SIZE, DB_KEEP_CACHE_SIZE, and DB_RECYCLE_CACHE_SIZE of over 2.5GB. The predominant part of the Variable Size category is the shared pool. (The shared pool for this SGA was slightly over 200MB.) This SGA is using about 3GB of the actual physical system memory in Listing 12-11. This information is also given in the Statspack report (see Chapter 14) and can be displayed by issuing an SHO SGA command as the SYS superuser.

TIP

Access the V$SGA view to get a baseline idea of the system's physical memory allocated for data, shared pool, large pool, java pool, and log buffering of Oracle.

Detail of Memory Allocated (V$SGASTAT)

A more detailed V$ view query to retrieve the information about memory allocation for the SGA is in the V$SGASTAT view. This view provides dynamic information about SGA and memory resources. (It changes as the database is accessed.) This statement describes the SGA sizes at a detailed level. The records FIXED_SGA, BUFFER_CACHE, and LOG_BUFFER are the same values for both the V$SGA and V$SGASTAT. The remaining records in V$SGASTAT make up the only other V$SGA record (the Variable Size or Shared Pool record).

Fixed Size (V$SGA)	= fixed_sga (V$SGASTAT)
Database Buffers (V$SGA)	= buffer_cache (V$SGASTAT)
Redo Buffers (V$SGA)	= log_buffer (V$SGASTAT)
Variable Size (V$SGA)	= 39 Other Records (V$SGASTAT)

In Oracle9.2, the V$SGASTAT has 43 total records, as shown in Listing 12-12:

```
select *
from    v$sgastat;

POOL          NAME                           BYTES
-----------   --------------------------   ----------
              buffer_cache                 2667577344
              fixed_sga                        734080
              log_buffer                      1311744
shared pool   1M buffer                       2098176
shared pool   Checkpoint queue              30725120
shared pool   DML lock                         100408
shared pool   FileIdentificatonBlock          5243896
shared pool   FileOpenBlock                  16267744
shared pool   KGK heap                          96600
shared pool   KGLS heap                        598208
...etc.
43 rows selected
```

Listing 12-12: Detail of memory allocated

This information is also given in the Statspack report (see Chapter 14), along with the starting and ending values over the duration of the Statspack report.

TIP
Accessing V$SGASTAT gives you a detailed breakdown for the Oracle SGA and breaks down all buckets for the Shared Pool allocation.

Finding init.ora Settings in V$PARAMETER

The script in Listing 12-13 displays the init.ora parameters for your system. It also provides information on each parameter that identifies whether the current value was the default value (ISDEFAULT=TRUE). It also shows whether the parameter is modifiable with the alter session command, and with the alter system command (ISSYS_MODIFIABLE=IMMEDIATE). These can be modified with the alter session and alter system commands vs. modifying the initializat file and shutting down and restarting the instance. The example in Listing 12-13 (from Oracle9.2) displays some of the initializat parameters that can be modified with one of the alter commands. (IMMEDIATE means it can be modified and it will take effect immediately.)

```
select    name, value, isdefault, isses_modifiable,
          issys_modifiable
from      v$parameter
order by  name;
```

Listing 12-13: Initialization parameters that can be modified with an alter command

Query of V$PARAMETER:

```
NAME                             VALUE                  ISDEFAULT ISSES ISSYS_MOD
-------------------------------  ---------------------  --------- ----- ---------
O7_DICTIONARY_ACCESSIBILITY      FALSE                  TRUE      FALSE FALSE
active_instance_count                                   TRUE      FALSE FALSE
aq_tm_processes                  1                      FALSE     FALSE IMMEDIATE
archive_lag_target               0                      TRUE      FALSE IMMEDIATE
audit_sys_operations             FALSE                  TRUE      FALSE FALSE
audit_trail                      NONE                   TRUE      FALSE FALSE
background_core_dump             partial                TRUE      FALSE FALSE
...partial output listing)
```

Version-dependent columns are also available.

TIP
Query V$PARAMETER and find out the current values for the init.ora parameters. It also shows which init.ora parameters have been changed from their original defaults: ISDEFAULT = FALSE. It also shows which parameters may be changed only for a given session, if ISSES_MODIFIABLE = TRUE. Lastly, it shows which parameters may be changed without shutting down and restarting the database for ISSYS_MODIFIABLE = IMMEDIATE as well as ISSYS_MODIFIABLE = DEFERRED for a parameter that is enforced for all new logins but not currently logged on sessions. If the parameter ISSYS_MODIFIABLE = FALSE, then the instance must be shut down and restarted for the parameter to take effect.

Determining Hit Ratio for Data (V$SYSSTAT)

Query V$SYSSTAT (as in Listing 12-14) to see how often your data is being read from memory. It gives the hit ratio for the setting of the database block buffers. This information can help you identify when your system needs more data buffers (DB_CACHE_SIZE) or when a system is not tuned very well. (Both lead to low hit ratios.) Generally, you should ensure the read hit ratio is greater than 95 percent. Increasing the hit ratio on your system from 98 percent to 99 percent could mean performance that is 100+ percent faster (depending on what is causing the disk reads).

```
select 1-(sum(decode(name, 'physical reads', value,0))/
          (sum(decode(name, 'db block gets', value,0)) +
          (sum(decode(name, 'consistent gets', value,0)))))
          "Read Hit Ratio"
from      v$sysstat;

Read Hit Ratio
--------------
    .996558641
```

Listing 12-14: Querying V$SYSSTAT for a data block buffer hit ratio

The hit ratio in Listing 12-14 is very good, but that does not mean the system is perfectly tuned. A high hit ratio could mean that overly indexed queries are being used. If this hit ratio is well below 95 percent, you may need to increase the init.ora parameter, DB_CACHE_SIZE, or tune some of the queries that are causing disk reads (if possible and efficient to do so). One exception to this is when the distribution of data within the individual blocks is greatly skewed. Despite this possibility, hit ratios below 90 percent almost always involve systems that are poorly tuned, other than those that are built in a Petri dish by someone who has built an extremely rare balance of data within each block. (See Chapter 4 for additional information on data hit ratios.)

You can also use the new V$DB_CACHE_ADVICE view to help you resize the data cache if you feel it is necessary. The query in Listing 12-15 creates a list of values that shows you the effect of a larger and smaller data cache.

```
column buffers_for_estimate format 999,999,999 heading 'Buffers'
column estd_physical_read_factor format 999.90 heading 'Estd Phys|Read Fact'
column estd_physical_reads format 999,999,999 heading 'Estd Phys| Reads'

SELECT  size_for_estimate, buffers_for_estimate,
        estd_physical_read_factor, estd_physical_reads
FROM    V$DB_CACHE_ADVICE
WHERE   name = 'DEFAULT'
AND     block_size =
            (SELECT value
             FROM   V$PARAMETER
             WHERE  name = 'db_block_size')
AND     advice_status = 'ON';
```

Listing 12-15: Checking the effect of a larger and smaller data cache

Determining Hit Ratio for the Data Dictionary (V$ROWCACHE)

You use the V$ROWCACHE view (as in Listing 12-16) to find how often the data dictionary calls are effectively hitting the memory cache allocated by the SHARED_POOL_SIZE init.ora parameter. This is discussed in Chapter 4 in detail. The only goal here is to review the V$ view access. If the dictionary hit ratio is not adequate, the overall system performance suffers greatly.

```
select  sum(gets), sum(getmisses),(1 - (sum(getmisses) / (sum(gets)
        + sum(getmisses)))) * 100 HitRate
from    v$rowcache;

SUM(GETS)    SUM(GETMISSES)      HITRATE
---------    --------------    ----------
   110673               670   99.3982558
```

Listing 12-16: Querying V$ROWCACHE for the dictionary hit ratio

The recommended hit ratio is 95 percent or higher. If the hit ratio falls below this percentage, it indicates that the SHARED_POOL_SIZE init.ora parameter may need to be increased. But remember, you saw in the V$SGASTAT view that the shared pool is made up of many pieces, of which this is only one. Note: Environments that make heavy use of public synonyms may struggle to get their dictionary cache hit rate above 75 percent even if the shared pool is huge. This is because Oracle must often check for the existence of non-existent objects.

Determining Hit Ratio for the Shared SQL and PL/SQL (V$LIBRARYCACHE)

Accessing the V$LIBRARYCACHE view shows how well the actual statements (SQL and PL/SQL) are accessing memory. If the SHARED_POOL_SIZE in the init.ora is too small, enough room may not be available to store all of the statements into memory. If the shared pool becomes extremely fragmented, large PL/SQL routines may not fit into the shared pool. If statements are not reused effectively, an enlarged shared pool may cause more harm than good. (See Chapter 4 for additional details.)

There is an execution (pinhitratio) and a reload hit ratio. The recommended hit ratio for pin hits is 95+ percent, and the reload hit ratio should be 99+ percent (less than 1 percent reloads). Reloads occur when a statement has been parsed previously, but the shared pool is usually not large enough to hold it in memory as other statements are parsed. The body of the statement is pushed out of memory (the head is still there); when the statement is again needed, a reload is recorded to reload the body. This could also occur if the execution plan for the statement changes. If either of the hit ratios falls below these percentages, it indicates that the shared pool should be investigated in greater detail. Listing 12-17 shows how to query for all of the information discussed above.

```
select   sum(pins) "Executions", sum(pinhits) "Hits",
         ((sum(pinhits) / sum(pins)) * 100) "PinHitRatio",
         sum(reloads) "Misses", ((sum(pins) / (sum(pins)
         + sum(reloads))) * 100)  "RelHitRatio"
from     v$librarycache;


Executions      Hits PinHitRatio    Misses RelHitRatio
---------- ---------- ----------- ---------- -----------
    202288    201304  99.5135648        15  99.9925854
```

Listing 12-17: Execution (pinhitratio) and reload hit ratio

TIP
Query V$LIBRARYCACHE to see how often your SQL and PL/SQL are being read from memory. The pinhitratio should generally be 95 percent or higher, and the number of reloads should not be greater than 1 percent.

Identifying PL/SQL Objects That Need to Be Kept (Pinned)

Fragmentation that causes several small pieces to be available in the shared pool, and not enough large contiguous pieces, is a common occurrence in the shared pool. The key to eliminating shared pool errors (see Chapters 4 and 13 for more information) is to understand which objects can cause problems. Once you know the potential problem PL/SQL objects, you can then pin this code when the database is started (and the shared pool is completely contiguous). You can query the V$DB_OBJECT_CACHE view to determine PL/SQL that is both large and currently not marked *kept*. This query shows only the current statements in the cache. The example in Listing 12-18 searches for those objects requiring greater than 100KB.

```
select  name, sharable_mem
from    v$db_object_cache
where   sharable_mem > 100000
and     type in ('PACKAGE', 'PACKAGE BODY',
            'FUNCTION', 'PROCEDURE')
and     kept = 'NO';
NAME                                    SHARABLE_MEM
------------------------------------    ------------
STANDARD                                      377236
```

Listing 12-18: Objects requiring more than 100KB

TIP
Query the V$DB_OBJECT_CACHE view to find objects that are not pinned and are also potentially large enough to cause problems.

Finding Problem Queries by Querying V$SQLAREA

V$SQLAREA provides a means of identifying the *potential* problem SQL statements or SQL statements needing optimization to improve overall database optimization by reducing disk access. The disk_reads signify the volume of disk reads that are being performed on the system. This combined with the executions (disk_reads/executions) returns the SQL statements that have the most disk hits per statement execution. The disk_reads was set to 100000 in Listing 12-18, but it could be set much larger or smaller on production systems (depending on the database) to reveal only the greater problem statements on your system. Once identified, the top statements should be reviewed and optimized to improve overall performance. Typically, the statement is not using an index or the execution path is forcing the statement not to use the proper indexes.

One potentially misleading part of the query in Listing 12-19 is the rds_exec_ratio. This is the number of disk reads divided by the executions. In reality, a statement may be read once using 100 disk reads and then forced out of memory (if memory is insufficient). If it is read again, then it will read 100 disk reads again and the rds_exec_ratio will be 100 (or 100 + 100 reads divided by 2 executions). But, if the statement happens to be in memory the second time (memory is sufficient), the disk reads will be zero (the second time) and the rds_exec_ratio will be only 50 (or 100 + 0 divided by 2 executions). Any statement that makes the top of this list is a problem and needs to be tuned—period!

NOTE
The following code was formatted for ease of reading.

```
select      b.username username, a.disk_reads reads,
            a.executions exec, a.disk_reads /decode
            (a.executions, 0, 1,a.executions) rds_exec_ratio,
            a.command_type, a.sql_text Statement
```

```
from       v$sqlarea a, dba_users b
where      a.parsing_user_id = b.user_id
and        a.disk_reads       > 100000
order by   a.disk_reads desc;

USERNAME   READS      EXEC   RDS_EXEC_RATIO   STATEMENT
--------   -------    ----   --------------   ---------
ADHOC1     7281934     1           7281934    select  custno, ordno
                                              from    cust, orders
ADHOC5     4230044     4           1057511    select  ordno
                                              from    orders
                                              where   trunc(ordno) = 721305
ADHOC1     801715      2            499858    select  custno, ordno
                                              from    cust
                                              where   decode(custno,1,6) = 314159
```

Listing 12-19: Querying V$SQLAREA

The DISK_READS column in the preceding statement can be replaced with the BUFFER_GETS column to provide information on SQL statements that may not possess the large disk hits (although they usually do), but possess a large number of memory hits (higher than normally desired). These are statements that are using a large amount of memory that is allocated for the data (DB_CACHE_SIZE). The problem is not that the statement is being executed in memory (which is good), but that the statement is hogging up a lot of the memory. Many times, this problem is attributable to a SQL statement using an index when it should be doing a full tablescan or a join. These types of SQL statements can also involve a join operation that is forcing the path to use a different index than desired, or using multiple indexes and forcing index merging or volumes of data merging. Remember, the bulk of system performance problems are attributable to poorly written SQL and PL/SQL statements.

TIP
Query the V$SQLAREA to find problem queries (and users).

Finding Out What Users Are Doing and Which Resources They Are Using

Joining V$SESSION and V$SQLTEXT displays the SQL statement that is currently being executed by each session, as shown in Listing 12-20. It is extremely useful when a DBA is trying to determine what is happening in the system at a given point in time.

```
select     a.sid, a.username, s.sql_text
from       v$session a, v$sqltext s
where      a.sql_address    = s.address
and        a.sql_hash_value = s.hash_value
order by a.username, a.sid, s.piece;

SID  USERNAME      SQL_TEXT
---  ----------    ------------------------------------
 11  PLSQL_USER    update s_employee set salary = 10000
```

```
 9  SYS            select a.sid, a.username, s.sql_text
 9  SYS            from v$session a, v$sqltext
 9  SYS            where a.sql_address  = s.address
 9  SYS            and a.sql_hash_value  = s.hash_value
 9  SYS            order by a.username, a.sid, s.piece
(...partial output listing)
```

Listing 12-20: SQL statement currently being executed by each session

The SQL_TEXT column displays the entire SQL statement, but the statement is stored in the V$SQLTEXT view as a VARCHAR2(64) datatype and therefore spans multiple records. The PIECE column is used to order the statement. To view the resources being used by each of the users, simply use the query in Listing 12-21. The goal of this statement is to highlight the physical disk and memory hits for each session. It is very easy to recognize users who are performing a large number of physical disk or memory reads.

```
select    a.username, b.block_gets, b.consistent_gets,
          b.physical_reads, b.block_changes, b.consistent_changes
from      v$session a, v$sess_io b
where     a.sid = b.sid
order by  a.username;
```

USERNAME	BLOCK_GETS	CONSISTENT_GETS	PHYSICAL_READS	BLOCK_ CHANGES	CONSISTENT_CHANGES
PLSQL_USER	39	72	11	53	1
SCOTT	11	53	12	0	0
SYS	14	409	26	0	0
SYSTEM	8340	10197	291	2558	419

Listing 12-21: Resources being used by each user

TIP
Query V$SESSION, V$SQLTEXT, and V$SESS_IO to find the problem users and what they are executing at a given point in time.

Finding Out Which Objects a User Is Accessing

Querying V$ACCESS can point you to potential problem objects (potentially missing indexes) once you have found the problem user or query on your system. It can also be helpful when you want to modify a particular object and need to know who is using it at a given point in time, as shown in Listing 12-22.

```
select a.sid, a.username, b.owner, b.object, b.type
from   v$session a, v$access b
where  a.sid = b.sid;
```

SID	USERNAME	OWNER	OBJECT	TYPE
8	SCOTT	SYS	DBMS_APPLICATION_INFO	PACKAGE
9	SYS	SYS	DBMS_APPLICATION_INFO	PACKAGE
9	SYS	SYS	X$BH	TABLE

```
10   SYSTEM     PUBLIC   V$ACCESS                  SYNONYM
10   SYSTEM     PUBLIC   V$SESSION                 SYNONYM
10   SYSTEM     SYS      DBMS_APPLICATION_INFO     PACKAGE
10   SYSTEM     SYS      V$ACCESS                  VIEW
10   SYSTEM     SYS      V$SESSION                 VIEW
10   SYSTEM     SYS      V_$ACCESS                 VIEW
```

Listing 12-22: Identifying who is using a particular object at a given point in time

This script displays all objects being accessed, including synonyms, views, stored source code, etc.

TIP
Query V$ACCESS to find all objects that are being accessed by a user at a given time. This can help to pinpoint problem objects, while also being helpful when modifying a particular object (find out who is accessing it). However, this would be a very expensive operation on a system with a large shared pool and hundreds of users.

Getting Detailed User Information

A method for analyzing user statistics is extremely valuable when a new or updated application module is being tested to determine the overhead. It also provides a window to a user who is having performance problems, because it provides statistics on a variety of areas for each user. In addition, it can serve as a guideline for setting profiles to limit a particular user. The script in Listing 12-23 limits the statistics only to areas that have a value (b.value != 0).

```
select    a.username, c.name, sum(b.value) value
from      v$session a, v$sesstat b, v$statname c
where     a.sid         = b.sid
and       b.statistic#  = c.statistic#
and       b.value       != 0
group by  name, username;
USERNAME        NAME                                    VALUE
----------      ------------------------------------    -----
PLSQL_USER      logons cumulative                           1
PLSQL_USER      opened cursors cumulative                  14
PLSQL_USER      session uga memory max                  31508
PLSQL_USER      table fetch by rowid                       10
PLSQL_USER      SQL*Net roundtrips to/from client          64
PLSQL_USER      bytes received via SQL*Net from client   5441
PLSQL_USER      bytes sent via SQL*Net to client         2632
PLSQL_USER      db block changes                           53
PLSQL_USER      physical reads                             11
PLSQL_USER      consistent gets                            72
PLSQL_USER      db block gets                              39
PLSQL_USER      enqueue requests                            2
PLSQL_USER      session pga memory max                   76592
PLSQL_USER      session pga memory                       76592
```

```
PLSQL_USER    session uga memory                    31508
PLSQL_USER    recursive calls                          69
PLSQL_USER    user calls                               57
PLSQL_USER    opened cursors current                    1
PLSQL_USER    logons current                            1
...etc.
```

Listing 12-23: Detailed user information with limited statistics

Using Indexes

Oracle9*i* introduced the ability to monitor the use of indexes. This new view signifies whether the index was used but not how often it was used. Indexes that you want to monitor need to be individually turned ON and OFF. You initiate monitoring with the alter index command, and index use is then tracked by querying the V$OBJECT_USAGE view. Listing 12-25 provides a description of the V$OBJECT_USAGE view.

```
SQL> desc v$object_usage

Name                     Null?      Type
----------------------   --------   ---------------------------
INDEX_NAME               NOT NULL   VARCHAR2(30)
TABLE_NAME               NOT NULL   VARCHAR2(30)
MONITORING                          VARCHAR2(3)
USED                                VARCHAR2(3)
START_MONITORING                    VARCHAR2(19)
END_MONITORING                      VARCHAR2(19)
```

Listing 12-25: V$OBJECT_USAGE view

Before any index is monitored, the view has no records:

```
select   *
from     v$object_usage;

no rows selected
```

You start monitoring on four indexes:

```
alter index HRDT_INDEX1 monitoring usage;
alter index HRDT_INDEX2 monitoring usage;
alter index HRDT_INDEX3 monitoring usage;
alter index HRDT_INDEX4 monitoring usage;
```

The view now shows the four indexes with a start time but no use yet:

```
select index_name, table_name, monitoring, used,
       start_monitoring, end_monitoring
from   v$object_usage;

INDEX_NAME    TABLE_NAME MON USE START_MONITORING     END_MONITORING
-----------   ---------- --- --- -------------------- --------------------
HRDT_INDEX1 HRS_DETAIL YES NO  10/13/2002 03:11:34
```

```
HRDT_INDEX2 HRS_DETAIL YES NO  10/13/2002 03:11:38
HRDT_INDEX3 HRS_DETAIL YES NO  10/13/2002 03:11:46
HRDT_INDEX4 HRS_DETAIL YES NO  10/13/2002 03:11:52
```

If you query using HRDT_INDEX1, the view now shows that this index has been used:

```
select index_name, table_name, monitoring, used,
       start_monitoring, end_monitoring
from   v$object_usage;


INDEX_NAME   TABLE_NAME  MON USE START_MONITORING      END_MONITORING
-----------  ----------- --- --- -------------------   -------------------
HRDT_INDEX1 HRS_DETAIL YES YES 10/13/2002 03:11:34
HRDT_INDEX2 HRS_DETAIL YES NO  10/13/2002 03:11:38
HRDT_INDEX3 HRS_DETAIL YES NO  10/13/2002 03:11:46
HRDT_INDEX4 HRS_DETAIL YES NO  10/13/2002 03:11:52
```

You end the monitoring on HRDT_INDEX4 and the view now shows an end monitoring time:

```
alter index HRDT_INDEX4 nomonitoring usage;
select index_name, table_name, monitoring, used,
       start_monitoring, end_monitoring
from   v$object_usage;


INDEX_NAME   TABLE_NAME  MON USE START_MONITORING      END_MONITORING
-----------  ----------- --- --- -------------------   -------------------
HRDT_INDEX1 HRS_DETAIL YES YES 10/13/2002 03:11:34
HRDT_INDEX2 HRS_DETAIL YES NO  10/13/2002 03:11:38
HRDT_INDEX3 HRS_DETAIL YES NO  10/13/2002 03:11:46
HRDT_INDEX4 HRS_DETAIL NO  NO  10/13/2002 03:11:52 10/13/2002 03:16:01
```

TIP
Use V$OBJECT_USAGE view to find out if indexes are being used.
Perhaps some indexes are not needed.

Identifying Locking Issues

Identifying locking issues is instrumental in locating the user who is waiting for someone or something else. You can use this strategy to identify users who are currently being locked in the system. This allows DBAs to ensure whether an Oracle-related process is truly locked or just running slow. You can also identify the current statement that the locked user(s) are currently executing. Listing 12-26 provides an example of identifying locking issues.

NOTE
These statements were not tuned in the previous version of the book.
(Now that's embarrassing.)

```
select    /*+ ordered */ b.username, b.serial#, d.id1, a.sql_text
from      v$lock d, v$session b, v$sqltext a
```

```
where      b.lockwait    = d.kaddr
and        a.address     = b.sql_address
and        a.hash_value  = b.sql_hash_value;

USERNAME      SERIAL#          ID1  SQL_TEXT
--------   ----------   ----------- ------------------------------------------
AUTHUSER          53        393242  update emp set salary = 5000
```

Listing 12-26: Identifying locking issues

You also need to identify the user in the system who is causing the problem of locking the previous user, as in Listing 12-27. (Usually, this is the user/developer who presses CTRL-ALT-DEL as you approach his or her desk.)

```
select     /*+ ordered */ a.serial#, a.sid, a.username, b.id1, c.sql_text
from       v$lock b, v$session a, v$sqltext c
where      b.id1 in
(select    /*+ ordered */ distinct e.id1
from       v$lock e, v$session d
where      d.lockwait    = e.kaddr)
and        a.sid         = b.sid
and        c.hash_value  = a.sql_hash_value
and        b.request     = 0;

SERIAL#    SID    USERNAME     ID1    SQL_TEXT
-------    ---    --------   ------   ------------------------------------------
     18    11     JOHNSON    393242   update authuser.emp set salary=90000
```

Listing 12-27: Identifying user who is causing the locking

In Listing 12-27, JOHNSON will make almost everyone happy by forgetting a crucial WHERE clause. Unfortunately, JOHNSON has locked the authorized user of this table.

Killing the Problem Session

A user may have run something that he or she really didn't want to run, or a problem query may need to be eliminated during business hours and rerun at night. If the operation in the previous section needed to be aborted, you could execute the statements in Listing 12-28 (to find and then kill the session).

```
select username, sid, serial#, program, terminal
from   v$session;

alter system kill session '11,18';
```

Listing 12-28: Finding and killing the session

The order of the parameters is SID, then SERIAL#. Make sure you DESCribe V$SESSION, because it has many columns that are helpful. In previous versions of Oracle, you could kill the current user session. Thankfully, you can no longer kill your own session accidentally, as shown in Listing 12-29.

```
alter system kill session '10,4';
*
ERROR at line 1:
ORA-00027: cannot kill current session
```

Listing 12-29: Unable to kill your own session

TIP
*Identify users who are locking others and kill their session
(if necessary).*

Finding Users with Multiple Sessions

At times, users enjoy using multiple sessions to accomplish several tasks at once, and this can be a problem. The problem may also be a developer who has built a poor application that begins spawning multiple processes. Either of these could degrade the system's overall performance. The query to the V$SESSION view in Listing 12-30 displays these types of issues.

```
select    username, count(*)
from      v$session
group by  username;

USERNAME        COUNT(*)
-----------     --------
PLSQL_USER          1
SCOTT               1
JOHNSON             9
SYS                 1
SYSTEM              1
                    8
```

Listing 12-30: Finding users with multiple sessions

On certain O/S platforms, if a user starts a session and reboots his or her PC, oftentimes the process will continue in the background as the user starts another session. If the user is running multiple reports on multiple terminals or PCs, this could also affect the system's overall performance.

NOTE
The NULL username and count are the Oracle background processes.

TIP
*Identify users who are holding multiple sessions and determine
whether it is an administrative problem (the user is using multiple
terminals) or a system problem (sessions are not being cleaned or
are spawning runaway processes).*

Querying for Current Profiles

Profiles are limits on a given schema (user). To view the profiles for your system, execute the query in Listing 12-31.

```
select    substr(profile,1,10) Profile,
          substr(resource_name,1,30) "Resource Name",
          substr(limit,1,10) Limit
from      dba_profiles
group by  substr(profile,1,10), substr(resource_name,1,30),
          substr(limit,1,10);
```

Listing 12-31: Viewing profiles for your system

Finding Disk I/O Issues

The views V$DATAFILE, V$FILESTAT, and DBA_DATA_FILES provide file I/O activity across all datafiles and disks of your database. Ideally, the physical reads and writes should be distributed equally. If the system is not configured properly, overall performance suffers. The script in Listing 12-32 identifies the actual distribution and makes it easy to identify where an imbalance exists. Chapter 3 looks at this topic in great detail; this section just shows the quick-hit query to get a baseline.

```
select    a.file#, a.name, a.status, a.bytes,
          b.phyrds, b.phywrts
from      v$datafile a, v$filestat b
where     a.file# = b.file#;
```

Listing 12-32: Identifying the actual distribution

The queries in Listings 12-33 and 12-34 give an improved formatted report for file and data distribution issues. The first gets the data file I/O and the second gets the disk I/O.

```
Set TrimSpool On
Set Line      142
Set Pages      57
Set NewPage     0
Set FeedBack Off
Set Verify    Off
Set Term      On
TTitle        Off
BTitle        Off
Clear Breaks
Break On Tablespace_Name
Column TableSpace_Name For A12     Head "Tablespace"
Column Name      For A45           Head "File Name"
Column Total     For 999,999,990   Head "Total"
Column Phyrds    For 999,999,990   Head "Physical|Reads  "
Column Phywrts   For 999,999,990   Head "Physical| Writes "
Column Phyblkrd For 999,999,990    Head "Physical  |Block Reads"
Column Phyblkwrt For 999,999,990   Head "Physical  |Block Writes"
Column Avg_Rd_Time  For 90.9999999 Head "Average  |Read Time|Per Block"
Column Avg_Wrt_Time For 90.9999999 Head "Average  |Write Time|Per Block"
```

```
Column Instance          New_Value _Instance   NoPrint
Column Today             New_Value _Date       NoPrint
select   Global_Name Instance, To_Char(SysDate, 'FXDay, Month DD, YYYY HH:MI') Today
from     Global_Name;
TTitle On
TTitle Left 'Date Run: ' _Date Skip 1-
Center 'Data File I/O' Skip 1 -
      Center 'Instance Name: ' _Instance Skip 1
select   C.TableSpace_Name, B.Name, A.Phyblkrd +
         A.Phyblkwrt Total, A.Phyrds, A.Phywrts,
         A.Phyblkrd, A.Phyblkwrt
from     V$FileStat A, V$DataFile B, Sys.DBA_Data_Files C
where    B.File# = A.File#
and      B.File# = C.File_Id
order by TableSpace_Name, A.File#
/
```

Listing 12-33: Getting the data file I/O

```
Column TableSpace_Name For A12      Head "Tablespace"
Column Total      For 9,999,999,990 Head "Total"
Column Phyrds     For 9,999,999,990 Head "Physical|Reads   "
Column Phywrts    For 9,999,999,990 Head "Physical| Writes "
Column Phyblkrd   For 9,999,999,990 Head "Physical  |Block Reads"
Column Phyblkwrt  For 9,999,999,990 Head "Physical  |Block Writes"
Column Avg_Rd_Time   For 9,999,990.9999   Head "Average |Read Time|Per Block"
Column Avg_Wrt_Time  For 9,999,990.9999   Head "Average |Write Time|Per Block"
Clear Breaks
Break on Disk Skip 1
Compute Sum Of Total On Disk
Compute Sum Of Phyrds On Disk
Compute Sum Of Phywrts On Disk
Compute Sum Of Phyblkrd On Disk
Compute Sum Of Phyblkwrt On Disk
TTitle Left 'Date Run: ' _Date Skip 1-
      Center 'Disk I/O' Skip 1 -
      Center 'Instance Name: ' _Instance Skip 2
select   SubStr(B.Name, 1, 13) Disk, C.TableSpace_Name,
         A.Phyblkrd + A.Phyblkwrt Total, A.Phyrds, A.Phywrts,
         A.Phyblkrd, A.Phyblkwrt, ((A.ReadTim /
         Decode(A.Phyrds,0,1,A.Phyblkrd))/100) Avg_Rd_Time,
         ((A.WriteTim / Decode(A.PhyWrts,0,1,A.PhyblkWrt)) /
         100) Avg_Wrt_Time
from     V$FileStat A, V$DataFile B, Sys.DBA_Data_Files C
where    B.File# = A.File#
and      B.File# = C.File_Id
order by Disk,C.Tablespace_Name, A.File#
/
Set FeedBack On
Set Verify  On
Set Term    On
Ttitle      Off
Btitle      Off
```

Listing 12-34: Getting the disk I/O

Finding Disk I/O Issues

TIP
*The views V$DATAFILE, V$FILESTAT, and DBA_DATA_FILES
provide file I/O activity across all datafiles and disks of your database.
Ensure that both datafiles and disks are properly balanced for optimal
performance.*

Finding Rollback Segment Contention

This helpful query shows the actual waits on a rollback segment. You can display rollback
information (including automatic undo) and determine whether more segments are needed. If
the waits-to-gets ratio goes over 1 percent regularly, add more rollback segments. Shrinks and
wraps can also be queried from the views in Listing 12-35.

```
select    a.name, b.extents, b.rssize, b.xacts,
          b.waits, b.gets, optsize, status
from      v$rollname a, v$rollstat b
where     a.usn = b.usn;
```

Listing 12-35: Querying for rollback shrinks and wraps

TIP
*Querying V$ROLLNAME, V$ROLLSTAT, and V$TRANSACTION
can provide information on how users are using rollback segments.
Generally, more than one person should not be accessing a rollback
segment at one time (although this is allowed).*

NOTE
*If using Automatic Undo Management, the previous query is
usually not needed.*

The query in Listing 12-36 shows the waits on the entire system as a whole.

```
Set TrimSpool On
Set NewPage    0
Set Pages      57
Set Line       132
Set FeedBack Off
Set Verify     Off
Set Term       On
TTitle         Off
BTitle         Off
Clear Breaks
Column Event       For A40 Heading "Wait Event"
Column Total_Waits For 999,999,990 Head "Total Number| Of Waits   "
Column Total_Timeouts For 999,999,990 Head "Total Number|Of TimeOuts"
Column Tot_Time    For 999,999,990 Head "Total Time|Waited   "
```

```
Column Avg_Time     For  99,990.999 Head "Average Time|Per Wait  "
Column Instance New_Value _Instance     NoPrint
Column Today     New_Value _Date        NoPrint
select    Global_Name Instance, To_Char(SysDate,
          'FXDay DD, YYYY HH:MI') Today
from      Global_Name;
TTitle On
TTitle Left 'Date Run: ' _Date Skip 1-
      Center 'System Wide Wait Events' Skip 1 -
      Center 'Instance Name: ' _Instance Skip 2
select    event, total_waits, total_timeouts,
          (time_waited / 100)  tot_time, (average_wait / 100)
          Avg_time
from      v$system_event
order by  total_waits desc
/
```

Listing 12-36: Querying for the system waits for the entire system

Determining Whether Freelists Is Sufficient

If you have multiple processes doing large inserts, using the default value of 1 for freelists (list of free database blocks) may not be enough. If you are not using Automatic Space Segment Management (ASSM), you may need to increase freelists and/or freelist groups. See Chapter 14 for additional information. To check if the *freelist groups* storage parameter is sufficient, run the report shown in Listing 12-37.

```
Set TrimSpool On
Set Line 132
Set Pages 57
Set NewPage 0
Set FeedBack Off
Set Verify Off
Set Term Off
TTitle Off
BTitle Off
Column Pct Format 990.99 Heading "% Of      |Free List Waits"
Column Instance New_Value _Instance NoPrint
Column Today    New_Value _Date NoPrint
select  Global_Name Instance, To_Char
        (SysDate, 'FXDay DD, YYYY HH:MI') Today
from    Global_Name;
TTitle On
TTitle Left 'Date Run: ' _Date Skip 1-
      Center 'Free list Contention' Skip 1 -
      Center 'If Percentage is Greater than 1%' Skip 1 -
      Center 'Consider increasing the number of free lists' Skip 1 -
      Center 'Instance Name: ' _Instance
select   ((A.Count / (B.Value + C.Value)) * 100) Pct
```

```
from       V$WaitStat A, V$SysStat B, V$SysStat C
where      A.Class = 'free list'
and        B.Statistic# =  (select    Statistic#
                            from      V$StatName
                            where     Name = 'db block gets')
and        C.Statistic# =  (select    Statistic#
                            from      V$StatName
                            where     Name = 'consistent gets')
/
```

Listing 12-37: Checking the freelist groups storage parameter

If the activity rate is greater than 1 percent, then freelist groups needs to be increased.

TIP

Ensure that freelists and freelist groups is sufficient when using multiple processes to do inserts. The default storage value for freelists is only 1. If you use ASSM, Oracle manages this for you, but a high transaction environment should be well-tested prior to employing ASSM.

Checking Privileges and Roles

This section contains several V$ scripts that show various security privileges. The titles of each script in Listings 12-38 through 12-45 give you a quick idea of what it would retrieve for you.

```
select b.owner || '.' || b.table_name obj,
       b.privilege what_granted, b.grantable,
       a.username
from   sys.dba_users a, sys.dba_tab_privs b
where  a.username = b.grantee
order by 1,2,3;
```

Listing 12-38: Object-level privileges that have been granted by username

```
Select    owner || '.' || table_name obj,
          privilege what_granted, grantable, grantee
from      sys.dba_tab_privs
where     not exists
          (select  'x'
          from sys.dba_users
          where   username = grantee)
order by 1,2,3;
```

Listing 12-39: Object-level privileges that have been granted by grantee

```
select    b.privilege what_granted,
          b.admin_option, a.username
from      sys.dba_users a, sys.dba_sys_privs b
where     a.username = b.grantee
order by  1,2;
```

Listing 12-40: System-level grants by username

```
select    privilege what_granted,
          admin_option, grantee
from      sys.dba_sys_privs
where     not exists
            (select  'x' from sys.dba_users
              where username = grantee)
order by  1,2;
```

Listing 12-41: System-level grants by grantee

```
select    b.granted_role ||
          decode(admin_option, 'YES',
      ' (With Admin Option)',
          null) what_granted, a.username
from      sys.dba_users a, sys.dba_role_privs b
where     a.username = b.grantee
order by  1;
```

Listing 12-42: Roles granted by username

```
select    granted_role  ||
          decode(admin_option, 'YES',
      ' (With Admin Option)', null) what_granted,
          grantee
from      sys.dba_role_privs
where     not exists
          (select 'x'
          from sys.dba_users
          where username = grantee)
order by 1;
```

Listing 12-43: Roles granted by grantee

```
select a.username,
b.granted_role || decode(admin_option,'YES',
    ' (With Admin Option)',null) what_granted
from   sys.dba_users a, sys.dba_role_privs b
where  a.username = b.grantee
UNION
```

Checking Privileges
and Roles

```
select a.username,
b.privilege || decode(admin_option,'YES',
    ' (With Admin Option)', null) what_granted
from   sys.dba_users a, sys.dba_sys_privs b
where  a.username = b.grantee
UNION
select   a.username,
         b.table_name || ' - ' || b.privilege
         || decode(grantable,'YES',
      ' (With Grant Option)',null) what_granted
from     sys.dba_users a, sys.dba_tab_privs b
where    a.username = b.grantee
order by 1;
```

Listing 12-44: Usernames with corresponding granted privileges

TIP
*Document the privileges that you have for your system so you can be
ready for any type of security situation.*

```
Select   username, profile, default_tablespace,
         temporary_tablespace, created
from     sys.dba_users
order by username;
```

Listing 12-45: Usernames with corresponding profile, default tablespace, and temporary tablespace

V$ View Categories

The views in this section are categorized according to their primary function. You will often need
to join one category to another category to retrieve the desired information. The V$ views can be
queried the same as any other Oracle view, but keep in mind that the information in these tables
changes rapidly. You can insert the information from the V$ views into a pre-created table to
allow for the compilation of data over a period of time, to be analyzed later or to build statistical
reports and alerts based on different conditions in your database.

The V$ view (and X$ table) information is used by most DBA monitoring tools on the market
today. Querying this database information without a DBA monitoring tool requires that you have
an in-depth understanding of the information stored in each view and how to query the view
properly. Table 12-1 contains a list of V$ views categorized according to their primary function.
The views are listed in categories related to the operation that they monitor. This list is not exhaustive.
It contains only the most commonly used views. Some views have changed from Oracle8*i* to
Oracle9*i*; I have noted any views that are completely new in Oracle9*i*. This is the information
that is contained on the TUSC V$ Poster.

Category	Description and Associated V$ Views
Backup/recovery	Information related to database backups and recovery, including last backup, archive logs, state of files for backup, and recovery **V$ Views:** V$ARCHIVE, V$ARCHIVED_LOG, V$ARCHIVE_DEST, V$ARCHIVE_DEST_STATUS (V9*i*), V$ARCHIVE_GAP (V9*i*), V$ARCHIVE_PROCESSES, V$BACKUP, V$BACKUP_ASYNC_IO, V$BACKUP_CORRUPTION, V$BACKUP_DATAFILE, V$BACKUP_DEVICE, V$BACKUP_PIECE, V$BACKUP_REDOLOG, V$BACKUP_SET, V$BACKUP_SYNC_IO, V$COPY_CORRUPTION, V$DATABASE_BLOCK_CORRUPTION, V$DATABASE_INCARNATION, V$DATAFILE_COPY, V$DELETED_OBJECT, V$FAST_START_SERVERS, V$FAST_START_TRANSACTIONS, V$INSTANCE_RECOVERY, V$MTTR_TARGET_ADVICE(V9*i*), V$PROXY_ARCHIVEDLOG, V$PROXY_DATAFILE, V$RMAN_CONFIGURATION (V9*i*), V$RECOVERY_FILE_STATUS, V$RECOVERY_LOG, V$RECOVERY_PROGRESS(V9*i*), V$RECOVERY_STATUS, V$RECOVER_FILE
Caches	Information related to the various caches, including objects, library, cursors, and the dictionary **V$ Views:** V$BUFFER_POOL, V$BUFFER_POOL_STATISTICS(V9*i*), V$DB_CACHE_ADVICE(V9*i*), VDB_OBJECT_CACHE, VLIBRARYCACHE, V$LIBRARY_CACHE_MEMORY(V9*i*), V$PGASTAT, V$PGA_TARGET_ADVICE(V9*i*), V$PGA_TARGET_ADVICE_HISTOGRAM(V9*i*), V$ROWCACHE, V$ROWCACHE_PARENT, V$ROWCACHE_SUBORDINATE, V$SGA, V$SGASTAT, V$SGA_CURRENT_RESIZE_OPS(V9*i*), V$SGA_DYNAMIC_COMPONENTS(V9*i*), V$SGA_DYNAMIC_FREE_MEMORY(V9*i*), V$SGA_RESIZE_OPS(V9*i*), V$SHARED_POOL_ADVICE(V9*i*), V$SHARED_POOL_RESERVED, V$SYSTEM_CURSOR_CACHE(V9*i*), V$SUBCACHE
Control files	Information related to instance control files **V$ Views:** V$CONTROLFILE, V$CONTROLFILE_RECORD_SECTION
Cursors/SQL statements	Information related to cursors and SQL statements, including the open cursors, statistics, and actual SQL text **V$ Views:** V$OPEN_CURSOR, V$SQL, V$SQLAREA, V$SQLTEXT, V$SQLTEXT_WITH_NEWLINES, V$SQL_BIND_DATA, V$SQL_BIND_METADATA, V$SQL_CURSOR, V$SQL_PLAN(V9*i*), V$SQL_PLAN_STATISTICS(V9*i*), V$SQL_PLAN_STATISTICS_ALL(V9*i*), V$SQL_REDIRECTION(V9*i*), V$RESERVED_WORDS, V$SQL_SHARED_CURSOR(V9*i*), VSQL_SHARED_MEMORY, VSQL_WORKAREA(V9*i*), V$SQL_WORKAREA_ACTIVE(V9*i*), V$SQL_WORKAREA_HISTOGRAM(V9*i*)
Database instances	Information related to the actual database instance **V$ Views:** V$ACTIVE_INSTANCES, V$BGPROCESS, V$COMPATIBILITY, V$COMPATSEG, V$DATABASE, V$DATAFILE, V$DATAFILE_HEADER, V$DBFILE, V$DBLINK, V$DB_PIPES, V$INSTANCE, V$LICENSE, V$OFFLINE_RANGE, V$OPTION, VSGA, VSGASTAT, V$TABLESPACE, V$VERSION **RAC Views:** V$BH

TABLE 12-1. *V$ Views Categories*

Category	Description and Associated V$ Views
Direct loader	Information related to the SQL*Loader direct load option **V$ Views:** V$LOADISTAT(V9*i*), V$LOADPSTAT
Fixed view	Information related to the v$ tables themselves **V$ Views:** V$FIXED_TABLE, V$FIXED_VIEW_DEFINITION, V$INDEXED_FIXED_COLUMN
General	General information related to various system information **V$ Views:** V$CONTEXT, V$GLOBALCONTEXT(V9*i*), V$RESERVED_WORDS, V$TIMER, V$TIMEZONE_NAMES(V9*i*), V$TYPE_SIZE, V$_SEQUENCES
I/O	Information related to I/O, including files and statistics **V$ Views:** V$FILESTAT, V$WAITSTAT, V$TEMPSTAT
Latches/locks	Information related to latches and locks **V$ Views:** V$CLASS_CACHE_TRANSFER(V9*i*), V$CLASS_PING, V$DLM_ALL_LOCKS, V$DLM_CONVERT_LOCAL, V$DLM_CONVERT_REMOTE, VDLM_LATCH, VDML_LOCKS, VDLM_MISC, VDLM_RESS, V$DLM_TRAFFIC_CONTROLLER(V9*i*), V$ENQUEUE_LOCK, V$ENQUEUE_STAT, V$EVENT_NAME, V$FILE_CACHE_TRANSFER(V9*i*), V$FILE_PING, V$GLOBAL_BLOCKED_LOCKS, V$LATCH, V$LATCHHOLDER, V$LATCHNAME, V$LATCH_CHILDREN, V$LATCH_MISSES, V$LATCH_PARENT, V$LOCK, V$LOCK_ACTIVITY, V$LOCK_ELEMENT, V$LOCKED_OBJECT, V$LOCKS_WITH_COLLISIONS, V$RESOURCE, V$RESOURCE_LIMIT, V$TEMP_CACHE_TRANSFER(V9*i*), V$TEMP_PING, V$TRANSACTION_ENQUEUE, V$_LOCK, V$_LOCK1 **RAC Views:** V$CR_BLOCK_SERVER(V9*i*), V$GCSHVMASTER_INFO(V9*i*), V$GCSPFMASTER_INFO(V9*i*), V$GC_ELEMENT(V9*i*), V$GC_ELEMENTS_WITH_COLLISIONS(V9*i*), V$GES_BLOCKING_ENQUEUE(V9*i*), V$GES_ENQUEUE(V9*i*), V$HVMASTER_INFO(V9*i*), V$LOCK_ACTIVITY, V$LOCK_ELEMENT, V$LOCKS_WITH_COLLISIONS
Log Miner	Information related to Log Miner **V$ Views:** V$LOGMNR_CALLBACK(V9*i*), V$LOGMNR_CONTENTS, V$LOGMNR_DICTIONARY, V$LOGMNR_LOGFILE, V$LOGMNR_LOGS, V$LOGMNR_PARAMETERS, V$LOGMNR_PROCESS, V$LOGMNR_REGION(V9*i*), V$LOGMNR_SESSION(V9*i*), V$LOGMNR_STATS, V$LOGMNR_TRANSACTION(V9*i*)
Multithreaded/ shared servers	Information related to multithreaded and parallel servers, including connections, queues, dispatchers, and shared servers **V$ Views:** V$CIRCUIT, V$DISPATCHER, V$DISPATCHER_RATE, V$PARALLEL_DEGREE_LIMIT_MTH, V$QUEUE, V$QUEUEING_MTH(V9*i*), V$REQDIST, V$SHARED_SERVER, V$SHARED_SERVER_MONITOR, V$THREAD

TABLE 12-1. *V$ Views Categories (continued)*

Category	Description and Associated V$ Views
Overall system	Information related to the overall system performance **V$ Tables:** V$GLOBAL_TRANSACTION, V$OBJECT_DEPENDENCY, V$OBJECT_USAGE(V9*i*), V$SHARED_POOL_RESERVED, V$RESUMABLE(V9*i*), V$SORT_SEGMENT, V$SORT_USAGE, V$STATNAME, V$SYSSTAT, V$SYSTEM_CURSOR_CACHE, V$SYSTEM_EVENT, V$TEMPFILE, V$TEMPORARY_LOBS, V$TEMP_EXTENT_MAP, V$TEMP_EXTENT_POOL, V$TEMP_SPACE_HEADER, V$TRANSACTION
Parallel Query	Information related to the Parallel Query option **V$ Views:** V$EXECUTION, V$PQ_SESSTAT, VPQ_SLAVE, VPQ_SYSSTAT, VPQ_TQSTAT, VPX_PROCESS, V$PX_PROCESS_SYSSTAT, V$PX_SESSION, V$PX_SESSTAT
Parameters	Information related to various Oracle parameters, including initialization and NLS per session **V$ Views:** V$NLS_PARAMETERS, V$NLS_VALID_VALUES, V$OBSOLETE_PARAMETER, V$PARAMETER, V$PARAMETER2, V$SPPARAMETER(V9*i*), V$SYSTEM_PARAMETER, V$SYSTEM_PARAMETER2
Redo logs	Information related to redo logs, including statistics and history **V$ Views:** VLOG, VLOGFILE, V$LOGHIST, V$LOG_HISTORY
Replication and materialized views	Information related to replication and materialized views **V$ Views:** V$MVREFRESH (V9*i*), V$REPLPROP(V9*i*), V$REPLQUEUE(V9*i*)
Rollback segments	Information on rollback segments, including statistics and transactions **V$ Views:** V$ROLLNAME, V$ROLLSTAT, V$TRANSACTION, V$UNDOSTAT(V9*i*)
Security/privileges	Information related to security **V$ Views:** V$ENABLEDPRIVS, V$PWFILE_USERS, V$VPD_POLICY(V9*i*)
Sessions (includes some replication information and heterogeneous services)	Information related to a session, including object access, cursors, processes, and statistics **V$ Views:** V$ACCESS, V$ACTIVE_SESS_POOL_MTH, VHS_AGENT, VHS_PARAMETER(V9*i*), V$HS_SESSION, V$MAX_ACTIVE_SESS_TARGET_MTH, V$MYSTAT, V$PROCESS, V$RSRC_CONSUMER_GROUP, V$RSRC_CONSUMER_GROUP_CPU_MTH, V$RSRC_PLAN, V$RSRC_PLAN_CPU_MTH, V$SESSION, V$SESSION_CONNECT_INFO, V$SESSION_CURSOR_CACHE, V$SESSION_EVENT, V$SESSION_LONGOPS, V$SESSION_OBJECT_CACHE, V$SESSION_WAIT, V$SESSTAT, V$SESS_IO
Standby databases (Data Guard)	Information related to standby databases **V$ Views:** V$DATAGUARD_STATUS, V$LOGSTDBY(V9*i*), V$LOGSTDBY_STATS(V9*i*), V$MANAGED_STANDBY(V9*i*), V$STANDBY_LOG(V9*i*)

V$ View Categories

TABLE 12-1.   *V$ Views Categories* (continued)

Category	Description and Associated V$ Views
File mapping interface	Information related to file mapping **V$ Views:** V$MAP_COMP_LIST(V9*i*), V$MAP_ELEMENT(V9*i*), V$MAP_EXT_ELEMENT(V9*i*), V$MAP_FILE(V9*i*), V$MAP_FILE_EXTENT(V9*i*), V$MAP_FILE_IO_STACK(V9*i*), V$MAP_LIBRARY(V9*i*), and V$MAP_SUBELEMENT(V9*i*)
Streams	Information related to streams **V$ Views:** V$STREAMS_APPLY_COORDINATOR(V9*i*), V$STREAMS_APPLY_READER(V9*i*), V$STREAMS_APPLY_SERVER(V9*i*), V$STREAMS_CAPTURE(V9*i*)
Statistics	Information related to statistics in general **V$ Views:** V$SEGMENT_STATISTICS, V$SEGSTAT, V$SEGSTAT_NAME, V$STATISTICS_LEVEL

TABLE 12-1. *V$ Views Categories* (continued)

Also note that the V$ROLLNAME and V$MLS_PARAMETERS views are created slightly differently than the other V$ views. The V$ROLLNAME is a join of an X$ table and the undo$ table. The V$MLS_PARAMETERS view is a subset of the V$NLS_PARAMETERS view. Note some of the V$ TIMING fields are dependent on the TIMED_STATISTICS init.ora parameter being set to TRUE; otherwise, there will be no timing in these fields.

Tips Review

- The V$ views that are accessed by SYSTEM are actually synonyms that point to the v_$ views that are views of the original V$ views based on the X$ tables. (Better read that one again.)

- When other DBAs need access to the V$ view information, but *not* the SYS or SYSTEM passwords, grant the user access to the v_$ views. The user may then access the V$ views that have public synonyms to the v_$ views.

- In Oracle9*i*, query V$FIXED_TABLE to get a listing of all GV$ and V$ views in the database. The GV$ views are exactly the same as the V$ views except the instance ID contains an identifier.

- Query V$FIXED_VIEW_DEFINITION to retrieve the query that creates the V$ and GV$ views from the X$ tables.

- The DBA_ views are *not* derived from the X$ tables or V$ views. The fact that you can delete rows from obj$ is a great reason to *never* be the SYS superuser.

- Query the V$DATABASE view to find out when your database was created and also to determine basic archiving information.

■   Query the V$LICENSE view to see the maximum sessions you are allowed. You can also set warnings when you get close to the maximum.

■   Query the V$OPTION view to retrieve the Oracle options you have installed. The V$VERSION view gives you the actual versions of products installed.

■   Access the V$SGA view to get a baseline idea of the system's physical memory that is allocated for Data, Shared Pool, and Log Buffering of Oracle.

■   Accessing V$SGASTAT gives you a detailed breakdown for the Oracle SGA and breaks down all buckets for the Shared Pool allocation.

■   Query V$PARAMETER and find out the current values for the init.ora parameters. It also shows which init.ora parameters have been changed from their original defaults (ISDEFAULT = FALSE) and which parameters may be changed without shutting down and restarting the database.

■   Query V$LIBRARYCACHE to see how often your SQL and PL/SQL is being read from memory. The pinhitratio should optimally be at 95 percent or better, and the number of reloads should not be greater than 1 percent.

■   Query the V$DB_OBJECT_CACHE view to find objects that are not pinned and are also large enough to potentially cause problems.

■   Query the V$SQLAREA to find problem queries (and users).

■   Query V$SESSION, V$SQLTEXT, and V$SESS_IO to find the problem users and what they are executing at a given point in time.

■   Query V$ACCESS to find all objects that are being accessed by a user at a given time. This can help to pinpoint problem objects, while also being helpful when modifying a particular object (find out who is accessing it).

■   Identify users who are locking others and kill their session (if necessary).

■   Identify users who are holding multiple sessions and determine whether it is an administrative problem (the user is using multiple terminals) or a system problem (sessions are not being cleaned or they are spawning runaway processes).

■   The views V$DATAFILE, V$FILESTAT, and DBA_DATA_FILES provide file I/O activity across all data files and disks of your database.

■   Querying V$ROLLNAME, V$ROLLSTAT, and V$TRANSACTION can provide information on how users are using rollback segments. V$UNDOSTAT gives you UNDO information. (Rollback segments are quickly becoming passé.)

■   Ensure that freelists is sufficient when using multiple processes to do inserts. The default storage value is 1.

■   Document the privileges that you have for your system so you can be ready for any type of security situation.

References

Trezzo, J. C., The V$ Arsenal: Key V$ Scripts Every DBA Should Use Regularly
Oracle Corporation, *Oracle7 Server: SQL Language Reference Manual*
Oracle Corporation, *Oracle7 Server: Application Developer's Guide*
Trezzo, J. C., TUSC, 1997 IOUG-A Proceedings: The V$ Views—A DBA's Best Friend
Niemiec R. & K. Loney, *How I Broke into Your Database*; COUG, 2001

Many thanks to Joe Trezzo, who wrote the majority of this chapter for the original book. Also, thanks to Allen Peterson, Robert Freeman, Kevin Gilpin, Bob Yingst, and Greg Pucka, who contributed to this chapter. To obtain a poster that contains the V$ view definitions grouped by category, call TUSC at (630) 960-2909 and request one. As of this writing, this poster is currently a listing of the Oracle9*i* V$ views.

CHAPTER
13

The X$ Tables
(Advanced DBA)

Why do people climb mountains? Because they are there! Why do people open the hood of their car and look at what's inside? Because they can! Why do DBAs look at the X$ tables? Because they are there and they can!

The X$ tables are the last frontier for the expert DBA to explore and analyze the deepest cavern of the Oracle database. Querying the X$ tables can give secrets to undocumented features and parameters, information about future Oracle versions, and shorter or faster routes to database information. The X$ tables are rarely mentioned in the Oracle documentation or the Oracle user community. Therefore, I am including them in this book as one of the only references available. The queries in this chapter were tested accessing version 9.2.0.1.0 of the database.

The topics covered in this chapter include the following:

- Introducing the X$ tables

- Creating V$ views and X$ tables

- Obtaining a list of all the X$ tables

- Obtaining a list of all the X$ indexes

- Using hints with X$ tables and indexes

- Shared pool

- Queries to monitor the shared pool

- Redo

- Initialization parameters

- Buffer cache/data blocks

- Instance/database

- Effective X$ Table Use and Strategy

- Related Oracle internals topics

- X$ table groups

- X$ table and non-V$ fixed view associations

- Common X$ table joins

Introducing the X$ Tables

The X$ tables are intriguing to mischievously curious DBAs. The Oracle dynamic tables are designed like many robust Oracle application data models. A set of tables is available to users (DBAs) via a set of synonyms on a set of views based on these tables. The synonym names start with *V$* and are the object names published in the reference manual of the Oracle documentation set. These synonyms on the V$ views are used as the primary method of querying data from these tables. Interested DBAs, however, keep and use a toolkit of practical X$ table queries that supplement their V$ view queries.

The X$ tables contain instance-specific information spanning a variety of areas. They contain information about the current configuration of the instance, the sessions connected to the instance, and a gold mine of performance information. The X$ tables are platform-specific. The documented column definitions of the V$ views may be consistent from platform to platform, but the underlying SQL statements referencing the X$ tables may differ. The Oracle kernel consists of layers. The X$ table names contain an abbreviation for the particular kernel layer to which they pertain.

The X$ tables are not permanent or even temporary tables that reside in database datafiles. The X$ tables reside only in memory. When you start up your instance, they are created. They exist even before you create your control file. When you shut down your instance, they are destroyed. All 394 X$ tables are defined right after the instance is started (before mount). They are defined, but they cannot all be queried. Many of them require at least a mounted, if not open, database. To observe this, query the X$KQFTA & X$KQFDT table after starting your instance with the nomount option.

The X$ tables are owned by the SYS database user and are read-only, which is why they are referred to as *fixed tables* and the V$ views are referred to as *fixed views*. This statement might be a juicy invitation for you to try to verify this read-only property. Any attempt to alter these tables with a DDL or DML statement is met with an ORA-02030 error.

Oracle has extensively used the decode function in the underlying SQL statements of the data dictionary views. If you compare the V$ view underlying SQL statements from version to version, you will likely find differences in the implementation of some V$ views. The columns of the V$ views may stay more constant in their name and meaning, which allows Oracle RDBMS engineers to change the X$ tables from version to version while not disrupting too much of the Oracle user community's use of the V$ views. The fact that the V$ views are accessed through synonyms allows another level of flexibility for Oracle engineers to alter the underlying structures, also with little or no impact on the user community's use of the V$ views. Oracle's extensive use of the decode function in the underlying V$ view SQL statements also facilitates the platform-specific implementation of a query returning the generic data that a user of a particular V$ view expects from platform to platform. Consequently, it is important to run the correct scripts when upgrading a database—to make sure the dictionary views are created in a way that matches the underlying X$ tables.

NOTE
Application designers and developers may save themselves some development and maintenance pain by adopting a similar strategy. They can employ views and synonyms for application software access to an application's underlying tables and stored programmatic objects (Java, PL/SQL). DBAs should investigate whether designers and developers can benefit from using this strategy. In some cases, the costs will be higher than the benefits.

Although this section is by no means a complete treatment of useful X$ table queries, it introduces some of the commonly used X$ table queries, grouped by the major tuning areas to which they pertain. Because X$ table queries are a supplement to queries of fixed views rather than a replacement for them, this section includes queries of both X$ tables and related fixed views.

Misconceptions About the X$ Tables

Do not use the X$ tables if you have a heart condition or are an inexperienced DBA, or you may ruin the entire database. (At least this is what some people will tell you. Sounds pretty scary.)

The most common misconception about the X$ tables is that the DBA can drop one or update one, thus ruining the database. However, X$ tables cannot be ruined. The only user who can select from these tables is the SYS user. A SELECT statement is the only command available to be performed on these X$ tables. An error occurs if you attempt to grant SELECT access to a user. Consider the following attempts to drop or alter an X$ table in Listings 13-1 and 13-2.

```
connect sys/change_on_install as sysdba
drop table X$ksppi;
ORA-02030: can only select from fixed tables/views
```

Listing 13-1: You will not be able to drop any of the X$ tables (even as the SYS user)

```
update   X$ksppi
set      ksppidf = 'FALSE'
where    ksppidf = 'TRUE';
ORA-02030: can only select from fixed tables/views
```

Listing 13-2: You will not be able to update, insert, or delete any data in the X$ tables (even as the SYS user)

TIP
When you mention the X$ tables, most people say "Ooh, pretty scary. I would never touch those tables." The fact is, DML commands (UPDATE, INSERT, DELETE) are not allowed on the X$ tables, even as the SYS superuser.

TIP
Only the SYS superuser can select from the X$ tables. An error occurs if an attempt is made to grant SELECT access to a user.

Granting Access to View the X$ Tables

You cannot grant access to the X$ tables even if you are the SYS user. You will get the error in Listing 13-3 if you try to make grants to the X$ tables.

```
connect sys/manager as sysdba
grant select on X$ksppi to richn;
ORA-02030: can only select fixed from fixed tables/views
```

Listing 13-3: You cannot grant access to the X$ tables (even as the SYS user)

Although the error message for attempting to grant access to X$KSPPI in the previous code is a little cryptic at first, it clarifies that you can perform only a SELECT and that the grant will not be allowed. However, you may build your own X$ views from the original X$ tables and then grant access to those views. Consider the following examples in Listings 13-4 through 13-9, which give access to the X$KSPPI table via a view called X$_KSPPI and a synonym called X$KSPPI.

```
Connect sys/change_on_install as sysdba
Connected.
```

Listing 13-4: Connecting to the SYS superuser

```
create view x$_ksppi as
select      *
from        X$ksppi;
View created.
```

Listing 13-5: Creating a view mirroring the X$KSPPI table

```
create public synonym X$_ksppi for x$_ksppi;
Synonym created.
```

Listing 13-6: Creating a synonym for the newly created view

```
grant select on X$_ksppi to richn;
Grant succeeded.
```

Listing 13-7: Granting to the desired user access to the newly created view

```
conn richn/tusc
Connected.
```

Listing 13-8: Connecting as the desired user

```
select      count(*)
from        X$_ksppi;

COUNT(*)
797
```

Listing 13-9: Accessing the X$_KSPPI view via the synonym created for X$_ksppi

You can now give access to the X$ table information without giving the password to the SYS account. The key is creating a view that references the original SYS-owned X$ tables.

TIP
A DBA may need access to the X$ table information, but not the SYS password. Create a view under a different name that mirrors the desired tables. Name these tables according to the appropriate synonyms of the original tables.

Creating V$ Views and X$ Tables

The X$ tables are virtual or fixed tables, which are created in memory at database startup and maintained real-time in memory. These tables store up-to-date information on the current activity of the database at the current point in time, or since the last database startup. In the SGA, V$ views are created (see Chapter 12) on these X$ tables to allow users to view this information in a more readable format. The X$ tables are fixed tables, and because they have been created in memory, access to these tables is very limited.

The V$ views are known as the virtual tables, fixed tables, V$ tables, dynamic performance tables, and a half-dozen other names. The first hurdle to understanding the X$ tables is to become familiar with their creation, security, content, and relationship to the V$ views.

In addition, these X$ tables are very cryptic in nature. They are similar to the underlying table construction of the Oracle Data Dictionary. Therefore, Oracle creates V$ views that are more readable and practical. In addition, Oracle has built other views (USER, DBA, ALL) within the catalog.sql script for easier use. Oracle has also created a public synonym on V_$ views in the catalog.sql file that changes the name back to a view with a prefix of v$. Listing 13-10 shows an example of a V_$ view and v$ public synonym creation in the CATALOG.SQL.

```
create or replace view v_$datafile
as select * from v$datafile;
create or replace public synonym v$datafile for v_$datafile;
```

Listing 13-10: Creating a V_$ view and v$ public synonym in CATALOG.SQL

TIP
See Chapter 12 and Appendix B for detailed V$ view information and Appendix C for detailed X$ information.

Once the catalog.sql file has been executed, the V$ views are available only to the SYS user. At this point, access can be granted to V$ views by granting SELECT on the V$ view. Therefore, all SELECTs performed against the V$ views are actually retrieving information out of the SGA; more specifically, out of the X$ tables. DBAs cannot modify X$ tables in any manner, and they cannot create indexes on these tables. Oracle began providing indexes on the X$ tables in version 8. In addition, the V$ views are the underlying views that are used for Oracle monitoring tools. Listing 13-11 shows how to get a listing of all V$ views.

```
select     kqfvinam name
from       x$kqfvi
order by   kqfvinam;
```

Listing 13-11: Getting a listing of all V$ views

Partial output:

```
NAME
GV$ACCESS
GV$ACTIVE_INSTANCES
GV$ACTIVE_SESS_POOL_MTH
```

```
GV$AQ1
GV$ARCHIVE
GV$ARCHIVED_LOG
GV$ARCHIVE_DEST
GV$ARCHIVE_DEST_STATUS
GV$ARCHIVE_GAP
...
V$ACCESS
V$ACTIVE_INSTANCES
V$ACTIVE_SESS_POOL_MTH
V$AQ1
V$ARCHIVE
...
```

Note that the GV$ views are the same as the V$ tables except that you can see multiple instances with Oracle Parallel Server or RAC. The only difference between the GV$ and V$ tables is a column that shows the instance ID.

Obtaining a List of the X$ Tables That Make Up the V$ Views

To obtain a list of the X$ tables that make up the V$ views, you must access the V$FIXED_VIEW_DEFINITION view. This view shows how the V$ views were created. By knowing which X$ tables make up a V$ view, you may be able to build a faster query that goes directly to the X$ tables, as in Listing 13-12.

```
select    *
from      v$fixed_view_definition
where     view_name = 'GV$FIXED_TABLE';
```

Listing 13-12: Viewing the X$ tables that make up a GV$ view

Output:

```
VIEW_NAME          VIEW_DEFINITION
GV$FIXED_TABLE     select  inst_id,kqftanam, kqftaobj, 'TABLE', indx
                   from    X$kqfta
                   union all
                   select  inst_id,kqfvinam, kqfviobj, 'VIEW', 65537
                   from    X$kqfvi
                   union all
                   select  inst_id,kqfdtnam, kqfdtobj, 'TABLE', 65537
                   from    X$kqfdt
```

TIP
Access the X$KQFVI table for a listing of all V$ and GV$ views.

TIP
Access the V$FIXED_VIEW_DEFINITION view to get all of the
information of the underlying X$ tables that make up a V$ view.

Obtaining a List of All the X$ Tables

The names of the X$ tables are in the X$KQFTA table (contains 381 of the X$ V9.2 tables) and
X$KQFTD table (contains another 13 of the X$ V9.2 tables). The v$ names can be found in the
X$KQFDT table. The V$FIXED_TABLE view combines all three of these tables so that you can
obtain a listing of any desired grouping. The query in Listing 13-13 shows how to obtain a listing
of the X$ tables.

```
select     name
from       v$fixed_table
where      name like 'X%'
order by   name;
```

Listing 13-13: Query V$FIXED_TABLE for the names of the X$ tables

Partial output:

```
NAME
X$ACTIVECKPT
X$BH
X$BUFQM
X$CKPTBUF
X$CLASS_STAT
X$CONTEXT
X$DUAL
X$ESTIMATED_MTTR
X$GLOBALCONTEXT
X$HOFP
X$HS_SESSION
… (there are 394 in Oracle9.2)
```

The query in Listing 13-14 shows output from x$kqfdt which is a partial listing of the X$ tables.

```
select     kqfdtnam, kqfdtequ
from       x$kqfdt;
KQFDTNAM                              KQFDTEQU
------------------------------        ---------
X$KCVFHONL                            X$KCVFH
X$KCVFHMRR                            X$KCVFH
X$KCVFHALL                            X$KCVFH
X$KGLTABLE                            X$KGLOB
X$KGLBODY                             X$KGLOB
X$KGLTRIGGER                          X$KGLOB
X$KGLINDEX                            X$KGLOB
X$KGLCLUSTER                          X$KGLOB
X$KGLCURSOR                           X$KGLOB
```

```
X$JOXFS                      X$JOXFT
X$JOXFC                      X$JOXFT
X$JOXFR                      X$JOXFT
X$JOXFD                      X$JOXFT
13 rows selected.
```

Listing 13-14: Querying X$KQFDT for a partial group of X$ tables

TIP
Query V$FIXED_TABLE for the names of the X$ tables, or you can also access the two X$ tables X$KQFTA and X$KQFTD for partial listings that when combined make up the full list.

Obtaining a List of All the X$ Indexes

If you often query the V$ views or X$ tables for information, it is helpful to understand which indexes are being used, as shown in Listing 13-15.

```
select     table_name, index_number, column_name
from       gv$indexed_fixed_column
order by   table_name, index_number, column_name, column_position;
```

Listing 13-15: Viewing the X$ table indexes

Partial output:

```
TABLE_NAME                          INDEX_NUMBER COLUMN_NAME
--------------------------------    ------------ ------------
X$CLASS_STAT                                   1 ADDR
X$CLASS_STAT                                   2 INDX
X$DUAL                                         1 ADDR
X$DUAL                                         2 INDX
X$JOXFM                                        1 OBN
X$JOXFT                                        1 JOXFTOBN
X$KCBBES                                       1 ADDR
X$KCBBES                                       2 INDX
X$KCBBF                                        1 ADDR
X$KCBBF                                        2 INDX
X$KCBBHS                                       1 ADDR
X$KCBBHS                                       2 INDX
X$KCBFWAIT                                     1 ADDR
X$KCBFWAIT                                     2 INDX
...
```

Only one X$ table has a multicolumn index, as shown in Listing 13-16.

```
SELECT    DISTINCT a.table_name, a.index_number,
          a.column_name,a.column_position
FROM      v$indexed_fixed_column a, v$indexed_fixed_column b
WHERE     a.table_name = b.table_name
```

Obtaining a List of All the X$ Indexes

```
AND       a.index_number = b.index_number
AND       a.column_name != b.column_name
ORDER BY a.table_name,a.index_number, a.column_position;


TABLE_NAME    INDEX_NUMBER COLUMN_NAME            COLUMN_POSITION
------------  ------------ ---------------------  ---------------
X$KTFBUE                 1 KTFBUESEGTSN                         0
X$KTFBUE                 1 KTFBUESEGFNO                         1
X$KTFBUE                 1 KTFBUESEGBNO                         2
```

Listing 13-16: Only one X$ table with a multicolumn index

To see the data concerning from which X$ tables the information is retrieved, perform the query to the V$FIXED_VIEW definition table (Listing 13-16).

```
select   *
from     v$fixed_view_definition
where    view_name = 'GV$INDEXED_FIXED_COLUMN';
```

Listing 13-16: Querying the V$FIXED_VIEW definition table

Output:

```
VIEW_NAME                     VIEW DEFINITION
-----------                   ---------------
V$INDEXED_FIXED_COLUMN        select   c.inst_id,    kqftanam,    kqfcoidx,
                                       kqfconam,     kqfcoipo
                              from      X$kqfco c,    X$kqftat
                              where     t.indx = c.kqfcotab
                              and       kqfcoidx != 0
```

TIP
Access the V$INDEXED_FIXED_COLUMN view for a listing of all X$TABLE indexes.

Using Hints with X$ Tables and Indexes

As with other tables, you can also use hints with the X$ tables to achieve greater performance. The queries shown in Listings 13-17 and 13-18 show the explain plan and statistics while changing the driving table using an ORDERED hint. Note that I am using aliases for the tables and must hint the alias and not the table.

```
select   /*+ ordered */ p.ksbdppro, p.ksbdpnam,
         d.ksbdddsc,p.ksbdperr
from     X$ksbdd d, X$ksbdp p
where    p.indx = d.indx;


Execution Plan
----------------------------------------------------------------
   0        SELECT STATEMENT Optimizer=CHOOSE (Cost=23 Card=100…
   1    0     HASH JOIN (Cost=23 Card=100 Bytes=8100)
```

```
    2     1        FIXED TABLE (FULL) OF 'X$KSBDD' (Cost=11 Card=100 …
    3     1        FIXED TABLE (FULL) OF 'X$KSBDP' (Cost=11 Card=100 ….
```

Listing 13-17: Forcing the X$KSBDP table as the driving table

```
select    /*+ ordered  */ p.ksbdppro, p.ksbdpnam,
          d.ksbdddsc,p.ksbdperr
from      X$ksbdp p, X$ksbdd d
where     p.indx = d.indx;
Execution Plan
-------------------------------------------------------------
    0        SELECT STATEMENT Optimizer=CHOOSE (Cost=23 Card=100 Bytes=81
    1     0   HASH JOIN (Cost=23 Card=100 Bytes=8100)
    2     1     FIXED TABLE (FULL) OF 'X$KSBDP' (Cost=11 …
    3     1     FIXED TABLE (FULL) OF 'X$KSBDD' (Cost=11 …
```

Listing 13-18: Using the ordered hint to force the driving table to be X$KSBDP

TIP
*Oracle generally uses the indexes as needed, but from time to time,
you may use hints to achieve a desired result.*

Shared Pool

You can use the X$KSMLRU table to monitor space allocations in the shared pool that may be causing space allocation contention. The relevant columns in this table are as follows:

Column	Definition
ADDR	Address of this row in the array of fixed tables
INDX	Index number of this row in the array of fixed tables
INST_ID	Oracle instance number
KSMLRCOM	Description of allocation type
KSMLRSIZ	Size in bytes of the allocated chunk
KSMLRNUM	Number of items flushed from the shared pool to allocate space
KSMLRHON	Name of the object being loaded
KSMLROHV	Hash value of the object being loaded
KSMLRSES	Session performing the allocation, joins to V$SESSION.SADDR

You can use the X$KSMSP table to examine the current contents of the shared pool. Each row represents a chunk of memory in the shared pool. The relevant columns in this table are as follows:

ADDR	Address of this row in the array of fixed tables
INDX	Index number of this row in the array of fixed tables

INST_ID	Oracle instance number
KSMCHCOM	Description of the allocated chunk of memory
KSMCHPTR	Physical address of this chunk of memory
KSMCHSIZ	The size of this chunk of allocated shared memory
KSMCHCLS	The class of this chunk of allocated shared memory, which has the following possible values:

recr   An allocated chunk of shared memory that is flushable if the shared pool is low on memory

freeabl   A freeable, but not flushable, chunk of shared memory that is currently in use

free   A free chunk of shared memory

perm   A permanently allocated, nonfreeable chunk of shared memory

R-free   Free memory in the reserved pool

R-freea   A freeable chunk in the reserved pool

R-recr   A recreatable chunk in the reserved pool

R-perm   A permanent chunk in the reserved pool

Queries to Monitor the Shared Pool

The shared pool is often a key area of performance impact. This section will focus on queries that will help you investigate the shared pool.

ORA-04031 Errors

V$SHARED_POOL_RESERVED.REQUEST_FAILURES (or X$KGHLU.KGHLUNFU) gives the number of ORA-04031 errors that have occurred since the instance was started. If any ORA-04031 errors are occurring, then SHARED_POOL_SIZE and/or JAVA_POOL_SIZE are too small, the shared pool is fragmented, or application code may not be being shared optimally. The query in Listing 13-19 checks the ORA-04031 errors that have occurred since the instance was started.

```
Number of Failed Shared Pool Allocations (ORA-04031 errors) Since Instance
Startup
   -- Number of ORA-04031 errors since instance startup.
SELECT request_failures
  FROM v$shared_pool_reserved;
```

Listing 13-19: Checking the ORA-04031 errors

If there are any ORA-04031 errors that have occurred then some SHARED_POOL_SIZE, JAVA_POOL_SIZE, and/or application tuning are in order. Consider one or more of the following:

- Pin large, high-use (high values for X$KSMLRU.KSMLRSIZ, COUNT(X$KSMLRU.KSMLRHON), and/or X$KSMLRU.KSMLRNUM) PL/SQL packages in memory with DBMS_SHARED_POOL.KEEP:

```
EXECUTE dbms_shared_pool.keep('PACKAGENAME');
```

■ Pin large, high-use Java classes, also with DBMS_SHARED_POOL.KEEP. You can pin a Java class by enclosing it in double quotes:

```
EXECUTE dbms_shared_pool.keep('"FullJavaClassName"', 'JC');
```

TIP
Enclose the class in double quotes if it contains a slash (/); otherwise, you will get an ORA-00995 error.

■ Increase the size of the shared pool by increasing the shared_pool_size initialization parameter if the percentage of SHARED_POOL free memory is low *and* there is contention for library cache space allocation and/or more than zero occurrences of the ORA-04031 error. The "Shared Pool" section later in this chapter notes that increasing the shared pool is *not* always recommended if a low amount of shared pool memory is observed. If you are increasing the size of the shared pool, you might also need to raise the value of the parameter SGA_MAX_SIZE.

■ Increase the size of the shared pool reserved area by increasing the SHARED_POOL_RESERVED_SIZE initialization parameter (the default is 5 percent of shared_pool_size).

■ Promote the sharing of SQL, PL/SQL, and Java code by application developers.

Large Allocations Causing Contention

The object being loaded (X$KSMLRU.KSMLRHON) is a *keep* candidate (consider keeping it with DBMS_SHARED_POOL.KEEP) if the X$KSMLRU.KSMLRCOM value is MPCODE or PLSQL%.

If you use features such as MTS, Recovery Manager, or Parallel Query, you should configure a larger shared pool and also configure a large pool that is bigger than the default. These features will create large allocations in the shared pool. These features will use the large pool instead if it is large enough. Contention on the shared pool latch (Listing 13-20) will be reduced if the large pool is used because the shared pool latch is not used for allocations in the large pool.

```
Amount of Each Type of Shared Pool Allocation Causing Contention
        -- Amount of each type of shared pool allocation causing contention.
SELECT   ksmlrcom, SUM(ksmlrsiz)
FROM     x$ksmlru
GROUP BY ksmlrcom;
```

Listing 13-20: Contention on the shared pool latch

TIP
If X$KSMLRU.KSMLRCOM is similar to Fixed UGA, then a high amount of session-specific allocation is occurring, which suggests that OPEN_CURSORS may be set too high. This is relevant only in cases where MTS is being used.

Queries to Monitor the Shared Pool

Fragmentation

This section takes a closer look at the shared pool with a plethora of queries to help you investigate in detail when needed. (The shared pool is also discussed in detail in Chapter 4.) The shared pool may be fragmented if you observe a large number of entries in X$KSMLRU, particularly a large number of them with small KSMLRSIZ values, or if there are a lot of chunks of type "free" in X$KSMSP. This may be contrasted with a large number of entries in X$KSMLRU with medium to high values of KSMLRSIZ, which is not likely to be a symptom of the shared pool being too fragmented; rather, it indicates that large PL/SQL packages and/or Java classes need to be kept in the shared pool, and possibly also that the shared pool itself is too small, and perhaps that application code is not being effectively shared (or some combination thereof). In identifying the problem, take the time to monitor the application code use over time to find out which code the user sessions are attempting to load. It is beneficial to network with application users, developers, designers, and application vendors. The four queries in Listings 13-21 and 13-22 will help you find contention and fragmentation issues.

```
Names of and Sessions for Shared Pool Allocations Causing Contention
    -- Names of and sessions for shared pool allocations causing contention.
  SELECT ksmlrhon, ksmlrsiz, ksmlrses
    FROM x$ksmlru
   WHERE ksmlrsiz > 1000
ORDER BY ksmlrsiz;
Shared Pool Memory Allocated
    -- Shared pool memory allocated.
SELECT sum(ksmchsiz)||' bytes' "TotSharPoolMem"
  FROM x$ksmsp;
Fragmentation of Shared Pool
    -- Fragmentation of Shared Pool.
    SET VERIFY off
  COLUMN PctTotSPMem for a11
  SELECT ksmchcls      "ChnkClass",
         SUM(ksmchsiz) "SumChunkTypeMem",
         MAX(ksmchsiz) "LargstChkofThisTyp",
         COUNT(1)      "NumOfChksThisTyp",
         ROUND((SUM(ksmchsiz)/tot_sp_mem.TotSPMem),2)*100||'%' "PctTotSPMem"
    FROM x$ksmsp,
         (select sum(ksmchsiz) TotSPMem from x$ksmsp) tot_sp_mem
GROUP BY ksmchcls, tot_sp_mem.TotSPMem
ORDER BY SUM(ksmchsiz);
```

Listing 13-21: Finding contention and fragmentation issues

```
    -- Information regarding shared_pool_reserved_size.
SELECT free_space,free_count,max_free_size,max_used_size,
       request_misses,max_miss_size
  FROM v$shared_pool_reserved;
```

Listing 13-22: Information about SHARED_POOL_RESERVED_SIZE

Low Free Memory in Shared and Java Pools

If a low percentage of the shared or java pools' memory is free, then the shared and/or java pools may have crossed the fine line between an optimal amount of free memory and not enough free memory. To determine this, consider how many free chunks exist, what the largest one is, whether there is a high number of reloads, and whether there have been any ORA-04031 errors. The two queries in Listing 13-23 will help.

```
Amount of Shared Pool Free Memory
    -- Amount of shared pool free memory.
SELECT *
  FROM v$sgastat
 WHERE name = 'free memory'
   AND pool = 'shared pool';
Amount of Java Pool Free Memory
    -- Amount of java pool free memory.
SELECT *
  FROM v$sgastat
 WHERE name = 'free memory'
   AND pool = 'java pool';
```

Listing 13-23: Shared pool free memory

Library Cache Hit Ratio

A low library cache hit ratio is a symptom of one of several problems. The shared and/or java pools may be too small, the SHARED_POOL_RESERVED_SIZE may be too small, CURSOR_SHARING may need to be set to FORCE, there may be inefficient sharing of SQL, PL/SQL, or Java code, or there may be insufficient use of bind variables. Investigate which application code is being used over time and how efficiently it is used (code sharing). Monitor the shared and java pool freespace over time. If the amount of free memory in the shared and java pools is relatively high, no ORA-04031 errors are occurring, and the library cache hit ratio is low, then poor code sharing is probably occurring. The queries in Listing 13-24 will help you investigate this area. (Note that I included some V$ view queries here due to the applicable nature to this subject.)

```
Library Cache Hit Ratio
    -- Library cache hit ratio.
  SELECT ROUND(SUM(pinhits)/SUM(pins),2)*100||'%' "Library Cache Hit Ratio"
    FROM v$librarycache
ORDER BY namespace;
Library Cache Reload Ratio
    -- Library cache reload ratio.
SELECT namespace,
       ROUND(DECODE(pins,0,0,reloads/pins),2)*100||'%' "Reload Ratio"
  FROM v$librarycache;
Library Cache High-Use Objects
    -- Library cache high-use objects.
  SELECT name,type
```

```
       FROM v$db_object_cache
ORDER BY executions;
Library Cache Object Sizes
    -- Library cache object sizes.
  SELECT *
    FROM v$db_object_cache
ORDER BY sharable_mem;
Shared Pool Object Sharing Efficiency
Column name format a40
Column type format a15
       -- Execute counts for currently cached objects.
  SELECT name, type, COUNT(executions) ExecCount
    FROM v$db_object_cache
GROUP BY name, type
ORDER BY ExecCount;
       -- Currently cached objects that have execute counts of just 1.
       -- Consider converting these objects to use bind variables.
  SELECT distinct name, type
    FROM v$db_object_cache
GROUP BY name, type
  HAVING COUNT(executions) = 1;
       -- Currently unkept, cached objects that have execute counts > 1.
       -- Consider pinning these objects.
  SELECT distinct name, type, COUNT(executions)
    FROM v$db_object_cache
   WHERE kept = 'NO'
GROUP BY name, type
  HAVING COUNT(executions) > 1
ORDER BY COUNT(executions);
-- Currently unkept, cached objects that are similar. Each of these
-- statements has at least 10 versions currently cached, but has only
-- been executed less than 5 times each. Consider converting these
-- objects to use bind variables and possibly also pinning them.
  SELECT SUBSTR(sql_text,1,40) "SQL", COUNT(1) , SUM(executions) "TotExecs"
    FROM  v$sqlarea
   WHERE executions < 5
     AND kept_versions = 0
GROUP BY SUBSTR(sql_text,1,40)
  HAVING COUNT(1) > 10
ORDER BY COUNT(1) ;
Clear columns
```

Listing 13-24: Library cache queries

A high percentage of reloads indicates that the shared and/or java pools are too small, code sharing is insufficient, and possibly also large code objects are repeatedly being used. Monitor the application code used over time. If particular large code objects are identified as frequently used, consider pinning them and/or increasing the size of the SHARED_POOL_RESERVED_SIZE.

If features such as MTS, Recovery Manager, or Parallel Query are used, consider a larger
SHARED_POOL_SIZE and/or larger LARGE_POOL_SIZE.

High Number of Hard Parses

You should review similar queries with low numbers of executions to uncover opportunities to
combine them into statements using bind variables. A high ratio of hard parses may mean that
the shared pool itself is too small or perhaps a SQL statement is repeatedly nudging other code
out of the precious shared pool or java pool cache space. Identify these statements and consider
pinning. Consider also setting the CURSOR_SHARING parameter = FORCE. Listing 13-25 shows
various queries to view parse activity.

```
Parse Activity
    -- Overall Parse Activity.
SELECT name, value
  FROM v$sysstat
 WHERE name = 'parse count (total)'
    OR name = 'parse count (hard)';
    -- Ratio of hard parses to total parses.
SELECT ROUND((b.value/a.value),2)*100||'%' HardParseRatio
  FROM v$sysstat a, v$sysstat b
 WHERE a.name = 'parse count (total)'
   AND b.name = 'parse count (hard)';
    -- SQL Statements experiencing a high amount of parse activity.
SELECT sql_text, parse_calls, executions
  FROM v$sqlarea
 WHERE parse_calls > 100
   AND kept_versions = 0
   AND executions < 2*parse_calls;
```

Listing 13-25: Parse activity queries

Latch Waits and/or Sleeps

If latch waits are high but shared and java pool freespace is also high, consider reducing the size
of the shared and/or java pools. This could indicate that sessions are having to spend time scanning
the unnecessarily large list of free shared pool chunks. Monitor the amount of shared and java
pool freespace over time. If ample freespace is available in these pools and no ORA-04031 errors
are occurring, consider reducing the sizes of these pools. Investigate when the miss ratio and
sleeps are high for any of the latches in the following list:

- Row cache objects
- Library cache
- Shared pool
- Shared java pool

Queries to Monitor
the Shared Pool

If freespace in the shared and java pools is low, then you should consider the other tuning areas, such as increasing the shared and/or java pools, pinning objects, and combining similar SQL statements to use bind variables. The query in Listing 13-26 will help you acquire some of these metrics.

```
Shared Pool Latch Efficiency
Column name for a20
   -- Shared pool latch efficiency.
SELECT name,
       ROUND(misses/decode(gets,0,1,gets),2)*100||'%' as "WillToWaitMissRatio",
       ROUND(immediate_misses/decode(immediate_gets,0,1,
       immediate_gets),2)*100 ||'%' "ImmMissRatio",
       sleeps
  FROM v$latch
 WHERE name in ('library cache', 'row cache objects', 'shared pool', 'shared java pool');
Clear columns
```

Listing 13-26: Shared pool latch efficiency

Remember that before increasing the SHARED_POOL_SIZE, you should consider whether there are any shared pool latch waits. Depending on what you observe, it may actually be more appropriate to reduce the size of the shared pool. This will be the case if there is a sufficient amount of free shared pool memory available, a low number of reloads, and a high number of shared pool latch waits. The reason to consider reducing the shared pool in this case is that with an oversized shared pool, sessions will hold the shared pool latch slightly longer than would be needed otherwise because the shared pool needs to scan a larger amount of space to determine exactly where to allocate the space it is requesting.

Miscellaneous

After exhausting previously discussed shared and java pool tuning options, you should consider increasing the _KGL_LATCH_COUNT parameter. This undocumented parameter sets the number of library cache latches: the latches that allow protected access to library cache objects for execution. Although only one shared pool latch existed prior to Oracle 9.0, seven shared pool latches are available in Oracle 9.0 and later. These enable Oracle to perform a protected memory allocation on behalf of a session. With this parameter you can create additional latches, allowing increased concurrent library cache object execution access. Consider prime values between 1 and the smallest prime number greater than twice the number of database server CPUs for the _KGL_LATCH_ COUNT parameter. The maximum allowed value for this parameter is 66.

Adjusting this parameter is, as with all undocumented parameters, unsupported by Oracle. Implement such changes only under the direction of Oracle Support and after thoroughly testing under direct simulation of production conditions.

Note that any particular database may experience conditions that are a combination of two or more of the previous conditions. Frequently, you must evaluate multiple conditions and decide on two or more potential corrective measures.

Also note that after each query on X$KSMLRU, the values in this table are reset back to zero. To effectively monitor the table, consider capturing the contents of it to a permanent table with an INSERT INTO ... AS SELECT ... statement or by simply spooling the output to a file. Furthermore, whenever you query X$KSMLRU, you might want to always select all of the columns instead of just one or a few you might be interested in at a particular moment; otherwise, you may miss some information that you later decide you wanted to see.

CAUTION
When "resetting" the X$KSMLRU table, there may still be rows in this table after each query. Do not interpret the remaining rows appearing after each query as entries pertaining to contention-causing code, but rather to preallocated entries in this table. If no problem statements are in X$KSMLRU, then the KSMLRHON and KSMLRSIZ values will be NULL and zero, respectively. If they are non-NULL, then these rows pertain to contention-causing code. Make sure multiple DBAs do not simultaneously query X$KSMLRU because each of them may observe misleading results.

Remember that when you decide to alter initialization parameters to remedy performance problems, you can now alter many of them by using an `alter system` command in Oracle9*i*. Despite the ease of doing this, you should first test such changes on a test system. For example, if you attempt to alter the SHARED_POOL_SIZE too small, the SQL*Plus session may hang and/or consume a large amount of memory and CPU resources during the execution of the `alter system` command. Or, prior to Oracle9*i*, if you set the _KGL_LATCH_COUNT parameter too high, you will get an ORA-600 [17038] error when you next try to start up the database.

Redo

The X$KCCCP table contains information about the current redo log file. The X$KCCLE table contains information about all redo log files, as shown in Listing 13-27.

```
Percentage Full of the Current Redo Log File
    -- Percentage full of the current redo log file.
SELECT ROUND((cpodr_bno/lesiz),2)*100||'%' PctCurLogFull
  FROM X$kcccp a, X$kccle b
 WHERE a.cpodr_seq = leseq;
```

Listing 13-27: Redo log level

If you are observing in V$LOG_HISTORY or in the "log file space waits" statistic that log switches are occurring more frequently than is appropriate for your database, you may decide to alter the redo log file configuration. This task can be performed while the database is open to users and all tablespaces are online. If you wish to minimize the impact on database performance while this or other similar maintenance is performed that involves a DBA-induced log switch with the alter system switch logfile command, you can use the query in Listing 13-27 to measure how much redo log information will have to be copied to complete the archive of the current log file. This is particularly relevant in cases of databases with large redo log files (100MB or larger).

You can also use this query as a tuning aid to measure how much redo activity is created by a particular transaction or process, if it is possible to isolate a particular database to one session that will be guaranteed as the only creator of redo records, other than Oracle itself. It may be useful to capture before and after results of this query when testing such a transaction. You can use this as an alternative or supplement to the *redo blocks written* statistic of V$SESSTAT.

Initialization Parameters

Oracle9*i* introduced the concept of the server parameter file, or spfile. This file allows DBAs to make persistent initialization parameter changes with the `alter system` command without having to manually incorporate these changes into a traditional parameter file, or pfile, to implement the persistence of the parameter change. This also allows the DBA to instantaneously save the current instance configuration to a file for archival or backup purposes. This flexibility introduces a bit of initialization parameter management complexity in that the Oracle instance can be started with either a pfile or an spfile. This complexity raises a few questions for the DBA when managing initialization parameters. The DBA must know what Oracle will use as an initialization parameter file at instance startup time, where the initialization parameters will be saved when an alter system ... scope=spfile or alter system ... scope=both command is issued, and whether a currently running Oracle instance was started using a pfile, an spfile, or both.

If the spfile in the platform-specific default location with the platform-specific default name exists, then Oracle will use it to start the instance. To get Oracle to use an spfile other than the one residing in the default location with the default filename, you must first rename, relocate, or delete this default spfile and then relocate and/or rename the desired spfile from the nondefault location to the default location and name. Alternatively, you can specify this nondefault spfile in the spfile initialization parameter in a pfile that is used to start up the instance.

Note that there is still the concept of the platform-specific default name and location for the pfile, which is used if no spfile is in the spfile default location and name. As in pre-Oracle9*i* versions, a nondefault pfile can be used to start an instance with the pfile option of the startup command. These are the only ways that Oracle will use a nondefault parameter file to start up the instance. There is no startup spfile command. Spfiles and pfiles are not interchangeable. Spfiles are (mostly) binary files that can be altered only with alter system commands and can be created only with create spfile commands.

As in pre-Oracle9*i* versions, pfiles are simply text files that may be created and altered with a text editor. An attempt to use an spfile in the startup pfile command will be met with an ORA-01078 error. If an instance was started with an spfile, then any changes made using the alter system ... scope=spfile or alter system ... scope=both commands will be saved to the spfile that was used to start the instance, even if the default spfile exists and was not used to start the instance. If both a pfile and an spfile are used to start an Oracle instance, Oracle overrides any parameters specified in the pfile with those specified in the spfile, if there are any conflicts.

The question of which file was used to start an Oracle instance has five possible answers:

- On startup, the database first looks for spfile<SID>.ora in the default location, and then looks for spfile.ora in the default location. Spfile in the default location is used with the default name and no pfile was used.

- A pfile in the default location with the default name was used and a nondefault spfile was used.

- A nondefault pfile was used and a nondefault spfile was used.

- A pfile in the default location with the default name was used and no spfile was used.

- A nondefault pfile was used and no spfile was used.

Note that it is possible that both an spfile and a pfile may have been used to start an instance. Check the following queries in the order listed to answer the question of which files may have been used for the initialization parameters to start the instance.

Case 1
Run the query in Listing 13-28.

```
Check for spfile-specified initialization parameters
    -- Check for spfile-specified initialization parameters.
SELECT count(1)
  FROM v$spparameter
 WHERE isspecified = 'TRUE';
```

Listing 13-28: Spfile-specified initialization parameters

Or just use the SQL*Plus command show parameter spfile as shown in Listing 13-29. This will show you exactly which spfile is used to start the database (gets set automatically when the database is started without specifying a pfile or spfile). If you start the database with the PFILE option, then this parameter is NULL. This is the equivalent to the query in Listing 13-28 but involves less typing.

```
SQL> SHOW PARAMETER SPFILE
```

Listing 13-29: The show parameter spfile command

Case 2
Run the query in Listing 13-30.

```
Determine which spfile was used to start the instance
    -- Determine which spfile was used to start the instance.
SELECT value
  FROM v$parameter
 WHERE name = 'spfile';
```

Listing 13-30: The SPFILE used to start the instance

Look for a pfile in the default location. If the spfile parameter value from the query in Listing 13-30 (to V$PARAMETER) is non-NULL and the value is not the default value for the spfile, then a pfile was used and it specified an alternate spfile in the spfile parameter. If this is the case and if the default pfile exists, then it was used to start the instance.

Case 3
If the spfile parameter value from the query in Listing 13-30 (to V$PARAMETER) is non-NULL and the value is not the default value for the spfile, then a pfile was used and it specified an alternate spfile in the spfile parameter. If this is the case and if the default pfile does not exist, then you must determine the location of the nondefault pfile. See Case 5.

Initialization Parameters

Case 4

If the spfile parameter value from the query in Listing 13-30 (to V$PARAMETER) is NULL, then a pfile was used and no spfile was used. If this is the case and if the default pfile exists, then it was used to start the instance.

Case 5

If it is determined from cases 1 through 3 that no spfile was used at all, and that the default pfile was not used, then the remaining possibility is that a nondefault pfile was used and no spfile was used. There are many site-specific possibilities for a nondefault pfile. A database startup, shutdown, or backup script, a third-party backup or database management software package, or a site-specific Oracle software directory structure may give a clue to what this file is. If there is uncertainty about this file, you can save the existing configuration initialization parameters by querying some of the Oracle X$ tables pertinent to initialization parameters. There is also the possibility that OEM, which can store a local copy of the parameter file, started the database.

Several X$ tables are relevant to initialization parameters: X$KSPSPFILE, X$KSPPSV, X$KSPPSV2, X$KSPPCV, X$KSPPCV2, X$KSPPI, and X$KSPPO. The X$KSPSPFILE table lists the contents of the spfile. The V$SPPARAMETER view, which is based on the X$KSPSPFILE table, excludes parameter names that start with an underscore, unless such "underscore" or "undocumented" parameters were explicitly specified in an spfile, a pfile, or with an alter system command and/or Oracle had to modify the DBA-specified value to fit a functional requirement of the parameter, such as a requirement that a particular parameter value be a prime number or a multiple of another DBA-specified parameter value, for example. To see all the parameter names, including those that the V$SPPARAMETER view excludes, query the X$KSPSPFILE table.

Note that if an spfile was not used to start an instance, then all of the values in the KSPSPFFTCTXSPVALUE column of X$KSPSPFILE will be NULL and all of the values in the KSPSPFFTCTXISSPECIFIED column will be FALSE. Conversely, if an spfile was used to start an instance, the values in the KSPSPFFTCTXISSPECIFIED column for which the particular parameter was specified in the spfile will be TRUE and the value in the KSPSPFFTCTXSPVALUE column for such parameters will be a non-NULL value.

The X$KSPPSV table lists the parameter names and values that are currently in effect for the instance. The V$SYSTEM_PARAMETER view, which is based on the X$KSPPSV table, excludes parameters that start with an underscore and have not been modified from their default value.

The X$KSPPSV2 table is very similar to the X$KSPPSV table. The difference is in how parameter values are stored that consist of lists of values. This table, like the X$KSPPSV table, lists parameters and parameter values that are currently in effect for this Oracle instance. A new session inherits parameter values from the system values. Each list parameter value appears as a separate row in the table. Presenting the list parameter values in this format enables you to quickly determine the values for a list parameter. For example, if a parameter value is "a,b," looking at X$KSPPSV does not tell you whether the parameter has two values ("a" and "b") or one value ("a, b"). X$KSPPSV2 makes the distinction between the list parameter values clear. Correspondingly, the V$SYSTEM_PARAMETER2 view is based on the X$KSPPSV2 table.

The X$KSPPCV and X$KSPPCV2 tables are similar to the X$KSPPSV and X$KSPPSV2 tables, except that the X$KSPPCV and X$KSPPCV2 tables apply to the current session, not necessarily the whole instance. If a parameter is changed with an alter session command, the change is reflected in the X$KSPPCV and X$KSPPCV2 tables. The V$PARAMETER and V$PARAMETER2 fixed views are based on the X$KSPPCV and X$KSPPCV2 tables, respectively.

The X$KSPPI table lists the initialization parameter names, types, and statuses. The V$PARAMETER, V$PARAMETER2, V$SYSTEM_PARAMETER, and V$SYSTEM_PARAMETER2 fixed views are based on the X$KSPPCV, X$KSPPCV2, X$KSPPSV, and X$KSPPSV2 tables; each of these X$ tables is joined with the X$KSPPI table in these fixed views to get the associated parameter names and other information. The query in Listing 13-31 is the query on which V$SYSTEM_PARAMETER is based, excluding the line in V$SYSTEM_PARAMETER that excludes parameter names that start with an underscore. The underlying SQL statements of the V$PARAMETER, V$PARAMETER2, and V$SYSTEM_PARAMETER2 fixed views have the same structure as the query in Listing 13-30.

```
All initialization parameter settings in effect for the instance.
    -- All initialization parameter settings in effect for the instance.
  SELECT x.indx+1 InstanceNum,
         ksppinm ParamName,
         ksppity ParamType,
         ksppstvl ParamValue,
         ksppstdf IsDefaultVal,
         DECODE(bitand(ksppiflg/256,1),
                1,'TRUE',
                  'FALSE') IsSessModifiable,
         DECODE (bitand(ksppiflg/65536,3),
                1,'IMMEDIATE',
                2,'DEFERRED',
                  'FALSE') IsSysModifiable,
         DECODE (bitand(ksppstvf,7),
                1,'MODIFIED',
                  'FALSE') IsModified,
         DECODE (bitand(ksppstvf,2),
                  2,'TRUE',
                    'FALSE') IsAdjusted,
         ksppdesc Description,
         ksppstcmnt UpdateComment
    FROM X$ksppi x, X$ksppsv y
   WHERE (x.indx = y.indx)
ORDER BY ParamName;
```

Listing 13-31: Query upon which V$SYSTEM_PARAMETER is based

The V$OBSOLETE_PARAMETER fixed view, which is based on the X$KSPPO table, lists obsolete initialization parameters. For some of these, such as SPIN_COUNT, you may note that they are now undocumented parameters.

Buffer Cache/Data Blocks

Four key performance-related buffer cache topics are the current buffer statuses, the identification of segments that are occupying the block buffers, the detection of hot (popular, or high contention) data blocks, and the cause of buffer-cache-related latch contention and wait events. These topics are relevant to buffer cache tuning in all Oracle versions, but there are additional considerations in Oracle8, 8*i*, and 9*i*. Oracle8 introduced the concept of multiple buffer pools. Oracle9*i* introduced the concept of multiple data block sizes and therefore the need for multiple buffer cache buffer sizes.

The following X$ tables are used in the buffer-cache-related queries that follow.

X$ Table	Definition
X$BH	Status and number of pings for every buffer in the SGA
X$KCBWDS	Statistics on all buffer pools available to the instance
X$KCBWBPD	Statistics on all buffer pools available to the instance, including buffer pool names
X$KCBWAIT	Number of and time spent in waits for buffer pool classes
X$KCBFWAIT	Buffer cache wait count and time

The following queries are relevant to these topics.

Buffer Statuses

A low number of buffers with a status of "Free" in X$BH does not necessarily mean that the buffer cache is undersized. It may, in fact, mean that the buffer cache is optimally sized such that Oracle will not have to perform frequent organization and maintenance on a superfluous number of buffers. Unfortunately, this same thought process leads many DBAs to undersize the buffer cache and leave memory sitting idle on their system. Similarly, if a large percentage of buffers are consistently free, then perhaps the buffer cache is oversized. See the subsequent sections discussing buffer cache contents, latches, and wait events for a better indication of the proper sizing and configuration of the buffer cache as it relates to the segments that are being used. The query in Listing 13-32 shows how to see the state of the buffers in the buffer cache.

```
Buffer Cache Buffer Statuses
        -- Buffer cache buffer statuses.
        SET VERIFY off
  COLUMN PctTotBCMem for a11
  SELECT /*+ ordered */
         tot_bc_mem.TotBCMem,
         decode(state,
                   0,'Free',
                   1,'Exclusive',
                   2,'SharedCurrent' ,
                   3,'ConsistentRead',
                   4,'BeingRead',
                   5,'InMediaRecoveryMode',
                   6,'InInstanceRecoveryMode',
                   7,'BeingWritten',
                   8,'Pinned') "BlockState",
       SUM(blsiz) "SumStateTypeMem",
       COUNT(1)   "NumOfBlksThisTyp",
       ROUND(SUM(blsiz)/tot_bc_mem.TotBCMem,2)*100||'%' "PctTotBCMem"
    FROM (SELECT sum(blsiz) TotBCMem
```

```
        FROM X$bh) tot_bc_mem,
           X$bh
GROUP BY tot_bc_mem.TotBCMem,
          decode(state,
                 0,'Free',
                 1,'Exclusive',
                 2,'SharedCurrent' ,
                 3,'ConsistentRead',
                 4,'BeingRead',
                 5,'InMediaRecoveryMode',
                 6,'InInstanceRecoveryMode',
                 7,'BeingWritten',
                 8,'Pinned')
ORDER BY SUM(blsiz);
CLEAR COLUMNS
```

Listing 13-32: Viewing the state of buffers in the data buffer cache

Here is a quick reference for the states of the buffers in X$BH:

Buffer State	Meaning
0	Free
1	Exclusive
2	Shared Current
3	Consistent Read
4	Being Read
5	In Media Recovery Mode
6	In Instance Recovery Mode
7	Being Written
8	Pinned

Segments Occupying Block Buffers

It is useful to note the distribution of segment owners, types, and names among the occupied buffers. Note in particular which objects occupy the most buffers. Observe the indexes currently in the cache. Question whether these indexes are appropriate. If they are nonselective indexes being used by selective queries (or vice versa), these indexes could be occupying precious buffers that could be used more effectively by the corresponding table blocks or by the blocks of other segments experiencing "buffer busy waits" wait events. Query V$SQLTEXT to observe the SQL statements currently using the segments occupying the highest percentages of the buffers and determine whether index usage in these statements is appropriate. The two queries in

Listings 13-33 and 13-34 show you the segments occupying block buffers and also the percentage of buffers occupied by segments in the buffer cache.

```
All Segments Occupying Block Buffers
    -- Segments Occupying Block Buffers.
SELECT o.*, d_o.owner, d_o.object_name, object_type, o.buffers, o.avg_touches
FROM (     SELECT obj object, count(1) buffers, AVG(tch) avg_touches
                    FROM X$bh
              GROUP BY obj) o,
dba_objects d_o
WHERE o.object = d_o.data_object_id
ORDER BY owner, object_name;
Percentage of Buffers Occupied by Segments in the Buffer Cache
    -- Percentage of Buffers Occupied by Segments in the Buffer Cache.
    -- Note that this percentage is the percentage of the number of
    -- occupied buffers, not the percentage of the number of allocated
    -- buffers.
    SELECT tot_occ_bufs.TotOccBufs,o.*,d_o.owner, d_o.object_name, object_type,
           ROUND((o.buffers/tot_occ_bufs.TotOccBufs)*100,2) || '%' PctOccBufs
    FROM   (SELECT obj object, count(1) buffers, AVG(tch) avg_touches
              FROM X$bh
           GROUP BY obj) o,
           (SELECT COUNT(1) TotOccBufs
              FROM X$bh
             WHERE  state != 0) tot_occ_bufs,
         dba_objects d_o
    WHERE o.object = d_o.data_object_id
ORDER BY round((o.buffers/tot_occ_bufs.TotOccBufs)*100,2),owner, object_name;
```

Listing 13-33: Determining the segments occupying block buffers

Note also that only segments that are of the same block size as the block size of the default pool (the default block size) may be assigned to the keep or recycle pools. As of the first release of Oracle9*i*, the keep and recycle pools are not available for use by segments that are not the default block size. This defeats some of the strategy involved with tuning segments that are either high or low access and are not the default block size. However, other tuning options are available for such segments, such as partitioning.

```
Pool Specific Buffer Cache Buffer Occupation
    -- Pool Specific Buffer Cache Buffer Occupation
 SELECT DECODE(wbpd.bp_id,1,'Keep',
                         2,'Recycle',
                         3,'Default',
                         4,'2K Pool',
                         5,'4K Pool',
                         6,'8K Pool',
                         7,'16K Pool',
                         8,'32K Pool',
                             'UNKNOWN') Pool,
        bh.owner,
        bh.object_name object_name,
```

```
            count(1) NumOfBuffers
    FROM X$kcbwds wds, X$kcbwbpd wbpd,
         (SELECT set_ds,x.addr,o.name object_name,
                 u.name owner
            fROM sys.obj$ o,
                 sys.user$ u,
                 X$bh x
          WHERE o.owner# = u.user#
            AND o.dataobj# = x.obj
            AND x.state !=0
            AND o.owner# !=0 ) bh
    WHERE wds.set_id >= wbpd.bp_lo_sid
      AND wds.set_id <= wbpd.bp_hi_sid
      AND wbpd.bp_size != 0
      AND wds.addr=bh.set_ds
    GROUP BY
      DECODE(wbpd.bp_id,1,'Keep',
                        2,'Recycle',
                        3,'Default',
                        4,'2K Pool',
                        5,'4K Pool',
                        6,'8K Pool',
                        7,'16K Pool',
                        8,'32K Pool',
                          'UNKNOWN'),
      bh.owner,
      bh.object_name
ORDER BY 1,4,3,2;
```

Listing 13-34: Buffers occupied by segments in the buffer cache

Hot Data Blocks/Latch Contention and Wait Events

The blocks of the segments returned by the query in Listing 13-35 are ones that are being accessed frequently, particularly if the value of the tch (touch count) column changes (higher *and* lower) between consecutive executions of this query. The tch column value is incremented every time a particular buffer is "touched" or "visited" by a transaction. This value can fluctuate as a buffer is moved up and down the LRU list. The reason for the fluctuation is that Oracle internally adjusts the tch value according to its position in the LRU list and other factors, such as how long it has been since the buffer was last touched. In some scenarios of this algorithm, Oracle internally resets the tch value back to 1.

```
Segments Occupying Hot Buffers
    -- Segments Occupying Hot Buffers.
    -- This query defines a "hot" buffer as a buffer that has
    -- a touch count greater than 10.
SELECT  /*+ use_hash(bh) */
              de.owner ||'.'|| de.segment_name  segment_name,
              de.segment_type  segment_type,
```

```
                de.extent_id  extent#,
                bh.dbablk - de.block_id + 1  block#,
                bh.tch
   FROM  dba_extents  de,
                X$bh  bh
WHERE  de.file_id = bh.file#
     AND  bh.dbablk between de.block_id and de.block_id + de.blocks - 1
     AND  bh.tch  > 10
ORDER BY bh.tch;
```

Listing 13-35: Segments occupying hot buffers

Capture the SQL statements involving these segments by querying V$SQLTEXT for SQL_TEXT lines that contain these segment names, and analyze their execution plans with the explain plan as described in Chapter 6. Consider the number of sessions accessing these blocks using the queries in this section, and whether these blocks are tables or appropriate indexes. Table blocks appearing in this list that are being accessed by multiple sessions are candidates for the keep pool. Table segments in this list that incur frequent full tablescans are candidates for being re-created in tablespaces that are configured for large block sizes (16K or larger). Conversely, table segments that incur single-row accesses are candidates for being re-created in tablespaces that are configured for smaller block sizes (2K, 4K, or 8K).

Note that you should balance rebuilding such single-row access tables in small block tablespaces with data locality considerations. If such a single-row access table is accessed *frequently* for similar data that is likely to be stored consecutively, then you should consider storing such segments in large block tablespaces instead of a small block tablespace. As a result, a lower number of physical block reads occurs because of the increased chance that the block containing the desired rows already resides in a buffer cache buffer from other recent queries.

Deciding how to size such objects depends on the default block size of the database and the amount of physical memory and SGA space available for creating a keep pool. Segments in buffers with a consistently low touch count should be candidates for the recycle pool, depending on the block size of the particular table versus the default block size. You should review the application SQL code, particularly the indexing strategy, to reconsider the logic of accessing such blocks frequently, in an effort to reduce contention on them. The queries in Listing 13-36 will help.

```
Segments Experiencing Waits on the Cache Buffers Chains Latch
    -- Segments Experiencing Waits on the Cache Buffers Chains Latch
  SELECT  /*+ ordered */
                de.owner ||'.'|| de.segment_name  segment_name,
                de.segment_type  segment_type,
                de.extent_id  extent#,
                bh.dbablk - de.block_id + 1  block#,
                bh.lru_flag,
                bh.tch,
                lc.child#
   FROM
                (SELECT MAX(sleeps) MaxSleeps
                    FROM v$latch_children
                 WHERE name='cache buffers chains') max_sleeps,
                v$latch_children  lc,
                X$bh  bh,
                dba_extents  de
WHERE  lc.name    = 'cache buffers chains'
```

```
      AND   lc.sleeps  > (0.8 * MaxSleeps)
      AND   bh.hladdr  = lc.addr
      AND   de.file_id = bh.file#
      AND   bh.dbablk between de.block_id and de.block_id + de.blocks - 1
ORDER BY bh.tch;
Segments Experiencing Waits on the Cache Buffers LRU Chain Latch
    -- Segments Experiencing Waits on the Cache Buffers LRU Chain Latch
SELECT  /*+ ordered */
                de.owner ||'.'|| de.segment_name  segment_name,
                de.segment_type  segment_type,
                de.extent_id  extent#,
                bh.dbablk - de.block_id + 1  block#,
                bh.lru_flag,
                bh.tch,
                lc.child#
  FROM   (SELECT MAX(sleeps) MaxSleeps
             FROM v$latch_children
               WHERE name='cache buffers lru chain') max_sleeps,
             v$latch_children  lc,
             X$bh  bh,
             dba_extents  de
WHERE  lc.name    = 'cache buffers lru chain'
    AND   lc.sleeps  > (0.8 * MaxSleeps)
    AND   bh.hladdr  = lc.addr
    AND   de.file_id = bh.file#
    AND   bh.dbablk between de.block_id and de.block_id + de.blocks - 1
ORDER BY bh.tch;
Sessions Experiencing Waits on the Buffer Busy Waits or Write Complete Waits Events
      -- Sessions Experiencing Waits on the Buffer Busy Waits or Write
      -- Complete Waits Events. Note that the values returned by the p1, p2,
      -- and p3 parameters disclose the file, block and reason for the wait.
      -- The cause disclosed by the p3 parameter is not externally published.
      -- The p3 parameter is a number that translates to one of several
      -- causes, among which are the buffer being read or written by
      -- another session.
  SELECT /*+ ordered */
        sid,event,owner,segment_name,segment_type,p1,p2,p3
    FROM v$session_wait sw, dba_extents de
   WHERE de.file_id = sw.p1
     AND sw.p2 between de.block_id and de.block_id + de.blocks - 1
     AND (event = 'buffer busy waits' OR event = 'write complete waits')
     AND p1 IS NOT null
ORDER BY event,sid;
```

Listing 13-36: Segments and sessions experiencing waits

Problem segments returned by queries in this section are likely to be the same as those returned by the query returning hot buffers earlier in this section. If they're not, a possible explanation may be that such a segment is accessed frequently by one session, as shown by the hot buffer query, but there may be no contention for it by other sessions, as may be shown by the absence of that segment from the result set of the other queries in this section. Other than that scenario, the segments returned by a hot buffers query are likely to also be returned by the other queries in this section that show the problem segment. Each of these queries conveniently includes the blocks of the particular segments associated with the latches or waits in question.

For table segments, you can use the DBMS_ROWID PL/SQL package to map the file and block numbers returned by these queries to the corresponding table rows. If one or a set of segments consistently shows up in the result sets of the queries in this section, then these are highly used segments. Investigate the application to reconsider the use of these popular segments. Ask questions like the following:

- Is the indexing scheme appropriate?

- Are there PL/SQL (or Java) loop exit conditions where they should be?

- Are superfluous tables included in join queries?

- Can any SQL code be reengineered to alter a join strategy, either with reengineered subqueries, inline views, or similar alternatives?

- Should some hints, like ordered, USE_HASH, etc., be used?

- Are statistics up-to-date?

- Do any of the involved tables have a high watermark that is well beyond the actual blocks that contain rows?

- Could a table or index make advantageous use of partitioning or histograms?

- Should a keep pool be used?

If a variety of different segments are repeatedly showing up in the result of the buffer-busy query, the buffer cache is probably undersized or the disk subsystem is not writing changed (dirty) buffers out to the datafiles fast enough for them to be reused (or both). If there does not seem to be contention on particular segments, but rather on a varying set of segments, this problem indicates that Oracle is having general trouble satisfying requests to load blocks into free buffers. Also consider increasing the number of pool-specific DB_BLOCK_LRU_LATCHES in this case.

If rollback segment blocks show up in the result sets of the queries in this section, then more rollback segments are probably needed due to rollback segment header block contention. Confirm this with a query on V$ROLLSTAT (check the WAITS column). Alternatively, you should consider whether the application is performing too many rollbacks and whether the physical rollback segment placement is optimal. Another option is to determine whether the rollback segment datafiles reside on physical disks with other high I/O datafiles or whether the physical disk configuration, such as a RAID5 configuration, will hinder rollback segment write performance and exacerbate these types of waits. A better option is to switch to Automatic Undo Management and avoid all of this.

You should also review the storage parameter configuration of the problem segments returned by the queries in this section. Consider whether there are sufficient freelists for the tables and indexes that can be classified as high concurrent update (multiple sessions updating them concurrently). You should probably set freelists to 2 or higher for these segments, but do not set freelists higher than the number of CPUs in the database server or use Automatic Segment Space Management (ASSM). You should review the data block size and PCT_FREE because different conditions call for blocks of a table or index to contain more rows or fewer rows. In situations in which a particular segment block is popular, you may want to reconstruct the segment with a higher PCT_FREE; thus, interblock contention for rows that were previously stored in the same block is reduced because the chance of those rows being stored in the same block has been reduced by simply reducing the number of rows that can be inserted into a block.

Obviously, more buffer cache buffers are required to accommodate a table reconstructed to have a larger pct_free and therefore consist of more row-containing blocks. The trade-off is that this can reduce the performance of full tablescan operations on such tables because more blocks must be visited to complete a full tablescan. In general, you must consider the overall use of these tables and indexes to judge whether it is more advantageous to have more or fewer rows in the blocks of the particular table or index. These points can be summarized as follows:

- **Condition**   Higher PCT_FREE and therefore fewer rows per block.
  - **Advantage**   Less contention on updates of popular blocks.
  - **Disadvantage**   The segment will consist of more blocks and therefore reduce full tablescan performance.

- **Condition**   Lower PCT_FREE and therefore more rows per block.
  - **Advantage**   There is a better chance that the block containing a requested row is already in a buffer cache buffer from a recent query. Full tablescans will need to visit fewer blocks.
  - **Disadvantage**   There may be more contention on blocks being updated. If a block contains a row to be updated, all the other rows (more of them) in that block are now in a copy of the block that is incompatible with other sessions requesting a read of other rows in that block; thus, another read-consistent copy of the block must be read into another buffer cache buffer.

Instance/Database

You can obtain some database and instance-specific information from the X$KCCDI table. Consider the following queries in Listing 13-37, which you can use to find overall instance- and database-specific information.

```
MAXLOGMEMBERS setting for a database.
    -- MAXLOGMEMBERS setting for a database.
SELECT dimlm
   FROM X$KCCDI;
Datafile creation times.
                -- Datafile creation times.
    SELECT indx file_id,
                fecrc_tim creation_date,
                file_name,
                tablespace_name
      FROM   X$kccfe int,
                dba_data_files dba
     WHERE dba.file_id = int.indx + 1
ORDER BY file_name;
Background process names and process ids.
-- Background process names and process ids.
   SELECT ksbdpnam ProcessName, ksbdppro OSPid
       FROM X$ksbdp
    WHERE  ksbdppro != '00' ;
Various instance resources .
-- Various instance resources.
```

```
SELECT kviival ResourceValue, kviidsc ResourceName
    FROM X$kvii;
```

Listing 13-37: Finding overall instance- and database-specific information

Note that the last query has different values returned for the resource values on different platforms.

Effective X$ Table Use and Strategy

Consider creating a separate X$ query user that has its own X$ views on the SYS X$ tables as described earlier in the chapter. This user could manually or with DBMS_JOB perform periodic queries to capture X$ table data into some other tables so that the contents of the X$ tables can be examined over time. If you do this, keep in mind that the data in the X$ tables is highly transient. Some scripts or jobs written to capture such information will likely miss a lot of it. On the other hand, you do not want to query these tables so frequently that these queries themselves and their associated activity information are a non-negligible percentage of the data in the tables.

In monitoring the X$KSMLRU table (and perhaps X$KSMSP and others), it may be prudent to capture the contents of the table to a permanent table for analysis and comparison over time.

Related Oracle Internals Topics

Alas, more toys for the mischievously curious DBAs. Except for traces, you should not use the utilities described in the following sections in production without the guidance of Oracle Support. You can take them and run with them in a sandbox database to learn what useful information they provide.

Traces

Database sessions can be traced to collect session information about the work performed in the session. Traces can be turned on by a variety of methods:

- Set SQL_TRACE = TRUE in the initialization parameter file.

- Set SQL_TRACE = TRUE with an alter session command.

- Execute the DBMS_SYSTEM.SET_SQL_TRACE_IN_SESSION( ) PL/SQL package for another session.

You can use these traces to find out the raw list of SQL statements and PL/SQL code objects executed by a particular session and performance information, such as the execution plans, related to each statement.

WARNING
If you set SQL_TRACE = TRUE in the parameter file, it generates traces for every process connected to the database, including the background processes.

Events

An *event* is similar to a system trigger in an Oracle instance. A trigger can capture pertinent information about the instance and individual database sessions to trace files. If an event is set in an initialization parameter file or with an alter system or alter session setting, then Oracle captures information to a trace file based on the conditions set in the event. Several events can be set. These can be described with the oerr command-line facility. Try the following command (in UNIX only):

```
oerr ora 10046
```

A particularly useful tuning tool is event 10046 (described in Chapter 9 in detail). This event can be enabled in the initialization parameter file with the following line (although this is not something that you generally want to set at the database level):

```
event = '10046 trace name context forever, level 8'
```

Or, it is more likely to be used at the session level with an alter session command:

```
alter session set events '10046 trace name context forever,level 12';
```

The trace information is captured to a file in the USER_DUMP_DEST directory specified in the initialization parameter file. This event is equivalent to setting SQL_TRACE = TRUE in the initialization parameter file. At level 12, this event setting includes the values of bind variables and the occurrences of wait events. Other events are useful in troubleshooting database and performance issues. Do not set events in production databases without first consulting with Oracle Support and testing them in a test database.

You can use the oradebug command (covered later in this chapter in the oradebug section) or DBMS_SUPPORT PL/SQL package to set events in sessions other than the current session.

Dumps

Several structures in an Oracle instance or database can be dumped to a trace file for low-level analysis, such as these:

- Control files
- Datafile headers
- Redo log file headers
- Instance state
- Process state
- Library cache
- Data blocks

Related Oracle Internals Topics

These dumps can be created with the commands in Listing 13-38.

```
alter session set events 'immediate trace name CONTROLF level 10';
alter session set events 'immediate trace name FILE_HDRS level 10';
alter session set events 'immediate trace name REDOHDR level 10';
alter session set events 'immediate trace name SYSTEMSTATE level 10';
alter session set events 'immediate trace name PROCESSSTATE level 10;'
alter session set events 'immediate trace name library_cache level 10';
alter system dump datafile 10 block 2057;   -- (This is covered in detail in
Chapter 9)
```

Listing 13-38: Creating dumps

The trace files containing this dump information are in the USER_DUMP_DEST directory.

Oradebug

You use the oradebug command for troubleshooting the instance or sessions. Oradebug can capture current instance state information, set events in sessions, and perform other low-level diagnostics. Type **oradebug help** from SQL*Plus to get the usage list shown in Listing 13-39.

```
SQL> oradebug help
HELP            [command]               Describe one or all commands
SETMYPID                                Debug current process
SETOSPID        <ospid>                 Set OS pid of process to debug
SETORAPID       <orapid> ['force']      Set Oracle pid of process to debug
DUMP            <dump_name> <level>     Invoke named dump
DUMPSGA         [bytes]                 Dump fixed SGA
DUMPLIST                                Print a list of available dumps
EVENT           <text>                  Set trace event in process
SESSION_EVENT   <text>                  Set trace event in session
DUMPVAR         <p|s|uga> <name> [level]  Print/dump a fixed PGA/SGA/UGA variable
SETVAR          <p|s|uga> <name> <value>  Modify a fixed PGA/SGA/UGA variable
PEEK            <addr> <len> [level]    Print/Dump memory
POKE            <addr> <len> <value>    Modify memory
WAKEUP          <orapid>                Wake up Oracle process
SUSPEND                                 Suspend execution
RESUME                                  Resume execution
FLUSH                                   Flush pending writes to trace file
CLOSE_TRACE                             Close trace file
TRACEFILE_NAME                          Get name of trace file
LKDEBUG                                 Invoke global enqueue service debugger
NSDBX                                   Invoke CGS name-service debugger
-G              <Inst-List | def | all> lkdebug cluster database command prefix
-R              <Inst-List | def | all> lkdebug cluster database command prefix
```

```
SETINST        <instance# .. | all>     Set instance list in double quotes
SGATOFILE      <SGA dump dir>           Dump SGA to file; dirname in double quotes
DMPCOWSGA      <SGA dump dir> Dump & map SGA as COW; dirname in double quotes
MAPCOWSGA      <SGA dump dir>           Map SGA as COW; dirname in double quotes
HANGANALYZE    [level]                  Analyze system hang
FFBEGIN                                 Flash Freeze the Instance
FFDEREGISTER                            FF deregister instance from cluster
FFTERMINST                              Call exit and terminate instance
FFRESUMEINST                            Resume the flash frozen instance
FFSTATUS                                Flash freeze status of instance
CORE                                    Dump core without crashing process
IPC                                     Dump ipc information
UNLIMIT                                 Unlimit the size of the trace file
PROCSTAT                                Dump process statistics
CALL           <func> [arg1] ... [argn] Invoke function with arguments
```

Listing 13-39: Usage list

X$ Table Groups

The X$ tables can be logically grouped as shown in Tables 13-1 through 13-44. The descriptions for these are updated to the best of my knowledge. I am unsure of the value where the description or other field is missing or blank. Oracle Corporation does not provide a full description list.

X$ Tables	Description
X$KCKCE	Features in use by the database instance that may prevent downgrading to a previous release
X$KCKFM	Some sort of information about the version of database or database parts
X$KCKTY	Features in use by the database instance that may prevent downgrading to a previous release
X$KSULL	Information about license limits
X$OPTION	Installed options
X$VERSION	Oracle RDBMS software version

TABLE 13-1. *Version/Installation*

X$ Tables	Description
X$KSUSGSTA	Instance statistics.
X$KCCDI	Main source of information for V$DATABASE.
X$KSMSD	SGA component sizes ("show sga").
X$KSMSS	Detailed SGA statistics (38 rows on Solaris and NT, 39 on Linux).
X$KSPPCV	Parameters and values that are in effect for the session.
X$KSPPCV2	Parameters and values that are in effect for the session. List parameter values appear as separate rows.
X$KSPPI	Parameters and values that are currently in effect for the session.
X$KSPPO	Obsolete parameters.
X$KSPPSV	Parameters and values that are in effect for the instance.
X$KSPPSV2	Parameters and values that are in effect for the instance. List parameter values appear as separate rows.
X$KSPSPFILE	Parameter names specified with an spfile (808 rows on Linux and Solaris, 799 rows on NT).
X$KSQDN	Database name.
X$OPTION	Installed options.
X$KVII	Instance limits and other instance metadata (includes miscellaneous information).
X$KVIS	Platform-specific block space information.
X$KVIT	State of various buffer cache conditions.
X$KSUXSINST	Main source of information for V$INSTANCE.
X$QUIESCE	Quiesce state of the instance.

TABLE 13-2. *Instance/Database*

X$ Tables	Description
X$KSULV	Valid values of NLS parameters
X$NLS_PARAMETERS	Current values of NLS parameters

TABLE 13-3. *NSL*

X$ Table	Description
X$TIMEZONE_NAMES	Time zone names

TABLE 13-4.   *Time Zones*

X$ Tables	Description
X$KCCAL	Information about archive log files from the control file
X$KCRRARCH	Information about the arch processes for the current instance
X$KCRRDEST	Describes, for the current instance, all the archive log destinations, their current value, mode, and status
X$KCRRDSTAT	Archive destination status

TABLE 13-5.   *Archive Log Files/Destinations/Processes*

X$ Tables	Description
X$KCCFE	File creation and other metadata
X$KCCTF	Temp file I/O information
X$KCVFH	Information source of V$DATAFILE
X$KCFIO	File I/O information
X$KCFTIO	Temp file I/O information
X$KCVFHALL	Datafile information similar to information in V$DATAFILE
X$KTFBFE	Free extents in files (ktfb free extents)
X$KTFBHC	Transaction information

TABLE 13-6.   *Data Files*

X$ Table Groups

X$ Tables	Description
X$KCCCF	Control file information
X$KCCOR	Datafile offline information from the control file
X$KCCRS	Information about the control file record sections
X$KCCRT	Log file information from the control files

TABLE 13-7.   *Control Files*

X$ Tables	Description
X$KCCCP	Redo log block information
X$KCCFN	Information about redo log files
X$KCCLE	Information about redo log files in need of archiving

TABLE 13-8.   *Redo Log Files*

X$ Table	Description
X$KCCTS	Tablespace information

TABLE 13-9.   *Tablespaces*

X$ Tables	Description
X$KTFTHC	Space usage in each temp tablespace
X$KTFTME	Status of each unit of all temp tablespaces (temp map extents/blocks)
X$KTSSO	Sort segment activity by session
X$KTSTFC	Temp segment usage: blocks used, cached, etc.
X$KTSTSSD	System temporary sort segment data

TABLE 13-10.   *Sort/Temp Segments*

X$ Tables	Description
X$KTFBUE	Rollback/undo segment block/extent usage
X$KTTVS	Rollback/undo segment stats
X$KTUGD	Global rollback/undo data
X$KTURD	Rollback/undo segment stats
X$KTUSMST	Rollback/undo segment stats
X$KTUXE	Rollback/undo segment activity: wraps, etc.

TABLE 13-11. *Rollback/Undo Segments*

X$ Tables	Description
X$KCVFHTMP	Tempfile information
X$KDLT	Temporary LOB information

TABLE 13-12. *Temporary Objects*

X$ Table	Description
X$UGANCO	Database link information

TABLE 13-13. *Database Links*

X$ Table	Description
X$KNSTMVR	Materialized view information

TABLE 13-14. *Materialized Views*

X$ Table Groups

X$ Tables	Description
X$KNSTRPP	Replication information
X$KNSTRQU	Replication information

TABLE 13-15. *Replication*

X$ Tables	Description
X$KCCBF	Information from the control file about datafiles and control files in backup sets (RMAN)
X$KCCBL	Information from the control file about archived logs in backup sets (RMAN)
X$KCCBP	Backup piece information from the control file (RMAN)
X$KCCBS	Backup set information from the control file (RMAN)
X$KCCCC	Datafile copy corruptions from the control file (RMAN)
X$KCCDC	Datafile copy information from the control file (RMAN)
X$KCCFC	Corruption in datafile backups (RMAN)
X$KCVFHONL	Backup status of all online datafiles
X$KSFHDVNT	Supported backup devices (RMAN)
X$KSFQP	Performance information about ongoing or recently completed backups
X$KSFVQST	Backup information
X$KSFVSL	Backup information
X$KSFVSTA	Backup information

TABLE 13-16. *Backup*

X$ Tables	Description
X$KCRFX	Statistics about the current recovery process
X$KCRMF	Statistics and status of files involved in recovery
X$KCRMX	Statistics and status of files involved in recovery

TABLE 13-17. *Recovery*

X$ Tables	Description
X$KCVFHMRR	Displays status of files during media recovery
X$KRVSLV	Recovery slave status
X$KRVSLVS	Recovery slave statistics
X$KTPRXRS	Information about recovery slaves performing parallel recovery
X$KTPRXRT	Information about transactions Oracle is currently recovering
X$ESTIMATED_MTTR	Estimates on the I/O work required if an instance recovery is needed right now
X$TARGETRBA	Target recovery block accesses or target redo block accesses

TABLE 13-17. *Recovery (continued)*

X$ Tables	Description
X$KCCDL	Information about deleted objects. Recovery catalog resync operation uses this to speed its optimize operation.
X$KCCPA	Descriptions of archivelog backups taken with proxy copy.
X$KCCPD	Descriptions of datafile and control file backups taken with proxy copy.
X$KCCRM	RMAN configuration.

TABLE 13-18. *RMAN*

X$ Table	Description
X$KCRRMS	Standby database status information
X$KCCSL	Undetermined standby information
X$NKSTACR	Standby database information: log standby coordinator
X$KNSTASL	Standby database information

TABLE 13-19. *Standby Databases*

X$ Table Groups

X$LOGMNR_ATTRIBUTE

X$LOGMNR_CALLBACK

X$LOGMNR_COL$

X$LOGMNR_COLTYPE$

X$LOGMNR_CONTENTS

X$LOGMNR_DICT$

X$LOGMNR_DICTIONARY

X$LOGMNR_ENCRYPTED_OBJ$

X$LOGMNR_ENCRYPTION_PROFILE$

X$LOGMNR_IND$

X$LOGMNR_INDPART$

X$LOGMNR_LOGFILE

X$LOGMNR_LOGS

X$LOGMNR_PARAMETERS

X$LOGMNR_PROCESS

X$LOGMNR_OBJ$

X$LOGMNR_REGION

X$LOGMNR_SESSION

X$LOGMNR_TAB$

X$LOGMNR_TABCOMPART$

X$LOGMNR_TABSUBPART$

X$LOGMNR_TRANSACTION

X$LOGMNR_TS$

X$LOGMNR_TYPE$

X$LOGNNR_TABPART$

X$LOGMNR_TABSUBPART$

X$LOGMNR_USER$

TABLE 13-20. *LogMiner*

X$ Tables	Description
X$MESSAGES	Messages that each background process processes
X$QESMMSGA	Limits, use, estimates, etc., of memory use by PGAs

TABLE 13-21. *Sessions/Processes*

X$ Tables	Description
X$KOCST	Object cache statistics for the current session
X$KSLES	Waits on event by sessions
X$KSQRS	Session resource usage
X$KSUSIO	I/O statistics for each session
X$KSULOP	Session information about long-running operations
X$KSUMYSTA	Statistics for the current session
X$KSUPL	Session information
X$KSUPR	Main source of information for V$PROCESS
X$KSUSE	Information in V$SESSION
X$KSUSECON	Information about how each session connected and authenticated
X$KSUSECST	Session waits, including wait parameters
X$KSUSESTA	Session performance statistics

TABLE 13-22. *Session Performance*

X$ Table	Description
X$KTCXB	Transaction information, including locks requested and held, rollback segments used by the transaction, and the type of transaction

TABLE 13-23. *Transactions*

X$ Table Groups

X$ Tables	Description
X$K2GTE	Information on the currently active global transactions
X$K2GTE2	Information on the currently active global transactions

TABLE 13-24. *Global Transactions*

X$ Tables	Description
X$KGSKASP	All available active session pool resource allocation methods
X$KGSKCFT	Data related to currently active resource consumer groups
X$KGSKCP	All resource allocation methods defined for resource consumer groups
X$KGSKDOPP	Available parallel degree limit resource allocation methods
X$KGSKPFT	Names of all currently active resource plans
X$KGSKQUEP	Available queue resource allocation methods
X$KSRMSGDES	Queue messages
X$KSRMSGO	Queue publisher/subscriber information
X$KWQSI	Read/write statistics on queues

TABLE 13-25. *Advanced Queuing (AQ)*

X$ Tables	Description
X$KCLCRST	Information about block server background processes used in cache fusion
X$KJBL	RAC DLM information
X$KJBLFX	RAC information
X$KJBR	RAC DLM information
X$KJDRHV	RAC instance information
X$KJDRPCMHV	RAC instance information
X$KJDRPCMPF	RAC instance information

TABLE 13-26. *Real Application Clusters*

X$ Tables	Description
X$KJICVT	RAC DLM information
X$KJILKFT	RAC DLM information
X$KJIRFT	RAC DLM information
X$KJISFT	RAC DLM information
X$KJITRFT	RAC DLM information
X$KJMDDP	RAC information
X$KJMSDP	RAC information
X$KJXM	RAC information
X$KSIMAT	RAC information
X$KSIMAV	RAC information
X$KSIMSI	Map of instance names to instance numbers for all instances mounting a particular database
X$LE	RAC lock element statistics (mode, blocks, releases, acquisitions, etc.)
X$LE_	RAC lock element status and activity

TABLE 13-26. *Real Application Clusters (continued)*

X$ Tables	Description
X$KGLCLUSTER	Likely currently loaded or recently referenced clusters.
X$KGLCURSOR	Statistics on shared SQL area without the GROUP BY clause and contains one row for each child of the original SQL text entered.
X$KGLNA	Text of SQL statements belonging to shared SQL cursors.
X$KGLNA1	Text of SQL statements belonging to shared SQL cursors: newlines and tabs not replaced with spaces.
X$KGLOB	Database objects that are cached in the library cache. Objects include tables, indexes, clusters, synonym definitions, PL/SQL procedures and packages, and triggers.
X$KGLST	Library cache performance and activity information.
X$KKSBV	Bind variable data (depending on setting of CURSOR_SHARING) for cursors owned by the current session.

TABLE 13-27. *Library Cache*

X$ Table Groups

X$ Tables	Description
X$KKSCS	Information about why nonshared child cursors are nonshared.
X$KKSSRD	Redirected SQL statements.
X$KQFVI	SQL statements of all the fixed views.
X$KQLFXPL	Execution plan for each child cursor loaded in the library cache.
X$KQLSET	Information about subordinate caches currently loaded in the library cache.
X$KSLEI	Wait statistics (totals) for each event.
X$KXSBD	SQL or session bind data.
X$KXSCC	Shared cursor cache. V$SQL_CURSOR debugging information for each cursor associated with the session querying this view. Memory use by each cursor of a session SQL cursor cache.
X$QESMMIWT	Shared memory management instantaneous working. Join to X$QKSMMWDS.
X$QKSMMWDS	Shared memory management working data size. Library cache memory use by child cursors.

TABLE 13-27.   *Library Cache (continued)*

X$ Tables	Description
X$KGHLU	Shared pool reserved list performance information
X$KGICC	Session cursor usage statistics: opens, hits, count, etc.
X$KGICS	Systemwide cursor usage statistics: opens, hits, count, etc.
X$KSMFSV	Shared memory information
X$KSMGV	SGA component names: buffer cache, java pool, large pool, shared pool
X$KSMHP	Shared memory information
X$KSMLRU	Shared memory: specific, loaded objects and their sizes, pin candidates
X$KSMFS	SGA sizes: fixed SGA, DB_BLOCK_BUFFERS, LOG_BUFFER
X$KSMSS	SGA size: shared pool (also listed in the "Instance/Database" section)

TABLE 13-28.   *Shared Memory*

X$ Tables	Description
X$KSMJS	SGA size: java pool
X$KSMLS	SGA size: large pool
X$KSMPP	Very similar to X$KSMSP, without DUR and IDX columns varying numbers on Linux, Solaris, and NT
X$KSMSP	Shared pool section sizes/values, etc.
X$KSMSPR	Shared pool reserved memory statistics/sizes
X$KSMSPR	Shared pool section sizes/values, etc.
X$KSMSP_DSNEW	Shared memory information
X$KSMSP_NWEXT	Shared memory information

TABLE 13-28. *Shared Memory* (continued)

X$ Tables	Description
X$ACTIVECKPT	Checkpoint statistics information
X$BH	Status and number of pings for every buffer in the SGA
X$CLASS_STAT	Number of blocks pinged per block class
X$KCBBHS	DBWR histogram statistics
X$KCBFWAIT	Buffer cache wait count and time
X$KCBKPFS	Buffer cache block prefetch statistics
X$KCBLSC	Buffer cache read/write/wait performance statistics
X$KCBSC	Buffer cache set read performance statistics
X$KCBWAIT	Number of and time spent in waits for buffer pool classes
X$KCBWBPD	Statistics on all buffer pools available to the instance, including buffer pool names
X$KCBWDS	Statistics on all buffer pools available to the instance

TABLE 13-29. *Buffer Cache*

X$ Tables	Description
X$KQRFP	Information about parent objects in the data dictionary
X$KQRFS	Information about subordinate objects in the data dictionary
X$KQRPD	Rowcache information
X$KQRSD	Rowcache information
X$KQRST	Rowcache performance statistics

TABLE 13-30.   *Rowcache*

X$ Tables	Description
X$KGLINDEX	Object names with currently held locks and other information about these locks
X$KGLLK	DDL locks currently held and requested
X$KSQEQ	Locks held by sessions
X$KSQST	Enqueue type, number of requests, number of waits, wait time, etc.
X$KTADM	Locks requested and held by sessions

TABLE 13-31.   *Locks/Enqueues*

X$ Tables	Description
X$KSLLD	Latch names and levels
X$KSLLT	Parent and child latch statistics
X$KSLLW	Statistics on latch waits, plus latch names
X$KSLPO	Latch posting
X$KSLWSC	Statistics on latch wait sleeps, plus latch names
X$KSUPRLAT	Information about current latch holders

TABLE 13-32.   *Latches*

X$ Tables	Description
X$KDXHS	Index histogram information
X$KDXST	Index statistics from the last `analyze index validate structure` command

TABLE 13-33. *Optimizer*

X$ Tables	Description
X$KMCQS	Multithread message queue information
X$KMCVC	Virtual circuit connection message transport statistical information
X$KMMDI	MTS dispatcher performance information
X$KMMDP	MTS dispatcher performance information
X$KMMRD	MTS dispatcher information
X$KMMSG	Shared servers process performance information
X$KMMSI	Shared servers process information

TABLE 13-34. *MTS*

X$ Table Groups

X$ Tables	Description
X$KSTEX	Information about parallel execution
X$KXFPCDS	PQ information very similar to X$KXFPSDS
X$KXFPCMS	PQ information very similar to X$KXFPSMS
X$KXFPCST	Performance statistics for all PQ sessions combined
X$KXFPDP	X$KXFPDP: metadata about current PQ sessions, such as number of degree of parallelism, etc.
X$KXFPPFT	Parallel query information
X$KQFPSDS	Selects a.type,b.reason from X$KXFPSMS a, X$KXFPSDS b, where a.indx = b.indx
X$KXFPSMS	Parallel query information

TABLE 13-35. *Parallel Query*

X$ Tables	Description
X$KXFPSST	Session statistics for parallel queries
X$KXFPYS	Parallel query system statistics
X$KXFPNS	Performance statistics for sessions running parallel execution
X$KXFQSROW	Statistics on parallel execution operations, query statistics row

TABLE 13-35. *Parallel Query* (continued)

X$ Tables	Description
X$KZDOS	Role-related security
X$KZRTPD	Fine-grained security policies and predicates associated with the cursors currently in the library cache
X$KZSPR	Privileges
X$KZSRO	Roles
X$KZSRT	List of users who have been granted SYSDBA and SYSOPER privileges

TABLE 13-36. *Security-Granted Privileges and Roles, Fine-Grained Security Policies*

X$ Tables	Description
X$KGSKPP	Available CPU resource allocation methods defined for resource plans
X$KGSKQUEP	Available queuing resource allocation methods
X$KGSKTE	Possibly rcg names
X$KGSKTO	Possibly rcg types and attributes

TABLE 13-37. *Resource/Consumer Groups*

X$ Tables	Description
X$CONTEXT	Context information
X$GLOBALCONTEXT	Context information

TABLE 13-38. *Contexts*

NOTE
"Contexts" has nothing to do with Oracle Text, which used to be called "Context."

X$ Tables	Description
X$HOFP	Init parameters in use by the hs server and agent
X$HS_SESSION	Information about the hs agents currently running on a given host

TABLE 13-39. *Heterogeneous Services*

X$ Table	Description
X$KWDDEF	PL/SQL reserved words

TABLE 13-40. *PL/SQL*

X$ Tables	Description
X$KLCIE	SQL*Loader load performance information
X$KLPT	SQL*Loader load performance information

TABLE 13-41. *SQL*Loader*

X$ Table Groups

X$ Tables	Description
X$JOXFC	Compile, resolve, reference information
X$JOXFD	Compile, resolve, reference information
X$JOXFR	Compile, resolve, reference information
X$JOXFS	Source name and/or code
X$JOXFT	Reference names, resolve information, compile information, class name information

TABLE 13-42. *Java Source*

X$ Tables	Description
X$DUAL	Everybody loves the permanent table DUAL, including Oracle. When the database is in a nomount or mount state, the permanent table DUAL is not available. For some operations, such as recovery, which Oracle needs to do when the database is in a nomount or mount state, Oracle queries X$DUAL.
X$KQFCO	Indexed columns of dynamic performance tables.
X$KQFDT	Fixed dynamic or derived tables.
X$KQFP	Fixed object names.
X$KQFSZ	Stores the sizes of various database component types.
X$KQFTA	Names of all the fixed tables.
X$KQFVI	Names of all the fixed views.
X$KSBDD	Descriptions of the background processes.
X$KSBDP	Background process names.
X$KSLED	Wait event names.
X$KSURLMT	System resource limits.
X$KSUSD	Statistics descriptions.
X$KSUTM	Lists the elapsed time in hundredths of seconds since the beginning of the epoch.

TABLE 13-43. *Miscellaneous*

Table Name	Probable Use
X$VINST	Unknown
X$RFMTE	Unknown
X$RFMP	Unknown
X$TRACE_EVENTS	Available events try to enable some of these events and see what shows up in X$TRACE. It seems that there are 1000 available events in 901 on NT, Linux, and Solaris.
X$TRACE	Enabled trace events.
X$LCR	RAC lock/enqueue information.
X$KZMAIE	Security.
X$KZEMAEA	Information about security encryption algorithm.
X$KTSPSTAT	Undo/rollback information.
X$KSXRSG	Unknown
X$KSRREPQ	Unknown
X$KSXRMSG	Unknown
X$KSXRCONQ	Unknown
X$KSXRCH	Unknown
X$KSXAFA	Unknown
X$KSUSEX	Session information.
X$KSURU	Resource usage.
X$KSUPGS	Unknown
X$KSUPGP	Unknown
X$KSUCF	Unknown
X$KSRMPCTX	Unknown
X$KSRCHDL	Unknown
X$KSRCDES	Unknown
X$KSRCCTX	Unknown
X$KSMNS	Shared memory information.
X$KSMNIM	Shared memory information.
X$KSMMEM	Shared memory information.

X$ Table Groups

TABLE 13-44. *Other X$ Tables*

Table Name	Probable Use
X$KSMJCH	Shared memory information.
X$KSMGST	Shared memory information.
X$KSMGOP	Shared memory information.
X$KSMDD	Shared memory information.
X$KRBAFF	Unknown
X$KQDPG	Dynamic performance information.
X$KKSAI	Unknown
X$KGLXS	Library cache information.
X$KGLTRIGGER	System trigger information.
X$KGLTR	Library cache information.
X$KGLTABLE	Table information.
X$KGLSN	Unknown
X$KGLLC	Unknown
X$KGLAU	Unknown
X$KGLRD	Unknown
X$KDNSSF	Lock information.
X$KCRMT	Cache fusion information.
X$KCLQN	Cache fusion information.
X$KCLLS	Cache fusion information.
X$KCLFX	Cache fusion information.
X$KCLFI	Cache fusion information.
X$KCLCURST	Cache fusion information.
X$KCBWH	Information about functions pertaining to the buffer cache.
X$KCBSW	Buffer cache information.
X$KCBSH	Buffer cache information.
X$KCBSDS	Buffer cache information.
X$KCBLDRHIST	Buffer cache information.
X$KCBKWRL	Buffer cache write list.
X$KCBBF	Unknown

TABLE 13-44. *Other X$ Tables* (continued)

Table Name	Probable Use
X$KCBBES	Unknown
X$CKPTBUF	Checkpoint information.

TABLE 13-44. *Other X$ Tables* (continued)

X$ Table and Non-V$ Fixed View Associations

Table 13-45 lists non-V$ fixed views (V$ views listed in Appendix B and C) that are based on at least one X$ table. Many of the fixed views are based on one or more X$ tables, plus other fixed views. You can use this list with the Oracle Reference manual and the $ORACLE_HOME/ rdbms/admin/sql.bsq and $ORACLE_HOME/rdbms/admin/migrate.bsq as an aid in deciphering the meaning of X$ table and column contents and in constructing queries that join X$ tables to other X$ tables or to fixed views.

Fixed View	Base X$ Tables and/or Fixed Views
COLUMN_PRIVILEGES	OBJAUTH$, COL$, OBJ$, USER$, X$KZSRO
DBA_BLOCKERS	V$SESSION_WAIT, X$KSQRS, V$_LOCK, X$KSUSE
DBA_DATA_FILES	FILE$, TS$, V$DBFILE, X$KTFBHC
DBA_DDL_LOCKS	V$SESSION, X$KGLOB, X$KGLLK
DBA_DML_LOCKS	V$_LOCK, X$KSUSE, X$KSQRS
DBA_EXTENTS	UET$ SYS_DBA_SEGS, FILE$, X$KTFBUE, FILE#
DBA_FREE_SPACE	TS$, FET$, FILE$, X$KTFBFE
DBA_FREE_SPACE_COALESCED	X$KTFBFE
DBA_KGLLOCK	X$KGLLK, X$KGLPN
DBA_LMT_FREE_SPAE	X$KTFBFE
DBA_LMT_USED_EXTENTS	X$KTFBUE
DBA_LOCK_INTERNAL	V$LOCK, V$PROCESS, V$SESSION, V$LATCHHOLDER, X$KGLOB, DBA_KGLLOCK
DBA_SOURCE	OBJ$, SOURCE$, USER$, X$JOXFS
DBA_TEMP_FILES	X$KCCFN, X$KTFTHC, TS$

TABLE 13-45. *X$ Table and Non-V$ Fixed View Associations*

Fixed View	Base X$ Tables and/or Fixed Views
DBA_UNDO_EXTENTS	UNDO$, TS$, X$KTFBUE, FILE$
DBA_WAITERS	V$SESSION_WAIT, X$KSQRS, V$_LOCK, X$KSUSE
DICTIONARY	V$ENABLED_PRIVS, OBJ$, COM$, SYN$, OBJAUTH$, X$KZSRO
DISK_AND_FIXED_OBJECTS	OBJ$, X$KQFP, X$KQFTA, X$KQFVI
EXU7FUL	X$KZSRO, USER$
EXU8FUL	X$KZSRO, USER$
EXU9FIL	FILE$, V$DBFILE, DBFILE$, X$KTFBHC, TS$, X$KCCFN, X$KTFTHC
EXU9TNEB	X$KTFBUE
IMP9TVOID	OBJ$, USER$, TYPE$, SESSION_ROLES, OBJAUTH$, X$KZSRO
INDEX_HISTOGRAM	X$KDXST, X$KDXHS
INDEX_STATS	OBJ$, IND$, SEG$, X$KDXST, INDPART$, INDSUBPART$
LOADER_DIR_OBJS	OBJ$, DIR$, V$ENABLEDPRIVS, X$KZSRO
LOADER_TAB_INFO	OBJ$, V$ENABLEDPRIVS, X$KZSRO, TAB$, USER$, OBJAUTH$
LOADER_TRIGGER_INFO	OBJ$, USER$, TRIGGER$, OBJAUTH$, V$ENABLED_PRIVS, X$KZSRO
LOADER_TRIGGER_INFO	OBJ$, USER$, TRIGGER$, X$KZSRO
ORA_KGLR7_DEPENDENCIES	OBJ$, DEPENDENCY$, USER$, X$KZSRO, V$FIXED_TABLE, OBJAUTH$
ORA_KGLR7_IDL_CHAR	ORA_KGLR7_OBJECTS, IDL_CHAR$, OBJAUTH$, X$KZSRO
ORA_KGLR7_IDL_SB4	ORA_KGLR7_OBJECTS, IDL_SB4$, OBJAUTH$, X$KZSRO, SYSAUTH$
ORA_KGLR7_IDL_UB1	ORA_KGLR7_OBJECTS, IDL_UB1$, OBJAUTH$, X$KZSRO, SYSAUTH$
ORA_KGLR7_IDL_UB2	ORA_KGLR7_OBJECTS, IDL_UB1$, OBJAUTH$, X$KZSRO, SYSAUTH$
QUEUE_PRIVILEGES	OBJAUTH$, OBJ$, USER$, X$KZSRO

TABLE 13-45. *X$ Table and Non-V$ Fixed View Associations* (continued)

Fixed View	Base X$ Tables and/or Fixed Views
ROLE_SYS_PRIVS	USER$, SYSTEM_PRIVILEGE_MAP, SYSAUTH$, X$KZDOS
ROLE_ROLE_PRIVS	USER$, SYSAUTH$, X$KZDOS
ROLE_TAB_PRIVS	USER$, TABLE_PRIVILEGE_MAP, OBJAUTH$, OBJ$, COL$, X$KZDOS, SYSAUTH$
SESSION_ROLES	X$KZSRO
TABLE_PRIVILEGES	OBJAUTH$, OBJ$, USER$, X$KZSRO

TABLE 13-45. *X$ Table and Non-V$ Fixed View Associations* (continued)

Common X$ Table Joins

Table 13-46 contains the X$ table column joins used in fixed views.

X$ Table and Column	Associated X$ Table and Column
X$BH.LE_ADDR	X$LE.LE_ADDR
X$KCCFN.FNFNO	X$KTFTHC.KTFTHCTFNO
X$HS_SESSION.FDS_INST_ID	X$HOFP.FDS_INST_ID
X$KCBSC.BPID	X$KCBWBPD.BP_ID
X$KCBSC.INST_ID	X$KCBWBPD.INST_ID
X$KCBWDS.SET_ID	X$KCBWBPD.BP_LO_SID
X$KCBWDS.SET_ID	X$KCBWBPD.BP_HI_SID
X$KCCFE.FEFNH	X$KCCFN.FNNUM
X$KCCFE.FENUM	X$KCCFN.FNFNO
X$KCCFE.FENUM	X$CFIO.KCFIOFNO
X$KCCFE.FENUM	X$KCCFN.FNFNO
X$KCCFE.FEPAX	X$KCCFN.FNNUM
X$KCCFN.FNFNO	X$KCVFHTMP.HTMPXFIL
X$KCCFN.FNFNO	X$KCVFH.HCFIL

TABLE 13-46. *Common Table Joins*

X$ Table and Column	Associated X$ Table and Column
X$KCCFN.FNFNO	X$KTFTHC.KTFTHCTFNO
X$KCCLE.INST_ID	X$KCCRT.INST_ID
X$KCCLE.LETHR	X$KCCRT.RTNUM
X$KCCTF.TFFNH	X$KCCFN.FNNUM
X$KCCTF.TFNUM	X$KCCFN.FNFNO
X$KCFTIO.KCFTIOFNO	X$KCCTF.TFNUM
X$KCRMF.FNO	X$KCCFN.FNFNO
X$KCRMF.FNO	X$KCCFN.FNFNO
X$KCRMX.THR	X$KCRFX.THR
X$KGLCRSOR.KGLHDADR	X$KZRTPD.KZRTPDAD
X$KGLCRSOR.KGLHDPAR	X$KZRTPD.KZRTPDPA
X$KGLCURSOR.KGLHDPAR	X$KZRTPD.KZRTPDPA
X$KGLCURSOR.KGLHDPAR	X$KKSSRD.PARADDR
X$KGLCURSOR.KGLOBHD6	X$KSMHP.KSMCHDS
X$KGLCURSOR.KGLOBHD6	X$KSMHP.KSMCHDS
X$KGLLK.KGLLKHDL	X$KGLDP.KGLHDADR
X$KGLLK.KGLLKUSE	X$KSUSE.ADDR
X$KGLLK.KGLNAHSH	X$KGLDP.KGLNAHSH
X$KGLOB.KGLHDADR	X$KGLDP.KGLRFHDL
X$KGLOB.KGLHDADR	X$KGLLK.KGLLKHDL
X$KGLOB.KGLNAHSH	X$KGLDP.KGLRFHSH
X$KQFVI.INDX	X$KQFVT.INDX
X$KSBDP.INDX	X$KSBDD.INDX
X$KSLEI.INDX	X$KSLED.INDX
X$KSLEI.INDX	X$KSLED.INDX
X$KSLES.KSLESENM	X$KSLED.INDX
X$KSLLD.INDX	X$KSLLT.LATCH#
X$KSLLT.KSLLTNUM	X$KSLLD.INDX
X$KSLLT.LATCH#	X$KSLLD.INDX

TABLE 13-46. *Common Table Joins* (continued)

X$ Table and Column	Associated X$ Table and Column
X$KSLLW.INDX	X$KSLWSC.INDX
X$KSLWSC.INDX	X$KSLLW.INDX
X$KSPPI.INDX	X$KSPPSV.INDX
X$KSPPI.INDX	X$KSPPCV.INDX
X$KSPPI.INDX	X$KSPPCV2.INDX
X$KSPPI.INDX	X$KSPPSV2.KSPFTCTXPN
X$KSQEQ.KSQLKRES	X$KSQRS.ADDR
X$KSQEQ.KSQLKSES	X$KSUSE.ADDR
X$KSUSE.INDX	X$KXUSESTA.INDX
X$KSUSE.KSUSEPRO	X$KXFPDP.KXFPDPPRO
X$KSUSECST.KSUSSOPC	X$KSLED.INDX
X$KSUSECST.KSUSSOPC	X$KSLED.INDX
X$KSUXSINST	Joined with X$KVIT and X$QUIESCE to create V$INSTANCE, but with no specific column joins
X$KSXTMPT.KGLHDADR	X$KGLCURSOR.KGLHDADR
X$KSXTMPT.KGLNAHSH	X$KGLCRSOR.KGLNAHSH
X$KTCXB.KSQLKRES	X$KSQRS.ADDR
X$KTCXB.KSQLKRES	X$KSQRS.DDR
X$KTCXB.KSQLKSES	X$KSUSE.ADDR
X$KTCXB.KSQLKSES	X$KSUSE.ADDR
X$KTCXB.KTCXBSES	X$KSUSE.ADDR
X$KTCXB.KTCXBSES	X$KSUSE.ADDR
X$KTCXB.KTCXBXBA	X$KTADM.KSSOBOWN
X$KTCXB.KTCXBXBA	X$KTADM.KSSOBOWN
X$TARGETRBA.INST_ID	X$SUSGSTA.INST_ID
X$TARGETRBA.INST_ID	X$ESTIMATED_MTTR.INST_ID

TABLE 13-46. *Common Table Joins* (continued)

Common X$ Table Joins

New 9i X$ Tables

The following X$ tables are new in Oracle9i:

- X$ESTIMATED_MTTR
- X$GLOBALCONTEXT
- X$KCBKPFS
- X$KCBKWRL
- X$KCBLDRHIST
- X$KCCRM
- X$KCCSL
- X$KCLCURST
- X$KCRRDSTAT
- X$KCRRMS
- X$KGSKQUEP
- X$KJBL
- X$KJBLFX
- X$KJBR
- X$KJBRFX
- X$KJDRHV
- X$KJDRPCMHV
- X$KJDRPCMPF
- X$KJMDDP
- X$KJMSDP
- X$KJXM
- X$KKSSRD
- X$KNSTACR
- X$KNSTASL
- X$KNSTMVR
- X$KNSTRPP
- X$KNSTRQU
- X$KQLFXPL
- X$KRVSLV
- X$KRVSLVS
- X$KSMDD
- X$KSMGOP
- X$KSMGST
- X$KSMGV
- X$KSMSP_DSNEW
- X$KSPSPFILE
- X$KSXRCH
- X$KSXRCONQ
- X$KSXRMSG
- X$KSXRREPQ
- X$KSXRSG
- X$KTRSO
- X$KTSPSTAT
- X$KTUGD
- X$KTUSMST
- X$KXFPPFT
- X$KZEMAEA
- X$KZEMAIE
- X$KZRTPD
- X$LCR
- X$LOGMNR_ATTRIBUTE$
- X$LOGMNR_CALLBACK
- X$LOGMNR_COL$
- X$LOGMNR_COLTYPE$
- X$LOGMNR_DICT$
- X$LOGMNR_ENCRYPTED_OBJ$

- X$LOGMNR_ENCRYPTION_PROFILE$
- X$LOGMNR_IND$
- X$LOGMNR_INDPART$
- X$LOGMNR_LOGFILE
- X$LOGMNR_OBJ$
- X$LOGMNR_PROCESS
- X$LOGMNR_REGION
- X$LOGMNR_ROOT$
- X$LOGMNR_SESSION
- X$LOGMNR_TAB$
- X$LOGMNR_TABCOMPART$
- X$LOGMNR_TABPART$
- X$LOGMNR_TABSUBPART$

- X$LOGMNR_TRANSACTION
- X$LOGMNR_TS$
- X$LOGMNR_TYPE$
- X$LOGMNR_USER$
- X$QESMMIWT
- X$QESMMSGA
- X$QKSMMWDS
- X$QUIESCE
- X$RFMP
- X$RFMTE
- X$TIMEZONE_NAMES
- X$TRACE_EVENTS
- X$VINST

Undocumented Fixed Views

The fixed views in Table 13-47 are not described in the Oracle Reference manuals, but there are some other references to check following this table.

Note that V$REQDIST , V$REPLQUEUE , V$REPLPROP , V$MVREFRESH , V$MANAGED_ STANDBY , V$LOGSTDBY_STATS , V$LOGSTDBY, V$HVMASTER_INFO, and V$GCSPFMASTER_ INFO are documented in the Oracle9202 Database Reference manual (Part No. A96536-02). Also, V$MANAGED_STANDBY, V$LOGSTDBY, and V$LOGSTDBY_STATS are documented in

View Name	Probable Use
V$AQ1	Advanced queuing
V$GCSPFMASTER_INFO	Unknown
V$HVMASTER_INFO	Unknown
V$LOGSTDBY	Logical standby databases
V$LOGSTDBY_APPLY	Logical standby databases
V$LOGSTDBY_STATS	Logical standby databases
V$MANAGED_STANDBY	Hot standby databases
V$MVREFRESH	Materialized views

TABLE 13-47.   *Fixed Views*

the Data Guard Concepts and Administration manual. Lastly, V$REPLQUEUE ,V$REPLPROP, and V$MVREFRESH are documented in the Replication Management API Reference manual.

> **NOTE**
> *See Appendixes B and C for detailed listings of all V$ views and X$ tables. There are 394 X$ tables in Oracle9.2. Appendix C lists all X$ tables along with all indexes. There is also a cross listing of X$ to V$ tables, and the X$ tables used in the V$ creation scripts are also detailed in Appendix C.*

Future Version Impact

As noted several times in this chapter, the V$ views and X$ tables are constantly being enhanced as more and more features are added to Oracle. Based on information obtained currently on Oracle version 8, the V$ views and X$ tables have changed from version 6. Performance of SELECTs on V$ views and X$ tables has improved as Oracle has added indexes (in V8) on the underlying X$ tables. More changes will certainly come in the future!

Tips Review

- When you mention the X$ tables, most people say "Ooh, pretty scary, I would never touch those tables." The fact is that DML commands (UPDATE, INSERT, DELETE) are not allowed on the X$ tables, even as the SYS superuser.

- Only the SYS superuser can SELECT from the X$ tables. An error occurs if an attempt is made to grant SELECT access to a user. A DBA may need access to the X$ table information, but *not* the SYS password. Create a view under a different name that mirrors the desired tables. Name these tables according to the appropriate synonyms of the original tables.

- Access the X$KQFVI table for a listing of all V$ and GV$ views.

- Access the V$FIXED_VIEW_DEFINITION view to obtain all of the information of the underlying X$ tables that make up a V$ view.

- Query V$FIXED_TABLE for the names of the X$ tables, or you may also access the two X$ tables X$KQFTA and X$KQFTD for partial listings which when combined make up the full list.

- Access the V$INDEXED_FIXED_COLUMN view for a listing of all X$TABLE indexes.

- Oracle generally uses the indexes and uses the correct driving table as needed for accessing the X$ tables, but from time to time, you may use hints to achieve a desired result.

References

Journey to the Center of the X$ tables; Joe Trezzo, TUSC
Oracle7 Server: SQL Language Reference Manual; Oracle Corporation

Oracle7 Server: Application Developer's Guide; Oracle Corporation
Get the Most out of Your Money: Utilize the v$ Tables; IOUG 1994, Joseph Trezzo
Monitoring Oracle Database: The Challenge; IOUG 1994, Eyal Aronoff & Noorali Sonawalla
Frank Naude's underground Oracle web page
Tony Jambu, Select Magazine column
Oracle Performance Tuning Tips & Techniques, by Rich Niemiec
Oracle8i Internal Services for Waits, Latches, Locks, and Memory, by Steve Adams
http://www.ixora.com.au (Oracle dump information)
http://www.orafaq.com/faqdbain.htm
Kevin Gilpin did the incredible job of updating this chapter. (Please read it quietly.)

Metalink Notes:

- 186859.995
- 1066346.6
- 153334.995
- 258597.999
- 235412.999
- 135223.1
- 221860.999
- 104933.1
- 83222.996
- 43600.1
- 129813.999
- 10630.996
- 86661.999
- 4256.997
- 2497.997
- 102925.1
- 95420.1
- 14848.997
- 235412.999

- 62172.1
- 135223.1
- 221860.999
- 83222.996
- 163424.1
- 104397.1
- 33883.1
- 346576.999
- 96845.1
- 73582.1
- 221860.999
- 212629.995
- 162866.1
- 138119.1
- 137483.1
- 186859.995
- 1066346.6
- 153334.995
- 258597.999

- 235412.999
- 135223.1
- 221860.999
- 104933.1
- 83222.996
- 43600.1
- 129813.999
- 10630.996
- 86661.999
- 4256.997
- 2497.997
- 102925.1
- 210375.995
- 39366.1
- 62294.1
- 187913.1
- 171647.1
- 39817.1

CHAPTER
14

Using STATSPACK
to Tune Waits and
Latches (Advanced DBA)

TIPS

COVERED

I f you could choose just two Oracle utilities to monitor and find performance problems of your system, those two utilities would be Enterprise Manager (Chapter 5) and STATSPACK (this chapter). In Oracle9*i* (as of Oracle 8.1.6), you can use the STATSPACK utility (available since Oracle 8.1.6) to monitor the performance of your database. STATSPACK replaces the UTLBSTAT/UTLESTAT scripts available with earlier versions of Oracle and offers several significant enhancements to those scripts. In this chapter, you will see how to install STATSPACK, how to manage it, and how to run and interpret the reports generated. STATSPACK includes data for both proactive and reactive tuning and is probably the best way to query most of the relevant V$ views and X$ tables and view the results in a single report.

The topics covered in this chapter include the following:

- Installing STATSPACK

- Interpreting the STATSPACK output

- Top 10 Things to Look for in STATSPACK output

Installing STATSPACK

STATSPACK must be installed in every database to be monitored. Prior to installing STATSPACK, you should create a tablespace to hold the STATSPACK data. During the installation process, you will be prompted for the name of the tablespace to hold the STATSPACK database objects. You should also designate a temporary tablespace that will be large enough to support the large inserts and deletes STATSPACK may perform.

The installation script, named spcreate.sql, is found in the /rdbms/admin subdirectory under the Oracle software home directory. The spcreate.sql script creates a user named PERFSTAT and creates a number of objects under that schema.

TIP
Allocate at least 100MB for the initial creation of the PERFSTAT schema's objects.

To start the spcreate.sql script, change your directory to the ORACLE_HOME/rdbms/admin directory and log in to SQL*Plus in an account with SYSDBA privileges:

```
SQL> connect system/manager as SYSDBA
SQL> @spcreate
```

During the installation process, you will be prompted for a default tablespace for the PERFSTAT user. (A list of available tablespaces will be displayed along with this prompt.) You will also be asked to specify a temporary tablespace for the user. Once you have provided a default and temporary tablespace for the PERFSTAT account, the account will be created and the installation script will log in as PERFSTAT and continue to create the required objects. If there is not sufficient space to create the PERFSTAT objects in the specified default tablespace, the script will return an error.

The spcreate.sql script calls for three scripts: spcusr.sql to create the user, spctab.sql to create the underlying tables, and spcpkg.sql to create the packages. When run, each of these scripts generates a listing file (spcusr.lis, etc.). Although you start the installation script while logged in as a SYSDBA-privileged user, the conclusion of the installation script will leave you logged in as the PERFSTAT user. If you want to drop the PERFSTAT user later, you can run the spdrop.sql script (which calls spdusr.sql and spdtab.sql) located in the ORACLE_HOME/rdbms/admin directory.

Security of the PERFSTAT Account

The spcusr.sql script creates the PERFSTAT account with the default password of PERFSTAT. The STATSPACK utility does not need to use the PERFSTAT default password; change the password after the installation process completes.

The HS_ADMIN_ROLE role is granted the SELECT_CATALOG_ROLE. The PERFSTAT use is granted several system privileges (CREATE/ALTER SESSION, CREATE TABLE, CREATE/DROP PUBLIC SYNONYM, CREATE SEQUENCE, and CREATE PROCEDURE). Any user who can access your PERFSTAT account can select from all of the dictionary views. For example, such a user could query all of the database account usernames from DBA_USERS, all the segment owners from DBA_SEGMENTS, and the currently logged in sessions from V$session. The PERFSTAT account, if left unprotected, provides a security hole that allows intruders to browse through your data dictionary and select targets for further intrusion.

In addition to the privileges it receives during the installation process, the PERFSTAT account will also have any privileges that have been granted to PUBLIC. If you use PUBLIC grants instead of roles for application privileges, you must secure the PERFSTAT account. You can lock database accounts and unlock them as needed. To lock the PERFSTAT account when you are not using STATSPACK, use the `alter user` command:

```
alter user PERFSTAT account lock;
```

When you need to gather statistics or access the STATSPACK data, you can unlock the account:

```
alter user PERFSTAT account unlock;
```

Post-Installation

Once the installation process is complete, the PERFSTAT account will own (in Oracle9*i*) 36 tables, 37 indexes, a sequence, and a package. You will use the package, named STATSPACK, to manage the statistics collection process and the data in the tables. The collection tables, whose names all begin with *STATS$,* will have column definitions based on the V$ view definitions. For example, the columns in STATS$WAITSTAT are the columns found in V$waitstat with three identification columns added at the top:

```
desc stats$waitstat

Name                          Null?    Type
----------------------------- -------- -----------
SNAP_ID                       NOT NULL NUMBER(6)
```

DBID	NOT NULL	NUMBER
INSTANCE_NUMBER	NOT NULL	NUMBER
CLASS	NOT NULL	VARCHAR2(18)
WAIT_COUNT		NUMBER
TIME		NUMBER

The CLASS, WAIT_COUNT, and TIME columns are based on the CLASS, COUNT, and TIME columns from V$waitstat. STATSPACK has added three identification columns:

Column	Definition
SNAP_ID	An identification number for the collection. Each collection is called a *snapshot* and is assigned an integer value.
DBID	A numeric identifier for the database.
INSTANCE_NUMBER	A numeric identifier for the instance, for Real Application Cluster installations.

TIP
Do not use both STATSPACK and UTLBSTAT/UTLESTAT in the same database. The UTLBSTAT/UTLESTAT scripts provided with earlier versions of Oracle also created a table named STATS$WAITSTAT, and you may encounter errors if you attempt to use both unless UTLESTAT is run as the PERFSTAT user.

Each collection you perform is given a new SNAP_ID value that is consistent across the collection tables. You will need to know the SNAP_ID values when executing the statistics report provided with STATSPACK.

Gathering Statistics

Each collection of statistics is called a *snapshot*. Snapshots of statistics have no relation to snapshots or materialized views used in replication. Rather, they are a point-in-time collection of the statistics available via the V$ views, and are given a SNAP_ID value to identify the snapshot. You can generate reports on the changes in the statistics between any two snapshots. This is a significant advantage over the UTLBSTAT/UTLESTAT reports available with prior releases of Oracle. With STATSPACK, you can collect as many snapshots as you need and then generate reports against any combination of them. As with the UTLBSTAT/UTLESTAT reports, the STATSPACK report will be valid only if the database was *not* shut down and restarted between the snapshots evaluated.

TIP
Be sure the TIMED_STATISTICS database initialization parameter is set to TRUE prior to gathering statistics.

To generate a snapshot of the statistics, execute the SNAP procedure of the STATSPACK package, as shown in Listing 14-1. You must be logged in as the PERFSTAT user to execute this procedure.

```
execute STATSPACK.SNAP;
PL/SQL procedure successfully completed.
```

Listing 14-1: Generating STATSPACK.SNAP

When you execute the SNAP procedure, Oracle populates your STATS$ tables with the current statistics. You can then query those tables directly, or you can use the standard STATSPACK report (to see the change in statistics between snapshots).

Snapshots should be taken in one of two ways:

■ To evaluate performance during specific tests of the system. For these tests, you can execute the SNAP procedure manually, as shown in the prior example.

■ To evaluate performance changes over a long period of time. To establish a baseline of the system performance, you may generate statistics snapshots on a scheduled basis. For these snapshots, you should schedule the SNAP procedure execution via Oracle's internal DBMS_JOB scheduler or via an operating system scheduler.

For the snapshots related to specific tests, you may wish to increase the collection level, which lets you gather more statistics. As noted in the "Managing the STATSPACK Data" section later in this chapter, each snapshot has a cost in terms of space usage and query performance. For example, because V$sysstat has 255 rows (in Oracle 9.0.1 on NT), every snapshot generates 255 rows (232 on Windows) in STATS$SYSSTAT. Avoid generating thousands of rows of statistical data with each snapshot unless you plan to use them.

To support differing collection levels, STATSPACK provides a level parameter. By default, the level value is set to 5. Prior to changing the level value, generate several snapshots and evaluate the reports generated. The default level value is adequate for most reports. Table 14-1 lists alternative level values.

Level	Description
0 to 4	General performance statistics on all memory areas, latches, pools, and events, and segment statistics, such as rollback and undo segments.
5	Same statistics from the lower levels, plus the most resource-intensive SQL statements.
6 to 9	Introduced in Oracle 9.0.1; level 6 includes the level 5 results plus SQL plans.
10 and greater	Same statistics from level 6 plus parent/child latch data.

TABLE 14-1.   *Alternative Level Values*

Gathering Statistics

The greater the collection level, the longer the snapshot will take. The default value (5) offers a significant degree of flexibility during the queries for the most resource-intensive SQL statements. The parameters used for the resource-intensive SQL portion of the snapshot are stored in a table named STATS$STATSPACK_PARAMETER. You can query STATS$STATSPACK_PARAMETER to see the settings for the different thresholds during the SQL statement gathering. Its columns include SNAP_LEVEL (the snapshot level), EXECUTIONS_TH (the threshold value for the number of executions), DISK_READS_TH (the threshold value for the number of disk reads), and BUFFER_GETS_TH (the threshold value for the number of disk reads).

For a level 5 snapshot using the default thresholds, SQL statements are stored if they meet any of the following criteria:

- The SQL statement has been executed at least 100 times.

- The number of disk reads performed by the SQL statement exceeds 1000.

- The number of parse calls performed by the SQL statement exceeds 1000.

- The number of buffer gets performed by the SQL statement exceeds 10,000.

- The sharable memory used by the SQL statement exceeds 1MB.

- The version count for the SQL statement exceeds 20.

When evaluating the snapshot's data and the performance report, keep in mind that the SQL threshold parameter values are cumulative. A very efficient query, if executed enough times, will exceed 10,000 buffer gets. Compare the number of buffer gets and disk reads to the number of executions to determine the activity each time the query is executed.

To modify the default settings for the thresholds, use the MODIFY_STATSPACK_PARAMETER procedure of the STATSPACK package. Specify the snapshot level via the I_SNAP_LEVEL parameter, along with the parameters to change. Table 16-2 lists the available parameters for the MODIFY_STATSPACK_PARAMETER procedure.

To increase the Buffer_Gets threshold for a level 5 snapshot to 100,000, issue the following command:

```
EXECUTE STATSPACK.MODIFY_STATSPACK_PARAMETER -
  (i_snap_level=>5, i_buffer_gets_th=>100000, -
  i_modify_parameter=>'true');
```

If you plan to run the SNAP procedure on a scheduled basis, you should pin the STATSPACK package following database startup. Listing 14-2 shows a trigger that will be executed each time the database is started. The KEEP procedure of the DBMS_SHARED_POOL package pins the STATSPACK package in the shared pool. As an alternative to pinning, you can use the SHARED_POOL_RESERVED_SIZE initialization parameter to reserve shared pool area for large packages.

Parameter Name	Range of Values	Default	Description
I_SNAP_LEVEL	0, 5, 6, 10	5	Snapshot level
I_UCOMMENT	Any text	blank	Comment for the snapshot
I_EXECUTIONS_TH	Integer >= 0	100	Threshold for the cumulative number of executions
I_DISK_READS_TH	Integer >= 0	1000	Threshold for the cumulative number of disk reads
I_PARSE_CALLS_TH	Integer >= 0	1000	Threshold for the cumulative number of parse calls
I_BUFFER_GETS_TH	Integer >= 0	10000	Threshold for the cumulative number of buffer gets
I_SHARABLE_MEM_TH	Integer >= 0	1048576	Threshold for the amount of sharable memory allocated
I_VERSION_COUNT_TH	Integer >= 0	20	Threshold for the number of versions of the SQL statement
I_SESSION_ID	Valid SID from V$session	0	Session ID of an Oracle session, if you wish to gather session-level statistics
I_MODIFY_PARAMETER	TRUE or FALSE	FALSE	Set to TRUE if you wish to save your changes for future snapshots

TABLE 14-2. *Modification Parameters*

```
create or replace trigger PIN_ON_STARTUP
after startup on database
begin
   DBMS_SHARED_POOL.KEEP ('PERFSTAT.STATSPACK', 'P');
end;
/
```

Listing 14-2: Creating a trigger on database startup

TIP
Pin the STATSPACK package following database startup if you plan to run the SNAP procedure on a scheduled basis.

Gathering Statistics

Running the Statistics Report

If you have generated more than one snapshot, you can report on the statistics for the period between the two snapshots. The database must not have been shut down between the times the two snapshots were taken. When you execute the report, you will need to know the SNAP_ID values for the snapshots. If you run the report interactively, Oracle will provide a list of the available snapshots and the times they were created.

To execute the report, go to the /rdbms/admin directory under the Oracle software home directory. Log in to SQL*Plus as the PERFSTAT user and run the spreport.sql file found there:

```
SQL> @ORACLE_HOME/rdbms/admin/spreport
```

Oracle displays the database and instance identification information from V$instance and V$database and then calls a second SQL file, sprepins.sql.

The sprepins.sql script generates the report of the changes in the statistics during the snapshot time interval. The available snapshots will be listed, and you will be prompted to enter a beginning and ending snapshot ID. Unless you specify otherwise, the output will be written to a file named sp_*beginning_ending*.lst (sp_1_2.lst for a report between SNAP_ID values of 1 and 2).

TIP
You can use a second report, sprepsql.sql, for additional research into the problem SQL statements identified via the spreport.sql report.

Interpreting the STATSPACK Output

Several sections are included in a STATSPACK output report. We'll cover each of the main sections and information on what to look for and how to move forward based on information that appears to be a problem. Most information must be combined with additional research to solve an issue and lead to an optimal system.

The Header Information

The first section of the report includes information about the database itself, including information on the database name, ID, release number, and host. Following this information is information on when the snapshot was started and ended and how many sessions were active. Generally, a STATSPACK report should cover at least an hour of time and should be strategically timed to measure periods of time that are problematic. You may also want to look at an entire day so that you can compare days over a period time. The cache sizes section shows the values of the Buffer Cache (DB_CACHE_SIZE in the initialization file), Shared Pool Size (SHARED_POOL_SIZE), Std Block Size (DB_BLOCK_SIZE), and the Log Buffer (LOG_BUFFER). An example of the header information is displayed in Listing 14-3.

DB Name	DB Id	Instance	Inst Num	Release	Cluster	Host
ORA9I	2249715753	ora9i	1	9.0.1.1.1	NO	RJNMOBILE

	Snap Id	Snap Time	Sessions
Begin Snap:	280	12-Jul-02 23:00:05	10
End Snap:	281	13-Jul-02 06:00:01	10
Elapsed:		419.93 (mins)	

Cache Sizes (end)			
Buffer Cache:	160M	Std Block Size:	8K
Shared Pool Size:	64M	Log Buffer:	512K

Listing 14-3: STATSPACK report header information

The Load Profile

The next portion of the report output, following the basic information, provides per-second and per-transaction statistics of the load profile. This is an excellent section to monitor throughput and load variations on your system. As the load on the system increases, you will see larger numbers for per second. As you tune the system for maximum efficiency, you will usually receive lower numbers for the per transaction statistic. Listing 14-4 shows sample output for the load profile section.

Load Profile	Per Second	Per Transaction
Redo size:	97,586.68	3,134.84
Logical reads:	11,667.83	374.81
Block changes:	565.40	18.16
Physical reads:	552.02	17.73
Physical writes:	59.03	1.90
User calls:	948.91	30.48
Parses:	56.54	1.82
Hard parses:	1.56	0.05
Sorts:	38.11	1.22
Logons:	0.01	0.00
Executes:	691.24	22.21
Transactions:	31.13	

% Blocks changed per Read:	4.85	Recursive Call %:	13.13
Rollback per transaction %:	2.28	Rows per Sort:	11.09

Listing 14-4: Load profile section sample output

The load profile helps to identify both the load and type of activity being performed. In this example, the activity recorded included a large amount of both logical and physical activity.

Look for the following clues in the load profile:

■ An increase in redo size, block changes, and % Blocks changed per Read indicates increased DML (insert/update/delete) activity.

■ A hard parse occurs when a SQL statement is executed and is *not* currently in the shared pool. A hard parse rate greater than 100/second could indicate that bind variables are not being used effectively, the CURSOR_SHARING initialization parameter should be used, or there is a shared pool sizing problem. (See Chapter 4 on sizing the shared pool for a detailed discussion related to this.)

■ A soft parse occurs when a SQL statement is executed and it *is* currently in the shared pool. A soft parse rate greater than 300/second could indicate program inefficiencies where statements are being parsed over and over again instead of the program efficiently parsing the statement only once per session.

TIP
Get to know your system by reviewing and knowing the regular Load Profile of your system. Significant changes to the Load Profile during what should be similar workloads or common times during the day may warrant further investigation.

Instance Efficiency

The Instance Efficiency section shows information for many of the common hit ratios. DBAs generally measure these so they can be alerted of significant changes in system behavior when compared historically. Hit ratios (when managed regularly) are a great way to be alerted of potential problems or potential wastes that should be addressed before becoming serious problems. Waits are another common way to see the problem, usually after it has become a larger issue.

Monitoring hit ratios is just one part of the thousands of pieces of your tuning arsenal. The reason so many tuning tips are provided is that in writing about tuning, I am writing about all of the turns the optimizer will make. Although I don't believe you could capture it all in a book (you'd be *un*-writing the hardest part of Oracle—the optimizer), I do believe this compilation helps solve many tuning problems. Some DBAs reduce the importance of hit ratios (proactive tuning) and focus completely on waits (reactive tuning), because focusing on waits is a great way to quickly solve the current burning problems. By monitoring the Instance Efficiency section (and using all of STATSPACK and Enterprise Manager), the DBA moves from reactive to proactive tuning and experiences less burning problems. Hit ratios are one important piece of the puzzle (as are waits). Listing 14-5 shows how well this STATSPACK section reveals all of the common hit ratios at once.

```
Instance Efficiency Percentages (Target 100%)
~~~~~~~~~~~~~~~~~~~~~~~~~~~~~~~~~~~~~~~~~~~~~~~~
            Buffer Nowait %:   99.99      Redo NoWait %:  100.00
            Buffer  Hit   %:   95.27   In-memory Sort %:  100.00
            Library Hit   %:   99.67       Soft Parse %:   97.24
         Execute to Parse %:   91.82        Latch Hit %:   99.60
Parse CPU to Parse Elapsd %:   73.48     % Non-Parse CPU:   99.82
```

Listing 14-5: Viewing all common hit ratios

Look for these things:

- **A Buffer NoWait % of less than 99 percent.**   This is the ratio of hits on a request for a specific buffer, where the buffer was immediately available in memory. If the ratio is low, there is a (hot) block(s) being contended for that should be found in the Buffer Wait section.

- **A Buffer Hit % of less than 95 percent.**   This is the ratio of hits on a request for a specific buffer, and the buffer was in memory instead of needing to do a physical I/O. Although originally one of the few methods of measuring memory efficiency, it is still an excellent method for showing how often you need to do a physical I/O, which merits further investigation as to the cause. Unfortunately, if you have unselective indexes that are frequently accessed, it will drive your hit ratio higher, which can be a misleading indication of good performance. When you effectively tune your SQL and have effective indexes on your entire system, this issue is not encountered as frequently and the hit ratio is a better performance indicator.

- **A Library Hit % of less than 95 percent.**   A lower library hit ratio usually indicates that SQL is being pushed out of the shared pool early (could be due to a shared pool that is too small). A lower ratio could also indicate that bind variables are not used or some other issue is causing SQL not to be reused (in which case, a smaller shared pool may be only a band-aid that will potentially fix a library latch problem that may result). You must fix the problem (use bind variables or CURSOR_SHARING) and then appropriately size the shared pool.

- **An In-Memory Sort % of less than 95 percent in OLTP.**   In an OLTP system, you really don't want to do disk sorts. Setting the PGA_AGGREGATE_TARGET (or SORT_AREA_SIZE) initialization parameter effectively eliminates this problem.

- **A Soft Parse % of less than 95 percent.**   As covered in the Load Profile section (last section), a soft parse ratio that is below around 80 percent indicates that SQL is not being reused and needs to be investigated.

- **A Latch Hit % of less than 99 percent is usually a big problem.**   Finding the specific latch leads you to solving this issue. I will cover this in detail in the "Top Wait Events" section.

If you regularly run STATSPACK, comparing hit ratios from one day to another can be a great barometer as to whether something drastic has changed. If an index was dropped on a frequently accessed column, the buffer hit ratio could drop greatly, giving you an indication to investigate. If an index was added to a table, it could cause the buffer hit ratio to soar if it causes a table join to occur in the wrong order, causing massive buffers to be read. A library hit ratio that rises or falls greatly from one day to the next will give you indications of changing SQL patterns. Latch hit ratio changes can reveal contention issues that need to be investigated more. Hit ratios can be a very proactive tool for a DBA who regularly monitors and understands a given production system, whereas many of the other tuning tools are reactive to problems that have already occurred.

TIP
Hit ratios are a great barometer of your system's health. A large increase or drop from day to day is an indicator of a major change that needs to be investigated. Investigating waits is like investigating an accident that has already occurred, whereas investigating a change in hit ratios is like looking into the intersection with a changing traffic pattern that may cause an accident in the future if something is not adjusted. Generally, buffer and library cache hit ratios should be greater than 95 percent for OLTP, but could be lower for a data warehouse that may do many full tablescans.

It is also important to remember that a system with very high ratios in this section of the report may still have performance problems. As just described, a poorly written query can cause volumes of index searches to join to other indexes, causing a high hit ratio (with lots of buffer gets), which is not good in this case. The database is doing most of its work in memory, but it shouldn't be doing so much work. Good hit ratios don't show the whole picture either. There are always cases where the database is working very efficiently, but this report shows only the database operations, not the application operations, server actions, or networking issues that also impact the performance of the application.

The Shared Pool statistics that follow the Instance Efficiency section show the percentage of the shared pool in use and the percentage of SQL statements that have been executed multiple times (as desired). Combining this data with the library, parse and latch data will help you to size the shared pool. Listing 14-6 shows sample shared pool statistics from the report.

Shared Pool Statistics	Begin	End
Memory Usage %:	28.37	29.17
% SQL with executions>1:	27.77	30.45
% Memory for SQL w/exec>1:	56.64	67.74

Listing 14-6: Sample shared pool statistics

Based on the data in the preceding listing, at the time of the second snapshot, 29.17 percent of the shared pool's memory was in use. Of the statements in the shared pool, only 30 percent had been executed more than once, indicating a potential need to improve cursor sharing in the application. The section of the report showing the percentage of shared pool memory in use is new with the Oracle9*i* version of STATSPACK.

Top Wait Events

This section of STATSPACK is probably the most revealing section in the entire report when you are trying to quickly eliminate bottlenecks on your system. This section of the report shows the top five wait events, the full list of wait events, and the background wait events. Identifying major wait events may help to target your tuning efforts to the most burning issues on your system. If TIMED_STATISTICS is TRUE, then the events are ordered in time waited; if FALSE, then the events are ordered by the number of waits. (In testing on NT, this was still ordered by wait time.)

For example, Listing 14-7 shows the top 5 wait events for a report interval.

```
Top 5 Wait Events
~~~~~~~~~~~~~~~~~~
                                                    Wait      % Total
Event                                  Waits     Time (cs)    Wt Time
-------------------------------------  --------  -----------  -------
SQL.NET data to client                    499          12      37.50
log buffer space                            2          11      34.38
log file sync                               1           5      15.63
db file sequential read                     1           3       9.38
control file sequential read               30           1       3.13
```

Listing 14-7: Top 5 wait events

In this example, none of the wait events has accounted for significant wait time, but there are some potential issues. The SQL*Net more data to client event is occurring because of the size of the data being requested by application users. If you can reduce the amount of data sent to the users, you can eliminate many of these waits. The log file sync event occurs with each commit, so you may need to alter your application's commit frequency if this wait event impacts your database performance. Although this listing does not show any major problems, Listing 14-8 depicts what you would more likely see on a high-volume system experiencing some problems.

```
Top 5 Wait Events
~~~~~~~~~~~~~~~~~~
                                                     Wait      % Total
Event                                  Waits      Time (cs)    Wt Time
-------------------------------------  -----------  -----------  -------
db file sequential read                18,977,104   22,379,571   82.29
latch free                              4,016,773    2,598,496    9.55
log file sync                           1,057,224      733,490    2.70
log file parallel write                 1,054,006      503,695    1.85
db file parallel write                  1,221,755      404,230    1.49
```

Listing 14-8: Problems on a high-volume system

In this listing, we see a large number of waits related to reading a single block (db file sequential reads) and also waits for latches (latch free). We also see some pretty high waits for some of the writing to both datafiles and log files, as well as other potential issues with log file contention. To solve these issues (identify which ones are truly major issues), we must narrow them down by investigating the granular reports within other sections of STATSPACK.

In Listing 14-9, we see a sample listing of waits on this very intense system. After the listing, we will investigate some of the common events that cause problems. This is only a partial listing, but I've included many of the most common problems.

```
                                                                   Avg
                                                     Total Wait   wait    Waits
Event                       Waits      Timeouts     Time (cs)     (ms)    /txn
--------------------------  -----------  ----------  -----------  ------  ------
db file sequential read     18,977,104           0   22,379,571      12    17.4
latch free                   4,016,773   2,454,622    2,598,496       6     3.7
log file sync                1,057,224          10      733,490       7     1.0
enqueue                         90,140       1,723       67,611       8     0.1
library cache pin                3,062           0       29,272      96     0.0
db file scattered read          21,110           0       26,313      12     0.0
```

buffer busy waits	29,640	2	22,739	8	0.0
log file sequential read	31,061	0	18,372	6	0.0
row cache lock	22,402	0	3,250	1	0.0
LGWR wait for redo copy	4,436	45	183	0	0.0
SQL*Net more data to client	15,937	0	156	0	0.0
file identify	125	0	12	1	0.0
wait for inquiry response	76	0	10	1	0.0
SQL*Net message to client	35,427,781	0	6,599	0	32.5

Listing 14-9: Waits on high-volume system

Here are some of the most common problems. This section is very important and worth its weight in gold!

■ **DB file scattered read** This generally indicates waits related to full tablescans. As full tablescans are pulled into memory, they are scattered throughout the buffer cache because it is usually unlikely that they fall into contiguous buffers. A large number indicates that indexes may be missing or suppressed. This could also be preferred because it may be more efficient to perform a full tablescan than an index scan. Check to ensure full tablescans are necessary when you see these waits. Try to cache small tables to avoid reading them in over and over again.

■ **DB file sequential read** This generally indicates a single block read (an index read, for example). A large number could indicate poor joining orders of tables or unselective indexing. This number will certainly be large (normally) for a high-transaction, well-tuned system. You should correlate this wait with other known issues within the STATSPACK report, such as inefficient SQL. Check to ensure index scans are necessary and check join orders for multiple table joins. The DB_CACHE_SIZE is also a determining factor in how often these waits show up; hash-area joins causing problems should show up in the PGA memory, but they are memory hogs that could cause high wait numbers for sequential reads or they can also show up as direct path read/write waits.

■ **Buffer busy wait** This is a wait for a buffer that is being used in an unshareable way or is being read into the buffer cache. Buffer busy waits should not be greater than 1 percent. Check the buffer wait statistics section (or V$waitstat) to find out if the wait is on a segment header. If so, increase the freelists and/or groups or increase the pctused to pctfree gap. (If you are using ASSM, Oracle does this for you by using bitmap freelists. This also removes the need to set pct_used.) If the wait is on an undo header, you can address this by adding rollback segments; if it's on an undo block, you need to reduce the data density on the table driving this consistent read or increase the DB_CACHE_SIZE. If the wait is on a data block, you can move data to another block to avoid this hot block, increase the freelists on the table, or use Locally Managed Tablespaces (LMTs). If it's on an index block, you should rebuild the index, partition the index, or use a reverse key index. To prevent buffer busy waits related to data blocks, you can also use a smaller block size: fewer records fall within a single block in this case, so it's not as "hot." When a DML (insert/update/delete) occurs, Oracle Database writes information into the block, including all users who are interested in the state of the block (Interested Transaction List (ITL)). To decrease waits in this area, you can increase the initrans, which will create the space in the block to allow multiple ITL slots. You can also increase the pctfree on the table where this block exists.

(This writes the ITL information up to the number of specified by maxtrans, when there are not enough slots built with the specified initrans.)

■ **Latch free**   Latches are low-level queueing mechanisms (they're accurately referred to as mutual exclusion mechanisms) used to protect shared memory structures in the System Global Area (SGA). Latches are like locks on memory that are very quickly obtained and released. Latches are used to prevent concurrent access to a shared memory structure. If the latch is not available, a latch free miss is recorded. Most latch problems are related to the failure to use bind variables (library cache latch), redo generation issues (redo allocation latch), buffer cache contention issues (cache buffers lru chain), and hot blocks in the buffer cache (cache buffers chain). There are also latch waits related to bugs; check Metalink for bug reports if you suspect this is the case (oracle.com/support). When latch miss ratios are greater than 0.5 percent, you should investigate the issue.

■ **Enqueue**   An *enqueue* is a lock that protects a shared resource. Locks protect shared resources such as data in a record, to prevent two people from updating the same data at the same time. It includes a queueing mechanism, which is first in, first out (FIFO). Note that Oracle's latching mechanism is not FIFO. Enqueue waits usually point to the *ST* enqueue, *HW* enqueue, and the *TX4* enqueue. The ST enqueue is used for space management and allocation for dictionary-managed tablespaces. Use LMTs, or try to preallocate extents or at least make the next extent larger for problematic dictionary-managed tablespaces. HW enqueues are used with the high water mark of a segment; manually allocating the extents can circumvent this wait. TX4 are the most common enqueue waits. TX4 enqueue waits are usually the result of one of three issues. The first issue is duplicates in a unique index; you need to commit/rollback to free the enqueue. The second is multiple updates to the same bitmap index fragment. Because a single bitmap fragment may contain multiple ROWIDS, you need to issue a commit or rollback to free the enqueue when multiple users are trying to update the same fragment. The third and most likely issue is when multiple users are updating the same block. If there are no free ITL slots, a block level lock could occur. You can easily avoid this scenario by increasing the initrans and/or maxtrans to allow multiple ITL slots and/or by increasing the pctfree on the table. Finally, there is a way to get TM locks, which are table locks. If you have foreign keys, be sure to index them to avoid this general locking issue. You could also use a smaller block size so that there are fewer rows in the block; thus, greater concurrency on the data is allowed.

■ **Logfile switch**   All commit requests are waiting for logfile switch (archiving needed) or logfile switch (chkpt. Incomplete). Ensure that the archive disk is not full or slow. DBWR may be too slow due to I/O. You may need to add more or larger redo logs, and you may potentially need to add database writers if the DBWR is the problem.

■ **Log buffer space**   This wait occurs because you are writing the log buffer faster than LGWR can write it to the redo logs, or because log switches are too slow. To address this problem, increase the size of the log files, increase the size of the log buffer, or get faster disks to write to. You might even consider using solid-state disks for their high speed.

■ **Log file sync**   When a user commits or rolls back data, the session's redo is flushed to the Redo Logs from the Log Buffer by LGWR. The user's process must wait for this flush to successfully complete. To reduce Log File Sync waits, try to commit more records. (Try to commit a batch of 50 instead of one at a time if possible.) Put Redo Logs on a faster disk or alternate Redo Logs on different physical disks to reduce the archiving effect on LGWR. Don't use RAID 5 because it is very slow for applications that write a lot; potentially consider using file system direct I/O or raw devices, which are very fast at writing information.

■ **Idle events** There are also several idle wait events in Listing 14-9 that can be ignored. Idle events are generally listed at the bottom of each section and include things like SQL*Net message to/from client and other background-related timings. Idle events are listed in the STATS$IDLE_EVENT table.

Wait Problem	Potential Fibx
Sequential read	Indicates many index reads. Tune the code (especially joins).
Scattered read	Indicates many full tablescans. Tune the code; cache small tables.
Free buffer	Increase the DB_CACHE_SIZE; shorten the checkpoint; tune the code.
Buffer busy – Segment Header	Add freelists or freelist groups.
Buffer busy – Data Block	Separate "hot" data; use reverse key indexes; smaller blocks. OR Increase initrans and/or maxtrans.
Buffer busy – Undo Header	Add rollback segments or areas.
Buffer busy – Undo Block	Commit more; larger rollback segments or areas.
Latch free	Investigate the detail.
Enqueue – ST	Use LMTs or preallocate large extents.
Enqueue – HW	Preallocate extents above high water mark.
Enqueue – TX	Increase initrans and/or maxtrans on the table or index.
Enqueue – TM	Index foreign keys; check application locking of tables.
Log buffer space	Increase the Log Buffer; faster disks for the Redo Logs.
Log file switch	Archive destination slow or full; add more or larger Redo Logs.
Log file sync	Commit more records at a time; faster Redo Log disks; raw devices.
Write complete waits	Add database writers; checkpoint more often; buffer cache too small.
Idle event	Ignore it.

Listing 14-10 is a partial listing of waits.

Event	Waits	Timeouts	Total Wait Time (cs)	Avg wait (ms)	Waits /txn
log file parallel write	1,054,094	92	503,743	5	1.0
db file parallel write	1,221,839	0	404,260	3	1.1
latch free	103,364	41,184	34,398	3	0.1
log file sequential read	31,061	0	18,372	6	0.0
control file parallel write	12,250	0	3,188	3	0.0
enqueue	21,025	37	2,165	1	0.0
db file scattered read	589	0	959	16	0.0
db file sequential read	174	0	207	12	0.0
pmon timer	15,288	10,782	3,498,255	2288	0.0
lock manager wait for remote	2,739,586	535,444	3,401,939	12	2.5

Listing 14-10: Partial listing of waits

The following list shows common idle events (type of idle event):

- Dispatcher timer (shared server idle event)

- Listen endpoint status (waiting for registration or unregistration to complete)

- Lock manager wait for remote message (RAC idle event)

- Pipe get (user process idle event)

- pmon timer (background process idle event)

- PX Idle Wait: (parallel query idle event)

- PX Deq: need buffer (parallel query idle event)

- PX Deq: execute msg (parallel query idle event)

- rdbms ipc message (background process idle event)

- smon timer (background process idle event)

- SQL*Net message from client (user process idle event)

- Virtual Circuit status (shared server idle event)

TIP
The top 5 wait events reveal to you the largest issues on your system at the macro level. Rarely do they point you to a specific problem. Other parts of STATSPACK will tell you why you are receiving the top 5 waits.

Interpreting the STATSPACK Output

Here is a nice breakdown of the life of an Oracle shadow process. This comes from Oracle Doc ID: 61998 and provides nice insight about what's happening in less than 1 second with Oracle.

State	Notes
IDLE	Waiting for SQL*Net message from client (waiting for the user). Receives the SQL*Net packet requesting parse/execute of a statement.
ON CPU	Decodes the SQL*Net packet.
WAITING	Waits for latch free to obtain the library cache latch. Gets the library cache latch.
ON CPU	Scans the shared pool for the SQL statement, finds match, frees latch. Sets up links to the shared cursor, etc. and begins to execute.
WAITING	Waits for db file sequential read; we need a block not in the cache (wait for I/O).
ON CPU	Block read from disk complete. Execution continues. Construct SQL*Net packet with first row of data to send to client and sends.
WAITING	Waits on SQL*Net message from client for acknowledgment packet received.
IDLE	Waits for next SQL*Net message from client.

Top SQL Statements

The most resource-intensive SQL statements in the database are listed next, in descending order of buffer gets. Because the buffer gets statistic is cumulative, the query with the most buffer gets may not be the worst performing query in the database; it may just have been executed enough times to earn the highest ranking. Compare the cumulative number of buffer gets to the cumulative number of disk reads for the queries; if the numbers are close, then you should evaluate the EXPLAIN PLAN for the query to find out why it is performing so many disk reads. If the disk reads are not high, but the buffer gets are high and the executions are low, then the query is either using a bad index or performing a join in the wrong order. This is also a problem for your system because you would be using a lot of your memory unnecessarily. Listing 14-11 shows an example.

```
SQL ordered by Gets for DB
-> End Buffer Gets Threshold:    10000
-> Note that resources reported for PL/SQL includes the resources used by
   all SQL statements called within the PL/SQL code. As individual SQL
   statements are also reported, it is possible and valid for the summed
   total % to exceed 100
  Buffer Gets     Executions   Gets per Exec   % Total   Hash Value
--------------- ------------- --------------- ------- ------------
   166,697,520         6,514        25,590.7     2.5   1577170159

SELECT DISTINCT USERNAME    FROM USER_TEST A, SALES B,CUSTOMER C
```

```
WHERE A.USERNAME_TYPE = :b1  AND A.ITEMNO = :b2 C.NAME =
A.NAME  AND B.TYPE = C.TYPE  AND NVL(C.STARTDATE,'31-DEC-2002')
> :b3 ORDER BY NAME
     101,306,038        6,510      15,561.6    1.5   613844091
SELECT A.ITEMNO, B.LINEITEM, C.LINEITEM_AMT FROM LINES A, LINE_ITEMS B,
LINE_ORDERS C WHERE A.LINENO = B.LINENO AND A.LINENO = C.LINENO AND
A.ORDERDATE = '31-DEC-2002' AND B.TYPE = 'CURRENT' ORDER BY CUSTOMERNO
```

Listing 14-11: Low disk reads but high buffer gets and low executions

After listing the SQL commands with the most cumulative buffer gets, a second listing of the commands is provided, this time ordered by the greatest number of physical reads. A third listing of commands orders the executions and then a fourth orders by parse calls. As part of these sections, you may also see the internal Oracle data dictionary operations listed. Your application commands commonly account for the majority of the buffer gets and disk reads performed by the database. If the shared pool is flushed between the execution times of the two snapshots, the SQL portion of the output report will not necessarily contain the most resource-intensive SQL executed during the period.

TIP
Tuning the top 25 buffer get and top 25 physical get queries has yielded system performance gains of anywhere from 5 percent to 5000 percent. The SQL section of the STATSPACK report tells you which queries to potentially tune first. The top 10 percent of your SQL statements should not be more than 10 percent of your buffer gets or disk reads.

Instance Activity Statistics

Following the SQL statement listing, you will see the list of changes to statistics from V$sysstat, entitled "Instance Activity Stats." The V$sysstat statistics are useful for identifying performance issues not shown in the prior sections. Listing 14-12 is a partial listing with some of the key sections shown.

Instance Activity Stats Statistic	Total	per Second	per Trans
CPU used by this session	3,876,875	110.8	3.6
DBWR buffers scanned	6,775,741	193.6	6.2
consistent gets	366,674,801	10,476.4	336.5
db block changes	19,788,834	565.4	18.2
db block gets	41,812,892	1,194.7	38.4
dirty buffers inspected	1,204,544	34.4	1.1
enqueue waits	87,613	2.5	0.1
free buffer requested	20,053,136	573.0	18.4
index fast full scans (full)	28,686	0.8	0.0
leaf node splits	21,066	0.6	0.0

Top SQL Statements

logons cumulative	186	0.0	0.0
parse count (hard)	54,681	1.6	0.1
parse count (total)	1,978,732	56.5	1.8
physical reads	19,320,574	552.0	17.7
physical writes non checkpoint	2,027,920	57.9	1.9
recursive calls	5,020,246	143.4	4.6
sorts (disk)	2	0.0	0.0
sorts (memory)	1,333,831	38.1	1.2
sorts (rows)	14,794,401	422.7	13.6

Listing 14-12: Instance Activity Stats

Things to look for:

Compare the number of sorts performed on disk to the number performed in memory; increase the PGA_AGGREGATE_TARGET (or sort area size) to reduce disk sorts. (See Chapter 4 for more information.) If physical reads are high, you are probably performing full tablescans. If there is a significant number of full tablescans of large tables, evaluate the most-used queries and try to reduce this inefficiency by using indexes. A large number for consistent gets signals potentially overindexed or nonselective index use. If dirty buffers inspected is high (over 5 percent) relative to free buffers requested, the DB_CACHE_SIZE may be too small or you may not be checkpointing often enough. If leaf node splits are high, consider rebuilding indexes that have grown and fragmented. The following sections will look at a few of these scenarios.

Listing 14-13 shows the four applicable rows from this section of the report.

Statistic	Total	per Second	per Trans
sorts (disk)	89	0.3	44.5
sorts (rows)	7,659	26.1	3,829.5
table scans (long tables)	0	0.0	0.0
table scans (short tables)	10	0.0	5.0

Listing 14-13: Sort and table scan statistics

In this example, the database performed 89 sorts on disk during the reporting interval. Of the tablescans performed, all were of very small tables. In the high volume example in Listing 14-14, we see a well-tuned memory-sorting area where almost 15 million records were sorted in memory, whereas only 2 sorts were done on disk.

Statistic	Total	per Second	per Trans
sorts (disk)	2	0.0	0.0
sorts (memory)	1,333,831	38.1	1.2
sorts (rows)	14,794,401	422.7	13.6

Listing 14-14: Well-tuned memory-sorting area

TIP
If many sorts are being performed to disk (greater than 1–5 percent of the total number of rows being sorted), you may need to increase the initialization parameters associated with sorting. See Chapter 4 for more information on these.

Consider these key areas:

■ **Consistent gets**   The number of blocks accessed in the buffer cache for queries without the SELECT FOR UPDATE clause. The value for this statistic plus the value of the db block gets statistic constitute what is referred to as a logical read.

■ **DB block gets**   The number of blocks in the buffer cache that were accessed for INSERT, UPDATE, DELETE, or SELECT FOR UPDATE statements.

■ **Physical reads**   The number of data blocks that were read from disks to satisfy SELECT, SELECT FOR UPDATE, INSERT, UPDATE, or DELETE statements.

By adding the consistent gets and db block gets, you get the number of Logical Reads (memory reads). Using the following equation, you can calculate the Data Cache Hit Ratio.

```
Hit Ratio = (Logical Reads - Physical Reads) / Logical Reads
```

TIP
The buffer hit ratio should be above 95 percent. If it is less than 95 percent, you should consider increasing the size of the data cache by increasing the DB_CACHE_SIZE initialization parameter (given that physical memory is available to do this).

■ **Dirty buffers inspected**   The number of dirty (modified) data buffers that were aged out on the LRU list. A value here indicates that the DBWR is not keeping up. You may benefit by adding more DBWRs.

TIP
If the number of dirty buffers inspected is greater than zero, consider increasing the database writers as detailed in Chapter 3.

■ **Enqueue timeouts**   The number of times an enqueue (lock) was requested and the specific one that was requested was not available. If this statistic is above zero, investigate the locking issues.

■ **Free buffers inspected**   The buffers that were skipped because they were dirty, pinned, or busy. If you subtract those values (dirty buffers inspected and buffer is pinned count)

Top SQL Statements

from this statistic, it will leave the buffers that could not be reused due to latch contention. A large number would be a good indicator of a buffer cache that is too small.

- **Parse count**   The number of times a SQL statement was parsed (total count).

- **Recursive calls**   The number of recursive calls to the database. This type of call occurs for a few reasons—misses in the dictionary cache, dynamic storage extension, and when PL/SQL statements are executed. Generally, if the number of recursive calls is more than four per process, you should check the dictionary cache hit ratio and see if there are tables or indexes with a large number of extents. Unless there is a significant use of PL/SQL, the ratio of recursive calls to user calls should be 10 percent or less.

- **Redo size**   The size in bytes of the amount of redo information that was written to the redo logs. This information can be used to help size the redo logs. Chapter 3 contains additional information for redo sizing.

- **Sorts (disk)**   The number of sorts that were unable to be performed in memory and therefore required the creation of a temp segment in the temporary tablespace. This statistic divided by the sorts (memory) should not be above 5 percent. If it is, you should increase the SORT_AREA_SIZE or PGA_AGGREGATE_TARGET parameter in the init.ora.

- **Sorts (memory)**   The number of sorts that were performed in memory.

- **Sorts (rows)**   The total number of rows that were sorted.

 TIP
The sorts (disk) statistic divided by the sorts (memory) should not be above 1–5 percent. If it is, you should increase the PGA_AGGREGATE_TARGET (or SORT_AREA_SIZE) parameter in the initialization file (given that physical memory is available to do this). Remember that the memory allocated for SORT_AREA_SIZE is a per-user value and PGA_AGGREGATE_TARGET is across all sessions.

- **table fetch by rowid**   The number of rows that were accessed by using a ROWID. This ROWID either came from an index or a WHERE ROWID = statement. A high number usually indicates a well-tuned application as far as fetching the data goes.

- **table fetch continued row**   The number of rows that were fetched, that were chained, or migrated.

 TIP
If chained rows are indicated in the previous parameter, the problem needs to be fixed as soon as possible. Chained rows can cause severe degradation to performance if a large number of rows are chained. See Chapter 3 for tips on chaining.

NOTE
The following parameter has a different meaning in Oracle9i, Oracle8i, and in Oracle8.0 and earlier. In Oracle9i, this is the number of db blocks up to which the table is considered small. This threshold is used to determine the cutover point for direct-read operations. Any object that is smaller than it will not be worth performing direct read for and thus will be read through the buffer cache. If the number of tablescans per transaction is above zero, you may wish to review the application SQL statements to try and increase the use of indexes.

- **table scans (long tables)** A table that is larger than _SMALL_TABLE_THRESHOLD (hidden) with no CACHE clause. The default value of _SMALL_TABLE_THRESHOLD is 2 percent of the buffer cache, or 20 blocks in 9i. _SMALL_TABLE_THRESHOLD is a dangerous parameter to modify without careful benchmarking of the effects. Because this affects all tables that access it, it is unwise to increase this significantly, if at all: it can cause blocks to age more quickly and reduce your hit ratio.

TIP
If full tablescans are being performed, serious performance issues may result and data hit ratios will be distorted. These tables need to be identified so the appropriate indexes are created or used. See Chapters 8 and 9 on query tuning for more information.

- **table scans (short tables)** A table that is shorter than _SMALL_TABLE_THRESHOLD (hidden) with no CACHE clause. The default value of _SMALL_TABLE_THRESHOLD is 2 percent of the buffer cache, or 20 blocks in 9i. Full tablescans on short tables are preferred.

Tablespace and File I/O Statistics

The next section of the report provides the I/O statistics first listed by I/Os and then listed by tablespace and by datafile. If the I/O is not properly distributed among your files, you may encounter performance bottlenecks during periods of high activity. As a rule, you don't want more than 100 I/Os per second per 10,000-RPM disk (even with RAID array). You can use this section of the report to identify such bottlenecks and to measure how effectively you have resolved those problems. The parameter that can be set in the init.ora to help improve the read time is the DB_FILE_MULTIBLOCK_READ_COUNT parameter. The DB_FILE_MULTIBLOCK_READ_COUNT parameter controls the number of blocks that can be read in one I/O when a full tablescan is being performed. This can reduce the number of I/Os needed to scan a table, thus improving the performance of the full tablescan. Unfortunately, the optimizer might do more full tablescans as a result of setting DB_FILE_MULTIBLOCK_READ_COUNT (you don't want this behavior), so you may also need to set the OPTIMIZER_INDEX_COST_ADJ to a number, such as ten, to eliminate this problem and drive the use of indexes. Listing 14-15 is an example listing from this section of the report.

```
Tablespace IO Stats for DB: ORA9I   Instance: ora9i   Snaps: 1 -2
->ordered by IO's (Reads + Writes) desc
Tablespace
------------------------------

                   Av      Av     Av                       Av        Buffer Av Buf
       Reads  Reads/s Rd(ms) Blks/Rd        Writes Writes/s    Waits Wt(ms)
-------------- ------- ------ ------- ------------- -------- ---------- ------
TS_ORDERS
     1,108,981      32   12.1     1.0     1,006,453       29      6,445    4.9
TS_ORDER_SUM
       967,108      28   12.5     1.0       675,647       19         51    7.6
TS_ORDER_LINES
     1,389,292      40   10.1     1.0        22,930        1      1,753    3.9
```

Listing 14-15: Tablespace I/O statistics

The following table provides definitions for some of the terms shown in the output in Listing 14-15.

Term	Definition
Tablespace	The name of the tablespace.
Reads	The number of physical reads that were performed on the datafile to retrieve data.
Av Blks/Rd	The number of blocks per read that were read from the datafile to satisfy an average read.
Writes	The number of writes to the datafile.

Following the tablespace I/O statistics is a file I/O section breakdown. This is a very granular look at how the I/O is being distributed across the datafiles. If one of the datafiles is getting a majority of the reads and writes, you may be able to improve performance by creating multiple datafiles on separate disks or by striping the datafile across multiple disks. Also, stay away from RAID 5 (Chapter 3 has more on this), or you'll get very slow write times.

TIP
If the number of physical reads is heavier on one physical disk, proper balancing of data will probably increase performance. See Chapter 3 for tips on fixing I/O problems with either datafiles or tablespaces.

Additional Memory Statistics

Following the I/O statistics, the report lists the buffer cache statistics by pool (default, keep, and recycle), instance recovery statistics (the number of redo blocks), and the PGA memory statistics. Listing 14-16 shows a sample listing of these three sections.

```
Buffer Pool Statistics for DB: ORA9I  Instance: ora9i  Snaps: 1 -2
-> Standard block size Pools  D: default,  K: keep,  R: recycle
-> Default Pools for otherblock sizes: 2k, 4k, 8k, 16k, 32k
                                                      Free    Write  Buffer
         Number of Cache     Buffer    Physical  Physical  Buffer Complete   Busy
  P      Buffers  Hit %        Gets       Reads     Writes   Waits    Waits  Waits
 ---  ----------- -----  -----------  ----------  ---------- -------  -------- ------
  D      5,898 100.0       4,721            0        208        0         0     0
         --------------------------------------------------------------
Instance Recovery Stats for DB: ORA9I   Instance: ora9i   Snaps: 1 -2
-> B: Begin snapshot,   E: End snapshot
   Targt Estd                                 Log File   Log Ckpt   Log Ckpt
   MTTR  MTTR  Recovery    Actual    Target      Size    Timeout    Interval
   (s)   (s)   Estd IO's  Redo Blks Redo Blks  Redo Blks Redo Blks  Redo Blks
 - ----- ----- ---------- --------- ---------- ---------- ---------- ----------
 B   33   18     5898        706      13546      184320      13546  ##########
 E   33   24     5898        717      14524      184320      14524  ##########
         --------------------------------------------------------------

PGA Memory Stats for DB: ORA9I   Instance: ora9i   Snaps: 1 -2
-> WorkArea (W/A) memory is used for: sort, bitmap merge, and hash join ops
Statistic                             Begin (M)         End (M)     % Diff
-------------------------------- ---------------- ---------------- ----------
maximum PGA allocated                  10.587           10.587        .00
```

Listing 14-16: Additional memory statistics

Although much of this information is shown in other sections, the section on buffer pool statistics is very detailed in this section of the report. It shows individual buffer pools for the keep and recycle pools if they are used. (Chapter 4 provides more information on buffer pools.) It also shows information for the different block sizes if you use multiple block sizes.

TIP
In Oracle9i, multiple data block sizes are allowed, and STATSPACK shows statistics for each of these block sizes individually.

Rollback/UNDO Statistics

The next section provides rollback segment statistics. First, it lists the activity in the rollback segment (writes, wraps, shrinks, extends) and the waits encountered, as shown in Listing 14-17.

```
Rollback Segment Stats for DB: ORA9I   Instance: ora9i   Snaps: 1 -2
->A high value for "Pct Waits" suggests more rollback segments may be required
->RBS stats may not be accurate between begin and end snaps when using Auto Undo
  management, as RBS may be dynamically created and dropped as needed
           Trans Table      Pct    Undo Bytes
RBS No       Gets          Waits    Written        Wraps   Shrinks  Extends
------  --------------   -------  ---------------  -------- -------- --------
```

0	3.0	0.00	0	0	0	0
1	5.0	0.00	122	0	0	0
2	5.0	0.00	0	0	0	0
3	119.0	0.00	156,786	4	0	3
4	11.0	0.00	198	0	0	0
5	11.0	0.00	1,780	0	0	0
6	13.0	0.00	0	0	0	0
7	5.0	0.00	0	0	0	0
8	9.0	0.00	122	0	0	0
9	16.0	0.00	198	0	0	0
10	9.0	0.00	0	0	0	0

Listing 14-17: Rollback segment activity and waits encountered

In this output, you can see that the number of bytes written per rollback segment was not even; in general, the longer the time interval for the STATSPACK report, the more even the rollback segment undo bytes written statistics will be. Rollback segment wraps do not cause significant performance problems, but extends indicate that the rollback segment was not large enough to support a transaction and incurred a performance penalty while extending itself. If rollback segment waits exceed 5 percent, you may need to add more rollback segments to your database.

The following table contains definitions for some of the terms shown in the output in Listing 14-17.

Term	Definition
RBS No	The rollback segment number.
Shrinks	The number of times the rollback segment eliminated one or more extents because it was larger than the optimal size.
Wraps	The number of times the rollback segment wrapped from one extent to another.

Listing 14-18 shows the rollback segment storage section of the report.

```
Rollback Segment Storage for DB: ORA9I   Instance: ora9i   Snaps: 1 -2
->Optimal Size should be larger than Avg Active
RBS No    Segment Size       Avg Active      Optimal Size      Maximum Size
------  ---------------  ---------------  ---------------  ---------------
     0          425,984                0                            425,984
     1          126,976           17,018                            192,512
     2          258,048           17,428                            258,048
     3          454,656           67,203                            454,656
     4          192,512           12,083                            192,512
     5          192,512           41,593                            258,048
     6          323,584           26,235                            323,584
     7          258,048           41,593                            258,048
```

8	454,656	31,016	454,656
9	389,120	33,090	389,120
10	651,264	6,645,804	13,627,392

Listing 14-18: Rollback segment statistics

The next section after the rollback segment statistics shows the storage allocations for your rollback segments, providing a guideline for the creation of additional rollback segments.

Following the rollback segment sections, the report lists the undo segment statistics for environments using system-managed undo. If you use automatic undo management mode, then there will be ten rollback segments and one system rollback segment (segment #0).

TIP
If you use automatic undo, ten rollback segments will be created in addition to the single system rollback segment (used only for database creation).

Latch Statistics

Latches are low-level queueing mechanisms (they're accurately referred to as mutual exclusion mechanisms) used to protect shared memory structures in the SGA (memory). Latches are like locks on memory that are very quickly obtained and released. Latches are used to prevent concurrent access to a shared memory structure. If the latch is not available, then a latch free miss is recorded. Most latch problems are related to *not* using bind variables (library cache latch), redo generation issues (redo allocation latch), buffer cache contention issues (cache buffers lru chain), and hot blocks in the buffer cache (cache buffers chain). There are also latch waits related to bugs, so check Metalink as well. When latch miss ratios are greater than 0.5 percent, you should investigate the issue.

Two types of latches exist: a willing-to-wait latch and a not-willing-to-wait latch. A latch that is willing to wait tries to acquire a latch. If none are available, it spins and then requests the latch again. It continues to do this up to the _SPIN_COUNT initialization parameter. (Note that spinning costs CPU.) If it can't obtain a latch after spinning up to the _SPIN_COUNT, it goes to sleep. It doesn't do anything for a while, and then it wakes up after 1 centisecond (one hundredth of a second). It does this twice. It then repeats this process, spinning up to the _SPIN_COUNT and then sleeping for twice as long (2 centiseconds). After doing this again, it doubles again. So the pattern is 1, 1, 2, 2, 4, 4, etc. It repeats this process until it gets the latch. Every time the latch sleeps, it creates a latch sleep wait. An example of a willing-to-wait latch is a library cache latch.

Some latches are not willing to wait. This type of latch does not wait for the latch to become available. It immediately times out and retries to obtain the latch. A redo copy latch is an example of a not-willing-to-wait latch. It generates information for the IMMEDIATE_GETS and the IMMEDIATE_MISSES columns of the V$latch view and also in the STATSPACK report. The hit ratio for these latches should also approach 99 percent and the misses should never fall below 1 percent.

By viewing this section of STATSPACK or querying the V$latch view, you can see how many processes had to wait (a latch miss) or sleep (a latch sleep) and the number of times they had to sleep. V$latchholder, V$latchname, and V$latch_children are also helpful in investigating latch issues. Listing 14-19 is a partial listing of the latch activity section; there are three sections (latch activity, latch sleep, and latch miss) of the STATSPACK report. (This one has a library cache problem.)

```
Latch Activity for DB: ORA9I  Instance: ora9i  Snaps: 1 -2
->"Get Requests", "Pct Get Miss" and "Avg Slps/Miss" are statistics for
  willing-to-wait latch get requests
->"NoWait Requests", "Pct NoWait Miss" are for no-wait latch get requests
->"Pct Misses" for both should be very close to 0.0
-> ordered by Wait Time desc, Avg Slps/Miss, Pct NoWait Miss desc
```

Latch	Get Requests	Pct Get Miss	Avg Slps /Miss	Wait Time (s)	NoWait Requests	Pct NoWait Miss
KCL freelist latch	4,924	0.0			0	
cache buffer handles	968,992	0.0	0.0		0	
cache buffers chains	761,708,539	0.0	0.4		21,519,841	0.0
cache buffers lru chain	8,111,269	0.1	0.8		19,834,466	0.1
library cache	67,602,665	2.2	2.0		213,590	0.8
redo allocation	12,446,986	0.2	0.0		0	
redo copy	320	0.0			10,335,430	0.1
user lock	1,973	0.3	1.2		0	

```
Latch Sleep breakdown for DB:
-> ordered by misses desc
```

Latch Name	Get Requests	Misses	Sleeps	Spin & Sleeps 1->4
library cache	67,602,665	1,474,032	2,935,368	199143/28003 6/582413/412 440/0
cache buffers chains	761,708,539	192,942	83,559	110054/82239 /628/21/0
redo allocation	12,446,986	25,444	1,135	24310/1133/1 /0/0
cache buffers lru chain	8,111,269	6,285	4,933	1378/4881/26 /0/0
process allocation	177	7	7	0/7/0/0/0

```
Latch Miss Sources for DB:
-> only latches with sleeps are shown
-> ordered by name, sleeps desc
```

Latch Name	Where	NoWait Misses	Sleeps	Waiter Sleeps
KCL lock element parent	kclulb	0	431	248
batching SCNs	kcsl01	0	3,836	3,099
batching SCNs	kcsl02	0	474	1,206
cache buffers chains	kcbgtcr: kslbegin	0	63,446	47,535

cache buffers chains	kcbgcur: kslbegin	0	9,820	7,603
cache buffers lru chain	kcbzgb: multiple sets nowa	0	4,859	0
enqueues	ksqdel	0	106,769	12,576
library cache	kglhdgn: child:	0	1,973,311	#######
library cache	kglpnal: child: alloc spac	0	279,254	#######
redo allocation	kcrfwr: redo allocation	0	942	1,032
redo allocation	kcrfwi: before write	0	191	53
redo allocation	kcrfwi: more space	0	2	39

Listing 14-19: Latch activity statistics

One point to remember about processes that are sleeping: these processes may also be holding other latches that will not be released until the process is finished with them. This will cause even more processes to sleep, waiting for those latches. Therefore, you can see how important it is to reduce contention as much as possible.

The following table contains terms found in this section of the report and their definitions.

Term	Definition
Latch Name	The name of the latch.
Gets	The number of times a willing-to-wait request for a latch was requested and it was available.
Misses	The number of times a willing-to-wait request for a latch was initially requested but was not available.
Sleeps	The number of a willing-to-wait request for a latch failed over and over until the spin count was exceeded and the process went to sleep. The number of sleeps may be higher than the misses. Processes may sleep multiple times before obtaining the latch.
NoWait Misses	The number of times an immediate (not willing-to-wait) request for a latch was unsuccessful.

Look for and remember the following tips:

- **Latch free** When latch free is high in the wait events section of the report, problems need to be investigated in the latch section of the report. This section helps you look for which latches are a problem. A sleeping latch (couldn't get the latch and sleeping until the next try) or spinning latch (waiting and retrying based on spin count) latches.

- **Library cache and shared pool** The library cache latch serializes access to objects in the library cache. Every time a SQL or PL/SQL procedure, package, function, or trigger is executed, this latch is used. It is also used intensively during parse operations. A single shared pool latch protected the allocation of memory in the library cache in Oracle8*i*; since Oracle9*i*, there are seven children latches for this. Contention for the shared pool, library cache pin, or library cache latches primarily occur when the shared pool is too small or when statements are not reused. Statements are not usually reused when bind variables are not used. Common but not exact SQL floods the shared pool. Increasing the size of the shared pool only makes the latch problem worse. You can also set the CURSOR_SHARING=FORCE (or SIMILAR in 9i) initialization parameter to help fix this issue and to reduce problems when bind variables are not used. But the shared pool and library cache latch issues also occur when space is needed in the library cache when it is set too small for the number of SQL statements that need to be processed. Although space is being freed up to load a SQL or PL/SQL statement, the latch is being held exclusively and other users must wait. You can help to reduce contention by increasing the shared pool or by pinning large SQL and PL/SQL statements in memory using the DBMS_Shared_Pool.Keep procedures.

- **Redo copy**   The number of redo copy latches has a default of 2*CPU_COUNT, but it can be set using the _LOG_SIMULTANEOUS_COPIES initialization parameter. Increasing this parameter may help to reduce contention for the redo copy latch, but Oracle found a global optimal default value as of 8.1.7 and it generally should not be altered. The redo copy latch is used to copy redo records from the PGA into the redo log buffer.

- **Redo allocation**   The redo allocation latch (allocates the space in the redo log buffer) contention can be reduced by using the NOLOGGING feature, which reduces the load on the redo log buffer. You should also try to avoid unnecessary commits.

- **Row cache objects**   The row cache objects latch contention usually means that there is contention in the data dictionary. This may also be a symptom of excessive parsing of SQL statements that depend on public synonyms. Increasing the shared pool usually solves this latch problem. You usually increase the shared pool for a library cache latch problem well before this one is a problem.

- **Cache buffers chains**   The cache buffers chains latch is needed to scan the SGA buffer cache for database cache buffers. Hot blocks (often accessed) in the buffer cache causes cache buffers chains latch issues. Hot blocks may also be a symptom of poorly tuned SQL statements. A hot record creates a hot block that can cause issues for other records inside that block as well as any block hashed to the same chain. To find the hot block, query V$latch_children for the address and join it to V$BH to identify the blocks protected by this latch. (This will show all blocks that are affected by the hot block.) You can identify the object by querying DBA_EXTENTS based on the file# and dbablk found from V$BH. If the hot block is on an index, using a reverse-key index moves sequential records to other blocks so that they are not locked up by the hot block in the chain. If the hot block is the index root block, a reverse-key index won't help. Setting _DB_BLOCK_HASH_BUCKETS to twice the number of buffers (DB_CACHE_SIZE/DB_BLOCK_SIZE) and then up to the next prime number larger than that usually eliminates this problem. Prior to Oracle9i, this parameter had a default that caused tremendous contention for this latch; the default is correctly set to a prime number in Oracle9i.

- **Cache buffers lru chain**   The cache buffers lru chain latch is used to scan the Least Recently Used (LRU) chain containing all of the blocks in the buffer cache. A small buffer cache, excessive buffer cache throughput, many cache-based sorts, and DBWR not keeping up with the workload are all culprits that can cause this problem. Try to fix the queries that are causing the excessive logical reads. You can increase the initialization parameter DB_BLOCK_LRU_LATCHES to have multiple LRU latches reduce contention. Generally, non-SMP (symmetric multiprocessor) machines need only a single LRU latch. Oracle automatically sets this to half the number of CPUs on SMP machines. You must have at least one LRU latch for each database writer; make sure you increase this number if you add database writers.

Latch Problem	Potential Fix
Library cache	Use bind variables; adjust the SHARED_POOL_SIZE.
Shared pool	Use bind variables; adjust the SHARED_POOL_SIZE.
Redo allocation	Minimize redo generation and avoid unnecessary commits.
Redo copy	Increase the _LOG_SIMULTANEOUS_COPIES.
Row cache objects	Increase the shared pool.
Cache buffers chain	_DB_BLOCK_HASH_BUCKETS needs to be increased or prime.
Cache buffers lru chain	Set DB_BLOCK_LRU_LATCHES or use multiple buffer pools.

You should configure LRU latches so that each buffer pool has NCPUs worth of latches. For example, if the system has eight CPUs, they should set:

db_block_lru_latches=24 (i.e., 3 * ncpus)

buffer_pool_keep = buffers:XXXX, lru_latches=8

buffer_pool_recycle = buffers:YYYY, lru_latches=8

XXXX and *YYYY* are the desired number of buffers in the keep and recycle pools, respectively. There is really no reason to have more LRU latches than the number of processes that may be concurrently executing.

Some latch problems have often been bug-related in the past, so make sure you check Metalink for issues related to latches. Investigate any latches that have a hit ratio below 99 percent. Some of the more common latches include the cache buffers chains, redo copy, library cache, and the cache buffers lru chain.

TIP
Latches are like locks on pieces of memory (or memory buffers). If the latch hit ratio is below 99 percent, there is a serious problem because not even the lock to get memory could be obtained.

Dictionary and Library Cache Statistics

The next two sections contain the dictionary and library cache information. Listed first is all of the data dictionary information. This data pertains to all of the objects in the database. This information is accessed for every SQL that gets parsed and again when the statement is executed. The activity in this area can be very heavy. Maintaining a good hit ratio is very important to prevent recursive calls back to the database to verify privileges. You can also evaluate the efficiency of the dictionary cache by querying the V$rowcache view. The query in Listing 14-20 shows the information that the STATSPACK report lists for this section of the report.

```
Dictionary Cache Stats for DB: ORA9I   Instance: ora9i   Snaps: 1 -2
->"Pct Misses"  should be very low (< 2% in most cases)
->"Cache Usage" is the number of cache entries being used
->"Pct SGA"     is the ratio of usage to allocated size for that cache
                      Get     Pct   Scan  Pct     Mod      FinalPct
Cache             Requests   Miss   Reqs  Miss    Reqs     UsageSGA
---------------- ---------- ------ ------ ----- -------- ---------- --
dc_constraints            0           0            0        0   0
dc_objects          170,317   1.0     0            4      841  77
dc_outlines               0           0            0        0   0
dc_profiles             175   0.0     0            0        1  14
dc_segments         451,486   0.3     0           33    1,525 100
dc_sequences          8,622   1.1     0        8,218       37  93
dc_synonyms          51,702   0.3     0            0      174  98
dc_tablespaces       40,925   0.1     0            0       22  76
dc_used_extents          33  60.6     0           33        7  64
dc_user_grants       18,533   0.0     0            0       25  66
dc_usernames         62,263   0.0     0            0       16  62
```

Listing 14-20: Dictionary and Library Cache statistics

The second part of this section of the report deals with the performance of the library cache. These statistics are generated from the V$librarycache view. The library cache contains the shared SQL and PL/SQL areas. These areas are represented by the BODY, SQL AREA, TABLE/ PROCEDURE, and the TRIGGER. They contain all of the SQL and PL/SQL statements that are cached in memory. The other names are areas that Oracle uses. If your Pct Miss value is high in this section of the report, you may need to improve cursor sharing in your application or increase the size of the shared pool. Listing 14-21 shows example data for this section.

```
Library Cache Activity for DB: ORA9I   Instance: ora9i   Snaps: 1 -2
->"Pct Misses"  should be very low
                   Get     Pct      Pin       Pct              Invali-
Namespace      Requests   Miss  Requests      Miss   Reloads   dations
-------------- --------- ------ ------------- ------ --------- --------
BODY                 102   2.0           104    4.8        3        0
CLUSTER              108   0.0           167    0.0        0        0
INDEX              3,586   1.9         2,327    3.1        0        0
OBJECT                 0                  0                0        0
PIPE                   0                  0                0        0
SQL AREA         924,407   5.4    27,307,859    0.3    3,621       61
TABLE/PROCEDURE  244,185   0.6     1,861,627    0.2      461        0
TRIGGER              173   4.6           173    7.5        5        0
```

Listing 14-21: Performance of the library cache

The following table contains terms found in this section of the report and their definitions.

Term	Definition
Namespace	The name of the library name space.
Get Requests	The number of times the system requested a handle to an object in this name space.
Pct Miss (Get Miss Ratio)	The number of GETHITS divided by the number of gets is the get hit ratio. The GETHITS are the number of times a request was made for an object and the object was already in the cache. The hit ratio should be as close to .99 percent as possible. The PCT MISS should be less than 1 percent.
Pin Requests	The number of times an item in the cache was executed. A high number is what you are after.
Pct Miss (Pin Miss Ratio)	The number of PINHITS divided by the number of pins shows the hit ratio. PINHITS are the number of times that objects the system is pinning are already in the cache. This ratio should be as close to 1 percent as possible. The miss ratio should be less than 1 percent.
Reloads	The number of library cache misses on an execution step. The number of reloads divided by the number of pins should be around 0 percent. If the ratio between this is greater than 1 percent, you should probably increase the size of the shared pool.
Invalidations	The total number of times objects in this name space were marked invalid because a dependent object was modified.

TIP
If the PINHITRATIO is less than .95 when the report is run for an extended period of time, the SHARED_POOL_SIZE is probably too small for your best system performance. If the reloads are greater than 1 percent, this also points to a SHARED_POOL_SIZE that is too small.

SGA Memory Statistics

Following an SGA memory summary (from V$SGA) and a listing of the memory changes during the snapshot interval, the report lists the database initialization parameters in use at the beginning and end of the report.

Taken as a whole, the report generates a significant amount of data, allowing you to develop a profile of the database and its usage. Based on the initialization, file I/O, and SGA data, you can develop an understanding of the major components in the database configuration. Listing 14-22 is a sample listing of this section of the report.

```
SGA Memory Summary for DB: ORA7  Instance: ORA7A  Snaps: 164 -194
SGA regions                      Size in Bytes
-------------------------------- -----------------
```

Dictionary and Library Cache Statistics

```
Database Buffers              1,572,864,000
Fixed Size                          103,396
Redo Buffers                     41,959,424
Variable Size                 3,854,102,528
                             ----------------
sum                           5,469,029,348
         ------------------------------------------------------------------

SGA breakdown difference for DB: ORA9I  Instance: ora9i  Snaps: 1 -2
Pool   Name                          Begin value        End value  % Diff
------ ----------------------------- ----------------  ----------------  ------
java   free memory                     27,934,720        27,934,720    .00
java   memory in use                    5,619,712         5,619,712    .00
shared 1M buffer                        1,049,088         1,049,088    .00
shared Checkpoint queue                   141,152           141,152    .00
shared DML lock                           100,408           100,408    .00
shared FileIdentificatonBlock             323,292           323,292    .00
shared FileOpenBlock                      695,504           695,504    .00
shared KGK heap                             3,756             3,756    .00
shared KGLS heap                        1,325,688         1,355,676    .26
shared KSXR pending messages que          226,636           226,636    .00
shared KSXR receive buffers             1,060,000         1,060,000    .00
shared PL/SQL DIANA                     2,882,084         2,882,084    .00
shared PL/SQL MPCODE                      257,108           290,300   2.91
shared PLS non-lib hp                       2,068             2,068   0.00
shared VIRTUAL CIRCUITS                   266,120           266,120   0.00
shared character set object               315,704           315,704   0.00
shared db_handles                          93,000            93,000   0.00
shared dictionary cache                   925,680           938,100   1.34
shared enqueue                            171,860           171,860   0.00
shared errors                              64,344            64,344   0.00
shared event statistics per sess        1,356,600         1,356,600   0.00
shared fixed allocation callback               60                60   0.00
shared free memory                     23,924,812        21,787,064  -8.94
shared joxlod: in ehe                     317,060           317,060   0.00
shared joxlod: in phe                     114,024           114,024   0.00
shared joxs heap init                       4,220             4,220   0.00
shared ksm_file2sga region                148,652           148,652   0.00
shared library cache                    3,832,604         4,238,528   0.59
shared message pool freequeue             772,672           772,672   0.00
shared miscellaneous                    2,318,632         2,324,904   0.27
shared parameters                           8,228            13,904   8.98
shared processes                          127,800           127,800   0.00
shared sessions                           395,760           395,760   0.00
shared simulator trace entries             98,304            98,304   0.00
shared sql area                         2,626,452         4,269,888   2.57
shared table definiti                         952             1,792  88.24
shared transaction                        182,376           182,376   0.00
shared trigger defini                       2,324             2,324   0.00
```

```
shared trigger inform                    1,108           1,108   0.00
shared trigger source                    1,212           1,212   0.00
        db_block_buffers           25,165,824      25,165,824   0.00
        fixed_sga                     282,536         282,536   0.00
        log_buffer                    524,288         524,288   0.00
        ------------------------------------------------------------
```

Listing 14-22: Major components in the database configuration

Nondefault init.ora Parameters

This last section shows the parameters in the initialization file that are set to a value other than the default. The list is generated by querying the V$parameter view where the default column is equal to FALSE. This list can be used as a reference. While you are tuning the database, these parameters can provide a record of how the database performed with certain values. The output in Listing 14-23 shows this section of the report.

```
init.ora Parameters for DB: ORA9I  Instance: ora9i  Snaps: 1 -2

                                                           End value
Parameter Name              Begin value                   (if different)
--------------------------  ------------------------------ --------------
background_dump_dest        f:\ora9i\admin\ora9i\bdump
compatible                  9.0.0
control_files               f:\ora9i\oradata\ora9i\CONTROL01.
core_dump_dest              f:\ora9i\admin\ora9i\cdump
db_block_size               4096
db_cache_size               25165824
db_create_file_dest         F:\ORA9I\ORADATA\ORA9I
db_domain                   world
db_name                     ora9i
dispatchers                 (PROTOCOL=TCP)(SER=MODOSE), (PROT
fast_start_mttr_target      300
instance_name               ora9i
java_pool_size              33554432
large_pool_size             1048576
open_cursors                300
processes                   150
remote_login_passwordfile   EXCLUSIVE
shared_pool_size            46137344
sort_area_size              524288
timed_statistics            TRUE
undo_management             AUTO
undo_tablespace             UNDOTBS
user_dump_dest              f:\ora9i\admin\ora9i\udump
        ------------------------------------------------------------
End of Report
```

Listing 14-23: Parameters in the initialization file set to a value other than the default

Top 10 Things to Look for in STATSPACK Output

Many DBAs already know how to use STATSPACK, but they are not always sure what to check regularly. Remember to separate OLTP and Batch activity when you run STATSPACK because they usually generate different types of waits. You can use the SQL script spauto.sql to run STATSPACK every hour on the hour. See the script in $ORACLE_HOME/rdbms/admin/spauto.sql for more information. (Note that JOB_QUEUE_PROCESSES must be set > 0.) Because every system is different, this is only a general list of things that you should *regularly* check in your STATSPACK output.

1. Top 5 wait events

2. Load profile

3. Instance efficiency hit ratios

4. Wait events

5. Latch waits

6. Top SQL

7. Instance activity

8. File I/O

9. Memory allocation

10. Buffer waits

Managing the STATSPACK Data

You should manage the data generated by STATSPACK to guarantee that the space usage and performance of the STATSPACK application meets your requirements as the application data grows. Managing STATSPACK data includes the following steps:

1. Regularly analyze the STATSPACK data. At a minimum, you should analyze the STATSPACK schema prior to running the spreport.sql report:

   ```
   execute DBMS_UTILITY.ANALYZE_SCHEMA('PERFSTAT','COMPUTE');
   ```

2. Purge old data. Because you cannot generate valid interval reports across database shutdown/startup actions, data prior to the last database startup may not be as useful as the most current data. When the data is no longer needed, purge it from the tables. Oracle provides a script, sppurge.sql, to facilitate purges. The sppurge.sql script, located in the /rdbms/admin directory under the Oracle software home directory, lists the currently stored snapshots and prompts you for two input parameters: the beginning and ending

snapshot numbers for the purge. The related records in the STATS$ tables will then be deleted. Due to the size of the transactions involved, databases using rollback segments should force the session to use a large rollback segment during the deletes (if automatic UNDO is not used):

```
SQL> commit;
SQL> set transaction use rollback segment roll_large;
SQL> @sppurge
```

The sppurge script prompts you to back up your old statistics before purging them. You can back up the data by exporting the PERFSTAT schema.

3. Truncate the STATSPACK tables when the data is not needed. Old statistical data may no longer be relevant, or you may have imported the old statistics during database migrations or creations. To truncate the old tables, execute the sptrunc.sql SQL*Plus script from within the PERFSTAT account. The script is located in the /rdbms/admin directory under the Oracle software home directory.

4. Include the STATSPACK tables in your backup scheme. If you are using Export, Oracle provides a parameter file named spuexp.par to assist you.

5. Include the STATSPACK tables in your space-monitoring procedures.

Upgrading STATSPACK

To upgrade old STATSPACK data to a new version of the database, execute the scripts provided by Oracle. Oracle does not support upgrading STATSPACK directly from 8.1.6 to 9.0.1; you must go through a few steps:

1. Upgrade from 8.1.6 to the 8.1.7 version of STATSPACK by executing the spup816.sql script.

2. Upgrade from the 8.1.7 STATSPACK objects to 9.0.1 by executing the spup817.sql script.

Uninstalling STATSPACK

Because STATSPACK includes public synonyms as well as private objects, you should remove the application via a SYSDBA privileged account. Oracle provides a script, spdrop.sql, to automate the process. From within the /rdbms/admin directory under the Oracle software home directory, log in to SQL*Plus and execute the script, as shown here:

```
SQL> connect system/manager as SYSDBA
SQL> @spdrop
```

The spdrop.sql script calls scripts (spdtab.sql, spdusr.sql) that will drop the tables, package, public synonyms, and the PERFSTAT user. To reinstall STATSPACK, execute the spcreate.sql script as shown in the "Installing STATSPACK" section earlier in this chapter.

Tips Review

- The files needed to create, manage, and drop the STATSPACK objects are all in the /rdbms/admin subdirectory under the Oracle software home directory, and they all start with the letters *sp*.

- Create a tablespace to hold the STATSPACK data apart from your application and SYSTEM objects.

- Change the PERFSTAT account's password and consider locking the account when it is no longer in use.

- Select the proper level for your reporting. In general, start with level 5 and use a higher level for further investigation.

- Avoid running STATSPACK reports for intervals that include database shutdowns.

- Actively manage the STATSPACK data, analyzing and purging it as needed. Monitor its space usage and include it in your backup and upgrade plans.

- Get to know your system by reviewing and knowing the regular load profile of your system. Significant changes to the load profile during what should be similar workloads or common times during the day may warrant further investigation.

- Hit ratios are a great barometer of your system's health. A large increase or drop from day to day indicates a major change that needs to be investigated.

- Generally, buffer and library cache hit ratios should be greater than 95 percent for OLTP, but could be lower for a data warehouse that may do many full tablescans.

- The top 5 wait events reveal to you the largest issues on your system at the macro level. Rarely do they point you to a specific problem. Other parts of STATSPACK tell you why you are receiving the top 5 waits.

- Tuning the top 25 buffer get and top 25 physical get queries has yielded system performance gains of anywhere from 5 to 5000 percent. The SQL section of the STATSPACK report tells you which queries to potentially tune first.

- The top 10 percent of your SQL statements should not be more than 10 percent of your buffer gets or disk reads.

- If the free buffers inspected divided by the free buffer scans are less than one, the DB_CACHE_SIZE parameter may need to be increased.

- The sorts (disk) statistic divided by the sorts (memory) should not be above 1–5 percent. If it is, you should increase the PGA_AGGREGATE_TARGET (or SORT_AREA_SIZE) parameter in the initialization file (given that physical memory is available to do this). Remember that the memory allocated for SORT_AREA_SIZE is a per-user value and PGA_AGGREGATE_TARGET is across all sessions.

- If you use automatic undo, ten rollback segments will be created in addition to the single system rollback segment (used only for database creation).

- Latches are like locks on pieces of memory (or memory buffers). If the latch hit ratio is below 99 percent, there is a serious problem because not even the lock to get memory could be gotten.

- If the PINHITRATIO is less than 95 percent when the report is run for an extended period of time, the SHARED_POOLSIZE is probably too small for your best system performance. If the reloads are greater than 1 percent, this also points to a SHARED_POOL_SIZE that is too small.

References

Oracle8i Internal Services for Waits, Latches, Locks, and Memory: Steve Adams (excellent)
Greg Pucka for the original chapter on estat/bstat
Oracle Doc ID: 61998.1, 39017.1
"Performance Tuning with STATSPACK" white paper, 2000; Connie Dialeris and Graham Wood
Notes from Richard Powell, Cecilia Gervasio, Russell Green, and Patrick Tearle
STATSPACK checklist; Randy Swanson and Bob Yingst, 2002
IOUG Masters Tuning Class; Rich Niemiec, 2002
Oracle 9i High-Performance Tuning with STATSPACK, Don Burleson, Oracle Press, 2002

Thank you to Kevin Loney for the entire installation portion of this chapter to STATSPACK and some added notes. This chapter took more than a month to write, so make sure you benefit from it. Steve Adams and Don Burleson helped edit some of the information. A big thank-you goes to them, too.

CHAPTER
15

Performing a Quick
System Review (DBA)

N obody seems to like tests or evaluations, yet performing simple evaluations can help to point out future performance problems and/or current issues. One of the key approaches to improving and maintaining excellent system health requires an annual review—either an internal or external review of your system performance. Many companies have developed methods of measuring system performance and overall system speed. This chapter does not present the six-month process that many of the more detailed evaluations propose; instead, it serves as a simple barometer of how your system rates as compared to others in the industry. Variations in your business processes may influence your score results using this simple review. Therefore, you will need to adjust these scales for your unique system.

The topics covered in this chapter include the following:

- The Total Performance Index (TPI)

- The Education Performance Index (EPI)

- The System Performance Index (SPI)

- The Memory Performance Index (MPI)

- The Disk Performance Index (DPI)

- The Total Performance Index (TPI)

- An overall system review example

- The system information list

The Total Performance Index (TPI)

I created the Total Performance Index (TPI) as a most basic tool for Oracle DBAs to measure their system and compare it to other systems, using a quick and simple scoring method. This index is meant to be only a barometer to see whether improvements might be beneficial. Many systems differ in categories based on their business case, but this index tells you how close or far your system is from others in the industry. There are four categories: Education, System, Memory, and Disk, as shown in Table 15-1. This chapter shows you how to measure your TPI using several simple queries. For detailed information on a particular category, please refer to the chapter in this book related to that issue. To help identify how your system is progressing, use your TPI to compare future growth in the number of users or changes in hardware and software.

Category Index	Maximum Score
Education Performance Index (EPI)	250
System Performance Index (SPI)	250
Memory Performance Index (MPI)	250
Disk Performance Index (DPI)	250
Total Performance Index (TPI)	1000

TABLE 15-1. *Measuring Your Total Performance Index*

Category	Level Required	Maximum Score
DBAs required to tune database	Yes	30
Developers required to tune code written	Yes	30
DBAs last trained in tuning	< 1 year	30
Developers last trained in tuning	< 1 year	30
DBAs proficient in V$ views	Yes	30
DBAs proficient in Enterprise Manager	Yes	20
DBAs trained in EXPLAIN PLAN	Yes	20
Developers trained in EXPLAIN PLAN	Yes	20
DBAs trained in use of hints	Yes	20
Developers trained in use of hints	Yes	20
Education Performance Index (EPI)	Section Total	250

TABLE 15-2.   *Receiving a Perfect Education Performance Index Score*

The Education Performance Index (EPI)

This index measures the knowledge and education of your technical staff members.
Table 15-2 illustrates how to receive a perfect EPI score. This rating system is not meant to
be an all-encompassing benchmark of knowledge and education, but rather, a barometer to
see whether educational improvements could be beneficial.

Rate your system:

Questions	Answers	Points	Score
Are DBAs *required* to tune the database?	Yes No	30 points 0 points	30
Are developers *required* to tune the code they write?	Yes No	30 points 0 points	0
When was the last time your DBAs attended a training course that included tuning?	< 1 year 1–2 years > 2 years	30 points 20 points 0 points	20
When was the last time your developers attended a training course that included tuning?	< 1 year 1–2 years > 2 years	30 points 20 points 0 points	20
Are DBAs proficient at using the V$ views?	Yes No	20 points 0 points	20

Education Performance Index (EPI)

Questions	Answers	Points	Score
Are DBAs proficient at using Enterprise Manager or an equivalent performance tool?	Yes No	20 points 0 points	20
Have DBAs been trained to use the EXPLAIN PLAN? (See Chapter 6.)	Yes No	20 points 0 points	20
Have developers been trained to use the EXPLAIN PLAN?	Yes No	20 points 0 points	0
Have DBAs been trained to use hints? (See Chapter 7.)	Yes No	20 points 0 points	20
Have developers been trained to use hints?	Yes No	20 points 0 points	0
Example Education Performance Index (EPI)		Total Score	150 (B)

Grade your system:

EPI Grade	Comments	Score
A+	Top 10 percent of most systems	250
A	Top 20 percent of most systems	210–249
B	Top 40 percent of most systems	150–209
C	Top 70 percent of most systems	90–149
Needs help now	Bottom 30 percent of most systems	< 90

TIP
Measuring your Education Performance Index (EPI) can help you identify beneficial educational improvements.

The System Performance Index (SPI)

This index measures overall system issues. Table 15-3 illustrates how to receive a perfect SPI score. This rating system is not meant to be an all-encompassing benchmark of overall system issues; rather, it is a barometer to see whether improvements could be beneficial.

Category	Level Required	Maximum Score
Inside party database review	< 1 year	50
Ran Statspack last	< 1 month	30
Users asked about performance issues	< 2 months	30
Backup tested for recovery speed	Yes	30
Outside party database review	< 1 year	30
Outside party operating system review	< 1 year	30
Optimizer used	Cost-based	20
Design is strictly or partially denormalized	Denormalized	20
Parallel Query used or tested for gains	Yes	10
System Performance Index (SPI)	Section Total	250

TABLE 15-3.   *Receiving a Perfect SPI Score*

Rate your system:

Questions	Level Required	Maximum	Score
When was your database last reviewed by an inside party other than the DBA?	< 1 year 1–2 years > 2 years	50 points 30 points 0 points	50 points
When did you last run *and* analyze Statspack? (See Chapter 14 on Statspack.)	< 1 month 1-3 months 4-6 months > 6 months	30 points 20 points 10 points 0 points	20 points
When were your system users last asked about system performance or where improvements could be made?	< 2 months 3-6 months 7-12 months > 1 year	30 points 20 points 10 points 0 points	20 points
Has your backup plan been tested to determine how long it will take to recover?	Yes No	30 points 0 points	30 points
When was your database last reviewed by an outside party?	< 1 year 1-2 years > 2 years	30 points 20 points 0 points	20 points
When was your operating system last reviewed by an outside party?	< 1 year 1-2 years > 2 years	30 points 20 points 0 points	30 points

System Performance Index (SPI)

Questions	Level Required	Maximum	Score
Which optimizer do you use?	Cost-based Rule-based Unsure	20 points 10 points 0 points	20 points
Do designers adhere strictly to third normal form or higher in their design of the database?	Yes *Denormalize No designer *Denormalized only where needed	10 points 20 points 0 points	20 points
Has parallel query been evaluated and is it in use where advantageous?	Yes Not needed Not tested	10 points 10 points 0 points	10 points
Example System Performance Index (SPI)		Total Score	220 (A+)

Grade your system:

SPI Grade	Comments	Score
A+	Top 10 percent of most systems	> 210
A	Top 20 percent of most systems	180–210
B	Top 40 percent of most systems	140–179
C	Top 70 percent of most systems	80–139
Needs help now	Bottom 30 percent of most systems	< 80

TIP
Measuring your System Performance Index (SPI) can help you identify beneficial overall system improvements.

The Memory Performance Index (MPI)

This index measures memory use and allocation. Table 15-4 illustrates how to receive a perfect MPI score. This rating system is not meant to be an all-encompassing benchmark of memory use and allocation; rather, it is a barometer to see whether memory use and allocation improvements could be beneficial.

Buffer Hit Ratio

The buffer hit ratio displays the percentage of data memory hits versus disk reads, as shown in Listing 15-1. Although a very high hit ratio could mean overindexing and poorly run queries doing many buffer reads, this assumes you've tuned the top queries to eliminate this issue and that the distribution of data within each block is generally balanced.

Category	Level Required	Maximum Score
Buffer hit ratio	> 98 percent	30
Dictionary hit ratio	> 98 percent	30
Library hit ratio	> 98 percent	30
Sorts in memory	> 98 percent	30
Buffers in X$BH at state = 0	10–25 percent	30
Top 10 statements memory use	< 5 percent	60
Top 25 (worst memory) statements tuned	Yes	30
Pin/cache frequently used objects	Yes	10
Memory Performance Index (MPI)	Section Total	250

TABLE 15-4. *Receiving a Perfect MPI Score*

```
select    (1 - (sum(decode(name, 'physical reads',value,0)) /
          (sum(decode(name, 'db block gets',value,0)) +
          sum(decode(name, 'consistent gets',value,0)))))) * 100 "Hit Ratio"
from      v$sysstat;
```

Listing 15-1: Query for buffer hit ratio

Sample output:

```
Hit Ratio
99.1373288
```

Rate your system:

Question	Level Required	Maximum	Score
What is your buffer hit ratio?	< 90 percent	0 points	30 points
	90–94 percent	10 points	
	95–98 percent	20 points	
	> 98 percent	30 points	

You can also expand the query in Listing 15-1 to include the actual ratings in your result. The query in Listing 15-2 shows how this task is accomplished by using the DECODE function. You can also apply this strategy to the remainder of the queries in this chapter if you would like the score in your results. At TUSC, we use a PL/SQL procedure to accomplish the results. (We also display them graphically.)

Memory Performance Index (MPI)

```
select (1 - (sum(decode(name, 'physical reads',value,0)) /
(sum(decode(name, 'db block gets',value,0)) +
sum(decode(name, 'consistent gets',value,0))))) * 100 "Hit Ratio",
decode(sign((1-(sum(decode(name, 'physical reads',value,0)) /
(sum(decode(name, 'db block gets',value,0)) +
sum(decode(name, 'consistent gets',value,0))))) * 100 - 98),1,30,
decode(sign((1-(sum(decode(name, 'physical reads',value,0)) /
(sum(decode(name, 'db block gets',value,0)) +
sum(decode(name, 'consistent gets',value,0))))) * 100 - 95),1,20,
decode(sign((1-(sum(decode(name, 'physical reads',value,0)) /
(sum(decode(name, 'db block gets',value,0)) +
sum(decode(name, 'consistent gets',value,0))))) * 100 - 90),1,10,0)))
"Score"
from v$sysstat
/
```

Listing 15-2: Alternate query for buffer hit ratio (includes the rating)

Sample output:

```
Hit Ratio      Score
99.1975576       30
```

Dictionary Cache Hit Ratio

The dictionary cache hit ratio displays the percentage of memory reads for the data dictionary and other objects, as shown in Listing 15-3.

```
select     (1-(sum(getmisses)/sum(gets))) * 100 "Hit Ratio"
from       v$rowcache;
```

Listing 15-3: Query for dictionary cache hit ratio

Sample output:

```
Hit Ratio
95.4630137
```

Rate your system:

Question	Level Required	Maximum	Score
What is your dictionary cache hit ratio?	< 85 percent	0 points	20 points
	86–92 percent	10 points	
	92–98 percent	20 points	
	> 98 percent	30 points	

Library Cache Hit Ratio

The library cache hit ratio reveals the percentage of memory reads for actual statements and PL/SQL objects, as shown in Listing 15-4. Note that a high hit ratio is not *always* good. See Chapter 4 for a detailed explanation.

```
select    Sum(Pins) / (Sum(Pins) + Sum(Reloads)) * 100  "Hit Ratio"
from      V$LibraryCache;
```

Listing 15-4: Query for library hit ratio

Sample output:

```
Hit Ratio
99.967065
```

Rate your system:

Question	Level Required	Maximum	Score
What is your library cache hit ratio?	< 90 percent	0 points	<u>30 points</u>
	90–94 percent	10 points	
	95–98 percent	20 points	
	> 98 percent	30 points	

Sorting in Memory Hit Ratio

Based on the value of the initialization parameter PGA_AGGREGATE_TARGET (or SORT_AREA_SIZE for backward compatibility), user sorts may fit into memory or be performed on disk in a specified temporary tablespace.

You can receive specific sorting statistics (memory, disk, and rows) by running the queries shown in Listing 15-5, or go to the STATSPACK output file (report.txt) to receive these statistics. (See Chapter 14 for more information on STATSPACK.)

```
select    a.value "Disk Sorts", b.value "Memory Sorts",
          round((100*b.value)/decode((a.value+b.value),0,1,(a.value+b.value)),2)
          "Pct Memory Sorts"
from      v$sysstat a, v$sysstat b
where     a.name = 'sorts (disk)'
and       b.name = 'sorts (memory)';
```

Listing 15-5: Query to get memory and disk sorts

Sample output:

```
Disk Sorts    Memory Sorts  Pct Memory Sorts
        16           66977             99.98
```

Rate your system:

Question	Level Required	Maximum	Score
What percentage of sorts are performed in memory?	< 90 percent	0 points	30 points
	90–94 percent	10 points	
	95–98 percent	20 points	
	> 98 percent	30 points	

Percent of Data Buffers Still Free

When you start the Oracle database at the beginning of the day, users begin using memory for their queries. Although this memory is reusable when the user's query is complete, when the query shown in Listing 15-6 runs on a system after two hours of processing, it is a good indication of how quickly the buffers are being used up. The number of free records divided by the total number of records in X$BH (which is the total number of data block buffers allocated) is the percentage. Also note that you have to run this query as SYS. Furthermore, having a lot of free buffers is not necessarily the best situation. See Chapter 13 on queries to this table for more information.

```
select    decode(state,0, 'FREE',
          1,decode(lrba_seq,0,'AVAILABLE','BEING USED'),
          3, 'BEING USED', state) "BLOCK STATUS",
          count(*)
from      x$bh
group by decode(state,0,'FREE',1,decode(lrba_seq,0,'AVAILABLE',
          'BEING USED'),3, 'BEING USED', state);
```

Listing 15-6: Query for free data buffers

Sample output:

```
BLOCK STATUS    COUNT(*)
AVAILABLE       7790
BEING USED      1540
FREE            1670
```

Rate your system:

Question	Level Required	Maximum	Score
What percentage of buffers in X$BH are at a state = 0 (free) after two hours of running in production?	< 5 percent	0 points	30 points
	5–19 percent	30 points	
	20–25 percent	20 points	
	> 25 percent	0 points	

NOTE

The reason you get 0 points for greater than 25 percent free is because the data buffers are probably oversized and potentially wasting memory. Remember, this is only a general guideline— one that you definitely need to tailor to your system.

Top 10 Memory Abusers as a Percent of All Statements

When left untuned, the top 10 SQL statements accessed on most systems make up over 50 percent of all memory reads for the entire system. The code in Listing 15-7 measures how severe the most harmful statements are as a percentage of the entire system.

```
set serverout on
DECLARE
 CURSOR c1 is
  select   buffer_gets
  from     v$sqlarea
  order by buffer_gets DESC;
 CURSOR c2 is
  select   sum(buffer_gets)
  from     v$sqlarea;

 sumof10 NUMBER:=0;
 mybg NUMBER;
 mytotbg NUMBER;

BEGIN
 dbms_output.put_line('Percent');
 dbms_output.put_line('-------');
 OPEN c1;
 FOR i IN 1..10 LOOP
  FETCH c1 INTO mybg;
  sumof10 := sumof10 + mybg;
 END
 LOOP;
 CLOSE c1;
 OPEN c2;
 FETCH c2 INTO mytotbg;
 CLOSE c2;
 dbms_output.put_line(sumof10/mytotbg*100);
END;
/
```

Listing 15-7: Script to retrieve this percentage

Sample output:

```
Percent
7.1415926
```

Listing 15-8 shows alternative SQL, which is faster (Oracle9*i* only).

```
select sum(pct_bufgets)
from  (select rank() over ( order by buffer_gets desc ) as rank_bufgets,
              to_char(100 * ratio_to_report(buffer_gets) over (), '999.99')
```

Percent of Data Buffers Still Free

```
            pct_bufgets
      from   v$sqlarea )
where  rank_bufgets < 11;
```

Listing 15-8: Alternative SQL

Rate your system:

Question	Level Required	Maximum	Score
Take your top 10 memory read statements in the V$SQLAREA view. Which percentage are they of all memory reads?	> 25 percent	0 points	60 points
	20–25 percent	30 points	
	5–19 percent	50 points	
	< 5 percent	60 points	

Top 25 Memory Abusers Statements Tuned

When left untuned, the top 25 statements accessed on most systems make up over 75 percent of all memory reads of the entire system. The code shown in Listing 15-9 rates and illustrates how to find the greatest 25 memory abusers.

```
set serverout on size 1000000
declare
 top25 number;
 text1 varchar2(4000);
 x number;
 len1 number;
cursor c1 is
  select buffer_gets, substr(sql_text,1,4000)
  from v$sqlarea
  order by buffer_gets desc;
begin
 dbms_output.put_line('Gets'||'     '||'Text');
 dbms_output.put_line('----------'||' '||'----------------------');
 open c1;
 for i in 1..25 loop
  fetch c1 into top25, text1;
  dbms_output.put_line(rpad(to_char(top25),9)||' '||substr(text1,1,66));
  len1:=length(text1);
  x:=66;
  while len1 > x-1 loop
   dbms_output.put_line('"         '||substr(text1,x,66));
  x:=x+66;
  end loop;
 end loop;
end;
/
```

Listing 15-9: Query to get the 25 worst memory abusers

Partial sample output:

```
SQL> @p14
Gets    Text
16409      select f.file#, f.block#, f.ts#, f.length from fet$ f, ts$ t where
"        e t.ts#=f.ts# and t.dflextpct!=0
6868       select job from sys.job$  where next_date < sysdate  order by next
"        t_date, job
6487       SELECT BUFFER_GETS,SUBSTR(SQL_TEXT,1,3500)   FROM V$SQLAREA ORDER
"           BY BUFFER_GETS DESC
3450       SELECT BUFFER_GETS,SUBSTR(SQL_TEXT,1,4000)   FROM V$SQLAREA ORDER
"           BY BUFFER_GETS DESC
(…Simplistic Partial Listing Displayed)
```

Rate your system:

Question	Level Required	Maximum	Score
How many of your top 25 memory statements in the V$SQLAREA view have you attempted to tune?	0	0 points	30 points
	1–5	10 points	
	6–15	20 points	
	16–25	30 points	

Pinning/Caching Objects

You can pin objects into memory if they are often-used objects, as shown in Chapter 10. You can also pin tables into memory by caching the table when it is created, or by using the alter command to cache a table. See Chapter 7 for more information on caching tables.

I recommended you pin the following packages:

- DBMS_ALERT
- DBMS_DDL
- DBMS_OUTPUT
- DBMS_SESSION
- DBMS_STANDARD
- STANDARD
- DBMS_DESCRIBE
- DBMS_LOCK
- DBMS_PIPE
- DBMS_SHARED_POOL
- DBMS_UTILITY

Pinning/Caching Objects

Rate your system:

Question	Level Required	Maximum	Score
Do you pin PL/SQL objects or cache tables when needed?	Yes/No need No	10 points 0 points	10 points
Example Memory Performance Index (MPI)	Total Score		230 (A)

Grade your system:

MPI Grade	Comments	Score
A+	Top 10 percent of most systems	> 230
A	Top 20 percent of most systems	200–230
B	Top 40 percent of most systems	160–199
C	Top 70 percent of most systems	100–159
Needs help now	Bottom 30 percent of most systems	< 100

TIP

Measuring your Memory Performance Index (MPI) can help you identify potential beneficial memory allocation and usage improvements.

The Disk Performance Index (DPI)

This index measures disk use. Table 15-5 illustrates how to receive a perfect DPI score. This rating system is not meant to be an all-encompassing benchmark of disk use; rather, it is a barometer to see whether disk use improvements could be beneficial. With the advent of SANs and other disk and disk-caching technology, you may need to alter this rating to be more appropriate for your system.

Category	Level Required	Maximum Score
Top 25 (worst disk) statements tuned	Yes	40
Top 10 statements disk use	< 5 percent	60
Tables/indexes collocated	No	30
Mission-critical tables with chaining	No	30
Redo logs/undo/data separated	Yes	30
Disks used for rollback segments	> 4	30
Disks used for temporary tablespaces	> 2	30
Disk Performance Index (DPI)	Section Total	250

TABLE 15-5. *Receiving a Perfect DPI Score*

Top 25 Disk-Read Abuser Statements Tuned

When left untuned, the top 25 SQL statements accessed on most systems make up over 75 percent of all disk reads for the entire system. This section measures how severe the most harmful statements are as a percentage of the entire system. Listing 15-10 shows a tuned system in which only data dictionary queries show up.

```
set serverout on size 1000000
declare
 top25 number;
 text1 varchar2(4000);
 x number;
 len1 number;
cursor c1 is
  select disk_reads, substr(sql_text,1,4000)
  from v$sqlarea
  order by disk_reads desc;
begin
 dbms_output.put_line('Reads'||'   '||'Text');
 dbms_output.put_line('----------'||' '||'---------------------');
 open c1;
 for i in 1..25 loop
  fetch c1 into top25, text1;
  dbms_output.put_line(rpad(to_char(top25),9)||' '||substr(text1,1,66));
  len1:=length(text1);
  x:=66;
  while len1 > x-1 loop
    dbms_output.put_line('"             '||substr(text1,x,66));
  x:=x+66;
  end loop;
 end loop;
end;
/
```

Listing 15-10: Query to get the 25 worst disk-read abusers

Partial sample output:

```
Reads    Text
1156     select file#, block#, ts# from seg$ where type# = 3
122      select distinct d.p_obj#,d.p_timestamp from sys.dependency$ d, obj
"        j$ o where d.p_obj#>=:1 and d.d_obj#=o.obj# and o.status!=5
111      BEGIN sys.dbms_ijob.remove(:job); END;
(...Simplistic Partial Listing Displayed)
```

Rate your system:

Question	Level Required	Maximum	Score
How many of your top 25 disk read statements in the V$SQLAREA view have you attempted to tune?	0 1–5 6–15 16–25	0 points 10 points 20 points 40 points	40 points

Top 10 Disk-Read Abusers as Percent of All Statements

When left untuned, the top 10–25 SQL statements accessed on most systems make up over 75 percent of all disk reads for the entire system. This section measures how severe the most harmful statements are as a percentage of the entire system, as shown in Listing 15-11.

```
Set serverout on;
DECLARE
 CURSOR c1 is
  select    disk_reads
  from      v$sqlarea
  order by  disk_reads DESC;
 CURSOR c2 is
  select    sum(disk_reads)
  from      v$sqlarea;
 Sumof10 NUMBER:=0;
 mydr NUMBER;
 mytotdr NUMBER;
BEGIN
 dbms_output.put_line('Percent');
 dbms_output.put_line('-------');
 OPEN c1;
 FOR i IN 1..10 LOOP
  FETCH c1 INTO mydr;
  sumof10 := sumof10 + mydr;
 END LOOP;
 CLOSE c1;
 OPEN c2;
 FETCH c2 INTO mytotdr;
 CLOSE c2;
 dbms_output.put_line(sumof10/mytotdr*100);
END;
/
```

Listing 15-11: Script to retrieve this percentage

Sample output:

```
Percent
5.5183036
```

Listing 15-12 shows alternative/tuned SQL.

```
select sum(pct_bufgets) from
  ( select rank() over ( order by disk_reads desc ) as rank_bufgets,
          to_char(100 * ratio_to_report(disk_reads) over (), '999.99') pct_bufgets
    from   v$sqlarea )
where rank_bufgets < 11;
```

Listing 15-12: Alternative SQL

Rate your system:

Question	Level Required	Maximum	Score
Take your top 10 disk read statements in the V$SQLAREA view. What percentage are they of all disk reads?	> 25 percent	0 points	50 points
	20–25 percent	30 points	
	5–19 percent	50 points	
	< 5 percent	60 points	

Tables/Indexes Separated

Tables and their corresponding indexes should be located on separate physical disks to decrease file I/O. Chapter 3 covers this topic and provides queries to assist in this matter.

Rate your system:

Question	Level Required	Maximum	Score
Are tables and their corresponding indexes located on the same physical disk or array?	Yes	0 points	30 points
	Disk array	20 points	
	No	30 points	

Chaining in Mission-Critical Tables

When a table is updated and the block of the record updated does not have enough room to fit the changes, a record is "chained" to another block. In other words, a record spans more than one block. By analyzing a table for chained rows and querying the CHAINED_ROWS table, you identify tables that are chained. Then you must decide which tables are mission-critical.

NOTE
You must first run the utlchain.sql script located in the /rdbms/admin subdirectory of your Oracle software home directory to build the CHAINED_ROWS table.

Chaining in
Mission-Critical Tables

Rate your system:

Question	Level Required	Maximum	Score
Are there mission-critical tables with records that are chained?	Yes No	0 points 30 points	30 points

Key Oracle Files Separated

It is important to keep data that is used for recovery separate from data that may need to be recovered. This section outlines a rating system for some of the important files to keep separate.

Rate your system:

Question	Level Required	Maximum	Score
Are redo logs on a different disk from undo segments? Are both separate from DML data?	Yes Disk array No	30 points 20 points 0 points	20 points

Rollback Segment Balance

Undo segments should be separated from each other and, optimally, from the disks that hold the tables and indexes on which they are performing operations. If your system is very small, then separating undo segments may not be possible. Also, the number of DML statements users are executing should determine the optimal number of undo segments. My rule of thumb is that you should choose the number of rollback undo segments so that more than one user is never (or extremely rarely) using a single undo segment at the same time. My rule varies greatly from others' rules. (Please use whichever rule is best for your system.) Adjust the scoring in this section based on your system size and the number of users who use rollback segments. The query shown in Listing 15-13 retrieves information on rollback segments and their locations if you are not using automatic undo management.

> **NOTE**
> *This rule is not applicable with Automatic Undo Management as described in Chapter 3, and it applies only to a heavy DML environment.*

```
select    segment_name, file_name
from      dba_data_files, dba_rollback_segs
where     dba_data_files.file_id = dba_rollback_segs.file_id;
```

Listing 15-13: Query to retrieve information on rollback segments and their locations

Sample output:

```
SEGMENT NAME    FILE NAME
RBS1            /disk1/oracle/rbs1.dbf
RBS2            /disk2/oracle/rbs2.dbf
RBS3            /disk3/oracle/rbs3.dbf
```

```
RBS4          /disk4/oracle/rbs4.dbf
RBS5          /disk1/oracle/rbs1.dbf
RBS6          /disk2/oracle/rbs2.dbf
RBS7          /disk3/oracle/rbs3.dbf
RBS8          /disk4/oracle/rbs4.dbf
```

Rate your system:

Question	Level Required	Maximum	Score
How many different disks do rollback segments occupy?	1	0 points	20 points
	2	10 points	
	3–4	20 points	
	> 4	30 points	

Temporary Segment Balance

When the SORT_AREA_SIZE specified in the init.ora is not sufficient for sorting, users will sort in their predefined temporary tablespace. If a large amount of sorting on disk is prevalent, you need to ensure that users are sorting on different disks. If you use a TEMPFILE, then you must query DBA_TEMP_FILES instead of DBA_DATA_FILES to get the output shown in Listing 15-14.

```
select    username, file_name
from      dba_data_files, dba_users
where     dba_data_files.tablespace_name = dba_users.temporary_tablespace;
```

Listing 15-14: Querying DBA_TEMP_FILES

Sample output:

```
USERNAME    FILE_NAME
SYS         /disk1/oracle/sys1orcl.dbf
TEDP        /disk1/oracle/tmp1orcl.dbf
SANDRA      /disk1/oracle/tmp1orcl.dbf
TEDR        /disk1/oracle/tmp2orcl.dbf
ROB         /disk1/oracle/tmp2orcl.dbf
DIANNE      /disk1/oracle/tmp2orcl.dbf
RICH        /disk1/soracle/tmp2orcl.dbf
DONNA       /disk1/oracle/tmp3orcl.dbf
DAVE        /disk1/oracle/tmp3orcl.dbf
ANDREA      /disk1/oracle/tmp3orcl.dbf
MIKE        /disk1/oracle/tmp3ora.dbf
```

Rate your system:

Question	Level Required	Maximum	Score
The users in your system can be altered to use a temporary tablespace for sorting. How many disks are used for this?	All in system	0 points	10 points
	1	10 points	
	2	20 points|	
	> 2	30 points	
Example Disk Performance Index (DPI)		Total Score	200 (B)

Grade your system:

DPI Grade	Comments	Score
A+	Top 10 percent of most systems	> 235
A	Top 20 percent of most systems	205–235
B	Top 40 percent of most systems	170–204
C	Top 70 percent of most systems	110–169
Needs help now	Bottom 30 percent of most systems	< 110

TIP
Measuring your Disk Performance Index (DPI) can help you identify potential beneficial disk improvements.

The Total Performance Index (TPI)

The Total Performance Index is the composite score of the Memory, Disk, Education, and System indices, as shown in Table 15-6.

Rate your system:

Index	Total Score
Example Education Performance Index (EPI)	150 (B)
Example System Performance Index (SPI)	220 (A+)
Example Memory Performance Index (MPI)	230 (A)
Example Disk Performance Index (DPI)	200 (B)
Example Total Performance Index (SPI)	800 (A)

Category Index	Maximum Score
Education Performance Index (EPI)	250
System Performance Index (SPI)	250
Memory Performance Index (MPI)	250
Disk Performance Index (DPI)	250
Total Performance Index (TPI)	1000

TABLE 15-6. *Measuring the Total Performance Index*

Grade your system:

TPI Grade	Comments	Score
A+	Top 10 percent of most systems	> 925
A	Top 20 percent of most systems	795–924
B	Top 40 percent of most systems	620–794
C	Top 70 percent of most systems	380–619
Needs help now	Bottom 30 percent of most systems	< 380

TIP
Measuring your Total Performance Index (TPI) can help you identify bottlenecks; it is a simple barometer that rates your overall system performance.

An Overall System Review Example

You can use the following rating scale to generate a yearly review for your system. Some of the items (such as backup and recovery ratings) are not covered in depth. The goal of this section is to help you consider the areas you might review. This is not an actual client system review, but a slightly modified version of several reviews to help generate discussion items for your review template. The objective is to give you a feel of a review. The parameters for the DBA rating and backup and recovery rating are listed in *Oracle DBA Tips & Techniques* (Sumit Sarin, 2000, Oracle Press).

Rating System

Use the following example rating report as a guideline as you detail an overall review and ratings. If your review includes a rating for items that desperately need improvement or attention (where appropriate), you will more easily generate manager support. In many cases, a DBA needs managerial support to receive the time to address major issues with the system. At times, if the system is up and running, upper management does realize that a change is necessary. This review can be a catalyst for needed change as issues are identified.

Grade	Comments	Score
A+	Excellent	Top 5 percent of systems reviewed
A	Very good to excellent	Top 10 percent
A-	Very good	Top 15 percent
B, B+, B-	Good/could be improved	Top 25 percent
C, C+, C-	Requires improvement	Top 50 percent
D, D+, D-	Desperately requires improvement	Bottom 50 percent
F	Immediately needs to be corrected	Bottom 10 percent

TIP
Have your system reviewed annually by an outside party, or at the minimum, by someone inside your company.

Example System Review Rating *Categories*

Table 15-7 summarizes the results of the system review. Although some of the categories of the TPI are discussed, this section is an addition to the TPI that goes into greater depth. An overview of the recommended changes should follow this section, and the TPI rating could precede or follow this section. This section is more subjective, so an experienced person whom you respect should make these judgments. The ratings should include more detailed comments than those given here as an example. The recommended changes should be detailed with supporting documentation.

NOTE
This is an example, not an actual review.

Category	Grade	Comments
Overall review	C-	The system is running very poorly due to an insufficient amount of memory allocated for the data processing. Several areas need to be corrected immediately to substantially improve system performance, especially as additional users are added.
Architecture	B	The overall architecture is good, but a SAN with onboard cache should be investigated to improve I/O issues.
Hardware sizing	A-	The hardware is well sized for the business activity, but the system is not tuned to take full advantage of the hardware.
Security	F	The passwords are never changed, even when employees leave the company. Several unprotected files have hard-coded passwords. The SYSTEM password is MANAGER and the SYS password is CHANGE_ON_INSTALL. This is unacceptable!
Memory allocation	B+	Of the 2GB of memory, more of the memory can be allocated for the DB_CACHE_SIZE.

TABLE 15-7. *Sample System Review Results*

Category	Grade	Comments
Database tuning	D-	The top 25 queries make up 98 percent of all resource usage. No effort has been made to tune these queries.
Disk configuration	B	Disk I/O is reasonably balanced, but it could be improved by partitioning a few of the hardest hit tables and indexes.
Redo logs	B+	Redo logs are sized well, but you may want to add a few more of them for batch processing when they switch much faster.
Archived log files	A+	File systems containing the archive log files are independent of other Oracle file systems. Archives are archived to tape, but also kept on disk for fast recoveries.
Rollback segments	A+	Automatic UNDO has been implemented and tuned.
Control files	A-	Multiple control files are located on different physical disks, but a backup of control file to TRACE does not exist.
Initialization parameters	C+	2GB of memory is available on the system. The database is 2TB (terabytes), and there are 1000 users on the system. The DB_CACHE_SIZE should be increased. You should be using multiple buffer pools to better balance the good users from the ad-hoc users.
Table design	C-	There is no database-level referential integrity.
Tables	C-	Tables are not partitioned as they should be, and parallel should be set on some of the larger tables. Some of the smaller tables need to be altered so that they will be cached in memory.
Indexes	C-	Indexes should be partitioned more. Bitmap indexes are not being employed for the low-cardinality (few unique rows) columns of query-only tables.
Tablespaces	C+	Tablespaces are severely undersized for future growth.

TABLE 15-7.   *Sample System Review Results* (continued)

NOTE
With Oracle9iR2, when you use DBCA to create a database, you cannot specify MANAGER or CHANGE_ON_INSTALL as the passwords for SYSTEM and SYS. You are forced to choose new passwords. You can always alter these users later.

Example System Review
Rating Categories

Items Requiring Immediate Action

Once you have reviewed your system, you need to make a comprehensive list of items that need to be addressed immediately. The following list is a partial summary of some of the actions to take immediately:

- Change the SYS and SYSTEM passwords immediately!

- Change all other default passwords. Change all user passwords because the security is currently compromised.

- Increase DB_CACHE_SIZE immediately! This can be done with the system up in Oracle9i if the SGA_MAX_SIZE is large enough.

- Tune the top 25 queries causing disk and memory reads.

> **TIP**
> *A system review should always include immediate action items. This ensures that the time and money needed for improvements will be allocated.*

Other Items Requiring Action

The second list you should make includes items needing attention after the most pressing issues have been addressed. A summary example list follows. Your list should include more detail on how to correct the action.

- Monitor the items detailed in this document at least once per quarter with the current growth rate of the system.

- Be sure SYSTEM and SYS passwords in production are different in development.

- Resize the database objects that are currently oversized and undersized.

- Change all passwords at least once per quarter.

- Fix file protection so that users are unable to delete Oracle software.

- Remove hard-coded passwords from scripts and backup jobs.

- Consider adding additional indexes for the top 25 worst disk-read queries to improve query performance.

If init.ora changes are to be made, you should compile a list with both the current and suggested values. Refer to Appendix A for a complete list of init.ora parameters with detailed descriptions.

The System Information List

This section describes some of the system information you should gather and keep with the review. As you look back on a review, you need to know what the parameters of the system were at the time of the review. Any ratings of specific items (such as backup and recovery) could be placed in this section. I have also included a sample DBA review that illustrates some of the areas that may be reviewed. It is wise to have someone else rate your DBA skills so that you can continue to improve. This section has been greatly simplified for the book. It is a quick list designed to provide a picture of the system as whole.

Memory-Related Values

Ask the following memory-related questions about the system. (I have also provided some sample answers.)

- What is the current memory for the hardware? 4GB.
- What is the current number of users? 500 total/50 concurrent.
- What will be the future number of users? 100–150 concurrent in the next three months.
- What other software is used on the system? None that is a major influence.
- Is the system client/server or browser/server? Browser/server.
- What response times are required? Subsecond. OLTP transactions make up main mix.
- How large is the database? Currently 9.5TB with 100GB free in the database.
- How large are often-accessed tables? One million rows is the average.
- Which future software will affect memory? None.
- Will you be implementing any other features/options? Oracle Streams in six months.

Disk-Related Values

Ask the following disk-related questions. (Sample answers are provided.)

- What is the maximum disk capacity for the hardware? Eight times current capacity.
- What disk sizes are available? Unknown.
- What will be the size of the database in one year? Ten percent larger than current.
- Is there a RAID (striping) level for database files/OS? Yes; RAID 1+0.
- Will there be multiplexed redo logs? Yes.
- What new software will be installed? No additions in near future.
- Which system utilities will be installed? Quest Utilities, Veritas DBE /AC 3.5.
- What EDI transfers will happen nightly? Bulk order transfers.

Other Items Requiring Action

CPU-Related Values

Answer the following CPU-related questions. (Sample answers are provided.)

- What's the maximum number of processors for the hardware? Six currently/12 maximum.

- Is there a future upgrade path? Yes; Path to 64 processors.

- What is the transaction processing load? Sixty percent CPU average/90 percent sustained maximum.

- What is the batch load? Some heavy at night/OK during the day.

- Are hot backups employed? Omniback cold backups are employed with archiving.

- Are batch processes running during the day? None that are affecting performance.

- Will parallel query be used in the future? Currently being used on some processes.

- Will there be a future distributed setup? Yes, with Oracle Streams.

Backup and Recovery–Related Information

Ask the following backup and recovery–related questions. (Sample answers are provided.)

- Does the system require 7/24 use? No, it is 6/24.

- How fast will recovery need to be made (on disk backup)? 12-hour maximum.

- Are there "standby" disks in case of failure? No, 4-hour turnaround from HP.

- How much data is "backed up"? Is it being "tape-striped" with parity? Unknown.

- Has the UPS been established? Yes.

- Are export files also taken? No.

- What is the condition of cold backup procedures? Excellent.

- What is the condition of export procedures? Needs improvement.

- What is the condition of hot backup procedures? Not applicable.

- What is the condition of disaster recovery procedures? Needs improvement.

The following is an example of some of the areas that you may evaluate in a backup and recovery rating. The *Oracle DBA Tips and Techniques* book goes into this rating in depth. The layout should be identical to your system review.

Category	Grade	Comments
Backup and recovery overall	A	Script to replace all backed up files should also be generated
Backup procedures	A	Excellent
Archiving procedures	A	Excellent
Recovery procedures	A-	Should have scripts ready to go for a recovery
Backup knowledge	A	Very good
Recovery knowledge	A	Very good
Disaster backup	A+	Excellent
Disaster recovery	A	Very good, rolling forward was still being worked on

Naming Conventions and/or OFA Standards and Security Information

Good system maintenance procedures are a key item to lower your future maintenance costs. Naming conventions will help make a system easier to maintain. Using OFA standards helps the entire team more easily find things in a commonly known directory structure. Having security procedures, including healthy password maintenance is essential to a well-maintained system. Ask the following questions related to these areas.

- What is the condition of the naming conventions used? Excellent, but not OFA.

- What is the condition of file protections on key Oracle files? Poor.

- What is the condition of the database security procedures? Poor.

- What is the condition of the password procedures? Poor.

DBA Knowledge Rating

Having all DBAs reviewed by an impartial expert is paramount to identifying and improving the skills for a DBA. Often, the primary DBA is too busy to attend training sessions or improve skills on new versions of Oracle. This rating will help identify areas of strengths and weaknesses. This process will fail if this review is used against a person. It *must* be used with the goal of identifying and improving.

Category	Rating
DBA knowledge overall	A
Oracle architecture	A-
Oracle objects	B+
Oracle internals	B+
Oracle initialization parameters	B+
Oracle query tuning	A
Oracle database tuning	A
Oracle backup	A
Oracle recovery	A
Oracle utilities	A
Operating system	B+

TIP
You should review a DBA's ability only if the review will be used as a means of improving the DBA's skills. Reviewing a person is a very sensitive issue and must be done by someone who has the goal of improvement first and foremost.

Tips Review

- Measuring your Memory Performance Index (MPI) can help you identify potential memory allocation and usage improvements that could be beneficial.

- Measuring your Disk Performance Index (DPI) can help you identify potential disk improvements that could be beneficial.

- Measuring your Education Performance Index (EPI) can help you identify educational improvements that could be beneficial.

- Measuring your System Performance Index (SPI) can help you identify overall system improvements that could be beneficial.

- Measuring your Total Performance Index (TPI) can help you identify bottlenecks and is a simple barometer rating your overall system performance as it compares to others in the industry.

- Have your system reviewed annually by an outside party or, at a minimum, by someone inside your company.

- A system review should always include immediate action items. This ensures that the time needed for improvements will be allocated.

■ You should review a DBA's ability only if the review will be used as a means of improving the DBA's skills. Reviewing a person is a very sensitive issue and must be done by someone who has the goal of improvement first and foremost.

■ If you can't effectively monitor your own system, then contract someone who can. The cost of maintaining a database is usually far less than the cost of downtime when problems occur.

References

Oracle9i SQL Language Reference Manual Versions, Oracle Corporation.
Memory Performance Index, Disk Performance Index, Education Performance Index, Total Performance Index, MPI, DPI, EPI, SPI, and TPI; Copyright TUSC 1998–2003.
Tuning Secrets from the Dark Room of the DBA; Maurice Aelion, Dr. Oleg Zhooravlev, and Arie Yuster.

Many thanks to Randy Swanson, Judy Corley, Sean McGuire, and Greg Pucka of TUSC for contributions to this chapter.

CHAPTER
16

Monitoring the System Using UNIX Utilities (DBA)

Part of being able to solve performance problems includes being able to effectively use operating system utilities. Using the correct utilities to find CPU, memory, and disk I/O issues is crucial to identifying where performance problems exist. This chapter focuses on UNIX utilities and shell scripts that you can use to find these problems.

The topics covered in this chapter include the following:

■ UNIX utilities

■ Tip review

■ References

UNIX Utilities

This chapter focuses on tools that monitor CPU, memory, and disk issues. Most of the utilities discussed are UNIX utilities.

The following tips are discussed in this chapter:

■ Using sar to monitor CPU usage

■ Using top to find the worst user on the system

■ Using uptime to monitor the CPU load

■ Using mpstat to identify CPU bottlenecks

■ Combining ps with selected V$ views

■ Using sar to monitor disk I/O problems

■ Using iostat to identify disk I/O bottlenecks

■ Using sar and vmstat to monitor paging/swapping

■ Determining shared memory usage using ipcs

■ Monitoring system load using vmstat

■ Monitoring disk freespace

■ Monitoring network performance

Using sar to Monitor CPU Usage

The sar command has many different switches that you can set to display different pieces of performance information. With the -u switch, you can use sar to monitor CPU usage. The sar command gives you a quick snapshot of how heavily the CPU is bogged down. Run this utility regularly to get a baseline for your system; it enables you to identify when your system is running poorly. Of the two numbers following the switch for sar (-u in the following example), the first is used to display the number of seconds between readings; the second is the number of times you want sar to run.

Report CPU Utilization (Default)

%usr   Percent of CPU running in user mode

%sys   Percent of CPU running in system mode

%wio   Percent of CPU running idle with a process waiting for block I/O

%idle   Percent of CPU that is idle

```
# sar -u 10 8
HP-UX sch1p197 B.10.20 E 9000/893    01/23/02
            usr    %sys    %wio    %idle
11:55:53    80     14      3       3
11:56:03    70     14      12      4
11:56:13    72     13      21      4
11:56:23    76     14      6       3
11:56:33    73     10      13      4
11:56:43    71     8       17      4
11:56:53    67     9       20      4
11:57:03    69     10      17      4
Average     73     11      13      4
```

Listing 16-1: Report CPU utilization (default)

A low %idle time points to a CPU-intensive job or an underpowered CPU. Use the ps or top command to find a CPU-intensive job. A poorly written query requiring a lot of disk access can also cause a lot of CPU usage.

The large values being returned for %wio (waiting for block I/O) vs. actual heavy CPU usage in the following sar output is cause for concern:

```
# sar -u 5 4
            %usr    %sys    %wio    %idle
14:29:58    20      20      60      0
14:30:03    17      23      60      0
14:30:08    19      14      67      0
14:30:13    22      11      67      0
Average     21      16      64      0
```

Listing 16-2: sar output showing large values returned for %wio vs. actual heavy CPU usage

This list shows a high %wio (waiting for I/O time), which points toward a disk contention problem. Use the iostat command to pinpoint disk contention.

TIP

Use the sar -u command to see how heavily the CPU is bogged down. Run sar regularly to get a baseline for your system so that you can identify when your system is running poorly. Keep in mind, however, that low CPU idle time can be an I/O issue and not a CPU issue.

Idle Percentage for the CPU

What's a good idle percentage for the CPU? It really depends on the system size and variation in time accessed. For instance, a system that is accessed with heavy CPU usage for short periods of time may have an 80 percent average CPU idle time. In contrast, a system with a lot of very small jobs may have the same 80 percent average CPU idle time. The idle percentage is not as important as what is available when you run a job that must complete immediately (and is very important to the business). A 50 percent idle CPU may be a problem for the company with a large CPU-bound job that must complete quickly, while a 10 percent idle CPU may be more than enough for a company that has a very small job (requiring little CPU) that must complete quickly. Oracle generally tries to use the entire CPU available to complete a job.

It is useful to run sar at regularly scheduled intervals throughout the day. The overhead is minimal and can be a great help in determining what was happening when the problem actually started occurring. You have the ability to keep information in report format for 30 days by default. The following entries in root's crontab produces a snapshot of the system state every 20 minutes during working hours:

```
20,40 8-17 * * 1-5 /usr/lib/sa/sa1
```

Listing 16-3: Crontab entry producing system state snapshot every 20 minutes during working hours

> **NOTE**
> *For further information about scheduling programs via cron, refer to your system's man pages on crontab.*

The next entry produces an hourly report of important activities throughout the workday:

```
5 18 * * 1-5 /usr/lib/sa/sa2 -s 8:00 -e 18:01 -i 1200 -A
```

Listing 16-4: Crontab entry producing hourly report of important activities throughout workday

To access the report at any time, simply type **sar** with the appropriate switches and you will see output for each sampling period.

> **NOTE**
> *For further information, see your man pages for sar, sa1, and sa2. The command to see the man page for crontab is man crontab.*

Using top to Find the Worst User on the System

The top command shows a continuous display of the most active processes. DBAs and operations experts often run this (or similar utilities) at the first sign of system performance issues. This display automatically updates itself onscreen every few seconds. The first lines give general system information, while the rest of the display is arranged in order of decreasing current CPU usage. (The worst user is on top.) If your system does not have top installed, it is available from sunfreeware.com or various other sources on the Web. Simply do a search for **top program download AND Unix** and you will find multiple locations from which to download the program.

```
# top
Cpu states:  0.0% idle, 81.0% user, 17.7% kernel,  0.8% wait,  0.5% swap
Memory: 765M real, 12M free, 318M swap, 1586M free swap
PID   USERNAME  PRI  NICE   SIZE    RES  STATE  TIME    WCPU     CPU   COMMAND
23626 psoft     -25    2   208M   4980K  cpu    1:20   22.47%  99.63%  oracle
15819 root      -15    4  2372K    716K  sleep 22:19    0.61%   3.81%  pmon
20434 oracle     33    0   207M   2340K  sleep  2:47    0.23%   1.14%  oracle
20404 oracle     33    0    93M   2300K  sleep  2:28    0.23%   1.14%  oracle
23650 root       33    0  2052K   1584K  cpu    0:00    0.23%   0.95%  top
23625 psoft      27    2  5080K   3420K  sleep  0:17    1.59%   0.38%  sqr
23554 root       27    2  2288K   1500K  sleep  0:01    0.06%   0.38%  brxpu2.1.adm
15818 root       21    4  6160K   2416K  sleep  2:05    0.04%   0.19%  proctool
  897 root       34    0  8140K   1620K  sleep 55:46    0.00%   0.00%  Xsun
20830 psoft      -9    2  7856K   2748K  sleep  7:14    0.67%   0.00%  PSRUN
20854 psoft      -8    2   208M   4664K  sleep  4:21    0.52%   0.00%  oracle
  737 oracle     23    0  3844K   1756K  sleep  2:56    0.00%   0.00%  tnslsnr
 2749 root       28    0  1512K    736K  sleep  1:03    0.00%   0.00%  lpNet
18529 root       14   10  2232K   1136K  sleep  0:56    0.00%   0.00%  xlock
    1 root       33    0   412K    100K  sleep  0:55    0.00%   0.00%  init
```

Listing 16-5: Output from top command

The results show the top user to be psoft with a PID of 23626. This user is using 99.63 percent of one CPU. If this output persisted for any length of time, it would be imperative to find out who this is and what he or she is doing.

TIP
Use the top command to find the worst user on the system at a given time (the kill command usually follows for many DBAs). If the worst query lasts only a short time, it may not be a problem; but if it persists, additional investigation may be necessary.

Monitoring Tools

On most platforms, GUI monitoring tools are available that either come bundled with the software or are accessible on the Internet. The Task Manager Process Monitor is available on Windows NT, Windows 2000, and ProcTool (primarily for older versions of Solaris, although an unsupported version exists on Solaris 7 and 8); the sdtprocess and Management Console tools are available for later versions of Solaris (once again, sunfreeware.com has a plethora of free tools); and tools like the Superdome Support Management Station (SMS), HP OpenView, and the servicecontrol suite are available for HP.

Using uptime to Monitor CPU Load

The uptime command is an excellent utility to find a quick 1-, 5-, and 15-minute CPU load of all jobs (including those currently running). You want to look at the load average: the number of jobs in the CPU run queue for the last 1, 5, and 15 minutes. [1]

NOTE
This is not the percentage of CPU being used.

```
# uptime
  3:10pm  up 5 day(s), 19:04,  2 users,  load average: 2.10, 2.50, 2.20
```

Listing 16-6: Output from uptime command

A system with an average run queue of 2-3 is generally acceptable. If you add the following script to your cron table to run every hour, you will be e-mailed your average system load every two hours.

```
{uptime; sleep 120; uptime; sleep 120; uptime;} | mailx -s uptime you@company.com
```

Listing 16-7: Chrontab script producing email notification of average system load

TIP
Use cron and uptime to get your system load mailed to you regularly.

Using mpstat to Identify CPU Bottlenecks

The mpstat command is a Sun Solaris tool that reports per-processor statistics in tabular form. Each row of the table represents the activity of one processor. The first table shows the summary of activity since boot time. Pay close attention to the smtx measurement; it measures the number of times the CPU failed to obtain a mutual exclusion lock (mutex). Mutex stalls waste CPU time and degrade multiprocessor scaling. In the following example, there are four processors numbered 0-3, and a system that is heading toward disaster.

```
# mpstat 10 5
CPU minf mjf xcal intr ithr csw icsw migr smtx srw syscl usr sys wt  idl
0   1    0   0    110  9    75  2    2    9    0   302   4   4   11  81
1   1    0   0    111  109  72  2    2    11   0   247   3   4   11  82
2   1    0   0    65   63   73  2    2    9    0   317   4   5   10  81
3   1    0   0    2    0    78  2    2    9    0   337   4   5   10  81
```

---

[1] This is a system-specific timing statistic. Sun is 1, 5, and 15 minutes; Digital UNIX is 5, 30, and 60 seconds.

CPU	minf	mjf	xcal	intr	ithr	csw	icsw	migr	smtx	srw	syscl	usr	sys	wt	idl
0	2	8	0	198	12	236	113	35	203	60	1004	74	26	0	0
1	1	17	0	371	286	225	107	39	194	48	1087	60	40	0	0
2	0	22	0	194	82	267	127	38	227	49	1197	63	37	0	0
3	0	14	0	103	0	218	107	35	188	46	1075	71	29	0	0
CPU	minf	mjf	xcal	intr	ithr	csw	icsw	migr	smtx	srw	syscl	usr	sys	wt	idl
0	17	22	0	247	12	353	170	26	199	21	1263	54	46	0	0
1	8	14	0	406	265	361	165	27	200	25	1242	53	47	0	0
2	6	15	0	408	280	306	151	23	199	24	1229	56	44	0	0
3	10	19	0	156	0	379	174	28	163	27	1104	63	37	0	0
CPU	minf	mjf	xcal	intr	ithr	csw	icsw	migr	smtx	srw	syscl	usr	sys	wt	idl
0	0	19	0	256	12	385	180	24	446	19	1167	48	52	0	0
1	0	13	0	416	279	341	161	24	424	20	1376	45	55	0	0
2	0	13	0	411	290	293	144	22	354	15	931	54	46	0	0
3	0	14	0	140	0	320	159	22	362	14	1312	58	42	0	0
CPU	minf	mjf	xcal	intr	ithr	csw	icsw	migr	smtx	srw	syscl	usr	sys	wt	idl
0	23	15	0	264	12	416	194	31	365	25	1146	52	48	0	0
1	20	10	0	353	197	402	184	29	341	25	1157	41	59	0	0
2	24	5	0	616	486	360	170	30	376	20	1363	41	59	0	0
3	20	9	0	145	0	352	165	27	412	26	1359	50	50	0	0

Listing 16-8: mpstat command and output

TIP
If the smtx column for the mpstat output is greater than 200, you are heading toward CPU bottleneck problems.

Combining ps with Selected V$ Views

Which process is using the most CPU? The following UNIX command lists the top nine CPU users in reverse order (much like the top command). Note that the actual output puts the text header at the bottom of the listing.

```
ps -e -o pcpu² ,pid,user,args | sort -k 0,0 -r | tail
%CPU   PID    USER      COMMAND
0.3    1337   oracle    oraclePRD
0.3    4888   oracle    oraclePRD (LOCAL=NO)
0.4    3      root      fsflush
0.4    1333   psoft     PSRUN PTPUPRCS
0.4    3532   root      ./pmon
0.4    4932   oracle    oraclePRD (DESCRIPTION=(LOCAL=NO) (ADDRESS=PROTOCOL=beq)))
0.4    4941   oracle    oraclePRD (LOCAL=NO)
2.6    4943   oracle    oraclePRD (LOCAL=NO)
16.3   4699   oracle    oraclePRD
```

Listing 16-9: ps command and output

---

² This command should work on any POSIX-compatible version of UNIX.

Using top to Find the Worst User

This command lists the %CPU[3] used, the PID, the UNIX username, and the command that was executed. If the top user was an Oracle user, you could use the following queries to get the information on the process from Oracle. The system PID obtained from the ps command is passed into these queries:

```
ps_view.sql
col username format a15
col osuser       format a10
col program    format a20
set verify off
select     a.username, a.osuser, a.program, spid, sid, a.serial#
from       v$session a, v$process b
where      a.paddr  =  b.addr
and        spid      = '&pid';
ps_sql.sql
set verify off
column username format a15
column sql_text    format a60
undefine sid
undefine serial#
accept sid prompt 'sid: '
accept serial prompt 'serial#: '
select     'SQL Currently Executing: '
from       dual;
select     b.username, a.sql_text
from       v$sql a, v$session b
where      b.sql_address        = a.address
and        b.sql_hash_value = a.hash_value
and        b.sid        = &sid
and        b.serial# = '&serial';
select     'Open Cursors:'
from       dual;
select     b.username, a.sql_text
from       v$open_cursor a, v$session b
where      b.sql_address        = a.address
and        b.sql_hash_value = a.hash_value
and        b.sid        = &sid
and        b.serial# = '&serial';
```

Listing 16-10: ps command queries

---

[3]   SunOS 5.5 defines pcpu as "The ratio of CPU time used recently to CPU time available in the same period, expressed as a percentage. The meaning of 'recently' in this context is unspecified. The CPU time available is determined in an unspecified manner."

Running an example (one step at a time)

```
$ ps -e -o pcpu,pid,user,args | sort -k 0,0 -r | tail
%CPU    PID    USER      COMMAND
0.4     650    nobody    /opt/SUNWsymon/sbin/sm_logscand
0.4     3242   oracle    ora_d000_DM6
0.4     3264   oracle    ora_d000_DMO
0.4     3316   oracle    ora_d000_CNV
0.4     4383   oracle    ora_d000_QAT
0.5     3      root      fsflush
0.8     654    root      /opt/SUNWsymon/sbin/sm_krd -i 10
1.7     652    root      /opt/SUNWsymon/sbin/sm_configd -i 10
3.6     4602   oracle    oracleCNV (LOCAL=NO)
$ sqlplus system/manager
SQL> @ps_view
Enter value for pid: 4602
```

Listing 16-11: ps command query example—part 1

Note that we use 4602 as the input because it is the PID for the worst CPU from the ps command.

```
old   4:          and spid='&pid'
new   4:          and spid='4602'
USERNAME   OSUSER   PROGRAM              SPID     SID     SERIAL#
DBAENT     mag      sqlplus@hrtest       4602     10      105
SQL> @ps_sql
sid: 10
serial#: 105
```

Listing 16-12: ps command query example—part 2

Note that we use 10 as the SID and 105 as the SERIAL# because they were the values retrieved in the preceding query (ps_view.sql).

```
'SQLCURRENTLYEXECUTING:'
-----------------------
SQL Currently Executing:
old    5: and b.sid=&sid
new    5: and b.sid=10
old    6: and b.serial#='&serial'
new    6: and b.serial#='105'
USERNAME    SQL_TEXT
DBAENT      select sum(bytes),sum(blocks) from dba_segments
'OPENCURSORS:'
Open Cursors:
old    5: and b.sid=&sid
new    5: and b.sid=10
old    6: and b.serial#='&serial'
new    6: and b.serial#='105'
USERNAME    SQL_TEXT
DBAENT      select sum(bytes),sum(blocks) from dba_segments
```

Listing 16-13: ps command query example - part 3

Putting it all together (setting headings off)

```
DBAENT      mag      sqlplus@hrtest      4602    10      105
SQL Currently Executing:
DBAENT      select sum(bytes),sum(blocks) from dba_segments
Open Cursors:
DBAENT      select sum(bytes),sum(blocks) from dba_segments
```

Listing 16-14: ps command query example - part 4 - putting it all together

If you had an ad-hoc query user problem and problem queries showed up in this result regularly, you could add an automated kill command at the end to completely automate the job.

TIP
Combine operating system utilities with Oracle utilities to quickly and effectively find problem users.

CPU/Memory-Monitoring Tool on NT

Task Manager can be used for monitoring CPU and memory use on Windows NT. Figure 16-1 shows a two-processor system on NT.

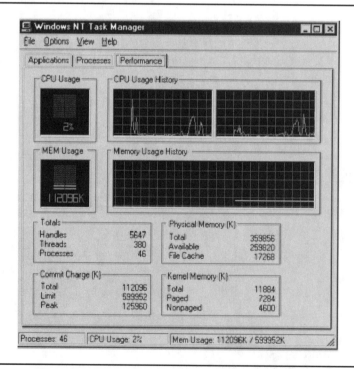

FIGURE 16-1. *Monitoring Tool on NT*

Using sar to Monitor Disk I/O Problems

Using sar with the -d switch shows potential disk I/O bottlenecks. This command lists the %busy, avque (average queue length), r+w/s (read and write activity), blks/s (number of blocks transferred), avwait, and avserv. A high %busy and high avque indicates a disk I/O bottleneck. Consider the following output, where disk sd17 is a problem. (It is 100 percent busy.) If this condition persisted, an analysis of disk sd17 should lead to a reorganization of information from sd17 to a less-used disk. The sar command allows two significant numerical inputs; the first is the number of seconds between running sar, and the second is how many times to run it. (Below 5 is 5 seconds, and 2 tells sar to run twice.)

```
# sar  -d 5 2
          device   %busy   avque   r+w/s   blks/s   avwait   avserv
13:37:11    fd0       0     0.0       0        0      0.0      0.0
            sd1       0     0.0       0        0      0.0      0.0
            sd3       0     0.0       0        0      0.0      0.0
            sd6       0     0.0       0        0      0.0      0.0
            sd15      0     0.0       0        0      0.0      0.0
            sd16     13     0.1       5      537      0.0     26.4
            sd17    100     6.1      84     1951      0.0     72.4
            sd18      0     0.0       0        0      0.0      0.0
13:37:16    fd0       0     0.0       0        0      0.0      0.0
            sd1       0     0.0       0        0      0.0      0.0
            sd3       1     0.0       1       16      0.0     32.7
            sd6       0     0.0       0        0      0.0      0.0
            sd15      3     0.1       1       22      0.0     92.3
            sd17    100     6.1      85     1955      0.0     71.5
            sd18      0     0.0       0        0      0.0      0.0
Average     fd0       0     0.0       0        0      0.0      0.0
            sd1       0     0.0       0        0      0.0      0.0
            sd3       0     0.0       0        3      0.0     32.7
            sd6       0     0.0       0        0      0.0      0.0
            sd15      1     0.0       0        4      0.0     92.3
            sd16     13     0.1       5      570      0.0     25.3
            sd17    100     6.1      85     1962      0.0     71.2
            sd18      0     0.0       0        0      0.0      0.0
```

Listing 16-15: sar command syntax and output

NOTE
Refer to Chapter 3 for additional information on tuning disk I/O when it is at the database level.

Using iostat to Identify Disk I/O Bottlenecks

The UNIX tool iostat can also be used to identify a disk bottleneck; it reports terminal and disk I/O activity, as well as CPU utilization. The first line of the output displays the I/O statistics since the system was started, as well as CPU utilization. Each subsequent line shows only the prior interval specified.

Depending on the flavor of UNIX, this command has several options (switches). The most useful switches are -d, -x, -D, and -c (cpu load).

```
Format:    iostat [option] [disk] [interval] [count]
```

Listing 16-16: iostat command syntax

Use the -d switch to see a list of the number of kilobytes transferred per second, the number of transfers per second, and the average service time in milliseconds. Using -d displays only I/O; it doesn't distinguish between reads and writes.

Using the -d switch of iostat

```
# iostat -d sd15 sd16 sd17 sd18 5 5
```

sd15			sd16			sd17			sd18		
Kps	tps	serv	Kps	tps	serv	Kps	tps	serv	Kps	tps	serv
1	0	53	57	5	145	19	1	89	0	0	14
140	14	16	0	0	0	785	31	21	0	0	0
8	1	15	0	0	0	814	36	18	0	0	0
11	1	82	0	0	26	818	36	19	0	0	0
0	0	0	1	0	22	856	37	20	0	0	0

Listing 16-17: iostat -d switch command and output

This output shows that sd17 is severely overloaded compared to the other drives. Moving information from sd17 to one of the other drives would be a good idea if this information is consistently representative of disk I/O.

Using the -D Switch of iostat
The -D switch reports the reads per second, writes per second, and percentage of disk utilization.

```
# iostat -D sd15 sd16 sd17 sd18 5 5
```

sd15			sd16			sd17			sd18		
rps	wps	util	rps	wps	util	rps	wps	util	rps	wps	util
0	0	0.3	4	0	6.2	1	1	1.8	0	0	0.0
0	0	0.0	0	35	90.6	237	0	97.8	0	0	0.0
0	0	0.0	0	34	84.7	218	0	98.2	0	0	0.0
0	0	0.0	0	34	88.3	230	0	98.2	0	0	0.0
0	2	4.4	0	37	91.3	225	0	97.7	0	0	0.0

Listing 16-18: iostat -D switch command and output

This report shows that the activity on sd17 is strictly read activity, while the activity on sd16 is strictly write activity. Both drives are at a peak level of utilization, and there may be I/O problems. These statistics were gathered during a backup of sd17 to sd16. Your system should never look this bad!

Using the -x Switch of iostat (Extended Disk Statistics)

The -x switch reports extended disk statistics for all disks. It combines many of the switches previously discussed.

```
# iostat -x
device r/s    w/s    kr/s    kw/s    wait   actv   svc_t    %w    %b
fd0     0.0    0.0    0.0     0.0     0.0    0.0    0.0      0     0
sd1     0.0    0.2    0.0     23.2    0.0    0.0    37.4     0     1
sd3     0.0    1.2    0.0     8.4     0.0    0.0    31.3     0     1
sd6     0.0    0.0    0.0     0.0     0.0    0.0    0.0      0     0
sd15    0.0    1.6    0.0     12.8    0.0    0.1    93.3     0     3
sd16    0.0    5.8    0.0     315.2   0.0    0.1    25.0     0     15
sd17    73.0   2.8    941.1   117.2   0.0    6.9    90.8     0     100
sd18    0.0    0.0    0.0     0.0     0.0    0.0    0.0      0     0
```

Listing 16-19: iostat -x switch command and output

Once again, disks sd16 and sd17 need to be investigated and monitored further.

Combining -x Switch of iostat with Logic in a Shell Script

The following script takes the iostat -x output, sorts it by the %busy field, and prints out the ten busiest disks for the listed interval. Some options for this script are listed next, followed by the script example and output.

- This is the diskbusy script built on 1/1/2000.

- The shell this example is running in is !/bin/ksh.

- This script gets an iostat -x listing and sorts it by the %busy field.

- Change print $10 to sort by a different field.

- Change iostat -x 5 5 to get a different interval and count.

- Change tail to tail -20 to get the top 20 busiest disks.

```
iostat -x | awk '/^disk/'
iostat -x 5 5|grep -v '^   ' |grep -v '^disk'| awk '{
        print $10 ", " $0
        }' $* |
sort -n |
awk -F, '{
        print $2
        }' |
tail
```

Listing 16-20: Shell script showing iostat -x switch and logic

The previous shell script produces the following output (less the headers):

```
# ./diskbusy
disk     r/s     w/s    Kr/s    Kw/s    wait    actv    svc_t    %w    %b
sd6      0.0     0.0     0.0     0.0     0.0     0.0      0.0     0     0
sd3      0.2     0.6     0.2     2.0     0.0     0.0      8.1     0     1
sd6      0.1     0.0     2.0     0.0     0.0     0.0    176.3     0     1
sd1      3.0     0.1    11.9    10.4     6.0     1.9   2555.3     3     3
sd17     3.4     0.7    37.4    17.2     0.0     0.2     54.6     0     4
sd16     4.1     0.8    38.6    26.0     0.0     0.6    129.5     0     6
sd17    99.0    14.2   790.8   795.2     0.0     3.6     31.4     0    99
sd17   100.0    14.0   798.8   784.0     0.0     3.5     30.8     0   100
sd17    95.0    14.2   760.0   772.8     0.0     3.6     32.7     0   100
sd17    95.5    14.0   764.3   762.7     0.0     3.5     31.6     0   100
```

Listing 16-21: Output of shell script showing iostat -x switch and logic

In the previous example, iostat runs five times, and the top ten busiest disks are displayed over all five runs. Disk sd17 is listed five times because it hits the combined top ten all five times iostat is run.

TIP
You can use the sar and iostat commands to find potential disk I/O problem areas. Using the capabilities of shell scripting with these commands embedded can further enhance these commands.

Using sar and vmstat to Monitor System Paging/Swapping

A quick way to determine whether any swapping activity has occurred since the system booted is to issue the vmstat -S command. If the swp/in and swp/out columns have a nonzero value, it's a good indicator of a possible problem. You can delve into more detail using the sar command.

You can also use the sar command to check for system paging/swapping. Depending on the system, any paging and swapping could be a sign of trouble. In a virtual memory system, paging occurs when users not currently active are moved from memory to disk (a small issue). Swapping occurs when currently active users are moved to disk due to insufficient memory (a very large issue). Swapping and paging could easily take an entire book due to the depth of the subject. This section provides simple and fast commands to get a general picture of your system's state.

Using the -p switch of sar to report paging activities

The following table describes fields that are displayed with the sar command's -p switch.

Field	Description
atch/s	Page faults per second that are satisfied by reclaiming a page currently in memory (attaches per second)
pgin/s	Pagein requests per second
ppgin/s	Pages paged in per second

Field	Description
pflt/s	Page faults from protection errors per second (illegal access to page) or copy-on-writes
vflt/s	Address translation page faults per second (valid page not in memory)
slock/s	Faults per second caused by software lock requests requiring physical I/O

```
#sar -p 5 4
          atch/s   pgin/s   ppgin/s   pflt/s   vflt/s   slock/s
14:37:41   13.15    20.12    179.08    11.16    2.19     58.57
14:37:46   34.33    20.56    186.23     4.19    1.40     57.49
14:37:51   22.36    19.56    151.30     2.20    0.00     60.88
14:37:56   24.75    22.36    147.90     1.80    0.00     60.28
Average    27.37    20.11    161.81     7.58    8.14     60.85
```

Listing 16-22: sar -p switch command and output

The key statistic to look for is an inordinate amount of page faults of any kind. This problem usually indicates a high degree of paging. Remember that paging is not nearly as bad as swapping, but as paging increases, swapping soon follows. You can review the daily reports from the sar command to see if paging is steadily increasing during a specific time. The sar -p command without any time intervals will show you the paging statistics from the entire day if you have enabled periodic automatic monitoring.

Using the -w Switch of sar to Report Swapping and Switching Activities

The -w switch of sar shows swapping activity. This command displays the fields swpin/s, swpot/s, bswin/s, and bswot/s, which are the number of transfers and number of 512-byte units transferred for swapins and swapouts (including initial loading of some programs). The field pswch/s shows process switches.

```
#sar -w 5 4
SunOS hrdev 5.8  Generic sun4u    07/15/02
          swpin/s   bswin/s   swpot/s   bswot/s   pswch/s
14:45:22   0.00       0.0      0.00       0.0       294
14:45:27   0.00       0.0      0.00       0.0       312
14:45:32   0.00       0.0      0.00       0.0       322
14:45:37   0.00       0.0      0.00       0.0       327
Average    0.00       0.0      0.00       0.0       315
```

Listing 16-23: sar -w switch command and output

A high count for process switching points toward a memory deficiency, because actual process memory is being paged. There is not a problem with swapping in the example above.

Using the -r Switch of sar to Report Free Memory and Free Swap

```
# sar -r 5 4
          freemem   freeswap
14:45:21   517      1645911
14:45:26   294      1645907
```

sar & vmstat: System Paging/Swapping

```
14:45:36     378        1645919
14:45:41     299        1642633
Average      367        1644597
```

Listing 16-24: sar -r switch command and output

When freemem (free memory—listed in 512-byte blocks) falls below a certain level, the system starts to page. If it continues to fall, the system then starts the swapout processes. This is a sign of a rapidly degrading system. Look for processes taking an extreme amount of memory or an excessive number of processes.

Using the -g Switch of sar to Report Paging Activities

The following table describes the fields that are displayed with the sar command's -g switch.

Fields	Description
pgout/s	Pageout requests per second.
ppgout/s	Pages paged out per second.
pgfree/s	Pages per second placed on the freelist by the page-stealing daemon.
pgscan/s	Pages per second scanned by the page-stealing daemon.
%ufs_ipf	The percentage of UFS inodes taken off the freelist by iget that had reusable pages associated with them. These pages are flushed and cannot be reclaimed by processes. Thus, this is the percentage of igets with page flushes.

```
#sar -g 5 5
           pgout/s   ppgout/s   pgfree/s   pgscan/s   %ufs_ipf
14:58:34     2.40      74.40     132.80     466.40      0.00
14:58:39     1.80      55.69      90.62     263.87      0.00
14:58:44     2.20      62.32      98.00     298.00      0.00
14:58:49     4.59     142.32     186.43     465.07      0.00
14:58:54     0.80      24.75      24.15       0.00      0.00
```

Listing 16-25: sar -g switch command and output

TIP
A high ppgout (pages being moved out of memory) also points toward a memory deficiency.

TIP
Use the sar command to monitor and evaluate memory use and a potential need for additional memory. Paging is generally the movement of inactive processes from memory to disk. A high degree of paging is usually the predecessor to swapping. Swapping is the movement of active processes from memory to disk. If swapping starts to escalate, your system begins the downward death spiral. Fixing memory hogs or adding memory is the correct solution.

Using ipcs to Determine Shared Memory

The ipcs command is another helpful memory command that you can use to monitor the Oracle SGA. The ipcs command shows the size of each shared memory segment for the SGA. If there is not enough memory for the entire SGA to fit in a contiguous piece of memory, the SGA is built in noncontiguous memory segments. In the event of an instant crash, there is a possibility that the memory will not be released. If this happens, note that the ipcrm command will remove the segments (ipcrm -m for memory segments and ipcrm -s for semaphore segments).

```
# ipcs -b
IPC status from <running system> as of Sun Jul 14 19:46:03 2002
T        ID    KEY         MODE          OWNER     GROUP QBYTES
Message Queues:
q         0    0x0000000a -Rrw------- usupport     udba   4096
T        ID    KEY         MODE          OWNER     GROUP    SEGSZ
Shared Memory:
m    204 0x171053d8 --rw-r-----       oracle       dba     65536
m    205 0x1f1053d8 --rw-r-----       oracle       dba 100659200
m    206 0x271053d8 --rw-r-----       oracle       dba   1740800
Semaphores:
s 393218 00000000    --ra-r-----       oracle       dba     300
```

Listing 16-26: ipcs -b switch command and output

In this example, the SGA is built in three noncontiguous segments (making up the 100MB+ SGA). The instance is then shut down and started with a smaller SGA (so that contiguous pieces of memory will make up the SGA). The SGA has been lowered to 70MB. The ipcs command is issued again.

```
# ipcs -b
Shared Memory:
m   4403 0x0f1053d8 --rw-r-----       oracle       dba 71118848
Semaphores:
s 393218 00000000    --ra-r-----       oracle       dba     300
```

Listing 16-27: ipcs -b switch command and output against smaller SGA

It is usually preferable to have the entire SGA fit into a single shared memory segment because of the overhead that can be required to track more than one segment and the time required to switch back and forth between those segments. You can increase the maximum size of a single shared memory segment by increasing the SHMMAX setting in the /etc/system files. See the Oracle installation documentation for more specific information for your platform.

TIP
*Use the ipcs command to see if your SGA is built using multiple noncontiguous pieces of memory. If your database crashes, a problem can occur with releasing the memory. Use the ipcrm command (only if the SGA pieces are not released after a database crash) to then remove the SGA pieces from memory. Do **not** issue the ipcrm command with a running database.*

Using vmstat to Monitor System Load

The vmstat command is a conglomeration of many of the other commands listed in this chapter. The difference with vmstat is you get to see everything at once. The problem with vmstat is that you see everything at once and must evaluate it.

Procs

The vmstat command shows the following processes:

R	Processes that are currently running
B	Processes that are able to run but are waiting on a resource
W	Processes that are able to run but have been swapped out

CPU information

The vmstat command shows the following CPU information:

Us	Percentage of user time for normal and priority processes
Sy	Percentage of system time
Id	Percentage of idle time

```
#vmstat 5 3
procs      memory            page            disk          faults        cpu
r  b w  swap    free re  mf  pi po fr de sr s0 s1 s6 s9   in    sy    cs us sy id
19 5 0 1372992 26296 0   2 363  0  0  0  0 70 31  0  0   703  4846   662 64 36  0
23 3 0 1372952 27024 0  42 287  0  0  0  0 68 22  0  0   778  4619   780 63 37  0
16 4 0 1381236 36276 0  43 290  0  0  0  0 59 23  0  0  1149  4560  1393 56 44  0
```

Listing 16-28: vmstat command and output

Having any process in the *b* or *w* column is usually a sign of a problem system. (The previous system has a problem if this continues.) If processes are blocked from running, the CPU is likely to be overburdened. The CPU idle time of 0 is a reflection of the overburdening processes that are running and is a serious problem because some processes are blocked and people are waiting for CPU time. On the reverse side, if the idle time is high, you may not be using your system to its full capacity (not balancing activities efficiently), or the system may be oversized for the task. An idle time of 5-20 percent is appropriate for a static system (not adding new users).

As the amount of time the system is waiting on I/O requests increases, the amount of idle time on the CPU decreases: system resources have to be expended to track those waiting I/O requests. So just make sure you look at the whole picture before making your decisions. Eliminating an I/O bottleneck may free up significant amounts of CPU time. Time spent tracking I/O is reflected as sy, or system time in the output of vmstat.

You can also use the vmstat command to view system paging and swapping. The pageout (po) and pagein (pi) indicate the amount of paging that is occurring on your system. A small amount of paging is acceptable during a heavy usage cycle, but it should not occur for a prolonged period of time. On most systems, paging occurs during Oracle startup.

TIP
Use the vmstat command to find blocked processes (users waiting for CPU time) and also for paging or swapping problems. Using the vmstat command is a great way to see many of the sar options in one screen.

Monitoring Disk Freespace

It is often important for DBAs, especially those without inhouse system administrators, to closely monitor disk freespace. For example, if the file system containing your archived redo logs fills, all activity on your database will come to a halt.

The following script allows you to easily monitor disk freespace and receive e-mails if there is an issue.You would generally schedule this script to run about every 15 minutes, but you can also run it more or less frequently; the choice is yours.

You schedule a program to run at specified intervals through the cron process. You add or remove entries with the crontab -e command. This command brings up your crontab file in a vi editor. An example that checks disk freespace every 15 minutes looks like this:

```
0,15,30,45 * * * * /usr/local/bin/diskfreespace.sh
```

Listing 16-29: Script for monitoring disk freespace

This runs the diskfreespace.sh program every 15 minutes, every day.

Finally, the following example script checks file system freespace on the host and e-mails the user if there is less than 5 percent freespace. You can edit this script for more or less freespace by changing the string **$PERC -gt 95**; for example, if you change it to **$PERC -gt 90**, an alert is sent when the system has less than 10 percent freespace.

NOTE
This script is designed for Linux and runs unmodified on Solaris. To run it on HP, change the command df -kl to df -kP.

```
#!/bin/sh
# script name: diskfreespace.sh
#
#
df -kl | grep -iv filesystem | awk '{ print $6" "$5}' | while read LINE; do
        PERC=`echo $LINE | awk '{ print $2 }'`
        if [ $PERC -gt 95 ]; then
            echo "`date` - ${LINE} space used on `hostname` " | mailx -s "${LINE} on
 `hostname` at ${CLIENT} is almost full" vincenzoj@tusc.com
        fi
        done
```

Listing 16-30: Checking host file system freespace and e-mailing user

Monitoring Network Performance

Occasionally, you will notice a performance drop that can be attributed only to network performance. You will know this because you will have tuned every other aspect of the system, and network problems are all that is left. Network tuning can be very difficult and has many variables with which to contend. I usually consider it "tuning of last resort." That's not to say that the network settings out of the box cannot be improved upon for your environment—they can. But you will usually see a much larger percentage improvement by tuning your SQL statements than you will by tuning your TCP stack.

The settings that we will look at here are Solaris-specific, but there are analogs in Linux, HP, and AIX. Any UNIX-based system that communicates using the TCP protocol uses some or all of the settings in some way.

Making any changes to the settings requires that you are the superuser (or root). You can view the settings if you are not, but you cannot make any changes.

The following simple Perl script lists /dev/tcp parameters and their current values:

```perl
#!/usr/bin/perl
#get all tunable tcp parameters
use strict;
#get all of the possible parameters
my $ndd = '/usr/sbin/ndd /dev/tcp \?';
my @tcp = qx/$ndd/;
foreach (@tcp) {
  (my $parameter,  my $junk)= split(/\(/, $_);
  (my $parameter,   my $junk2)= split(/ /, $parameter);
  chomp ($junk);
  chomp ($parameter);
  #now disregard parameters that we cannot change
  if ( $junk eq "read and write)" ) {
    (my $type, my $junk)=split(/_/, $parameter);
    my $nddstat = "/usr/sbin/ndd /dev/tcp $parameter";
    #print "$nddstat\n";
    my $result = qx/$nddstat/;
    chomp ($result);
    print "$parameter\t";
    print "$result\n";
  }
}
```

Listing 16-31: Perl script listing /dev/tcp parameters and their current values

Now that you have a listing of your TCP settings, we can take a look at tuning some of them.

First, you have to determine whether anything actually needs to be tuned. The output of netstat -s helps you determine where possible problems are. The following example of normal output has been truncated to allow us to focus on certain areas.

```
TCP
        tcpRtoMax           =  60000     tcpMaxConn           =     -1
        tcpActiveOpens      =138398      tcpPassiveOpens      =157734
        tcpCurrEstab        =     96     tcpOutSegs           =761862710
        tcpOutDataSegs      =737025936   tcpOutDataBytes      =974079802
        tcpRetransSegs      =  56784     tcpRetransBytes      =16421938
        tcpOutAck           =24835587    tcpOutAckDelayed     =3487354
        tcpInInorderSegs    =95997710    tcpInInorderBytes    =3154946802
        tcpInUnorderSegs    =  54135     tcpInUnorderBytes    =3265601
        tcpListenDrop       =     11     tcpListenDropQ0      =      0
        tcpHalfOpenDrop     =      0     tcpOutSackRetrans    =    319
```

Listing 16-32: TCP normal output

Here we see a relatively high number of tcpActiveOpens and tcpPassiveOpens because the system has been up for only 25 hours.

Incoming calls are PassiveOpens and outgoing calls are ActiveOpens. This seems to indicate that there is a high amount of network traffic on this box. This assumption is reinforced by the size of tcpOutdataBytes. To determine whether you are possibly reaching the maximum on your network interface, use the following simple calculation:

```
TcpRetransBytes/tcpOutDataBytes=retransmission %.
```

Listing 16-33: Calculation of throughput

If this number is greater than 10 percent, you most likely have a serious throughput problem. You should almost definitely add more bandwidth or reduce the amount of traffic coming and going to the box.

Also, remember that only so much traffic can go through a network card and only so many users can be connected or establishing connections at once. You can determine whether you are having a problem with user connections by looking at tcpListenDrop.

If you have a value greater than 0, connections are being dropped and you need to increase the size of the listen queue. Just increase the parameter tcp_conn_req_max_q0. The default on Solaris is 1024. I recommend changing this default to 10,000.

Here's the command to make the change on a running system:

```
ndd -set /dev/tcp tcp_conn_req_max_q0 10000
```

Listing 16-34: Command to increase tcp_conn_req_max_q0

A simple way to drastically improve the efficiency of managing *active* TCP connections is to increase the tcp_connection_hash_size parameter. This improves the efficiency of hash table lookups on your system quite a bit. Additional memory will be required to manage the increased size of the hash table, but if you are expecting many connections, it is well worth the cost. To make this point clearer, the system defaults to 512, and Sun engineers set this default to **262144** when they are benchmarking their systems! There must quite a benefit if they change the default so drastically. Because this parameter is read-only, it must be set in the /etc/system file and requires a system reboot.

Another interesting phenomenon is the slow start bug. This was intended to avoid congesting the network by using a delayed ACK: the application can piggyback its response onto the first response back to the server. This seems like a great idea until a sender request can't fit into a single packet. TCP will break the packet up before sending an ACK and send a partial packet. The receiver is waiting for the completion of the packet before sending any more data, which it will not do until it receives a full packet. But the slow start phase allows only one packet. The sender needs to send more than one packet. This deadlock eventually times out and the receiver sends the ACK needed to establish the connection.

This problem doesn't normally occur unless you have many short-lived connections that are experiencing the deadlock. For example, a web server may have serious performance problems due to this issue.

As of Solaris 2.6, the tcp_slow_start_initial parameter was added to bypass this problem. It defaults to 1, which is the normal behavior just mentioned. I recommend that you change this default to either 2 or 4.

NOTE
As of Solaris 8, this changes to 4 for the default, so no action should be needed.

```
ndd -set /dev/tcp tcp_slow_start_initial 4
```

Listing 16-35: Changing value of tcp_slow_start_initial

You can set several timers to improve performance as well. The most important one, in my opinion, is tcp_keepalive_interval. This timer sets how long the system waits to verify that a connection is still valid. On a web server, which can have many short-lived connections, this setting can be critical. The default is **7200000**. On a busy web server, you want to clean up dead connections much faster than that.

```
ndd -set /dev/tcp tcp_keepalive_interval 10000
```

Listing 16-36: Changing the value of tcp_keepalive_interval

Sometimes the output of netstat shows a lot of connections that are in FIN_WAIT_2. This is a connection that is essentially waiting to die. If an application does not close a connection actively or a browser crashes, a connection ends up in FIN_WAIT_2, using resources that should be allocated to new connections. The default is **675000**, which is a pretty large number. Ten percent of that seems to be a much more reasonable amount of time to wait before cleaning up the connections, but you can investigate this more within your documentation and test your system to find the appropriate value.

```
ndd -set /dev/tcp tcp_fin_wait_2_flush_interval 67500
```

Listing 16-37: Changing the value of tcp_fin_wait_2_flush_interval

TIP
Use ndd and netstat to tune network performance issues.

Tips Review

- Use the sar -u command to see a quick snapshot of how heavily the CPU is bogged down.

- Use the top command to find the worst user on the system at a given time.

- Use cron and uptime to get your system load mailed to you regularly.

- If the smtx column for the mpstat output is greater than 200, you are heading toward CPU bottleneck problems.

- Combine operating system utilities with Oracle V$ views.

- Use the sar and iostat commands to find potential disk I/O problem areas. These commands are further enhanced by using the capabilities of shell scripting.

- Use the sar command to monitor and evaluate memory use and a potential need for additional memory.

- Paging is generally the movement of inactive processes from memory to disk. A high degree of paging is usually the predecessor to swapping. Swapping is the movement of active processes from memory to disk. If swapping starts to escalate, your system begins the downward death spiral. Fixing memory hogs or adding memory is the correct solution.

- Use the ipcs command to see whether your SGA is built using multiple noncontiguous pieces of memory. If your database crashes, you could have a problem releasing the memory.

- Use the ipcrm command (only if the SGA pieces are not released after a database crash) to remove the SGA pieces from memory. Do not issue the ipcrm command with a running database.

- Use the vmstat command to find blocked processes (users waiting for CPU time) and also for paging or swapping problems. The vmstat command is a great way to see many of the sar options in one screen.

- Use the ndd and netstat commands to tune network performance issues.

References

Oracle Performance Tuning, Mark Gurry and Peter Corrigan
Sun Performance and Tuning, Adrian Cockcroft

APPENDIX
A

Key init.ora
Parameters (DBA)

There are 257 different documented and 540 different undocumented initialization (init.ora/spfile.ora) parameters in Oracle9*i* (9.2.0.1). Even these numbers vary on different versions of Oracle9*i*. The init.ora parameters vary (in both name and number) based on the database version and release used. Run the queries at the end of this appendix (accessing the V$PARAMETER view and the x$ksppi table) on your version of the database to get the number of parameters and details for your specific version.

The topics covered in this appendix include the following:

- Desupported init.ora parameters

- Deprecated init.ora parameters

- Top twenty-five init.ora parameters

- Top ten init.ora parameters to remember

- Top thirteen undocumented init.ora parameters (as I see it)

- Listing of documented init.ora parameters (V$PARAMETER)

- Listing of undocumented init.ora parameters (x$ksppi/x$ksppcv)

- Top ten reasons not to write a book

Because every system is set up differently, my top 25 may not be the same as your top 25. Hopefully, this will give you a place to start until someone writes the 1000-page book on *all* 797 init.ora parameters. Please refer to Chapter 4 for a detailed look at the most important parameters.

Desupported init.ora Parameters

The following are Oracle9*i*R2 desupported initialization parameters. This means that these are no longer available, although they sometimes become undocumented parameters (which some of these are).

- ALWAYS_ANTI_JOIN

- ALWAYS_SEMI_JOIN

- DB_BLOCK_LRU_LATCHES

- DB_BLOCK_MAX_DIRTY_TARGET

- DB_FILE_DIRECT_IO_COUNT

- DISTRIBUTED_TRANSACTIONS GC_DEFER_TIME

- GC_RELEASABLE_LOCKS

- GC_ROLLBACK_LOCKS

- HASH_MULTIBLOCK_IO_COUNT

- INSTANCE_NODESET

- JOB_QUEUE_INTERVAL
- MAX_TRANSACTION_BRANCHES
- OPS_INTERCONNECTS
- OPTIMIZER_PERCENT_PARALLEL
- PARALLEL_BROADCAST_ENABLED
- SORT_MULTIBLOCK_READ_COUNT
- STANDBY_PRESERVES_NAMES
- TEXT_ENABLE
- USE_INDIRECT_DATA_BUFFERS

Deprecated init.ora Parameters

The following are Oracle9*i*R2 deprecated initialization parameters. This means that you can use them for backward compatibility, but they probably will not be available in the future.

- BUFFER_POOL_KEEP
- BUFFER_POOL_RECYCLE
- DB_BLOCK_BUFFERS
- DRS_START
- FAST_START_IO_TARGET
- LOG_ARCHIVE_DEST
- LOG_ARCHIVE_DUPLEX_DEST
- LOG_CHECKPOINT_INTERVAL (reinterpreted in Oracle9*i*)
- MTS_CIRCUITS
- MTS_DISPATCHERS
- MTS_MAX_DISPATCHERS
- MTS_MAX_SERVERS
- MTS_SERVERS
- MTS_SESSIONS
- PARALLEL_SERVER
- PARALLEL_SERVER_INSTANCES
- ROLLBACK_SEGMENTS
- TRANSACTIONS_PER_ROLLBACK_SEGMENT

Deprecated init.ora
Parameters

Top Twenty-Five init.ora Parameters

The following list is *my* list of the top 25 most important init.ora parameters, in order of importance. Your top 25 may vary somewhat from my top 25 because everyone has unique businesses, applications, and experiences.

1. DB_CACHE_SIZE   Initial memory allocated to data cache

2. PGA_AGGREGATE_TARGET   Soft memory cap for total of all users' PGA

3. SHARED_POOL_SIZE   Memory allocated for data dictionary, SQL, and PL/SQL

4. SGA_MAX_SIZE   Maximum memory to which the SGA can dynamically grow

5. OPTIMIZER_MODE   CHOOSE, RULE, FIRST_ROWS FIRST_ROWS_*n,* or ALL_ROWS

6. CURSOR_SHARING   Converts literal SQL to SQL with bind variables reducing parse overhead

7. OPTIMIZER_INDEX_COST_ADJ   Course adjustment between the cost of an index scan and the cost of a full table scan

8. QUERY_REWRITE_ENABLED   Used to enable materialized view and function-based index capabilities

9. DB_FILE_MULTIBLOCK_READ_COUNT   For full table scans to perform I/O more efficiently

10. LOG_BUFFER   Buffer for uncommitted transactions in memory

11. DB_KEEP_CACHE_SIZE   Memory allocated to keep pool

12. DB_RECYCLE_CACHE_SIZE   Memory allocated to recycle pool

13. DBWR_IO_SLAVES (also DB_WRITER_PROCESSES, if you have asynch I/O)   Number of writers from SGA to disk for simulated asynch I/O

14. LARGE_POOL_SIZE   Total blocks in the large pool allocation for large PL/SQL

15. STATISTICS_LEVEL   Used to enable advisory information and optionally keep additional OS statistics to refine optimizer decisions

16. HASH_JOIN_ENABLED   Enables hash joining for fast table joins

17. JAVA_POOL_SIZE   Memory allocated to the JVM for Java stored procedures

18. JAVA_MAX_SESSIONSPACE_SIZE   Upper limit on memory that is used to keep track of user session state of Java classes

19. MAX_SHARED_SERVERS   Upper limit on shared servers when MTS is enabled

20. PARALLEL_AUTOMATIC_TUNING   Enable parallel query automatic tuning capabilities

NOTE
*The PARALLEL_AUTOMATIC_TUNING parameter is also used
by the database to automatically calculate the settings for
PARALLEL_ADAPTIVE_MULTI_USER, PARALLEL_MAX_SERVERS,
PROCESSES, SESSIONS, and TRANSACTIONS.*

21. WORKAREA_SIZE_POLICY   Used to enable automatic PGA size management

22. FAST_START_MTTR_TARGET   Bounds time to complete a crash recovery

23. LOG_CHECKPOINT_INTERVAL   How often a checkpoint is forced

24. OPEN_CURSORS   Holds user statements to be processed (private area)

25. DB_BLOCK_SIZE   Size of the blocks

TIP
*Setting certain init.ora parameters correctly could make the difference
between a report taking two seconds and two hours. Test changes
on a test system thoroughly before implementing those changes in
a production environment.*

Top Ten init.ora Parameters to Remember

This section details some other important init.ora parameters. However, these parameters may
be important only in certain cases or only if you are using a certain feature or version of Oracle.

- CONTROL_FILES   This is the location of your control files.
- COMPATIBLE   Set this to the correct version or you'll miss features in the new version.
- OPTIMIZER_FEATURES_ENABLED   If not set, you are missing out on new features.
- UNDO_MANAGEMENT   Set this to AUTO for automatic UNDO management.
- UNDO_TABLESPACE   Set this to the tablespace to use for UNDO management.
- JOB_QUEUE_PROCESSES   If you want to use DBMS_JOB, you must set this parameter.
- UTL_FILE_DIR   This must be set to use the utl_file package.
- RECOVERY_PARALLELISM   Recover using the Parallel Query Option, a faster solution.
- LICENSE_MAX_SESSIONS and LICENSE_MAX_USERS   These limit concurrent and
  named users.
- LICENSE_SESSIONS_WARNING   Here, you specify at which session you get a warning.

Top Ten init.ora Parameters
to Remember

TIP
There are some excellent options within Oracle. Unfortunately, some of them do not work unless you have the init.ora parameter set correctly.

Top Thirteen Undocumented init.ora Parameters

WARNING
These 13 parameters are not supported by Oracle, nor do I recommend them on a production system. Use them only if you have thoroughly tested them on your crash-and-burn system (and your closest friend has been using them for years). Undocumented init.ora parameters can lead to database corruption (although some of them can get your database back up when you have corruption). Try to use these only when all other choices have failed, and only with the help of Oracle Support.

1. **_ALLOW_RESETLOGS_CORRUPTION** This saves you when you have corrupted redo logs.

The _ALLOW_RESETLOGS_CORRUPTION parameter can force the database open after a failed recovery, but at a very high cost. Setting _ALLOW_RESETLOGS_CORRUPTION allows the database to open with the datafiles at different SCN synchronization levels. This means some datafiles may contain changes that other datafiles do not (like the RBS or UNDO tablespace). This parameter may allow you to get to your data, but there is no easy way to determine if the data that is available after using these parameters is logically consistent. Regardless of data consistency, the DBA will have to rebuild the database afterwards. Failure to do so results in multiple ORA-600's occurring within the database at a later time.

2. **_CORRUPTED_ROLLBACK_SEGMENTS** This can be a means of last resort when you have corrupted rollback segments.

_CORRUPTED_ROLLBACK_SEGMENTS allows the database to open by assuming every transaction in the rollback segments is a complete, committed transaction. This leads to logical corruption throughout the database, and can easily corrupt the data dictionary. When creating a table, think of all the individual dictionary objects that are updated: fet$, uet$, tab$, ind$, col$, etc. By setting this parameter, you allow the table creation to succeed, even if only fet$ was updated, but not uet$, or tab$ was updated, but not col$. Use it when there is no other means of recovery, and export/import/rebuild soon after.

Also, these first two parameters do not always work or may corrupt the database so badly that an export cannot be taken once the database is open. If you use them and they do not work, Oracle Support cannot salvage the database; however, you can take some precautions *before* using these parameters that will allow other recovery methods to be used afterwards. Therefore, if you must use these parameters, please ensure that you use them with the help of Oracle Support. Another good reason to use Oracle Support in this effort is because the _ALLOW_RESETLOGS_CORRUPTION parameter is problematic, often requiring an event to be set as well, to get the database open.

3. CPU_COUNT   This is the number of CPUs that you have (causes bugs with Parallel Query Option).

4. _INIT_SQL_FILE (where the SQL.BSQ file is)   This is the file to execute upon database creation.

5. _TRACE_FILES_PUBLIC   This allows users to see the trace output without major privileges.

6. _FAST_FULL_SCAN_ENABLED   This allows index fast full scans if only an index is needed.

7. _KSMG_GRANULE_SIZE   This is the multiple for SGA pieces of memory, such as SHARED_POOL_SIZE and DB_CACHE_SIZE.

8. _HASH_MULTIBLOCK_IO_COUNT   This is the number of blocks that a hash join will read/write at once.

9. _INDEX_JOIN_ENABLED   Use this to disable the use of index joins.

10. _OPTIMIZER_ADJUST_FOR_NULLS   Adjust this selectivity for null values.

11. _ORACLE_TRACE_EVENTS   These are Oracle trace event flags.

12. _TRACE_EVENTS   Trace events are enabled at startup.

13. _UNNEST_SUBQUERY   Use this to unnest a correlated subquery.

The following three parameters are used for latch contention:

■ _KGL_LATCH_COUNT   This is the number of library cache latches (set to next prime number higher than 2*CPU). Setting this parameter too high can lead to ORA-600 errors (Bug 1381824).

■ _DB_BLOCK_HASH_BUCKETS   This must be prime (set to next prime number higher than 2* Cache buffers).

■ _SPIN_COUNT   This is how often the processor will take a new request (reduce CPU timeouts).

The following seven parameters are listed as required for Oracle11*i* applications:

■ _LIKE_WITH_BIND_AS_EQUALITY   Treat LIKE predicate with bind as an equality predicate.

■ _SHARED_POOL_RESERVED_MIN_ALLOC   Minimum allocation size in bytes for reserved area of shared pool.

Top Thirteen Undocumented init.ora Parameters

- **_TABLE_SCAN_COST_PLUS_ONE**   Bump estimated full table scan and index ffs cost by one.

- **_SYSTEM_TRIG_ENABLED**   Determines whether system triggers are enabled.

The next parameters apply only to Oracle 8.1.5 and 8.1.6:

- **_OPTIMIZER_MODE_FORCE**   Forces setting of optimizer mode for user recursive SQL also.

- **_OPTIMIZER_UNDO_CHANGES**   Undo changes to query optimizer.

- **_SORT_ELIMINATION_COST_RATIO**   Cost ratio for sort elimination under FIRST_ROWS mode.

For a query that will give you a complete listing of all undocumented parameters, their default values, and descriptions, see "Listing of Undocumented init.ora Parameters (x$ksppi/x$ksppcv)" later in this chapter.

Listing of Documented init.ora Parameters (V$PARAMETER)

The following query retrieves the listing below on 9iR2 under NT.

```
Col name format a25
Col value for a10
Col ismodified for a5
Col description for a35
select     name, value, ismodified,  description
from       v$parameter
order by   name;
```

The following table contains the output of the above query, and includes the parameter names, values, whether the parameter can be modified, and a brief description.

Name	Val	Is Modified	Description
o7_dictionary_accessibility	FALSE	FALSE	Version 7 dictionary accessibility support
active_instance_count		FALSE	Number of active instances in the cluster database
aq_tm_processes	1	FALSE	Number of aq time managers to start
archive_lag_target	0	FALSE	Maximum number of seconds of redos the standby could lose

TABLE A-I.   *Documented init.ora Parameters (V$PARAMETER)*

Name	Val	Is Modified	Description
audit_sys_operations	FALSE	FALSE	Enable system auditing
audit_trail	NONE	FALSE	Enable system auditing
background_core_dump	Partial	FALSE	Core size for background processes
background_dump_dest	C:\oracle\admin\ora92\bdump	FALSE	Detached process dump directory
backup_tape_io_slaves	FALSE	FALSE	Backup tape I/O slaves
bitmap_merge_area_size	1048576	FALSE	Maximum memory allowed for bitmap merge
blank_trimming	FALSE	FALSE	Blank trimming semantics parameter
buffer_pool_keep		FALSE	Number of database blocks/latches to keep in the buffer pool
buffer_pool_recycle		FALSE	Number of database blocks/latches in recycle buffer pool
circuits	170	FALSE	Maximum number of circuits
cluster_database	FALSE	FALSE	If true, start up in cluster database mode
cluster_database_instances	1	FALSE	Number of instances to use for sizing cluster db sga structures
cluster_interconnects		FALSE	Interconnects for rac use
commit_point_strength	1	FALSE	Bias this node has toward not preparing in a two-phase commit
compatible	9.2.0.0.0	FALSE	Database will be completely compatible with this software version
control_file_record_keep_time	7	FALSE	Control file record keeps time in days
control_files	C:\oracle\oradata\ora92\CONTROL01.CTL, C:\ORACLE\ORADATA\ORA92\control02.ctl, c:\oracle\oradata\ora92\CONTROL03.CTL	FALSE	Control filenames list
core_dump_dest	C:\oracle\admin\ora92\cdump	FALSE	Core dump directory
cpu_count	1	FALSE	Initial number of CPUs for this instance
create_bitmap_area_size	8388608	FALSE	Creates bitmap buffer size of create bitmap buffer for bitmap index

Listing of Documented init.ora Parameters (V$PARAMETER)

TABLE A-I.   *Documented init.ora Parameters (V$PARAMETER)* (continued)

Name	Val	Is Modified	Description
cursor_sharing	EXACT	FALSE	Cursor sharing mode
cursor_space_for_time	FALSE	FALSE	Uses more memory to get faster execution
db_16k_cache_size	0	FALSE	Size of cache for 16KB buffers
db_2k_cache_size	0	FALSE	Size of cache for 2KB buffers
db_32k_cache_size	0	FALSE	Size of cache for 32 KB buffers
db_4k_cache_size	0	FALSE	Size of cache for 4 KB buffers
db_8k_cache_size	0	FALSE	Size of cache for 8 KB buffers
db_block_buffers	0	FALSE	Number of db blocks cached in memory
db_block_checking	FALSE	FALSE	Data and index block checking
db_block_checksum	TRUE	FALSE	Stores checksum in db blocks and check during reads
db_block_size	8192	FALSE	Size of database block in bytes
db_cache_advice	ON	FALSE	Buffer cache sizing advisory
db_cache_size	25165824	FALSE	Size of default buffer pool for standard block size buffers
db_create_file_dest		FALSE	Default database location
db_create_online_log_dest_1		FALSE	Online log/control file destination #1
db_create_online_log_dest_2		FALSE	Online log/control file destination #2
db_create_online_log_dest_3		FALSE	Online log/control file destination #3
db_create_online_log_dest_4		FALSE	Online log/control file destination #4
db_create_online_log_dest_5		FALSE	Online log/control file destinations #5
db_domain	World	FALSE	Directory part of global database name stored with create database
db_file_multiblock_read_count	16	FALSE	DB blocks to be read on each I/O
db_file_name_convert		FALSE	Datafile name convert patterns and strings for standby/clone db
db_files	200	FALSE	Maximum allowable number of db files
db_keep_cache_size	0	FALSE	Size of keep buffer pool for standard block size buffers
db_name	ora92	FALSE	Database name specified in create database
db_recycle_cache_size	0	FALSE	Size of recycle buffer pool for standard block size buffers

TABLE A-1. *Documented init.ora Parameters (V$PARAMETER)* (continued)

Name	Val	Is Modified	Description
db_writer_processes	1	FALSE	Number of background database writer processes to start
dblink_encrypt_login	FALSE	FALSE	Enforces password for distributed login to always be encrypted
dbwr_io_slaves	0	FALSE	dbwr I/O slaves
dg_broker_config_file1	%ORACLE_ HOME%\ DATABASE\ DR1%ORACLE_ SID%.DAT	FALSE	Data guard broker configuration file #1
dg_broker_config_file2	%ORACLE_ HOME%\ DATABASE\ DR2%ORACLE_ SID%.DAT	FALSE	Data guard broker configuration file #2
dg_broker_start	FALSE	FALSE	Starts data guard broker framework (dmon process)
disk_asynch_io	TRUE	FALSE	Uses asynch I/O for random access devices
dispatchers	(PROTOCOL= TCP) (SERVICE= ora92xDB)	FALSE	Specifications of dispatchers
distributed_lock_timeout	60	FALSE	Number of seconds a distributed transaction waits for a lock
dml_locks	748	FALSE	dml locks: one for each table modified in a transaction
drs_start	FALSE	FALSE	Starts dg broker monitor (dmon process)
enqueue_resources	968	FALSE	Resources for enqueues
event		FALSE	Debugs event control: default null string
fal_client		FALSE	FAL client
fal_server	FALSE	FALSE	FAL server list
fast_start_io_target	0	FALSE	Upper bound on recovery reads
fast_start_mttr_target	300	FALSE	mttr target of forward crash recovery in seconds
fast_start_parallel_rollback	LOW	FALSE	Maximum number of parallel recovery slaves that may be used
file_mapping	FALSE	FALSE	Enables file mapping

TABLE A-I.   *Documented init.ora Parameters (V$PARAMETER)* (continued)

Listing of Documented init.ora Parameters (V$PARAMETER)

Name	Val	Is Modified	Description
filesystemio_options		FALSE	I/O operations on file system files
fixed_date		FALSE	Fixed sysdate value
gc_files_to_locks		FALSE	Mapping between file numbers and global cache locks (dfs)
global_context_pool_size		FALSE	Global application context pool size in bytes
global_names	FALSE	FALSE	Enforces that database links have same name as remote database
hash_area_size	1048576	FALSE	Size of in-memory hash work area
hash_join_enabled	TRUE	FALSE	Enables/disables hash join
hi_shared_memory_address	0	FALSE	sga starting address (high order 32 bits on 64-bit platforms)
hs_autoregister	TRUE	FALSE	Enables automatic server dd updates in hs agent self-registration
ifile		FALSE	Includes file in init.ora
instance_groups		FALSE	List of instance group names
instance_name	ora92	FALSE	Instance name supported by the instance
instance_number	0	FALSE	Instance number
java_max_sessionspace_size	0	FALSE	Maximum allowed size in bytes of a Java sessionspace
java_pool_size	33554432	FALSE	Size in bytes of the Java pool
java_soft_sessionspace_limit	0	FALSE	Warning limit on size in bytes of a Java sessionspace
job_queue_processes	10	FALSE	Number of job queue slave processes
large_pool_size	8388608	FALSE	Size in bytes of the large allocation pool
license_max_sessions	0	FALSE	Maximum number of nonsystem user sessions allowed
license_max_users	0	FALSE	Maximum number of named users that can be created in the database
license_sessions_warning	0	FALSE	Warning level for number of nonsystem user sessions
local_listener		FALSE	Local listener
lock_name_space		FALSE	Lock name space used for generating lock names for standby/clone
lock_sga	FALSE	FALSE	Lock entire sga in physical memory

TABLE A-1. *Documented init.ora Parameters (V$PARAMETER)* (continued)

Name	Val	Is Modified	Description
log_archive_dest		FALSE	Archival destination text string
log_archive_dest_1		FALSE	Archival destination #1 text string
log_archive_dest_10		FALSE	Archival destination #10 txt string
log_archive_dest_2		FALSE	Archival destination #2 text string
log_archive_dest_3		FALSE	Archival destination #3 text string
log_archive_dest_4		FALSE	Archival destination #4 text string
log_archive_dest_5		FALSE	Archival destination #5 text string
log_archive_dest_6		FALSE	Archival destination #6 text string
log_archive_dest_7		FALSE	Archival destination #7 text string
log_archive_dest_8		FALSE	Archival destination #8 text string
log_archive_dest_9		FALSE	Archival destination #9 text string
log_archive_dest_state_1	Enable	FALSE	Archival dest #1 state text string
log_archive_dest_state_10	Enable	FALSE	Archival dest #10 state text string
log_archive_dest_state_2	Enable	FALSE	Archival dest #2 state text string
log_archive_dest_state_3	Enable	FALSE	Archival dest #3 state text string
log_archive_dest_state_4	Enable	FALSE	Archival dest #4 state text string
log_archive_dest_state_5	Enable	FALSE	Archival dest #5 state text string
log_archive_dest_state_6	Enable	FALSE	Archival dest #6 state text string
log_archive_dest_state_7	Enable	FALSE	Archival dest #7 state text string
log_archive_dest_state_8	Enable	FALSE	Archival dest #8 state text string
log_archive_dest_state_9	Enable	FALSE	Archival dest #9 state text string
log_archive_duplex_dest		FALSE	Duplex archival destination text string
log_archive_format	ARC%S.%T	FALSE	Archival destination format
log_archive_max_processes	2	FALSE	Maximum number of active archive processes
log_archive_min_succeed_dest	1	FALSE	Minimum number of archive destinations that must succeed
log_archive_start	FALSE	FALSE	Start archival process on sga initialization
log_archive_trace	0	FALSE	Establish archivelog operation tracing level
log_buffer	524288	FALSE	Redo circular buffer size
log_checkpoint_interval	0	FALSE	Number of redo blocks checkpoint threshold

TABLE A-1.   *Documented init.ora Parameters (V$PARAMETER)* (continued)

Listing of Documented init.ora Parameters (V$PARAMETER)

Name	Val	Is Modified	Description
log_checkpoint_timeout	1800	FALSE	Maximum time interval between checkpoints in seconds
log_checkpoints_to_alert	FALSE	FALSE	Log checkpoint begin/end to alert file
log_file_name_convert		FALSE	Logfile name convert patterns and strings for standby/clone db
log_parallelism	1	FALSE	Number of log buffer strands
logmnr_max_persistent_sessions	1	FALSE	Maximum number of threads to mine
max_commit_propagation_delay	700	FALSE	Maximum age of new snapshot in .01 seconds
max_dispatchers	5	FALSE	Maximum number of dispatchers
max_dump_file_size	UNLIMITED	FALSE	Maximum size (blocks) of dump file
max_enabled_roles	30	FALSE	Maximum number of roles a user can have enabled
max_rollback_segments	37	FALSE	Maximum number of rollback segments in sga cache
max_shared_servers	20	FALSE	Maximum number of shared servers
mts_circuits	170	FALSE	Maximum number of circuits
mts_dispatchers	(PROTOCOL= TCP) (SERVICE= ora92XDB)	FALSE	Specifications of dispatchers
mts_listener_address		FALSE	Address(es) of network listener
mts_max_dispatchers	5	FALSE	Maximum number of dispatchers
mts_max_servers	20	FALSE	Maximum number of shared servers
mts_multiple_listeners	FALSE	FALSE	Determines whether multiple listeners are enabled
mts_servers	1	FALSE	Number of shared servers to start
mts_service	ora92	FALSE	Service supported by dispatchers
mts_sessions	165	FALSE	Maximum number of shared server sessions
nls_calendar		FALSE	nls calendar system name
nls_comp		FALSE	nls comparison
nls_currency		FALSE	nls local currency symbol
nls_date_format		FALSE	nls Oracle date format
nls_date_language		FALSE	nls date language name
nls_dual_currency		FALSE	Dual currency symbol

TABLE A-1. *Documented init.ora Parameters (V$PARAMETER)* (continued)

Name	Val	Is Modified	Description
nls_iso_currency		FALSE	nls iso currency territory name
nls_language	AMERICAN	FALSE	nls language name
nls_length_semantics	BYTE	FALSE	Creates columns using byte or char semantics by default
nls_nchar_conv_excp	FALSE	FALSE	NLS raises an exception instead of allowing implicit conversion
nls_numeric_characters		FALSE	nls numeric characters
nls_sort		FALSE	nls linguistic definition name
nls_territory	AMERICA	FALSE	nls territory name
nls_time_format		FALSE	Time format
nls_time_tz_format		FALSE	Time with timezone format
nls_timestamp_format		FALSE	Timestamp format
nls_timestamp_tz_format		FALSE	Timestamp with timezone format
object_cache_max_size_percent	10	FALSE	Percentage of maximum size over optimal of the user session's object
object_cache_optimal_size	102400	FALSE	Optimal size of the user session's object cache in bytes
olap_page_pool_size	33554432	FALSE	Size of the olap page pool in bytes
open_cursors	300	FALSE	Maximum number of cursors per session
open_links	4	FALSE	Maximum number of open links per session
open_links_per_instance	4	FALSE	Maximum number of open links per instance
optimizer_dynamic_sampling	1	FALSE	Optimizer dynamic sampling
optimizer_features_enable	9.2.0	FALSE	Optimizer plan compatibility parameter
optimizer_index_caching	0	FALSE	Optimizer percent index caching
optimizer_index_cost_adj	100	FALSE	Optimizer index cost adjustment
optimizer_max_permutations	2000	FALSE	Optimizer maximum join permutations per query block
optimizer_mode	CHOOSE	FALSE	Optimizer mode
oracle_trace_collection_name		FALSE	Oracle trace default collection name
oracle_trace_collection_path	%ORACLE_HOME%\ OTRACE\ ADMIN\CDF\	FALSE	Oracle trace collection path

TABLE A-I. *Documented init.ora Parameters (V$PARAMETER) (continued)*

Name	Val	Is Modified	Description
oracle_trace_collection_size	5242880	FALSE	Trace collection file maximum size
oracle_trace_enable	FALSE	FALSE	Oracle trace enabled/disabled
oracle_trace_facility_name	Oracled	FALSE	Oracle trace default facility name
oracle_trace_facility_path	%ORACLE_ HOME%\ OTRACE\ ADMIN\FDF\	FALSE	Oracle trace facility path
os_authent_prefix	OPS$	FALSE	Prefix for auto-logon accounts
os_roles	FALSE	FALSE	Retrieve roles from the operating system
parallel_adaptive_multi_user	FALSE	FALSE	Enables adaptive setting of degree for multiple user streams
parallel_automatic_tuning	FALSE	FALSE	Enables intelligent defaults for parallel execution parameters
parallel_execution_message_size	2148	FALSE	Message buffer size for parallel execution
parallel_instance_group		FALSE	Instance group to use for all parallel operations
parallel_max_servers	5	FALSE	Maximum parallel query servers per instance
parallel_min_percent	0	FALSE	Minimum percent of threads required for parallel query
parallel_min_servers	0	FALSE	Minimum parallel query servers per instance
parallel_server	FALSE	FALSE	If true, start up in parallel server mode
parallel_server_instances	1	FALSE	Number of instances to use for sizing ops sga structures
parallel_threads_per_cpu	2	FALSE	Number of parallel execution threads per CPU
partition_view_enabled	FALSE	FALSE	Enables/disables partitioned views
pga_aggregate_target	25165824	FALSE	Target size for the aggregate pga memory consumed by the instance
plsql_compiler_flags	INTERPRETED	FALSE	plsql compiler flags
plsql_native_c_compiler		FALSE	plsql native c compiler
plsql_native_library_dir		FALSE	plsql native library dir
plsql_native_library_subdir_ count	0	FALSE	plsql native library number of subdirectories

TABLE A-1. *Documented init.ora Parameters (V$PARAMETER)* (continued)

Name	Val	Is Modified	Description
plsql_native_linker		FALSE	plsql native linker
plsql_native_make_file_name		FALSE	plsql native compilation make file
plsql_native_make_utility		FALSE	plsql native compilation make utility
plsql_v2_compatibility	FALSE	FALSE	plsql version 2.x compatibility flag
pre_page_sga	FALSE	FALSE	Prepage sga for process
processes	150	FALSE	User processes
query_rewrite_enabled	FALSE	FALSE	Allows rewrite of queries using materialized views if enabled
query_rewrite_integrity	Enforced	FALSE	Performs rewrite using materialized views with desired integrity
rdbms_server_dn		FALSE	rdbms' distinguished name
read_only_open_delayed	FALSE	FALSE	If true, delays opening of read-only files until first access
recovery_parallelism	0	FALSE	Number of server processes to use for parallel recovery
remote_archive_enable	True	FALSE	Remote archival enable setting
remote_dependencies_mode	TIMESTAMP	FALSE	Remote-procedure-call dependencies mode parameter
remote_listener		FALSE	Remote listener
remote_login_passwordfile	EXCLUSIVE	FALSE	Password file usage parameter
remote_os_authent	FALSE	FALSE	Allows nonsecure remote clients to use auto-logon accounts
remote_os_roles	FALSE	FALSE	Allows nonsecure remote clients to use os roles
replication_dependency_tracking	TRUE	FALSE	Tracking dependency for replication parallel propagation
resource_limit	FALSE	FALSE	Master switch for resource limit
resource_manager_plan		FALSE	Resource mgr top plan
rollback_segments		FALSE	Undo segment list
row_locking	Always	FALSE	Row-locking
serial_reuse	DISABLE	FALSE	Reuse the frame segments
serializable	FALSE	FALSE	Serializable
service_names	ora92.world	FALSE	Service names supported by the instance

Listing of Documented init.ora Parameters (V$PARAMETER)

TABLE A-1. *Documented init.ora Parameters (V$PARAMETER)* (continued)

Name	Val	Is Modified	Description
session_cached_cursors	0	FALSE	Number of cursors to save in the session cursor cache
session_max_open_files	10	FALSE	Maximum number of open files allowed per session
sessions	170	FALSE	User and system sessions
sga_max_size	135338868	FALSE	Maximum total sga size
shadow_core_dump	Partial	FALSE	Core size for shadow processes
shared_memory_address	0	FALSE	sga starting address (low order 32 bits on 64-bit platforms)
shared_pool_reserved_size	2516582	FALSE	Size in bytes of reserved area of shared pool
shared_pool_size	50331648	FALSE	Size in bytes of shared pool
shared_server_sessions	165	FALSE	Maximum number of shared server sessions
shared_servers	1	FALSE	Number of shared servers to start
sort_area_retained_size	0	FALSE	Size of in-memory sort work area retained between fetch calls
sort_area_size	524288	FALSE	Size of in-memory sort work area
spfile	%ORACLE_ HOME%\ DATABASE\ SPFILE%ORACLE_ SID%.ORA	FALSE	Server parameter file
sql92_security	FALSE	FALSE	Require select privilege for searched update/delete
sql_trace	FALSE	FALSE	Enable sql trace
sql_version	NATIVE	FALSE	SQL language version parameter for compatibility issues
standby_archive_dest	%ORACLE_ HOME%\ RDBMS	FALSE	Standby database archivelog destination text string
standby_file_management	MANUAL	FALSE	If auto, then files are created/dropped automatically on standby
star_transformation_enabled	FALSE	FALSE	Enables the use of star transformation

TABLE A-I. *Documented init.ora Parameters (V$PARAMETER)* (continued)

Name	Val	Is Modified	Description
statistics_level	TYPICAL	FALSE	Statistics level
tape_asynch_io	TRUE	FALSE	Uses asynch I/O requests for tape devices
thread	0	FALSE	Redo thread to mount
timed_os_statistics	0	FALSE	Internal os statistic gathering interval in seconds
timed_statistics	TRUE	FALSE	Maintains internal timing statistics
trace_enabled	TRUE	FALSE	Enables kst tracing
tracefile_identifier		FALSE	Traces file custom identifier
transaction_auditing	TRUE	FALSE	Transaction auditing records generated in the redo log
transactions	187	FALSE	Maximum number of concurrent active transactions
transactions_per_rollback_segment	5	FALSE	Number of active transactions per rollback segment
undo_management	AUTO	FALSE	Instance runs in smu mode if true, or else in rbu mode
undo_retention	10800	FALSE	Undo retention in seconds
undo_suppress_errors	FALSE	FALSE	Suppresses rbu errors in smu mode
undo_tablespace	UNDOTBS1	FALSE	Uses/switches undo tablespace
use_indirect_data_buffers	FALSE	FALSE	Enables indirect data buffers (very large sga on 32-bit platforms)
user_dump_dest	C:\oracle\admin \ora92\udump	FALSE	User process dump directory
utl_file_dir		FALSE	utl_file accessible directories list
workarea_size_policy	AUTO	FALSE	Policy used to size sql working areas (manual/auto)

TABLE A-1.   *Documented init.ora Parameters (V$PARAMETER)* (continued)

Listing of Documented init.ora Parameters (V$PARAMETER)

Listing of Undocumented init.ora Parameters (x$ksppi/x$ksppcv)

WARNING
Oracle does not support these undocumented parameters, nor do I recommend using them on a production system. Use them only if you have thoroughly tested them on your crash-and-burn system. Undocumented init.ora parameters can lead to database corruption (although a few of them can get your database back up when you have corruption). Use at your own risk.

The following query retrieves the undocumented parameters. No output is displayed due to space considerations.

```
select    a.ksppinm, b.ksppstvl, b.ksppstdf, a.ksppdesc
from      x$ksppi a, x$ksppcv b
where     a.indx = b.indx
and       substr(ksppinm,1,1) = '_'
order     by ksppinm;
```

TIP
Undocumented init.ora parameters often show a glimpse of what's to come in the next version of Oracle. However, some of them don't work or cause severe problems.

Top Ten Reasons Not to Write a Book

1. You like sleep, and caffeine-enhanced water clogs your coffee maker.

2. You have enough trouble getting the time to read books, let alone write one.

3. You enjoy getting together with your family from time to time.

4. You're tired of being the first one in the office (actually you've been there all night).

5. Your hobby is golf, and you'd like to play more than once a year.

6. You enjoy noticing the world around you vs. a purple haze all through your mind.

7. Kevin Loney will write on that subject eventually—you'll wait for his book.

8. You don't want to show off how much you know—you're far too humble.

9. Your PC is out of disk space already—you've just loaded Windows 99.1415926.

10. You just got your life back after the last Oracle conversion.

TIP
Retirement is a good time to write a book, not during the most painful economic conditions since 1929.

Tips Review

■ Setting certain init.ora parameters correctly could be the difference between a report taking two seconds and two hours. Try changes out on a test system thoroughly *before* implementing those changes in a production environment!

■ There are some excellent options within Oracle. Unfortunately, some of them do *not* work unless the init.ora parameter is set correctly.

■ Undocumented init.ora parameters can corrupt your database! Some of them can also salvage a corrupted database. Try to use these only when all other choices have failed, and use them with the help of Oracle Support.

■ Undocumented init.ora parameters often show a glimpse of what's coming in the next version of Oracle, but many of them don't work at all.

■ Retirement is a good time to write a book. Writing a book during the most painful economic conditions since 1929 is *not*.

References

Oracle7, 8 Server Tuning; Oracle Corporation
Oracle9i Performance Tuning; Oracle Corporation
Performance Tuning Guide Version 7.0; Oracle Corporation
Oracle9i DBA Handbook; Kevin Loney
Oracle8 Advanced Tuning & Administration; Aronoff, Loney, Sonawalla
Oracle8 Tuning; Corey, Abbey, Dechichio, and Abramson

Thanks to Brad Brown, Joe Trezzo, Randy Swanson, Sean McGuire, Greg Pucka, Mike Broullette, and Kevin Loney for their contributions to this chapter.

APPENDIX B

The V$ Views
(DBA and Developer)

The V$ views are very helpful in analyzing database issues. This appendix lists all views and creation scripts used to actually build the V$ and GV$ views. The V$ views vary in structure and number based on the database version and release used. Run the queries on your version of the database to get the number of views and structure for your specific version.

The topics covered in this appendix include the following:

- Creation of V$ and GV$ views and *X$* tables

- The Oracle9i (9.2.0.1.0) GV$ views

- The Oracle9i (9.2.0.1.0) V$ views

- The Oracle9i scripts of the *X$* tables used to create the V$ views

NOTE
Appendix C includes V$ to X$ and X$ to V$ cross references.

Creation of V$ and GV$ Views and X$ Tables

V$ and data dictionary views can be crucial to fully comprehending the intricacies of Oracle. Although knowing how to use the views and tables is critical to your career, their creation has remained somewhat of a painstaking mystery.

Figure B-1 illustrates the creation of the *X$* tables and the V$ views.

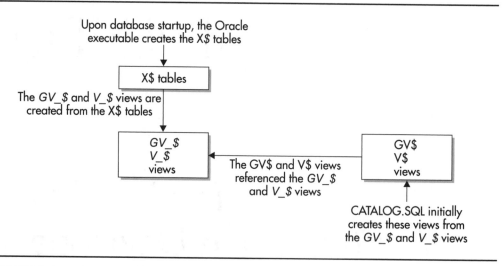

FIGURE B-1. *Creation of the X$ tables and the V$ views*

The Oracle9i (9.2.0.1.0) GV$ Views

NOTE
The Oracle9i V$ views are the same as the GV$ views, less INST_ID.

The following Oracle9i query produces this listing of 259 views:

```
select    name
from      v$fixed_table
where     name like 'GV%'
order by  name;
```

GV$LOCK	GV$LOCKED_OBJECT
GV$LOCKS_WITH_COLLISIONS	GV$LOCK_ACTIVITY
GV$LOGFILE	GV$LOGHIST
GV$LOGMNR_CALLBACK	GV$LOGMNR_CONTENTS
GV$LOGMNR_DICTIONARY	GV$LOGMNR_LOGFILE
GV$LOGMNR_LOGS	GV$LOGMNR_PARAMETERS
GV$LOGMNR_PROCESS	GV$LOGMNR_REGION
GV$LOGMNR_SESSION	GV$LOGMNR_STATS
GV$LOGMNR_TRANSACTION	GV$LOGSTDBY
GV$LOGSTDBY_STATS	GV$LOG_HISTORY
GV$ACCESS	GV$ACTIVE_INSTANCES
GV$ACTIVE_SESS_POOL_MTH	GV$AQ1
GV$ARCHIVE	GV$ARCHIVED_LOG
GV$ARCHIVE_DEST	GV$ARCHIVE_DEST_STATUS
GV$ARCHIVE_GAP	GV$ARCHIVE_PROCESSES
GV$AW_CALC	GV$AW_OLAP
GV$AW_SESSION_INFO	GV$BACKUP
GV$BACKUP_ASYNC_IO	GV$BACKUP_CORRUPTION
GV$BACKUP_DATAFILE	GV$BACKUP_DEVICE
GV$BACKUP_PIECE	GV$BACKUP_REDOLOG
GV$BACKUP_SET	GV$BACKUP_SPFILE
GV$BACKUP_SYNC_IO	GV$BGPROCESS
GV$BH	GV$BSP
GV$BUFFER_POOL	GV$BUFFER_POOL_STATISTICS
GV$CIRCUIT	GV$CLASS_CACHE_TRANSFER
GV$CLASS_PING	GV$COMPATIBILITY
GV$COMPATSEG	GV$CONTEXT
GV$CONTROLFILE	GV$CONTROLFILE_RECORD_SECTION
GV$COPY_CORRUPTION	GV$CR_BLOCK_SERVER

GV$DATABASE	GV$DATABASE_BLOCK_CORRUPTION
GV$DATABASE_INCARNATION	GV$DATAFILE
GV$DATAFILE_COPY	GV$DATAFILE_HEADER
GV$DATAGUARD_STATUS	GV$DBFILE
GV$DBLINK	GV$DB_CACHE_ADVICE
GV$DB_OBJECT_CACHE	GV$DB_PIPES
GV$DELETED_OBJECT	GV$DISPATCHER
GV$DISPATCHER_RATE	GV$DLM_ALL_LOCKS
GV$DLM_CONVERT_LOCAL	GV$DLM_CONVERT_REMOTE
GV$DLM_LATCH	GV$DLM_LOCKS
GV$DLM_MISC	GV$DLM_RESS
GV$DLM_TRAFFIC_CONTROLLER	GV$ENABLEDPRIVS
GV$ENQUEUE_LOCK	GV$ENQUEUE_STAT
GV$EVENT_NAME	GV$EXECUTION
GV$FAST_START_SERVERS	GV$FAST_START_TRANSACTIONS
GV$FILESTAT	GV$FILE_CACHE_TRANSFER
GV$FILE_PING	GV$FIXED_TABLE
GV$FIXED_VIEW_DEFINITION	GV$GCSHVMASTER_INFO
GV$GCSPFMASTER_INFO	GV$GC_ELEMENT
GV$GC_ELEMENTS_WITH_COLLISIONS	GV$GES_BLOCKING_ENQUEUE
GV$GES_ENQUEUE	GV$GLOBALCONTEXT
GV$GLOBAL_BLOCKED_LOCKS	GV$GLOBAL_TRANSACTION
GV$HS_AGENT	GV$HS_PARAMETER
GV$HS_SESSION	GV$HVMASTER_INFO
GV$INDEXED_FIXED_COLUMN	GV$INSTANCE
GV$INSTANCE_RECOVERY	GV$LATCH
GV$LATCHHOLDER	GV$LATCHNAME
GV$LATCH_CHILDREN	GV$LATCH_MISSES
GV$LATCH_PARENT	GV$LIBRARYCACHE
GV$LIBRARY_CACHE_MEMORY	GV$LICENSE
GV$LOADISTAT	GV$LOADPSTAT
GV$LOCK	GV$LOCKED_OBJECT
GV$LOCKS_WITH_COLLISIONS	GV$LOCK_ACTIVITY
GV$LOCK_ELEMENT	GV$LOG
GV$LOGFILE	GV$LOGHIST
GV$LOGMNR_CALLBACK	GV$LOGMNR_CONTENTS
GV$LOGMNR_DICTIONARY	GV$LOGMNR_LOGFILE
GV$LOGMNR_LOGS	GV$LOGMNR_PARAMETERS
GV$LOGMNR_PROCESS	GV$LOGMNR_REGION
GV$LOGMNR_SESSION	GV$LOGMNR_STATS
GV$LOGMNR_TRANSACTION	GV$LOGSTDBY
GV$LOGSTDBY_STATS	GV$LOG_HISTORY

GV$MANAGED_STANDBY

GV$MAP_ELEMENT

GV$MAP_FILE

GV$MAP_FILE_IO_STACK

GV$MAP_SUBELEMENT

GV$MTTR_TARGET_ADVICE

GV$MYSTAT

GV$NLS_VALID_VALUES

GV$OBSOLETE_PARAMETER

GV$OPEN_CURSOR

GV$PARALLEL_DEGREE_LIMIT_MTH

GV$PARAMETER2

GV$PGA_TARGET_ADVICE

GV$PQ_SESSTAT

GV$PQ_SYSSTAT

GV$PROCESS

GV$PROXY_DATAFILE

GV$PX_PROCESS

GV$PX_SESSION

GV$QUEUE

GV$RECOVERY_FILE_STATUS

GV$RECOVERY_PROGRESS

GV$RECOVER_FILE

GV$REPLQUEUE

GV$RESERVED_WORDS

GV$RESOURCE_LIMIT

GV$RMAN_CONFIGURATION

GV$ROWCACHE

GV$ROWCACHE_SUBORDINATE

GV$RSRC_CONSUMER_GROUP_CPU_MTH

GV$RSRC_PLAN_CPU_MTH

GV$SEGSTAT

GV$SESSION

GV$SESSION_CURSOR_CACHE

GV$SESSION_LONGOPS

GV$SESSION_WAIT

GV$SESS_IO

GV$SGASTAT

GV$SGA_DYNAMIC_COMPONENTS

GV$SGA_RESIZE_OPS

GV$SHARED_POOL_RESERVED

GV$SHARED_SERVER_MONITOR

GV$MAP_COMP_LIST

GV$MAP_EXT_ELEMENT

GV$MAP_FILE_EXTENT

GV$MAP_LIBRARY

GV$MAX_ACTIVE_SESS_TARGET_MTH

GV$MVREFRESH

GV$NLS_PARAMETERS

GV$OBJECT_DEPENDENCY

GV$OFFLINE_RANGE

GV$OPTION

GV$PARAMETER

GV$PGASTAT

GV$PGA_TARGET_ADVICE_HISTOGRAM

GV$PQ_SLAVE

GV$PQ_TQSTAT

GV$PROXY_ARCHIVEDLOG

GV$PWFILE_USERS

GV$PX_PROCESS_SYSSTAT

GV$PX_SESSTAT

GV$QUEUEING_MTH

GV$RECOVERY_LOG

GV$RECOVERY_STATUS

GV$REPLPROP

GV$REQDIST

GV$RESOURCE

GV$RESUMABLE

GV$ROLLSTAT

GV$ROWCACHE_PARENT

GV$RSRC_CONSUMER_GROUP

GV$RSRC_PLAN

GV$SEGMENT_STATISTICS

GV$SEGSTAT_NAME

GV$SESSION_CONNECT_INFO

GV$SESSION_EVENT

GV$SESSION_OBJECT_CACHE

GV$SESSTAT

GV$SGA

GV$SGA_CURRENT_RESIZE_OPS

GV$SGA_DYNAMIC_FREE_MEMORY

GV$SHARED_POOL_ADVICE

GV$SHARED_SERVER

GV$SORT_SEGMENT

GV$ Views

GV$SORT_USAGE	GV$SPPARAMETER
GV$SQL	GV$SQLAREA
GV$SQLTEXT	GV$SQLTEXT_WITH_NEWLINES
GV$SQL_BIND_DATA	GV$SQL_BIND_METADATA
GV$SQL_CURSOR	GV$SQL_PLAN
GV$SQL_PLAN_STATISTICS	GV$SQL_PLAN_STATISTICS_ALL
GV$SQL_REDIRECTION	GV$SQL_SHARED_CURSOR
GV$SQL_SHARED_MEMORY	GV$SQL_WORKAREA
GV$SQL_WORKAREA_ACTIVE	GV$SQL_WORKAREA_HISTOGRAM
GV$STANDBY_LOG	GV$STATISTICS_LEVEL
GV$STATNAME	GV$STREAMS_APPLY_COORDINATOR
GV$STREAMS_APPLY_READER	GV$STREAMS_APPLY_SERVER
GV$STREAMS_CAPTURE	GV$SUBCACHE
GV$SYSSTAT	GV$SYSTEM_CURSOR_CACHE
GV$SYSTEM_EVENT	GV$SYSTEM_PARAMETER
GV$SYSTEM_PARAMETER2	GV$TABLESPACE
GV$TEMPFILE	GV$TEMPORARY_LOBS
GV$TEMPSTAT	GV$TEMP_CACHE_TRANSFER
GV$TEMP_EXTENT_MAP	GV$TEMP_EXTENT_POOL
GV$TEMP_PING	GV$TEMP_SPACE_HEADER
GV$THREAD	GV$TIMER
GV$TIMEZONE_NAMES	GV$TRANSACTION
GV$TRANSACTION_ENQUEUE	GV$TYPE_SIZE
GV$UNDOSTAT	GV$VERSION
GV$VPD_POLICY	GV$WAITSTAT
GV$_LOCK	GV$_LOCK1
GV$_SEQUENCES	

The Oracle9*i* (9.2.0.1.0) V$ Views

The following Oracle9*i* query produces this listing of 259 views:

```
select    name
from      v$fixed_table
where     name like 'V%'
order by  name;
```

V$ACCESS	V$ACTIVE_INSTANCES
V$ACTIVE_SESS_POOL_MTH	V$AQ1
V$ARCHIVE	V$ARCHIVED_LOG
V$ARCHIVE_DEST	V$ARCHIVE_DEST_STATUS
V$ARCHIVE_GAP	V$ARCHIVE_PROCESSES
V$AW_CALC	V$AW_OLAP
V$AW_SESSION_INFO	V$BACKUP

V$BACKUP_ASYNC_IO	V$BACKUP_CORRUPTION
V$BACKUP_DATAFILE	V$BACKUP_DEVICE
V$BACKUP_PIECE	V$BACKUP_REDOLOG
V$BACKUP_SET	V$BACKUP_SPFILE
V$BACKUP_SYNC_IO	V$BGPROCESS
V$BH	V$BSP
V$BUFFER_POOL	V$BUFFER_POOL_STATISTICS
V$CIRCUIT	V$CLASS_CACHE_TRANSFER
V$CLASS_PING	V$COMPATIBILITY
V$COMPATSEG	V$CONTEXT
V$CONTROLFILE	V$CONTROLFILE_RECORD_SECTION
V$COPY_CORRUPTION	V$CR_BLOCK_SERVER
V$DATABASE	V$DATABASE_BLOCK_CORRUPTION
V$DATABASE_INCARNATION	V$DATAFILE
V$DATAFILE_COPY	V$DATAFILE_HEADER
V$DATAGUARD_STATUS	V$DBFILE
V$DBLINK	V$DB_CACHE_ADVICE
V$DB_OBJECT_CACHE	V$DB_PIPES
V$DELETED_OBJECT	V$DISPATCHER
V$DISPATCHER_RATE	V$DLM_ALL_LOCKS
V$DLM_CONVERT_LOCAL	V$DLM_CONVERT_REMOTE
V$DLM_LATCH	V$DLM_LOCKS
V$DLM_MISC	V$DLM_RESS
V$DLM_TRAFFIC_CONTROLLER	V$ENABLEDPRIVS
V$ENQUEUE_LOCK	V$ENQUEUE_STAT
V$EVENT_NAME	V$EXECUTION
V$FAST_START_SERVERS	V$FAST_START_TRANSACTIONS
V$FILESTAT	V$FILE_CACHE_TRANSFER
V$FILE_PING	V$FIXED_TABLE
V$FIXED_VIEW_DEFINITION	V$GCSHVMASTER_INFO
V$GCSPFMASTER_INFO	V$GC_ELEMENT
V$GC_ELEMENTS_WITH_COLLISIONS	V$GES_BLOCKING_ENQUEUE
V$GES_ENQUEUE	V$GLOBALCONTEXT
V$GLOBAL_BLOCKED_LOCKS	V$GLOBAL_TRANSACTION
V$HS_AGENT	V$HS_PARAMETER
V$HS_SESSION	V$HVMASTER_INFO
V$INDEXED_FIXED_COLUMN	V$INSTANCE
V$INSTANCE_RECOVERY	V$LATCH
V$LATCHHOLDER	V$LATCHNAME
V$LATCH_CHILDREN	V$LATCH_MISSES
V$LATCH_PARENT	V$LIBRARYCACHE

V$ Views

V$LIBRARY_CACHE_MEMORY	V$LICENSE
V$LOADISTAT	V$LOADPSTAT
V$LOCK	V$LOCKED_OBJECT
V$LOCKS_WITH_COLLISIONS	V$LOCK_ACTIVITY
V$LOCK_ELEMENT	V$LOG
V$LOGFILE	V$LOGHIST
V$LOGMNR_CALLBACK	V$LOGMNR_CONTENTS
V$LOGMNR_DICTIONARY	V$LOGMNR_LOGFILE
V$LOGMNR_LOGS	V$LOGMNR_PARAMETERS
V$LOGMNR_PROCESS	V$LOGMNR_REGION
V$LOGMNR_SESSION	V$LOGMNR_STATS
V$LOGMNR_TRANSACTION	V$LOGSTDBY
V$LOGSTDBY_STATS	V$LOG_HISTORY
V$MANAGED_STANDBY	V$MAP_COMP_LIST
V$MAP_ELEMENT	V$MAP_EXT_ELEMENT
V$MAP_FILE	V$MAP_FILE_EXTENT
V$MAP_FILE_IO_STACK	V$MAP_LIBRARY
V$MAP_SUBELEMENT	V$MAX_ACTIVE_SESS_TARGET_MTH
V$MTTR_TARGET_ADVICE	V$MVREFRESH
V$MYSTAT	V$NLS_PARAMETERS
V$NLS_VALID_VALUES	V$OBJECT_DEPENDENCY
V$OBSOLETE_PARAMETER	V$OFFLINE_RANGE
V$OPEN_CURSOR	V$OPTION
V$PARALLEL_DEGREE_LIMIT_MTH	V$PARAMETER
V$PARAMETER2	V$PGASTAT
V$PGA_TARGET_ADVICE	V$PGA_TARGET_ADVICE_HISTOGRAM
V$PQ_SESSTAT	V$PQ_SLAVE
V$PQ_SYSSTAT	V$PQ_TQSTAT
V$PROCESS	V$PROXY_ARCHIVEDLOG
V$PROXY_DATAFILE	V$PWFILE_USERS
V$PX_PROCESS	V$PX_PROCESS_SYSSTAT
V$PX_SESSION	V$PX_SESSTAT
V$QUEUE	V$QUEUEING_MTH
V$RECOVERY_FILE_STATUS	V$RECOVERY_LOG
V$RECOVERY_PROGRESS	V$RECOVERY_STATUS
V$RECOVER_FILE	V$REPLPROP
V$REPLQUEUE	V$REQDIST
V$RESERVED_WORDS	V$RESOURCE
V$RESOURCE_LIMIT	V$RESUMABLE
V$RMAN_CONFIGURATION	V$ROLLSTAT
V$ROWCACHE	V$ROWCACHE_PARENT

V$ROWCACHE_SUBORDINATE

V$RSRC_CONSUMER_GROUP_CPU_MTH

V$RSRC_PLAN_CPU_MTH

V$SEGSTAT

V$SESSION

V$SESSION_CURSOR_CACHE

V$SESSION_LONGOPS

V$SESSION_WAIT

V$SESS_IO

V$SGASTAT

V$SGA_DYNAMIC_COMPONENTS

V$SGA_RESIZE_OPS

V$SHARED_POOL_RESERVED

V$SHARED_SERVER_MONITOR

V$SORT_USAGE

V$SQL

V$SQLTEXT

V$SQL_BIND_DATA

V$SQL_CURSOR

V$SQL_PLAN_STATISTICS

V$SQL_REDIRECTION

V$SQL_SHARED_MEMORY

V$SQL_WORKAREA_ACTIVE

V$STANDBY_LOG

V$STATNAME

V$STREAMS_APPLY_READER

V$STREAMS_CAPTURE

V$SYSSTAT

V$SYSTEM_EVENT

V$SYSTEM_PARAMETER2

V$TEMPFILE

V$TEMPSTAT

V$TEMP_EXTENT_MAP

V$TEMP_PING

V$THREAD

V$TIMEZONE_NAMES

V$TRANSACTION_ENQUEUE

V$UNDOSTAT

V$VPD_POLICY

V$_LOCK

V$_SEQUENCES

V$RSRC_CONSUMER_GROUP

V$RSRC_PLAN

V$SEGMENT_STATISTICS

V$SEGSTAT_NAME

V$SESSION_CONNECT_INFO

V$SESSION_EVENT

V$SESSION_OBJECT_CACHE

V$SESSTAT

V$SGA

V$SGA_CURRENT_RESIZE_OPS

V$SGA_DYNAMIC_FREE_MEMORY

V$SHARED_POOL_ADVICE

V$SHARED_SERVER

V$SORT_SEGMENT

V$SPPARAMETER

V$SQLAREA

V$SQLTEXT_WITH_NEWLINES

V$SQL_BIND_METADATA

V$SQL_PLAN

V$SQL_PLAN_STATISTICS_ALL

V$SQL_SHARED_CURSOR

V$SQL_WORKAREA

V$SQL_WORKAREA_HISTOGRAM

V$STATISTICS_LEVEL

V$STREAMS_APPLY_COORDINATOR

V$STREAMS_APPLY_SERVER

V$SUBCACHE

V$SYSTEM_CURSOR_CACHE

V$SYSTEM_PARAMETER

V$TABLESPACE

V$TEMPORARY_LOBS

V$TEMP_CACHE_TRANSFER

V$TEMP_EXTENT_POOL

V$TEMP_SPACE_HEADER

V$TIMER

V$TRANSACTION

V$TYPE_SIZE

V$VERSION

V$WAITSTAT

V$_LOCK1

V$ Views

The Oracle9i Scripts of the *X$* Tables Used to Create the V$ Views

Use the following Oracle9i query to get one of the listings detailed in the following sections:

```
select 'View Name: '||view_name,substr(view_definition,1,(instr(view_definition,'from')
     -1)) def1,substr(view_definition,(instr(view_definition,'from')))||';' def2
from   v$fixed_view_definition
         order by view_name;
```

View Name: GV$ACCESS

```
select distinct s.inst_id,s.ksusenum,o.kglnaown,o.kglnaobj, decode(o.kglobtyp, 0,
     'CURSOR',1,'INDEX',2,'TABLE',3,'CLUSTER',4,'VIEW',5,'SYNONYM',6,
     'SEQUENCE',7,'PROCEDURE',8,'FUNCTION',9,'PACKAGE',10,'NON-EXISTENT',11,
     'PACKAGE BODY',12,'TRIGGER',13,'TYPE',14,'TYPE BODY',15,'OBJECT',16,
     'USER',17,'DBLINK',18,'PIPE',19,'TABLE PARTITION',20,'INDEX PARTITION',21,
     'LOB',22,'LIBRARY',23,'DIRECTORY',24, 'QUEUE',25,'INDEX-ORGANIZED TABLE',26,
     'REPLICATION OBJECT GROUP',27,'REPLICATION PROPAGATOR',28,'JAVA SOURCE',29,
     'JAVA CLASS',30,'JAVA RESOURCE',31,'JAVA JAR','INVALID TYPE')
from   x$ksuse s,x$kglob o,x$kgldp d,x$kgllk l
where  l.kgllkuse=s.addr and
       l.kgllkhdl=d.kglhdadr and l.kglnahsh=d.kglnahsh and o.kglnahsh=d.kglrfhsh
       and o.kglhdadr=d.kglrfhdl;
```

View Name: V$ACCESS

```
select SID, OWNER, OBJECT, TYPE
from   GV$ACCESS where inst_id = USERENV('Instance');
```

View Name: GV$ACTIVE_INSTANCES

```
select inst_id, ksiminum, rpad(ksimstr,60)
from   x$ksimsi;
```

View Name: V$ACTIVE_INSTANCES

```
select INST_NUMBER, INST_NAME
from   GV$ACTIVE_INSTANCES
where  inst_id = USERENV('Instance');
```

View Name: GV$ACTIVE_SESS_POOL_MTH

```
select inst_id, policy_name_kgskasp
from   x$kgskasp;
```

View Name: V$ACTIVE_SESS_POOL_MTH

```
select name
from   gv$active_sess_pool_mth
where  inst_id = userenv('instance');
```

View Name: GV$AQI

```
select INST_ID,KWQSIQID,KWQSINWT,KWQSINRD,KWQSINEX,KWQSINCO,KWQSITWT,
     DECODE(KWQSINCO,0,0,KWQSITWT/KWQSINCO)
from   X$KWQSI;
```

View Name: **V$AQ1**

```
select QID,WAITING,READY,EXPIRED,TOTAL_CONSUMERS,TOTAL_WAIT, AVERAGE_WAIT
from GV$AQ1;
```

View Name: **GV$ARCHIVE**

```
select le.inst_id,le.lenum,le.lethr,le.leseq,decode(bitand(le.leflg,8),0,'NO','YES'),
       decode(bitand(le.leflg,8),0,'NO','YES'),to_number(le.lelos)
from   x$kccle le,x$kccdi di
       where bitand(di.diflg,1)!=0 and le.ledup!=0 and
       bitand(le.leflg,1)=0 and (to_number(le.lelos)<=to_number(di.difas) or
       bitand(le.leflg,8)=0);
```

View Name: **V$ARCHIVE**

```
select GROUP#, THREAD#, SEQUENCE#, ISCURRENT, "CURRENT", FIRST_CHANGE#
from   GV$ARCHIVE
where inst_id = USERENV('Instance');
```

View Name: **GV$ARCHIVED_LOG**

```
select inst_id,alrid,alstm,alnam,aldst,althp,alseq,to_number(alrls),
       to_date(alrlc,'MM/DD/RR HH24:MI:SS','NLS_CALENDAR=Gregorian'),
       to_number(allos),to_date(allot,'MM/DD/RR HH24:MI:SS','NLS_CALENDAR=Gregorian'),
       to_number(alnxs),to_date(alnxt,'MM/DD/RR HH24:MI:SS','NLS_CALENDAR=Gregorian'),
       albct,albsz,decode(bitand(alflg,16+32+64+128+256),16,'ARCH',32,'FGRD',64,
       'RMAN',128,'SRMN',256,'LGWR','UNKNOWN'),decode(bitand(alflg,4),4,'RFS',
       decode(bitand(alflg,16+32+64+128+256),16,'ARCH',32,'FGRD',64,'RMAN',128,
       'SRMN',256,'LGWR','UNKNOWN')),decode(bitand(alflg,8),0,'NO','YES'),
       decode(bitand(alflg,2),0,'NO','YES'),decode(bitand(alflg,1024),0, 'NO','YES'),
       decode(bitand(alflg,1),0,'NO','YES'),decode(bitand(alflg,1+2048+4096),
       0,'A',1,'D',2048,'X',4096,'U','?'),to_date(altsm,'MM/DD/RR HH24:MI:SS',
       'NLS_CALENDAR=Gregorian'),decode(bitand(alflg,8192), 0,'NO','YES'),
       decode(bitand(alflg,16384),0,'NO','YES'),decode(bitand(alflg,32768),
       0,'NO','YES'),to_number(bitand(alfl2,15)),altoa,alacd
from   x$kccal;
```

View Name: **V$ARCHIVED_LOG**

```
select RECID,STAMP,NAME,DEST_ID,THREAD#,SEQUENCE#,RESETLOGS_CHANGE#,RESETLOGS_TIME,
       FIRST_CHANGE#,FIRST_TIME,NEXT_CHANGE#,NEXT_TIME,BLOCKS,BLOCK_SIZE,
       CREATOR,REGISTRAR,STANDBY_DEST,ARCHIVED,APPLIED,DELETED,STATUS,
       COMPLETION_TIME,DICTIONARY_BEGIN,DICTIONARY_END,END_OF_REDO,BACKUP_COUNT,
       ARCHIVAL_THREAD#,ACTIVATION#
from   GV$ARCHIVED_LOG
where  inst_id = USERENV('Instance');
```

View Name: **GV$ARCHIVE_DEST**

```
select inst_id,to_number(ADDID),ADDXX,decode(ADSTS,1,'VALID',2,'INACTIVE',3,
       'DEFERRED',4,'ERROR',5,'DISABLED',6,'BADPARAM',7,'ALTERNATE',8,'FULL',
       'UNKNOWN'),decode(ADMND,0,'OPTIONAL','MANDATORY'),decode(ADSES,0,
       'SYSTEM','SESSION'),decode(ADRMT,0,'PRIMARY',1,'STANDBY',2,'LOCAL',3,
       'REMOTE','UNKNOWN'),decode(ADPRC,0,'ARCH',1,'LGWR',2,'FOREGROUND',3,
       'RFS','UNKNOWN'),decode(ADSCH,0,'INACTIVE',1,'PENDING',2,'ACTIVE',3,
       'LATENT','UNKNOWN'),ADDNM,to_number(ADLSQ),to_number(ADROP),
       to_number(ADDLY),to_number(ADNTT),decode(ADWHO,0,'ARCH',1,'LGWR',2,
       'FOREGROUND',3,'RFS','UNKNOWN'),decode(ADREG,0,'NO','YES'),
       to_date(ADFDT,'MM/DD/RR HH24:MI:SS','NLS_CALENDAR=Gregorian'),
```

```
        to_number(ADFSQ),to_number(ADFBK),to_number(ADFCT),to_number(ADMXF),
        ADFER,ADALT,ADDPD,ADRFT,to_number(ADQSZ),to_number(ADQSD),ADMID,decode
        (ADLAB,0,decode(ADPAR,0,'SYNCHRONOUS','PARALLELSYNC'),'ASYNCHRONOUS'),
        to_number(ADLAB),decode(ADAFF,0,'NO','YES'),decode(ADDTG,0,'PUBLIC','PRIVATE')
from    x$kcrrdest;
```

View Name: V$ARCHIVE_DEST

```
select DEST_ID,DEST_NAME,STATUS,BINDING,NAME_SPACE,TARGET,ARCHIVER,SCHEDULE,
        DESTINATION,LOG_SEQUENCE,REOPEN_SECS,DELAY_MINS,NET_TIMEOUT,PROCESS,
        REGISTER,FAIL_DATE,FAIL_SEQUENCE,FAIL_BLOCK,FAILURE_COUNT,MAX_FAILURE,ERROR,
        ALTERNATE,DEPENDENCY,REMOTE_TEMPLATE,QUOTA_SIZE,QUOTA_USED,MOUNTID,
        TRANSMIT_MODE,ASYNC_BLOCKS,AFFIRM,TYPE
from    GV$ARCHIVE_DEST
where   inst_id = USERENV('Instance');
```

View Name: GV$ARCHIVE_DEST_STATUS

```
select inst_id,to_number(DSDID),DSDXX,decode(DSSTS,1,'VALID',2,'INACTIVE',3,
        'DEFERRED',4,'ERROR',5,'DISABLED',6,'BAD PARAM','UNKNOWN'),decode(DSTYP,1,
        'LOCAL',2,'PHYSICAL',3,'LOGICAL',4,'CROSS-INSTANCE','UNKNOWN'),decode(DSDMD,1,
        'STARTED',2,'MOUNTED',3,'MOUNTED-STANDBY',4,'OPEN',5,'OPEN-READ-ONLY','UNKNOWN'),
        decode(DSRMD,1,'IDLE',2,'MANUAL',3,'MANAGED','UNKNOWN'),decode(DSPRT,0,
        'MAXIMUM PERFORMANCE',1,'MAXIMUM PROTECTION',2,'MAXIMUM AVAILABILITY',3,
        'RESYNCHRONIZATION','UNKNOWN'),DSDNM,to_number(DSCNT),to_number(DSACT),
        to_number(DSLTA),to_number(DSLSA),to_number(DSLTR),to_number(DSLSR),DSERR,
        decode(DSSRL,0,'NO','YES')
from    x$kcrrdstat;
```

View Name: V$ARCHIVE_DEST_STATUS

```
select DEST_ID,DEST_NAME,STATUS,TYPE,DATABASE_MODE,RECOVERY_MODE,PROTECTION_MODE,
        DESTINATION,STANDBY_LOGFILE_COUNT,STANDBY_LOGFILE_ACTIVE,ARCHIVED_THREAD#,
        ARCHIVED_SEQ#,APPLIED_THREAD#,APPLIED_SEQ#,ERROR, SRL
from    GV$ARCHIVE_DEST_STATUS  where inst_id = USERENV('Instance');
```

View Name: GV$ARCHIVE_GAP

```
select USERENV('Instance'),high.thread#,"LOW_SEQUENCE#","HIGH_SEQUENCE#"
from
  (select thread#,min(sequence#)-1 "HIGH_SEQUENCE#"
   from
    (select a.thread#, a.sequence#
     from
      (select thread#, sequence#
       from   v$archived_log) a,
      (select thread#,max(sequence#) gap1
       from   v$log_history
       group  by thread#) b
     where a.thread# = b.thread#
     and    a.sequence# > gap1)
   group by thread#) high,
    (select thread#, min(gap2) "LOW_SEQUENCE#"
     from
      (select thread#, sequence#+1 gap2
       from   v$log_history h, v$datafile d
       where  checkpoint_change# <= next_change#
       and    checkpoint_change# >= first_change#
```

```
        and     enabled = 'READ WRITE')
    group by thread# ) low
where low.thread# = high.thread#
and   "LOW_SEQUENCE#" <= "HIGH_SEQUENCE#"
and   "HIGH_SEQUENCE#" <
 (select MAX(sequence#)
  from   v$archived_log);
```

View Name: V$ARCHIVE_GAP

```
select THREAD#,LOW_SEQUENCE#,HIGH_SEQUENCE#
from   GV$ARCHIVE_GAP where inst_id = USERENV('Instance');
```

View Name: GV$ARCHIVE_PROCESSES

```
select inst_id,to_number(kcrrxpid),decode(kcrrxsts,1,'SCHEDULED',2,'STARTING',3,
       'ACTIVE',4,'STOPPING',5,'TERMINATED','STOPPED'),to_number(kcrrxseq),
       decode(kcrrxsta,1,'BUSY','IDLE')
from   x$kcrrarch;
```

View Name: V$ARCHIVE_PROCESSES

```
select PROCESS,STATUS,LOG_SEQUENCE,STATE
from   GV$ARCHIVE_PROCESSES where inst_id = USERENV('Instance');
```

View Name: GV$AW_CALC

```
select inst_id,agcachhit,agcachmiss,scachesuccess,scachefailure,pgcachhit,
       pgcachmiss,pgnewpage,pgscrounge,pgcachewrite,pgpoolsize
from   x$xsaggr;
```

View Name: V$AW_CALC

```
select AGGREGATE_CACHE_HITS,AGGREGATE_CACHE_MISSES,SESSION_CACHE_HITS,
       SESSION_CACHE_MISSES,POOL_HITS,POOL_MISSES,POOL_NEW_PAGES,
       POOL_RECLAIMED_PAGES,CACHE_WRITES,POOL_SIZE
from   gv$aw_calc where inst_id = USERENV('Instance');
```

View Name: GV$AW_OLAP

```
select a.inst_id,s.ksusenum,a.awnum,decode(mod(a.at_mode,128),1,'READ WRITE',
       'READ ONLY'),a.gen_xsawso,a.temp_lob_count,a.temp_lob_read,a.perm_lob_read,
       a.changed_cache,a.unchanged_cache
from   x$ksuse s, x$xsawso a  where s.addr = a.KSSOBOWN and a.at_mode < 128;
```

View Name: V$AW_OLAP

```
select session_id,aw_number,attach_mode,generation,temp_space_pages,temp_space_reads,
       lob_reads,pool_changed_pages,pool_unchanged_pages
from   gv$aw_olap
where  inst_id = USERENV('Instance');
```

View Name: GV$AW_SESSION_INFO

```
select inst_id,client,state,sesshandle,userid,cdmlcmd,pdmlcmd,tottrns,tottrntime,
       avgtrntime,trncputime,tottrncputime,avgtrncputime
from   x$xssinfo;
```

**Scripts of X$ Tables Used
to Create V$ Views**

View Name: **V$AW_SESSION_INFO**

```
select CLIENT_TYPE,SESSION_STATE,SESSION_HANDLE,USERID,CURR_DML_COMMAND,
       PREV_DML_COMMAND,TOTAL_TRANSACTION,TOTAL_TRANSACTION_TIME,
       AVERAGE_TRANSACTION_TIME,TRANSACTION_CPU_TIME,TOTAL_TRANSACTION_CPU_TIME,
       AVERAGE_TRANSACTION_CPU_TIME
from   gv$aw_session_info where inst_id = USERENV('Instance');
```

View Name: **GV$BACKUP**

```
select inst_id,hxfil,decode(hxerr,0,decode(bitand(fhsta,1),0,'NOT ACTIVE',
       'ACTIVE'),1,'FILE MISSING',2,'OFFLINE NORMAL',3,'NOT VERIFIED',4,
       'FILE NOT FOUND',5,'CANNOT OPEN FILE',6,'CANNOT READ HEADER',7,
       'CORRUPT HEADER',8,'WRONG FILE TYPE',9,'WRONG DATABASE',10,'WRONG FILE NUMBER',11,
       'WRONG FILE CREATE',12,'WRONG FILE CREATE',16,'DELAYED OPEN','UNKNOWN ERROR'),
       to_number(fhbsc),to_date(fhbti,'MM/DD/RR HH24:MI:SS','NLS_CALENDAR=Gregorian')
from   x$kcvfhonl;
```

View Name: **V$BACKUP**

```
select FILE#,STATUS,CHANGE#,TIME
from   GV$BACKUP
where  inst_id = USERENV('Instance');
```

View Name: **GV$BACKUP_ASYNC_IO**

```
select inst_id,sid,ser,setid,devtype,decode(type,1,'INPUT',2,'OUTPUT',3,'AGGREGATE',
       'UNKNOWN'),decode(status,1,'NOT STARTED',2,'IN PROGRESS',3,'FINISHED',
       'UNKNOWN'),filename,set_count,set_stamp,block_size * buffer_size,buffer_count,
       decode(total_blocks,0,null,total_blocks) * block_size,to_date
       (open_time,'MM/DD/RR HH24:MI:SS','NLS_CALENDAR=Gregorian'),
       to_date(close_time,'MM/DD/RR HH24:MI:SS','NLS_CALENDAR=Gregorian'),
       (to_date(close_time,'MM/DD/RR HH24:MI:SS','NLS_CALENDAR=Gregorian') -
       to_date(open_time,'MM/DD/RR HH24:MI:SS','NLS_CALENDAR=Gregorian')) *
       8640000,decode(aggregate_count,0,null,aggregate_count) * 1,blocks *
       block_size,decode(instr(open_time,close_time),1,null,round((blocks *
       block_size) / ((to_date(close_time,'MM/DD/RR HH24:MI:SS',
       'NLS_CALENDAR=Gregorian') - to_date(open_time,'MM/DD/RR HH24:MI:SS',
       'NLS_CALENDAR=Gregorian')) * 86400))) * 1,async_short_count +
       async_long_count + async_ready,async_ready,async_short_count,
       async_short_tottime,async_short_maxtime,async_long_count,
       async_long_tottime,async_long_maxtime
from   x$ksfqp
where  bitand(flags,2) = 2;
```

View Name: **V$BACKUP_ASYNC_IO**

```
select SID, SERIAL, USE_COUNT, DEVICE_TYPE, TYPE, STATUS, FILENAME, SET_COUNT,
       SET_STAMP, BUFFER_SIZE, BUFFER_COUNT, TOTAL_BYTES, OPEN_TIME,
       CLOSE_TIME, ELAPSED_TIME, MAXOPENFILES, BYTES, EFFECTIVE_BYTES_PER_SECOND,
       IO_COUNT, READY, SHORT_WAITS, SHORT_WAIT_TIME_TOTAL, SHORT_WAIT_TIME_MAX,
       LONG_WAITS, LONG_WAIT_TIME_TOTAL, LONG_WAIT_TIME_MAX
from   gv$backup_async_io
where  inst_id = userenv('Instance');
```

View Name: **GV$BACKUP_CORRUPTION**

```
select inst_id,fcrid,fcstm,fcbss,fcbsc,fcpno,fcdfp,fcblk,fccnt,to_number(fcscn),
       decode(bitand(fcflg,1),1,'YES','NO'),decode(bitand(fcflg,30),2,'ALL ZERO',4,
```

```
        'FRACTURED',8,'CHECKSUM',16,'CORRUPT','LOGICAL')
from    x$kccfc;
```

View Name: **V$BACKUP_CORRUPTION**

```
select  RECID,STAMP,SET_STAMP,SET_COUNT,PIECE#,FILE#,BLOCK#,BLOCKS,CORRUPTION_CHANGE#,
        MARKED_CORRUPT,CORRUPTION_TYPE
from    GV$BACKUP_CORRUPTION
where   inst_id = USERENV('Instance');
```

View Name: **GV$BACKUP_DATAFILE**

```
select  inst_id,bfrid,bfstm,bfbss,bfbsc,bfdfp,to_number(bfcrs),to_date(bfcrt,
        'MM/DD/RR HH24:MI:SS','NLS_CALENDAR=Gregorian'),to_number(bfrls),
        to_date(bfrlc,'MM/DD/RR HH24:MI:SS','NLS_CALENDAR=Gregorian'),
        decode(bitand(bfflg,1),1,bflvl,NULL),to_number(bfics),to_number(bfcps),
        to_date(bfcpt,'MM/DD/RR HH24:MI:SS','NLS_CALENDAR=Gregorian'),to_number(bfafs),
        bfncb,bfmcb,bflcb,bffsz,bfbct,bfbsz,bflor,to_date(bftsm,
        'MM/DD/RR HH24:MI:SS','NLS_CALENDAR=Gregorian'),decode(bfdfp, 0, decode
        (bitand(bfflg,2),2,'S','B'), NULL)
from    x$kccbf;
```

View Name: **V$BACKUP_DATAFILE**

```
select  RECID,STAMP,SET_STAMP,SET_COUNT,FILE#,CREATION_CHANGE#,CREATION_TIME,
        RESETLOGS_CHANGE#,RESETLOGS_TIME,INCREMENTAL_LEVEL,INCREMENTAL_CHANGE#,
        CHECKPOINT_CHANGE#,CHECKPOINT_TIME,ABSOLUTE_FUZZY_CHANGE#,MARKED_CORRUPT,
        MEDIA_CORRUPT,LOGICALLY_CORRUPT,DATAFILE_BLOCKS,BLOCKS,BLOCK_SIZE,
        OLDEST_OFFLINE_RANGE,COMPLETION_TIME,CONTROLFILE_TYPE
from    GV$BACKUP_DATAFILE
where   inst_id = USERENV('Instance');
```

View Name: **GV$BACKUP_DEVICE**

```
select  inst_id, devtype, devname
from    x$ksfhdvnt;
```

View Name: **V$BACKUP_DEVICE**

```
select  DEVICE_TYPE, DEVICE_NAME
from    GV$BACKUP_DEVICE
where   INST_ID = USERENV('Instance');
```

View Name: **GV$BACKUP_PIECE**

```
select  inst_id,bprid,bpstm,bpbss,bpbsc,bpnum,bitand(bpflg, 12)/4 + (bitand(bpext,
        64-1) * 4) + 1,bpdev,bphdl,bpcmt,bpmdh,bitand(bpflg, 4080) / 16,decode(bitand
        (bpflg,2),1,'YES','NO'),bptag,decode(bitand(bpflg, 1+4096+8192),0,'A',1,'D',
        4096,'X',8192,'U','?'),decode(bitand(bpflg,1),1,'YES','NO'),to_date(bptsm,
        'MM/DD/RR HH24:MI:SS','NLS_CALENDAR=Gregorian'),to_date(bptim,'MM/DD/RR
        HH24:MI:SS','NLS_CALENDAR=Gregorian'),(to_date(bptim,'MM/DD/RR
        HH24:MI:SS','NLS_CALENDAR=Gregorian')- to_date(bptsm,'MM/DD/RR
        HH24:MI:SS','NLS_CALENDAR=Gregorian'))*86400
from    x$kccbp;
```

View Name: **V$BACKUP_PIECE**

```
select  RECID,STAMP,SET_STAMP,SET_COUNT,PIECE#,COPY#,DEVICE_TYPE,HANDLE,COMMENTS,
        MEDIA,MEDIA_POOL,CONCUR,TAG,STATUS,START_TIME,COMPLETION_TIME,
```

Scripts of X$ Tables Used to Create V$ Views

```
       ELAPSED_SECONDS,DELETED
from   GV$BACKUP_PIECE
where  inst_id = USERENV('Instance');
```

View Name: GV$BACKUP_REDOLOG

```
select inst_id,blrid,blstm,blbss,blbsc,blthp,blseq,to_number(blrls),to_date(blrlc,
       'MM/DD/RR HH24:MI:SS','NLS_CALENDAR=Gregorian'),to_number(bllos),to_date
       (bllot,'MM/DD/RR HH24:MI:SS','NLS_CALENDAR=Gregorian'),to_number(blnxs),
       to_date(blnxt,'MM/DD/RR HH24:MI:SS','NLS_CALENDAR=Gregorian'),blbct,blbsz
from   x$kccbl;
```

View Name: V$BACKUP_REDOLOG

```
select RECID,STAMP,SET_STAMP,SET_COUNT,THREAD#,SEQUENCE#,RESETLOGS_CHANGE#,
       RESETLOGS_TIME, FIRST_CHANGE#, FIRST_TIME, NEXT_CHANGE#, NEXT_TIME,
       BLOCKS, BLOCK_SIZE
from   GV$BACKUP_REDOLOG
where  inst_id = USERENV('Instance');
```

View Name: GV$BACKUP_SET

```
select inst_id,bsrid,bsstm,bsbss,bsbsc,decode(bitand(bstyp,11),1,'D',2,'I',8,'L'),
       decode(bitand(bstyp,4+64),4,'YES',68,'SBY','NO'),decode(bitand(bstyp,16),16,
       bslvl,NULL),bspct,to_date(bsbst,'MM/DD/RR HH24:MI:SS','NLS_CALENDAR=Gregorian'),
       to_date(bstsm,'MM/DD/RR HH24:MI:SS','NLS_CALENDAR=Gregorian'),
       (to_date(bstsm,'MM/DD/RR HH24:MI:SS','NLS_CALENDAR=Gregorian')-
       to_date(bsbst,'MM/DD/RR HH24:MI:SS','NLS_CALENDAR=Gregorian'))*86400,bsbsz,
       decode(bitand(bstyp,128),128,'YES','NO'),decode(bitand(bstyp, 1792), 0, 'NO',
       'YES'),to_date(bskpt,'MM/DD/RR HH24:MI:SS','NLS_CALENDAR=Gregorian'),
       decode(bitand(bstyp,1792),256,'LOGS',512,'NOLOGS',1024,'CONSISTENT',NULL)
from   x$kccbs;
```

View Name: V$BACKUP_SET

```
select RECID,STAMP,SET_STAMP,SET_COUNT,BACKUP_TYPE,CONTROLFILE_INCLUDED,
       INCREMENTAL_LEVEL, PIECES, START_TIME, COMPLETION_TIME, ELAPSED_SECONDS,
       BLOCK_SIZE, INPUT_FILE_SCAN_ONLY, KEEP, KEEP_UNTIL, KEEP_OPTIONS
from   GV$BACKUP_SET
where  inst_id = USERENV('Instance');
```

View Name: GV$BACKUP_SPFILE

```
select inst_id,birid,bistm,bibss,bibsc,to_date(bimdt, 'MM/DD/RR HH24:MI:SS',
       'NLS_CALENDAR=Gregorian'), bifsz, to_date(bitsm, 'MM/DD/RR HH24:MI:SS',
       'NLS_CALENDAR=Gregorian')
from   x$kccbi;
```

View Name: V$BACKUP_SPFILE

```
select RECID,STAMP,SET_STAMP,SET_COUNT,MODIFICATION_TIME,BYTES,COMPLETION_TIME
from   GV$BACKUP_SPFILE
where  inst_id = USERENV('Instance');
```

View Name: GV$BACKUP_SYNC_IO

```
select inst_id,sid,ser,setid,devtype,decode(type,1,'INPUT',2,'OUTPUT',3,
       'AGGREGATE','UNKNOWN'),decode(status,1,'NOT STARTED',2,'IN PROGRESS',3,
       'FINISHED','UNKNOWN'),filename,set_count,set_stamp,block_size *
```

```
        buffer_size,buffer_count,decode(total_blocks,0,null,total_blocks) *
        block_size,to_date(open_time,'MM/DD/RR HH24:MI:SS','NLS_CALENDAR=Gregorian'),
        to_date(close_time,'MM/DD/RR HH24:MI:SS','NLS_CALENDAR=Gregorian'),
        (to_date(close_time,'MM/DD/RR HH24:MI:SS','NLS_CALENDAR=Gregorian') -
        to_date(open_time,'MM/DD/RR HH24:MI:SS','NLS_CALENDAR=Gregorian')) *
        8640000,decode(aggregate_count,0,null,aggregate_count) * 1,blocks * block_size,
        decode(instr(open_time,close_time),1,null,round((blocks * block_size)
        / ((to_date(close_time,'MM/DD/RR HH24:MI:SS','NLS_CALENDAR=Gregorian') -
        to_date(open_time,'MM/DD/RR HH24:MI:SS','NLS_CALENDAR=Gregorian')) *
        86400))) * 1,sync_count,sync_tottime,sync_maxtime,decode(sync_tottime,0,
        NULL,round((blocks * block_size) / sync_tottime * 100)) * 1
from    x$ksfqp
where   bitand(flags,2) = 0;
```

View Name: **V$BACKUP_SYNC_IO**

```
select SID,SERIAL,USE_COUNT,DEVICE_TYPE,TYPE,STATUS,FILENAME,SET_COUNT,SET_STAMP,
       BUFFER_SIZE,BUFFER_COUNT,TOTAL_BYTES,OPEN_TIME,CLOSE_TIME,ELAPSED_TIME,
       MAXOPENFILES,BYTES,EFFECTIVE_BYTES_PER_SECOND,IO_COUNT,IO_TIME_TOTAL,
       IO_TIME_MAX,DISCRETE_BYTES_PER_SECOND
from   gv$backup_sync_io
where  inst_id = userenv('Instance');
```

View Name: **GV$BGPROCESS**

```
select p.inst_id,p.ksbdppro,p.ksbdpnam,d.ksbdddsc,p.ksbdperr
from   x$ksbdp p,x$ksbdd d
where  p.indx=d.indx;
```

View Name: **V$BGPROCESS**

```
select paddr,name,description,error
from gv$bgprocess
where inst_id = USERENV('Instance');
```

View Name: **GV$BH**

```
select bh.inst_id,file#,dbablk,class,decode(state,0,'free',1,'xcur',2,'scur',
       3,'cr',4,'read',5,'mrec',6,'irec',7,'write',8,'pi'),x_to_null,forced_reads,
       forced_writes,bh.le_addr,name,le_class,decode(bitand(flag,1),0,'N','Y'),
       decode(bitand(flag,16),0,'N','Y'),decode(bitand(flag,1536),0,'N','Y'),
       decode(bitand(flag,16384),0,'N','Y'),decode(bitand(flag,65536),0,'N','Y'),
       'N',obj,ts#
from   x$bh bh, x$le le
where  bh.le_addr = le.le_addr (+);
```

View Name: **V$BH**

```
select file#,block#,class#,status,xnc,forced_reads,forced_writes,lock_element_addr,
       lock_element_name,lock_element_class,dirty,temp,ping,stale,direct,new,objd,ts#
from   gv$bh
where  inst_id = USERENV('Instance');
```

View Name: **GV$BSP**

```
select inst_id,reqcr,reqcur,reqdata,requndo,reqtx,rescur,respriv,reszero,resdisk,
       resfail,fairdc,faircl,freedc,flush,flushq,flushf,flushmx,light,error
from   x$kclcrst;
```

View Name: V$BSP

```
select cr_requests,current_requests,data_requests,undo_requests,tx_requests,
       current_results,private_results,zero_results,disk_read_results,fail_results,
       fairness_down_converts,fairness_clears,free_lock_elements,flushes,
       flushes_queued,flush_queue_full,flush_max_time,light_works,errors
from   gv$bsp
where  inst_id = USERENV('Instance');
```

View Name: GV$BUFFER_POOL

```
select inst_id,bp_id,bp_name,bp_blksz,decode(bp_state, 0, 'STATIC',1,'ALLOCATING',
       2,'ACTIVATING',3,'SHRINKING'),bp_currgrans * bp_gransz,bp_size,bp_tgtgrans *
       bp_gransz,bp_tgtgrans * bp_bufpergran,bp_prevgrans * bp_gransz,bp_prevgrans *
       bp_bufpergran,0,0,bp_lo_sid,bp_hi_sid,bp_set_ct
from   x$kcbwbpd
where  bp_id > 0 and bp_currgrans > 0 and bp_tgtgrans > 0;
```

View Name: V$BUFFER_POOL

```
select id,name,block_size,resize_state,current_size,buffers,target_size,
       target_buffers,prev_size,prev_buffers,lo_bnum,hi_bnum,lo_setid,hi_setid,
       set_count
from   gv$buffer_pool
where  inst_id = USERENV('Instance');
```

View Name: GV$BUFFER_POOL_STATISTICS

```
select kcbwbpd.inst_id,kcbwbpd.bp_id,kcbwbpd.bp_name,kcbwbpd.bp_blksz,
       sum(kcbwds.cnum_set),sum(kcbwds.cnum_repl),sum(kcbwds.cnum_write),
       sum(kcbwds.cnum_set),sum(kcbwds.buf_got),sum(kcbwds.sum_wrt),
       sum(kcbwds.sum_scn),sum(kcbwds.fbwait),sum(kcbwds.wcwait),
       sum(kcbwds.bbwait),sum(kcbwds.fbinsp),sum(kcbwds.dbinsp),
       sum(kcbwds.dbbchg),sum(kcbwds.dbbget),sum(kcbwds.conget),sum(kcbwds.pread),
       sum(kcbwds.pwrite)
from   x$kcbwds kcbwds,x$kcbwbpd kcbwbpd
where  kcbwds.set_id >= kcbwbpd.bp_lo_sid and kcbwds.set_id <= kcbwbpd.bp_hi_sid
       and kcbwbpd.bp_size != 0 group by kcbwbpd.inst_id,kcbwbpd.bp_id,
       kcbwbpd.bp_name,kcbwbpd.bp_blksz;
```

View Name: V$BUFFER_POOL_STATISTICS

```
select id,name,block_size,set_msize,cnum_repl,cnum_write,cnum_set,buf_got,
       sum_write,sum_scan,free_buffer_wait,write_complete_wait,buffer_busy_wait,
       free_buffer_inspected,dirty_buffers_inspected,db_block_change,db_block_gets,
       consistent_gets,physical_reads,physical_writes
from   gv$buffer_pool_statistics
where  inst_id = USERENV('Instance');
```

View Name: GV$CIRCUIT

```
select inst_id,addr,kmcvcdpc,decode(kmcvcpro,kmcvcdpc, hextoraw('00'),kmcvcpro),
       kmcvcwat,kmcvcses,kmcvcsta,kmcvcque,kmcvcsz0, kmcvcsz1,kmcvcsz2,kmcvcsz3,
       kmcvcnmg, kmcvcnmb,kmcvcbrk,kmcvcpre,kmcvcpvc
from   x$kmcvc
where  bitand(ksspaflg,1) != 0;
```

View Name: V$CIRCUIT

```
select  CIRCUIT,DISPATCHER,SERVER,WAITER,SADDR,STATUS,QUEUE,MESSAGE0,MESSAGE1,
        MESSAGE2,MESSAGE3,MESSAGES,BYTES,BREAKS,PRESENTATION,PCIRCUIT
from    GV$CIRCUIT
where   inst_id = USERENV('Instance');
```

View Name: GV$CLASS_CACHE_TRANSFER

```
select  inst_id,decode(indx,1,'data block',2,'sort block',3,'save undo block',4,
        'segment header',5,'save undo header',6,'free list',7,'extent map', 8,
        '1st level bmb',9,'2nd level bmb',10,'3rd level bmb',11,'bitmap block',12,
        'bitmap index block',13,'unused',14,'undo header',15,'undo block'),
        CLASS_X2NC,CLASS_X2NFWC,CLASS_X2NFSC,CLASS_X2SC,CLASS_X2SFWC,CLASS_S2NC,
        CLASS_S2NFSC,CLASS_N2XC,CLASS_S2XC,CLASS_N2SC
from    x$class_stat;
```

View Name: V$CLASS_CACHE_TRANSFER

```
select  class,x_2_null,x_2_null_forced_write,x_2_null_forced_stale,
        x_2_s,x_2_s_forced_write,s_2_null, s_2_null_forced_stale,null_2_x,
        s_2_x,null_2_s
from    gv$class_cache_transfer
where   inst_id = USERENV('Instance');
```

View Name: GV$CLASS_PING

```
select  inst_id,decode(indx,1,'data block',2,'sort block',3,'save undo block',4,
        'segment header',5,'save undo header',6,'free list',7,'extent map',8,Z
        '1st level bmb',9,'2nd level bmb',10,'3rd level bmb',11,'bitmap block',12,
        'bitmap index block',13,'unused',14,'undo header',15,'undo block'),
        CLASS_X2NC,CLASS_X2NFWC,CLASS_X2NFSC,CLASS_X2SC,CLASS_X2SFWC,0,0,
        CLASS_S2NC,CLASS_S2NFSC,0,0,0,CLASS_N2XC,CLASS_S2XC,0,CLASS_N2SC,0
from    x$class_stat;
```

View Name: V$CLASS_PING

```
select  class,x_2_null,x_2_null_forced_write,x_2_null_forced_stale,x_2_s,
        x_2_s_forced_write,x_2_ssx,x_2_ssx_forced_write,s_2_null,s_2_null_forced_stale,
        ss_2_null,ss_2_rls,op_2_ss,null_2_x,s_2_x,ssx_2_x,null_2_s,null_2_ss
from    gv$class_ping
where   inst_id = USERENV('Instance');
```

View Name: GV$COMPATIBILITY

```
select  inst_id,kcktyid,kcktyrls,kcktydsc
from    x$kckty;
```

View Name: V$COMPATIBILITY

```
select  TYPE_ID,RELEASE,DESCRIPTION
from    GV$COMPATIBILITY
where   inst_id = USERENV('Instance');
```

View Name: GV$COMPATSEG

```
select  inst_id,kckceid,kckcerl,kckcevsn
from    x$kckce;
```

View Name: V$COMPATSEG

```
select TYPE_ID,RELEASE,UPDATED
from   GV$COMPATSEG
where  inst_id = USERENV('Instance');
```

View Name: GV$CONTEXT

```
select namespace,attribute,value
from   x$context;
```

View Name: V$CONTEXT

```
select namespace,attribute,value
from   x$context;
```

View Name: GV$CONTROLFILE

```
select inst_id,decode(bitand(cfflg,1),0,'',1,'INVALID'),cfnam
from   x$kcccf;
```

View Name: V$CONTROLFILE

```
select STATUS,NAME
from   GV$CONTROLFILE
where  inst_id = USERENV('Instance');
```

View Name: GV$CONTROLFILE_RECORD_SECTION

```
select inst_id,decode(indx,0,'DATABASE',1, 'CKPT PROGRESS', 2, 'REDO THREAD',3,'
       REDO LOG',4,'DATAFILE',5,'FILENAME',6,'TABLESPACE',7,'TEMPORARY FILENAME',8,
       'RMAN CONFIGURATION',9,'LOG HISTORY',10,'OFFLINE RANGE',11,'ARCHIVED LOG',
       12,'BACKUP SET',13,'BACKUP PIECE',14,'BACKUP DATAFILE',15, 'BACKUP REDOLOG',
       16,'DATAFILE COPY',17,'BACKUP CORRUPTION',18,'COPY CORRUPTION',19,
       'DELETED OBJECT',20,'PROXY COPY',21,'BACKUP SPFILE',23,'DATABASE INCARNATION',
       'UNKNOWN'),rsrsz,rsnum,rsnus,rsiol,rsilw,rsrlw
from   x$kccrs
where  indx not in (22);
```

View Name: V$CONTROLFILE_RECORD_SECTION

```
select TYPE,RECORD_SIZE,RECORDS_TOTAL,RECORDS_USED,FIRST_INDEX, LAST_INDEX,LAST_RECID
from   GV$CONTROLFILE_RECORD_SECTION
where  inst_id = USERENV('Instance');
```

View Name: GV$COPY_CORRUPTION

```
select inst_id,ccrid,ccstm,ccdcp,ccdcs,ccdfp,ccblk,cccnt,to_number(ccscn),
       decode(bitand(ccflg,1),1,'YES','NO'),decode(bitand(ccflg,30),2,'ALL ZERO',4,
       'FRACTURED',8,'CHECKSUM',16,'CORRUPT','LOGICAL')
from   x$kcccc;
```

View Name: V$COPY_CORRUPTION

```
select RECID,STAMP,COPY_RECID,COPY_STAMP,FILE#,BLOCK#,BLOCKS,CORRUPTION_CHANGE#,
       MARKED_CORRUPT,CORRUPTION_TYPE
from   GV$COPY_CORRUPTION
where  inst_id = USERENV('Instance');
```

View Name: GV$CR_BLOCK_SERVER

```
select inst_id,reqcr,reqcur,reqdata,requndo,reqtx,rescur,respriv,reszero,
       resdisk,resfail,fairdc,faircl,freedc,flush,flushq,flushf,flushmx,light,error
from   x$kclcrst;
```

View Name: V$CR_BLOCK_SERVER

```
select cr_requests,current_requests,data_requests,undo_requests,tx_requests,
       current_results,private_results, zero_results, disk_read_results,fail_results,
       fairness_down_converts, fairness_clears,free_gc_elements, flushes,
       flushes_queued,flush_queue_full, flush_max_time, light_works, errors
from   gv$cr_block_server
where  inst_id = USERENV('Instance');
```

View Name: GV$DATABASE

```
select inst_id,didbi,didbn,to_date(dicts,'MM/DD/RR HH24:MI:SS',
       'NLS_CALENDAR=Gregorian'),to_number(dirls),to_date(dirlc,
       'MM/DD/RR HH24:MI:SS','NLS_CALENDAR=Gregorian'),to_number(diprs),
       to_date(diprc,'MM/DD/RR HH24:MI:SS','NLS_CALENDAR=Gregorian'),
       decode(bitand(diflg,1),0,'NOARCHIVELOG','ARCHIVELOG'),to_number(discn),
       to_number(difas),decode(bitand(diflg,256),256,'CREATED',
       decode(bitand(diflg,1024),1024,'STANDBY',decode(bitand(diflg,32768),
       32768,'CLONE',decode(bitand(diflg,4096),4096,'BACKUP','CURRENT')))),
       to_date(dicct,'MM/DD/RR HH24:MI:SS','NLS_CALENDAR=Gregorian'),
       dicsq,to_number(dickp_scn),to_date(dickp_tim,'MM/DD/RR HH24:MI:SS',
       'NLS_CALENDAR=Gregorian'),decode(bitand(diflg,4),4,'REQUIRED',decode(diirs,0,
       'NOT ALLOWED','ALLOWED')),to_date(divts,'MM/DD/RR HH24:MI:SS',
       'NLS_CALENDAR=Gregorian'),decode(didor,0,'MOUNTED',decode(didor,1,
       'READ WRITE','READ ONLY')),decode(bitand(diflg,65536),65536,'MAXIMUM
       PROTECTION',decode(bitand(diflg,128),128,'MAXIMUM AVAILABILITY',
       decode(bitand(diflg,134217728),134217728,'RESYNCHRONIZATION',
       decode(bitand(diflg,8),8,'UNPROTECTED','MAXIMUM PERFORMANCE')))),
       decode(diprt,1,'MAXIMUM PROTECTION',2,'MAXIMUM AVAILABILITY',3,
       'RESYNCHRONIZATION',4,'MAXIMUM PERFORMANCE',5,'UNPROTECTED','UNKNOWN'),
       decode(dirae,0,'DISABLED',1,'SEND',2,'RECEIVE',3,'ENABLED','UNKNOWN'),
       to_number(diacid),decode(bitand(diflg,33554432),33554432,'LOGICAL STANDBY',
       decode(bitand(diflg,1024),1024,'PHYSICAL STANDBY','PRIMARY')),to_number(diars),
       decode(disos,0,'IMPOSSIBLE',1,'NOT ALLOWED',2,'SWITCHOVER LATENT',3,
       'SWITCHOVER PENDING',4,'TO PRIMARY',5,'TO STANDBY',6,'RECOVERY NEEDED',7,
       'SESSIONS ACTIVE','UNKNOWN'),decode(didgd,0,'DISABLED','ENABLED'),
       decode(bitand(diflg,1048576),1048576,'ALL',decode(bitand(diflg,2097152),
       2097152,'STANDBY','NONE')),decode(bitand(diflg,1073741824),1073741824,
       'YES','NO'),decode(bitand(diflg,131072),131072,'YES','NO'),
       decode(bitand(diflg,262144),262144,'YES','NO'),decode(bitand(diflg,268435456),
       268435456,'YES','NO')
from   x$kccdi;
```

View Name: V$DATABASE

```
select DBID,NAME,CREATED,RESETLOGS_CHANGE#,RESETLOGS_TIME,PRIOR_RESETLOGS_CHANGE#,
       PRIOR_RESETLOGS_TIME,LOG_MODE,CHECKPOINT_CHANGE#,ARCHIVE_CHANGE#,
       CONTROLFILE_TYPE,CONTROLFILE_CREATED,CONTROLFILE_SEQUENCE#,CONTROLFILE_CHANGE#,
       CONTROLFILE_TIME,OPEN_RESETLOGS,VERSION_TIME,OPEN_MODE,PROTECTION_MODE,
       PROTECTION_LEVEL,REMOTE_ARCHIVE,ACTIVATION#,DATABASE_ROLE,ARCHIVELOG_CHANGE#,
       SWITCHOVER_STATUS,DATAGUARD_BROKER,GUARD_STATUS,SUPPLEMENTAL_LOG_DATA_MIN,
       SUPPLEMENTAL_LOG_DATA_PK,SUPPLEMENTAL_LOG_DATA_UI,FORCE_LOGGING
from   GV$DATABASE
where  inst_id = USERENV('Instance');
```

View Name: GV$DATABASE_BLOCK_CORRUPTION

```
select distinct userenv('Instance'),file#,block#,blocks,corruption_change#,
       corruption_type
from
  (select file#,block#,blocks,corruption_change#,copy_stamp stamp,corruption_type
   from    v$copy_corruption
   union
   select file#, block#,blocks,corruption_change#,bs.stamp,corruption_type
   from    v$backup_corruption bc,v$backup_set bs
   where   bc.set_count = bs.set_count and bc.set_stamp = bs.set_stamp) outer
where  not exists
  (select 1
   from    v$datafile_copy
   where   scanned = 'YES'
   and     outer.file# = file#
   and     outer.stamp < stamp
   union
   select 1
   from    v$backup_datafile bdf, v$backup_set bs
   where   bdf.set_count = bs.set_count
   and     bdf.set_stamp = bs.set_stamp
   and     outer.file# = file#
   and     outer.stamp < bs.stamp);
```

View Name: V$DATABASE_BLOCK_CORRUPTION

```
select FILE#, BLOCK#, BLOCKS, CORRUPTION_CHANGE#, CORRUPTION_TYPE
from    GV$DATABASE_BLOCK_CORRUPTION
where   inst_id = USERENV('Instance');
```

View Name: GV$DATABASE_INCARNATION

```
select userenv('Instance'),to_number(icrls),to_date(icrlc,'MM/DD/RR HH24:MI:SS',
       'NLS_CALENDAR=Gregorian'),to_number(icprs),to_date(icprc,'MM/DD/RR HH24:MI:SS',
       'NLS_CALENDAR=Gregorian')
from    x$kccic;
```

View Name: V$DATABASE_INCARNATION

```
select resetlogs_change#,resetlogs_time,prior_resetlogs_change#,prior_resetlogs_time
from    GV$DATABASE_INCARNATION
where   inst_id = USERENV('Instance');
```

View Name: GV$DATAFILE

```
select fe.inst_id,fe.fenum,to_number(fe.fecrc_scn),to_date
       (fe.fecrc_tim,'MM/DD/RR HH24:MI:SS','NLS_CALENDAR=Gregorian'),
       fe.fetsn,fe.ferfn,decode(fe.fetsn,0,decode(bitand(fe.festa,2),0,
       'SYSOFF','SYSTEM'),decode(bitand(fe.festa,18),0,'OFFLINE',2,
       'ONLINE','RECOVER')),decode(fe.fedor,2,'READ ONLY',
       decode(bitand(fe.festa, 12),0,'DISABLED',4,'READ ONLY',12,'READ WRITE',
       'UNKNOWN')),to_number(fe.fecps),to_date(fe.fecpt,'MM/DD/RR HH24:MI:SS',
       'NLS_CALENDAR=Gregorian'),to_number(fe.feurs),to_date(fe.feurt,
       'MM/DD/RR HH24:MI:SS','NLS_CALENDAR=Gregorian'),to_number(fe.fests),
       decode(fe.fests,NULL,to_date(NULL),to_date(fe.festt,'MM/DD/RR HH24:MI:SS',
       'NLS_CALENDAR=Gregorian')),to_number(fe.feofs),to_number(fe.feonc_scn),
       to_date(fe.feonc_tim,'MM/DD/RR HH24:MI:SS','NLS_CALENDAR=Gregorian'),
       fh.fhfsz*fe.febsz,fh.fhfsz,fe.fecsz*fe.febsz,fe.febsz,fn.fnnam,fe.fefdb,
       fn.fnbof,decode(fe.fepax, 0,'UNKNOWN', 65535,'NONE',fnaux.fnnam)
```

```
from   x$kccfe fe,x$kccfn fn,x$kccfn fnaux,x$kcvfh fh
where  ((fe.fepax!=65535 and fe.fepax!=0 and fe.fepax=fnaux.fnnum) or
       ((fe.fepax=65535 or fe.fepax=0) and fe.fenum=fnaux.fnfno and fnaux.fntyp=4
       and fnaux.fnnam is not null and fnaux.fnfno=fh.hxfil and fe.fefnh=fnaux.fnnum))
       and fn.fnfno=fe.fenum and fn.fnfno=fh.hxfil and fe.fefnh=fn.fnnum and
       fe.fedup!=0 and fn.fntyp=4 and fn.fnnam is not null;
```

View Name: **V$DATAFILE**

```
select FILE#,CREATION_CHANGE#,CREATION_TIME,TS#,RFILE#,STATUS,ENABLED,
       CHECKPOINT_CHANGE#,CHECKPOINT_TIME,UNRECOVERABLE_CHANGE#,UNRECOVERABLE_TIME,
       LAST_CHANGE#,LAST_TIME,OFFLINE_CHANGE#,ONLINE_CHANGE#,ONLINE_TIME,
       BYTES,BLOCKS,CREATE_BYTES,BLOCK_SIZE,NAME,PLUGGED_IN,BLOCK1_OFFSET,AUX_NAME
from   GV$DATAFILE
where  inst_id = USERENV('Instance');
```

View Name: **GV$DATAFILE_COPY**

```
select inst_id,dcrid,dcstm,dcnam,dctag,dcdfp,dcrfn,to_number(dccrs),
       to_date(dccrt,'MM/DD/RR HH24:MI:SS','NLS_CALENDAR=Gregorian'),
       to_number(dcrls),to_date(dcrlc,'MM/DD/RR HH24:MI:SS',
       'NLS_CALENDAR=Gregorian'),decode(bitand(dcflg,8),8,0,NULL),
       to_number(dccps),to_date(dccpt,'MM/DD/RR HH24:MI:SS','NLS_CALENDAR=Gregorian'),
       to_number(dcafs),to_number(dcrfs),to_date(dcrft,'MM/DD/RR HH24:MI:SS',
       'NLS_CALENDAR=Gregorian'),decode(bitand(dcflg,2),0,'NO','YES'),
       decode(bitand(dcflg, 4),0,'NO','YES'),dcncb,dcmcb,dclcb,dcbct,dcbsz,
       dclor,decode(bitand(dcflg, 1),0,'NO','YES'),decode(bitand(dcflg,1+32+64),
       0,'A',1,'D',32,'X',64,'U','?'),to_date(dctsm,'MM/DD/RR HH24:MI:SS',
       'NLS_CALENDAR=Gregorian'),decode(dcdfp, 0, decode(bitand(dcflg,16),
       16,'S','B'),NULL),decode(bitand(dcflg,1792),0,'NO','YES'),
       to_date(dckpt,'MM/DD/RR HH24:MI:SS','NLS_CALENDAR=Gregorian'),
       decode(bitand(dcflg,1792),256,'LOGS',512,'NOLOGS',1024,'CONSISTENT',NULL),
       decode(bitand(dcflg, 128),0,'NO','YES')
from   x$kccdc;
```

View Name: **V$DATAFILE_COPY**

```
select RECID,STAMP,NAME,TAG,FILE#,RFILE#,CREATION_CHANGE#,CREATION_TIME,
       RESETLOGS_CHANGE#,RESETLOGS_TIME,INCREMENTAL_LEVEL,CHECKPOINT_CHANGE#,
       CHECKPOINT_TIME,ABSOLUTE_FUZZY_CHANGE#,RECOVERY_FUZZY_CHANGE#,
       RECOVERY_FUZZY_TIME,ONLINE_FUZZY,BACKUP_FUZZY,MARKED_CORRUPT,MEDIA_CORRUPT,
       LOGICALLY_CORRUPT,BLOCKS,BLOCK_SIZE,OLDEST_OFFLINE_RANGE,DELETED,STATUS,
       COMPLETION_TIME,CONTROLFILE_TYPE,KEEP,KEEP_UNTIL,KEEP_OPTIONS,SCANNED
from   GV$DATAFILE_COPY
where  inst_id = USERENV('Instance');
```

View Name: **GV$DATAFILE_HEADER**

```
select inst_id,hxfil,decode(hxons, 0, 'OFFLINE', 'ONLINE'),decode(hxerr, 0, NULL,1,
       'FILE MISSING',2,'OFFLINE NORMAL',3,'NOT VERIFIED',4,'FILE NOT FOUND',5,
       'CANNOT OPEN FILE',6,'CANNOT READ HEADER',7,'CORRUPT HEADER',8,
       'WRONG FILE TYPE',9,'WRONG DATABASE',10,'WRONG FILE NUMBER',11,
       'WRONG FILE CREATE',12,'WRONG FILE CREATE',16,'DELAYED OPEN',14,
       'WRONG RESETLOGS',15,'OLD CONTROLFILE','UNKNOWN ERROR'),hxver,
       decode(hxnrcv, 0,'NO',1,'YES', NULL),decode(hxifz,0,'NO',1,'YES',
       NULL),to_number(fhcrs),to_date(fhcrt,'MM/DD/RR HH24:MI:SS',
       'NLS_CALENDAR=Gregorian'),fhtnm,fhtsn,fhrfn,to_number(fhrls),
       to_date(fhrlc,'MM/DD/RR HH24:MI:SS','NLS_CALENDAR=Gregorian'),
       to_number(fhscn),to_date(fhtim,'MM/DD/RR HH24:MI:SS','NLS_CALENDAR=Gregorian'),
       fhcpc,fhfsz*fhbsz,fhfsz,hxfnm
from   x$kcvfh;
```

View Name: V$DATAFILE_HEADER

```
select FILE#,STATUS,ERROR,FORMAT,RECOVER,FUZZY,CREATION_CHANGE#,CREATION_TIME,
       TABLESPACE_NAME,TS#,RFILE#,RESETLOGS_CHANGE#,RESETLOGS_TIME,CHECKPOINT_CHANGE#,
       CHECKPOINT_TIME,CHECKPOINT_COUNT,BYTES,BLOCKS,NAME
from   GV$DATAFILE_HEADER
where  inst_id = USERENV('Instance');
```

View Name: GV$DATAGUARD_STATUS

```
select   inst_id,decode(agfac,1,'Crash Recovery',2,'Log Transport Services',3,
         'Log Apply Services',4,'Role Management Services',5,'Remote File Server',6,
         'Fetch Archive Log',7,'Data Guard',8,'Network Services','UNKNOWN'),
         decode(agsev,1,'Informational',2,'Warning',3,'Error',4,'Fatal',5,'Control',
         'UNKNOWN'),agdid,agseq,agoer,decode(bitand(agflg, 1),0,'NO','YES'),
         to_date(agdat,'MM/DD/RR HH24:MI:SS','NLS_CALENDAR=Gregorian'),agtxt
from     x$kcrralg
order by agseq;
```

View Name: V$DATAGUARD_STATUS

```
select FACILITY,SEVERITY,DEST_ID,MESSAGE_NUM,ERROR_CODE,CALLOUT,TIMESTAMP,MESSAGE
from   GV$DATAGUARD_STATUS
where  inst_id = USERENV('Instance');
```

View Name: GV$DBFILE

```
select inst_id,fnfno,fnnam
from   x$kccfn
where  fnnam is not null and fntyp=4;
```

View Name: V$DBFILE

```
select FILE#, NAME
from   GV$DBFILE
where  inst_id = USERENV('Instance');
```

View Name: GV$DBLINK

```
select inst_id,nconam,ncouid,decode(bitand(hstflg, 32),0,'NO','YES'),
       decode(bitand(hstflg,8),0,'NO','YES'),decode(hstpro,1,'V5',2,'V6',3,'V6_NLS',
       4,'V7','UNKN'),ncouct, decode(bitand(ncoflg, 2),0,'NO','YES'),
       decode(bitand(ncoflg,8),0,'NO','YES'),nco2pstr
from   x$uganco
where  bitand(hstflg, 1) != 0;
```

View Name: V$DBLINK

```
select DB_LINK,OWNER_ID,LOGGED_ON,HETEROGENEOUS,PROTOCOL,OPEN_CURSORS,IN_TRANSACTION,
       UPDATE_SENT,COMMIT_POINT_STRENGTH
from   GV$DBLINK
where  inst_id = USERENV('Instance');
```

View Name: GV$DB_CACHE_ADVICE

```
select   A.inst_id,A.bpid,B.bp_name,A.blksz,decode (A.status,2,'ON','OFF'),A.poolsz,
         round((A.poolsz / A.actual_poolsz),4),A.nbufs,decode(A.base_preads,0,
         to_number(null),round((A.preads / A.base_preads),4)),decode(A.base_preads,0,
         A.preads,round((A.preads * (A.actual_preads / A.base_preads)),0))
```

```
from    x$kcbsc A, x$kcbwbpd B
where   A.bpid = B.bp_id and A.inst_id = B.inst_id
order by A.inst_id,A.bpid,A.poolsz;
```

View Name: V$DB_CACHE_ADVICE

```
select  id,name,block_size,advice_status,size_for_estimate,size_factor,
        buffers_for_estimate,estd_physical_read_factor,estd_physical_reads
from    gv$db_cache_advice
where   inst_id = userenv('instance');
```

View Name: GV$DB_OBJECT_CACHE

```
select  inst_id,kglnaown,kglnaobj,kglnadlk,decode(kglhdnsp,0,'CURSOR',1,
        'TABLE/PROCEDURE',2,'BODY',3,'TRIGGER',4,'INDEX',5,'CLUSTER',6,'OBJECT',13,
        'JAVA SOURCE',14,'JAVA RESOURCE',15,'REPLICATED TABLE OBJECT',16,
        'REPLICATION INTERNAL PACKAGE',17,'CONTEXT POLICY',18,'PUB_SUB',19,
        'SUMMARY',20,'DIMENSION',21,'APP CONTEXT',22,'STORED OUTLINE',23,'RULESET',24,
        'RSRC PLAN',25,'RSRC CONSUMER GROUP',26,'PENDING RSRC PLAN',27,
        'PENDING RSRC CONSUMER GROUP',28,'SUBSCRIPTION',29,'LOCATION',30,
        'REMOTE OBJECT',31,'SNAPSHOT METADATA',32,'JAVA SHARED DATA',33,
        'SECURITY PROFILE','INVALID NAMESPACE'),decode(bitand(kglobflg,3),0,
        'NOT LOADED',2,'NON-EXISTENT',3,'INVALID STATUS',decode(kglobtyp,0,'CURSOR',1,
        'INDEX',2,'TABLE',3,'CLUSTER',4,'VIEW',5,'SYNONYM',6,'SEQUENCE',7,
        'PROCEDURE',8,'FUNCTION',9,'PACKAGE',10,'NON-EXISTENT',11,
        'PACKAGE BODY',12,'TRIGGER',13,'TYPE',14,'TYPEBODY',15,'OBJECT',16,
        'USER',17,'DBLINK',18,'PIPE',19,'TABLE PARTITION',20,'INDEX PARTITION',21,
        'LOB',22,'LIBRARY',23,'DIRECTORY',24,'QUEUE',25,'INDEX-ORGANIZED TABLE',26,
        'REPLICATION OBJECT GROUP',27,'REPLICATION PROPAGATOR',28,'JAVA SOURCE',29,
        'JAVA CLASS',30,'JAVA RESOURCE',31,'JAVA JAR',32,'INDEX TYPE',33,'OPERATOR',34,
        'TABLE SUBPARTITION',35,'INDEX SUBPARTITION',36,'REPLICATED TABLE OBJECT',37,
        'REPLICATION INTERNAL PACKAGE',38,'CONTEXT POLICY',39,'PUB_SUB',40,
        'LOB PARTITION',41,'LOB SUBPARTITION',42,'SUMMARY',43,'DIMENSION',44,
        'APP CONTEXT',45,'STORED OUTLINE',46,'RULESET',47,'RSRC PLAN',48,
        'RSRC CONSUMER GROUP',49,'PENDING RSRC PLAN',50,'PENDING RSRC CONSUMER GROUP',51,
        'SUBSCRIPTION',52,'LOCATION',53,'REMOTE OBJECT',54,'SNAPSHOT METADATA',55,
        'IFS',56,'JAVA SHARED DATA',57,'SECURITY PROFILE','INVALID TYPE')),
        kglobhs0+kglobhs1+kglobhs2+kglobhs3+kglobhs4+kglobhs5+kglobhs6,
        kglhdldc,kglhdexc,kglhdlkc,kglobpc0,decode(kglhdkmk,0,'NO','YES'),kglhdclt
from    x$kglob;
```

View Name: V$DB_OBJECT_CACHE

```
select  OWNER,NAME,DB_LINK,NAMESPACE,TYPE,SHARABLE_MEM,LOADS,EXECUTIONS,LOCKS,PINS,KEPT,
        CHILD_LATCH
from    GV$DB_OBJECT_CACHE
where   inst_id = USERENV('Instance');
```

View Name: GV$DB_PIPES

```
select  inst_id,decode(kglobt00,1,kglobt17,null),kglnaobj,decode(kglobt00,1,'PRIVATE',
        'PUBLIC'),kglobhs0+kglobhs1+kglobhs2+kglobhs3+kglobhs4+kglobhs5+kglobhs6
from    x$kglob
where   kglhdnsp=7 and kglobsta != 0;
```

View Name: V$DB_PIPES

```
select  OWNERID,NAME,TYPE,PIPE_SIZE
from    GV$DB_PIPES
where   inst_id = USERENV('Instance');
```

View Name: **GV$DELETED_OBJECT**

```
select inst_id,dlrid,dlstm,decode(dltyp,11,'ARCHIVED LOG',13,'BACKUP PIECE',16,'
    DATAFILE COPY',20,'PROXY COPY',255,'BACKUP PIECE AVAILABLE',254,
    'BACKUP PIECE EXPIRED',253,'PROXY COPY AVAILABLE',252,'PROXY COPY EXPIRED',251,
    'BACKUP PIECE UNAVAILABLE',250,'PROXY COPY UNAVAILABLE',249,
    'DATAFILE COPY AVAILABLE',248,'DATAFILE COPY EXPIRED',247,'DATAFILE COPY
    UNAVAILABLE',246,'ARCHIVED LOG AVAILABLE',245,'ARCHIVED LOG EXPIRED',244,
    'ARCHIVED LOG UNAVAILABLE',243,'BACKUP SET KEEP OPTIONS',242,'BACKUP SET KEEP
    UNTIL',241,'PROXY COPY KEEP OPTIONS',240,'PROXY COPY KEEP UNTIL',239,
    'DATAFILE COPY KEEP OPTIONS',238,'DATAFILE COPY KEEP UNTIL','UNKNOWN'),
    dlobp,dlosm,dltsd
from    x$kccdl;
```

View Name: **V$DELETED_OBJECT**

```
select RECID,STAMP,TYPE,OBJECT_RECID,OBJECT_STAMP,OBJECT_DATA
from    GV$DELETED_OBJECT
where   inst_id = USERENV('Instance');
```

View Name: **GV$DISPATCHER**

```
select inst_id,kmmdinam,kmmdiadd,kmmdipro,kmmdista,decode(kmmdiacc,0,'NO','YES'),
    kmmdinmg,kmmdinmb,kmmdibrk,  kmmdinvo,kmmditnc,kmmdiidl,kmmdibsy,kmmdiler,
    kmmdidci
from    x$kmmdi
where   kmmdiflg != 0;
```

View Name: **V$DISPATCHER**

```
select NAME,NETWORK,PADDR,STATUS,ACCEPT,MESSAGES,BYTES,BREAKS,OWNED,CREATED,IDLE,BUSY,
    LISTENER, CONF_INDX
from    GV$DISPATCHER
where   inst_id = USERENV('Instance');
```

View Name: **GV$DISPATCHER_RATE**

```
select inst_id,kmmdinam,kmmdipro,kmmdicrle,kmmdicre,kmmdicep1,kmmdicrm,kmmdicrus,
    kmmdicrys,kmmdicyus,kmmdicruc,kmmdicryc,kmmdicyuc,kmmdicru,  kmmdicry,kmmdicyu,
    kmmdicic,kmmdicoc,kmmdicrr,kmmdimrle,kmmdimre,kmmdimep1,  kmmdimrm,kmmdimrus,
    kmmdimrys,kmmdimyus,kmmdimruc,kmmdimryc,kmmdimyuc,  kmmdimru,kmmdimry,kmmdimyu,
    kmmdimic,kmmdimoc,kmmdimrr,kmmdiarle,kmmdiare,kmmdiaep1,kmmdiarm,kmmdiarus,
    kmmdiarys,kmmdiayus,kmmdiaruc,kmmdiaryc,  kmmdiayuc,kmmdiaru,kmmdiary,kmmdiayu,
    kmmdiaic,kmmdiaoc,kmmdiarr,  kmmdinrle,kmmdinrm,kmmdinrus,kmmdinruc,
    kmmdinru,kmmdinic,kmmdinoc,kmmdinrr,  kmmdisrle,kmmdisrm,kmmdisrus,kmmdisruc,
    kmmdisru,kmmdisic,kmmdisoc,kmmdisrr
from    x$kmmdi where kmmdiflg!=0;
```

View Name: **V$DISPATCHER_RATE**

```
select NAME,PADDR,CUR_LOOP_RATE,CUR_EVENT_RATE,CUR_EVENTS_PER_LOOP,CUR_MSG_RATE,
    CUR_SVR_BUF_RATE,CUR_SVR_BYTE_RATE,CUR_SVR_BYTE_PER_BUF,CUR_CLT_BUF_RATE,
    CUR_CLT_BYTE_RATE,CUR_CLT_BYTE_PER_BUF,CUR_BUF_RATE,CUR_BYTE_RATE,
    CUR_BYTE_PER_BUF,CUR_IN_CONNECT_RATE,CUR_OUT_CONNECT_RATE,CUR_RECONNECT_RATE,
    MAX_LOOP_RATE,MAX_EVENT_RATE,MAX_EVENTS_PER_LOOP,MAX_MSG_RATE,MAX_SVR_BUF_RATE,
    MAX_SVR_BYTE_RATE,MAX_SVR_BYTE_PER_BUF,MAX_CLT_BUF_RATE,MAX_CLT_BYTE_RATE,
    MAX_CLT_BYTE_PER_BUF,MAX_BUF_RATE,MAX_BYTE_RATE,MAX_BYTE_PER_BUF,
    MAX_IN_CONNECT_RATE,MAX_OUT_CONNECT_RATE,MAX_RECONNECT_RATE,AVG_LOOP_RATE,
    AVG_EVENT_RATE,AVG_EVENTS_PER_LOOP,AVG_MSG_RATE,AVG_SVR_BUF_RATE,
    AVG_SVR_BYTE_RATE,AVG_SVR_BYTE_PER_BUF,AVG_CLT_BUF_RATE,AVG_CLT_BYTE_RATE,
```

```
        AVG_CLT_BYTE_PER_BUF,AVG_BUF_RATE,AVG_BYTE_RATE,AVG_BYTE_PER_BUF,
        AVG_IN_CONNECT_RATE,AVG_OUT_CONNECT_RATE,AVG_RECONNECT_RATE,TTL_LOOPS,
        TTL_MSG,TTL_SVR_BUF,TTL_CLT_BUF,TTL_BUF,TTL_IN_CONNECT,TTL_OUT_CONNECT,
        TTL_RECONNECT,SCALE_LOOPS,SCALE_MSG,SCALE_SVR_BUF,SCALE_CLT_BUF,SCALE_BUF,
        SCALE_IN_CONNECT,SCALE_OUT_CONNECT,SCALE_RECONNECT
from    GV$DISPATCHER_RATE
where   inst_id = USERENV('Instance');
```

View Name: **GV$DLM_ALL_LOCKS**

```
select USERENV('Instance'),HANDLE,GRANT_LEVEL,REQUEST_LEVEL,RESOURCE_NAME1,
        RESOURCE_NAME2,PID,TRANSACTION_ID0,TRANSACTION_ID1,GROUP_ID,OPEN_OPT_DEADLOCK,
        OPEN_OPT_PERSISTENT,OPEN_OPT_PROCESS_OWNED,OPEN_OPT_NO_XID,CONVERT_OPT_GETVALUE,
        CONVERT_OPT_PUTVALUE,CONVERT_OPT_NOVALUE,CONVERT_OPT_DUBVALUE,
        CONVERT_OPT_NOQUEUE,CONVERT_OPT_EXPRESS,CONVERT_OPT_NODEADLOCKWAIT,
        CONVERT_OPT_NODEADLOCKBLOCK,WHICH_QUEUE,STATE,AST_EVENT0,OWNER_NODE,BLOCKED,
        BLOCKER
from    V$GES_ENQUEUE;
```

View Name: **V$DLM_ALL_LOCKS**

```
select LOCKP,GRANT_LEVEL,REQUEST_LEVEL,RESOURCE_NAME1,RESOURCE_NAME2,PID,
        TRANSACTION_ID0,TRANSACTION_ID1,GROUP_ID,OPEN_OPT_DEADLOCK,OPEN_OPT_PERSISTENT,
        OPEN_OPT_PROCESS_OWNED,OPEN_OPT_NO_XID,CONVERT_OPT_GETVALUE,CONVERT_OPT_PUTVALUE,
        CONVERT_OPT_NOVALUE,CONVERT_OPT_DUBVALUE,CONVERT_OPT_NOQUEUE,CONVERT_OPT_EXPRESS,
        CONVERT_OPT_NODEADLOCKWAIT,CONVERT_OPT_NODEADLOCKBLOCK,WHICH_QUEUE,LOCKSTATE,
        AST_EVENT0,OWNER_NODE,BLOCKED,BLOCKER
from    GV$DLM_ALL_LOCKS
where   INST_ID = USERENV('Instance');
```

View Name: **GV$DLM_CONVERT_LOCAL**

```
select inst_id,kjicvtnam,kjicvtalt,kjicvtalc
from    x$kjicvt;
```

View Name: **V$DLM_CONVERT_LOCAL**

```
select INST_ID,CONVERT_TYPE,AVERAGE_CONVERT_TIME,CONVERT_COUNT
from    GV$DLM_CONVERT_LOCAL
where   INST_ID = USERENV('Instance');
```

View Name: **GV$DLM_CONVERT_REMOTE**

```
select inst_id,kjicvtnam,kjicvtart,kjicvtarc
from    x$kjicvt;
```

View Name: **V$DLM_CONVERT_REMOTE**

```
select INST_ID,CONVERT_TYPE,AVERAGE_CONVERT_TIME,CONVERT_COUNT
from    GV$DLM_CONVERT_REMOTE
where   INST_ID = USERENV('Instance');
```

View Name: **GV$DLM_LATCH**

```
select USERENV('Instance'),addr,latch#,level#,name,gets,misses,sleeps,immediate_gets,
        immediate_misses,waiters_woken,waits_holding_latch,spin_gets,sleep1,sleep2,
        sleep3,sleep4,sleep5,sleep6,sleep7,sleep8,sleep9,sleep10,sleep11,wait_time
from    V$LATCH
where   NAME like 'ges %' or NAME like 'gcs %';
```

Scripts of X$ Tables Used
to Create V$ Views

View Name: V$DLM_LATCH

```
select addr,latch#,level#,name,gets,misses,sleeps,immediate_gets,immediate_misses,
       waiters_woken,waits_holding_latch,spin_gets,sleep1,sleep2,sleep3,sleep4,sleep5,
       sleep6,sleep7,sleep8,sleep9,sleep10,sleep11,wait_time
from   GV$DLM_LATCH
where  INST_ID = USERENV('Instance');
```

View Name: GV$DLM_LOCKS

```
select USERENV('Instance'),HANDLE,GRANT_LEVEL,REQUEST_LEVEL,RESOURCE_NAME1,
       RESOURCE_NAME2,PID,TRANSACTION_ID0,TRANSACTION_ID1,GROUP_ID,OPEN_OPT_DEADLOCK,
       OPEN_OPT_PERSISTENT,OPEN_OPT_PROCESS_OWNED,OPEN_OPT_NO_XID,CONVERT_OPT_GETVALUE,
       CONVERT_OPT_PUTVALUE,CONVERT_OPT_NOVALUE,CONVERT_OPT_DUBVALUE,
       CONVERT_OPT_NOQUEUE,CONVERT_OPT_EXPRESS,CONVERT_OPT_NODEADLOCKWAIT,
       CONVERT_OPT_NODEADLOCKBLOCK,WHICH_QUEUE,STATE,AST_EVENT0,OWNER_NODE,BLOCKED,
       BLOCKER
from   V$GES_BLOCKING_ENQUEUE;
```

View Name: V$DLM_LOCKS

```
select LOCKP,GRANT_LEVEL,REQUEST_LEVEL,RESOURCE_NAME1,RESOURCE_NAME2,PID,
       TRANSACTION_ID0,TRANSACTION_ID1,GROUP_ID,OPEN_OPT_DEADLOCK,OPEN_OPT_PERSISTENT,
       OPEN_OPT_PROCESS_OWNED,OPEN_OPT_NO_XID,CONVERT_OPT_GETVALUE,CONVERT_OPT_PUTVALUE,
       CONVERT_OPT_NOVALUE,CONVERT_OPT_DUBVALUE,CONVERT_OPT_NOQUEUE,CONVERT_OPT_EXPRESS,
       CONVERT_OPT_NODEADLOCKWAIT,CONVERT_OPT_NODEADLOCKBLOCK,WHICH_QUEUE,LOCKSTATE,
       AST_EVENT0,OWNER_NODE,BLOCKED,BLOCKER
from   GV$DLM_LOCKS
where  INST_ID = USERENV('Instance');
```

View Name: GV$DLM_MISC

```
select inst_id,indx,kjisftdesc,kjisftval
from   x$kjisft;
```

View Name: V$DLM_MISC

```
select STATISTIC#,NAME,VALUE
FROM   GV$DLM_MISC
where  INST_ID = USERENV('Instance');
```

View Name: GV$DLM_RESS

```
select inst_id,kjirftrp,kjirftrn,kjirftcq,kjirftgq,kjirftpr,kjirftmn,kjirftncl,
       kjirftvs, kjirftvb
from   x$kjirft union all
select inst_id,kjbrresp,kjbrname,decode(kjbrcvtq,'00',0,1),decode(kjbrgrantq,'00',0,1),
       1,kjbrmaster,kjbrncvl,'KJUSERVS_NOVALUE','0x0'
from   x$kjbr;
```

View Name: V$DLM_RESS

```
select RESP,RESOURCE_NAME,ON_CONVERT_Q,ON_GRANT_Q,PERSISTENT_RES,MASTER_NODE,
       NEXT_CVT_LEVEL,VALUE_BLK_STATE,VALUE_BLK
from   GV$DLM_RESS
where  INST_ID = USERENV('Instance');
```

View Name: GV$DLM_TRAFFIC_CONTROLLER

```
select inst_id,kjitrftlid,kjitrftrid,kjitrftrrd,kjitrftinc,kjitrftta,kjitrfttl,
       kjitrfttr,decode(kjitrfttw,0,'NO','YES'),kjitrftss,kjitrftsr, kjitrftsql,
       kjitrftsqm,kjitrftsqt,kjitrftqtb,kjitrftqtw,kjitrftst,kjitrftpxy
from   x$kjitrft;
```

View Name: V$DLM_TRAFFIC_CONTROLLER

```
select LOCAL_NID,REMOTE_NID,REMOTE_RID,REMOTE_INC,TCKT_AVAIL,TCKT_LIMIT,
       TCKT_RCVD,TCKT_WAIT,SND_SEQ_NO,RCV_SEQ_NO,SND_Q_LEN,SND_Q_MAX,SND_Q_TOT,
       SND_Q_TM_BASE,SND_Q_TM_WRAP,STATUS,SND_PROXY
from   GV$DLM_TRAFFIC_CONTROLLER
where  INST_ID = userenv('instance');
```

View Name: GV$ENABLEDPRIVS

```
select inst_id,-indx
from   x$kzspr
where  x$kzspr.kzsprprv=1;
```

View Name: V$ENABLEDPRIVS

```
select PRIV_NUMBER
from   GV$ENABLEDPRIVS
where  inst_id = USERENV('Instance');
```

View Name: GV$ENQUEUE_LOCK

```
select /*+ ordered use_nl(l),use_nl(s),use_nl(r) +*/  s.inst_id,l.addr,l.ksqlkadr,
       s.ksusenum,r.ksqrsidt,r.ksqrsid1,r.ksqrsid2, l.ksqlkmod, l.ksqlkreq,
       l.ksqlkctim,l.ksqlklblk
from   x$ksqeq l,x$ksuse s,x$ksqrs r
where  l.ksqlkses=s.addr
and    bitand(l.kssobflg,1)!=0
and    (l.ksqlkmod!=0 or l.ksqlkreq!=0)
and    l.ksqlkres=r.addr;
```

View Name: V$ENQUEUE_LOCK

```
select ADDR,KADDR,SID,TYPE,ID1,ID2,LMODE,REQUEST,CTIME,BLOCK
from   GV$ENQUEUE_LOCK
where  inst_id = USERENV('Instance');
```

View Name: GV$ENQUEUE_STAT

```
select inst_id,ksqsttyp,ksqstreq,ksqstwat,ksqstsgt,ksqstfgt,ksqstwtm
from   X$KSQST
where  ksqstreq > 0;
```

View Name: V$ENQUEUE_STAT

```
select INST_ID,EQ_TYPE,TOTAL_REQ#,TOTAL_WAIT#,SUCC_REQ#,FAILED_REQ#,CUM_WAIT_TIME
from   GV$ENQUEUE_STAT
where  inst_id = USERENV('Instance');
```

**Scripts of X$ Tables Used
to Create V$ Views**

View Name: GV$EVENT_NAME

```
select  inst_id,indx,kslednam,ksledp1,ksledp2,ksledp3
from    x$ksled;
```

View Name: V$EVENT_NAME

```
select  event#,name,parameter1,parameter2,parameter3
from    gv$event_name
where   inst_id = USERENV('Instance');
```

View Name: GV$EXECUTION

```
select  inst_id,pid,val0,func,decode(id,1,'call',2,'return',3,'longjmp'),nvals,val2,
        val3,seqh,seql
from    x$kstex where op=10;
```

View Name: V$EXECUTION

```
select  PID,DEPTH,FUNCTION,TYPE,NVALS,VAL1,VAL2,SEQH,SEQL
from    GV$EXECUTION
where   inst_id = USERENV('Instance');
```

View Name: GV$FAST_START_SERVERS

```
SELECT  inst_id,state,wdone,pid
from    x$ktprxrs;
```

View Name: V$FAST_START_SERVERS

```
SELECT  STATE,UNDOBLOCKSDONE,PID
from    GV$FAST_START_SERVERS
where   inst_id = USERENV('Instance');
```

View Name: GV$FAST_START_TRANSACTIONS

```
SELECT  inst_id,usn,slt,seq,state,wkd,twk,pid,etime,parentusn,parentslt,parentseq
from    x$ktprxrt;
```

View Name: V$FAST_START_TRANSACTIONS

```
SELECT  USN,SLT,SEQ,STATE,UNDOBLOCKSDONE,UNDOBLOCKSTOTAL,PID,CPUTIME,PARENTUSN,
        PARENTSLT,PARENTSEQ
from    GV$FAST_START_TRANSACTIONS
where   INST_ID = USERENV('Instance');
```

View Name: GV$FILESTAT

```
select  k.inst_id,k.kcfiofno,k.kcfiopyr,k.kcfiopyw,k.kcfiopbr,k.kcfiopbw,k.kcfiosbr,
        k.kcfioprt,k.kcfiopwt,k.kcfiosbt,k.kcfioavg,k.kcfiolst,k.kcfiomin,
        k.kcfiormx,k.kcfiowmx
from    x$kcfio k,x$kccfe f
where   f.fedup <> 0
and     f.fenum=k.kcfiofno;
```

View Name: V$FILESTAT

```
select  FILE#,PHYRDS,PHYWRTS,PHYBLKRD,PHYBLKWRT,SINGLEBLKRDS,READTIM,WRITETIM,
        SINGLEBLKRDTIM,AVGIOTIM,LSTIOTIM,MINIOTIM,MAXIORTM,MAXIOWTM
from    GV$FILESTAT
where   inst_id = USERENV('Instance');
```

View Name: GV$FILE_CACHE_TRANSFER

```
select  x.inst_id,kcfiofno,KCFIOX2NC,KCFIOX2NFWC,KCFIOX2NFSC,KCFIOX2SC,KCFIOX2SFWC,
        KCFIOS2NC,KCFIOS2NFSC,KCFIORBRC,KCFIORBRFWC,KCFIORBRFSC,KCFION2XC,KCFIOS2XC,
        KCFION2SC,KCFIOCRTR,KCFIOCURTR
from    x$kcfio x, x$kccfe fe
where   x.kcfiofno = fe.fenum;
```

View Name: V$FILE_CACHE_TRANSFER

```
select  file_number,x_2_null,x_2_null_forced_write,x_2_null_forced_stale,x_2_s,
        x_2_s_forced_write,s_2_null,s_2_null_forced_stale,rbr,rbr_forced_write,
        rbr_forced_stale,null_2_x,s_2_x,null_2_s,cr_transfers,cur_transfers
from    gv$file_cache_transfer
where   inst_id = USERENV('Instance');
```

View Name: GV$FILE_PING

```
select  x.inst_id,kcfiofno,0,KCFIOX2NC,KCFIOX2NFWC,KCFIOX2NFSC,KCFIOX2SC,KCFIOX2SFWC,
        0,0,KCFIOS2NC,KCFIOS2NFSC,0,0,0,0,KCFIORBRC,KCFIORBRFWC,KCFIORBRFSC,0,0,
        KCFION2XC,KCFIOS2XC,0,KCFION2SC,0,0
from    x$kcfio x,x$kccfe fe
where   x.kcfiofno = fe.fenum;
```

View Name: V$FILE_PING

```
select  file_number,frequency,x_2_null,x_2_null_forced_write,x_2_null_forced_stale,
        x_2_s, x_2_s_forced_write,x_2_ssx,x_2_ssx_forced_write,s_2_null,
        s_2_null_forced_stale,ss_2_null,ss_2_rls,wrb,wrb_forced_write,rbr,
        rbr_forced_write,rbr_forced_stale,cbr,cbr_forced_write,null_2_x,s_2_x,
        ssx_2_x,null_2_s,null_2_ss,op_2_ss
from gv$file_ping
where inst_id = USERENV('Instance');
```

View Name: GV$FIXED_TABLE

```
select  inst_id,kqftanam,kqftaobj,'TABLE',indx
from    x$kqfta union all
            select inst_id,kqfvinam,kqfviobj,'VIEW',65537
            from   x$kqfvi union all
                select inst_id,kqfdtnam, kqfdtobj, 'TABLE', 65537
                from  x$kqfdt;
```

View Name: V$FIXED_TABLE

```
select  NAME,OBJECT_ID,TYPE,TABLE_NUM
from    GV$FIXED_TABLE
where   inst_id = USERENV('Instance');
```

View Name: GV$FIXED_VIEW_DEFINITION

```
select i.inst_id,kqfvinam,kqftpsel
from   x$kqfvi i,x$kqfvt t
where  i.indx = t.indx;
```

View Name: V$FIXED_VIEW_DEFINITION

```
select VIEW_NAME,VIEW_DEFINITION
from   GV$FIXED_VIEW_DEFINITION
where  inst_id = USERENV('Instance');
```

View Name: GV$GCSHVMASTER_INFO

```
select inst_id,KJDRPCMHVID,KJDRPCMHVCMAS,KJDRPCMHVPMAS,KJDRPCMHVRMCNT
from   x$kjdrpcmhv;
```

View Name: V$GCSHVMASTER_INFO

```
select HV_ID,CURRENT_MASTER,PREVIOUS_MASTER,REMASTER_CNT
from   GV$GCSHVMASTER_INFO
where  inst_id = USERENV('Instance');
```

View Name: GV$GCSPFMASTER_INFO

```
select inst_id,KJDRPCMPFID,KJDRPCMPFCMAS,KJDRPCMPFPMAS,KJDRPCMPFRMCNT
from   x$kjdrpcmpf;
```

View Name: V$GCSPFMASTER_INFO

```
select FILE_ID,CURRENT_MASTER,PREVIOUS_MASTER,REMASTER_CNT
from   GV$GCSPFMASTER_INFO
where  inst_id = USERENV('Instance');
```

View Name: GV$GC_ELEMENT

```
select inst_id,le_addr,indx,le_class,name,le_mode,le_blks,le_rls,le_acq,le_write,
       le_recovery,le_local,le_flags
from   x$le;
```

View Name: V$GC_ELEMENT

```
select gc_element_addr,indx,class,gc_element_name,mode_held,block_count,releasing,
       acquiring,writing,recovering,local,flags
from   gv$gc_element
where  inst_id = USERENV('Instance');
```

View Name: GV$GC_ELEMENTS_WITH_COLLISIONS

```
select    USERENV('Instance'),lock_element_addr
from      v$bh
where     (forced_writes + forced_reads) > 10
group by  lock_element_addr having count(*) >= 2;
```

View Name: **V$GC_ELEMENTS_WITH_COLLISIONS**

```
select  gc_element_addr
from    gv$gc_elements_with_collisions
where   inst_id = USERENV('Instance');
```

View Name: **GV$GES_BLOCKING_ENQUEUE**

```
select  USERENV('Instance'),HANDLE,GRANT_LEVEL,REQUEST_LEVEL,RESOURCE_NAME1,
        RESOURCE_NAME2,PID,TRANSACTION_ID0,TRANSACTION_ID1,GROUP_ID,
        OPEN_OPT_DEADLOCK,OPEN_OPT_PERSISTENT,OPEN_OPT_PROCESS_OWNED,OPEN_OPT_NO_XID,
        CONVERT_OPT_GETVALUE,CONVERT_OPT_PUTVALUE,CONVERT_OPT_NOVALUE,
        CONVERT_OPT_DUBVALUE,CONVERT_OPT_NOQUEUE,CONVERT_OPT_EXPRESS,
        CONVERT_OPT_NODEADLOCKWAIT,CONVERT_OPT_NODEADLOCKBLOCK, WHICH_QUEUE,
        STATE,AST_EVENT0,OWNER_NODE,BLOCKED,BLOCKER
from    V$GES_ENQUEUE
where   (REQUEST_LEVEL != 'KJUSERNL')
and     (BLOCKED = 1 or BLOCKER = 1);
```

View Name: **V$GES_BLOCKING_ENQUEUE**

```
select  HANDLE,GRANT_LEVEL,REQUEST_LEVEL,RESOURCE_NAME1,RESOURCE_NAME2,PID,
        TRANSACTION_ID0,TRANSACTION_ID1,GROUP_ID,OPEN_OPT_DEADLOCK,
        OPEN_OPT_PERSISTENT,OPEN_OPT_PROCESS_OWNED,OPEN_OPT_NO_XID,
        CONVERT_OPT_GETVALUE,CONVERT_OPT_PUTVALUE,CONVERT_OPT_NOVALUE,
        CONVERT_OPT_DUBVALUE,CONVERT_OPT_NOQUEUE,CONVERT_OPT_EXPRESS,
        CONVERT_OPT_NODEADLOCKWAIT,CONVERT_OPT_NODEADLOCKBLOCK,WHICH_QUEUE,STATE,
        AST_EVENT0,OWNER_NODE,BLOCKED,BLOCKER
from    GV$GES_BLOCKING_ENQUEUE
where   INST_ID = USERENV('Instance');
```

View Name: **GV$GES_ENQUEUE**

```
select  inst_id,kjilkftlkp,kjilkftgl,kjilkftrl,kjilkftrn1,kjilkftrn2,kjilkftpid,
        kjilkftxid0,kjilkftxid1,kjilkftgid,kjilkftoodd,kjilkftoopo,kjilkftoopt,
        kjilkftoonxid,kjilkftcogv,kjilkftcopv,kjilkftconv,kjilkftcodv,kjilkftconq,
        kjilkftcoep,kjilkftconddw,kjilkftconddb,kjilkftwq,kjilkftls,kjilkftaste0,
        kjilkfton,kjilkftblked,kjilkftblker
from    x$kjilkft union all
            select inst_id, kjbllockp, kjblgrant, kjblrequest,kjblname,
                   kjblname2,0,0,0,0,0,1,0,1,0,0,0,0,0,0,0,0,kjblqueue,kjbllockst,0,
                   kjblowner,kjblblocked,kjblblocker
            from   x$kjbl;
```

View Name: **V$GES_ENQUEUE**

```
select  HANDLE,GRANT_LEVEL,REQUEST_LEVEL,RESOURCE_NAME1,RESOURCE_NAME2,PID,
        TRANSACTION_ID0,TRANSACTION_ID1,GROUP_ID,OPEN_OPT_DEADLOCK,
        OPEN_OPT_PERSISTENT,OPEN_OPT_PROCESS_OWNED,OPEN_OPT_NO_XID,
        CONVERT_OPT_GETVALUE,CONVERT_OPT_PUTVALUE,CONVERT_OPT_NOVALUE,
        CONVERT_OPT_DUBVALUE,CONVERT_OPT_NOQUEUE,CONVERT_OPT_EXPRESS,
        CONVERT_OPT_NODEADLOCKWAIT,CONVERT_OPT_NODEADLOCKBLOCK,WHICH_QUEUE,STATE,
        AST_EVENT0,OWNER_NODE,BLOCKED,BLOCKER
from    GV$GES_ENQUEUE
where   INST_ID = USERENV('Instance');
```

Scripts of X$ Tables Used to Create V$ Views

View Name: GV$GLOBALCONTEXT

```
select namespace,attribute,value,username,clientidentifier
from   x$globalcontext
where  upper(namespace) not like 'SYS_%';
```

View Name: V$GLOBALCONTEXT

```
select namespace,attribute,value,username,clientidentifier
from   gv$globalcontext;
```

View Name: GV$GLOBAL_BLOCKED_LOCKS

```
select USERENV('instance'),addr,kaddr,sid,type,id1,id2,lmode,request,ctime
from   v$lock l
where exists
  (select *
   from   v$dlm_locks d
   where  substr(d.resource_name2,1,instr(d.resource_name2, ',',1,1)-1) = id1
   and    substr(d.resource_name2,instr(d.resource_name2,',',1,1)+1,
          instr(d.resource_name2, ',',1,2)-instr(d.resource_name2,',',1,1)-1) = id2
   and    substr(d.resource_name2,instr(d.resource_name2,',',-1,1)+1,2) = type);
```

View Name: V$GLOBAL_BLOCKED_LOCKS

```
select ADDR,KADDR,SID,TYPE,ID1,ID2,LMODE,REQUEST,CTIME
from   gv$global_blocked_locks
where  inst_id = userenv('instance');
```

View Name: GV$GLOBAL_TRANSACTION

```
select inst_id,K2GTIFMT,K2GTITID_EXT,K2GTIBID,K2GTECNT,K2GTERCT,K2GTDPCT,
       decode (K2GTDFLG,0,'ACTIVE',1,'COLLECTING',2,'FINALIZED',4,'FAILED',8,
       'RECOVERING',16,'UNASSOCIATED',32,'FORGOTTEN',64,'READY FOR RECOVERY',
       'COMBINATION'),K2GTDFLG,decode (K2GTETYP,0,'FREE',1,'LOOSELY COUPLED',2,
       'TIGHTLY COUPLED')
from   X$K2GTE2;
```

View Name: V$GLOBAL_TRANSACTION

```
select FORMATID,GLOBALID,BRANCHID,BRANCHES,REFCOUNT,PREPARECOUNT,STATE,FLAGS,
       COUPLING
from   GV$GLOBAL_TRANSACTION
where  INST_ID = USERENV('Instance');
```

View Name: GV$HS_AGENT

```
select unique INST_ID,AGENT_ID,MACHINE,PROCESS,PROGRAM,OSUSER,AGT_STARTTIME,
       AGENT_TYPE,decode(AGENT_TYPE,1,to_number(NULL),FDS_CLASS_ID),
       decode(AGENT_TYPE,1,to_number(NULL),FDS_INST_ID)
from   X$HS_SESSION;
```

View Name: V$HS_AGENT

```
select unique AGENT_ID,MACHINE,PROCESS,PROGRAM,OSUSER,STARTTIME,AGENT_TYPE,
       FDS_CLASS_ID,FDS_INST_ID
from   GV$HS_AGENT
where  INST_ID = USERENV('Instance');
```

View Name: GV$HS_PARAMETER

```
select  A.INST_ID,HS_SESSION_ID,PARAMETER,VALUE,SOURCE,ENV
from    X$HS_SESSION A,X$HOFP B
where   A.FDS_INST_ID = B.FDS_INST_ID;
```

View Name: V$HS_PARAMETER

```
select  HS_SESSION_ID,PARAMETER,VALUE,SOURCE,ENV
from    GV$HS_PARAMETER
where   INST_ID = userenv('instance');
```

View Name: GV$HS_SESSION

```
select  INST_ID,HS_SESSION_ID,AGENT_ID,SID,decode(AGENT_TYPE,1,NULL,DB_LINK),
        decode(AGENT_TYPE,1,to_number(NULL),DB_LINK_OWNER),SES_STARTTIME
from    X$HS_SESSION;
```

View Name: V$HS_SESSION

```
select  HS_SESSION_ID,AGENT_ID,SID,DB_LINK,DB_LINK_OWNER,STARTTIME
from    GV$HS_SESSION
where   INST_ID = USERENV('Instance');
```

View Name: GV$HVMASTER_INFO

```
select  inst_id,KJDRHVID,KJDRHVCMAS,KJDRHVPMAS,KJDRHVRMCNT
from    x$kjdrhv;
```

View Name: V$HVMASTER_INFO

```
select  HV_ID,CURRENT_MASTER,PREVIOUS_MASTER,REMASTER_CNT
from    GV$HVMASTER_INFO
where   inst_id = USERENV('Instance');
```

View Name: GV$INDEXED_FIXED_COLUMN

```
select  c.inst_id,kqftanam,kqfcoidx,kqfconam,kqfcoipo
from    x$kqfco c,x$kqfta t
where   t.indx = c.kqfcotab
and     kqfcoidx != 0;
```

View Name: V$INDEXED_FIXED_COLUMN

L B-177

```
select  TABLE_NAME,INDEX_NUMBER,COLUMN_NAME,COLUMN_POSITION
from    GV$INDEXED_FIXED_COLUMN
where   inst_id = USERENV('Instance');
```

View Name: GV$INSTANCE

```
select  ks.inst_id,ksuxsins,ksuxssid,ksuxshst,ksuxsver,ksuxstim,
        decode(ksuxssts,0,'STARTED',1,'MOUNTED',2,'OPEN',3,'OPEN MIGRATE','UNKNOWN'),
        decode(ksuxsshr,0,'NO',1,'YES',2,NULL),ksuxsthr,
        decode(ksuxsarc,0,'STOPPED',1,'STARTED','FAILED'),
        decode(ksuxslsw,0,NULL,2,'ARCHIVE LOG',3,'CLEAR LOG',4,'CHECKPOINT'),
        decode(ksuxsdba,0,'ALLOWED','RESTRICTED'),
        decode(ksuxsshp,0,'NO','YES'),
```

```
        decode(kvitval,0,'ACTIVE',2147483647,'SUSPENDED','INSTANCE RECOVERY'),
        decode(ksuxsrol,1,'PRIMARY_INSTANCE',2,'SECONDARY_INSTANCE','UNKNOWN'),
        decode(qui_state,0,'NORMAL',1,'QUIESCING',2,'QUIESCED','UNKNOWN')
from    x$ksuxsinst ks, x$kvit kv, x$quiesce qu
where   kvittag = 'kcbwst';
```

View Name: V$INSTANCE

```
select  INSTANCE_NUMBER,INSTANCE_NAME,HOST_NAME,VERSION,STARTUP_TIME,STATUS,PARALLEL,
        THREAD#,ARCHIVER,LOG_SWITCH_WAIT,LOGINS,SHUTDOWN_PENDING,DATABASE_STATUS,
        INSTANCE_ROLE,ACTIVE_STATE
from    GV$INSTANCE
where   inst_id = USERENV('Instance');
```

View Name: GV$INSTANCE_RECOVERY

```
select  T.INST_ID,to_number
        (decode(CUR_EST_RCV_READS,-1,NULL,CUR_EST_RCV_READS)),ACTUAL_REDO_BLKS,
        to_number(decode(MIN_LAG,-1,NULL,MIN_LAG)),
        to_number(decode(LOGFILESZ,-1,NULL,LOGFILESZ)),
        to_number(decode(CT_LAG,-1,NULL,CT_LAG)),
        to_number(decode(CI_LAG,-1,NULL,CI_LAG)),
        to_number(decode(ACTUAL_REDO_BLKS,0,NULL,NULL)),
        INUSE_EST_MTTR_SEC, CUR_EST_MTTR_SEC,
    (select ksusgstv -
      (select ksusgstv
       from   X$KSUSGSTA
       where  ksusdnam='physical writes non checkpoint'
       and    inst_id=t.inst_id)
     from   X$KSUSGSTA
     where  ksusdnam = 'physical writes'
     and    inst_id=t.inst_id)
from    X$TARGETRBA T, X$ESTIMATED_MTTR E
where   T.INST_ID=E.INST_ID;
```

View Name: V$INSTANCE_RECOVERY

```
select  RECOVERY_ESTIMATED_IOS,ACTUAL_REDO_BLKS,TARGET_REDO_BLKS,
        LOG_FILE_SIZE_REDO_BLKS,LOG_CHKPT_TIMEOUT_REDO_BLKS,
        LOG_CHKPT_INTERVAL_REDO_BLKS,FAST_START_IO_TARGET_REDO_BLKS,
        TARGET_MTTR, ESTIMATED_MTTR,CKPT_BLOCK_WRITES
from    GV$INSTANCE_RECOVERY
where   INST_ID = USERENV('Instance');
```

View Name: GV$LATCH

```
select  d.inst_id,d.kslldadr,la.latch#,d.kslldlvl,d.kslldnam,la.gets,la.misses,
        la.sleeps,la.immediate_gets,la.immediate_misses,la.waiters_woken,
        la.waits_holding_latch,la.spin_gets,la.sleep1,la.sleep2, la.sleep3,la.sleep4,
        la.sleep5,la.sleep6,la.sleep7,la.sleep8,la.sleep9,la.sleep10,la.sleep11,
        la.wait_time
from    x$kslld d,
        (select kslltnum latch#,sum(kslltwgt)gets,sum(kslltwff)misses,
        sum(kslltwsl) sleeps,sum(kslltngt) immediate_gets,
        sum(kslltnfa) immediate_misses,sum(kslltwkc) waiters_woken,
        sum(kslltwth) waits_holding_latch,sum(ksllthst0) spin_gets,
        sum(ksllthst1) sleep1,sum(ksllthst2) sleep2,sum(ksllthst3) sleep3,
        sum(ksllthst4) sleep4,sum(ksllthst5) sleep5, sum(ksllthst6) sleep6,
        sum(ksllthst7) sleep7,sum(ksllthst8) sleep8,sum(ksllthst9) sleep9,
        sum(ksllthst10) sleep10,sum(ksllthst11) sleep11,sum(kslltwtt) wait_time
```

```
       from   x$ksllt group by kslltnum) la
       where  la.latch# = d.indx;
```

View Name: V$LATCH

```
select addr,latch#,level#,name,gets,misses,sleeps,immediate_gets,immediate_misses,
       waiters_woken,waits_holding_latch,spin_gets,sleep1,sleep2,sleep3,sleep4,
       sleep5,sleep6,sleep7,sleep8,sleep9,sleep10,sleep11,wait_time
from   gv$latch
where  inst_id = USERENV('Instance');
```

View Name: GV$LATCHHOLDER

```
select inst_id,ksuprpid,ksuprsid,ksuprlat,ksuprlnm
from   x$ksuprlat;
```

View Name: V$LATCHHOLDER

```
select PID,SID,LADDR,NAME
from   GV$LATCHHOLDER
where  inst_id = USERENV('Instance');
```

View Name: GV$LATCHNAME

```
select inst_id,indx,kslldnam
from   x$kslld;
```

View Name: V$LATCHNAME

```
select latch#,name
from   gv$latchname
where  inst_id = userenv('Instance');
```

View Name: GV$LATCH_CHILDREN

```
select t.inst_id,t.addr,t.kslltnum,t.kslltcnm,n.kslldlvl,n.kslldnam,t.kslltwgt,
       t.kslltwff,t.kslltwsl,t.kslltngt,t.kslltnfa,t.kslltwkc,t.kslltwth,
       t.ksllthst0,t.ksllthst1,t.ksllthst2,t.ksllthst3,t.ksllthst4,t.ksllthst5,
       t.ksllthst6,t.ksllthst7,t.ksllthst8,t.ksllthst9,t.ksllthst10,t.ksllthst11,
       t.kslltwtt
from   x$ksllt t,x$kslld n
where  t.kslltcnm > 0
and    t.kslltnum = n.indx;
```

View Name: V$LATCH_CHILDREN

```
select ADDR,LATCH#,CHILD#,LEVEL#,NAME,GETS,MISSES,SLEEPS,IMMEDIATE_GETS,
       IMMEDIATE_MISSES,WAITERS_WOKEN,WAITS_HOLDING_LATCH,SPIN_GETS,SLEEP1,SLEEP2,
       SLEEP3,SLEEP4,SLEEP5,SLEEP6,SLEEP7,SLEEP8,SLEEP9,SLEEP10,SLEEP11,
       WAIT_TIME
from   GV$LATCH_CHILDREN
where  inst_id = USERENV('Instance');
```

View Name: GV$LATCH_MISSES

```
select t1.inst_id,t1.ksllasnam,t2.ksllwnam,t1.kslnowtf,t1.kslsleep,t1.kslwscwsl,
       t1.kslwsclthg,t2.ksllwnam
from   x$ksllw t2,x$kslwsc t1
where  t2.indx = t1.indx;
```

View Name: V$LATCH_MISSES

```
select PARENT_NAME,LOCATION,NWFAIL_COUNT,SLEEP_COUNT,WTR_SLP_COUNT,LONGHOLD_COUNT,
       LOCATION
from   GV$LATCH_MISSES
where  inst_id = USERENV('Instance');
```

View Name: GV$LATCH_PARENT

```
select t.inst_id,t.addr,t.kslltnum,n.kslldlvl,n.kslldnam,t.kslltwgt,t.kslltwff,
       t.kslltwsl,t.kslltngt,t.kslltnfa,t.kslltwkc,t.kslltwth,t.kslthst0,
       t.kslthst1,t.kslthst2,t.kslthst3,t.kslthst4,t.kslthst5,t.kslthst6,
       t.kslthst7,t.kslthst8,t.kslthst9,t.kslthst10,t.kslthst11,t.kslltwtt
from   x$ksllt t,x$kslld n
where  t.kslltcnm = 0
and    t.kslltnum = n.indx;
```

View Name: V$LATCH_PARENT

```
select ADDR,LATCH#,LEVEL#,NAME,GETS,MISSES,SLEEPS,IMMEDIATE_GETS,IMMEDIATE_MISSES,
       WAITERS_WOKEN,WAITS_HOLDING_LATCH,SPIN_GETS,SLEEP1,SLEEP2,SLEEP3,SLEEP4,
       SLEEP5,SLEEP6,SLEEP7,SLEEP8,SLEEP9,SLEEP10,SLEEP11,WAIT_TIME
from   GV$LATCH_PARENT
where  inst_id = USERENV('Instance');
```

View Name: GV$LIBRARYCACHE

```
select inst_id,decode(indx,0,'SQL AREA',1,'TABLE/PROCEDURE',2,'BODY',3,
       'TRIGGER',4,'INDEX',5,'CLUSTER',6,'OBJECT',7,'PIPE',13,'JAVA SOURCE',14,
       'JAVA RESOURCE',32,'JAVA DATA','?'),kglstget,kglstght,
       decode(kglstget,0,1,kglstght/kglstget),kglstpin,kglstpht,
       decode(kglstpin,0,1,kglstpht/kglstpin),kglstrld,kglstinv,kglstlrq,
       kglstprq,kglstprl,kglstirq,kglstmiv
from   x$kglst
where  indx<8 or indx=13 or indx=14 or indx=32;
```

View Name: V$LIBRARYCACHE

```
select NAMESPACE,GETS,GETHITS,GETHITRATIO,PINS,PINHITS,PINHITRATIO,RELOADS,
       INVALIDATIONS,DLM_LOCK_REQUESTS,DLM_PIN_REQUESTS,DLM_PIN_RELEASES,
       DLM_INVALIDATION_REQUESTS,DLM_INVALIDATIONS
from   GV$LIBRARYCACHE
where  inst_id = USERENV('Instance');
```

View Name: GV$LIBRARY_CACHE_MEMORY

```
select inst_id,decode(kglsim_namespace,0,'SQL AREA',1,'TABLE/PROCEDURE',2,
       'BODY',3,'TRIGGER',4,'INDEX',5,'CLUSTER',6,'OBJECT',7,'PIPE',13,
       'JAVA SOURCE',14,'JAVA RESOURCE',32,'JAVA DATA','?'),kglsim_pincnt,
       kglsim_pinmem,kglsim_unpincnt,kglsim_unpinmem
from   x$kglmem
where  kglsim_namespace<8
or     kglsim_namespace=13
or     kglsim_namespace=14
or     kglsim_namespace=32
union
select inst_id,'OTHER/SYSTEM',sum(kglsim_pincnt) sum_pincnt,
       sum(kglsim_pinmem) sum_pinmem,sum(kglsim_unpincnt) sum_unpincnt,
```

```
      sum(kglsim_unpinmem) sum_unpinmem
from   x$kglmem
where  not (kglsim_namespace<8
or     kglsim_namespace=13
or     kglsim_namespace=14
or     kglsim_namespace=32)
group  by   inst_id;
```

View Name: V$LIBRARY_CACHE_MEMORY

```
select  lc_namespace,lc_inuse_memory_objects,lc_inuse_memorysize,
        lc_freeable_memory_objects,lc_freeable_memory_size
from    gv$library_cache_memory
where   inst_id = USERENV('Instance');
```

View Name: GV$LICENSE

```
select  inst_id,ksullms,ksullws,ksullcs,ksullhs,ksullmu
from    x$ksull;
```

View Name: V$LICENSE

```
select  sessions_max,sessions_warning,sessions_current,sessions_highwater,users_max
from    gv$license
where   inst_id = userenv('Instance');
```

View Name: GV$LOADISTAT

```
select  inst_id,klcieon,klcietn,klciein,klcieisn,klciemsg
from    x$klcie;
```

View Name: V$LOADISTAT

```
select  OWNER,TABNAME,INDEXNAME,SUBNAME,MESSAGE
from    GV$LOADISTAT
where   INST_ID = USERENV('Instance');
```

View Name: GV$LOADPSTAT

```
select  inst_id,klcpxon,klcpxtn,klcpxpn,klcpxrld
from    x$klpt;
```

View Name: V$LOADPSTAT

```
select  OWNER,TABNAME,PARTNAME,LOADED
from    GV$LOADPSTAT
where   inst_id = USERENV('Instance');
```

View Name: GV$LOCK

```
select /*+ ordered use_nl(l), use_nl(s), use_nl(r) +*/  s.inst_id,l.laddr,
       l.kaddr,s.ksusenum,r.ksqrsidt,r.ksqrsid1,r.ksqrsid2,l.lmode,l.request,
       l.ctime,decode(l.lmode,0,0,l.block)
from   v$_lock l,x$ksuse s,x$ksqrs r
where  l.saddr=s.addr
and    l.raddr=r.addr;
```

View Name: V$LOCK

```
select ADDR,KADDR,SID,TYPE,ID1,ID2,LMODE,REQUEST,CTIME,BLOCK
from   GV$LOCK
where  inst_id = USERENV('Instance');
```

View Name: GV$LOCKED_OBJECT

```
select x.inst_id,x.kxidusn,x.kxidslt,x.kxidsqn,l.ktadmtab,s.indx,s.ksuudlna,
       s.ksuseunm,s.ksusepid,l.ksqlkmod
from   x$ktcxb x,x$ktadm l,x$ksuse s
where  x.ktcxbxba = l.kssobown
and    x.ktcxbses = s.addr;
```

View Name: V$LOCKED_OBJECT

```
select xidusn,xidslot,xidsqn,object_id,session_id,oracle_username, os_user_name,
       process,locked_mode
from   gv$locked_object
where  inst_id = USERENV('Instance');
```

View Name: GV$LOCKS_WITH_COLLISIONS

```
select   USERENV('Instance'),lock_element_addr
from     v$bh
where    (forced_writes + forced_reads) > 10
group by lock_element_addr having count(*) >= 2;
```

View Name: V$LOCKS_WITH_COLLISIONS

```
select   lock_element_addr
from     v$bh
where    (forced_writes + forced_reads) > 10
group by lock_element_addr having count(*) >= 2;
```

View Name: GV$LOCK_ACTIVITY

```
select inst_id,decode(indx,0,'NULL',1,'NULL',2,'S',3,'S',4,'X',5,'X','?'),
       decode(indx,0,'S',1,'X',2,'NULL',3,'X',4,'NULL',5,'S','?'),
       decode(indx,0,'Lock buffers for read',1,'Lock buffers for write',2,
       'Make buffers CR (no write)',3,'Upgrade read lock to write',4,
       'Make buffers CR (write dirty buffers)',5,
       'Downgrade write lock to read (write dirty buffers)','Should not happen'),conv
from   x$le_stat
where  conv > 0;
```

View Name: V$LOCK_ACTIVITY

```
select FROM_VAL,TO_VAL,ACTION_VAL,COUNTER
from   GV$LOCK_ACTIVITY
where  INST_ID = USERENV('INSTANCE');
```

View Name: GV$LOCK_ELEMENT

```
select inst_id,le_addr,indx,le_class,name,le_mode,le_blks,le_rls,le_acq,0,le_flags
from   x$le;
```

View Name: **V$LOCK_ELEMENT**

```
select  lock_element_addr,indx,class,lock_element_name,mode_held,block_count,
        releasing,acquiring,invalid,flags
from    gv$lock_element
where   inst_id = USERENV('Instance');
```

View Name: **GV$LOG**

```
select  le.inst_id, le.lenum, le.lethr, le.leseq, le.lesiz*le.lebsz, ledup,
        decode(bitand(le.leflg,1),0,'NO','YES'),decode(bitand(le.leflg,24),8,
        decode(bitand(le.leflg,2),2,'INVALIDATED','CURRENT'),16,'CLEARING',24,
        'CLEARING_CURRENT',decode(sign(leseq),0,'UNUSED',
        decode(sign((to_number(rt.rtckp_scn)-to_number(le.lenxs))*
        bitand(rt.rtsta,2)),-1,'ACTIVE','INACTIVE'))),to_number(le.lelos),
        to_date(le.lelot,'MM/DD/RR HH24:MI:SS','NLS_CALENDAR=Gregorian')
from    x$kccle le,x$kccrt rt
where   le.ledup!=0
and     le.lethr=rt.rtnum
and     le.inst_id = rt.inst_id;
```

View Name: **V$LOG**

```
select  GROUP#,THREAD#,SEQUENCE#,BYTES,MEMBERS,ARCHIVED,STATUS,FIRST_CHANGE#,
        FIRST_TIME
from    GV$LOG
where   inst_id = USERENV('Instance');
```

View Name: **GV$LOGFILE**

```
select  inst_id,fnfno,decode(fnflg,0,'',decode(bitand(fnflg,1),1,'INVALID',
        decode(bitand(fnflg,2),2,'STALE',decode(bitand(fnflg,4),4,'DELETED',
        decode(bitand(fnflg,8),8,'','UNKNOWN')))))),
        decode(bitand(fnflg,8),0,'ONLINE','STANDBY'),fnnam
from    x$kccfn
where   fnnam is not null
and     fntyp=3;
```

View Name: **V$LOGFILE**

```
L B-217
```

```
select  GROUP#,STATUS,TYPE,MEMBER
from    GV$LOGFILE
where   inst_id = USERENV('Instance');
```

View Name: **GV$LOGHIST**

```
select  inst_id,lhthp,lhseq,to_number(lhlos),
        to_date(lhlot,'MM/DD/RR HH24:MI:SS','NLS_CALENDAR=Gregorian'),
        to_number(lhnxs)
from    x$kcclh;
```

View Name: **V$LOGHIST**

```
select  THREAD#,SEQUENCE#,FIRST_CHANGE#,FIRST_TIME,SWITCH_CHANGE#
from    GV$LOGHIST
where   inst_id = USERENV('Instance');
```

View Name: GV$LOGMNR_CALLBACK

```
select  inst_id,decode(state,0,'ENABLED',1,'DISABLED','UNKNOWN'),
        decode(type,0,'EVERY_CHANGE_RECORD',1,'ON_COMMIT',2,'ON_DDL',3,
        'ON_SPECIAL_MARKER','UNKNOWN'),
        decode(capability,0,'ANYORDER',1,'INORDER','UNKNOWN')
from    x$logmnr_callback;
```

View Name: V$LOGMNR_CALLBACK

```
select  state,type,capability
from    gv$logmnr_callback
where   inst_id = userenv('instance');
```

View Name: GV$LOGMNR_CONTENTS

```
select  INST_ID,SCN,CSCN,TIMESTAMP,COMMIT_TIMESTAMP,THREAD#,LOG_ID,XIDUSN,XIDSLT,
        XIDSQN,PXIDUSN,PXIDSLT,PXIDSQN,RBASQN,RBABLK,RBABYTE,UBAFIL,UBABLK,UBAREC,
        UBASQN,ABS_FILE#,REL_FILE#,DATA_BLK#,DATA_OBJ#,DATA_OBJD#,SEG_OWNER,SEG_NAME,
        SEG_TYPE,SEG_TYPE_NAME,TABLE_SPACE,ROW_ID,SESSION#,SERIAL#,USERNAME,
        SESSION_INFO,TX_NAME,ROLLBACK,OPERATION,OPERATION_CODE,SQL_REDO,SQL_UNDO,
        RS_ID,SEQUENCE#,SSN,CSF,INFO,STATUS,REDO_VALUE,UNDO_VALUE,SQL_COLUMN_TYPE,
        SQL_COLUMN_NAME,REDO_LENGTH,REDO_OFFSET,UNDO_LENGTH,UNDO_OFFSET
from    x$logmnr_contents
where   ROW_TYPE = 0;
```

View Name: V$LOGMNR_CONTENTS

```
select  SCN,CSCN,TIMESTAMP,COMMIT_TIMESTAMP,THREAD#,LOG_ID,XIDUSN,XIDSLT,
        XIDSQN,PXIDUSN,PXIDSLT,PXIDSQN,RBASQN,RBABLK,RBABYTE,UBAFIL,UBABLK,
        UBAREC,UBASQN,ABS_FILE#,REL_FILE#,DATA_BLK#,DATA_OBJ# ,DATA_OBJD#,
        SEG_OWNER,SEG_NAME,SEG_TYPE,SEG_TYPE_NAME,TABLE_SPACE,ROW_ID,SESSION#,
        SERIAL#,USERNAME,SESSION_INFO,TX_NAME,ROLLBACK,OPERATION,OPERATION_CODE,
        SQL_REDO,SQL_UNDO,RS_ID,SEQUENCE#,SSN,CSF,INFO,STATUS,REDO_VALUE,
        UNDO_VALUE,SQL_COLUMN_TYPE,SQL_COLUMN_NAME,REDO_LENGTH,REDO_OFFSET,
        UNDO_LENGTH,UNDO_OFFSET
from    GV$LOGMNR_CONTENTS
where   inst_id = userenv('instance');
```

View Name: GV$LOGMNR_DICTIONARY

```
select  INST_ID,TIMESTAMP,DB_ID,DB_NAME,FILENAME,DICTIONARY_SCN,RESET_SCN,
        RESET_SCN_TIME,ENABLED_THREAD_MAP,INFO,STATUS
from    x$logmnr_dictionary;
```

View Name: V$LOGMNR_DICTIONARY

```
select  TIMESTAMP,DB_ID,DB_NAME,FILENAME,DICTIONARY_SCN,RESET_SCN,RESET_SCN_TIME,
        ENABLED_THREAD_MAP,INFO,STATUS
from    GV$LOGMNR_DICTIONARY
where   inst_id = userenv('instance');
```

View Name: GV$LOGMNR_LOGFILE

```
select  inst_id,log_id,filename,low_time,next_time,db_id,db_name,reset_scnwrp,
        reset_scnbas,reset_scn_time,thread_id,thread_sqn,low_scnwrp,low_scnbas,
        next_scnwrp,next_scnbas,
        decode(state,0,'FILE_NOT_OPEN',1,'FILE_OPEN',2,'DONE')
from    x$logmnr_logfile;
```

View Name: **V$LOGMNR_LOGFILE**

```
select  log_id,filename,low_time,next_time,db_id,db_name,reset_scnwrp,
        reset_scnbas,reset_scn_time,thread_id,thread_sqn,low_scnwrp, low_scnbas,
        next_scnwrp,next_scnbas,file_state
from    gv$logmnr_logfile
where inst_id = userenv('instance');
```

View Name: **GV$LOGMNR_LOGS**

```
select  INST_ID,LOG_ID,FILENAME,LOW_TIME,HIGH_TIME,DB_ID,DB_NAME,RESET_SCN,
        RESET_SCN_TIME,THREAD_ID,THREAD_SQN,LOW_SCN,NEXT_SCN,DICTIONARY_BEGIN,
        DICTIONARY_END,INFO,STATUS
from    x$logmnr_logs;
```

View Name: **V$LOGMNR_LOGS**

```
select  LOG_ID,FILENAME,LOW_TIME,HIGH_TIME,DB_ID,DB_NAME,RESET_SCN,
        RESET_SCN_TIME,THREAD_ID,THREAD_SQN,LOW_SCN,NEXT_SCN,
        DICTIONARY_BEGIN,DICTIONARY_END,INFO,STATUS
from    GV$LOGMNR_LOGS
where   inst_id = userenv('instance');
```

View Name: **GV$LOGMNR_PARAMETERS**

```
select  INST_ID,START_DATE,END_DATE,START_SCN,END_SCN,INFO,STATUS
from    x$logmnr_parameters;
```

View Name: **V$LOGMNR_PARAMETERS**

```
select  START_DATE,END_DATE,START_SCN,END_SCN,INFO,STATUS
from    GV$LOGMNR_PARAMETERS
where   inst_id = userenv('instance');
```

View Name: **GV$LOGMNR_PROCESS**

```
select  a.inst_id,a.pid,b.spid,a.role,b.username,b.serial#,b.latchwait,b.latchspin
from    x$logmnr_process a,v$process b
where   a.pid = b.pid;
```

View Name: **V$LOGMNR_PROCESS**

```
select  pid,spid,role,username,serial#,latchwait,latchspin
from    gv$logmnr_process
where   inst_id = userenv('instance');
```

View Name: **GV$LOGMNR_REGION**

```
select  inst_id,memstate,
        decode(state,0,'INIT',1,'AVAIL',2,'ASSIGNED',3,'PREPARED',4,'ASSEMBLED'),
        owning_process
from    x$logmnr_region;
```

View Name: **V$LOGMNR_REGION**

```
select  memstate,state,owning_process
from    gv$logmnr_region
where   inst_id = userenv('instance');
```

Scripts of X$ Tables Used
to Create V$ Views

View Name: GV$LOGMNR_SESSION

```
select INST_ID,SESSION_ID,SESSION_NAME,
       decode(state,1,'READY',2,'STARTED',3,'ACTIVE',4,'DISCARDED',5,'DETACHED',
       'UNKNOWN'),start_scnwrp,start_scnbas,end_scnwrp,end_scnbas,spill_scnwrp,
       spill_scnbas,required_slave_num,eager_threshold,stopmining_threshold,
       memory_size,client_id,db_id,reset_scnwrp,reset_scnbas,callback_count,
       slave_count
from   x$logmnr_session;
```

View Name: V$LOGMNR_SESSION

```
select SESSION_ID,SESSION_NAME,session_state,start_scnwrp,start_scnbas,end_scnwrp,
       end_scnbas,spill_scnwrp,spill_scnbas,required_slave_num,eager_threshold,
       stopmining_threshold,memory_size,client_id,db_id,reset_scnwrp,
       reset_scnbas,callback_count,slave_count
from   GV$LOGMNR_SESSION
where  inst_id = userenv('instance');
```

View Name: GV$LOGMNR_STATS

```
select inst_id,session_id,name,value
from   x$krvxsv;
```

View Name: V$LOGMNR_STATS

```
select session_id,name,value
from   gv$logmnr_stats
where  inst_id = USERENV('Instance');
```

View Name: GV$LOGMNR_TRANSACTION

```
select inst_id,xidusn,xidslt,xidsqn,commit_scnwrp,commit_scnbas,num_change_record,
       flags,chunk_index,total_chunks
from   x$logmnr_transaction;
```

View Name: V$LOGMNR_TRANSACTION

```
select xidusn,xidslt,xidsqn,commit_scnwrp,commit_scnbas,num_change_record,flags,
       chunk_index,total_chunks
from   gv$logmnr_transaction
where inst_id = userenv('instance');
```

View Name: GV$LOGSTDBY

```
select     inst_id,serial#,logstdby_id,pid,type,status_code,status,high_scn
from       x$krvslv
where exists
    (select 1
     from v$session s,x$knstacr x
     where s.sid=x.sid_knst
     and s.serial#=x.serial_knst);
```

View Name: V$LOGSTDBY

```
select serial#,logstdby_id,pid,type,status_code,status,high_scn
from   gv$logstdby
where  inst_id = USERENV('Instance');
```

View Name: GV$LOGSTDBY_STATS

```
select inst_id, name,value
from
  (select inst_id, name,value
   from x$krvslvs
   union all
   select inst_id,name, to_char(value)
   from
     (select inst_id,session_id,name,value
      from   x$krvxsv)
     where   session_id =
        (select value
         from   system.logstdby$parameters
         where  name = 'LMNR_SID'))
where exists
  (select 1
   from   v$session s,x$knstacr x
   where  s.sid=x.sid_knst
   and    s.serial#=x.serial_knst);
```

View Name: V$LOGSTDBY_STATS

L B-245

```
select name,value
from   gv$logstdby_stats
where  inst_id = USERENV('Instance');
```

View Name: GV$LOG_HISTORY

```
select inst_id,lhrid,lhstm,lhthp,lhseq,to_number(lhlos),
       to_date(lhlot,'MM/DD/RR HH24:MI:SS','NLS_CALENDAR=Gregorian'),
       to_number(lhnxs)
from   x$kcclh;
```

View Name: V$LOG_HISTORY

```
select RECID,STAMP,THREAD#,SEQUENCE#,FIRST_CHANGE#,FIRST_TIME,NEXT_CHANGE#
from   GV$LOG_HISTORY
where  inst_id = USERENV('Instance');
```

View Name: GV$MANAGED_STANDBY

```
select inst_id,decode(MSTYP,1,'RFS',2,'MRP0',3,'MR(fg)',4,
     'ARCH',5,'FGRD',6,'LGWR','UNKNOWN'), to_number(MSPID),
       decode(MSSTS,0,'UNUSED',1,'ALLOCATED',2,'CONNECTED',3,'ATTACHED',4,
       'IDLE',5,'ERROR',6,'OPENING',7,'CLOSING',8,'WRITING',9,
       'RECEIVING',10,'ANNOUNCING',11,'REGISTERING',12,'WAIT_FOR_LOG',13,
       'WAIT_FOR_GAP',14,'APPLYING_LOG','UNKNOWN'),
       decode(MSPAR,0,'N/A',4,'ARCH',5,'Archival',6,'LGWR','UNKNOWN'),
       decode(MSPPID,0,'N/A',to_number(MSPPID)),
       decode(MSDBID,0,'N/A',to_number(MSDBID)),
       decode(MSLNO, 0,'N/A',to_number(MSLNO)),to_number(MSTHR),
       to_number(MSSEQ),to_number(MSBNO),to_number(MSBCT),
       to_number(MSDLY),to_number(MSRCLT),to_number(MSACLT)
from   x$kcrrms;
```

Scripts of X$ Tables Used to Create V$ Views

View Name: **V$MANAGED_STANDBY**

```
select PROCESS,PID,STATUS,CLIENT_PROCESS,CLIENT_PID,CLIENT_DBID,GROUP#,THREAD#,
       SEQUENCE#,BLOCK#,BLOCKS,DELAY_MINS,KNOWN_AGENTS,ACTIVE_AGENTS
from   GV$MANAGED_STANDBY
where  inst_id = USERENV('Instance');
```

View Name: **GV$MAP_COMP_LIST**

```
select inst_id,elem_idx,num_comp,comp1_name,comp1_val,comp2_name,comp2_val,
       comp3_name,comp3_val,comp4_name,comp4_val,comp5_name,comp5_val
from   x$ksfmcompl;
```

View Name: **V$MAP_COMP_LIST**

```
select ELEM_IDX,NUM_COMP,COMP1_NAME,COMP1_VAL, COMP2_NAME,COMP2_VAL,COMP3_NAME,
       COMP3_VAL, COMP4_NAME,COMP4_VAL,COMP5_NAME,COMP5_VAL
from   gv$map_comp_list
where  inst_id = USERENV('Instance');
```

View Name: **GV$MAP_ELEMENT**

```
select inst_id,elem_name,elem_idx,elem_cfgid,
       decode(elem_type,1,'MIRROR',2,'STRIPE',3,'RAID5', 4,'CONCATENATED',5,
       'PARTITION',6,'DISK',7,'NONE'),
       to_number(decode(elem_size,4294967295,NULL,elem_size)),
       elem_nsubelem,elem_descr,stripe_size,
       to_number(decode(lib_idx,4294967295,NULL,lib_idx))
from   x$ksfmelem;
```

View Name: **V$MAP_ELEMENT**

```
select ELEM_NAME,ELEM_IDX,ELEM_CFGID,ELEM_TYPE,ELEM_SIZE,ELEM_NSUBELEM,ELEM_DESCR,
       STRIPE_SIZE,LIB_IDX
from   gv$map_element
where  inst_id = USERENV('Instance');
```

View Name: **GV$MAP_EXT_ELEMENT**

```
select inst_id,elem_idx,num_attrb,attrb1_name,attrb1_val,attrb2_name,attrb2_val,
       attrb3_name,attrb3_val,attrb4_name,attrb4_val,attrb5_name,attrb5_val
from   x$ksfmextelem;
```

View Name: **V$MAP_EXT_ELEMENT**

```
select ELEM_IDX,NUM_ATTRB,ATTRB1_NAME,ATTRB1_VAL,ATTRB2_NAME,ATTRB2_VAL,
       ATTRB3_NAME,ATTRB3_VAL,ATTRB4_NAME,ATTRB4_VAL,ATTRB5_NAME,ATTRB5_VAL
from   gv$map_ext_element
where  inst_id = USERENV('Instance');
```

View Name: **GV$MAP_FILE**

```
select inst_id,file_idx,file_cfgid,decode(file_status,1,'VALID',2,'INVALID'),
       file_name,decode(file_type,1,'DATAFILE',2,'SPFILE',3,'TEMPFILE',4,
       'CONTROLFILE',5,'LOGFILE',6,'ARCHIVEFILE'),
       decode(file_struct,1,'FILE',2,'RAWVOLUME',3,'RAWDEVICE',4,'NONE'),
       file_size,file_nexts,to_number(decode(lib_idx,4294967295,NULL,lib_idx))
from   x$ksfmfile;
```

View Name: V$MAP_FILE

```
select FILE_MAP_IDX,FILE_CFGID,FILE_STATUS,FILE_NAME,FILE_TYPE,FILE_STRUCTURE,
       FILE_SIZE,FILE_NEXTS,LIB_IDX
from   gv$map_file
where  inst_id = USERENV('Instance');
```

View Name: GV$MAP_FILE_EXTENT

```
select inst_id,file_idx,ext_num,ext_dev_off,ext_size,ext_file_off,
       decode(ext_type,1,'DATA',2,'PARITY',3,'NONE'),elem_idx
from   x$ksfmfileext
where  elem_idx != 4294967295;
```

View Name: V$MAP_FILE_EXTENT

```
L B-259
```

```
select FILE_MAP_IDX,EXT_NUM,EXT_ELEM_OFF,EXT_SIZE,EXT_FILE_OFF,EXT_TYPE,ELEM_IDX
from   gv$map_file_extent
where  inst_id = USERENV('Instance');
```

View Name: GV$MAP_FILE_IO_STACK

```
select inst_id,file_idx,depth,elem_idx,cu_size,stride,num_cu,dev_offset,
       to_number(decode(file_offset,4294967295,NULL,file_offset)),
       decode(data_type,1,'DATA',2,'PARITY',3,'DATA AND PARITY'),
       parity_pos, parity_perd,row_id,prow_id
from   x$ksfmiost;
```

View Name: V$MAP_FILE_IO_STACK

```
select FILE_MAP_IDX,DEPTH,ELEM_IDX,CU_SIZE, STRIDE,NUM_CU,ELEM_OFFSET,FILE_OFFSET,
       DATA_TYPE, PARITY_POS,PARITY_PERIOD,ID,PARENT_ID
from   gv$map_file_io_stack
where  inst_id = USERENV('Instance');
```

View Name: GV$MAP_LIBRARY

```
select inst_id,lib_idx,lib_name,vendor_name,protocol_num, version_num,path_name,
       decode(bitand(cap_file,1),0,'N',1,'Y'),
       decode(bitand(cap_file,6),0,'NONE',6,'PERSISTENT',2,'NONPERSISTENT'),
       decode(bitand(cap_elem,1),0,'N',1,'Y'),
       decode(bitand(cap_elem,6),0,'NONE',6,'PERSISTENT',4,'NONPERSISTENT'),
       decode(cap_other,0,'N',1,'Y')
from   x$ksfmlib;
```

View Name: V$MAP_LIBRARY

```
select LIB_IDX,LIB_NAME,VENDOR_NAME,PROTOCOL_NUM,VERSION_NUM,PATH_NAME,MAP_FILE,
       FILE_CFGID,MAP_ELEM,ELEM_CFGID,MAP_SYNC
from   gv$map_library
where  inst_id = USERENV('Instance');
```

View Name: GV$MAP_SUBELEMENT

```
select inst_id,child_idx,parent_idx,sub_num,
       to_number(decode(sub_size,4294967295,NULL,sub_size)),
       to_number(decode(elem_offset,4294967295,NULL,elem_offset)),sub_flags
```

Scripts of X$ Tables Used to Create V$ Views

```
from    x$ksfmsubelem
where   child_idx != 4294967295;
```

View Name: V$MAP_SUBELEMENT

```
select  CHILD_IDX,PARENT_IDX,SUB_NUM,SUB_SIZE, ELEM_OFFSET,SUB_FLAGS
from    gv$map_subelement
where   inst_id = USERENV('Instance');
```

View Name: GV$MAX_ACTIVE_SESS_TARGET_MTH

```
select  inst_id,policy_name_kgskasp
from    x$kgskasp;
```

View Name: V$MAX_ACTIVE_SESS_TARGET_MTH

```
select  name
from    gv$max_active_sess_target_mth
where   inst_id = userenv('instance');
```

View Name: GV$MTTR_TARGET_ADVICE

```
select  distinct inst_id,mttr_v,decode(status,0,'OFF',4,'ON','READY'),
        decode(dirty_limit,0,to_number(NULL),dirty_limit),
        decode(factored_sim_writes,-1,to_number(NULL),factored_sim_writes),
        decode(base_real_nondirect_writes,0,to_number(NULL),
        decode(factored_sim_writes,-1,to_number(NULL),
        round((factored_sim_writes / base_real_nondirect_writes),4))),
        decode(total_writes,-1,to_number(NULL),total_writes),
        decode(base_total_writes,0,to_number(NULL),
        decode(total_writes,-1,to_number(NULL),
        round((total_writes / base_total_writes),4))),
        decode(total_ios,-1,to_number(NULL),total_ios),
        decode(base_total_ios,0,to_number(NULL),
        decode(total_ios,-1,to_number(NULL),round((total_ios / base_total_ios), 4)))
from    x$kcbmmav;
```

View Name: V$MTTR_TARGET_ADVICE

```
select  mttr_target_for_estimate,advice_status,dirty_limit,estd_cache_writes,
        estd_cache_write_factor,estd_total_writes,estd_total_write_factor,
        estd_total_ios, estd_total_io_factor
from    gv$mttr_target_advice
where   inst_id = userenv('instance');
```

View Name: GV$MVREFRESH

```
select      inst_id,sid_knst,serial_knst,currmvowner_knstmvr,currmvname_knstmvr
from        x$knstmvr x
where       type_knst=6
and exists  (select 1
             from   v$session s
             where  s.sid=x.sid_knst
             and    s.serial#=x.serial_knst);
```

View Name: V$MVREFRESH

```
select  SID,SERIAL#,CURRMVOWNER,CURRMVNAME
from    GV$MVREFRESH;
```

View Name: GV$MYSTAT

```
select  inst_id,ksusenum,ksusestn,ksusestv
from    x$ksumysta
where   bitand(ksspaflg,1)!=0
and     bitand(ksuseflg,1)!=0
and     ksusestn<
            (select ksusgstl
             from x$ksusgif);
```

View Name: V$MYSTAT

```
select  SID,STATISTIC#,VALUE
from    GV$MYSTAT
where   inst_id = USERENV('Instance');
```

View Name: GV$NLS_PARAMETERS

```
select  inst_id,parameter,value
from    x$nls_parameters
where   parameter != 'NLS_SPECIAL_CHARS';
```

View Name: V$NLS_PARAMETERS

```
select  PARAMETER,VALUE
from    GV$NLS_PARAMETERS
where   inst_id = USERENV('Instance');
```

View Name: GV$NLS_VALID_VALUES

```
select  inst_id,parameter,value
from    x$ksulv;
```

View Name: V$NLS_VALID_VALUES

```
select  PARAMETER,VALUE
from    GV$NLS_VALID_VALUES
where   inst_id = USERENV('Instance');
```

View Name: GV$OBJECT_DEPENDENCY

```
select  d.inst_id,d.kglhdpar,d.kglnahsh,o.kglnaown,o.kglnaobj,o.kglhdadr,o.kglnahsh,
            o.kglobtyp
from    x$kglob o,x$kgldp d
where   o.kglnahsh = d.kglrfhsh
and     o.kglhdadr = d.kglrfhdl;
```

View Name: V$OBJECT_DEPENDENCY

```
select  FROM_ADDRESS,FROM_HASH,TO_OWNER,TO_NAME,TO_ADDRESS,TO_HASH,TO_TYPE
from    GV$OBJECT_DEPENDENCY
where   inst_id = USERENV('Instance');
```

View Name: GV$OBSOLETE_PARAMETER

```
select  inst_id,kspponm,decode(ksppoval,0,'FALSE','TRUE')
from    x$ksppo;
```

View Name: **V$OBSOLETE_PARAMETER**

```
select NAME,ISSPECIFIED
from   GV$OBSOLETE_PARAMETER
where  inst_id = USERENV('Instance');
```

View Name: **GV$OFFLINE_RANGE**

```
select inst_id,orrid,orstm,ordfp,to_number(orofs),to_number(orons),
       to_date(oront,'MM/DD/RR HH24:MI:SS','NLS_CALENDAR=Gregorian')
from   x$kccor;
```

View Name: **V$OFFLINE_RANGE**

```
select RECID,STAMP,FILE#,OFFLINE_CHANGE#,ONLINE_CHANGE#,ONLINE_TIME
from   GV$OFFLINE_RANGE
where  inst_id = USERENV('Instance');
```

View Name: **GV$OPEN_CURSOR**

```
select inst_id,kgllkuse,kgllksnm,user_name,kglhdpar,kglnahsh,kglnaobj
from   x$kgllk
where  kglhdnsp = 0
and    kglhdpar != kgllkhdl;
```

View Name: **V$OPEN_CURSOR**

```
select SADDR,SID,USER_NAME,ADDRESS,HASH_VALUE,SQL_TEXT
from   GV$OPEN_CURSOR
where  inst_id = USERENV('Instance');
```

View Name: **GV$OPTION**

```
select inst_id,parameter,value
from   x$option;
```

View Name: **V$OPTION**

```
select PARAMETER,VALUE
from   GV$OPTION
where  inst_id = USERENV('Instance');
```

View Name: **GV$PARALLEL_DEGREE_LIMIT_MTH**

```
select inst_id,policy_name_kgskdopp
from   x$kgskdopp;
```

View Name: **V$PARALLEL_DEGREE_LIMIT_MTH**

```
select name
from   gv$parallel_degree_limit_mth
where  inst_id = userenv('instance');
```

View Name: **GV$PARAMETER**

```
select x.inst_id,x.indx+1,ksppinm,ksppity,ksppstvl,ksppstdf,
       decode(bitand(ksppiflg/256,1),1,'TRUE','FALSE'),
       decode(bitand(ksppiflg/65536,3),1,'IMMEDIATE',2,'DEFERRED',3,
```

```
        'IMMEDIATE','FALSE'),
        decode(bitand(ksppstvf,7),1,'MODIFIED',4,'SYSTEM_MOD','FALSE'),
        decode(bitand(ksppstvf,2),2,'TRUE','FALSE'),ksppdesc, ksppstcmnt
from    x$ksppi x,x$ksppcv y
where   (x.indx = y.indx)
and     ((translate(ksppinm,'_','#') not like '#%')
or      (ksppstdf = 'FALSE'));
```

View Name: V$PARAMETER

```
select  NUM,NAME,TYPE,VALUE,ISDEFAULT,ISSES_MODIFIABLE,ISSYS_MODIFIABLE,ISMODIFIED,
        ISADJUSTED,DESCRIPTION,UPDATE_COMMENT
from    GV$PARAMETER
where   inst_id = USERENV('Instance');
```

View Name: GV$PARAMETER2

```
select  x.inst_id,kspftctxpn,ksppinm,ksppity,kspftctxvl,kspftctxdf,
        decode(bitand(ksppiflg/256,1),1,'TRUE','FALSE'),
        decode(bitand(ksppiflg/65536,3),1,'IMMEDIATE',2,'DEFERRED',3,
        'IMMEDIATE','FALSE'),
        decode(bitand(kspftctxvf,7),1,'MODIFIED',4,'SYSTEM_MOD','FALSE'),
        decode(bitand(kspftctxvf,2),2,'TRUE','FALSE'),ksppdesc, kspftctxvn,
        kspftctxct
from    x$ksppi x,x$ksppcv2 y
where   ((x.indx+1) = kspftctxpn)
and     ((translate(ksppinm,'_','#') not like '#%')
or      (kspftctxdf = 'FALSE'));
```

View Name: V$PARAMETER2

```
select  NUM,NAME,TYPE,VALUE,ISDEFAULT,ISSES_MODIFIABLE,ISSYS_MODIFIABLE,ISMODIFIED,
        ISADJUSTED,DESCRIPTION,ORDINAL,UPDATE_COMMENT
from    GV$PARAMETER2
where   inst_id = USERENV('Instance');
```

View Name: GV$PGASTAT

```
select  INST_ID,QESMMSGANM,
        decode(QESMMSGAUN,3,(QESMMSGAVL*QESMMSGAMU)/100,QESMMSGAVL*QESMMSGAMU),
        decode(QESMMSGAUN,0,'bytes',1,'microseconds',3,'percent','')
from    X$QESMMSGA
where   QESMMSGAVS = 1;
```

View Name: V$PGASTAT

```
select  NAME,VALUE,UNIT
from    GV$PGASTAT
where   INST_ID = USERENV('Instance');
```

View Name: GV$PGA_TARGET_ADVICE

```
select  INST_ID,PAT_PRED * 1024,round(PAT_PRED/PAT_CURR,4),
        decode(status,0,'OFF','ON'),BYTES_PROCESSED * 1024,
        EXTRA_BYTES_RW * 1024,round(decode(BYTES_PROCESSED+EXTRA_BYTES_RW,0,0,
        (BYTES_PROCESSED*100)/(BYTES_PROCESSED+EXTRA_BYTES_RW))), OVERALLOC
from    X$QESMMAPADV;
```

Scripts of X$ Tables Used
to Create V$ Views

View Name: V$PGA_TARGET_ADVICE

```
select  PGA_TARGET_FOR_ESTIMATE,PGA_TARGET_FACTOR,ADVICE_STATUS,BYTES_PROCESSED,
        ESTD_EXTRA_BYTES_RW,ESTD_PGA_CACHE_HIT_PERCENTAGE,ESTD_OVERALLOC_COUNT
from    GV$PGA_TARGET_ADVICE
where   INST_ID = USERENV('Instance');
```

View Name: GV$PGA_TARGET_ADVICE_HISTOGRAM

```
select  INST_ID,PAT_PRED * 1024,round(PAT_PRED/PAT_CURR, 4),
        decode(status,0,'OFF','ON'),LOWBND * 1024,(HIBND * 1024)-1,
        OPTIMAL,ONEPASS,MPASS,MPASS+ONEPASS+OPTIMAL,IGNORED
from    X$QESMMAHIST;
```

View Name: V$PGA_TARGET_ADVICE_HISTOGRAM

```
select  PGA_TARGET_FOR_ESTIMATE,PGA_TARGET_FACTOR,ADVICE_STATUS,LOW_OPTIMAL_SIZE,
        HIGH_OPTIMAL_SIZE,ESTD_OPTIMAL_EXECUTIONS,ESTD_ONEPASS_EXECUTIONS,
        ESTD_MULTIPASSES_EXECUTIONS,ESTD_TOTAL_EXECUTIONS,IGNORED_WORKAREAS_COUNT
from    GV$PGA_TARGET_ADVICE_HISTOGRAM
where   INST_ID = USERENV('Instance');
```

View Name: GV$PQ_SESSTAT

```
select  inst_id,kxfpssnam,kxfpssval,kxfpsstot
from    x$kxfpsst;
```

View Name: V$PQ_SESSTAT

```
select  STATISTIC,LAST_QUERY,SESSION_TOTAL
from    GV$PQ_SESSTAT
where   inst_id = USERENV('Instance');
```

View Name: GV$PQ_SLAVE

```
select  inst_id,kxfpdpnam,decode(bitand(kxfpdpflg, 16), 0, 'BUSY', 'IDLE'),
        kxfpdpses,floor(kxfpdpcit / 6000),floor(kxfpdpcbt / 6000),
        floor(kxfpdpcct / 100),kxfpdpclsnt + kxfpdpcrsnt,
        kxfpdpclrcv + kxfpdpcrrcv,floor((kxfpdptit + kxfpdpcit) / 6000),
        floor((kxfpdptbt + kxfpdpcbt) / 6000),
        floor((kxfpdptct + kxfpdpcct) / 100),
        kxfpdptlsnt + kxfpdpclsnt + kxfpdptrsnt + kxfpdpcrsnt,
        kxfpdptlrcv + kxfpdpclrcv + kxfpdptrrcv + kxfpdpcrrcv
from    x$kxfpdp
where   bitand(kxfpdpflg, 8) != 0;
```

View Name: V$PQ_SLAVE

```
select  SLAVE_NAME,STATUS,SESSIONS,IDLE_TIME_CUR,BUSY_TIME_CUR,CPU_SECS_CUR,
        MSGS_SENT_CUR,MSGS_RCVD_CUR,IDLE_TIME_TOTAL,BUSY_TIME_TOTAL,CPU_SECS_TOTAL,
        MSGS_SENT_TOTAL,MSGS_RCVD_TOTAL
from    GV$PQ_SLAVE
where   inst_id = USERENV('Instance');
```

View Name: GV$PQ_SYSSTAT

```
select  inst_id,rpad(kxfpysnam,30),kxfpysval
from    x$kxfpys;
```

View Name: **V$PQ_SYSSTAT**

```
select STATISTIC,VALUE
from   GV$PQ_SYSSTAT
where  inst_id = USERENV('Instance');
```

View Name: **GV$PQ_TQSTAT**

```
select inst_id,kxfqsqn,kxfqsid,rpad(kxfqsty,10),kxfqscnt,kxfqslen,kxfqset,kxfqsavl,
       kxfqsdw,kxfqsdt,rpad(kxfqssid,10),kxfqsiid
from   x$kxfqsrow;
```

View Name: **V$PQ_TQSTAT**

```
select DFO_NUMBER,TQ_ID,SERVER_TYPE,NUM_ROWS,BYTES,OPEN_TIME,AVG_LATENCY,WAITS,
       TIMEOUTS,PROCESS,INSTANCE
from   GV$PQ_TQSTAT
where  inst_id = USERENV('Instance');
```

View Name: **GV$PROCESS**

```
select inst_id,addr,indx,ksuprpid,ksuprunm,ksuprser,ksuprtid,ksuprpnm,ksuprtfi,
       decode(bitand(ksuprflg,2),0,null,1), decode(ksllawat,hextoraw('00'),
       null,ksllawat),decode(ksllaspn,hextoraw('00'),null,ksllaspn),
       ksuprpum,ksuprpnam+ksuprpram,ksuprpfm,
case
  when ksuprpnam+ksuprpram > ksuprpmm
  then ksuprpnam+ksuprpram
  else ksuprpmm end
from   x$ksupr
where  bitand(ksspaflg,1)!=0;
```

View Name: **V$PROCESS**

```
select addr,pid,spid,username,serial#,terminal,program,traceid,background,latchwait,
       latchspin,pga_used_mem,pga_alloc_mem,pga_freeable_mem,pga_max_mem
from   gv$process
where  inst_id = USERENV('Instance') ;
```

View Name: **GV$PROXY_ARCHIVEDLOG**

```
select inst_id,pcrid,pcstm,pcdev,pchdl,pccmt,pcmdh,pcmpl,
       decode(bitand(pcflg, 1+2+4),0,'A',1,'D',2,'X',4,'U','?'),
       decode(bitand(pcflg,1),1,'YES','NO'),pathp,paseq,
       to_number(parls),to_date(parlc,'MM/DD/RR HH24:MI:SS',
       'NLS_CALENDAR=Gregorian'),to_number(palos),
       to_date(palot,'MM/DD/RR HH24:MI:SS','NLS_CALENDAR=Gregorian'),
       to_number(panxs),to_date(panxt,'MM/DD/RR HH24:MI:SS',
       'NLS_CALENDAR=Gregorian'),pabct,pabsz,
       to_date(pctsm,'MM/DD/RR HH24:MI:SS','NLS_CALENDAR=Gregorian'),
       to_date(pctim,'MM/DD/RR HH24:MI:SS','NLS_CALENDAR=Gregorian'),
       (to_date(pctim,'MM/DD/RR HH24:MI:SS','NLS_CALENDAR=Gregorian')-
       to_date(pctsm,'MM/DD/RR HH24:MI:SS','NLS_CALENDAR=Gregorian'))*86400
from   x$kccpa;
```

View Name: **V$PROXY_ARCHIVEDLOG**

```
select RECID,STAMP,DEVICE_TYPE,HANDLE,COMMENTS,MEDIA,MEDIA_POOL,STATUS,
       DELETED,THREAD#,SEQUENCE#,RESETLOGS_CHANGE#,RESETLOGS_TIME,
       FIRST_CHANGE#,FIRST_TIME,NEXT_CHANGE#,NEXT_TIME,BLOCKS,BLOCK_SIZE,
```

```
      START_TIME,COMPLETION_TIME,ELAPSED_SECONDS
from  GV$PROXY_ARCHIVEDLOG
where inst_id = USERENV('Instance');
```

View Name: GV$PROXY_DATAFILE

```
select inst_id,pcrid,pcstm,pcdev,pchdl,pccmt,pcmdh,pcmpl,pctag,
       decode(bitand(pcf lg,1+2+4),0,'A',1,'D',2,'X',4,'U','?'),
       decode(bitand(pcflg,1),1,'YES','NO'),pdd fp,to_number(pdcrs),
       to_date(pdcrt,'MM/DD/RR HH24:MI:SS','NLS_CALENDAR=Gregorian' ),
       to_number(pdrls),
       to_date(pdrlc,'MM/DD/RR HH24:MI:SS','NLS_CALENDAR=Gregorian') ,
       to_number(pdcps),
       to_date(pdcpt,'MM/DD/RR HH24:MI:SS','NLS_CALENDAR=Gregorian'),
       to_number(pdafs),to_number(pdrfs),
       to_date(pdrft,'MM/DD/RR HH24:MI:SS','NLS_CALEN DAR=Gregorian'),
       decode(bitand(pdflg,1),1,0,NULL),
       decode(bitand(pdflg,2),0,'NO' ,'YES'),
       decode(bitand(pdflg,4),0,'NO','YES'),pdfsz,pdbsz,pdlor,
       to_date(pctsm,'M M/DD/RR HH24:MI:SS','NLS_CALENDAR=Gregorian'),
       to_date(pctim,'MM/DD/RR HH24:MI:SS ','NLS_CALENDAR=Gregorian'),
       (to_date(pctim,'MM/DD/RR HH24:MI:SS','NLS_CALENDAR=G regorian')-
       to_date(pctsm,'MM/DD/RR HH24:MI:SS','NLS_CALENDAR=Gregorian'))*86400 ,
       decode(pddfp,0,decode(bitand(pcflg,8),8,'S','B'),NULL),
       decode(bitand(pdflg ,1792),0,'NO',   'YES'),
       to_ date(pdkpt,'MM/DD/RR HH24:MI:SS','NLS_CALENDAR=Gregorian'),
       decode(bitand(pdflg,1792),256,'LOGS',512,'NOLOGS',1024,'CONSISTENT',NULL)
from  x$kccpd;
```

View Name: V$PROXY_DATAFILE

```
select RECID,STAMP,DEVICE_TYPE,HANDLE,COMMENTS,MEDIA,MEDIA_POOL,TAG,STATUS,DELETED,
       FILE#,CREATION_CHANGE#,CREATION_TIME,RESETLOGS_CHANGE#,RESETLOGS_TIME,
       CHECKPOINT_CHANGE#,CHECKPOINT_TIME,ABSOLUTE_FUZZY_CHANGE#,
       RECOVERY_FUZZY_CHANGE#,RECOVERY_FUZZY_TIME,INCREMENTAL_LEVEL,ONLINE_FUZZY,
       BACKUP_FUZZY,BLOCKS,BLOCK_SIZE,OLDEST_OFFLINE_RANGE,START_TIME,
       COMPLETION_TIME,ELAPSED_SECONDS,CONTROLFILE_TYPE,KEEP,KEEP_UNTIL,KEEP_OPTIONS
from  GV$PROXY_DATAFILE
where inst_id = USERENV('Instance');
```

View Name: GV$PWFILE_USERS

```
select inst_id,username,decode(sysdba,1,'TRUE','FALSE'),
       decode(sysoper,1,'TRUE','FALSE')
from  x$kzsrt
where valid=1
and   username != 'INTERNAL' ;
```

View Name: V$PWFILE_USERS

```
select USERNAME,SYSDBA,SYSOPER
from  GV$PWFILE_USERS
where inst_id = USERENV('Instance');
```

View Name: GV$PX_PROCESS

```
select a.inst_id,a.kxfpdpnam,
       decode(bitand(a.kxfpdpflg, 16),0,'IN USE','AVAILABLE'),
       b.pid,a.kxfpdpspid,c.sid,c.serial#
from  x$kxfpdp a,V$PROCESS b,V$SESSION c
```

```
where   bitand(kxfpdpflg, 8) != 0
and     a.kxfpdpspid = b.SPID
and     a.kxfpdpspid = c.PROCESS(+);
```

View Name: **V$PX_PROCESS**

```
select  SERVER_NAME,STATUS,PID,SPID,SID,SERIAL#
from    GV$PX_PROCESS
where   inst_id = USERENV('Instance');
```

View Name: **GV$PX_PROCESS_SYSSTAT**

```
select  inst_id,rpad(kxfpnsnam,30),kxfpnsval
from    x$kxfpns;
```

View Name: **V$PX_PROCESS_SYSSTAT**

```
select  STATISTIC,VALUE
from    GV$PX_PROCESS_SYSSTAT
where   inst_id = USERENV('Instance');
```

View Name: **GV$PX_SESSION**

```
select  a.inst_id,a.addr,a.indx,a.ksuseser,
        decode(b.kxfpdpqcsid,NULL,a.indx,b.kxfpdpqcsid),
        b.kxfpdpqcser,b.kxfpdpcin,b.kxfpdpsvgrp,b.kxfpdpsvset,b.kxfpdpsvnum,
        b.kxfpdpadg,b.kxfpdprdg
from    x$ksuse a,x$kxfpdp b
where   bitand(a.ksspaflg,1)!=0
and     bitand(a.ksuseflg,1)!=0
and     a.ksuseqcsid > 0
and     a.ksusepro = b.kxfpdppro(+);
```

View Name: **V$PX_SESSION**

```
select  saddr,sid,serial#,qcsid,qcserial#,qcinst_id,server_group,server_set,
        server#,degree,req_degree
from    GV$PX_SESSION
where   inst_id = USERENV('Instance');
```

View Name: **GV$PX_SESSTAT**

```
select  a.inst_id,a.addr,a.indx,a.ksuseser,
        decode(b.kxfpdpqcsid,NULL,a.indx,b.kxfpdpqcsid),
        b.kxfpdpqcser,b.kxfpdpcin,b.kxfpdpsvgrp,b.kxfpdpsvset,
        b.kxfpdpsvnum,b.kxfpdpadg,b.kxfpdprdg,c.ksusestn,c.ksusestv
from    x$ksuse a,x$kxfpdp b,x$ksusesta c
where   bitand(a.ksspaflg,1)!=0
and     bitand(a.ksuseflg,1)!=0
and     a.KSUSEQCSID > 0
and     a.ksusepro = b.kxfpdppro(+)
and     a.indx = c.indx
and     c.ksusestn < (select  ksusgstl from x$ksusgif);
```

View Name: **V$PX_SESSTAT**

```
select  saddr,sid,serial#,qcsid,qcserial#,qcinst_id,server_group,server_set,
        server#,degree,req_degree,statistic#,value
from    GV$PX_SESSTAT
where   inst_id = USERENV('Instance');
```

Scripts of X$ Tables Used to Create V$ Views

View Name: GV$QUEUE

```
select inst_id,kmcqspro,decode(indx,0,'COMMON','DISPATCHER'),kmcqsncq,kmcqswat,
       kmcqstnc
from   x$kmcqs
where  indx=0 or kmcqspro!=hextoraw('00');
```

View Name: V$QUEUE

```
select PADDR,TYPE,QUEUED,WAIT,TOTALQ
from   GV$QUEUE
where  inst_id = USERENV('Instance');
```

View Name: GV$QUEUEING_MTH

```
select inst_id,policy_name_kgskquep
from   x$kgskquep;
```

View Name: V$QUEUEING_MTH

```
select name
from   gv$queueing_mth
where  inst_id = userenv('instance');
```

View Name: GV$RECOVERY_FILE_STATUS

```
select fn.inst_id,fn.fnfno,fn.fnnam,
       decode(nvl(mf.cps,0),0,'NOT RECOVERED',281474976710655,'CURRENT',
       'IN RECOVERY')
from   x$kcrmx mx,x$kccfn fn,x$kccfe fe,x$kcrmf mf
where  fn.fntyp = 4
       and mf.fno(+) = fn.fnfno
       and ((bitand(mx.flg,2) != 0
and    fe.fedup != 0)
or     mf.fno = fn.fnfno)
and    fe.fenum = fn.fnfno;
```

View Name: V$RECOVERY_FILE_STATUS

```
select FILENUM,FILENAME,STATUS
from   GV$RECOVERY_FILE_STATUS
where  inst_id = USERENV('Instance');
```

View Name: GV$RECOVERY_LOG

```
select inst_id,lhthp,lhseq,
       to_date(lhlot,'MM/DD/RR HH24:MI:SS','NLS_CALENDAR=Gregorian'),lhnam
from   x$kcclh
where  to_number(lhnxs) >
          (select min(to_number(fhscn))
           from x$kcvfhmrr
           where hxerr = 0)
          and lhseq not in
             (select leseq
              from x$kccle
              where lethr = lhthp)
           and to_number(lhlos) <
              (select max(to_number(hxsts))
               from x$kcvfhmrr
               where hxerr = 0);
```

View Name: **V$RECOVERY_LOG**

```
select THREAD#,SEQUENCE#,TIME,ARCHIVE_NAME
from   GV$RECOVERY_LOG
where  inst_id = USERENV('Instance');
```

View Name: **GV$RECOVERY_PROGRESS**

```
select USERENV('Instance'),OPNAME,TARGET_DESC,SOFAR,TOTALWORK
from   V$SESSION_LONGOPS
where  opname like '% Recovery';
```

View Name: **V$RECOVERY_PROGRESS**

```
select TYPE,ITEM,SOFAR,TOTAL
from   GV$RECOVERY_PROGRESS
where  INST_ID = USERENV('Instance');
```

View Name: **GV$RECOVERY_STATUS**

```
select fx.inst_id,to_date(mx.ckptim,'MM/DD/RR HH24:MI:SS','NLS_CALENDAR=Gregorian'),
       mx.thr,mx.seq,mx.los,
       to_date(mx.tim,'MM/DD/RR HH24:MI:SS','NLS_CALENDAR=Gregorian'),
       nvl(mx.nam, 'NONE'),decode(bitand(mx.mrs,256 + 128 + 64 + 8),8,'RELEASE',64,
       'WRONG LOG',128,'MISSING NAME',256,'UNNEEDED NAME','NONE'),
       decode(nvl(fx.err,3),1,'NEED LOG',3,'END OF THREAD',4,'LOG REUSED','UNKNOWN')
from   x$kcrmx mx,x$kcrfx fx
where  fx.thr(+) = mx.thr;
```

View Name: **V$RECOVERY_STATUS**

```
select RECOVERY_CHECKPOINT,THREAD,SEQUENCE_NEEDED,SCN_NEEDED,TIME_NEEDED,
       PREVIOUS_LOG_NAME,PREVIOUS_LOG_STATUS,REASON
from   GV$RECOVERY_STATUS
where  inst_id = USERENV('Instance');
```

View Name: **GV$RECOVER_FILE**

```
select inst_id,hxfil,decode(hxons,0,'OFFLINE','ONLINE'),
       decode(hxons,0,'OFFLINE', 'ONLINE'),
       decode(hxerr, 0,'',1,'FILE MISSING',2,'OFFLINE NORMAL',3,
       'NOT VERIFIED',4,'FILE NOT FOUND',5,'CANNOT OPEN FILE',6,
       'CANNOT READ HEADER',7,'CORRUPT HEADER',8,'WRONG FILE TYPE',9,
       'WRONG DATABASE',10,'WRONG FILE NUMBER',11,'WRONG FILE CREATE',12,
       'WRONG FILE CREATE',16,'DELAYED OPEN','UNKNOWN ERROR'),
       to_number(fhscn),to_date(fhtim,'MM/DD/RR HH24:MI:SS',
       'NLS_CALENDAR=Gregorian')
from   x$kcvfhmrr;
```

View Name: **V$RECOVER_FILE**

```
select FILE#,"ONLINE",ONLINE_STATUS,ERROR,CHANGE#,TIME
from   GV$RECOVER_FILE
where  inst_id = USERENV('Instance');
```

View Name: **GV$REPLPROP**

```
select      inst_id,sid_knst,serial_knst,
            decode(type_knst,3,'Replication Parallel Prop Slave' ||
```

```
            slavenum_knstrpp,4,'Replication Parallel Prop Coordinator'),
            dblink_knstrpp,decode(state_knstrpp,0,NULL,1,'WAIT',2,
            'SLEEP',3,'PUSH',4,'PURGE',5,'CREATE ERROR',6,
            'SCHEDULE TXN'),decode(type_knst,4,NULL,xid_knstrpp),sequence_knstrpp
from        x$knstrpp x
where       type_knst in (3,4)
and exists

            (select 1
             from v$session s
             where s.sid=x.sid_knst
             and s.serial#=x.serial_knst);
```

View Name: V$REPLPROP

```
select  SID,SERIAL#,NAME,DBLINK,STATE,XID,SEQUENCE
from    GV$REPLPROP
where   INST_ID = USERENV('Instance');
```

View Name: GV$REPLQUEUE

```
select  inst_id,txns_enqueued_knstrqu,calls_enqueued_knstrqu,txns_purged_knstrqu,
        last_enqueue_time_knstrqu,last_purge_time_knstrqu
from    x$knstrqu;
```

View Name: V$REPLQUEUE

```
select  TXNS_ENQUEUED,CALLS_ENQUEUED,TXNS_PURGED,LAST_ENQUEUE_TIME,LAST_PURGE_TIME
from    GV$REPLQUEUE
where   INST_ID = USERENV('Instance');
```

View Name: GV$REQDIST

```
select  inst_id,kmmrdbuc,sum(kmmrdcnt)
from    x$kmmrd
where   kmmrdpro!=hextoraw('00')
group by inst_id,kmmrdbuc;
```

View Name: V$REQDIST

```
select  BUCKET,COUNT
from    GV$REQDIST
where   inst_id = USERENV('Instance');
```

View Name: GV$RESERVED_WORDS

```
select  inst_id,keyword,length
from    x$kwddef;
```

View Name: V$RESERVED_WORDS

```
select  KEYWORD,LENGTH
from    GV$RESERVED_WORDS
where   inst_id = USERENV('Instance');
```

View Name: GV$RESOURCE

```
select  inst_id,addr,ksqrsidt,ksqrsid1,ksqrsid2
from    x$ksqrs
where   bitand(ksqrsflg,2)!=0;
```

View Name: **V$RESOURCE**

```
select ADDR,TYPE,ID1,ID2
from   GV$RESOURCE
where  inst_id = USERENV('Instance');
```

View Name: **GV$RESOURCE_LIMIT**

```
select inst_id,ksurlmnm,ksurlmcv,ksurlmmv,
       LPAD(decode(bitand(ksurlmfg, 1),0,to_char(ksurlmia),'UNLIMITED'),10),
       LPAD(decode(bitand(ksurlmfg, 2),0,to_char(ksurlmlv),'UNLIMITED'),10)
from   x$ksurlmt;
```

View Name: **V$RESOURCE_LIMIT**

```
select RESOURCE_NAME,CURRENT_UTILIZATION,MAX_UTILIZATION,INITIAL_ALLOCATION,
       LIMIT_VALUE
from   GV$RESOURCE_LIMIT
where  inst_id = USERENV('Instance');
```

View Name: **GV$RESUMABLE**

```
select inst_id,ktrsfaddr,ktrsfsid,decode (bitand(ktrsfflg,1),0,'NO','YES'),
       decode(ktrsfsta,0,'NORMAL',1,'SUSPENDED',2,'TIMEOUT',3,'ERROR',4,
       'ABORTED',''),ktrsftmo,ktrsfspt,ktrsfrst,ktrsfnam,ktrsferr,ktrsfep1,ktrsfep2,
       ktrsfep3,ktrsfep4,ktrsfep5,ktrsfems
from   x$ktrso;
```

View Name: **V$RESUMABLE**

```
select ADDR,SID,ENABLED,STATUS,TIMEOUT,SUSPEND_TIME,RESUME_TIME,NAME,ERROR_NUMBER,
       ERROR_PARAMETER1,ERROR_PARAMETER2,ERROR_PARAMETER3, ERROR_PARAMETER4,
       ERROR_PARAMETER5,ERROR_MSG
from   GV$RESUMABLE
where  inst_id = USERENV('Instance');
```

View Name: **GV$RMAN_CONFIGURATION**

```
select INST_ID,RMRNO,RMNAM,RMVAL
from   X$KCCRM
where  RMNAM is not null;
```

View Name: **V$RMAN_CONFIGURATION**

```
select CONF#,NAME,VALUE
from   GV$RMAN_CONFIGURATION
where  inst_id = USERENV('Instance');
```

View Name: **GV$ROLLSTAT**

```
select inst_id,kturdusn,kturdlat,kturdext,kturdsiz,kturdwrt,kturdnax,kturdget,
kturdwat,decode(kturdopt, -1,to_number(null),kturdopt),kturdhwm,kturdnsh,
       kturdnwp,kturdnex,kturdash,kturdaae,
       decode(bitand(kturdflg,127),0,'ONLINE',2,'PENDING OFFLINE',3,'OFFLINE',4,
       'FULL','UNKNOWN'),kturdcex, kturdcbk
from   x$kturd
where  kturdsiz != 0
and    bitand(kturdflg,127) != 3;
```

View Name: V$ROLLSTAT

```
select  USN,LATCH,EXTENTS,RSSIZE,WRITES,XACTS,GETS,WAITS,OPTSIZE,HWMSIZE,SHRINKS,
        WRAPS,EXTENDS,AVESHRINK,AVEACTIVE,STATUS,CUREXT,CURBLK
from    GV$ROLLSTAT
where   inst_id = USERENV('Instance');
```

View Name: GV$ROWCACHE

```
select  inst_id,kqrstcid,decode(kqrsttyp,1,'PARENT','SUBORDINATE'),
        decode(kqrsttyp,2,kqrstsno,null),kqrsttxt,kqrstcsz,kqrstusg,kqrstfcs,
        kqrstgrq,kqrstgmi,kqrstsrq,kqrstsmi,kqrstsco,kqrstmrq,kqrstmfl,
        kqrstilr,kqrstifr,kqrstisr
from    x$kqrst;
```

View Name: V$ROWCACHE

```
select  cache#,type,subordinate#,parameter,count,usage,fixed, gets,getmisses,scans,
        scanmisses,scancompletes,modifications,flushes,dlm_requests,dlm_conflicts,
        dlm_releases
from    gv$rowcache
where   inst_id = USERENV('Instance');
```

View Name: GV$ROWCACHE_PARENT

```
select  inst_id,indx,kqrfphsh,kqrfpadd,kqrfpcid,kqrfpcnm,
        decode(bitand(kqrfpflg,1),0,'Y','N'),kqrfpmod,kqrfpreq,kqrfptxn,kqrfpses,
        kqrfpirq, kqrfpirl, kqrfpity, kqrfpii1,kqrfpii2,kqrfpkey
from    x$kqrfp;
```

View Name: V$ROWCACHE_PARENT

```
select  indx,hash,address,cache#,cache_name,existent,lock_mode,lock_request,
        txn,saddr,inst_lock_request,inst_lock_release,inst_lock_type,inst_lock_id1,
        inst_lock_id2,key
from    gv$rowcache_parent
where   inst_id = USERENV('Instance');
```

View Name: GV$ROWCACHE_SUBORDINATE

```
select  inst_id,indx,kqrfshsh,kqrfsadd,kqrfscid,kqrfssid,kqrfssnm,
        decode(bitand(kqrfsflg,1),0,'Y','N'),kqrfspar,kqrfskey
from x$kqrfs;
```

View Name: V$ROWCACHE_SUBORDINATE

```
select  indx,hash,address,cache#,subcache#,subcache_name,existent,parent,key
from    gv$rowcache_subordinate
where   inst_id = USERENV('Instance');
```

View Name: GV$RSRC_CONSUMER_GROUP

```
select  inst_id,name_kgskcft,current_count_kgskcft,runnable_count_kgskcft,
        total_count_kgskcft,cpu_wait_kgskcft,cpu_waits_kgskcft,total_used_kgskcft,
        yields_kgskcft,num_queued_kgskcft,undo_consump_kgskcft
from    x$kgskcft;
```

View Name: **V$RSRC_CONSUMER_GROUP**

```
select  name,active_sessions,execution_waiters,requests,cpu_wait_time,cpu_waits,
        consumed_cpu_time,yields,queue_length,current_undo_consumption
from    gv$rsrc_consumer_group
where   inst_id = userenv('instance');
```

View Name: **GV$RSRC_CONSUMER_GROUP_CPU_MTH**

```
select  inst_id,policy_name_kgskcp
from    x$kgskcp;
```

View Name: **V$RSRC_CONSUMER_GROUP_CPU_MTH**

```
select  name
from    gv$rsrc_consumer_group_cpu_mth
where   inst_id = userenv('instance');
```

View Name: **GV$RSRC_PLAN**

```
select  inst_id,name_kgskpft
from    x$kgskpft;
```

View Name: **V$RSRC_PLAN**

```
select  name
from    gv$rsrc_plan
where   inst_id = userenv('instance');
```

View Name: **GV$RSRC_PLAN_CPU_MTH**

```
select  inst_id,policy_name_kgskpp
from    x$kgskpp;
```

View Name: **V$RSRC_PLAN_CPU_MTH**

```
select  name
from    gv$rsrc_plan_cpu_mth
where   inst_id = userenv('instance');
```

View Name: **GV$SEGMENT_STATISTICS**

```
select  s.inst_id,u.name,o.name,o.subname,ts.name,s.fts_tsn, o.obj#,o.dataobj#,
        decode(o.type#,0,'NEXT OBJECT',1,'INDEX',2,'TABLE',3,'CLUSTER',4,'VIEW',5,
        'SYNONYM',6,'SEQUENCE',7,'PROCEDURE',8,'FUNCTION',9,'PACKAGE',11,
        'PACKAGE BODY',12,'TRIGGER',13,'TYPE',14,'TYPE BODY',19,'TABLE PARTITION',20,
        'INDEX PARTITION',21,'LOB',22,'LIBRARY',23,'DIRECTORY',24,'QUEUE',28,
        'JAVA SOURCE',29,'JAVA CLASS',30,'JAVA RESOURCE',32,'INDEXTYPE',33,
        'OPERATOR',34,'TABLE SUBPARTITION',35,'INDEX SUBPARTITION',40,
        'LOB PARTITION',41,'LOB SUBPARTITION',42,'MATERIALIZED VIEW',43,
        'DIMENSION',44,'CONTEXT',47,'RESOURCE PLAN',48,'CONSUMER GROUP',51,
        'SUBSCRIPTION',52,'LOCATION',55,'XML SCHEMA',56,'JAVA DATA',57,
        'SECURITY PROFILE','UNDEFINED'),s.fts_statnam,s.fts_statid,s.fts_staval
from    obj$ o,user$ u,x$ksolsfts s,ts$ ts
where   o.owner# = u.user#
and     s.fts_inte = 0
```

Scripts of X$ Tables Used to Create V$ Views

```
and     s.fts_objn = o.obj#
and     s.fts_tsn = ts.ts#
and     s.fts_objd = o.dataobj#
and     o.linkname is null
and     (o.type# not in (1  /* INDEX - handled below */,10 /* NON-EXISTENT */)
or      (o.type# = 1 and 1 = (select 1 from ind$  i
                                where  i.obj# = o.obj# and i.type# in (1,2,3,4,6,7,9))))
and     o.name != '_NEXT_OBJECT'
and     o.name != '_default_auditing_options_';
```

View Name: V$SEGMENT_STATISTICS

```
select  owner,object_name,subobject_name,tablespace_name,ts#,obj#,dataobj#,
        object_type,statistic_name,statistic#,value
from    gv$segment_statistics
where   inst_id = userenv('instance');
```

View Name: GV$SEGSTAT

```
select  inst_id,fts_tsn,fts_objn,fts_objd,fts_statnam,fts_statid,fts_staval
from    x$ksolsfts
where   fts_inte = 0;
```

View Name: V$SEGSTAT

```
select  ts#,obj#,dataobj#,statistic_name,statistic#,value
from    gv$segstat
where   inst_id = userenv('instance');
```

View Name: GV$SEGSTAT_NAME

```
select  inst_id,st_statid,st_colname,decode(st_samp,0,'NO',1,'YES')
from    x$ksolsstat where st_inte = 0;
```

View Name: V$SEGSTAT_NAME

```
select  statistic#,name,sampled
from    gv$segstat_name
where   inst_id = userenv('instance');
```

View Name: GV$SESSION

```
select  inst_id,addr,indx,ksuseser,ksuudses,ksusepro, ksuudlui,ksuudlna,ksuudoct,
        ksusesow, decode(ksusetrn,hextoraw('00'),null,ksusetrn),
        decode(ksqpswat,hextoraw('00'),null,ksqpswat),
        decode(bitand(ksuseidl,11),1,'ACTIVE',0,decode(bitand(ksuseflg,4096),0,
        'INACTIVE','CACHED'),2,'SNIPED',3,'SNIPED','KILLED'),
        decode(ksspatyp,1,'DEDICATED',2,'SHARED',3,'PSEUDO','NONE'),
        ksuudsid,ksuudsna,ksuseunm,ksusepid,ksusemnm,ksusetid,ksusepnm,
        decode(bitand(ksuseflg,19),17,'BACKGROUND',1,'USER',2,'RECURSIVE','?'),
        ksusesql,ksusesqh,ksusepsq,ksusepha,ksuseapp,ksuseaph,ksuseact,ksuseach,
        ksusecli,ksusefix,ksuseobj,ksusefil,ksuseblk,ksuseslt,ksuseltm,
        ksusectm,decode(bitand(ksusepfl,16),0,'NO','YES'),
        decode(ksuseft,2,'SESSION',4,'SELECT',8,'TRANSACTIONAL','NONE'),
        decode(ksusefm,1,'BASIC',2,'PRECONNECT',4,'PREPARSE','NONE'),
        decode(ksusefs,1,'YES','NO'), ksusegrp,decode(bitand(ksusepfl,16),16,
        'ENABLED', decode(bitand(ksusepfl,32),32,'FORCED','DISABLED')),
        decode(bitand(ksusepfl,64),64,'FORCED',
        decode(bitand(ksusepfl,128),128,'DISABLED','ENABLED')),
```

```
          decode(bitand(ksusepfl,512),512,'FORCED',
          decode(bitand(ksusepfl,256),256,'DISABLED','ENABLED')),ksusecqd, ksuseclid
from      x$ksuse
where     bitand(ksspaflg,1)!=0 and bitand(ksuseflg,1)!=0;
```

View Name: V$SESSION

```
select SADDR,SID,SERIAL#,AUDSID,PADDR,USER#,USERNAME,COMMAND,OWNERID,TADDR,
       LOCKWAIT,STATUS,SERVER,SCHEMA#,SCHEMANAME,OSUSER,PROCESS,MACHINE,TERMINAL,
       PROGRAM,TYPE,SQL_ADDRESS,SQL_HASH_VALUE,PREV_SQL_ADDR,PREV_HASH_VALUE,
       MODULE,MODULE_HASH,ACTION,ACTION_HASH,CLIENT_INFO,FIXED_TABLE_SEQUENCE,
       ROW_WAIT_OBJ#,ROW_WAIT_FILE#,ROW_WAIT_BLOCK#,ROW_WAIT_ROW#,LOGON_TIME,
       LAST_CALL_ET,PDML_ENABLED,FAILOVER_TYPE,FAILOVER_METHOD,FAILED_OVER,
       RESOURCE_CONSUMER_GROUP,PDML_STATUS,PDDL_STATUS,PQ_STATUS,
       CURRENT_QUEUE_DURATION,CLIENT_IDENTIFIER
from   GV$SESSION
where  inst_id = USERENV('Instance');
```

View Name: GV$SESSION_CONNECT_INFO

```
select inst_id,ksusenum,decode(ksuseaty,0,'DATABASE',1,'OS',2,'NETWORK',3,
       'PROXY',4,'SERVER',5,'PASSWORD',6,'EXTERNAL ADAPTERS',7,'INTERNAL',8,
       'GLOBAL',9,'EXTERNAL',10,'PASSWORD BASED GLOBAL USER','?'),ksuseunm,ksuseban
from   x$ksusecon
where  bitand(ksuseflg,1)!=0
and bitand(ksuseflg,16)=0;
```

View Name: V$SESSION_CONNECT_INFO

```
select sid,authentication_type,osuser,network_service_banner
from   gv$session_connect_info
where  inst_id = USERENV('Instance');
```

View Name: GV$SESSION_CURSOR_CACHE

```
select inst_id,kgiccmax,kgicccnt,kgiccopd,kgiccope,kgiccopn,kgicchit,
       decode(kgiccopn,0,1,kgicchit/kgiccopn)
from   x$kgicc;
```

View Name: V$SESSION_CURSOR_CACHE

```
select MAXIMUM,COUNT,OPENED_ONCE,OPEN,OPENS,HITS,HIT_RATIO
from   GV$SESSION_CURSOR_CACHE
where  inst_id = USERENV('Instance');
```

View Name: GV$SESSION_EVENT

```
select s.inst_id,s.kslessid,d.kslednam,s.ksleswts,s.kslestmo,
       round(s.kslestim / 10000),round(s.kslestim / (10000 * s.ksleswts)),
       round(s.kslesmxt / 10000),s.kslestim
from   x$ksles s, x$ksled d
where  s.ksleswts != 0 and s.kslesenm = d.indx;
```

View Name: V$SESSION_EVENT

```
select sid,event,total_waits,total_timeouts,time_waited,average_wait,max_wait,
       time_waited_micro
from   gv$session_event
where  inst_id = USERENV('Instance');
```

View Name: GV$SESSION_LONGOPS

```
select inst_id,ksulosno,ksulosrn,ksulopna,ksulotna,ksulotde,ksulosfr,ksulotot,
       ksulouni,to_date(ksulostm,'MM/DD/RR HH24:MI:SS','NLS_CALENDAR=Gregorian'),
       to_date(ksulolut,'MM/DD/RR HH24:MI:SS','NLS_CALENDAR=Gregorian'),
       decode(sign(ksulotot-ksulosfr),-1,to_number(NULL),
       decode(ksulosfr,0,to_number(NULL),
       round(ksuloetm*((ksulotot-ksulosfr)/ksulosfr)))),ksuloetm,ksuloctx,ksulomsg,
       ksulounm,ksulosql,ksulosqh,ksuloqid
from   x$ksulop;
```

View Name: V$SESSION_LONGOPS

```
select SID,SERIAL#,OPNAME,TARGET,TARGET_DESC,SOFAR,TOTALWORK,UNITS,START_TIME,
       LAST_UPDATE_TIME,TIME_REMAINING,ELAPSED_SECONDS,CONTEXT,MESSAGE,USERNAME,
       SQL_ADDRESS,SQL_HASH_VALUE,QCSID
from   GV$SESSION_LONGOPS
where  inst_id = USERENV('Instance');
```

View Name: GV$SESSION_OBJECT_CACHE

```
select inst_id,kocstpin,kocsthit,kocsttht,decode(kocstpin,0,1,kocsthit/kocstpin),
       decode(kocstpin,0,1,kocsttht/kocstpin),kocstorf,kocstrfs,kocstofs,
       kocstfls,kocstshr,kocstcnt,kocstpnd,kocstsiz,kocstopt,kocstmax
from   x$kocst;
```

View Name: V$SESSION_OBJECT_CACHE

```
select pins,hits,true_hits,hit_ratio,true_hit_ratio,object_refreshes,
       cache_refreshes,object_flushes,cache_flushes,cache_shrinks,
       cached_objects,pinned_objects,cache_size,optimal_size,maximum_size
from gv$session_object_cache
where inst_id=userenv('Instance');
```

View Name: GV$SESSION_WAIT

```
select s.inst_id,s.indx,s.ksussseq,e.kslednam, e.ksledp1,s.ksussp1,
       s.ksussp1r,e.ksledp2,s.ksussp2,s.ksussp2r,e.ksledp3,s.ksussp3,s.ksussp3r,
       decode(s.ksusstim,0,0,-1,-1,-2,-2,
       decode(round(s.ksusstim/10000),0,-1,round(s.ksusstim/10000))),
       s.ksusewtm,decode(s.ksusstim,0,'WAITING',-2,'WAITED UNKNOWN TIME',-1,
       'WAITED SHORT TIME','WAITED KNOWN TIME')
from x$ksusecst s, x$ksled e
where bitand(s.ksspaflg,1)!=0
and bitand(s.ksuseflg,1)!=0
and s.ksussseq!=0
and s.ksussopc=e.indx;
```

View Name: V$SESSION_WAIT

```
select sid,seq#,event,p1text,p1,p1raw,p2text,p2,p2raw,p3text, p3,p3raw,wait_time,
       seconds_in_wait,state
from   gv$session_wait
where  inst_id = USERENV('Instance');
```

View Name: GV$SESSTAT

```
select inst_id,indx,ksusestn,ksusestv
from   x$ksusesta
```

```
where   bitand(ksspaflg,1)!=0
and     bitand(ksuseflg,1)!=0
and     ksusestn<
   (select ksusgstl
    from x$ksusgif);
```

View Name: **V$SESSTAT**

```
select SID,STATISTIC#,VALUE
from   GV$SESSTAT
where  inst_id = USERENV('Instance');
```

View Name: **GV$SESS_IO**

```
select inst_id,indx,ksusesbg,ksusescg,ksusespr,ksusesbc,ksusescc
from   x$ksusio
where  bitand(ksspaflg,1)!=0
and    bitand(ksuseflg,1)!=0;
```

View Name: **V$SESS_IO**

```
select SID,BLOCK_GETS,CONSISTENT_GETS,PHYSICAL_READS,BLOCK_CHANGES,
       CONSISTENT_CHANGES
from   GV$SESS_IO
where  inst_id = USERENV('Instance');
```

View Name: **GV$SGA**

```
select inst_id,ksmsdnam,ksmsdval
from   x$ksmsd;
```

View Name: **V$SGA**

```
select NAME,VALUE
from   GV$SGA
where  inst_id = USERENV('Instance');
```

View Name: **GV$SGASTAT**

```
select inst_id,'',ksmssnam,ksmsslen
from   x$ksmfs
where  ksmsslen>1 union all
   select inst_id,'shared pool',ksmssnam,sum(ksmsslen)
   from x$ksmss
   where ksmsslen>1
   group by inst_id,'shared pool',ksmssnam union all
      select inst_id,'large pool',ksmssnam, sum(ksmsslen)
      from x$ksmls
      where ksmsslen>1
      group by inst_id, 'large pool', ksmssnam  union all
         select inst_id,'java pool',ksmssnam,ksmsslen
         from x$ksmjs
         where ksmsslen>1;
```

View Name: **V$SGASTAT**

```
select POOL,NAME,BYTES
from   GV$SGASTAT
where  inst_id = USERENV('Instance');
```

View Name: GV$SGA_CURRENT_RESIZE_OPS

```
select sc.inst_id,gv.component,decode(sc.opcode,1,'GROW',2,'SHRINK',NULL),
       decode(sc.opmode,1,'MANUAL',2,'AUTO',NULL),pn.name,sc.initsize * gv.gransize,
       sc.targsize * gv.gransize,sc.realsize * gv.gransize,sc.starttime,sc.lasttime
from   x$ksmgsc sc, x$ksmgv gv, v$parameter pn
where  (sc.grantype = gv.grantype)
and    (sc.parno = pn.num)
and    (sc.opcode <> 0)
and    (sc.starttime is not null);
```

View Name: V$SGA_CURRENT_RESIZE_OPS

```
select component,oper_type,oper_mode,parameter,initial_size,target_size,
       current_size,start_time,last_update_time
from   gv$sga_current_resize_ops
where  inst_id = USERENV('Instance');
```

View Name: GV$SGA_DYNAMIC_COMPONENTS

```
select st.inst_id,gv.component,st.cursize * gv.gransize,st.minsize * gv.gransize,
       st.maxsize * gv.gransize,st.opercnt,
       decode(st.lastoper,1,'GROW',2,'SHRINK',NULL),
       decode(st.lastmode,1,'MANUAL',2,'AUTO',NULL),st.lasttime,gv.gransize
from   x$ksmgst st,x$ksmgv gv
where  (st.grantype = gv.grantype);
```

View Name: V$SGA_DYNAMIC_COMPONENTS

```
select component,current_size,min_size,max_size,oper_count,last_oper_type,
       last_oper_mode,last_oper_time,granule_size
from   gv$sga_dynamic_components
where  inst_id = USERENV('Instance');
```

View Name: GV$SGA_DYNAMIC_FREE_MEMORY

```
select inst_id,gv.gransize *
         (select count(*)
          from x$ksmge
          where granstate = 'FREE' or granstate = 'INVALID')
from   x$ksmgv gv
where  rownum=1;
```

View Name: V$SGA_DYNAMIC_FREE_MEMORY

```
select current_size
from   gv$sga_dynamic_free_memory
where  inst_id = USERENV('Instance');
```

View Name: GV$SGA_RESIZE_OPS

```
select    op.inst_id,gv.component,decode(op.opcode,1,'GROW',2,'SHRINK',NULL),
          decode(op.opmode,1,'MANUAL',2,'AUTO',NULL),pn.name,
          op.initsize * gv.gransize,op.targsize * gv.gransize,
          op.realsize * gv.gransize,
          decode(op.status,1,'NORMAL',2,'CANCEL',3,'ERROR',NULL),
          op.starttime, op.endtime
from      x$ksmgop op,x$ksmgv gv,v$parameter pn
where     (op.grantype = gv.grantype)
```

```
and      (op.parno = pn.num)
order by op.starttime;
```

View Name: **V$SGA_RESIZE_OPS**

```
select component,oper_type,oper_mode,parameter,initial_size,target_size,final_size,
       status,start_time,end_time
from   gv$sga_resize_ops
where  inst_id = USERENV('Instance');
```

View Name: **GV$SHARED_POOL_ADVICE**

```
select inst_id,sp_size,round(sp_size / basesp_size, 4),kglsim_size,kglsim_objs,
       kglsim_timesave,decode(kglsim_basetimesave,0,to_number(null),
       round(kglsim_timesave / kglsim_basetimesave,4)),kglsim_hits
from   x$kglsim;
```

View Name: **V$SHARED_POOL_ADVICE**

```
select shared_pool_size_for_estimate,shared_pool_size_factor,estd_lc_size,
       estd_lc_memory_objects,estd_lc_time_saved,estd_lc_time_saved_factor,
       estd_lc_memory_object_hits
from   gv$shared_pool_advice
where  inst_id = USERENV('Instance');
```

View Name: **GV$SHARED_POOL_RESERVED**

```
select avg(x$ksmspr.inst_id),sum(decode(ksmchcls,'R-free',ksmchsiz,0)),
       avg(decode(ksmchcls,'R-free',ksmchsiz,0)),sum(decode(ksmchcls,'R-free',1,0)),
       max(decode(ksmchcls,'R-free',ksmchsiz,0)),
       sum(decode(ksmchcls,'R-free',0,ksmchsiz)),
       avg(decode(ksmchcls,'R-free',0,ksmchsiz)),
       sum(decode(ksmchcls,'R-free',0,1)),max(decode(ksmchcls,'R-free',0,ksmchsiz)),
       avg(kghlurcn),avg(kghlurmi),avg(kghlurmz),avg(kghlurmx),avg(kghlunfu),
       avg(kghlunfs),avg(kghlumxa),avg(kghlumer),avg(kghlumes)
from   x$ksmspr,x$kghlu
where  ksmchcom not like '%reserved sto%';
```

View Name: **V$SHARED_POOL_RESERVED**

```
select FREE_SPACE,AVG_FREE_SIZE,FREE_COUNT,MAX_FREE_SIZE,USED_SPACE,AVG_USED_SIZE,
       USED_COUNT,MAX_USED_SIZE,REQUESTS,REQUEST_MISSES,LAST_MISS_SIZE,
       MAX_MISS_SIZE,REQUEST_FAILURES,LAST_FAILURE_SIZE,ABORTED_REQUEST_THRESHOLD,
       ABORTED_REQUESTS,LAST_ABORTED_SIZE
from   GV$SHARED_POOL_RESERVED
where  inst_id = USERENV('Instance');
```

View Name: **GV$SHARED_SERVER**

```
select inst_id,kmmsinam,kmmsiprp,kmmsista,kmmsinmg,kmmsinmb,kmmsibrk,kmmsivcp,
       kmmsiidl,kmmsibsy,kmmsitnc
from   x$kmmsi
where  bitand(kmmsiflg,1)!=0;
```

View Name: **V$SHARED_SERVER**

```
select NAME,PADDR,STATUS,MESSAGES,BYTES,BREAKS,CIRCUIT,IDLE,BUSY,REQUESTS
from   GV$SHARED_SERVER
where  inst_id = USERENV('Instance');
```

Scripts of X$ Tables Used
to Create V$ Views

View Name: GV$SHARED_SERVER_MONITOR

```
select inst_id,kmmsgcmx,kmmsgmmx,kmmsgsta+kmmsgutr,kmmsgtrm,kmmsgsmx
from   x$kmmsg;
```

View Name: V$SHARED_SERVER_MONITOR

```
select MAXIMUM_CONNECTIONS,MAXIMUM_SESSIONS,SERVERS_STARTED,SERVERS_TERMINATED,
       SERVERS_HIGHWATER
from   GV$SHARED_SERVER_MONITOR
where  inst_id = USERENV('Instance');
```

View Name: GV$SORT_SEGMENT

```
select inst_id,tablespace_name,segment_file,segment_block,extent_size,
       current_users,total_extents,total_blocks,used_extents,used_blocks,
       free_extents,free_blocks,added_extents,extent_hits,freed_extents,
       free_requests,max_size,max_blocks,max_used_size,max_used_blocks,
       max_sort_size,max_sort_blocks,relative_fno
from   x$ktstssd;
```

View Name: V$SORT_SEGMENT

```
select TABLESPACE_NAME,SEGMENT_FILE,SEGMENT_BLOCK,EXTENT_SIZE,CURRENT_USERS,
       TOTAL_EXTENTS,TOTAL_BLOCKS,USED_EXTENTS,USED_BLOCKS,FREE_EXTENTS,FREE_BLOCKS,
       ADDED_EXTENTS,EXTENT_HITS,FREED_EXTENTS,FREE_REQUESTS,MAX_SIZE,MAX_BLOCKS,
       MAX_USED_SIZE,MAX_USED_BLOCKS,MAX_SORT_SIZE,MAX_SORT_BLOCKS,RELATIVE_FNO
from   GV$SORT_SEGMENT
where  inst_id = USERENV('Instance');
```

View Name: GV$SORT_USAGE

```
select x$ktsso.inst_id,username,username,ktssoses,ktssosno,prev_sql_addr,
       prev_hash_value,ktssotsn,decode(ktssocnt,0,'PERMANENT',1,'TEMPORARY'),
       decode(ktssosegt,1,'SORT',2,'HASH',3,'DATA',4,'INDEX',5,
       'LOB_DATA',6,'LOB_INDEX','UNDEFINED'),ktssofno,ktssobno,ktssoexts,
       ktssoblks,ktssorfno
from   x$ktsso,v$session
where  ktssoses = v$session.saddr
and    ktssosno = v$session.serial#;
```

View Name: V$SORT_USAGE

```
select USERNAME,"USER",SESSION_ADDR,SESSION_NUM,SQLADDR,SQLHASH,TABLESPACE,
       CONTENTS,SEGTYPE,SEGFILE#,SEGBLK#,EXTENTS,BLOCKS,SEGRFNO#
from   GV$SORT_USAGE
where  inst_id = USERENV('Instance');
```

View Name: GV$SPPARAMETER

```
select  INST_ID,KSPSPFFTCTXSPSID,KSPSPFFTCTXSPNAME,KSPSPFFTCTXSPVALUE,
        KSPSPFFTCTXISSPECIFIED,KSPSPFFTCTXORDINAL,KSPSPFFTCTXCOMMENT
from    x$kspspfile
where  ((translate(KSPSPFFTCTXSPNAME,'_','#') not like '#%')
or      KSPSPFFTCTXISSPECIFIED = 'TRUE');
```

View Name: **V$SPPARAMETER**

```
select SID,NAME,VALUE,ISSPECIFIED,ORDINAL,UPDATE_COMMENT
from   GV$SPPARAMETER
where  INST_id = USERENV('Instance');
```

View Name: **GV$SQL**

```
select inst_id,kglnaobj,
       kglobhs0+kglobhs1+kglobhs2+kglobhs3+kglobhs4+kglobhs5+k globhs6+kglobt16,
       kglobt08+kglobt11,kglobt10,kglobt01,decode(kglobhs6,0,0,1),
       decode(kglhdlmd,0,0,1),kglhdlkc,kglobt04,kglobt05,kglobpc6,kglhdldc,
       substr(to_char(kglnatim,'YYYY-MM-DD/HH24:MI:SS'),1,19),kglhdivc,kglobt12,
       kglobt13,kglobt14,kglobt15,kglobt02,
       decode(kglobt32,0,'NONE',1,'ALL_ROWS',2,'FIRST_ROWS',3,'RULE',4,
'CHOOSE','UNKNOWN'),kglobtn0,kglobt17,kglobt18,kglhdkmk,kglhdpar,
       kglobtp0,kglnahsh ,kglobt30,kglobt09,kglobts0,kglobt19,kglobts1,
       kglobt20,kglobt21,kglobts2 ,kglobt06,kglobt07,kglobt28,kglhdadr,
       kglobt29,decode(bitand(kglobt00,64),6 4,'Y','N'),
       decode(kglobsta,1,'VALID',2,'VALID_AUTH_ERROR',3,'VALID_COMPILE_ERROR',4,
'VALID_UNAUTH',5,'INVALID_UNAUTH',6,'INVALID'),kglobt31,
       substr(to_char(kglobtt0,'YYYY-MM-DD/HH24:MI:SS'),1,19),
       decode(kglobt33,1,'Y','N'),kglhdclt
from   x$kglcursor
where  kglhdadr != kglhdpar
and    kglobt02 != 0;
```

View Name: **V$SQL**

```
select SQL_TEXT,SHARABLE_MEM,PERSISTENT_MEM,RUNTIME_MEM,SORTS,LOADED_VERSIONS,
       OPEN_VERSIONS,USERS_OPENING,FETCHES,EXECUTIONS,USERS_EXECUTING,LOADS,
       FIRST_LOAD_TIME,INVALIDATIONS,PARSE_CALLS,DISK_READS,BUFFER_GETS,
       ROWS_PROCESSED,COMMAND_TYPE,OPTIMIZER_MODE,OPTIMIZER_COST,PARSING_USER_ID,
       PARSING_SCHEMA_ID,KEPT_VERSIONS,ADDRESS,TYPE_CHK_HEAP,HASH_VALUE,
       PLAN_HASH_VALUE,CHILD_NUMBER,MODULE,MODULE_HASH,ACTION,ACTION_HASH,
       SERIALIZABLE_ABORTS,OUTLINE_CATEGORY,CPU_TIME,ELAPSED_TIME,OUTLINE_SID,
       CHILD_ADDRESS,SQLTYPE,REMOTE,OBJECT_STATUS,LITERAL_HASH_VALUE,
       LAST_LOAD_TIME,IS_OBSOLETE,CHILD_LATCH
from GV$SQL
where inst_id = USERENV('Instance');
```

View Name: **GV$SQLAREA**

```
select    inst_id,kglnaobj,
          sum(kglobhs0+kglobhs1+kglobhs2+kglobhs3+kglobhs4+kglobhs5+kglobhs6),
          sum(kglobt08+kglobt11),sum(kglobt10),sum(kglobt01),count(*)-1,
          sum(decode(kglobhs6,0,0,1)),decode(sum(decode(kglhdlmd,0,0,1)),0,0,
          sum(decode(kglhdlmd,0,0,1))-1),sum(kglhdlkc)/2,sum(kglobt04),
          sum(kglobt05),sum(kglobpc6),sum(kglhdldc)-1,
          substr(to_char(kglnatim,'YYYY-MM-DD/HH24:MI:SS'),1,19),
          sum(kglhdivc),sum(kglobt12),sum(kglobt13),sum(kglobt14),
          sum(kglobt15),sum(decode(kglobt09,0,kglobt02,0)),decode(count(*)-1,1,
          decode(sum(decode(kglobt09,0,kglobt32,0)),0,'NONE',1,'ALL_ROWS',2,
'FIRST_ROWS',3,'RULE',4,'CHOOSE','UNKNOWN'),'MULTIPLE CHILDREN PRESENT'),
          sum(decode(kglobt09,0,kglobt17,0)),sum(decode(kglobt09,0,kglobt18,0)),
          decode(sum(decode(kglhdkmk,0,0,1)),0,0,sum(decode(kglhdkmk,0,0,1))-1),
          kglhdpar,kglnahsh,kglobts0,kglobt19,kglobts1,kglobt20,sum(kglobt21),
          sum(kglobt06),sum(kglobt07),decode(kglobt33,1,'Y','N'),kglhdclt
```

Scripts of X$ Tables Used
to Create V$ Views

```
from       x$kglcursor
group by   inst_id,kglnaobj,kglhdpar,kglnahsh,kglnatim,kglobts0,kglobt19,kglobts1,
           kglobt20,decode(kglobt33,1,'Y','N'),kglhdclt
having sum (decode(kglobt09,0,kglobt02,0)) != 0;
```

View Name: V$SQLAREA

```
select SQL_TEXT,SHARABLE_MEM,PERSISTENT_MEM,RUNTIME_MEM,SORTS,VERSION_COUNT,
       LOADED_VERSIONS,OPEN_VERSIONS,USERS_OPENING,FETCHES,EXECUTIONS,
       USERS_EXECUTING,LOADS,FIRST_LOAD_TIME,INVALIDATIONS,PARSE_CALLS,DISK_READS,
       BUFFER_GETS,ROWS_PROCESSED,COMMAND_TYPE,OPTIMIZER_MODE,PARSING_USER_ID,
       PARSING_SCHEMA_ID,KEPT_VERSIONS,ADDRESS,HASH_VALUE,MODULE,MODULE_HASH,
       ACTION,ACTION_HASH,SERIALIZABLE_ABORTS,CPU_TIME,ELAPSED_TIME,IS_OBSOLETE,
       CHILD_LATCH
from   GV$SQLAREA
where  inst_id = USERENV('Instance');
```

View Name: GV$SQLTEXT

```
select inst_id,kglhdadr,kglnahsh,kgloboct,piece,name
from   x$kglna where kgloboct != 0;
```

View Name: V$SQLTEXT

```
select ADDRESS,HASH_VALUE,COMMAND_TYPE,PIECE,SQL_TEXT
from   GV$SQLTEXT
where  inst_id = USERENV('Instance');
```

View Name: GV$SQLTEXT_WITH_NEWLINES

```
select inst_id,kglhdadr,kglnahsh,kgloboct,piece,name
from   x$kglna1 where kgloboct != 0;
```

View Name: V$SQLTEXT_WITH_NEWLINES

```
select ADDRESS,HASH_VALUE,COMMAND_TYPE,PIECE,SQL_TEXT
from   GV$SQLTEXT_WITH_NEWLINES
where  inst_id = USERENV('Instance');
```

View Name: GV$SQL_BIND_DATA

```
select inst_id,kxsbdcur,kxsbdbnd,kxsbddty,kxsbdmxl,kxsbdpmx,kxsbdmal,kxsbdpre,
       kxsbdscl,kxsbdof1,kxsbdof2,kxsbdbfp,kxsbdbln,kxsbdavl,kxsbdbfl,kxsbdind,
       kxsbdval
from   x$kxsbd;
```

View Name: V$SQL_BIND_DATA

```
select CURSOR_NUM,POSITION,DATATYPE,SHARED_MAX_LEN,PRIVATE_MAX_LEN,ARRAY_SIZE,
       PRECISION,SCALE,SHARED_FLAG,SHARED_FLAG2,BUF_ADDRESS,BUF_LENGTH,VAL_LENGTH,
       BUF_FLAG,INDICATOR,VALUE
from   GV$SQL_BIND_DATA
where  inst_id = USERENV('Instance');
```

View Name: GV$SQL_BIND_METADATA

```
select inst_id,kglhdadr,position,kkscbndt,kkscbndl,kkscbnda,kksbvnnam
from   x$kksbv;
```

View Name: **V$SQL_BIND_METADATA**

```
select ADDRESS,POS
ITION,DATATYPE,MAX_LENGTH,ARRAY_LEN,BIND_NAME
from   GV$SQL_BIND_METADATA
where  inst_id = USERENV('Instance');
```

View Name: **GV$SQL_CURSOR**

```
select inst_id,kxsccur,kxsccfl,
       decode(kxsccsta,0,'CURNULL',1,'CURSYNTAX',2,'CURPARSE',3,'CURBOUND',4,
       'CURFETCH',5,'CURROW','ERROR'),kxsccphd,kxsccplk, kxsccclk, kxscccpn,
       kxscctbm,kxscctwm,kxscctbv,kxscctdv,kxsccbdf,kxsccflg,kxsccfl2
from   x$kxscc;
```

View Name: **V$SQL_CURSOR**

```
select CURNO,FLAG,STATUS,PARENT_HANDLE,PARENT_LOCK,CHILD_LOCK,CHILD_PIN,
       PERS_HEAP_MEM,WORK_HEAP_MEM,BIND_VARS,DEFINE_VARS,BIND_MEM_LOC,INST_FLAG,
       INST_FLAG2
from   GV$SQL_CURSOR
where  inst_id = USERENV('Instance');
```

View Name: **GV$SQL_PLAN**

```
select inst_id,kqlfxpl_phad,kqlfxpl_hash,kqlfxpl_chno,
       substr(kqlfxpl_oper,1,30),substr(kqlfxpl_oopt,1,30),
       substr(kqlfxpl_tqid,1,10),
       to_number(decode(kqlfxpl_objn,0,NULL, kqlfxpl_objn)),
case      when kqlfxpl_objname is not null
          then 'SYS'
          else u.name
          end,
       nvl(p.kqlfxpl_objname,o.name),substr(kqlfxpl_opti, 1, 20),kqlfxpl_opid,
       to_number(decode(kqlfxpl_opid,0,NULL,kqlfxpl_paid)),
       kqlfxpl_depth,kqlfxpl_pos,kqlfxpl_scols,
       to_number(decode(kqlfxpl_cost,0,NULL,kqlfxpl_cost)),
       to_number(decode(kqlfxpl_card,0,NULL,kqlfxpl_card)),
       to_number(decode(kqlfxpl_size,0,NULL,kqlfxpl_size)),
       substr(kqlfxpl_otag,1,35),substr(kqlfxpl_psta,1,5),substr(kqlfxpl_psto,1,5),
       to_number(decode(kqlfxpl_pnid,0,NULL,kqlfxpl_pnid)),
       kqlfxpl_other,substr(kqlfxpl_dist,1,20),
       to_number(decode(kqlfxpl_cpuc,0,NULL,kqlfxpl_cpuc)),
       to_number(decode(kqlfxpl_ioct,0,NULL,kqlfxpl_ioct)),
       to_number(decode(kqlfxpl_temp,0,NULL,kqlfxpl_temp)),
       kqlfxpl_keys,kqlfxpl_filter
from   x$kqlfxpl p, obj$ o, user$ u
where  p.kqlfxpl_hadd != p.kqlfxpl_phad
and    p.kqlfxpl_objn = o.obj#(+)
and    o.owner# = u.user#(+);
```

View Name: **V$SQL_PLAN**

```
select ADDRESS,HASH_VALUE,CHILD_NUMBER,OPERATION,OPTIONS,OBJECT_NODE,OBJECT#,
       OBJECT_OWNER,OBJECT_NAME,OPTIMIZER,ID,PARENT_ID,DEPTH,POSITION,
       SEARCH_COLUMNS,COST,CARDINALITY,BYTES,OTHER_TAG,PARTITION_START,
       PARTITION_STOP,PARTITION_ID,OTHER,DISTRIBUTION,CPU_COST,IO_COST,TEMP_SPACE,
       ACCESS_PREDICATES,FILTER_PREDICATES
from   GV$SQL_PLAN
where  inst_id = USERENV('Instance');
```

Scripts of **X$** Tables Used to Create **V$** Views

View Name: **GV$SQL_PLAN_STATISTICS**

```
select inst_id, PHADD_QESRS,HASHV_QESRS,CHILDNO_QESRS,OPERID_QESRS, EXECS_QESRS,
       LSTARTS_QESRS, STARTS_QESRS,LOUTROWS_QESRS,OUTROWS_QESRS,LCRGETS_QESRS,
       CRGETS_QESRS,LCUGETS_QESRS,CUGETS_QESRS,LDREADS_QESRS,DREADS_QESRS,
       LDWRITES_QESRS,DWRITES_QESRS,LELAPTIME_QESRS,ELAPTIME_QESRS
from   X$QESRSTAT;
```

View Name: **V$SQL_PLAN_STATISTICS**

```
select ADDRESS,HASH_VALUE,CHILD_NUMBER,OPERATION_ID,EXECUTIONS,LAST_STARTS,STARTS,
       LAST_OUTPUT_ROWS,OUTPUT_ROWS,LAST_CR_BUFFER_GETS,CR_BUFFER_GETS,
       LAST_CU_BUFFER_GETS,CU_BUFFER_GETS,LAST_DISK_READS,DISK_READS,
       LAST_DISK_WRITES,DISK_WRITES,LAST_ELAPSED_TIME,ELAPSED_TIME
from   GV$SQL_PLAN_STATISTICS
where  inst_id = USERENV('Instance');
```

View Name: **GV$SQL_PLAN_STATISTICS_ALL**

```
select inst_id,PHADD_QESRS,HASHV_QESRS,CHILDNO_QESRS,substr(oper_qesrs,1,30),
       substr(oopt_qesrs,1,30),substr(tqid_qesrs,1,10),
       to_number(decode(objn_qesrs,0,NULL,objn_qesrs)),
case
  when objname_qesrs is not null
  then 'SYS'
  else u.name
       end,nvl(p.objname_qesrs, o.name),substr(opti_qesrs,1,20),opid_qesrs,
       to_number(decode(opid_qesrs,0,NULL,paid_qesrs)),depth_qesrs,pos_qesrs,
       scols_qesrs,to_number(decode(cost_qesrs,0,NULL,cost_qesrs)),
       to_number(decode(card_qesrs,0,NULL,card_qesrs)),
       to_number(decode(size_qesrs,0,NULL,size_qesrs)),substr(otag_qesrs,1,35),
       substr(psta_qesrs,1,5),substr(psto_qesrs,1,5),
       to_number(decode(pnid_qesrs,0,NULL,pnid_qesrs)),other_qesrs,
       substr(dist_qesrs,1,20),to_number(decode(cpuc_qesrs,0,NULL,cpuc_qesrs)),
       to_number(decode(ioct_qesrs,0,NULL,ioct_qesrs)),
       to_number(decode(temp_qesrs,0,NULL,temp_qesrs)),KEYS_QESRS,
       FILTER_QESRS,EXECS_QESRS,LSTARTS_QESRS,STARTS_QESRS,LOUTROWS_QESRS,
       OUTROWS_QESRS,LCRGETS_QESRS,CRGETS_QESRS,LCUGETS_QESRS,CUGETS_QESRS,
       LDREADS_QESRS,DREADS_QESRS,LDWRITES_QESRS,DWRITES_QESRS,
       LELAPTIME_QESRS,ELAPTIME_QESRS,substr(SIZEPOLICY_QESRS,1,10),
       OPTIMAL_QESRS * 1024,ONEPASS_QESRS * 1024,LASTMEM_QESRS * 1024,
       substr(decode(LASTPASS_QESRS,0,'OPTIMAL',to_char(LASTPASS_QESRS) || 'PASS' ||
       decode(LASTPASS_QESRS,1,'','ES')),1,10),LASTDOP_QESRS,
       (OPTACTS_QESRS + SPAACTS_QESRS + MPAACTS_QESRS),OPTACTS_QESRS,SPAACTS_QESRS,
       MPAACTS_QESRS,ATIME_QESRS,
       to_number(decode(MAXTSEG_QESRS,0,NULL,MAXTSEG_QESRS)),
       to_number(decode(LASTTSEG_QESRS,0,NULL,LASTTSEG_QESRS))
from   X$QESRSTATALL p, obj$ o, user$ u
where  p.haddr_qesrs != p.phadd_qesrs
and    p.objn_qesrs = o.obj#(+)
and    o.owner# = u.user#(+);
```

View Name: **V$SQL_PLAN_STATISTICS_ALL**

```
select ADDRESS,HASH_VALUE,CHILD_NUMBER,OPERATION,OPTIONS,OBJECT_NODE,OBJECT#,
       OBJECT_OWNER,OBJECT_NAME,OPTIMIZER,ID,PARENT_ID,DEPTH,POSITION,
       SEARCH_COLUMNS,COST,CARDINALITY,BYTES,OTHER_TAG,PARTITION_START,
       PARTITION_STOP,PARTITION_ID,OTHER,DISTRIBUTION,CPU_COST,
       IO_COST,TEMP_SPACE,ACCESS_PREDICATES,FILTER_PREDICATES,EXECUTIONS,
       LAST_STARTS,STARTS,LAST_OUTPUT_ROWS,OUTPUT_ROWS,LAST_CR_BUFFER_GETS,
```

```
       CR_BUFFER_GETS,LAST_CU_BUFFER_GETS,CU_BUFFER_GETS,LAST_DISK_READS,
       DISK_READS,LAST_DISK_WRITES,DISK_WRITES,LAST_ELAPSED_TIME,ELAPSED_TIME,
       POLICY,ESTIMATED_OPTIMAL_SIZE,ESTIMATED_ONEPASS_SIZE,LAST_MEMORY_USED,
       LAST_EXECUTION,LAST_DEGREE,TOTAL_EXECUTIONS,OPTIMAL_EXECUTIONS,
       ONEPASS_EXECUTIONS,MULTIPASSES_EXECUTIONS,ACTIVE_TIME,
       MAX_TEMPSEG_SIZE,LAST_TEMPSEG_SIZE
from   GV$SQL_PLAN_STATISTICS_ALL
where  inst_id = USERENV('Instance');
```

View Name: **GV$SQL_REDIRECTION**

```
select c.inst_id,c.kglhdadr,c.kglhdpar,c.kglnahsh,c.kglobt09,c.kglobt17,c.kglobt18,
       c.kglobt02,
       decode(r.reason,1,'INVALID OBJECT',2,'ROWID',3,'QUERY REWRITE','READ ONLY'),
       r.error_code,r.position,r.sql_text_piece,r.error_msg
from   x$kglcursor c, x$kkssrd r
where  c.kglhdadr != c.kglhdpar
and    c.kglobt02 !=0
and    c.kglhdpar=r.parAddr
and    c.kglhdadr = r.kglhdadr;
```

View Name: **V$SQL_REDIRECTION**

```
select ADDRESS,PARENT_HANDLE,HASH_VALUE,CHILD_NUMBER,PARSING_USER_ID,
       PARSING_SCHEMA_ID,COMMAND_TYPE,REASON,ERROR_CODE,POSITION,SQL_TEXT_PIECE,
       ERROR_MESSAGE
from   GV$SQL_REDIRECTION
where  inst_id = USERENV('Instance');
```

View Name: **GV$SQL_SHARED_CURSOR**

```
select inst_id, kglhdadr, kglhdpar,
       decode(bitand(bitvector,POWER(2,0)),POWER(2,0),'Y','N'),
       decode(bitand(bitvector,POWER(2,1)),POWER(2,1),'Y','N'),
       decode(bitand(bitvector,POWER(2,2)),POWER(2,2),'Y','N'),
       decode(bitand(bitvector,POWER(2,3)),POWER(2,3),'Y','N'),
       decode(bitand(bitvector,POWER(2,4)),POWER(2,4),'Y','N'),
       decode(bitand(bitvector,POWER(2,5)),POWER(2,5),'Y','N'),
       decode(bitand(bitvector,POWER(2,6)),POWER(2,6),'Y','N'),
       decode(bitand(bitvector,POWER(2,7)),POWER(2,7),'Y','N'),
       decode(bitand(bitvector,POWER(2,8)),POWER(2,8),'Y','N'),
       decode(bitand(bitvector,POWER(2,9)),POWER(2,9),'Y','N'),
       decode(bitand(bitvector,POWER(2,10)),POWER(2,10),'Y','N'),
       decode(bitand(bitvector,POWER(2,11)),POWER(2,11),'Y','N'),
       decode(bitand(bitvector,POWER(2,12)),POWER(2,12),'Y','N'),
       decode(bitand(bitvector,POWER(2,13)),POWER(2,13),'Y','N'),
       decode(bitand(bitvector,POWER(2,14)),POWER(2,14),'Y','N'),
       decode(bitand(bitvector,POWER(2,15)),POWER(2,15),'Y','N'),
       decode(bitand(bitvector,POWER(2,16)),POWER(2,16),'Y','N'),
       decode(bitand(bitvector,POWER(2,17)),POWER(2,17),'Y','N'),
       decode(bitand(bitvector,POWER(2,18)),POWER(2,18),'Y','N'),
       decode(bitand(bitvector,POWER(2,19)),POWER(2,19),'Y','N'),
       decode(bitand(bitvector,POWER(2,20)),POWER(2,20),'Y','N'),
       decode(bitand(bitvector,POWER(2,21)),POWER(2,21),'Y','N'),
       decode(bitand(bitvector,POWER(2,22)),POWER(2,22),'Y','N'),
       decode(bitand(bitvector,POWER(2,23)),POWER(2,23),'Y','N'),
       decode(bitand(bitvector,POWER(2,24)),POWER(2,24),'Y','N'),
       decode(bitand(bitvector,POWER(2,25)),POWER(2,25),'Y','N'),
       decode(bitand(bitvector,POWER(2,26)),POWER(2,26),'Y','N'),
       decode(bitand(bitvector,POWER(2,27)),POWER(2,27),'Y','N'),
```

Scripts of X$ Tables Used to Create V$ Views

```
      decode(bitand(bitvector,POWER(2,28)),POWER(2,28),'Y','N'),
      decode(bitand(bitvector,POWER(2,29)),POWER(2,29),'Y','N'),
      decode(bitand(bitvector,POWER(2,30)),POWER(2,30),'Y','N')
from  x$kkscs;
```

View Name: V$SQL_SHARED_CURSOR

```
select ADDRESS,KGLHDPAR,UNBOUND_CURSOR,SQL_TYPE_MISMATCH,OPTIMIZER_MISMATCH,
       OUTLINE_MISMATCH,STATS_ROW_MISMATCH,LITERAL_MISMATCH,SEC_DEPTH_MISMATCH,
       EXPLAIN_PLAN_CURSOR,BUFFERED_DML_MISMATCH,PDML_ENV_MISMATCH,
       INST_DRTLD_MISMATCH,SLAVE_QC_MISMATCH,TYPECHECK_MISMATCH,AUTH_CHECK_MISMATCH,
       BIND_MISMATCH,DESCRIBE_MISMATCH,LANGUAGE_MISMATCH,TRANSLATION_MISMATCH,
       ROW_LEVEL_SEC_MISMATCH,INSUFF_PRIVS,INSUFF_PRIVS_REM,REMOTE_TRANS_MISMATCH,
       LOGMINER_SESSION_MISMATCH,INCOMP_LTRL_MISMATCH,OVERLAP_TIME_MISMATCH,
       SQL_REDIRECT_MISMATCH,MV_QUERY_GEN_MISMATCH,USER_BIND_PEEK_MISMATCH,
       TYPCHK_DEP_MISMATCH,NO_TRIGGER_MISMATCH,FLASHBACK_CURSOR
from   GV$SQL_SHARED_CURSOR
where  inst_id = USERENV('Instance');
```

View Name: GV$SQL_SHARED_MEMORY

```
select /*+use_nl(h,c)*/ c.inst_id,kglnaobj,kglnahsh,kglobhd6,
       rtrim(substr(ksmchcom,1,instr(ksmchcom, ':', 1, 1) - 1)),
       ltrim(substr(ksmchcom,-(length(ksmchcom) - (instr(ksmchcom,':',1,1))),
       (length(ksmchcom) - (instr(ksmchcom,':',1,1)) + 1))),ksmchcom,ksmchptr,
       ksmchsiz,ksmchcls,ksmchtyp,ksmchpar
from   x$kglcursor c, x$ksmhp h
where  ksmchds = kglobhd6
and    kglhdadr != kglhdpar;
```

View Name: V$SQL_SHARED_MEMORY

```
select SQL_TEXT,HASH_VALUE,HEAP_DESC,STRUCTURE,FUNCTION,CHUNK_COM,CHUNK_PTR,
       CHUNK_SIZE,ALLOC_CLASS,CHUNK_TYPE,SUBHEAP_DESC
from   GV$SQL_SHARED_MEMORY
where  inst_id = USERENV('Instance');
```

View Name: GV$SQL_WORKAREA

```
SELECT INST_ID,PHADD_QKSMM, HASHV_QKSMM, CHILDNO_QKSMM, WADDR_QKSMM,
       substr(OPERTYPE_QKSMM, 1, 20),
       to_number(decode(OPERTID_QKSMM, 65535, NULL, OPERTID_QKSMM)),
       substr(SIZEPOLICY_QKSMM, 1, 10),OPTIMAL_QKSMM * 1024, ONEPASS_QKSMM * 1024,
       LASTMEM_QKSMM * 1024,substr(decode(LASTPASS_QKSMM, 0, 'OPTIMAL',
       to_char(LASTPASS_QKSMM) || 'PASS' || decode(LASTPASS_QKSMM,1,'','ES')),1,10),
       LASTDOP_QKSMM,(OPTACTS_QKSMM + SPAACTS_QKSMM + MPAACTS_QKSMM),OPTACTS_QKSMM,
       SPAACTS_QKSMM,MPAACTS_QKSMM,ATIME_QKSMM,
       to_number(decode(MAXTSEG_QKSMM,0,NULL,MAXTSEG_QKSMM*1024)),
       to_number(decode(LASTTSEG_QKSMM,0,NULL,LASTTSEG_QKSMM*1024))
from   X$QKSMMWDS;
```

View Name: V$SQL_WORKAREA

```
select ADDRESS,HASH_VALUE,CHILD_NUMBER,WORKAREA_ADDRESS,OPERATION_TYPE,OPERATION_ID,
       POLICY,ESTIMATED_OPTIMAL_SIZE,ESTIMATED_ONEPASS_SIZE,LAST_MEMORY_USED,
       LAST_EXECUTION,LAST_DEGREE,TOTAL_EXECUTIONS,OPTIMAL_EXECUTIONS,
       ONEPASS_EXECUTIONS,MULTIPASSES_EXECUTIONS,ACTIVE_TIME,MAX_TEMPSEG_SIZE,
       LAST_TEMPSEG_SIZE
```

```
from   GV$SQL_WORKAREA
where  inst_id = USERENV('Instance');
```

View Name: GV$SQL_WORKAREA_ACTIVE

```
select INST_ID, WADDR, substr(OPER_TYPE,1,20),
       to_number(decode(OPID,65535,NULL,OPID)),
       substr(decode(bitand(MEM_FLAGS,1),0,'MANUAL','AUTO'),1,6),SID,
       to_number(decode(QCINSTID,65535,NULL,QCINSTID)),
       to_number(decode(QCSID,65535,NULL,QCSID)),ATIME,WA_SIZE * 1024,
       to_number(decode(bitand(MEM_FLAGS,1),0,NULL,EXP_SIZE*1024)),
       ACTUAL_MEM * 1024,MAX_MEM * 1024,PASSES,
       to_number(decode(KTSSOTSN,'',NULL,KTSSOSIZE*1024)),
       decode(KTSSOTSN,'',NULL,KTSSOTSN),
       to_number(decode(KTSSOTSN,'',NULL,KTSSORFNO)),
       to_number(decode(KTSSOTSN,'',NULL,KTSSOBNO))
from   x$qesmmiwt;
```

View Name: V$SQL_WORKAREA_ACTIVE

```
select WORKAREA_ADDRESS,OPERATION_TYPE,OPERATION_ID,POLICY,SID,QCINST_ID,QCSID,
       ACTIVE_TIME,WORK_AREA_SIZE,EXPECTED_SIZE,ACTUAL_MEM_USED,MAX_MEM_USED,
       NUMBER_PASSES,TEMPSEG_SIZE,TABLESPACE,SEGRFNO#,SEGBLK#
from   GV$SQL_WORKAREA_ACTIVE
where  INST_ID = USERENV('Instance');
```

View Name: GV$SQL_WORKAREA_HISTOGRAM

```
select INST_ID,LOWBND * 1024,(HIBND * 1024)-1,OPTIMAL,ONEPASS,MPASS,
       MPASS+ONEPASS+OPTIMAL
from   X$QESMMIWH;
```

View Name: V$SQL_WORKAREA_HISTOGRAM

```
select LOW_OPTIMAL_SIZE,HIGH_OPTIMAL_SIZE,OPTIMAL_EXECUTIONS,ONEPASS_EXECUTIONS,
       MULTIPASSES_EXECUTIONS,TOTAL_EXECUTIONS
from   GV$SQL_WORKAREA_HISTOGRAM
where  INST_ID = USERENV('Instance');
```

View Name: GV$STANDBY_LOG

```
select inst_id,slnum,slthr,slseq,slsiz*slbsz,slnab*slbsz,
       decode(bitand(slflg,1),0,'NO','YES'),
       decode(sign(slseq),0,'UNASSIGNED','ACTIVE'),
       to_number(sllos),to_date(sllot,'MM/DD/RR HH24:MI:SS',
       'NLS_CALENDAR=Gregorian'),to_number(slnxs),
       to_date(slnxt,'MM/DD/RR HH24:MI:SS','NLS_CALENDAR=Gregorian')
from   x$kccsl;
```

View Name: V$STANDBY_LOG

```
select GROUP#,THREAD#,SEQUENCE#,BYTES,USED,ARCHIVED,STATUS,FIRST_CHANGE#,
       FIRST_TIME,LAST_CHANGE#,LAST_TIME
from   GV$STANDBY_LOG
where  inst_id = USERENV('Instance');
```

Scripts of X$ Tables Used
to Create V$ Views

View Name: GV$STATISTICS_LEVEL

```
select  inst_id,name,description,
        decode(session_status,0,'DISABLED',1,'ENABLED','UNKNOWN'),
        decode(system_status,0,'DISABLED',1,'ENABLED', 'UNKNOWN'),
        decode(activation_level,0,'BASIC',1,'TYPICAL','ALL'),
        view_name,decode(session_changeable,0,'NO','YES')
from    x$prmsltyx;
```

View Name: V$STATISTICS_LEVEL

```
select  statistics_name,description,session_status,system_status,activation_level,
        statistics_view_name,session_settable
from    gv$statistics_level
where   inst_id = USERENV('Instance');
```

View Name: GV$STATNAME

```
select  inst_id,indx,ksusdnam,ksusdcls
from    x$ksusd;
```

View Name: V$STATNAME

```
select  STATISTIC#,NAME,CLASS
from    GV$STATNAME
where   inst_id = USERENV('Instance');
```

View Name: GV$STREAMS_APPLY_COORDINATOR

```
select      inst_id,sid_knst,serial_knst, applynum_knstacr, applyname_knstacr,
            decode(state_knstacr,0,'INITIALIZING',1,'APPLYING',2,
            'SHUTTING DOWN CLEANLY',3,'ABORTING'),
            total_applied_knstacr,total_waitdeps_knstacr,total_waitcommits_knstacr,
            total_admin_knstacr,total_assigned_knstacr,total_received_knstacr,
            total_errors_knstacr,lwm_time_knstacr, lwm_msg_num_knstacr,
            lwm_msg_time_knstacr,hwm_time_knstacr,hwm_msg_num_knstacr,
            hwm_msg_time_knstacr,startup_time_knstacr,elapsed_schedule_time_knstacr
from        x$knstacr x
where       type_knst=1
and exists
            (select 1
             from v$session s
             where s.sid=x.sid_knst
             and s.serial#=x.serial_knst);
```

View Name: V$STREAMS_APPLY_COORDINATOR

```
SELECT SID, SERIAL#, STATE,APPLY#,APPLY_NAME,TOTAL_APPLIED,TOTAL_WAIT_DEPS,
       TOTAL_WAIT_COMMITS,TOTAL_ADMIN,TOTAL_ASSIGNED,TOTAL_RECEIVED,
       TOTAL_ERRORS,LWM_TIME,LWM_MESSAGE_NUMBER,LWM_MESSAGE_CREATE_TIME,HWM_TIME,
       HWM_MESSAGE_NUMBER,HWM_MESSAGE_CREATE_TIME,STARTUP_TIME,
       ELAPSED_SCHEDULE_TIME
from   GV$STREAMS_APPLY_COORDINATOR
where  INST_ID = USERENV('Instance');
```

View Name: GV$STREAMS_APPLY_READER

```
select     inst_id,sid_knst,serial_knst,applynum_knstasl, applyname_knstasl,
           decode(state_knstasl,0,'IDLE',8,'DEQUEUE MESSAGES',10,
           'SCHEDULE MESSAGES'),total_msg_knstasl,last_rcv_time_knstasl,
           last_rcv_msg_num_knstasl,last_rcv_msg_time_knstasl, sga_used_knstasl,
           elapsed_dequeue_time_knstasl, elapsed_schedule_time_knstasl
from       x$knstasl x
where      type_knst=7
and exists
   (select 1
    from   v$session s
    where  s.sid=x.sid_knst
    and    s.serial#=x.serial_knst);
```

View Name: V$STREAMS_APPLY_READER

```
select SID,SERIAL#,APPLY#,APPLY_NAME,STATE,TOTAL_MESSAGES_DEQUEUED,DEQUEUE_TIME,
       DEQUEUED_MESSAGE_NUMBER,DEQUEUED_MESSAGE_CREATE_TIME,SGA_USED,
       ELAPSED_DEQUEUE_TIME,ELAPSED_SCHEDULE_TIME
from   GV$STREAMS_APPLY_READER
where  INST_ID = USERENV('Instance');
```

View Name: GV$STREAMS_APPLY_SERVER

```
select inst_id,sid_knst,serial_knst,applynum_knstasl, applyname_knstasl,
       slavid_knstasl,decode(state_knstasl,0,'IDLE',1,'POLL SHUTDOWN',2,
       'RECORD LOW-WATERMARK',3,'ADD PARTITION',4,'DROP PARTITION',5,
       'EXECUTE TRANSACTION',6,'WAIT COMMIT',7,'WAIT DEPENDENCY',8,
       'GET TRANSACTIONS',9,'WAIT FOR NEXT CHUNK'),
       xid_usn_knstasl,xid_slt_knstasl,xid_sqn_knstasl,cscn_knstasl,
       depxid_usn_knstasl,depxid_slt_knstasl,depxid_sqn_knstasl,
       depcscn_knstasl,msg_num_knstasl,total_assigned_knstasl,
       total_admin_knstasl,total_msg_knstasl, last_apply_time_knstasl,
       last_apply_msg_num_knstasl,last_apply_msg_time_knstasl,
       elapsed_dequeue_time_knstasl, elapsed_apply_time_knstasl
from   x$knstasl x
where  type_knst=2
and exists
   (select 1
    from v$session s
    where s.sid=x.sid_knst
    and s.serial#=x.serial_knst);
```

View Name: V$STREAMS_APPLY_SERVER

```
select SID,SERIAL#,APPLY#,APPLY_NAME,SERVER_ID,STATE,XIDUSN,XIDSLT,XIDSQN,
       COMMITSCN,DEP_XIDUSN,DEP_XIDSLT,DEP_XIDSQN,DEP_COMMITSCN,MESSAGE_SEQUENCE,
       TOTAL_ASSIGNED,TOTAL_ADMIN,TOTAL_MESSAGES_APPLIED,APPLY_TIME,
       APPLIED_MESSAGE_NUMBER,APPLIED_MESSAGE_CREATE_TIME,ELAPSED_DEQUEUE_TIME,
       ELAPSED_APPLY_TIME
from   GV$STREAMS_APPLY_SERVER
where  INST_ID = USERENV('Instance');
```

Scripts of X$ Tables Used to Create V$ Views

View Name: GV$STREAMS_CAPTURE

```
select inst_id,sid_knst,serial_knst,capnum_knstcap,capname_knstcap,
       startup_time_knstcap,decode(state_knstcap,0,'INITIALIZING',1,
    'CAPTURING CHANGES',2,'EVALUATING RULE',3,'ENQUEUING MESSAGE',4,
    'SHUTTING DOWN',5,'ABORTING',6,'CREATING LCR'),total_captured_knstcap,
       recent_time_knstcap,recent_msg_num_knstcap,recent_msg_time_knstcap,
       total_msg_enq_knstcap,enqueue_time_knstcap,enqueue_msg_num_knstcap,
       enqueue_msg_time_knstcap,elapsed_capture_time_knstcap,
       elapsed_rule_time_knstcap,elapsed_enqueue_time_knstcap,
       elapsed_lcr_time_knstcap
from   x$knstcap x
where  type_knst=8
and    exists
  (select 1
   from   v$session s
   where  s.sid=x.sid_knst
   and    s.serial#=x.serial_knst);
```

View Name: V$STREAMS_CAPTURE

```
select SID,SERIAL#,CAPTURE#,CAPTURE_NAME,STARTUP_TIME,STATE,TOTAL_MESSAGES_CAPTURED,
       CAPTURE_TIME,CAPTURE_MESSAGE_NUMBER,CAPTURE_MESSAGE_CREATE_TIME,
       TOTAL_MESSAGES_ENQUEUED,ENQUEUE_TIME,ENQUEUE_MESSAGE_NUMBER,
       ENQUEUE_MESSAGE_CREATE_TIME,ELAPSED_CAPTURE_TIME,ELAPSED_RULE_TIME,
       ELAPSED_ENQUEUE_TIME,ELAPSED_LCR_TIME
from   GV$STREAMS_CAPTURE
where  INST_ID = USERENV('Instance');
```

View Name: GV$SUBCACHE

```
select inst_id,kglnaown,kglnaobj,kglobtyp,kqlfshpn,kqlfscid,kqlfsscc,kqlfsesp,
       kqlfsasp, kqlfsusp
from   x$kqlset;
```

View Name: V$SUBCACHE

```
select OWNER_NAME,NAME,TYPE,HEAP_NUM,CACHE_ID,CACHE_CNT,HEAP_SZ,HEAP_ALOC,HEAP_USED
from   GV$SUBCACHE
where  inst_id = USERENV('Instance');
```

View Name: GV$SYSSTAT

```
select inst_id,indx,ksusdnam,ksusdcls,ksusgstv
from   x$ksusgsta;
```

View Name: V$SYSSTAT

```
select STATISTIC#,NAME,CLASS,VALUE
from   GV$SYSSTAT
where  inst_id = USERENV('Instance');
```

View Name: GV$SYSTEM_CURSOR_CACHE

```
select inst_id,kgicsopn,kgicshit,decode(kgicsopn,0,1,kgicshit/kgicsopn)
from   x$kgics;
```

View Name: V$SYSTEM_CURSOR_CACHE

```
select OPENS,HITS,HIT_RATIO
from   GV$SYSTEM_CURSOR_CACHE
where  inst_id = USERENV('Instance');
```

View Name: GV$SYSTEM_EVENT

```
select d.inst_id,d.kslednam,s.ksleswts,s.kslestmo,round(s.kslestim / 10000),
       round(s.kslestim / (10000 * s.ksleswts)),s.kslestim
from   x$kslei s,x$ksled d
where  s.ksleswts != 0
and    s.indx = d.indx;
```

View Name: V$SYSTEM_EVENT

```
select event,total_waits,total_timeouts,time_waited,average_wait,time_waited_micro
from   gv$system_event
where  inst_id = USERENV('Instance');
```

View Name: GV$SYSTEM_PARAMETER

```
select x.inst_id,x.indx+1,ksppinm,ksppity,ksppstvl,ksppstdf,
       decode(bitand(ksppiflg/256,1),1,'TRUE','FALSE'),
       decode(bitand(ksppiflg/65536,3),1,'IMMEDIATE',2,'DEFERRED','FALSE'),
       decode(bitand(ksppstvf,7),1,'MODIFIED','FALSE'),
       decode(bitand(ksppstvf,2),2,'TRUE','FALSE'),ksppdesc, ksppstcmnt
from   x$ksppi x, x$ksppsv y
where  (x.indx = y.indx)
and    ((translate(ksppinm,'_','#') not like '#%')
or     (ksppstdf = 'FALSE'));
```

View Name: V$SYSTEM_PARAMETER

```
select NUM,NAME,TYPE,VALUE,ISDEFAULT,ISSES_MODIFIABLE,ISSYS_MODIFIABLE,ISMODIFIED,
       ISADJUSTED,DESCRIPTION,UPDATE_COMMENT
from   GV$SYSTEM_PARAMETER
where  inst_id = USERENV('Instance');
```

View Name: GV$SYSTEM_PARAMETER2

```
select  x.inst_id,kspftctxpn,ksppinm,ksppity,kspftctxvl,kspftctxdf,
        decode(bitand(ksppiflg/256,1),1,'TRUE','FALSE'),
        decode(bitand(ksppiflg/65536,3),1,'IMMEDIATE',2,'DEFERRED','FALSE'),
        decode(bitand(kspftctxvf,7),1,'MODIFIED','FALSE'),
        decode(bitand(kspftctxvf,2),2,'TRUE','FALSE'),ksppdesc,kspftctxvn,kspftctxct
```

```
from    x$ksppi x, x$ksppsv2 y
where  ((x.indx+1) = kspftctxpn)
and    ((translate(ksppinm,'_','#') not like '#%')
or     (kspftctxdf = 'FALSE'));
```

View Name: V$SYSTEM_PARAMETER2

```
select NUM,NAME,TYPE,VALUE,ISDEFAULT,ISSES_MODIFIABLE,ISSYS_MODIFIABLE,ISMODIFIED,
       ISADJUSTED,DESCRIPTION,ORDINAL,UPDATE_COMMENT
from   GV$SYSTEM_PARAMETER2
where  inst_id = USERENV('Instance');
```

View Name: GV$TABLESPACE

```
select inst_id,tstsn,tsnam,decode(bitand(tsflg, 2),2,'NO','YES')
from   x$kccts
where  tstsn != -1;
```

View Name: V$TABLESPACE

```
select TS#,NAME,INCLUDED_IN_DATABASE_BACKUP
from   GV$TABLESPACE
where  inst_id = USERENV('Instance');
```

View Name: GV$TEMPFILE

```
select tf.inst_id,tf.tfnum,to_number(tf.tfcrc_scn),to_date(tf.tfcrc_tim,
       'MM/DD/RR HH24:MI:SS','NLS_CALENDAR=Gregorian'),tf.tftsn,tf.tfrfn,
       decode(bitand(tf.tfsta,2),0,'OFFLINE',2,'ONLINE','UNKNOWN'),
       decode(bitand(tf.tfsta, 12), 0,'DISABLED',4,'READ ONLY',12,'READ WRITE',
       'UNKNOWN'),fh.fhtmpfsz*tf.tfbsz,fh.fhtmpfsz,tf.tfcsz*tf.tfbsz,tf.tfbsz,
       fn.fnnam
from   x$kcctf tf,x$kccfn fn,x$kcvfhtmp fh
where  fn.fnfno=tf.tfnum
and    fn.fnfno=fh.htmpxfil
and    tf.tffnh=fn.fnnum
and    tf.tfdup!=0
and    fn.fntyp=7
and    fn.fnnam is not null;
```

View Name: V$TEMPFILE

```
select FILE#,CREATION_CHANGE#,CREATION_TIME,TS#,RFILE#,STATUS,ENABLED,BYTES,BLOCKS,
       CREATE_BYTES,BLOCK_SIZE,NAME
from   GV$TEMPFILE
where  inst_id = USERENV('Instance');
```

View Name: GV$TEMPORARY_LOBS

```
select   inst_id,kdltsno,sum(kdltctmp),sum(kdltnctmp)
from     X$KDLT
group by inst_id,kdltsno
order by kdltsno;
```

View Name: **V$TEMPORARY_LOBS**

```
select SID,CACHE_LOBS,NOCACHE_LOBS
from   GV$TEMPORARY_LOBS
where  inst_id = USERENV('Instance');
```

View Name: **GV$TEMPSTAT**

```
select k.inst_id,k.kcftiofno,k.kcftiopyr,k.kcftiopyw,k.kcftiopbr,k.kcftiopbw,
       k.kcftiosbr,k.kcftioprt,k.kcftiopwt,k.kcftiosbt,k.kcftioavg,k.kcftiolst,
       k.kcftiomin,k.kcftiormx,k.kcftiowmx
from   x$kcftio k,x$kcctf f
where  f.tfdup <> 0
and    f.tfnum=k.kcftiofno;
```

View Name: **V$TEMPSTAT**

```
select FILE#,PHYRDS,PHYWRTS,PHYBLKRD,PHYBLKWRT,SINGLEBLKRDS,READTIM,WRITETIM,
       SINGLEBLKRDTIM,AVGIOTIM,LSTIOTIM,MINIOTIM,MAXIORTM,MAXIOWTM
from   GV$TEMPSTAT
where  inst_id = USERENV('Instance');
```

View Name: **GV$TEMP_CACHE_TRANSFER**

```
select x.inst_id,kcftiofno,KCFTIOX2NC,KCFTIOX2NFWC,KCFTIOX2NFSC,KCFTIOX2SC,
       KCFTIOX2SFWC,KCFTIOS2NC,KCFTIOS2NFSC,KCFTIORBRC,KCFTIORBRFWC,KCFTION2XC,
       KCFTIOS2XC,KCFTION2SC
from   x$kcftio x, x$kcctf tf
where  x.kcftiofno = tf.tfnum;
```

View Name: **V$TEMP_CACHE_TRANSFER**

```
select file_number,x_2_null, x_2_null_forced_write,x_2_null_forced_stale,x_2_s,
       x_2_s_forced_write,s_2_null,s_2_null_forced_stale,rbr,rbr_forced_write,
       null_2_x, s_2_x, null_2_s
from   gv$temp_cache_transfer
where  inst_id = USERENV('Instance');
```

View Name: **GV$TEMP_EXTENT_MAP**

```
select /*+ ordered use_nl(me) */ me.inst_id,ts.name,me.ktftmetfno,me.ktftmebno,
       me.ktftmeblks*ts.blocksize,me.ktftmeblks,me.ktftmeinst,me.ktftmefno
from   ts$ ts,x$ktftme me
where  ts.contents$ = 1
and    ts.bitmapped <> 0
and    ts.online$ = 1
and    ts.ts# = me.ktftmetsn;
```

View Name: **V$TEMP_EXTENT_MAP**

```
select TABLESPACE_NAME,FILE_ID,BLOCK_ID,BYTES,BLOCKS,OWNER,RELATIVE_FNO
from   GV$TEMP_EXTENT_MAP
where  inst_id = USERENV('Instance');
```

View Name: GV$TEMP_EXTENT_POOL

```
select /*+ ordered use_nl(fc) */ fc.inst_id,ts.name,fc.ktstfctfno,fc.ktstfcec,
       fc.ktstfceu,fc.ktstfcbc,fc.ktstfcbu,fc.ktstfcbc*ts.blocksize,
       fc.ktstfcbu*ts.blocksize,fc.ktstfcfno
from   ts$ ts,x$ktstfc fc
where  ts.contents$ = 1
and    ts.bitmapped <> 0
and    ts.online$ = 1
and    ts.ts# = fc.ktstfctsn;
```

View Name: V$TEMP_EXTENT_POOL

```
select TABLESPACE_NAME,FILE_ID,EXTENTS_CACHED,EXTENTS_USED,BLOCKS_CACHED,
       BLOCKS_USED,BYTES_CACHED,BYTES_USED,RELATIVE_FNO
from   GV$TEMP_EXTENT_POOL
where  inst_id = USERENV('Instance');
```

View Name: GV$TEMP_PING

```
select x.inst_id, kcftiofno,0,KCFTIOX2NC,KCFTIOX2NFWC,KCFTIOX2NFSC,KCFTIOX2SC,
       KCFTIOX2SFWC,0,0,KCFTIOS2NC,KCFTIOS2NFSC,0,0,0,0,KCFTIORBRC,KCFTIORBRF
       WC,0,0,0,KCFTION2XC,KCFTIOS2XC,0,KCFTION2SC,0,0
from   x$kcftio x,x$kcctf tf
where  x.kcftiofno = tf.tfnum;
```

View Name: V$TEMP_PING

```
select file_number,frequency,x_2_null,x_2_null_forced_write, x_2_null_forced_stale,
       x_2_s, x_2_s_forced_write,x_2_ssx,x_2_ssx_forced_write,s_2_null,
       s_2_null_forced_stale,ss_2_null,ss_2_rls,wrb,wrb_forced_write,rbr,
       rbr_forced_write,rbr_forced_stale,cbr,cbr_forced_write,null_2_x, s_2_x,
       ssx_2_x, null_2_s, null_2_ss, op_2_ss
from   gv$temp_ping
where  inst_id = USERENV('Instance');
```

View Name: GV$TEMP_SPACE_HEADER

```
select /*+ ordered use_nl(hc) */ hc.inst_id,ts.name,hc.ktfthctfno,
      (hc.ktfthcsz - hc.ktfthcfree)*ts.blocksize,(hc.ktfthcsz - hc.ktfthcfree),
      hc.ktfthcfree*ts.blocksize, hc.ktfthcfree, hc.ktfthcfno
from   ts$ ts, x$ktfthc hc
where  ts.contents$ = 1
and    ts.bitmapped <> 0
and    ts.online$ = 1
and    ts.ts# = hc.ktfthctsn
and    hc.ktfthccval = 0;
```

View Name: V$TEMP_SPACE_HEADER

```
select TABLESPACE_NAME,FILE_ID,BYTES_USED,BLOCKS_USED,BYTES_FREE,BLOCKS_FREE,
       RELATIVE_FNO
from   GV$TEMP_SPACE_HEADER
where  inst_id = USERENV('Instance');
```

View Name: GV$THREAD

```
select inst_id,rtnum,decode(bitand(rtsta,1),1,'OPEN','CLOSED'),
      decode(bitand(rtsta,6),0,'DISABLED',2,'PRIVATE',6,'PUBLIC','UNKNOWN'),
      rtnlf,rtsid,to_date(rtots,'MM/DD/RR HH24:MI:SS','NLS_CALENDAR=Gregorian'),
      rtcln,rtseq,to_number(rtckp_scn),to_date(rtckp_tim,'MM/DD/RR HH24:MI:SS',
      'NLS_CALENDAR=Gregorian'),to_number(rtenb),
      to_date(rtets,'MM/DD/RR HH24:MI:SS','NLS_CALENDAR=Gregorian'),
      to_number(rtdis), to_date(rtdit,'MM/DD/RR HH24:MI:SS',
      'NLS_CALENDAR=Gregorian')
from   x$kccrt
where  rtnlf!=0;
```

View Name: V$THREAD

```
select THREAD#,STATUS,ENABLED,GROUPS,INSTANCE,OPEN_TIME,CURRENT_GROUP#,SEQUENCE#,
      CHECKPOINT_CHANGE#,CHECKPOINT_TIME,ENABLE_CHANGE#,ENABLE_TIME,
      DISABLE_CHANGE#,DISABLE_TIME
from   GV$THREAD
where  inst_id = USERENV('Instance');
```

View Name: GV$TIMER

```
select inst_id,ksutmtim
from   x$ksutm;
```

View Name: V$TIMER

```
select HSECS
from   GV$TIMER
where  inst_id = USERENV('Instance');
```

View Name: GV$TIMEZONE_NAMES

```
select TZNAME,TZABBREV
from   X$TIMEZONE_NAMES;
```

View Name: V$TIMEZONE_NAMES

```
select TZNAME,TZABBREV
from   GV$TIMEZONE_NAMES;
```

View Name: GV$TRANSACTION

```
select inst_id,ktcxbxba,kxidusn,kxidslt,kxidsqn,ktcxbkfn,kubablk,kubaseq,kubarec,
      decode(ktcxbsta,0,'IDLE',1,'COLLECTING',2,'PREPARED',3,'COMMITTED',4,
      'HEURISTIC ABORT',5,'HEURISTIC COMMIT',6,'HEURISTIC DAMAGE',7,'TIMEOUT',9,
      'INACTIVE',10,'ACTIVE',11,'PTX PREPARED',12,'PTX COMMITTED','UNKNOWN'),
      ktcxbstm,ktcxbssb,ktcxbssw,ktcxbsen,ktcxbsfl,ktcxbsbk,ktcxbssq,ktcxbsrc,
      ktcxbses,ktcxbflg, decode(bitand(ktcxbflg,16),0,'NO','YES'),
      decode(bitand(ktcxbflg,32),0,'NO','YES'),decode(bitand(ktcxbflg,64),0,
      'NO','YES'), decode(bitand(ktcxbflg,8388608),0,'NO','YES'),ktcxbnam,
      ktcxbpus,ktcxbpsl,ktcxbpsq,ktcxbpxu,ktcxbpxs,ktcxbpxq,ktcxbdsb,ktcxbdsw,
      ktcxbubk,ktcxburc,ktcxblio,ktcxbpio,ktcxbcrg,ktcxbcrc
```

```
from    x$ktcxb
where   bitand(ksspaflg,1)!=0
and     bitand(ktcxbflg,2)!=0;
```

View Name: V$TRANSACTION

```
select ADDR,XIDUSN,XIDSLOT,XIDSQN,UBAFIL,UBABLK,UBASQN,UBAREC,STATUS,START_TIME,
       START_SCNB,START_SCNW,START_UEXT,START_UBAFIL,START_UBABLK,START_UBASQN,
       START_UBAREC,SES_ADDR,FLAG,SPACE,RECURSIVE,NOUNDO,PTX,NAME,PRV_XIDUSN,
       PRV_XIDSLT,PRV_XIDSQN,PTX_XIDUSN,PTX_XIDSLT,PTX_XIDSQN,"DSCN-B","DSCN-W",
       USED_UBLK,USED_UREC,LOG_IO,PHY_IO,CR_GET,CR_CHANGE
from    gv$transaction
where   inst_id = USERENV('Instance');
```

View Name: GV$TRANSACTION_ENQUEUE

```
select /*+ ordered use_nl(l), use_nl(s), use_nl(r) +*/ s.inst_id,l.ktcxbxba,
       l.ktcxblkp,s.ksusenum,r.ksqrsidt,r.ksqrsid1,r.ksqrsid2,l.ksqlkmod,l.ksqlkreq,
       l.ksqlkctim,l.ksqlklblk
from    x$ktcxb l,x$ksuse s,x$ksqrs r
where   l.ksqlkses=s.addr
and     bitand(l.ksspaflg,1)!=0
and     (l.ksqlkmod!=0
or      l.ksqlkreq!=0)
and     l.ksqlkres=r.addr;
```

View Name: V$TRANSACTION_ENQUEUE

```
select ADDR,KADDR,SID,TYPE,ID1,ID2,LMODE,REQUEST,CTIME,BLOCK
from    GV$TRANSACTION_ENQUEUE
where   inst_id = USERENV('Instance');
```

View Name: GV$TYPE_SIZE

```
select inst_id,kqfszcom,kqfsztyp,kqfszdsc,kqfszsiz
from    x$kqfsz;
```

View Name: V$TYPE_SIZE

```
select COMPONENT,TYPE,DESCRIPTION,TYPE_SIZE
from    GV$TYPE_SIZE
where   inst_id = USERENV('Instance');
```

View Name: GV$UNDOSTAT

```
select inst_id,to_date(KTUSMSTRBEGTIME,'MM/DD/RR HH24:MI:SS',
       'NLS_CALENDAR=Gregorian'),to_date(KTUSMSTRENDTIME,'MM/DD/RR HH24:MI:SS',
       'NLS_CALENDAR=Gregorian'),KTUSMSTTSN,KTUSMSTUSU,KTUSMSTTCT,KTUSMSTMQL,
       KTUSMSTMTC,KTUSMSTUAC,KTUSMSTUBS,KTUSMSTUBR,KTUSMSTXAC,KTUSMSTXBS,KTUSMSTXBR,
       KTUSMSTSOC, KTUSMSTOOS
from    X$KTUSMST;
```

View Name: V$UNDOSTAT

```
select to_date(KTUSMSTRBEGTIME,'MM/DD/RR HH24:MI:SS','NLS_CALENDAR=Gregorian'),
       to_date(KTUSMSTRENDTIME,'MM/DD/RR HH24:MI:SS','NLS_CALENDAR=Gregorian'),
       KTUSMSTTSN,KTUSMSTUSU,KTUSMSTTCT,KTUSMSTMQL,KTUSMSTMTC,
       KTUSMSTUAC,KTUSMSTUBS,KTUSMSTUBR,KTUSMSTXAC,KTUSMSTXBS,KTUSMSTXBR,KTUSMSTSOC,
```

```
        KTUSMSTOOS
from    X$KTUSMST
where   INST_ID = userenv('instance');
```

View Name: GV$VERSION

```
select inst_id,banner
from   x$version;
```

View Name: V$VERSION

```
select BANNER
from   GV$VERSION
where  inst_id = USERENV('Instance');
```

View Name: GV$VPD_POLICY

```
select c.inst_id,c.kglhdadr,c.kglhdpar,c.kglnahsh,c.kglobt09, p.kzrtpdow,p.kzrtpdon,
       p.kzrtpdgp,p.kzrtpdpy,p.kzrtpdpo,p.kzrtpdtx
from   x$kglcursor c, x$kzrtpd p
where  c.kglhdadr != c.kglhdpar
and    c.kglobt02 != 0
and    c.kglhdpar=p.kzrtpdpa
and    c.kglhdadr = p.kzrtpdad;
```

View Name: V$VPD_POLICY

```
select ADDRESS,PARADDR,SQL_HASH,CHILD_NUMBER,OBJECT_OWNER,OBJECT_NAME,
       POLICY_GROUP,POLICY,POLICY_FUNCTION_OWNER,PREDICATE
from   GV$VPD_POLICY
where  inst_id = USERENV('Instance');
```

View Name: GV$WAITSTAT

```
select inst_id,decode(indx,1,'data block',2,'sort block',3,'save undo block',4,
       'segment header',5,'save undo header',6,'free list',7,'extent map',8,
       '1st level bmb',9,'2nd level bmb',10,'3rd level bmb', 11,'bitmap block',12,
       'bitmap index block',13,'file header block',14,'unused',15,
       'system undo header',16,'system undo block', 17,'undo header',18,
       'undo block'), count,time
from   x$kcbwait
where  indx!=0;
```

View Name: V$WAITSTAT

```
select class,count,time
from   gv$waitstat
where  inst_id = USERENV('Instance');
```

View Name: GV$_LOCK

```
select USERENV('Instance'),laddr,kaddr,saddr,raddr,lmode,request,ctime,block
from   v$_lock1 union all
         select inst_id,addr,ksqlkadr,ksqlkses,ksqlkres,ksqlkmod,ksqlkreq,
                ksqlkctim,ksqlklblk
         from   x$ktadm
         where  bitand(kssobflg,1)!=0
         and (ksqlkmod!=0 or ksqlkreq!=0) union all
```

```
            select inst_id,ktcxbxba,ktcxblkp,ksqlkses,ksqlkres,ksqlkmod,ksqlkreq,
                   ksqlkctim,ksqlklblk
            from   x$ktcxb
            where  bitand(ksspaflg,1)!=0
            and    (ksqlkmod!=0 or ksqlkreq!=0);
```

View Name: V$_LOCK

```
select LADDR,KADDR,SADDR,RADDR,LMODE,REQUEST,CTIME,BLOCK
from   GV$_LOCK
where  inst_id = USERENV('Instance');
```

View Name: GV$_LOCK1

```
select inst_id,addr,ksqlkadr,ksqlkses,ksqlkres,ksqlkmod,ksqlkreq, ksqlkctim,ksqlklblk
from   x$kdnssf
where  bitand(kssobflg,1)!=0
and    (ksqlkmod!=0 or ksqlkreq!=0) union all
            select inst_id,addr,ksqlkadr,ksqlkses,ksqlkres,ksqlkmod,ksqlkreq,ksqlkctim,
                   ksqlklblk
            from   x$ksqeq
            where  bitand(kssobflg,1)!=0
            and    (ksqlkmod!=0 or ksqlkreq!=0);
```

View Name: V$_LOCK1

```
select LADDR,KADDR,SADDR,RADDR,LMODE,REQUEST,CTIME,BLOCK
from   GV$_LOCK1
where  inst_id = USERENV('Instance');
```

View Name: GV$_SEQUENCES

```
select inst_id,KGLNAOWN,KGLNAOBJ,KGLOBT08,decode(bitand(KGLOBT00,1),0,'N','Y'),
       decode(bitand(KGLOBT00,2),0,'N','Y'),decode(bitand(KGLOBT00,16),0,'N','Y'),
       KGLOBTN0,KGLOBTN2,KGLOBTN3,KGLOBTN1,decode(bitand(KGLOBT09,1),0,'N','Y'),
       decode(bitand(KGLOBT09,2),0,'N','Y'),KGLOBTN4,KGLOBTN5,
       decode(KGLOBT10,1,'Y','N'),decode(KGLOBT10,1,KGLOBT02,null)
from   X$KGLOB
where  KGLOBTYP = 6
and    KGLOBT11 = 1 ;
```

View Name: V$_SEQUENCES

```
select SEQUENCE_OWNER,SEQUENCE_NAME,OBJECT#,ACTIVE_FLAG,REPLENISH_FLAG,
       WRAP_FLAG, NEXTVALUE, MIN_VALUE, MAX_VALUE, INCREMENT_BY, CYCLE_FLAG,
       ORDER_FLAG, CACHE_SIZE, HIGHWATER, BACKGROUND_INSTANCE_LOCK,
       INSTANCE_LOCK_FLAGS
from   GV$_SEQUENCES
where  inst_id = USERENV('Instance');
```

APPENDIX
C

The X$ Tables (DBA)

The x$ tables are usually not mentioned or talked about in many Oracle books or even in the Oracle user community. For this reason, I am including them in this book as one of the only references available. The x$ tables vary in structure and number based on the database version and release used. Run the queries on your version of the database to get the number of views and structure for your specific version.

The topics covered in this appendix include the following:

- Oracle9i X$ tables ordered by name
- Oracle9i X$ indexes
- Oracle9i X$ tables cross referenced to V$ views
- Oracle9i GV$ views cross referenced to X$ tables
- Oracle9i X$ tables not referenced by a GV$ view

Oracle9i X$ Tables Ordered by Name

The following Oracle9i query produces this listing of 394 X$ tables, ordered by name:

```
select     name
from       v$fixed_table
where      name like 'X%'
order by   name;
```

X$ACTIVECKPT	X$BH	X$BUFQM
X$CKPTBUF	X$CLASS_STAT	X$CONTEXT
X$DUAL	X$ESTIMATED_MTTR	X$GLOBALCONTEXT
X$HOFP	X$HS_SESSION	X$JOXFC
X$JOXFD	X$JOXFM	X$JOXFR
X$JOXFS	X$JOXFT	X$K2GTE
X$K2GTE2	X$KCBBES	X$KCBBF
X$KCBBHS	X$KCBFWAIT	X$KCBKPFS
X$KCBKWRL	X$KCBLDRHIST	X$KCBLSC
X$KCBMMAV	X$KCBSC	X$KCBSDS
X$KCBSH	X$KCBSW	X$KCBVBL
X$KCBWAIT	X$KCBWBPD	X$KCBWDS
X$KCBWH	X$KCCAL	X$KCCBF
X$KCCBI	X$KCCBL	X$KCCBP
X$KCCBS	X$KCCCC	X$KCCCF
X$KCCCP	X$KCCDC	X$KCCDI

X$KCCDI2	X$KCCDL	X$KCCFC
X$KCCFE	X$KCCFN	X$KCCIC
X$KCCLE	X$KCCLH	X$KCCOR
X$KCCPA	X$KCCPD	X$KCCRM
X$KCCRS	X$KCCRT	X$KCCSL
X$KCCTF	X$KCCTS	X$KCFIO
X$KCFTIO	X$KCKCE	X$KCKFM
X$KCKTY	X$KCLCRST	X$KCLCURST
X$KCLFH	X$KCLFI	X$KCLFX
X$KCLLS	X$KCLQN	X$KCRFWS
X$KCRFX	X$KCRMF	X$KCRMT
X$KCRMX	X$KCRRALG	X$KCRRARCH
X$KCRRDEST	X$KCRRDSTAT	X$KCRRLNS
X$KCRRMS	X$KCVFH	X$KCVFHALL
X$KCVFHMRR	X$KCVFHONL	X$KCVFHTMP
X$KDLT	X$KDNSSF	X$KDXHS
X$KDXST	X$KGHLU	X$KGICC
X$KGICS	X$KGLAU	X$KGLBODY
X$KGLCLUSTER	X$KGLCURSOR	X$KGLDP
X$KGLINDEX	X$KGLLC	X$KGLLK
X$KGLMEM	X$KGLNA	X$KGLNA1
X$KGLOB	X$KGLPN	X$KGLRD
X$KGLSIM	X$KGLSN	X$KGLST
X$KGLTABLE	X$KGLTR	X$KGLTRIGGER
X$KGLXS	X$KGSKASP	X$KGSKCFT
X$KGSKCP	X$KGSKDOPP	X$KGSKPFT
X$KGSKPP	X$KGSKQUEP	X$KGSKTE
X$KGSKTO	X$KJBL	X$KJBLFX
X$KJBR	X$KJBRFX	X$KJCTFR
X$KJCTFRI	X$KJCTFS	X$KJDRHV
X$KJDRPCMHV	X$KJDRPCMPF	X$KJICVT
X$KJILFT	X$KJILKFT	X$KJIRFT

X$KJISFT	X$KJITRFT	X$KJMDDP
X$KJMSDP	X$KJXM	X$KKSAI
X$KKSBV	X$KKSCS	X$KKSSRD
X$KLCIE	X$KLPT	X$KMCQS
X$KMCVC	X$KMMDI	X$KMMDP
X$KMMRD	X$KMMSG	X$KMMSI
X$KNSTACR	X$KNSTASL	X$KNSTCAP
X$KNSTMVR	X$KNSTRPP	X$KNSTRQU
X$KOCST	X$KQDPG	X$KQFCO
X$KQFDT	X$KQFP	X$KQFSZ
X$KQFTA	X$KQFVI	X$KQFVT
X$KQLFXPL	X$KQLSET	X$KQRFP
X$KQRFS	X$KQRPD	X$KQRSD
X$KQRST	X$KRBAFF	X$KRVSLV
X$KRVSLVS	X$KRVXSV	X$KSBDD
X$KSBDP	X$KSFHDVNT	X$KSFMCOMPL
X$KSFMELEM	X$KSFMEXTELEM	X$KSFMFILE
X$KSFMFILEEXT	X$KSFMIOST	X$KSFMLIB
X$KSFMSUBELEM	X$KSFQP	X$KSFVQST
X$KSFVSL	X$KSFVSTA	X$KSIMAT
X$KSIMAV	X$KSIMSI	X$KSLECLASS
X$KSLED	X$KSLEI	X$KSLEMAP
X$KSLES	X$KSLLCLASS	X$KSLLD
X$KSLLT	X$KSLLW	X$KSLPO
X$KSLWSC	X$KSMDD	X$KSMFS
X$KSMFSV	X$KSMGE	X$KSMGOP
X$KSMGSC	X$KSMGST	X$KSMGV
X$KSMHP	X$KSMJCH	X$KSMJS
X$KSMLRU	X$KSMLS	X$KSMMEM
X$KSMNIM	X$KSMNS	X$KSMPP
X$KSMSD	X$KSMSP	X$KSMSPR
X$KSMSP_DSNEW	X$KSMSP_NWEX	X$KSMSS

X$KSMUP	X$KSOLSFTS	X$KSOLSSTAT
X$KSPPCV	X$KSPPCV2	X$KSPPI
X$KSPPO	X$KSPPSV	X$KSPPSV2
X$KSPSPFH	X$KSPSPFILE	X$KSQDN
X$KSQEQ	X$KSQRS	X$KSQST
X$KSRCCTX	X$KSRCDES	X$KSRCHDL
X$KSRMPCTX	X$KSRMSGDES	X$KSRMSGO
X$KSTEX	X$KSUCF	X$KSULL
X$KSULOP	X$KSULV	X$KSUMYSTA
X$KSUPGP	X$KSUPGS	X$KSUPL
X$KSUPR	X$KSUPRLAT	X$KSURLMT
X$KSURU	X$KSUSD	X$KSUSE
X$KSUSECON	X$KSUSECST	X$KSUSESTA
X$KSUSEX	X$KSUSGIF	X$KSUSGSTA
X$KSUSIO	X$KSUTM	X$KSUXSINST
X$KSXAFA	X$KSXRCH	X$KSXRCONQ
X$KSXRMSG	X$KSXRREPQ	X$KSXRSG
X$KTADM	X$KTCXB	X$KTFBFE
X$KTFBHC	X$KTFBUE	X$KTFTHC
X$KTFTME	X$KTPRXRS	X$KTPRXRT
X$KTRSO	X$KTSPSTAT	X$KTSSO
X$KTSTFC	X$KTSTSSD	X$KTTVS
X$KTUGD	X$KTURD	X$KTUSMST
X$KTUXE	X$KVII	X$KVIS
X$KVIT	X$KWDDEF	X$KWQPD
X$KWQPS	X$KWQSI	X$KXFPCDS
X$KXFPCMS	X$KXFPCST	X$KXFPDP
X$KXFPNS	X$KXFPPFT	X$KXFPSDS
X$KXFPSMS	X$KXFPSST	X$KXFPYS
X$KXFQSROW	X$KXSBD	X$KXSCC
X$KZDOS	X$KZEMAEA	X$KZEMAIE
X$KZRTPD	X$KZSPR	X$KZSRO

X$KZSRT	X$LCR	X$LE
X$LE_STAT	X$LOGMNR_ATTRIBUTE$	X$LOGMNR_CALLBACK
X$LOGMNR_COL$	X$LOGMNR_COLTYPE$	X$LOGMNR_CONTENTS
X$LOGMNR_DICT$	X$LOGMNR_DICTIONARY	X$LOGMNR_ENCRYPTED_OBJ$
X$LOGMNR_ENCRYPTION_PROFILE$	X$LOGMNR_IND$	X$LOGMNR_INDPART$
X$LOGMNR_LOGFILE	X$LOGMNR_LOGS	X$LOGMNR_OBJ$
X$LOGMNR_PARAMETERS	X$LOGMNR_PROCESS	X$LOGMNR_REGION
X$LOGMNR_ROOT$	X$LOGMNR_SESSION	X$LOGMNR_TAB$
X$LOGMNR_TABCOMPART$	X$LOGMNR_TABPART$	X$LOGMNR_TABSUBPART$
X$LOGMNR_TRANSACTION	X$LOGMNR_TS$	X$LOGMNR_TYPE$
X$LOGMNR_USER$	X$MESSAGES	X$NLS_PARAMETERS
X$NSV	X$OPTION	X$PRMSLTYX
X$QESMMAHIST	X$QESMMAPADV	X$QESMMIWH
X$QESMMIWT	X$QESMMSGA	X$QESRSTAT
X$QESRSTATALL	X$QKSMMWDS	X$QUIESCE
X$RFMP	X$RFMTE	X$TARGETRBA
X$TEMPORARY_LOB_REFCNT	X$TIMEZONE_NAMES	X$TRACE
X$TRACE_EVENTS	X$UGANCO	X$VERSION
X$VINST	X$XSAGGR	X$XSAWSO
X$XSSINFO		

Oracle9*i* X$ Indexes

The following Oracle9*i* query produces this listing of 326 X$ indexes, ordered by table name:

```
select     table_name, column_name, index_number
from       v$indexed_fixed_column
order by   table_name;
```

TABLE_NAME	COLUMN_NAME	INDEX_NUMBER
X$CLASS_STAT	ADDR	1
X$CLASS_STAT	INDX	2
X$DUAL	ADDR	1

TABLE_NAME	COLUMN_NAME	INDEX_NUMBER
X$DUAL	INDX	2
X$JOXFM	OBN	1
X$JOXFT	JOXFTOBN	1
X$KCBBES	ADDR	1
X$KCBBES	INDX	2
X$KCBBF	ADDR	1
X$KCBBF	INDX	2
X$KCBBHS	ADDR	1
X$KCBBHS	INDX	2
X$KCBFWAIT	ADDR	1
X$KCBFWAIT	INDX	2
X$KCBKWRL	ADDR	1
X$KCBKWRL	INDX	2
X$KCBLDRHIST	ADDR	1
X$KCBLDRHIST	INDX	2
X$KCBLSC	ADDR	1
X$KCBLSC	INDX	2
X$KCBSDS	ADDR	1
X$KCBSDS	INDX	2
X$KCBSW	ADDR	1
X$KCBSW	INDX	2
X$KCBWAIT	ADDR	1
X$KCBWAIT	INDX	2
X$KCBWBPD	ADDR	1
X$KCBWBPD	INDX	2
X$KCBWDS	ADDR	1
X$KCBWDS	INDX	2
X$KCBWH	ADDR	1
X$KCBWH	INDX	2
X$KCCAL	ALRID	1
X$KCCBF	BFRID	1

X$ Indexes

TABLE_NAME	COLUMN_NAME	INDEX_NUMBER
X$KCCBI	BIRID	1
X$KCCBL	BLRID	1
X$KCCBP	BPRID	1
X$KCCBS	BSRID	1
X$KCCCC	CCRID	1
X$KCCCP	CPTNO	1
X$KCCDC	DCRID	1
X$KCCDL	DLRID	1
X$KCCFC	FCRID	1
X$KCCFE	FENUM	1
X$KCCFN	FNNUM	1
X$KCCIC	ICRID	1
X$KCCLE	LENUM	1
X$KCCLH	LHRID	1
X$KCCOR	ORRID	1
X$KCCPA	PCRID	1
X$KCCPD	PCRID	1
X$KCCRM	RMRNO	1
X$KCCRT	RTNUM	1
X$KCCTF	TFNUM	1
X$KCCTS	TSRNO	1
X$KCFIO	INDX	1
X$KCFTIO	INDX	1
X$KCLCRST	ADDR	1
X$KCLCRST	INDX	2
X$KCLCURST	ADDR	1
X$KCLCURST	INDX	2
X$KCRFWS	ADDR	1
X$KCRFWS	INDX	2
X$KCVFH	HXFIL	1
X$KCVFHTMP	HTMPXFIL	1
X$KDNSSF	ADDR	1

TABLE_NAME	COLUMN_NAME	INDEX_NUMBER
X$KDNSSF	INDX	2
X$KDXHS	ADDR	1
X$KDXHS	INDX	2
X$KDXST	INDX	1
X$KGICC	ADDR	1
X$KGICC	INDX	2
X$KGICS	ADDR	1
X$KGICS	INDX	2
X$KGLDP	KGLNAHSH	1
X$KGLLC	ADDR	1
X$KGLLC	INDX	2
X$KGLLK	KGLNAHSH	1
X$KGLNA	KGLNAHSH	1
X$KGLNA1	KGLNAHSH	1
X$KGLOB	KGLNAHSH	1
X$KGLRD	KGLNACHV	1
X$KGLST	ADDR	1
X$KGLST	INDX	2
X$KGSKASP	ADDR	1
X$KGSKASP	INDX	2
X$KGSKCP	ADDR	1
X$KGSKCP	INDX	2
X$KGSKDOPP	ADDR	1
X$KGSKDOPP	INDX	2
X$KGSKPP	ADDR	1
X$KGSKPP	INDX	2
X$KGSKQUEP	ADDR	1
X$KGSKQUEP	INDX	2
X$KGSKTE	ADDR	1
X$KGSKTE	INDX	2
X$KGSKTO	ADDR	1
X$KGSKTO	INDX	2

X$ Indexes

TABLE_NAME	COLUMN_NAME	INDEX_NUMBER
X$KJMDDP	ADDR	1
X$KJMDDP	INDX	2
X$KJMSDP	ADDR	1
X$KJMSDP	INDX	2
X$KMCQS	ADDR	1
X$KMCQS	INDX	2
X$KMCVC	ADDR	1
X$KMCVC	INDX	2
X$KMMDI	ADDR	1
X$KMMDI	INDX	2
X$KMMDP	ADDR	1
X$KMMDP	INDX	2
X$KMMRD	ADDR	1
X$KMMRD	INDX	2
X$KMMRD	KMMRDBUC	3
X$KMMSG	ADDR	1
X$KMMSG	INDX	2
X$KMMSI	ADDR	1
X$KMMSI	INDX	2
X$KNSTACR	ADDR	1
X$KNSTACR	INDX	2
X$KNSTASL	ADDR	1
X$KNSTASL	INDX	2
X$KNSTCAP	ADDR	1
X$KNSTCAP	INDX	2
X$KNSTMVR	ADDR	1
X$KNSTMVR	INDX	2
X$KNSTRPP	ADDR	1
X$KNSTRPP	INDX	2
X$KNSTRQU	ADDR	1
X$KNSTRQU	INDX	2
X$KOCST	ADDR	1

TABLE_NAME	COLUMN_NAME	INDEX_NUMBER
X$KOCST	INDX	2
X$KQDPG	ADDR	1
X$KQDPG	INDX	2
X$KQFDT	ADDR	1
X$KQFDT	INDX	2
X$KQFP	ADDR	1
X$KQFP	INDX	2
X$KQFSZ	ADDR	1
X$KQFSZ	INDX	2
X$KQFTA	ADDR	1
X$KQFTA	INDX	2
X$KQFVI	ADDR	1
X$KQFVI	INDX	2
X$KQFVT	ADDR	1
X$KQFVT	INDX	2
X$KQLFXPL	KQLFXPL_HADD	1
X$KQLFXPL	KQLFXPL_PHAD	2
X$KQLFXPL	KQLFXPL_HASH	3
X$KQRFP	KQRFPHSH	1
X$KQRFS	KQRFSHSH	1
X$KQRPD	ADDR	1
X$KQRPD	INDX	2
X$KQRSD	ADDR	1
X$KQRSD	INDX	2
X$KQRST	ADDR	1
X$KQRST	INDX	2
X$KRBAFF	FNO	1
X$KSBDD	ADDR	1
X$KSBDD	INDX	2
X$KSBDP	INDX	1
X$KSFMIOST	FILE_IDX	1
X$KSFQP	SID	1

X$ Indexes

TABLE_NAME	COLUMN_NAME	INDEX_NUMBER
X$KSIMAT	ADDR	1
X$KSIMAT	INDX	2
X$KSLECLASS	ADDR	1
X$KSLECLASS	INDX	2
X$KSLED	ADDR	1
X$KSLED	INDX	2
X$KSLEI	ADDR	1
X$KSLEI	INDX	2
X$KSLEMAP	ADDR	1
X$KSLEMAP	INDX	2
X$KSLES	KSLESSID	1
X$KSLLCLASS	ADDR	1
X$KSLLCLASS	INDX	2
X$KSLLD	ADDR	1
X$KSLLD	INDX	2
X$KSLLW	ADDR	1
X$KSLLW	INDX	2
X$KSLPO	ADDR	1
X$KSLPO	INDX	2
X$KSLWSC	ADDR	1
X$KSLWSC	INDX	2
X$KSMDD	INDX	1
X$KSMFS	ADDR	1
X$KSMFS	INDX	2
X$KSMFSV	ADDR	1
X$KSMFSV	INDX	2
X$KSMHP	KSMCHDS	1
X$KSMJS	ADDR	1
X$KSMJS	INDX	2
X$KSMMEM	ADDR	1
X$KSMMEM	INDX	2

TABLE_NAME	COLUMN_NAME	INDEX_NUMBER
X$KSMSD	ADDR	1
X$KSMSD	INDX	2
X$KSMSP_DSNEW	ADDR	1
X$KSMSP_DSNEW	INDX	2
X$KSOLSFTS	FTS_OBJD	1
X$KSOLSSTAT	ADDR	1
X$KSOLSSTAT	INDX	2
X$KSPPCV	ADDR	1
X$KSPPCV	INDX	2
X$KSPPI	ADDR	1
X$KSPPI	INDX	2
X$KSPPSV	ADDR	1
X$KSPPSV	INDX	2
X$KSQDN	ADDR	1
X$KSQDN	INDX	2
X$KSQEQ	ADDR	1
X$KSQEQ	INDX	2
X$KSQRS	ADDR	1
X$KSQRS	INDX	2
X$KSQST	ADDR	1
X$KSQST	INDX	2
X$KSRCCTX	ADDR	1
X$KSRCCTX	INDX	2
X$KSRCDES	ADDR	1
X$KSRCDES	INDX	2
X$KSRMPCTX	ADDR	1
X$KSRMPCTX	INDX	2
X$KSRMSGDES	ADDR	1
X$KSRMSGDES	INDX	2
X$KSUCF	ADDR	1
X$KSUCF	INDX	2

X$ Indexes

TABLE_NAME	COLUMN_NAME	INDEX_NUMBER
X$KSUCF	KSUPLSTN	3
X$KSUMYSTA	ADDR	1
X$KSUMYSTA	INDX	2
X$KSUMYSTA	KSUSESTN	3
X$KSUPL	ADDR	1
X$KSUPL	INDX	2
X$KSUPL	KSUPLSTN	3
X$KSUPR	ADDR	1
X$KSUPR	INDX	2
X$KSURU	INDX	1
X$KSURU	KSURIND	3
X$KSUSD	ADDR	1
X$KSUSD	INDX	2
X$KSUSE	INDX	1
X$KSUSECST	INDX	1
X$KSUSESTA	INDX	1
X$KSUSESTA	KSUSESTN	3
X$KSUSEX	SID	1
X$KSUSGIF	ADDR	1
X$KSUSGIF	INDX	2
X$KSUSGSTA	ADDR	1
X$KSUSGSTA	INDX	2
X$KSUSIO	INDX	1
X$KSUTM	ADDR	1
X$KSUTM	INDX	2
X$KSXRCH	ADDR	1
X$KSXRCH	INDX	2
X$KSXRCONQ	ADDR	1
X$KSXRCONQ	INDX	2
X$KSXRMSG	ADDR	1
X$KSXRMSG	INDX	2

TABLE_NAME	COLUMN_NAME	INDEX_NUMBER
X$KSXRREPQ	ADDR	1
X$KSXRREPQ	INDX	2
X$KSXRSG	ADDR	1
X$KSXRSG	INDX	2
X$KTADM	ADDR	1
X$KTADM	INDX	2
X$KTFBFE	KTFBFETSN	1
X$KTFBHC	KTFBHCAFNO	1
X$KTFBUE	KTFBUESEGTSN	1
X$KTFBUE	KTFBUESEGFNO	1
X$KTFBUE	KTFBUESEGBNO	1
X$KTFTHC	KTFTHCTFNO	1
X$KTFTHC	KTFTHCTSN	2
X$KTFTME	KTFTMETSN	1
X$KTSTFC	KTSTFCTSN	1
X$KTTVS	ADDR	1
X$KTTVS	INDX	2
X$KTUGD	ADDR	1
X$KTUGD	INDX	2
X$KTUXE	KTUXEUSN	1
X$KVII	ADDR	1
X$KVII	INDX	2
X$KVIS	ADDR	1
X$KVIS	INDX	2
X$KVIT	ADDR	1
X$KVIT	INDX	2
X$KWDDEF	ADDR	1
X$KWDDEF	INDX	2
X$KWQSI	KWQSIQID	1
X$KXFPCDS	ADDR	1
X$KXFPCDS	INDX	2

X$ Indexes

TABLE_NAME	COLUMN_NAME	INDEX_NUMBER
X$KXFPCMS	ADDR	1
X$KXFPCMS	INDX	2
X$KXFPCST	ADDR	1
X$KXFPCST	INDX	2
X$KXFPDP	ADDR	1
X$KXFPDP	INDX	2
X$KXFPSDS	ADDR	1
X$KXFPSDS	INDX	2
X$KXFPSMS	ADDR	1
X$KXFPSMS	INDX	2
X$KXFPSST	ADDR	1
X$KXFPSST	INDX	2
X$KZDOS	ADDR	1
X$KZDOS	INDX	2
X$KZRTPD	KZRTPDPH	1
X$KZSPR	ADDR	1
X$KZSPR	INDX	2
X$KZSRO	ADDR	1
X$KZSRO	INDX	2
X$LE_STAT	ADDR	1
X$LE_STAT	INDX	2
X$MESSAGES	ADDR	1
X$MESSAGES	INDX	2
X$QESMMIWH	ADDR	1
X$QESMMIWH	INDX	2
X$QESRSTAT	HADDR_QESRS	1
X$QESRSTAT	PHADD_QESRS	2
X$QESRSTAT	HASHV_QESRS	3
X$QESRSTATALL	HADDR_QESRS	1
X$QESRSTATALL	PHADD_QESRS	2
X$QESRSTATALL	HASHV_QESRS	3
X$QKSMMWDS	HADDR_QKSMM	1

TABLE_NAME	COLUMN_NAME	INDEX_NUMBER
X$QKSMMWDS	PHADD_QKSMM	2
X$QKSMMWDS	HASHV_QKSMM	3
X$QUIESCE	ADDR	1
X$QUIESCE	INDX	2
X$RFMP	ADDR	1
X$RFMP	INDX	2
X$XSAWSO	ADDR	1
X$XSAWSO	INDX	2

Oracle9*i* X$ Tables Cross Referenced to V$ Views

The Oracle9*i* V$ views are the same as the GV$ views without the instance_id. I am showing the X$ table mapped back to the V$ view. You must go through the GV$ view to make this inference. The following V$ views are referenced by the ordered X$ table names:

X$ Table	Fixed View
x$bh	vbh, vgl_elements_with_collisions, v$locks_with_collisions
x$class_stat	v$class_cache_transfer, V$CLASS_PING
x$context	v$context
x$estimated_mttr	v$instance_recovery
x$globalcontext	v$globalcontext
x$hofp	v$hs_parameter
x$hs_session	vhs_agent, vhs_session, v$hs_parameter
x$k2gte2	v$global_transaction
x$kcbfwait	v_$filestatxs, v_$tempstatxs
X$kcbmmav	v$mttr_target_advice
x$kcbsc	v$db_cache_advice
x$kcbwait	v$waitstat
x$kcbwbpd	v$buffer_pool, v$buffer_pool_statistics, v$db_cache_advice
x$kcbwds	v$buffer_pool_statistics
x$kccal	v$archived_log

X$ Table	Fixed View
x$kccbf	v$backup_datafile
x$kccbl	v$backup_redolog, v$backup_spfile
x$kccbp	v$backup_piece
x$kccbs	v$backup_set
x$kcccc	v$copy_corruption
x$kcccf	v$controlfile
x$kccdc	v$datafile_copy
x$kccdi	v$archive, v$database
x$kccdl	v$deleted_object
x$kccfc	v$backup_corruption
x$kccfe	v_$kccfe, v$datafile, v$file_cache_transfer, v$file_ping, v$filestat, v$recovery_file_status
x$kccfn	v$datafile, v$dbfile, v$logfile, v$recovery_file_status, v$tempfile
x$kccic	v$database_incarnation
x$kccle	v$archive, v$log, v$recovery_log
x$kcclh	v$loghist, v$log_history, v$recovery_log
x$kccor	v$offline_range
x$kccpa	V$PROXY_ARCHIVEDLOG
x$kccpd	v$proxy_datafile
x$kccrm	v$rman_configuration
x$kccrs	v$controlfile_record_section
x$kccrt	vlog, vthread
x$kccsl	v$standby_log
x$kcctf	v$tempfile, v$temp_cache_transfer, v$temp_ping, v$tempstat
x$kccts	v$tablespace
x$kcfio	v$file_cache_transfer, v$file_ping, v$filestat
x$kcftio	v$temp_cache_transfer, v$temp_ping, v$tempstat
x$kckce	v$compatseg

X$ Table	Fixed View
x$kckty	v$compatibility
x$kclcrst	vbsp, vcr_block_server
x$klcie	v$loadistat
x$kcrfx	v$recovery_status
x$kcrmf	v$recovery_file_status
x$kcrmx	v$recovery_file_status, v$recovery_status
x$kcrralg	v$dataguard_status
x$kcrrarch	v$archive_processes
x$kcrrdest	v$archive_dest
x$kcrrdstat	v$archive_dest_status
x$kcrrms	v$managed_standby
x$kcvfh	v$datafile, v$datafile_header
x$kcvfhmrr	v$recovery_log, v$recover_file
x$kcvfhonl	v$backup
x$kcvfhtmp	v$tempfile
x$kdlt	v$temporary_lobs
x$kdnssf	v$_lock1
x$kghlu	v$shared_pool_reserved
x$kgicc	v$session_cursor_cache
x$kgics	v$system_cursor_cache
x$kglcursor	vsql, vsqlarea, v$sql_redirection, v$sql_shared_memory, v$vpd_policy
x$kgldp	v$access, v$object_dependency
x$kgllk	v$access, v$open_cursor
x$kglmem	v$library_cache_memory
x$kglna	v$sqltext
x$kglna1	v$sqltext_with_newlines
x$kglob	v$_sequences, v$access, vdb_object_cache, vdb_pipes, v$object_dependency
X$KGLSIM	v$shared_pool_advice
x$kglst	v$librarycache

X$ Table	Fixed View
x$kgskasp	v$active_sess_pool_mth, v$max_active_sess_target_mth
x$kgskcft	v$rsrc_consumer_group
x$kgskcp	v$rsrc_consumer_group_cpu_mth
x$kgskdopp	v$parallel_degree_limit_mth
x$kgskpft	v$rsrc_plan
x$kgskpp	v$rsrc_plan_cpu_mth
x$kgskquep	v$queueing_mth
x$kjbl	v$ges_enqueue
x$kjbr	v$dlm_ress
x$kjdrhv	v$hvmaster_info
x$kjdrpcmhv	v$gcshvmaster_info
x$kjdrpcmpf	v$gcspfmaster_info
x$kjicvt	v$dlm_convert_local, v$dlm_convert_remote
x$kjilkft	v$ges_enqueue
x$kjirft	v$dlm_ress
x$kjisft	v$dlm_misc
x$kjitrft	v$dlm_traffic_controller
x$kksbv	v$sql_bind_metadata
x$kkscs	v$sql_shared_cursor
x$kkssrd	v$sql_redirection
x$klpt	v$loadpstat
X$kmcqs	v$queue
x$kmcvc	v$circuit
x$kmmdi	v$dispatcher, v$dispatcher_rate
x$kmmrd	v$reqdist
x$kmmsg	v$shared_server_monitor
x$kmmsi	v$shared_server
x$knstacr	v$logstdby, v$logstdby_stats, v$streams_apply_coordinator
x$knstasl	v$streams_apply_reader, v$streams_apply_server

X$ Table	Fixed View
x$knstcap	v$streams_capture
x$knstmvr	v$mvrefresh
x$knstrpp	v$replprop
x$knstrqu	v$replqueue
x$kocst	v$sesssion_object_cache
x$kqfco	v$indexed_fixed_column
x$kqfsz	v$type_size
x$kqfdt	v$fixed_table
x$kqfta	v$indexed_fixed_column, v$fixed_table
x$kqfvi	v$fixed_table, v$fixed_view_definition
x$kqfvt	v$fixed_view_definition
x$kqlfxpl	v$sql_plan
x$kqlset	v$subcache
x$kqrfp	v$rowcache_parent
x$kqrfs	v$rowcache_subordinate
x$kqrst	v$rowcache
x$krvslv	v$logstdby
x$krvslvs	v$logstdby_stats
x$krvxsv	v$logstdby_stats, v$logmnr_stats
x$ksbdd	v$bgprocess
x$ksbdp	v$bgprocess
x$ksfhdvnt	v$backup_device
x$ksfmcompl	v$map_comp_list
x$ksfmelem	v$map_element
x$ksfmextelem	v$map_ext_element
x$ksfmfile	v$map_file
x$ksfmfileext	v$map_file_extent
x$ksfmiost	v$map_file_io_stack
x$ksfmlib	v$map_library
x$ksfmsubelem	v$map_subelement
x$ksfqp	v$backup_async_io, v$backup_sync_io

X$ Tables Cross-Referenced to V$ Views

X$ Table	Fixed View
x$ksimsi	v$active_instances
x$ksled	v$event_name, v$system_event, v$session_event, v$session_wait
x$kslei	v$system_event
x$ksles	v$session_event
x$kslld	v$latch, v$latchname, v$latch_children, v$latch_parent
x$ksllt	v$latch, v$latch_children, v$latch_parent
x$ksllw	v$latch_misses
x$kslwsc	v$latch_misses
x$ksmfs	v$sgastat
x$ksmge	v$sga_dynamic_free_memory
x$ksmgop	v$sga_resize_ops
x$ksmgsc	v$sga_current_resize_ops
x$ksmgst	v$sga_dynamic_components
x$ksmgv	v$sga_dynamic_free_memory, vsga_resize_ops, vsga_current_resize_ops, v$sga_dynamic_components
x$ksmhp	v$sql_shared_memory
x$ksmjs	v$sgastat
x$ksmls	v$sgastat
x$ksmsd	v$sga
x$ksmspr	v$shared_pool_reserved
x$ksmss	v$sgastat
x$ksolsfts	v$segment_statistics, v$segstat
x$ksolsstat	v$segstat_name
x$ksppcv	v$parameter
x$ksppcv2	v$parameter2
x$ksppi	v$parameter, v$parameter2, v$system_parameter, v$system_parameter2
x$ksppsv	v$system_parameter
x$ksppsv2	v$system_parameter2
x$ksppo	v$obsolete_parameter

X$ Table	Fixed View
x$kspspfile	v$spparameter
x$ksqeq	v$_lock1, v$enqueue_lock
x$ksqrs	v$enqueue_lock, v$resource, v$transaction_enqueue, v$lock
x$ksqst	v$enqueue_stat
x$kstex	v$execution
x$ksull	v$license
x$ksulop	v$session_longops
x$ksulv	v$nls_valid_values
x$ksumysta	v$mystat
x$ksupr	v$process
x$ksuprlat	v$latchholder
x$ksurlmt	v$resource_limit
x$ksusd	v$statname
x$ksuse	v$access, v$aw_olap, v$enqueue_lock, v$locked_object, v$px_session, v$session, v$px_sesstat, v$transaction_enqueue, v$lock
x$ksusecon	v$session_connect_info
x$ksusecst	v$session_wait
x$ksusesta	v$px_sesstat, v$sesstat
x$ksusgif	v$mystat, v$sesstat
x$ksusgsta	v$sysstat, v$instance_recovery
x$ksusio	v$sess_io
x$ksutm	v$timer
x$ksuxsinst	v$instance
X$KTADM	v$_lock, v$locked_object
x$ktcxb	v$_lock, v$locked_object, v$transaction, v$transaction_enqueue
x$ktfthc	v$temp_space_header
x$ktftme	v$temp_extent_map
x$ktprxrs	v$fast_start_servers
x$ktprxrt	v$fast_start_transactions
x$ktrso	v$resumable

X$ Table	Fixed View
x$ktsso	v$sort_usage
x$ktstfc	v$temp_extent_pool
x$ktstSSD	v$sort_segment
x$kturd	v_$rollname, v$rollstat
x$ktusmst	v$undostat
x$kvit	v$instance
x$kwddef	v$reserved_words
x$kwqsi	v$aq1
X$kxfpdp	vpq_slave, vpx_process, v$px_session, v$px_sesstat
x$kxfpns	v$px_process_sysstat
x$kxfpsst	v$pq_sesstat
x$kxfpys	v$pq_sysstat
x$kxfqsrow	v$pq_tqstat
x$kxsbd	v$sql_bind_data
x$kxscc	v$sql_cursor
x$kzspr	v$enabledprivs
x$kzrtpd	v$vpd_policy
x$kzsrt	v$pwfile_users
x$le	vbh, vgc_element, v$lock_element
x$le_stat	v$lock_activity
x$logmnr_callback	v$logmnr_callback
x$logmnr_contents	v$logmnr_contents
x$logmnr_dictionary	v$logmnr_dictionary
x$logmnr_logfile	v$logmnr_logfile
x$logmnr_logs	v$logmnr_logs
x$logmnr_parameters	v$logmnr_parameters
x$logmnr_process	v$logmnr_process
x$logmnr_region	v$logmnr_region
x$logmnr_session	v$logmnr_session
x$logmnr_transaction	v$logmnr_transaction
x$nls_parameters	v$nls_parameters

X$ Table	Fixed View
x$option	v$option
x$prmsltyx	v$statistics_level
x$qesmmahist	v$pga_target_advice_histogram
x$qesmmapadv	v$pga_target_advice
x$qesmmiwh	v$sql_workarea_histogram
x$qesmmiwt	v$sql_workarea_active
x$qesmmsga	v$pgastat
x$qesrstat	v$sql_plan_statistics
x$qesrstatall	v$sql_plan_statistics_all
x$qksmmwds	v$sql_workarea
x$quiesce	v$instance
x$ksusgsta	v$instance_recovery
x$targetrba	v$instance_recovery
x$timezone_names	v$timezone_names
x$uganco	v$dblink
x$version	v$version
x$xsaggr	v$aw_calc
x$xsawso	v$aw_olap
x$xssinfo	v$aw_session_info

Oracle9*i* GV$ Views Cross Referenced to X$ Tables

The Oracle9*i* V$ views are the same as the GV$ views without the instance_id. I am showing the X$ table mapped back to the V$ view. You must go through the GV$ view to make this inference. The following X$ tables are referenced ordered by the V$ view names (some are referenced only to limit the rows of the view in some way):

Fixed View	Referenced X$ Tables and/or Fixed Views
v$access	x$ksuse, x$kglob, x$kgldp, x$kgllk
v$active_instances	x$ksimsi
v$active_sess_pool_mth	x$kgskasp
v$aq1	x$kwqsi
v$archive	x$kccle, x$kccdi

Fixed View	Referenced X$ Tables and/or Fixed Views
v$archived_log	x$kccal
v$archive_dest	x$kcrrdest
v$archive_dest_status	x$kcrrdstat
v$archive_GAP	v$archived_log, v$log_history, v$datafile
v$archive_processes	x$kcrrarch
v$aw_calc	x$xsaggr
v$aw_olap	x$gksuse, x$xsawso
v$aw_session_info	x$xssinfo
v$backup	x$kcvfhonl
v$backup_async_io	x$ksfqp
v$backup_corruption	x$kccfc
v$backup_datafile	x$kccbf
v$backup_device	x$ksfhdvnt
v$backup_piece	x$kccbp
v$backup_redolog	x$kccbl
v$backup_set	x$kccbs
v$backup_spfile	x$kccbi
v$backup_sync_io	x$ksfqp
v$bgprocess	x$ksbdp, x$ksbdd
v$bh	xbh, xle
v$bsp	x$kclcrst
v$buffer_pool	x$kcbwbpd
v$buffer_pool_statistics	x$kcbwds, x$kcbwbpd
v$circuit	x$kmcvc
v$class_cache_transfer	x$class_stat
v$class_ping	x$class_stat
v$compatibility	x$kckty
v$compatseg	x$kckce
v$context	x$context
v$controlfile	x$kcccf
v$controlfile_record_section	x$kccrs

Fixed View	Referenced X$ Tables and/or Fixed Views
v$copy_corruption	x$kcccc
v$cr_block_server	x$kclcrst
v$database	x$kccdi
v$database_block_corruption	v$copy_corruption, v$backup_corruption, v$backup_set, v$datafile_copy, v$backup_datafile
v$database_incarnation	x$kccic
v$datafile	x$kccfe, x$kccfn, x$kcvfh
v$datafile_copy	x$kccdc
v$datafile_header	x$kcvfh
v$dataguard_status	x$kcrralg
v$dbfile	x$kccfn
v$dblink	x$uganco
v$db_cache_advice	x$kcbsc, x$kcbwbpd
v$db_object_cache	x$kglob
v$db_pipes	x$kglob
v$deleted_object	x$kccdl
v$dispatcher	x$kmmdi
v$dispatcher_rate	x$kmmdi
v$dlm_all_locks	v$ges_enqueue
v$dlm_convert_local	x$kjicvt
v$dlm_convert_remote	x$kjicvt
v$dlm_latch	v$latch
v$dlm_locks	v$ges_blocking_enqueue
v$dlm_misc	x$kjisft
v$dlm_ress	x$kjirft, x$kjbr
v$dlm_traffic_controller	x$kjitrft
v$enabledprivs	x$kzspr
v$enqueue_lock	x$ksqeq, x$ksuse, x$ksqrs
v$enqueue_stat	x$ksqst
v$event_name	x$ksled

Fixed View	Referenced X$ Tables and/or Fixed Views
v$execution	x$kstex
v$fast_start_servers	x$ktprxrs
v$fast_start_transactions	x$ktprxrt
v$filestat	x$kcfio, x$kccfe
v$file_cache_transfer	x$kcfio, x$kccfe
v$file_ping	x$kcfio, x$kccfe
v$fixed_table	x$kqfta, x$kqfvi, x$kqfdt
v$fixed_view_definition	x$kqfvi, x$kqfvt
v$gcshvmaster_info	x$kjdrpcmhv
v$gcspfmaster_info	x$kjdrpcmpf
v$gc_element	x$le
v$gc_elements_with_collisions	v$bh
v$ges_blocking_enqueue	v$ges_enqueue
v$ges_enqueue	x$kjilkft, x$kjbl
v$globalcontext	x$globalcontext
v$global_blocked_locks	v$lock, v$dlm_locks
V$global_transaction	x$k2gte2
v$hs_agent	x$hs_session
v$hs_parameter	x$hs_session, x$hofp
v$hs_session	x$hs_session
v$hvmaster_info	x$kjdrhv
v$indexed_fixed_column	x$kqfco, x$kqfta
v$instance	x$ksuxsinst, x$kvit, x$quiesce
v$instance_recovery	x$ksusgsta, x$targetrba, x$estimated_mttr
v$latch	x$kslld, x$ksllt
v$latchholder	x$ksuprlat
v$latchname	x$kslld
v$latch_children	x$ksllt, x$kslld
v$latch_misses	x$ksllw, x$kslwsc
v$latch_parent	x$ksllt, x$kslld
v$librarycache	x$kglst
v$library_cache_memory	x$kglmem

Fixed View	Referenced X$ Tables and/or Fixed Views
v$license	x$ksull
v$loadistat	x$klcie
v$loadpstat	x$klpt
v$lock	v$_lock, x$ksuse, x$ksqrs
v$locked_object	x$ktcxb, x$ktadm, x$ksuse
v$locks_with_collisions	v$bh
v$lock_activity	x$le_stat
v$lock_element	x$le
v$log	x$kccle, x$kccrt
v$logfile	x$kccfn
v$loghist	x$kcclh
v$logmnr_callback	x$logmnr_callback
v$logmnr_contents	x$logmnr_contents
v$logmnr_dictionary	x$logmnr_dictionary
v$logmnr_logfile	x$logmnr_logfile
v$logmnr_logs	x$logmnr_logs
v$logmnr_parameters	x$logmnr_parameters
v$logmnr_process	x$logmnr_process, V$process
v$logmnr_region	x$logmnr_region
v$logmnr_session	x$logmnr_session
v$logmnr_stats	x$krvxsv
v$logmnr_transaction	x$logmnr_transaction
v$logstdby	x$krvslv, v$session, x$knstacr
v$logstdby_stats	x$krvslvs, x$krvxsv, logstdby$parameters, v$session, x$knstacr
v$log_history	x$kcclh
v$managed_standby	x$kcrrms
v$map_comp_list	x$ksfmcompl
v$map_element	x$ksfmelem
v$map_ext_element	x$ksfmextelem
v$map_file	x$ksfmfile

GV$ Views Cross-Referenced to X$ Tables

Fixed View	Referenced X$ Tables and/or Fixed Views
v$map_file_extent	x$ksfmfileext
v$map_file_io_stack	x$ksfmiost
v$map_library	x$ksfmlib
v$map_subelement	x$ksfmsubelem
v$max_active_sess_target_mth	x$kgskasp
v$mttr_target_advice	x$kcbmmav
v$mvrefresh	x$knstmvr, v$session
v$mystat	x$ksumysta, x$ksusgif
v$nls_parameters	x$nls_parameters
v$nls_valid_values	x$ksulv
v$object_dependency	x$kglob, x$kgldp
v$obsolete_parameter	x$ksppo
v$offline_range	x$kccor
v$open_cursor	x$kgllk
v$option	x$option
v$parallel_degree_limit_mth	x$kgskdopp
v$parameter	x$ksppi, x$ksppcv
v$parameter2	x$ksppi, x$ksppcv2
v$pgastat	x$qesmmsga
v$pga_target_advice	x$qesmmapadv
v$pga_target_advice_histogram	x$qesmmahist
v$pq_sesstat	x$kxfpsst
v$pq_slave	x$kxfpdp
v$pq_sysstat	x$kxfpys
v$pq_tqstat	x$kxfqsrow
v$process	x$ksupr
v$proxy_archivedlog	x$kccpa
v$proxy_datafile	x$kccpd
v$pwfile_users	x$kzsrt
v$px_process	X$kxfpdp, v$process, v$session
v$px_process_sysstat	x$kxfpns

Fixed View	Referenced X$ Tables and/or Fixed Views
v$px_session	x$ksuse, x$kxfpdp
v$px_sesstat	x$ksuse, x$kxfpdp, x$ksusesta, x$ksusgif
v$queue	X$kmcqs
v$queueing_mth	x$kgskquep
v$recovery_file_status	x$kcrmx, x$kccfn, x$kccfe, x$kcrmf
v$recovery_log	x$kcclh, x$kcvfhmrr, x$kccle
v$recovery_progress	v$session_longops
v$recovery_status	x$kcrmx, x$kcrfx
v$recover_file	x$kcvfhmrr
v$replprop	x$knstrpp, v$session
v$replqueue	x$knstrqu
v$reqdist	x$kmmrd
v$reserved_words	x$kwddef
v$resource	x$ksqrs
v$resource_limit	x$ksurlmt
v$resumable	x$ktrso
v$rman_configuration	x$kccrm
v$rollstat	x$kturd
v$rowcache	x$kqrst
v$rowcache_parent	x$kqrfp
v$rowcache_subordinate	x$kqrfs
v$rsrc_consumer_group	x$kgskcft
v$rsrc_consumer_group_cpu_mth	x$kgskcp
v$rsrc_plan	x$kgskpft
v$rsrc_plan_cpu_mth	x$kgskpp
v$segment_statistics	obj$, user$, x$ksolsfts, ts$, ind$
v$segstat	x$ksolsfts
v$segstat_name	x$ksolsstat
v$session	x$ksuse
v$session_connect_info	x$ksusecon

GV$ Views Cross-Referenced to X$ Tables

Fixed View	Referenced X$ Tables and/or Fixed Views
v$session_cursor_cache	x$kgicc
v$session_event	x$ksles, x$ksled
v$session_longops	x$ksulop
v$sesssion_object_cache	x$kocst
v$session_wait	x$ksusecst, x$ksled
v$sesstat	x$ksusesta, x$ksusgif
v$sess_io	x$ksusio
v$sga	x$ksmsd
v$sgastat	x$ksmfs, x$ksmss, x$ksmls, x$ksmjs
v$sga_current_resize_ops	x$ksmgsc, x$ksmgv, v$parameter
v$sga_dynamic_components	x$ksmgst, x$ksmgv
v$sga_dynamic_free_memory	x$ksmge, x$ksmgv
v$sga_resize_ops	x$ksmgop, x$ksmgv, v$parameter
v$shared_pool_advice	x$kglsim
v$shared_pool_reserved	x$ksmspr, x$kghlu
v$shared_server	x$kmmsi
v$shared_server_monitor	x$kmmsg
v$sort_segment	x$ktstssd
v$sort_usage	x$ktsso, v$session
v$spparameter	x$kspspfile
v$sql	x$kglcursor
v$sqlarea	x$kglcursor
v$sqltext	x$kglna
v$sqltext_with_newlines	x$kglna1
v$sql_bind_data	x$kxsbd
v$sql_bind_metadata	x$kksbv
v$sql_cursor	x$kxscc
v$sql_plan	x$kqlfxpl, obj$, user$
v$sql_plan_statistics	x$qesrstat
v$sql_plan_statistics_all	x$qesrstatall, obj$, user$
v$sql_redirection	x$kglcursor, x$kkssrd

Fixed View	Referenced X$ Tables and/or Fixed Views
v$sql_shared_cursor	x$kkscs
v$sql_shared_memory	x$kglcursor, x$ksmhp
v$sql_workarea	x$qksmmwds
v$sql_workarea_active	x$qesmmiwt
v$sql_workarea_histogram	x$qesmmiwh
v$standby_log	x$kccsl
v$statistics_level	x$prmsltyx
v$statname	x$ksusd
v$streams_apply_coordinator	x$knstacr, v$session
v$streams_apply_reader	x$knstasl, v$session
v$streams_apply_server	x$knstasl, v$session
v$streams_capture	x$knstcap, v$session
v$subcache	x$kqlset
v$sysstat	x$ksusgsta
v$system_cursor_cache	x$kgics
v$system_event	x$kslei, x$ksled
v$system_parameter	x$ksppi, x$ksppsv
v$system_parameter2	x$ksppi, x$ksppsv2
v$tablespace	x$kccts
v$tempfile	x$kcctf, x$kccfn, x$kcvfhtmp
v$temporary_lobs	x$kdlt
v$tempstat	x$kcftio, x$kcctf
v$temp_cache_transfer	x$kcftio, x$kcctf
v$temp_extent_map	ts$, x$ktftme
v$temp_extent_pool	ts$, x$ktstfc
v$temp_ping	x$kcftio, x$kcctf
v$temp_space_header	ts$, x$ktfthc
v$thread	x$kccrt
v$timer	x$ksutm
v$timezone_names	x$timezone_names
v$transaction	x$ktcxb

Fixed View	Referenced X$ Tables and/or Fixed Views
v$transaction_enqueue	x$ktcxb, x$ksuse, x$ksqrs
v$type_size	x$kqfsz
v$undostat	x$ktusmst
v$version	x$version
v$vpd_policy	x$kglcursor, x$kzrtpd
v$waitstat	x$kcbwait
v_$filestatxs	x$kcbfwait, v$filestat, v$tablespace, v$datafile
v_$kccfe	x$kccfe
v_$kccdi	x$kccdi
v_$rollname	x$kturd, undo$
v_$tempstatxs	x$kcbfwait, v$tempstat, v$tablespace, v$tempfile
v$_lock	v$_lock1, x$ktadm, x$ktcxb
v$_lock1	x$kdnssf, x$ksqeq
v$_sequences	x$kglob

Oracle9i X$ Tables Not Referenced by a GV$ View

The following Oracle9i query produces this listing of 155 table names, ordered by X$:

```
select      name
from        v$fixed_table ft
where       not exists
    (select     'x'
     from       v$fixed_view_definition fv
     where      instr(lower(fv.view_definition),lower(ft.name)) > 0)
and name like 'X%'
order by name;
```

X$ACTIVECKPT	X$BUFQM	X$CKPTBUF
X$DUAL	X$JOXFC	X$JOXFD
X$JOXFM	X$JOXFR	X$JOXFS
X$JOXFT	X$KCBBES	X$KCBBF
X$KCBBHS	X$KCBFWAIT	X$KCBKPFS

X$KCBKWRL	X$KCBLDRHIST	X$KCBLSC
X$KCBSDS	X$KCBSH	X$KCBSW
X$KCBVBL	X$KCBWH	X$KCCCP
X$KCCDI2	X$KCKFM	X$KCLCURST
X$KCLFH	X$KCLFI	X$KCLFX
X$KCLLS	X$KCLQN	X$KCRFWS
X$KCRMT	X$KCRRLNS	X$KCVFHALL
X$KDXHS	X$KDXST	X$KGLAU
X$KGLBODY	X$KGLCLUSTER	X$KGLINDEX
X$KGLLC	X$KGLPN	X$KGLRD
X$KGLSN	X$KGLTABLE	X$KGLTR
X$KGLTRIGGER	X$KGLXS	X$KGSKTE
X$KGSKTO	X$KJBLFX	X$KJBRFX
X$KJCTFR	X$KJCTFRI	X$KJCTFS
X$KJILFT	X$KJMDDP	X$KJMSDP
X$KJXM	X$KKSAI	X$KMMDP
X$KQDPG	X$KQFP	X$KQRPD
X$KQRSD	X$KRBAFF	X$KSFVQST
X$KSFVSL	X$KSFVSTA	X$KSIMAT
X$KSIMAV	X$KSLECLASS	X$KSLEMAP
X$KSLLCLASS	X$KSLPO	X$KSMDD
X$KSMFSV	X$KSMJCH	X$KSMLRU
X$KSMMEM	X$KSMNIM	X$KSMNS
X$KSMPP	X$KSMSP_DSNEW	X$KSMSP_NWEX
X$KSMUP	X$KSPSPFH	X$KSQDN
X$KSRCCTX	X$KSRCDES	X$KSRCHDL
X$KSRMPCTX	X$KSRMSGDES	X$KSRMSGO
X$KSUCF	X$KSUPGP	X$KSUPGS
X$KSUPL	X$KSURU	X$KSUSEX
X$KSXAFA	X$KSXRCH	X$KSXRCONQ
X$KSXRMSG	X$KSXRREPQ	X$KSXRSG
X$KTFBFE	X$KTFBHC	X$KTFBUE

X$KTSPSTAT	X$KTTVS	X$KTUGD
X$KTUXE	X$KVII	X$KVIS
X$KWQPD	X$KWQPS	X$KXFPCDS
X$KXFPCMS	X$KXFPCST	X$KXFPPFT
X$KXFPSDS	X$KXFPSMS	X$KZDOS
X$KZEMAEA	X$KZEMAIE	X$KZSRO
X$LCR	X$LOGMNR_ATTRIBUTE$	X$LOGMNR_COL$
X$LOGMNR_COLTYPE$	X$LOGMNR_DICT$	X$LOGMNR_ENCRYPTED_OBJ$
X$LOGMNR_ENCRYPTION_PROFILE$	X$LOGMNR_IND$	X$LOGMNR_INDPART$
X$LOGMNR_OBJ$	X$LOGMNR_ROOT$	X$LOGMNR_TAB$
X$LOGMNR_TABCOMPART$	X$LOGMNR_TABPART$	X$LOGMNR_TABSUBPART$
X$LOGMNR_TS$	X$LOGMNR_TYPE$	X$LOGMNR_USER$
X$MESSAGES	X$NSV	X$RFMP
X$TEMPORARY_LOB_REFCNT	X$RFMTE	X$TRACE
X$TRACE_EVENTS	X$VINST	

Index

A

Administrative features, new Oracle9i, 3–11

Advanced tuning, table joins and other, 303–377

Aliases, using, 251–252

ALL_ROWS hints, 255

AND_EQUAL hints, 259

APPEND hints, 271–272

Architectural features, new Oracle9i, 11–14

Arrays, disk, 64–66

AUTOTRACE, using on parallel operations, 445–450

B

B-tree indexes, 49–50

Backup and recovery features, new Oracle9i, 21–23

Beginners, looking at some examples for, 422–425

Binary height, 43–45

Bitmap indexes, 50–53

Bitmap join indexes, 328–334

Books, top ten reasons not to write, 678–679

Bottlenecks
using iostat to identify disk I/O, 645–648
using mpstat to identifying CPU, 640–641

Buffer cache/data blocks, 523–531
buffer statuses, 524–525
hot data blocks/latch contention and wait events, 527–531
segments occupying block buffers, 525–527

Buffer pools, using Oracle multiple, 129–132
allocating memory for data, 130
allocating memory for statements, 131–132
modifying LRU algorithm, 131
pools related to DB_BLOCK_BUFFERS, 130
pools related to SHARED_POOL_SIZE, 131–132

Business impact reporting, 198–201
application health assessment, 199–201
Service-Level reporting, 198

C

CACHE hints, 272–273
Caching tables in memory, 293–294
Calls, reducing to SYSDATE, 395–397
Candidate rows, 321–322
CHOOSE hints, 252–253
CLUSTER hints, 274
Clustering factors, 42–43
Comparisons, performance, 457–459
Concatenated indexes, 36–37
Consoles, Enterprise Manager, 147
Contention
    avoiding disk, 73–83
    I/O disk, 68–70
Control theory, apply, 365–375
CPU bottlenecks, using mpstat to identify, 640–641
CPU, idle percentage for, 638
CPU load, using uptime to monitor, 640
CPU/memory-monitoring tool on NT, 644
CPU usage, using sar to monitor, 636–638
Creating
    enough dispatchers, 135–136
    table and index examples, 435–437
    V$ and GV$ views and x$ tables, 682
    V$ views, 506–508
    X$ tables, 506–508
Cursors, using rollback segments to open large, 418–420
CURSOR_SHARING_EXACT hints, 275

D

Data and index files, storing, 67–68
Data blocks; See also Buffer cache/data blocks
Data blocks, hot, 527–531
Data files across available hardware disks, 66–70
    avoiding I/O disk contention, 68–70
    moving data files to balance file I/Os, 70
    storing data and index files in separate locations, 67–68
Data files, moving to balance file I/Os, 70
Data, how optimization looks at, 135
Data reads, setting DB_BLOCK_SIZE to reflect size of, 119–141
    tuning SHARED_POOL_SIZE for optimal performance, 120–129
    using Oracle multiple buffer pools, 129–132
Data types
    comparing mismatched, 41
    standardizing on, 391–395
    using time components when working with DATE, 413–416
Database; See Instance/database
Database tables
    using log timing information in, 383–386
    using temporary, 420–421
Databases, tuning with initialization parameters, 107–143
    changing init.ora files without restart, 109–110
    identifying crucial init.ora parameters, 108–109
    increasing performance by tuning DB_CACHE_SIZE, 111–118
    setting DB_BLOCK_SIZE to reflect size of data reads, 119–141
    viewing init.ora parameters with Enterprise Manager, 110–111
DATE data types, using time components when working with, 413–416
DBA_OBJECT_SIZE, getting object information from, 404–405
DB_BLOCK_SIZE, setting to reflect size of data reads, 119–141
    creating enough dispatchers, 135–136
    cross-based verses rule-based optimization, 134–135
    finding undocumented init.ora parameters, 138–139

modeling typical servers, 140–141

modifying size of SGA, 132–134

optimal use of memory, 132

tuning PGA_AGGREGATE_
TARGET, 132

tuning SHARED_POOL_SIZE for
optimal performance, 120–129

twenty-five important initialization
parameters, 137–138

understanding OPTIMIZER_MODE,
134–135

understanding typical servers,
139–140

using Oracle multiple buffer pools,
129–132

DB_CACHE_SIZE, increasing performance
by tuning, 111–118

keeping hit ratio for data cache
above 95 percent, 115

monitoring V$QLAREA to find slow
queries, 115–118

using V$DB_CACHE_ADVICE in
tuning DB_CACHE_SIZE, 113–114

DB_CACHE_SIZE, using
V$DB_CACHE_ADVICE in tuning,
113–114

DBMS_APPLICATION_INFO, using for
real-time monitoring, 381–383

DBMS_SHARED_POOL.SIZES, using and
modifying, 402–404

DDL statements and operations, parallel
DML and, 430–431

Disabled triggers, finding, 406–408

Disk arrays, 64–66

Disk contention, avoiding by using
partitions, 73–83

getting more information about
partitions, 76–77

miscellaneous partitioning options,
80–83

miscellaneous types of partitions,
77–80

Disk contention, I/O, 68–70

Disk freespace, monitoring, 653

Disk I/O and fragmentation, 63–106

avoiding disk contention by using
partitions, 73–83

considering issues in planning stages,
104–105

data files across available hardware
disks, 66–70

disk arrays, 64–66

eliminating fragmentation, 84–92

examining miscellaneous disk I/O
precautions and tips, 104

exporting partitions, 84

having multiple control files on
different controllers, 103

having multiple control files on
different disks, 103

index partitioning, 83–84

killing problem sessions, 100–101

locally managed tablespaces, 71–73

rollback segments, 96–99

sorting in memory to reduce disk I/O,
101–103

UNDO management, 92–96

undo tablespaces, 99–100

using raw devices to improve I/O for
write-intensive data, 103–104

Disk I/O bottlenecks, using iostat to
identify, 645–648

Disk I/O problems, using sar to monitor, 645

Disk Performance Index (DPI), 618–624

Disks, data files across available hardware,
66–70

avoiding I/O disk contention, 68–70

storing data and index files in
separate locations, 67–68

Distributed queries, tuning, 338–340

DML and DDL statements and operations,
parallel, 430–431

DML statements and examples, parallel,
437–440

DML statements and operations since
Oracle9i, parallel, 431

DPI (Disk Performance Index), 618–624
  chaining in mission-critical tables,
    621–622
  key Oracle files separated, 622
  rollback segment balance, 622–623
  tables/indexes separated, 621
  temporary segment balance, 623–624
  top 10 disk-read abusers as percentage
    of all statements, 620–621
  top 25 disk-read abuser statements
    tuned, 619–620
DRIVING_SITE hints, 266

E

Education Performance Index (EPI),
  607–608
Enterprise Manager and Tuning pack,
  145–204
  business impact reporting, 198–201
  Enterprise Manager console, 147
  Index Tuning Wizard, 188–189
  Instance folder, 148–150
  Oracle SQL Scratchpad, 161–163
  Oracle Tuning pack-Oracle Expert,
    189–196
  Oracle Tuning pack-SQL Analyze,
    179–188
  Oracle Tuning pack-Tablespace Map,
    196–197
  Performance Manager, 163–179
  Schema folder, 150–157
  Security folder, 157–160
  SQL*Plus Worksheet, 161–163
  Storage folder, 160–161
Enterprise Manager console, 147
Enterprise Manager, viewing init.ora
  parameters with, 110–111
EPI (Education Performance Index), 607–608
Events, wait, 527–531
Examples
  for beginners, 422–425
  creating table and index, 435–437

  overall system review, 625–628
  parallel DML statements and, 437–440
  stored outlines, 238–241
  using tree approaches, 227–230
Execution locations, pinpoint, 421
EXISTS function, 300–301
EXPLAIN PLAN
  output method, 226–227
  reading, 220, 221–225
  using alone, 216–220
  using on parallel operations, 445–450
EXPLAIN, using, 205
Exporting partitions, 84

F

Fast full scans, 47
Fast index rebuilding, 60
Features, introduction to Oracle9i
  new, 1–32
  new Oracle9i administrative
    features, 3–11
  new Oracle9i architectural
    features, 11–14
  new Oracle9i backup and
    recovery features, 21–23
  new Oracle9i data warehousing
    features, 15–16
  new Oracle9i SQL and PL/SQL
    features, 16–21
  Real Application Clusters (RAC),
    23–31
Features, new Oracle9 administrative, 3–11
  Automatic Undo Management
    (AUM), 5–6
  cursor sharing, 10
  default temporary tablespaces, 7
  dynamic memory management, 8–9
  migration notes, 3–4
  miscellaneous administrative
    features, 11
  multiple database block size
    support, 9–10

online table redefinition, 10
Oracle-Managed Files (OMF), 7
resumable space allocation, 6–7
security enhancements with DBCA
    and SYS accounts, 4
self-tuning PGA, 10
server parameter files (SPFILE), 4–5
SVRMGRL and connect Internet
    desupport, 4
Features, new Oracle9i architectural, 11–14
    Automatic Segment Space
        Management (ASSM), 13
    extraction of object metadata, 12–13
    new indexing features, 13–14
    new partitioning options and
        features, 12
Features, new Oracle9i backup and
    recovery, 21–23
    fast start fault recovery (FSFR), 21
    flashback query, 22
    new log miner features, 23
    new RMAN features, 22–23
    Oracle9i Data Guard, 23
Features, new Oracle9i SQL and PL/SQL,
    16–21
    associative arrays, 17
    miscellaneous SQL and PL/SQL
        features, 19–21
    Oracle CASE statements and
        expressions, 17–18
    Oracle MERGE statements, 18
    support for ANSI/ISO 1999
        compliance, 18–19
Features, new Oracle9i warehousing,
    15–16
    external tables, 15
    multitable insert statements, 15–16
    view constraints, 15
Features, using parallel, 427–462
File I/Os, moving data files to balance, 70
Files
    data, 66–70
    storing data and index, 67–68

FIRST_ROWS hints, 254
Folders
    Instance, 148–150
    Schema, 150–157
    Security, 157–160
    Storage, 160–161
Fragmentation, disk I/O and, 63–106
Fragmentation, eliminating, 84–92
    avoiding chaining by setting
        percents correctly, 89–90
    creating new tablespaces, 86–88
    exporting and reimporting tables,
        88–89
    moving data to new tablespaces,
        86–88
    rebuilding databases, 90–92
    using correct extent size, 86
Freespace, monitoring disk, 653
FULL hints, 255–256
Function-based indexes, 56–57
Functions
    reducing use of MOD, 397–399
    using, 40
    using EXISTS, 300–301

G

Groupings, available hints and
    changing execution path, 248
    using access method hints, 249
    using joining operation hints, 249
    using miscellaneous hints, 250
    using parallel execution, 250
    using query transformation
        hints, 249
Groups, X$ table, 535–555
GV$ views
    creation of V$ and, 682
    cross referenced to X$ tables,
        791–800
    Oracle9i X$ tables not referenced
        by, 800–802
GV$ views, Oracle9i, 683–686

H

Hardware disks, data files across available, 66–70
HASH hints, 274
HASH indexes, 53–55
Height, binary, 43–45
High ppgout, 650
Hint syntax, basic, 245–280
    available hints and groupings, 248–250
    hints at a glance, 276–277
    problems with hints, 275–276
    specifying hints, 250–251
    specifying multiple hints, 251
    top hints used, 247–248
    using aliases, 251–252
    using hints, 252–275
Hints
    ALL_ROWS, 255
    AND_EQUAL, 259
    APPEND, 271–272
    CACHE, 272–273
    CHOOSE, 252–253
    CLUSTER, 274
    CURSOR_SHARING_EXACT, 275
    DRIVING_SITE, 266
    FIRST_ROWS, 254
    FULL, 255–256
    at a glance, 276–277
    HASH, 274
    INDEX, 256–257
    INDEX_ASC, 260
    INDEX_COMBINE, 259–260
    INDEX_DESC, 260–261
    INDEX_FFS, 261
    INDEX_JOIN, 258
    LEADING, 263
    NOAPPEND, 272
    NOCACHE, 273
    NO_EXPAND, 265–266
    NO_INDEX, 257–258
    NOPARALLEL, 271
    ORDERED, 261–262

    ORDERED_PREDICATES, 263–264
    PARALLEL, 270–271
    problems with, 275–276
    PUSH_SUBQ, 269
    ROWID, 264–265
    RULE, 253
    specifying, 250–251
    specifying multiple, 251
    USE_HASH, 268–269
    USE_MERGE, 267
    USE_NL, 267–268
    using, 252–275
Hints and groupings, available
    changing execution pack, 248
    using access method hints, 249
    using joining operation hints, 249
    using miscellaneous hints, 250
    using parallel execution, 250
    using query transformation hints, 249
Hints used, top, 247–248
Histograms, 45–47
Hit ratio distortions, miscellaneous, 118
Hit ratios, 116, 117, 117–118
Hot data blocks/latch contention and wait events, 527–531

I

I/O bottlenecks, using iostat to identify disk, 645–648
I/O disk contention, avoiding, 68–70
I/O problems, using sar to monitor disk, 645
I/Os
    disk, 63–106
    moving data files to balance file, 70
IF statement order, standardizing on, 391–395
Index concepts, basic, 34–36
Index examples, creating table and, 435–437
Index files, storing data and, 67–68
INDEX hints, 256–257
Index merge, 296–297

Index-organized tables, 55
Index partitioning, 83–84
Index principles, basic, 33–62
    basic index concepts, 34–36
    binary height, 43–45
    clustering factors, 42–43
    concatenated indexes, 36–37
    fast full scans, 47
    fast index rebuilding, 60
    Oracle ROWID, 37–38
    selectivity, 41–42
    skip-scans, 47–49
    suppressing indexes, 38–41
    types of indexes, 49–59
    using histograms, 45–47
Index rebuilding, fast, 60
Index Tuning Wizard, 188–189
INDEX_ASC hints, 260
INDEX_COMBINE hints, 259–260
INDEX_DESC hints, 260–261
Indexes
    B-tree, 49–50
    bitmap, 50–53
    bitmap join, 328–334
    checking on tables, 287
    concatenated, 36–37
    creating, 286–287
    determining when to use, 285
    fixing bad, 288–289
    forgetting, 285–286
    function-based, 56–57
    handling suppressed, 297–298
    HASH, 53–55
    local, 58–59
    obtaining list of all X$, 509–510
    Oracle9i X$, 772–783
    partitioned, 57–59
    reverse key, 55–56
    using function-based, 298–299
    using hints with X$ tables and,
        510–511
    using multiple, 294–296

Indexes, suppressing, 38–41
    using IS NOT NULL, 39–40
    using IS NULL, 39–40
    using NOT EQUAL operators, 38
Indexes, types of, 49–59
    B-tree indexes, 49–50
    bitmap indexes, 50–53
    function-based indexes, 56–57
    HASH indexes, 53–55
    index-organized tables, 55
    partitioned indexes, 57–59
    reverse key indexes, 55–56
INDEX_FFS hints, 261
Indexing properly, 287–288
Indexing SELECT and WHERE, 290–291
INDEX_JOIN hints, 258
Information list, system, 628–632
Initialization parameters, 520–523
    tuning Oracle9i, 450–456
Initialization parameters, tuning databases
    with, 107–143
    changing init.ora files without restart,
        109–110
    identifying crucial init.ora
        parameters, 108–109
    increasing performance by tuning
        DB_CACHE_SIZE, 111–118
    setting DB_BLOCK_SIZE to reflect
        size of data reads, 119–141
    viewing init.ora parameters with
        Enterprise Manager, 110–111
Initiation parameters, waits related to,
    128–129
Init.ora file, changing without restart,
    109–110
Init.ora parameters, 659–679
    deprecated, 661
    deprecated init.ora parameters, 661
    desupported, 660–661
    desupported init.ora parameters,
        660–661
    finding undocumented, 138–139

identifying crucial, 108–109
listing of documented, 666–677
listing of documented init.ora
parameters (V$PARAMETER),
666–677
listing of undocumented, 678
listing of undocumented init.ora
parameters (x$ksppi/x$ksppcv), 678
top ten init.ora parameters to
remember, 663–664
top ten reasons not to write books,
678–679
top thirteen undocumented, 664–666
top thirteen undocumented init.ora
parameters, 664–666
top twenty-five, 662–663
top twenty-five init.ora parameters,
662–663
for undocumented TRACE, 233–235
viewing with Enterprise Manager,
110–111
Init.ora parameters to remember, top ten,
663–664
Installing STATSPACK, 566–572
Instance/database, 531–532
Instance folder, 148–150
Inter- and intraoperation parallelization,
432–435
Intervals topics, related Oracle, 532–535
dumps, 533–534
events, 533
oradebug, 534–535
traces, 532
Intraoperation parallelization, inter- and,
432–435
Invalid objects, finding, 405–406
Iostat, using to identify disk I/O
bottlenecks, 645–648
Ipcs, using to determine shared memory, 651
IS NOT NULL, 39–40
IS NULL, 39–40
Iterations, reducing PL/SQL program unit,
386–389

Iterative processing, using ROWID for,
389–391

J

Join methods, 305–312
CLUSTER joins, 307–308
comparing primary, 312–313
HASH joins, 308
index joins, 308–312
NESTED LOOPS joins, 305–306
SORT-MERGE joins, 306–307
Joins, common X$ table, 557–562
future version impact, 562
new 9i X$ tables, 560–561
undocumented fixed views, 561–562
Joins, table, 303–377
apply control theory, 365–375
bitmap join indexes, 328–334
comparing primary join methods,
312–313
eliminating join records in multitable
joins, 321–322
equal-sized tables, 313–316
forcing specific join method,
319–321
join methods, 305–312
miscellaneous tuning snippets,
341–351
more mathematical techniques,
365–375
table join initialization parameters, 312
third-party product tuning, 334–338
three-table joins, 326–328
tuning distributed queries, 338–340
tuning using simple mathematical
techniques, 351–365
two-table INDEXED join, 316–318
two-table join, 313–316
two-table join between large and
small tables, 323–326
when you have everything tuned, 340
Joins, two-table, 313–316

L

Latches, using STATSPACK to tune waits and, 565–603
LEADING hints, 263
Lists, system information, 628–632
Load
    using uptime to monitor CPU, 640
    using vmstat to monitor system, 652–653
Loading, parallel, 456–457
Local indexes, 58–59
Locally managed tablespaces, 71–73
Locations
    examining implications of PL/SQL object, 417–418
    pinpoint execution, 421
Log timing information, using in database tables, 383–386

M

Manager, Performance, 163–179
Maps, Tablespace, 196–197
Mathematical techniques
    more, 365–375
    tuning using simple, 351–365
Memory
    allocating for statements, 131–132
    caching tables in, 293–294
    optimal use of, 132
    using ipcs to determine shared, 651
Memory-monitoring tool on NT; *See* CPU/memory-monitoring tool on NT
Memory Performance Index (MPI), 610–618
Merge, index, 296–297
Migration notes, 3–4
Mismatched data types, comparing, 41
MOD function, reducing use of, 397–399
Monitor CPU load, using uptime to, 640
Monitor system load, using vmstat to, 652–653

Monitor system paging/swapping
    using sar to, 648–650
    using vmstat to, 648–650
Monitoring
    disk freespace, 653
    network performance, 654–657
    parallel operations, 457–459
    parallel operations via V$ views, 440–445
    system using UNIX utilities, 635–657
    tools, 639
    using DBMS_APPLICATION_INFO for real-time, 381–383
MPI (Memory Performance Index), 610–618
    buffer hit ratio, 610–612
    dictionary cache hit ratio, 612
    library cache hit ratio, 613
    percent of data buffers still free, 614
    pinning/caching objects, 617–618
    sorting in memory hit ratio, 613–614
    top 10 memory abusers as percent of all statements, 615–616
    top 25 memory abusers statements tuned, 616–617
Mpstat, using to identify CPU bottlenecks, 640–641
Multiple hints, specifying, 251
Multiple indexes, 294–296

N

Names, Oracle9i X$ tables ordered by, 768–772
Network performance, monitoring, 654–657
New features, introduction to Oracle9i, 1–32
New Oracle9i
    administrative features, 3–11
    architectural features, 11–14
    backup and recovery features, 21–23
    data warehousing features, 15–16
    SQL and PL/SQL features, 16–21

NOAPPEND hints, 272
NOCACHE hints, 273
NO_EXPAND hints, 265–266
NO_INDEX hints, 257–258
Non-V$ fixed view associations, X$ table and, 555–557
NOPARALLEL hints, 271
Notes, miscellaneous parallel, 460
NT, CPU/memory-monitoring tool on, 644
NULL
    IS, 39–40
    IS NOT, 39–40

O

Object information, getting from DBA_OBJECT_SIZE, 404–405
Objects
    finding invalid, 405–406
    identifying PL/SQL, 401–402
    pinning in shared pool, 399–401
Operations
    basic concept of parallel, 428–430
    monitoring parallel, 440–445, 457–459
    using AUTOTRACE on parallel, 445–450
    using EXPLAIN PLAN on parallel, 445–450
    using parallel, 435–437
Optimization, how it looks at data, 135
OR, understanding curious, 299–300
Oracle
    multiple buffer pools, 129–132
    ROWID, 37–38
    SQL Scratchpad, 161–163
    TRACE utility, 206–241
    Tuning pack-Oracle, Expert, 189–196
    Tuning pack-SQL Analyze, 179–188
    Tuning pack-Tablespace Map, 196–197
Oracle Expert, Oracle Tuning pack, 189–196
    Oracle Expert-drilling down to recommendation detail, 194–195

Oracle Expert-focusing on schemas, 190–191
Oracle Expert-making changes, 192–193
Oracle Expert-recommended systemwide changes, 195–196
Oracle Expert-setting up rules for tuning sessions, 191–192
Oracle Expert-viewing recommendations, 193–194
Oracle9i
    GV$ views, 683–686
    initialization parameters, tuning, 450–456
    new features, 1–32
    parallel DML statements and operations since, 431
    scripts of x$ tables used to create V$ views, 690–766
    V$ views, 686–689
    X$ tables ordered by name, 768–772
ORDERED hints, 261–262
ORDERED_PREDICATES hints, 263–264
Outlines, dropping stored, 238
Outlines, using stored, 235–241
    creating and using stored outlines, 237–238
    dropping stored outlines, 238
    how OUTLINES are stored, 236–237
    setting up STORED OUTLINES, 235–236
    stored outlines example, 238–241
Output
    interpreting STATSPACK, 572–599
    things to look for in STATSPACK, 600–601

P

Paging, modifying size of SGA to avoid, 132–134
Paging/swapping
    using sar to monitor system, 648–650

using vmstat to monitor system,
648–650

Parallel DML
and DDL statements and operations,
430–431
statements and examples, 437–440
statements and operations since
Oracle9i, 431

Parallel execution, tuning, 450–456

Parallel features, using to improve
performance, 427–462
basic concepts of parallel operations,
428–430
creating table and index examples,
435–437
inter- and intraoperation
parallelization, 432–435
miscellaneous parallel notes, 460
monitoring parallel operations,
457–459
monitoring parallel operations via V$
views, 440–445
parallel DDL statements and
operations, 430–431
parallel DML statements and
examples, 437–440
parallel DML statements and
operations, 430–431
parallel DML statements and
operations since Oracle9i, 431
parallel loading, 456–457
parallelism and partitions, 432
performance comparisons, 457–459
tuning Oracle9i initialization
parameters, 450–456
tuning parallel execution, 450–456
using AUTOTRACE on parallel
operations, 445–450
using EXPLAIN PLAN on parallel
operations, 445–450
using parallel operations, 435–437

PARALLEL hints, 270–271

Parallel loading, 456–457

Parallel notes, miscellaneous, 460

Parallel operations
basic concepts of, 428–430
monitoring, 440–445, 457–459
using, 435–437
using AUTOTRACE on, 445–450
using EXPLAIN PLAN on, 445–450

Parallelism and partitions, 432

Parallelization, inter- and intraoperation,
432–435

Parameters
desupported init.ora, 660–661
initialization, 520–523
INIT.ORA, 233–235
init.ora deprecated, 661
key init.ora, 659–679
listing of documented init.ora,
666–677
listing of undocumented init.ora, 678
top thirteen undocumented init.ora,
664–666
top twenty-five init.ora, 662–663
tuning databases with initialization,
107–143
tuning Oracle9i initialization,
450–456
waits related to initiation, 128–129

Parameters to remember, top ten init.ora,
663–664

Partitions
exporting, 84
parallelism and, 432

Partitions, avoiding disk contention by
using, 73–83
getting more information about
partitions, 76–77
miscellaneous partition options,
80–83
miscellaneous types of partitions,
77–80

Performance
comparisons, 457–459
monitoring network, 654–657

tuning SHARED_POOL_SIZE for
optimal, 120–129
using PL/SQL to enhance, 379–426
using temporary database tables for
increased, 420–421
Performance Manager, 163–179
buffer cache hit ratio, 165–167
building charts, 173–175
data dictionary cache hit ratio,
168–169
database health overview chart,
163–165
database instance information,
171–172
library cache hit ratio, 167–168
memory sort hit ratio, 169–170
SQL Area, 169
system I/O rate, 170–171
top charts and sessions, 175–179
Performance, using parallel features to
improve, 427–462
basic concepts of parallel operations,
428–430
creating table and index examples,
435–437
inter- and intraoperation
parallelization, 432–435
miscellaneous parallel notes, 460
monitoring parallel operations,
457–459
monitoring parallel operations via
V$ views, 440–445
parallel DDL statements and
operations, 430–431
parallel DML statements and
operations, 430–431
parallel DML statements and
operations since Oracle9i, 431
parallel loading, 456–457
parallelism and partitions, 432
performance comparisons, 457–459
tuning Oracle9i initialization
parameters, 450–456

tuning parallel execution, 450–456
using AUTOTRACE on parallel
operations, 445–450
using EXPLAIN PLAN on parallel
operations, 445–450
using parallel operations, 435–437
PGA_AGGREGATE_TARGET, 132
Pinned, identifying PL/SQL objects that
need to be, 401–402
Pinning objects in shared pool, 399–401
PL/SQL features, new Oracle9i SQL and,
16–21
PL/SQL object locations, examining
implications of, 417–418
PL/SQL objects, identifying that need to
be pinned, 401–402
PL/SQL program unit iterations and
iteration time, 386–389
PL/SQL tables, using for fast reference
table lookups, 408–410
PL/SQL, tuning and testing, 416–417
PL/SQL, using to enhance performance,
379–426
examining implications of PL/SQL
object locations, 417–418
finding disabled triggers, 406–408
finding invalid objects, 405–406
finding SQL when objects are used,
410–413
getting object information from
DBA_OBJECT_SIZE, 404–405
identifying PL/SQL objects that need
to be pinned, 401–402
integrating user tracking
mechanism, 421
limiting use of dynamic SQLs,
421–422
looking at some examples for
beginners, 422–425
modifying
DBMS_SHARED_POOL.SIZES,
402–404

pinning objects in shared pool, 399–401

pinpoint execution locations, 421

reducing calls to SYSDATE, 395–397

reducing PL/SQL program unit iterations, 386–389

reducing PL/SQL programming unit iteration time, 386–389

reducing use of MOD function, 397–399

standardizing on data types, 391–395

standardizing on IF statement order, 391–395

standardizing on PLS_INTEGER, 391–395

tuning and testing PL/SQL, 416–417

tuning SQL when objects are used, 410–413

using DBMS_APPLICATION_INFO for real-time monitoring, 381–383

using DBMS_SHARED_POOL.SIZES, 402–404

using log timing information in database tables, 383–386

using PL/SQL tables for fast reference table lookups, 408–410

using rollback segments to open large cursors, 418–420

using ROWID for iterative processing, 389–391

using temporary database tables for increased performance, 420–421

using time components when working with DATE data types, 413–416

PLAN_TABLE table, important columns in, 230–232

PLS_INTEGER, standardizing on, 391–395

Pools
    shared, 399–401, 511–512, 512–519
    using Oracle multiple buffer, 129–132

Ppgout, high, 650

Principles, basic index, 33–62

Processing, using ROWID for iterative, 389–391

Ps, combining with selected V$ views, 641–644

PUSH_SUBQ hints, 269

Q

Queries
    making magically faster, 292
    monitoring V$SQLAREA to find slow, 115–118
    slow, 117–118
    tuning distributed, 338–340

Query tuning, 281–302
    caching tables in memory, 293–294
    checking indexes on tables, 287
    creating indexes, 286–287
    determining when to use indexes, 285
    fixing bad indexes, 288–289
    forgetting indexes, 285–286
    handling suppressed indexes, 297–298
    indexing properly, 287–288
    indexing SELECT and WHERE, 290–291
    making queries magically faster, 292
    querying V$SQLAREA and V$SQL, 283–284
    understanding curious OR, 299–300
    using EXISTS function, 300–301
    using fast full scan, 291–292
    using function-based indexes, 298–299
    using index merge, 296–297
    using multiple indexes, 294–296

Querying V$SQLAREA and V$SQL, 283–284

R

RAC (Real Application Clusters), 23–31,
341–342
    architecture of Oracle RAC, 25–27
    internal workings of Oracle RAC
        system, 27–29
    parallel databases, 24
    SCN processing, 29–30
RAID levels, available, 65
Raw devices, using to improve I/O, 103–104
Reads, setting DB_BLOCK_SIZE to reflect
size of data, 119–141
Real-time monitoring, using DBMS_
APPLICATION_INFO for, 381–383
Rebuilding, fast index, 60
Recovery features, new Oracle9i backup
and, 21–23
Reference table lookups, using PL/SQL
tables for fast, 408–410
Reporting, business impact, 198–201
Restart, changing init.ora file without,
109–110
Reverse key indexes, 55–56
Review, performing quick system, 605–633
Rollback segments, 96–99
    using to open large cursors, 418–420
ROWID
    Oracle, 37–38
    using for iterative processing,
        389–391
ROWID hints, 264–265
Rows, candidate, 321–322
RULE hints, 253

S

Sar
    using to monitor CPU usage,
        636–638
    using to monitor disk I/O problem, 645
    using to monitor system
        paging/swapping, 648–650

Scans; *See also* Skip-scans
Scans, fast full, 47, 291–292
Schema folder, 150–157
Scratchpad, Oracle SQL, 161–163
Scripts, Oracle9i, 690–766
Security folder, 157–160
Selectivity, 41–42
Servers
    modeling typical, 140–141
    understanding typical, 139–140
Sessions, killing problem, 100–101
SGA, modifying size of, 132–134
SGA_MAX_SIZE, setting, 119
Shared memory, using ipcs to
determine, 651
Shared pools, 511–512
    pinning objects in, 399–401
Shared pools, queries to monitor, 512–519
    fragmentation, 514
    high number of hard parses, 517
    large allocation causing
        contention, 513
    latch waits and/or sleeps, 517–518
    library cache hit ratio, 515–517
    low free memory in shared and
        Java pools, 515
    miscellaneous, 518–519
    ORA-04031 errors cumin, 512–513
SHARED_POOL_SIZE, tuning for optimal
performance, 120–129
    shared SQL area, 120–122
Skip-scans, 47–49
Snippets, miscellaneous tuning, 341–351
SPI (System Performance Index), 608–610
SQL Analyze, Oracle Tuning pack, 179–188
    SQL Analyze-comparing different
        plans, 184–185
    SQL Analyze-execution statistics,
        182–184
    SQL Analyze-EXPLAIN PLAN,
        180–182
    SQL Analyze-Tuning Wizard,
        185–188

SQL and PL/SQL features, new Oracle9i,
16–21
SQL Scratchpad, Oracle, 161–163
SQL*Plus Worksheet, 161–163
SQLs
finding when objects are used,
410–413
limiting use of dynamic, 421–422
tuning when objects are used,
410–413
Statements, allocating memory for,
131–132
Statements and examples, parallel DML,
437–440
Statements and operations, parallel DML
and DDL, 430–431
STATSPACK, installing, 566–572
gathering statistics, 568–571
post-installation, 567–568
running statistics reports, 572
security of PERFSTAT account, 567
STATSPACK output, interpreting,
572–599
additional memory statistics,
588–589
dictionary and library cache statistics,
595–597
header information, 572–573
Instance Activity Statistics, 583–587
Instance Efficiency, 574–576
latch statistics, 591–595
load profile, 573–574
nondefault init.ora parameters, 599
rollback/UNDO statistics, 589–591
SGA memory statistics, 597–599
tablespace and file I/O statistics,
587–588
top SQL statements, 582–583
top wait events, 576–582
STATSPACK output, things to look for in,
600–601
managing STATSPACK data, 600–601

STATSPACK, using to tune waits and
latches, 565–603
installing STATSPACK, 566–572
interpreting STATSPACK output,
572–599
things to look for in STATSPACK
output, 600–601
Storage folder, 160–161
Stored outlines
dropping, 238
example, 238–241
Stored outlines, using, 205, 235–241
creating and using stored outlines,
237–238
dropping stored outlines, 238
how OUTLINES are stored, 236–237
setting up STORED OUTLINES,
235–236
stored outlines example, 238–241
Structure, building tree, 226–227
Swapping; See also Paging/swapping
Swapping, modifying size of SGA to avoid,
132–134
Syntax, basic hint, 245–280
available hints and groupings,
248–250
hints at a glance, 276–277
problems with hints, 275–276
specifying hints, 250–251
specifying multiple hints, 251
top hints used, 247–248
using aliases, 251–252
using hints, 252–275
SYSDATE, reducing calls to, 395–397
System, finding worst users on, 638–640
System information list, 628–632
backup and recovery, 630–631
CPU-related values, 630
DBA knowledge rating, 631–632
disk-related values, 629
memory-related values, 629
naming conventions, 631
OFA standards and security
information, 631

System load, using vmstat to monitor, 652–653
System, monitoring, 635–657
System paging/swapping
    using sar to monitor, 648–650
    using vmstat to monitor, 648–650
System Performance Index (SPI), 608–610
System review example, overall, 625–628
    example system review rating categories, 626–627
    items requiring immediate action, 628
    miscellaneous items requiring action, 628
    rating system, 625–626
System review, performing quick, 605–633
    Disk Performance Index (DPI), 618–624
    Education Performance Index (EPI), 607–608
    Memory Performance Index (MPI), 610–618
    overall system review example, 625–628
    system information list, 628–632
    System Performance Index (SPI), 608–610
    Total Performance Index (TPI), 606–607, 624–625

T

Table and index examples, creating, 435–437
Table groups, X$, 535–555
Table join initialization parameters, 312
Table joins and other advanced tuning, 303–377
    apply control theory, 365–375
    bitmap join indexes, 328–334
    comparing primary join methods, 312–313
    eliminating join records in multitable joins, 321–322
    equal-sized tables, 313–316
    forcing specific join method, 319–321
    join methods, 305–312
    miscellaneous tuning snippets, 341–351
    more mathematical techniques, 365–375
    table join initialization parameters, 312
    third-party product tuning, 334–338
    three-table joins, 326–328
    tuning distributed queries, 338–340
    tuning using simple mathematical techniques, 351–365
    two-table INDEXED join, 316–318
    two-table join, 313–316
    two-table join between large and small tables, 323–326
    when you have everything tuned, 340
Table joins, common X$, 557–562
Table lookups, using PL/SQL tables for fast reference, 408–410
Tables
    caching in memory, 293–294
    checking indexes on, 287
    creating X$, 506–508
    creation of x$, 682
    important columns in PLAN_TABLE, 230–232
    index-organized, 55
    introducing X$, 502–505
    Oracle9i GV$ views cross referenced to X$, 791–800
    Oracle9i X$, 800–802
    PL/SQL, 408–410
    using log timing information in database, 383–386
    using temporary database, 420–421
    X$, 501–563, 690–766, 767–802
    X$KSMSP, 127–128
Tables cross referenced to V$ views, Oracle9i X$, 783–791

Tablespace Map, Oracle Tuning pack, 196–197
    Oracle Expert analysis report, 197–198
Tablespaces, locally managed, 71–73
    creating tablespaces as locally managed, 71–72
    migrating dictionary-managed tablespaces to locally managed, 72–73
    viewing file/tablespace information using Enterprise Manager, 73
Tablespaces, undo, 99–100
    monitoring UNDO spaces, 100
Temporary database tables, using for increased performance, 420–421
Theory, apply control, 365–375
Three-table joins, 326–328
Time components, using when working with DATE data types, 413–416
Time, reducing PL/SQL programming unit iteration, 386–389
TKPROF, 205
TKPROF output
    digging into, 215–216
    more complex, 213–214
Tools
    CPU/memory-monitoring, 644
    monitoring, 639
Total Performance Index (TPI), 606–607, 624–625
TPI (Total Performance Index), 606–607, 624–625
TRACE
    INIT.ORA parameters for undocumented, 233–235
    using, 205
TRACE utility, Oracle, 206–241
    another EXPLAIN PLAN output method, 226–227
    building tree structure, 226–227
    digging into TKPROF output, 215–216
    example using tree approach, 227–230

    helpful Oracle-supplied packages, 232–233
    important columns in PLAN_TABLE table, 230–232
    INIT.ORA parameters for undocumented TRACE, 233–235
    more complex TKPROF output, 213–214
    reading EXPLAIN PLAN, 220, 221–225
    sections of TRACE output, 212–213
    simple steps for TRACE with simple query, 207–211
    tracing/EXPLAINing problem queries in developer products, 230
    using EXPLAIN PLAN alone, 216–220
    using stored outlines, 235–241
Tracking mechanism, integrating user, 421
Tree approach, example using, 227–230
Tree structure, building, 226–227
Triggers, finding disabled, 406–408
Tuned, when you have everything, 340
Tuning
    databases with initialization parameters, 107–143
    distributed queries, 338–340
    Oracle9i initialization parameters, 450–456
    parallel execution, 450–456
    SHARED_POOL_SIZE for optimal performance, 120–129
    table joins and other advanced, 303–377
    and testing PL/SQL, 416–417
    third-party product, 334–338
Tuning DB_CACHE_SIZE, increasing performance by
    keeping hit ratio for data cache above 95 percent, 115
    monitoring V$QLAREA to find slow queries, 115–118
    using V$DB_CACHE_ADVICE in tuning DB_CACHE_SIZE, 113–114

Tuning DB_CACHE_SIZE, using
  V$DB_CACHE_ADVICE in, 113–114
Tuning pack, Enterprise Manager and,
  145–204
    business impact reporting, 198–201
    Enterprise Manager console, 147
    Index Tuning Wizard, 188–189
    Instance folder, 148–150
    Oracle SQL Scratchpad, 161–163
    Oracle Tuning pack-Oracle Expert,
      189–196
    Oracle Tuning pack-SQL Analyze,
      179–188
    Oracle Tuning pack-Tablespace Map,
      196–197
    Performance Manager, 163–179
    Schema folder, 150–157
    Security folder, 157–160
    SQL*Plus Worksheet, 161–163
    Storage folder, 160–161
Tuning pack-Oracle Expert, Oracle,
  189–196
    Oracle Expert-measuring impact,
      192–193
Tuning pack-SQL Analyze, Oracle,
  179–188
Tuning, query, 281–302
    caching tables in memory, 293–294
    checking indexes on tables, 287
    creating indexes, 286–287
    determining when to use indexes, 285
    fixing bad indexes, 288–289
    forgetting indexes, 285–286
    handling suppressed indexes,
      297–298
    indexing properly, 287–288
    indexing SELECT and WHERE,
      290–291
    making queries magically faster, 292
    querying V$SQLAREA and V$SQL,
      283–284
    understanding curious OR, 299–300
    using EXISTS function, 300–301
    using fast full scan, 291–292

    using function-based indexes,
      298–299
    using index merge, 296–297
    using multiple indexes, 294–296
Tuning snippets, miscellaneous, 341–351
    block dumps, 350–351
    developer coding issue, 348
    external tables, 343–348
    Linux is making a move, 342–343
    Real Application Clusters (RAC),
      341–342
    Red Hot is red hot, 342–343
    set event to dump every wait,
      348–350
    snapshot too old, 348
Tuning SQL when objects are used,
  410–413
Tuning using simple mathematical
  techniques, 351–365
    mathematical techniques
      conclusions, 364–365
    pattern interpretation, 359–364
    seven-step methodology, 352–359
    traditional mathematical analysis, 352
Tuning Wizard, Index, 188–189
Two-table join, 313–316
    between large and small tables,
      323–326
Types
    standardizing on data, 391–395
    using time components when
      working with DATE data, 413–416

U

UNDO management, using
    committing after each batch, 96
    determining sizes of checkpoint
      intervals, 94–96
    determining sizes of log files, 94–96
    increasing chances of recovery, 96
    whether redo log file sizes are
      problems, 93

Undo tablespaces, 99–100
    monitoring UNDO spaces, 100
Undocumented init.ora parameters,
    listing of, 678
Unit iteration time, reducing PL/SQL
    program, 386–389
UNIX utilities, 636–657
    combining ps with selected
        V$ views, 641–644
    finding worst users on system,
        638–640
    monitoring disk freespace, 653
    monitoring network performance,
        654–657
    using iostat to identify disk I/O
        bottlenecks, 645–648
    using ipcs to determine shared
        memory, 651
    using mpstat to identify CPU
        bottlenecks, 640–641
    using sar to monitor CPU usage,
        636–638
    using sar to monitor disk I/O
        problems, 645
    using sar to monitor system
        paging/swapping, 648–650
    using uptime to monitor CPU
        load, 640
    using vmstat to monitor system
        load, 652–653
    using vmstat to monitor system
        paging/swapping, 648–650
UNIX utilities, monitoring system using,
    635–657
    UNIX utilities, 636–657
Uptime, using to monitor CPU load, 640
Usage, using sar to monitor CPU, 636–638
USE_HASH hints, 268–269
USE_MERGE hints, 267
USE_NL hints, 267–268
User tracking mechanism, integrating, 421
Users on system, worst, 638–640

Utilities
    monitoring system using UNIX,
        635–657
    Oracle TRACE, 206–241
    UNIX, 636–657

V

V$ and GV$ views and x$ tables,
    creation of, 682
V$ view creation and access, 465–498
    checking privileges and roles,
        492–494
    detail of memory allocated
        (V$SGASTAT), 475–476
    determining hit ratio for data
        dictionary (V$ROWCACHE),
        478–479
    determining hit ratio for data
        (V$SYSSTAT), 477–478
    determining hit ratio for
        shared SQL and PL/SQL
        (V$LIBRARYCACHE), 479
    determining whether freelists are
        sufficient, 491–492
    finding disk I/O issues, 488–490
    finding init.ora settings in
        V$PARAMETER, 476–477
    finding out what users are doing,
        481–482
    finding out which objects users are
        accessing, 482–484
    finding out which resources users
        are using, 481–482
    finding problem queries by querying
        V$SQLAREA, 480–481
    finding rollback segment contention,
        490–491
    finding underlying objects that make
        up DBA_views, 470–471
    finding users with multiple sessions,
        487–488

finding X$ table used to create V$
  views, 469
identifying locking issues, 485–486
identifying PL/SQL objects that need
  to be kept, 479–480
killing problem sessions, 486–487
obtaining count and listing of all V$
  views, 467–468
summary of memory allocated
  (V$SGA), 475
using helpful V$ scripts, 471–474
using indexes, 484–485
V$ view categories, 494–498
V$ views, 463–500, 681–766
  combining ps with selected, 641–644
  creating, 506–508
  creation of V$ and GV$ views and
    x$ tables, 682
  creation of x$ tables, 682
  monitoring parallel operations via,
    440–445
  Oracle9i, 686–689
  Oracle9i GV$ views, 683–686
  Oracle9i scripts of x$ tables used
    to create, 690–766
  Oracle9i scripts of x$ tables used
    to create V$ views, 690–766
  Oracle9i V$ views, 686–689
  Oracle9i X$ tables cross referenced
    to, 783–791
  V$ view creation and access,
    465–498
V$DB_CACHE_ADVICE, using in tuning
  DB_CACHE_SIZE, 113–114
View associations, X$ table and non-V$
  fixed, 555–557
Views
  combining ps with selected V#,
    641–644
  creating V$, 506–508
  GV$, 791–800
  monitoring parallel operations via V$,
    440–445
  monitoring V$QLAREA, 115–118

Oracle9i GV$, 683–686
Oracle9i V$, 686–689
Oracle9i X$ tables cross referenced
  to V$, 783–791
Oracle9i X$ tables not referenced
  by GV$, 800–802
V$, 463–500, 681–766
Vmstat
  using to monitor system load,
    652–653
  using to monitor system
    paging/swapping, 648–650
V$PO_SESSTAT, 444–445
V$PO_SYSSTAT, 441–444
V$PO_TQSTAT, 440–441
V$QLAREA view, monitoring, 115–118
V$SQL, querying V$SQLAREA and,
  283–284
V$SQLAREA and V$SQL, querying,
  283–284

W

Wait events, 527–531
Waits and latches, using STATSPACK
  to tune, 565–603
Waits related to initiation parameters,
  128–129
Warehousing features, new Oracle9i,
  15–16
Wizard, Index Tuning, 188–189
Worksheet, SQL*Plus, 161–163

X

X$ indexes, Oracle9i, 772–783
X$ table and non-V$ fixed view
  associations, 555–557
X$ table groups, 535–555
X$ table joins, common, 557–562
  future version impact, 562
  new 9i X$ tables, 560–561
  undocumented fixed views, 561–562

X$ tables, 501–563, 690–766, 767–802
    buffer cache/data blocks, 523–531
    common X$ table joins, 557–562
    creating, 506–508
    creating V$ views, 506–508
    creating X$ tables, 506–508
    creation of, 682
    cross referenced to V$ views,
      783–791
    effective X$ table use and
      strategy, 532
    groups, 535–555
    initialization parameters, 520–523
    instance/database, 531–532
    introducing X$ tables, 502–505
    and non-V$ fixed view associations,
      555–557
    not referenced by GV$ views,
      800–802
    obtaining list of all X$ indexes,
      509–510
    obtaining list of all X$ tables,
      508–509
    Oracle9i GV$ views cross
      referenced to, 791–800

Oracle9i GV$ views cross referenced
    to X$ tables, 791–800
Oracle9i X$ indexes, 772–783
Oracle9i X$ tables cross referenced
    to V$ views, 783–791
Oracle9i X$ tables not referenced by
    GV$ views, 800–802
Oracle9i X$ tables ordered by name,
    768–772
ordered by name, 768–772
queries to monitor shared pool,
    512–519
redo, 519
related Oracle intervals topics,
    532–535
shared pool, 511–512
using hints with X$ tables and
    indexes, 510–511
X$ tables, introducing, 502–505
    granting access to view X$ tables,
      504–505
    misconceptions about X$ tables, 504
X$KSMSP tables, 127–128

INTERNATIONAL CONTACT INFORMATION

AUSTRALIA
McGraw-Hill Book Company Australia Pty. Ltd.
TEL +61-2-9900-1800
FAX +61-2-9878-8881
http://www.mcgraw-hill.com.au
books-it_sydney@mcgraw-hill.com

CANADA
McGraw-Hill Ryerson Ltd.
TEL +905-430-5000
FAX +905-430-5020
http://www.mcgraw-hill.ca

**GREECE, MIDDLE EAST, & AFRICA
(Excluding South Africa)**
McGraw-Hill Hellas
TEL +30-210-6560-990
TEL +30-210-6560-993
TEL +30-210-6560-994
FAX +30-210-6545-525

MEXICO (Also serving Latin America)
McGraw-Hill Interamericana Editores S.A. de C.V.
TEL +525-117-1583
FAX +525-117-1589
http://www.mcgraw-hill.com.mx
fernando_castellanos@mcgraw-hill.com

SINGAPORE (Serving Asia)
McGraw-Hill Book Company
TEL +65-6863-1580
FAX +65-6862-3354
http://www.mcgraw-hill.com.sg
mghasia@mcgraw-hill.com

SOUTH AFRICA
McGraw-Hill South Africa
TEL +27-11-622-7512
FAX +27-11-622-9045
robyn_swanepoel@mcgraw-hill.com

SPAIN
McGraw-Hill/Interamericana de España, S.A.U.
TEL +34-91-180-3000
FAX +34-91-372-8513
http://www.mcgraw-hill.es
professional@mcgraw-hill.es

**UNITED KINGDOM, NORTHERN,
EASTERN, & CENTRAL EUROPE**
McGraw-Hill Education Europe
TEL +44-1-628-502500
FAX +44-1-628-770224
http://www.mcgraw-hill.co.uk
computing_europe@mcgraw-hill.com

ALL OTHER INQUIRIES Contact:
McGraw-Hill/Osborne
TEL +1-510-420-7700
FAX +1-510-420-7703
http://www.osborne.com
omg_international@mcgraw-hill.com

GET YOUR **FREE SUBSCRIPTION**
TO ORACLE MAGAZINE

Oracle Magazine is essential gear for today's information technology professionals. Stay informed and increase your productivity with every issue of *Oracle Magazine*. Inside each free bimonthly issue you'll get:

- Up-to-date information on Oracle Database, E-Business Suite applications, Web development, and database technology and business trends
- Third-party news and announcements
- Technical articles on Oracle Products and operating environments
- Development and administration tips
- Real-world customer stories

IF THERE ARE OTHER ORACLE USERS AT YOUR LOCATION WHO WOULD LIKE TO RECEIVE THEIR OWN SUBSCRIPTION TO ORACLE MAGAZINE, PLEASE PHOTOCOPY THIS FORM AND PASS IT ALONG.

Three easy ways to subscribe:

① Web

Visit our Web site at www.oracle.com/oraclemagazine. You'll find a subscription form there, plus much more!

② Fax

Complete the questionnaire on the back of this card and fax the questionnaire side only to +1.847.647.9735.

③ Mail

Complete the questionnaire on the back of this card and mail it to P.O. Box 1263, Skokie, IL 60076-8263

Oracle Publishing

ORACLE®

FREE SUBSCRIPTION

○ Yes, please send me a FREE subscription to *Oracle Magazine*   ○ **NO**

To receive a free subscription to *Oracle Magazine*, you must fill out the entire card, sign it, and date it (incomplete cards cannot be processed or acknowledged). You can also fax your application to +1.847.647.9735.

Or subscribe at our Web site at www.oracle.com/oraclemagazine/

○ From time to time, Oracle Publishing allows our partners exclusive access to our e-mail addresses for special promotions and announcements. To be included in this program, please check this box.

○ Oracle Publishing allows sharing of our mailing list with selected third parties. If you prefer your mailing address not to be included in this program, please check here. If at any time you would like to be removed from this mailing list, please contact Customer Service at +1.847.647.9630 or send an e-mail to oracle@halldata.com.

signature (required)

X

date

name   title

company   e-mail address

street/p.o. box

city/state/zip or postal code   telephone

country   fax

YOU MUST ANSWER ALL NINE QUESTIONS BELOW.

① WHAT IS THE PRIMARY BUSINESS ACTIVITY OF YOUR FIRM AT THIS LOCATION? (check one only)

- ☐ 01 Application Service Provider
- ☐ 02 Communications
- ☐ 03 Consulting, Training
- ☐ 04 Data Processing
- ☐ 05 Education
- ☐ 06 Engineering
- ☐ 07 Financial Services
- ☐ 08 Government (federal, local, state, other)
- ☐ 09 Government (military)
- ☐ 10 Health Care
- ☐ 11 Manufacturing (aerospace, defense)
- ☐ 12 Manufacturing (computer hardware)
- ☐ 13 Manufacturing (noncomputer)
- ☐ 14 Research & Development
- ☐ 15 Retailing, Wholesaling, Distribution
- ☐ 16 Software Development
- ☐ 17 Systems Integration, VAR, VAD, OEM
- ☐ 18 Transportation
- ☐ 19 Utilities (electric, gas, sanitation)
- ☐ 98 Other Business and Services

② WHICH OF THE FOLLOWING BEST DESCRIBES YOUR PRIMARY JOB FUNCTION? (check one only)

Corporate Management/Staff
- ☐ 01 Executive Management (President, Chair, CEO, CFO, Owner, Partner, Principal)
- ☐ 02 Finance/Administrative Management (VP/Director/ Manager/Controller, Purchasing, Administration)
- ☐ 03 Sales/Marketing Management (VP/Director/Manager)
- ☐ 04 Computer Systems/Operations Management (CIO/VP/Director/ Manager MIS, Operations)

IS/IT Staff
- ☐ 05 Systems Development/ Programming Management
- ☐ 06 Systems Development/ Programming Staff
- ☐ 07 Consulting
- ☐ 08 DBA/Systems Administrator
- ☐ 09 Education/Training
- ☐ 10 Technical Support Director/Manager
- ☐ 11 Other Technical Management/Staff
- ☐ 98 Other

③ WHAT IS YOUR CURRENT PRIMARY OPERATING PLATFORM? (select all that apply)

- ☐ 01 Digital Equipment UNIX
- ☐ 02 Digital Equipment VAX VMS
- ☐ 03 HP UNIX
- ☐ 04 IBM AIX

- ☐ 05 IBM UNIX
- ☐ 06 Java
- ☐ 07 Linux
- ☐ 08 Macintosh
- ☐ 09 MS-DOS
- ☐ 10 MVS
- ☐ 11 NetWare
- ☐ 12 Network Computing
- ☐ 13 OpenVMS
- ☐ 14 SCO UNIX
- ☐ 15 Sequent DYNIX/ptx
- ☐ 16 Sun Solaris/SunOS
- ☐ 17 SVR4
- ☐ 18 UnixWare
- ☐ 19 Windows
- ☐ 20 Windows NT
- ☐ 21 Other UNIX
- ☐ 98 Other
- 99 ☐ None of the above

④ DO YOU EVALUATE, SPECIFY, RECOMMEND, OR AUTHORIZE THE PURCHASE OF ANY OF THE FOLLOWING? (check all that apply)

- ☐ 01 Hardware
- ☐ 02 Software
- ☐ 03 Application Development Tools
- ☐ 04 Database Products
- ☐ 05 Internet or Intranet Products
- 99 ☐ None of the above

⑤ IN YOUR JOB, DO YOU USE OR PLAN TO PURCHASE ANY OF THE FOLLOWING PRODUCTS? (check all that apply)

Software
- ☐ 01 Business Graphics
- ☐ 02 CAD/CAE/CAM
- ☐ 03 CASE
- ☐ 04 Communications
- ☐ 05 Database Management
- ☐ 06 File Management
- ☐ 07 Finance
- ☐ 08 Java
- ☐ 09 Materials Resource Planning
- ☐ 10 Multimedia Authoring
- ☐ 11 Networking
- ☐ 12 Office Automation
- ☐ 13 Order Entry/Inventory Control
- ☐ 14 Programming
- ☐ 15 Project Management
- ☐ 16 Scientific and Engineering
- ☐ 17 Spreadsheets
- ☐ 18 Systems Management
- ☐ 19 Workflow

Hardware
- ☐ 20 Macintosh
- ☐ 21 Mainframe
- ☐ 22 Massively Parallel Processing

- ☐ 23 Minicomputer
- ☐ 24 PC
- ☐ 25 Network Computer
- ☐ 26 Symmetric Multiprocessing
- ☐ 27 Workstation

Peripherals
- ☐ 28 Bridges/Routers/Hubs/Gateways
- ☐ 29 CD-ROM Drives
- ☐ 30 Disk Drives/Subsystems
- ☐ 31 Modems
- ☐ 32 Tape Drives/Subsystems
- ☐ 33 Video Boards/Multimedia

Services
- ☐ 34 Application Service Provider
- ☐ 35 Consulting
- ☐ 36 Education/Training
- ☐ 37 Maintenance
- ☐ 38 Online Database Services
- ☐ 39 Support
- ☐ 40 Technology-Based Training
- ☐ 98 Other
- 99 ☐ None of the above

⑥ WHAT ORACLE PRODUCTS ARE IN USE AT YOUR SITE? (check all that apply)

Software
- ☐ 01 Oracle9i
- ☐ 02 Oracle9i Lite
- ☐ 03 Oracle8
- ☐ 04 Oracle8i
- ☐ 05 Oracle8i Lite
- ☐ 06 Oracle7
- ☐ 07 Oracle9i Application Server
- ☐ 08 Oracle9i Application Server Wireless
- ☐ 09 Oracle Data Mart Suites
- ☐ 10 Oracle Internet Commerce Server
- ☐ 11 Oracle interMedia
- ☐ 12 Oracle Lite
- ☐ 13 Oracle Payment Server
- ☐ 14 Oracle Video Server
- ☐ 15 Oracle Rdb

Tools
- ☐ 16 Oracle Darwin
- ☐ 17 Oracle Designer
- ☐ 18 Oracle Developer
- ☐ 19 Oracle Discoverer
- ☐ 20 Oracle Express
- ☐ 21 Oracle JDeveloper
- ☐ 22 Oracle Reports
- ☐ 23 Oracle Portal
- ☐ 24 Oracle Warehouse Builder
- ☐ 25 Oracle Workflow

Oracle E-Business Suite
- ☐ 26 Oracle Advanced Planning/Scheduling
- ☐ 27 Oracle Business Intelligence
- ☐ 28 Oracle E-Commerce
- ☐ 29 Oracle Exchange
- ☐ 30 Oracle Financials

- ☐ 31 Oracle Human Resources
- ☐ 32 Oracle Interaction Center
- ☐ 33 Oracle Internet Procurement
- ☐ 34 Oracle Manufacturing
- ☐ 35 Oracle Marketing
- ☐ 36 Oracle Order Management
- ☐ 37 Oracle Professional Services Automation
- ☐ 38 Oracle Projects
- ☐ 39 Oracle Sales
- ☐ 40 Oracle Service
- ☐ 41 Oracle Small Business Suite
- ☐ 42 Oracle Supply Chain Management
- ☐ 43 Oracle Travel Management
- ☐ 44 Oracle Treasury

Oracle Services
- ☐ 45 Oracle.com Online Services
- ☐ 46 Oracle Consulting
- ☐ 47 Oracle Education
- ☐ 48 Oracle Support
- ☐ 98 ther
- 99 ☐ None of the above

⑦ WHAT OTHER DATABASE PRODUCTS ARE IN USE AT YOUR SITE? (check all that apply)

- ☐ 01 Access   ☐ 08 Microsoft Access
- ☐ 02 Baan   ☐ 09 Microsoft SQL Server
- ☐ 03 dbase   ☐ 10 PeopleSoft
- ☐ 04 Gupta   ☐ 11 Progress
- ☐ 05 BM DB2   ☐ 12 SAP
- ☐ 06 Informix   ☐ 13 Sybase
- ☐ 07 Ingres   ☐ 14 VSAM
- ☐ 98 Other
- 99 ☐ None of the above

⑧ DURING THE NEXT 12 MONTHS, HOW MUCH DO YOU ANTICIPATE YOUR ORGANIZATION WILL SPEND ON COMPUTER HARDWARE, SOFTWARE, PERIPHERALS, AND SERVICES FOR YOUR LOCATION? (check only one)

- ☐ 01 Less than $10,000
- ☐ 02 $10,000 to $49,999
- ☐ 03 $50,000 to $99,999
- ☐ 04 $100,000 to $499,999
- ☐ 05 $500,000 to $999,999
- ☐ 06 $1,000,000 and over

⑨ WHAT IS YOUR COMPANY'S YEARLY SALES REVENUE? (please choose one)

- ☐ 01 $500, 000, 000 and above
- ☐ 02 $100, 000, 000 to $500, 000, 000
- ☐ 03 $50, 000, 000 to $100, 000, 000
- ☐ 04 $5, 000, 000 to $50, 000, 000
- ☐ 05 $1, 000, 000 to $5, 000, 000

123101

DATE DUE